Innovations in

TRANSPORTABLE HEALTHCARE

ARCHITECTURE

Innovations in Transportable Healthcare Architecture is the first book to examine the ways that healthcare architecture can provide better assistance in disaster-stricken communities.

Aimed at architects and other professionals working across the disaster relief sector, it provides:

- an overview of the need for rapid response healthcare facilities;
- global case studies which demonstrate real examples;
- historical perspectives on redeployables used in past military and civilian contexts;
- analysis of the advantages, challenges, and opportunities associated with offsite, premanufactured healthcare facilities and their component systems, for permanent installations or reuse on multiple sites;
- planning and design considerations for transportable offsite-built healthcare architecture;
- state-of-the-art research on pop-up clinics, truck-based configurations, ISO container-based outpatient clinical and trauma care centers, and modularized facilities for contemporary military and civilian contexts.

Innovations in Transportable Healthcare Architecture will be an invaluable reference source for architects, disaster mitigation planners, design and engineering practitioners, non-governmental medical aid organizations (NGOs), governmental health ministries, and policy specialists across the spectrum of disciplines engaged in disaster mitigation and the provision of healthcare in medically underserved communities globally.

Stephen Verderber is an award-winning scholar, researcher, and registered architect whose core specialty is architecture, design therapeutics, and health. He is a Professor at the John H. Daniels Faculty of Architecture, Landscape, and Design, and the Dalla Lana School of Public Health, at the University of Toronto. He holds a doctorate in architecture from the University of Michigan and is co-founder of R-2ARCH. His many publications include *Innovations in Hospice Architecture* (2005), *Innovations in Hospital Architecture* (2010), and *Sprawling Cities and Our Endangered Public Health* (2012).

Innovations in TRANSPORTABLE HEALTHCARE ARCHITECTURE

Stephen Verderber

Routledge
Taylor & Francis Group
LONDON AND NEW YORK

First published 2016 by Routledge

2 Park Square, Milton Park, Abingdon, Oxfordshire OX14 4RN
52 Vanderbilt Avenue, New York, NY 10017

Routledge is an imprint of the Taylor & Francis Group, an informa business

First issued in hardback 2019

British Library Cataloguing-in-Publication Data
A catalogue record for this book is available from the British Library

Library of Congress Cataloging-in-Publication Data
Verderber, Stephen author.
Innovations in transportable healthcare architecture / Stephen Verderber.
p. ; cm.
Includes bibliographical references and index.
I. Title.
[DNLM: 1. Facility Design and Construction--trends. 2. Mobile Health Units--trends. 3. Architecture as Topic--trends. WX 190]
RA967
725'.51--dc23
2015009426

ISBN: 978-1-138-84719-4 (hbk)

Typeset in Avenir
by Saxon Graphics Ltd, Derby

For my children, Elyssa Leigh Verderber
and Alexander Verderber

Contents

Illustration credits

FRONT COVER ILLUSTRATION

Seagull RTC Prototype, North Atlantic Ocean Deployment Scenario. Illustration: Ryan Ramsey/Stephen Verderber

BACK COVER PHOTOS

SmartPOD Prototype RTC, Washington, D.C. Deployment Scenario. Illustration: George Hughes

BLU-MED Installation, Haiti. Photo: BLU-MED Response Systems/Alaska Structures

Mobile Field Hospital Deployment Scenario, Morocco. Illustration: Hord Coplan Macht Architects, Baltimore

Combat Surgical Hospital Installation, Iraq. Photo: Weatherhaven/U.S. Army

CHAPTER 1

1.1	Source unknown/adapted by Stephen Verderber

CHAPTER 2

2.1–2.5	Photos: Courtesy of the National Museum of Civil War Medicine, Frederick, Maryland
2.6	Source unknown
2.7a–b, 2.8	Photos: Courtesy United States Army Medical Library, Washington, D.C.
2.9	Source unknown
2.10a–b–2.14a–b	Photos: Courtesy United States Army Medical Library, Washington, D.C.
2.15, 2.16	Source unknown
2.17	Photo: Courtesy Defense Industry Daily
2.18–2.23	Photos: Courtesy United States Army Medical Library, Washington, D.C.
2.24, 2.25a–b	Source unknown
2.26, 2.27	Photos: Courtesy United States Army Medical Library, Washington, D.C.
2.28a–b	Source unknown
2.29a–b–2.31a–b	Photos: Courtesy United States Army Medical Library, Washington, D.C.
2.32	Source unknown

2.33, 2.34a–c	Photos: Courtesy Medcoach Corporation, Oneonta, New York
2.35	Photo: Farber Specialty Vehicles, Columbus, Ohio
2.36	Drawing: Farber Specialty Vehicles, Columbus, Ohio
2.37	Photo: Farber Specialty Vehicles, Columbus, Ohio
2.38	Drawings: Dodgen Mobile Technologies, Humboldt, Iowa
2.39	Photo: Courtesy 'Clinic in a Can,' Wichita, Kansas
2.40	Drawings: Courtesy 'Clinic in a Can,' Wichita, Kansas
2.41	Diagram/illustration: Stephen Verderber

CHAPTER 3

3.1, 3.2a–c	Source unknown
3.3	Photo: Hugh Broughton Architects, London, U.K.
3.4	Source unknown
3.5a–b	Photos: Courtesy Sankyo Corporation Ltd., Tokyo, Japan
3.6a–c	Photo/illustrations: Courtesy Eggrock Modular/Pod Solutions, Telford, PA
3.7a–c	Drawings: Perkins+Will, Seattle, Washington
3.8	Drawing: Perkins+Will, Seattle, Washington
3.9a–b, 3.10a–b	Photos: Perkins+Will, Seattle, Washington
3.11a–b	Drawings/illustration: NBBJ, Columbus, Ohio
3.12a–d, 3.13a–c	Photos: NBBJ, Columbus, Ohio

CHAPTER 4

4.1, 4.2a–b	Photos/drawings: Stephen Verderber/Clemson University Team 899
4.3–4.6a–c	Drawings/Illustrations: Stephen Verderber/George Hughes and Valerie Or
4.7–4.12a–b	Photos/drawings: Stephen Verderber/Clemson University Team 899
4.13, 4.14a–b	Illustrations: Stephen Verderber/Yanwen Xiao and Kimberly Bandy
4.15–4.18a–b	Photos/drawings: Stephen Verderber/Clemson University Team 899

CHAPTER 5

5.6	Source unknown
5.9	Photo: Weatherhaven-North America
5.12, 5.13	Photos: Weatherhaven-North America
5.19	Source unknown
5.20	Photo: Courtesy Ashley Hamer Photography
5.25, 5.26	Photos: Robin Constable Hanson Photography
5.28	Drawing: George Hughes, Washington, D.C.
5.29	Source unknown
5.32	Photo: Courtesy Kamalini Lokuge, Canberra, Australia

CHAPTER 6

6.1.1–6.1.6	Drawings/illustrations: STANTEC/STACK Design, Boston, Massachusetts
6.2.1–6.2.2	Photos: Zeppelin Mobile Systems, Germany
6.2.4, 6.2.5	Photos: Zeppelin Mobile Systems, Germany
6.3.1–6.3.3	Photos: Courtesy Ganny Gozaly, Photography
6.3.4a–c	Drawings: Courtesy dpavilion Architects, Surabaya, Indonesia
6.3.5, 6.3.6	Photos: Courtesy Ganny Gozaly, Photography
6.4.1–6.4.3a–d	Photos: Courtesy BLU-MED Response Systems/Alaska Structures, Kirkland, Washington
6.4.5a–l, 6.4.6	Photos: BLU-MED Response Systems/Alaska Structures, Kirkland, Washington
6.5.1a–e–6.5.5	Photos/drawings: Quickspace, Ltd, Tokyo, Japan
6.6.1	Photo: Capital Health Edmonton Area/Alberta Health Services, Edmonton, Alberta, Canada
6.6.3a–l, 6.6.4a–j	Photos: Courtesy Capital Health Edmonton Area/Alberta Health Services, Edmonton, Alberta, Canada
6.7.1, 6.7.2	Photos: United States Army/Weatherhaven-North America
6.8.1a–d–6.8.7	Photos/drawings: Advanced Mobile Hospital Systems, Inc., Boulder, Colorado
6.9.1–6.9.6	Illustrations/drawings: Hord Coplan Macht Architects, Baltimore, Maryland
6.10.1–6.10.7	Illustrations/drawings: Jeff Gard/jag architecture, San Francisco, California
6.11.1a–d–6.11.2a–c	Photos: Toronto Rehabilitation Institute/iDAPT Centre, Toronto, Ontario, Canada

6.11.5a–d	Model photos: Toronto Rehabilitation Institute/ iDAPT Centre, Toronto, Ontario, Canada
6.12.1–6.12.6	Drawing: PmMt Arquitectura, Barcelona, Spain. Photos: Courtesy Sebastian Crespo, Fotografia, Spain
6.13.1–6.13.7	Drawings/Photos: Courtesy Perkins+Will, Seattle, Washington and Whitley Manufacturing Corp./ Modular Builders, Rochester, Indiana
6.14.1	Drawing: NBBJ, Seattle, Washington
6.14.2, 6.14.3	Photos: Courtesy Benjamin Benschneider Photography, Seattle, Washington
6.14.4a–b–6.14.6a–h	Drawings: NBBJ, Seattle, Washington
6.14.7–6.14.9	Photos: Courtesy Benjamin Benschneider Photography, Seattle, Washington
6.15.1–6.15.4	Drawing/illustrations: Gregory Swindon, South Carolina
6.15.6a–c	Drawings/illustration: Gregory Swindon, South Carolina
6.16.1–6.16.8a–c	Drawings/illustrations: George Hughes, Washington, D.C.
6.17.1–6.17.5a–b	Drawings/illustrations: Ryan Ramsey, Atlanta, Georgia
6.17.6	Illustration: Ryan Ramsey/Timothy Boll
6.17.7	Illustration: Ryan Ramsey, Atlanta, Georgia
6.18.1–6.18.2	Illustrations: Michael Bardin/Perkins+Will, San Francisco

APPENDICES

A1–A3	Photos/drawings: Stephen Verderber/Clemson University Team 899

Endpaper photo: RTC Installation: Stephen Verderber and Tim Boll

Note: Chapters 5 and 6 drawings/illustrations provided by Stephen Verderber: 5.1–5.5, 5.7, 5.8a–b, 5.10, 5.11, 5.14–5.18, 5.21a–b, 5.22–5.24, 5.27, 5.30. 5.31, 5.33a-c, 5.34–5.40, 6.1.7, 6.2.3, 6.2.6, 6.4.4, 6.4.7, 6.5.6a–b, 6.6.2, 6.6.5, 6.7.3–6.7.7, 6.11.3a–b, 6.11.4a–c, 6.15.5a–b, 6.18.3–6.18.5.

Preface

This book would not have been written were it not for Hurricane Katrina. Katrina struck New Orleans and the Mississippi Gulf Coast on 29 August 2005. A massive wall of water surged inland, destroying entire coastal communities. My wife, two children, and I evacuated our home in New Orleans at sunrise on Sunday 28 August. The previous night, we raced about the house in the dead of night to move our belongings out of harm's way, because a portion of our home, circa 1920, was an on-slab addition built in the mid-1950s. The four of us packed everything we could fit into our SUV and began our fifteen-hour, epic road trip westward to Houston. We packed clothing and all we could, including two laptops and a guitar. Under normal circumstances, it would have been a six-hour car trip. But as one of many thousands of vehicles all headed in the same direction, we were forced to slowly thread our way through a labyrinth of reverse-flow lanes, then were redirected through the rural countryside then back onto the Interstate. We were lucky to have booked in advance a hotel room in Houston. When we arrived there that Sunday evening we felt a mixture of relief and despair. Tens of thousands of other New Orleanians arrived in Texas that night.

The next day was uneventful. We assumed we would be returning home in no time. But by the early hours of Tuesday morning, as I lay in bed watching the cable news, I got the first glimpse of how our lives were to be radically upended. A news report from a hospital in downtown New Orleans showed a nurse who was asking the reporter on camera why the basement and parts of the first floor of her hospital were filling with water. Since it was still the dead of night, no confirmatory recognizance was possible until dawn. An unfolding catastrophe was revealed to us and to the world. New Orleans, much of which sits below sea level, was rapidly filling up with water pouring in from Lake Pontchartrain, which sits directly to the north of the city and is connected to the Gulf of Mexico. The hurricane's tidal surge swelled the lake to the point where the manmade levee system built by the U.S. Corps of Engineers began to fall apart. In all, the levees collapsed in twenty-three places, flooding 80 percent of Orleans Parish, all of St. Bernard Parish immediately to the east of the city, and portions of Jefferson Parish to the west. All eyes were transfixed on the TV screen for hours on end. The worst had happened.

We would not return to our home for nearly four months.

In the days after, times were rough. We owned a vehicle with gasoline in the tank, so we were among the fortunate. More than a million people fled to points near and far, with more than 250,000 evacuees obtaining refuge in Texas that first week. What came of those who lacked transportation, left stranded in the city, or those too stubborn to leave? On the world's stage, they were forced to fend for themselves. The Louisiana Superdome stadium became, by default, the city emergency shelter, although no plans had been made prior regarding any such designation. It was a makeshift operation. Without power, running water or food inside the cavernous stadium the conditions descended into chaos. The intense wind had ripped off a major portion of the stadium roof, allowing a large slice of daylight to bathe part of the football field. With the city in shambles and nowhere to turn for aid, stranded residents soon turned to the nearby Morial Convention Center as a place of last refuge.

I returned to the city in a first response role for the first time eight days after the levees broke. Tulane University, where I had been on the faculty for twenty years, was hit hard and the university would be closed for four months. The faculty and students were strewn about like fallen leaves across the continent. The cell phone system, and my University email account, vanished. I had been able to return to the nearly destroyed city only because of my continuing role as the lead-consulting architect with the State of Louisiana Department of Health and Hospital's Office of Public Health (DHH-OPH). Right after the storm, I was charged with conducting the damage assessment of every damaged DHH-OPH clinic in the disaster strike zone. Many had sustained significant damage (two weeks later the list of damaged clinics grew longer, in the aftermath of Hurricane Rita). The agency's administrative and main laboratory building in downtown New Orleans sustained sixteen feet of floodwater in its basement. I worked in consort with Federal Emergency Management Agency (FEMA) personnel as I completed damage assessment reports over the next two months. For each impacted clinic, a laborious FEMA report was required. Until the end of December I shuttled faithfully between New Orleans, Baton Rouge, and Austin, Texas. In Austin, we had rented a house so our children could attend school there through the fall 2005 term.

One morning, in the second week after the levees so spectacularly failed, I received a call from the DHH-OPH medical director. He needed to meet with me ASAP at the temporary Katrina morgue that had been quickly set up. There, the decreased were identified and 'processed': this was where most of the 1,800 persons who died in Katrina were taken. The DHH-OPH team was working alongside FEMA personnel in overcrowded FEMA travel trailers. These were but two units from the armada of 94,000 now-infamous, flimsy, toxic structures the federal government brought into the disaster zone to serve as disaster relief housing. The temperature in these flimsy, poorly insulated trailers was soaring by mid-afternoon. Working conditions were unbearable. The laptops were malfunctioning. It was hot and humid inside. What could I do? This godforsaken place was in the middle of nowhere. It was in fact eight miles south of Baton Rouge, a remote stretch on the River Road. As I drove into the dust-bowl parking lot it was impossible to not stare at the long row of eighteen-wheeler refrigeration trailers, one after another. Each was filled with corpses transported from New Orleans.

A large tent had been set up next to a large prefab metal farm structure with open sides. Corpses were being examined in this tent and under the metal shed, in open-air conditions. It was a crude operation by any standards. Could this be the United States in the twenty-first century? It all seemed so surreal. Was this really happening? I diagnosed one way to solve their problem—double the air conditioning capacity in these trailers and try to make the most of any natural ventilation possibilities. Some weeks later FEMA would erect a much larger, enclosed, prefab morgue, in Carville, a bit farther down the same road. That place cost $17 million to construct and featured a full decontamination unit and enough space to examine up to 150 bodies a day. It also provided living accommodations for up to 500 FEMA workers at once. One thing became clear from this: the mere construction of this center was proof that FEMA believed if a Katrina could happen once it could happen again. This center's capacity was decided in the days immediately after the storm when it was thought the death total might rise to over 5,000. This offsite prefab morgue was 70,000 total square feet (6,500 meters). It housed the new morgue, a supply and equipment warehouse, and a large office area filled with (unoccupied) cubicles. It had a large cafeteria, and even a physical fitness center! When it shut down in February 2006 all equipment used in the disaster response operation was placed in storage there, presumably, in anticipation of the next disaster. This FEMA morgue was documented in a February 2006 article in *The New York Times* by Shaila Dewan ('Morgue for Katrina Shuts Down').

It was a life altering experience. Being in the midst of it all as a first responder architect was unreal. The scope of this disaster had overwhelmed the public's ability to grasp what had really happened. At all levels, the governmental response had been a failure to that point (and beyond). Pre-planning protocols were proven woefully poor. What was happening around me stood as a textbook case for the need for a vastly more intelligent disaster mitigation planning process—including the failure of architecture. How could architecture, and architects, help? In the future, first response must center on being able to quickly deploy infirmaries and clinics where most needed immediately *after the event*, and for appropriate readiness staging *before the event*. I felt helpless. Architects could have done far better, I reasoned, had they been better educated and professionally predisposed to do so prior to a disaster of this magnitude.

In normal everyday circumstances, the healthcare needs of medically underserved populations call out for the interventional role of architecture. But in the aftermath of global disasters, often, tens of thousands of sick and injured victims are in urgent need of emergency medical care. This was certainly the case after Hurricane Katrina and this holds equally true in virulent infectious disease pandemics such as Ebola. Stationary hospitals are essential. But after a disaster the local hospitals may all be knocked out of commission. These institutions, for their part, must do far better from a disaster mitigation standpoint. But this continuing problem is not the main focus of this book. Traditional brick and mortar hospitals in disaster strike zones often themselves become victims of the disaster. And when these institutions go down, a second disaster is triggered. In Katrina, the hospitals in New Orleans and on the Mississippi Gulf Coast became dysfunctional. Their dedicated staff personnel remained "onboard" although the facilities themselves were overwhelmed by events that became, inexplicably, uncontrollable. Simply put, they lacked resiliency.

What to do? This book came from my very personal, and my professional, experience in coping with disaster. In Chapter 1, the fundamental thesis is presented and the discussion concludes with a typology of portable, offsite prefabricated structures for health. This typology is examined further in relation to disaster mitigation theory and practice. It seeks to address the needs of the medically underserved worldwide. In Chapter 2, a brief modern history of portable structures for health is presented, tracing the portable field hospital from its roots in the ancient yurt and tipi to high tech lightweight mobile buildings for health. From the Industrial Revolution to the current Information Revolution, key advancements have been driven by the necessities of war. This stems from the pioneering work of Florence Nightingale and military physicians who argued for the recuperative effects of fresh air for the recovering patient. With each military conflict, advancements in medicine and nursing care became directly expressed in the design and appearance of field hospitals, train infirmaries, and mobile vehicular clinics.

In Chapter 3, the focus shifts to offsite prefabricated buildings and components that are then transited to a permanent installation site, elsewhere. The first modern prefabricated hospital was constructed at Renkioi during the Crimean War in the 1850s. Since then, architects have been remarkably slow to embrace the merits of prefab modularity in the arena of healthcare. The unfortunate twentieth-century legacy of architects' repeated failure to effectively utilize offsite technology is discussed in this chapter. Recently, the situation has begun to change somewhat, within the global construction industry. Two recent U.S. healthcare case studies are examined in some detail, against the backdrop of Kieran and Timberlake's recent call for architects to become more committed to extending the reach and exploring the aesthetic possibilities of offsite prefab modularity.

In Chapter 4, the growing popularity of pop-up installations provides a backdrop to explore their applicability in the provision of mobile healthcare in both everyday routine circumstances and in the aftermath of disaster. Case studies and research carried out in two historic American cities, New Orleans, and Charleston, South Carolina, are reported. Both cities are located on large bodies of water and both are threatened annually by intense hurricanes and the slow but inexorable rise of the world's oceans. Both cities also happen to have colonial histories, and a large inventory of historic buildings and neighborhoods that are prime for this type of intervention.

In Chapter 5, a compendium of eighty planning and design considerations are presented on the subject of prefab modularity for mobile healthcare. The goal is to articulate central aesthetic, functional, tectonic, and socio-cultural aspects of offsite portable modular structures and their component systems for health. These considerations are structured into seven categories: (1) site and context; (2) transiting and commissioning; (3) arrival and semi-public spaces; (4) diagnostic and treatment functions; (5) pop-up clinics; (6) facility tectonics; and (7) administration/total environment. This set of considerations is viewed in relation to the typology presented in the first chapter. In the concluding chapter, Chapter 6, eighteen case studies of portable structures for health are presented. The architectural typology presented in Chapter 1 is reprised here again in relation to these case studies: (1) modular and containerized systems; (2) panelized and tent-based systems; (3) vehicular and guided systems; (4) prefab hospitals and clinics; and (5) RTC prognostications. A two-part Appendix section follows this chapter. Part 1 of the Appendix consists of additional case study pop-up clinic sites not reported in detail in Chapter 4. Part 2 consists of a series of interviews conducted with individuals who represent four key facets of the book's overarching narrative, particularly with regards to the future of this important, emerging area of interdisciplinary research and professional practice.

Thanks to Clemson University for its unwavering support of my teaching and research activities during the 2007–2013 period, after I departed Tulane University and New Orleans. I had taught at Tulane since 1985. Kate Schwennsen, Chair of the School of Architecture at Clemson, provided essential financial support for this project from its inception. I am equally indebted to the contributions of my trusted research assistants in Clemson's Graduate Program in Architecture + Health, Robert J. Schultz, Josh Boltinghouse, George Hughes, Ryan Ramsey, Kimberly Bandy, and Josh Domingo, and to all the members of Team 899, Scott Abernathy, Ashley Colquhoun, Valerie Or, Julie Randolph, Ervin Jose Riefkohl, and Yanwen Xiao.

In 2013, I relocated to the University of Toronto. In Toronto, I am indebted to Dean Richard Sommer for his support of the further development of this book and its completion. Invaluable support has been provided by my U of T lead Research Assistant, Timothy Boll, who has provided strong assistance, and to Jina S. Lee, Jasper Flores, Terri Peters, Samira Daneshvar and Meaghan Burke for their contributions. The seeds for this book have been ten years in the making. I am indebted to Gary T. Moore, my first mentor, who is now Professor Emeritus at the University of Sydney, to Robert Kronenburg, for his important research and writings on portable architecture, and Christopher Alexander, for his influence on my research, scholarship, and professional practice work. This book is for the architect, industrial designer, systems engineer, and the builder. It is for health policy specialists, elected officials, private humanitarian organizations, philanthropic organizations, emergency operations center teams, and disaster mitigation professionals. But it is especially for every physician, nurse, technician, and everyone else who devotes his or her time and energy, often in extremely difficult working circumstances, to meet the needs of the medically underserved, and the victims of disaster, worldwide.

The United States Senate would drag its feet until 2015, ten years after Hurricane Katrina, to acknowledge that climate change is real, bringing it up to speed with every major world scientific body (yet, quixotically, it declined to acknowledge that human activity plays any role). Against this, this book's publication, ten years after Katrina, is most befitting.

Stephen Verderber
TORONTO
2015

PART 1

Background

Introduction

CHAPTER 1

A recent Home Box Office (HBO) cable TV series set in south Louisiana provides insight as to how things get done in Louisiana. Parallels have been drawn between this series, *True Detective*, and a twentieth-century cosmic-horror tradition in literature that dates from H.P. Lovecraft's pulp fiction classic 'The Call of Cthulhu,' first published in 1926. Lovecraft's short story strongly influenced this series, as well as the tale of a surreal fictional northwestern backwoods Louisiana swamp-town, Bon Temps, depicted in another recent HBO series, *True Blood* (2008–2014).[1] In both series, this literary genre is interestingly entwined with Louisiana's quasi-surreal physical and cultural landscape. The characters accept as a *fait accompli* the disappearance of Louisiana's coast, the pollution that belches from its oil refineries, and the stark geography of its rural parishes along the Mississippi River, hemmed in by continuous, massive levees along its banks. Long prior to Hurricane Katrina in 2005, New Orleans and its surrounding region had captured the imagination of a broad swath of America. It was, and remains, a poetically dilapidated region fixated by the threat of the really Big One hitting someday, the effects of drastic land loss that has resulted from nearly a century of oil and gas drilling throughout its delicate wetlands, and the effects of pervasive subsidence, in large part attributable to the Mississippi Delta's spongy soil, not to mention the effects of global sea level rise.[2]

In Katrina's aftermath, the city, and outlying areas hit hardest looked and felt like virtual war zones.[3] In that first week, a pair of medical aid tents appeared in the parking roof deck of the Louisiana Superdome.[4] Adequate levels of supplies and federal troops would not reach the city for *five days* after the federally-built levees collapsed. Suffice to say, the governmental response at the local, regional, state, and federal levels was pathetic.[5] Federal and state agencies worked tirelessly alongside non-governmental organizations (NGOs) to assist those who had been unable to evacuate, while struggling to provide basic living resources to the trickle of refugees now starting to return to the few remaining non-flooded parts of the city. These were the neighborhoods situated nearest the Mississippi River—the narrow strip that, since Katrina, has become widely known as the 'Sliver by the River'.[6] The *American Red Cross* somewhat belatedly re-entered the city and by October was operating a number of relief centers across the strike zone.[7] These aid stations consisted of one truck and a portable tent, dispensing basic supplies such as infant diapers, mops, buckets, gloves, and facemasks to protect from the insidious mold that permeated the hot, humid air.

In time, most of these neighborhood relief centers were shut down, beginning with those in the most functioning parts of the city. The American Red Cross continued to provide meals although at a far reduced scale and into 2006. The USNS *Comfort* hospital naval ship was dispatched to New Orleans three days after the flood. Starting in Pascagoula, Mississippi and then sailing into New Orleans, the *Comfort* treated 1,956 patients in all before returning to its homeport at the conclusion of its seven-week deployment.[8] Federal, state, and local disaster planning had lacked a functional strategy to keep the local hospitals functioning. In Katrina's wake, the city's hospitals, lacking electricity, potable water, sewerage services, and gas, were virtually severed from any form of first response aid efforts.[9] It was by now crystal clear the entire disaster response healthcare system in the United States warranted a thorough reappraisal from top to bottom, and back.[10] Without adequate infrastructural support, it was impossible to provide any reasonable standard of care for the sickest of the sick—without even emergency power generation to operate the ventilators, bedside monitors, or kidney dialysis machines.[11]

At Memorial Medical Center in Uptown New Orleans, the scene became gruesome:

> The smell of death was overpowering the moment the relief worker cracked open one of the hospital chapel's wooden doors. Inside, more than a dozen bodies lay motionless on low cots and on the ground, shrouded in white sheets. Here, a wisp of grey hair peeked out. There, a knee was flung akimbo. A pallid hand reached across a blue gown. Within days, this grisly tableau became the focus of an investigation into what happened when the floodwaters of Hurricane Katrina marooned Memorial Medical Center in Uptown New Orleans. The hurricane knocked out power and running water and sent the temperature inside to well above 100 degrees. Still, investigators were surprised at the number of bodies in the makeshift morgue and were stunned when healthcare workers charged that a well-regarded doctor and two respected nurses had hastened the deaths of patients by injecting them with lethal doses of drugs. Mortuary workers eventually carried forty-five corpses from Memorial… the physician, Anna Pou, defended herself on national television, saying that her role was to 'help' patients through their pain.[12]

At St. Rita's nursing home in St. Bernard Parish, thirty-five aged residents drowned in their beds as Katrina's floodwaters burst through the levees, filing up the one-level nursing facility nearly to the ceiling, within no more than twenty minutes. Of the five nursing homes in St. Bernard Parish, St. Rita's was the only one that had not been evacuated *a priori*.[13] Sadly, no evacuation plan was in place, prior. Interestingly, the owners of this nursing home were found *not guilty* of negligent homicide.[14] Every hospital in the city experienced major security breaches as scavengers raided what was left of supplies and pharmaceuticals.[15] Offers of volunteer assistance came in from throughout North America in the storm's aftermath, from academic medical centers, the Medical Reserve Corps, professional medical associations, hospitals, trauma care teams, and from private individuals. Unfortunately, and shockingly, there existed no single federal database with the ability to register, track, or manage the many hundreds of medical volunteers who came (or had hoped to come) to the Gulf Coast to help, and as a result many physicians and nurses were turned away.[16] Medical centers outside the strike zone did have resources that might have helped in New Orleans and the Gulf Coast, but they too became ensnarled in intractable red tape. This was made all the worse by antiquated Louisiana laws.[17]

The response of Louisiana State University (LSU) stood out in stark contrast to the ineptitude playing out in New Orleans, with LSU successfully setting up an ad hoc field hospital in the Pete Maravich Assembly Center in Baton Rouge within hours of the levee breaches.[18] The sports arena became the site of the largest civilian-run, ad hoc, field hospital ever on U.S. soil following a disaster. It housed 800 cots and was staffed by over 1,700 volunteer medical and non-medical personnel. More than 6,000 patients were treated, or were housed overnight, and many students, university staff, and locals volunteered to assist evacuees by donating their time, houses, and apartments to the evacuees.[19] The city and region had been caught totally unprepared, especially from a healthcare facility standpoint. To this author, one thing was now clear: the future must not be anything like the past—not here, not anywhere.

A changing planet

The *Intergovernmental Panel on Climate Change* (IPCC) is a scientific, multinational body, working under the auspices of the

United Nations (UN). It was established in 1988 by two UN organizations, the World Meteorological Organization, and the UN Environment Program. The IPCC has produced five reports in support of the UN Framework Convention on Climate Change (UNFCCC), which functions as the main international treaty on the subject of global climate change. The aim of the UNFCCC is to stabilize greenhouse gas concentrations in the atmosphere at a level that would prevent dangerous anthropogenic, i.e. human-induced, interference with the earth's natural climatic systems.[20] The IPCC does not carry out its own research but instead bases its assessments on the published scientific literature, which includes peer-reviewed and certain non-peer-reviewed sources. Thousands of scientists and other experts contribute on a voluntary basis to its reports.[21] Each IPCC report contains a 'Summary for Policymakers,' which is subject to line-by-line approval by the delegates from all participating governmental jurisdictions and this rigorous protocol typically involves a total of 120 countries. The IPCC has become the preeminent internationally respected authority on global climate change, its causes, and its present and future directions and for this, in 2007, it garnered a share of the Nobel Peace Prize.

Its fifth assessment report was published in October 2014. More than 800 authors, selected from a pool of more than 3,000, were involved in its laborious writing and editing. Findings include the following: the warming of the global climate system is unequivocal, and since the 1950s many of the now-observed changes have been near unprecedented in history. Atmospheric concentrations of carbon dioxide, methane, and nitrous oxide have increased to levels higher than at any time in the past 800,000 years.[22] Human influence on the climate is an incontrovertible fact and it is a 95–100 percent probability that human influence was the dominant cause of global warming between 1951 and 2010. Many of the ills of the modern world—starvation, poverty, flooding, heat waves, droughts, war, and disease—are likely to worsen as the world warms from its human-induced climate alterations. The word 'exacerbates' was used repeatedly in the 2014 assessment report to describe climate change's effects on poverty, drought and accordant diminishing water supplies, the rise and spread of infectious disease pandemics, and even as a cause of intensified military conflict, such as water wars.[23]

Without new policies to mitigate vast changes underway, current scientific projections suggest an increase in global mean temperature by 2100 of 3.7 to 4.8 degrees Celsius, relative to pre-industrial (pre-1850) levels.[24] The 2014 report anticipates that throughout the twenty-first century, climate change impacts will exacerbate global desertification, and hence, serve to begin to dangerously erode food supplies, resulting in further magnified socio-economic inequalities. Key risks include an increasing number of deaths occurring from atmospheric warming, combined with sea level rise and attendant coastal flooding, especially in large metro areas situated on coasts and other vulnerable bodies of water. With an increase in famine in developing nations, infrastructure failures will mount because of the effects of various types of extreme weather events. Heat waves will become commonplace and marine ecosystems will be subject to total extinction.[25]

The collapse of large parts of the Antarctica ice sheet is well underway. This assessment, feared by some scientists for decades, could portend a rise in global sea levels of as much as ten feet over a period of many decades.[26] While this will occur gradually over the coming century, in time, it will reach a crisis level. The continued release of greenhouse gases will likely further destabilize the Greenland ice sheet as well.[27] By 2014, it had become clear the rate of Upper Ocean warming had been grossly underestimated.[28] The World Bank estimated that natural disasters had cost a total of $3.8 trillion since 1980.[29] The consequences of coastal flooding will cost coastal cities $60 billion per year by 2050 if current patterns are not mitigated or reversed. Of these projected losses, $52 billion will have been the result of continued unchecked sheer population growth. As much as 80 percent of the world's population will reside along coastlines by 2050. The remaining $8–$11 billion in required mitigation expenditures will have been directly attributable to a perverse trifecta of global sea level rise, coastal land subsidence, and intensified land use, i.e. overdevelopment, within coastal regions.[30]

Global climate change is redefining the rhythms of everyday life for tens of millions. Highly developed and developing societies alike are now experiencing the beginning of the massive changes ahead.[31] In Bangladesh in 2011, for instance, more than 60,000 internally displaced persons (IDPs, a United Nations designation) became homeless due to the rising sea and inland flooding decimating the region's healthcare infrastructure.[32] The number of global natural disasters reported each year rose steadily in the 1970–2004 period from 78 to 348.[33] Communities are now realizing they will need to learn to adapt to minimize the health-related consequences of these changes.[34] In 2013, 89 percent of the world's natural disaster victims were from Asia, and China alone represented 67 percent of all disaster victims worldwide. By contrast, North and South America, combined with Europe, accounted for only 6 percent of total disaster victims, worldwide.[35] Major disasters of the past decade include:

Hurricane Katrina (2005)—Katrina stands as the costliest American natural disaster, to date, and one of the five deadliest hurricanes in the whole history of the nation. It inflicted the loss of 1,837 lives due, as mentioned, to massive flooding of the New Orleans metro area and along the Gulf Coast. This storm incurred more than $200 billion in property damages.[36] Among recorded Atlantic hurricanes, it was sixth strongest in history. Most of the deaths occurred in New Orleans, due to the previously mentioned failure of the city's rag-tag levee system.[37] Large tracts of neighboring St. Bernard Parish, St. Tammany Parish, and Plaquemines Parish also experienced massive flooding. The toxic floodwaters lingered for weeks in the city of New Orleans due to being hemmed in by the ring of levees and floodwalls that surround the city proper. The military, and American Red Cross tent infirmaries, and the USNS *Comfort* hospital ship had a significant positive impact, but this was still not enough. This discussion is further referenced in Chapters 4 and 5.[38]

Haitian earthquake (2010)—This earthquake happened in January of that year, and was a catastrophic magnitude 7.0 event. Its epicenter was near the town of Léogâne, approximately sixteen miles (25 km) west of Port-au-Prince, Haiti's capital city. An estimated three million people were impacted by the quake, with 316,000 lives lost, 300,000 injured, and more than one million persons instantly becoming homeless IDPs.[39] The Haitian government estimated that 250,000 residences and 30,000 commercial buildings collapsed or were severely damaged. Overnight, tent cities sprang up, inhabited by the zombie-like victims. These encampments soon appeared virtually everywhere in the days and weeks following the catastrophe. Golf courses, vacant lots, parking lots—in short, anywhere with existing open space—were commandeered for conversion into makeshift encampments.[40] These parcels ranged in size from being able to house a few dozen families to thousands of families, tightly packed together in thoroughly inhumane, unhealthful conditions.

One of the hundreds of encampments was set up in Corail, eight miles north of the center of Port-au-Prince. Within days, thousands of skeptical refugees would agree to relocate to this desolate, remote place. In addition, the UN deployed a dozen portable field hospitals to the strike zone, and the USNS *Comfort* soon arrived in Port-au-Prince.[41] The government of Israel deployed one of its portable hospitals, its Israeli Defense Forces Medical Corps (IDF-MC) Field Hospital.[42] This facility treated a total of 1,100 quake victims, conducted 319 surgeries, delivered sixteen births, and its search and rescue operation recovered many victims from the rubble.[43] The local healthcare network was completely broken, and the assistance provided by this network of portable medical facilities, and the *Comfort* ship, made a significant difference.[44] Beyond this, donor major nations such as the United States, which donated $10 billion to the Haitian rebuilding effort, began to harbor deep fears of widespread corruption occurring at the local level, and this remains a major impediment in the rebuilding process, to this day.[45] In the throes of chaos in post-earthquake Haiti, it was mainly about just trying to do *something, anything*:

> They [in reference to portable emergency first aid stations] never seem to be where they are needed. The call comes through, 'We need a 40-bed unit ASAP—Emergency!' Lining up the trucks and drivers is enough of a challenge. When they arrive, the drivers all want to be paid up front or else they will feel free to pilfer food and whatever behind your back. The black market for supplies and food rations is tremendously robust, as one might imagine. This can happen on the front end. Along the route, pilfering continues. Who is in charge of security? The military? Volunteers? Some disaster relief agencies employ their own mercenary 'police'—excuse me—security teams, to accompany these transports.[46]

But these so-called security specialists may be supercilious, themselves succumbing to the temptations of the black market. And things often can get worse as the units get closer to their destination. Supplies can be dragged off of flatbed trucks, broken into and ransacked for any items perceived of value. Some transporters even desert their convoy en route to its destination. This happened in the days and weeks following the Haitian earthquake. Armed gangs waited patiently on the roadsides to spring their attacks at the most opportune moment, usually under cover of darkness. Some airlifted shipments were intercepted right at the airstrip, or from ad hoc holding warehouses set up post-haste at the airport and its immediate environs. It can be a staggering logistical challenge, obviously, to get things to where they need to be after an entire regional infrastructure has collapsed in a matter of minutes.

BP Deepwater Horizon (2010)—Late in the evening of 20 April, a massive explosion occurred in the Gulf of Mexico sixty miles off the coast of Louisiana. An immense ball of fire erupted high into the clear night sky, as eleven men lost their lives. An over-budget, problem-plagued deep water oil exploration platform had imploded and with it the limitations of extreme engineering technology were laid bare for the entire world to witness, as a massive oil rig fell 5,000 feet to the ocean floor where it lay in ruins.[47] For three months thereafter its ruptured wellbore continued to spew more than 200 million barrels of crude oil directly into the ocean on a 24/7 basis. The unprecedented damage inflicted upon this coastal region's delicate aquatic ecosystems, its seafood industry, tourism, and the lives of the residents in the communities directly impacted garnered extensive global media attention, and intense scrutiny by international environmental advocacy organizations such as Greenpeace and the Ocean Conservancy. Caught completely unprepared, so-called governmental 'oversight agencies' with supposed regulatory legal and planning oversight failed completely.[48] Tens of thousands of toxic tar balls washed up on the beaches across the disaster strike zone, a zone that stretched many hundreds of miles along the coastline to the east and west of the disaster site.[49]

Tohoku earthquake and tsunami (2011)—This earthquake occurred off the Pacific coast of Tohoku Prefecture, and was a magnitude 9.0 undersea mega thrust event. It was the most powerful known earthquake to have ever hit Japan, and one of the five most powerful earthquakes in the world, overall, since modern record keeping began in 1900.[50] It triggered powerful tsunami waves reaching heights of 40.5 meters in Iwate Prefecture, and these forcefully traveled six miles (10 km) inland throughout the Sendai Region. The NHK News Service in Japan reported that in addition to the loss of 15,800 lives, 5,900 injuries, 3,600 missing persons, and the total destruction of 45,000 buildings, damage to an additional 144,000 buildings, and massive destruction of infrastructural amenities, the tsunami itself inflicted multiple major nuclear reactor accidents. These accidents centered around an ongoing Level-7 meltdown occurring at three reactors within the Fukushima 1 Nuclear Power Plant complex, uprooting the lives of 300,000 persons due to the mandatory evacuation. With remediation and reconstruction exceeding $300 billion this is, at this writing, the costliest global disaster ever.[51]

Typhoon Haiyan (2013)—Known in the Philippines as Typhoon Yolanda, this was one of the fiercest Category-5 tropical cyclones on record, devastating portions of Southeast Asia and particularly the Philippines, in November that year. The typhoon killed more than 6,300 people there, alone. Haiyan was the strongest storm ever recorded at landfall there, with peak winds clocking at 160 miles per hour (250 kilometers per hour).[52] In its wake, the scope of the damage was jaw dropping.[53] The worst-hit places included Tacloban on the island of Leyte, where more than 600,000 became homeless. NGOs from around the world struggled to airlift food and medical supplies into the country while villagers, now homeless, lined the roadsides in search of food, clothing, and shelter.[54] In Tacloban, the situation soon became desperate. One NGO aid worker described it as 'worse than hell.' A week after the storm, aid slowly began to trickle in. Each morning, thousands would trek to the destroyed airport in search of anything, or a chance to get out. Most returned with nothing. Meanwhile, typhoid, cholera, and hepatitis outbreaks were taking root in the community.[55]

Reports came in of relief aid warehouses being ransacked by armed gangs alongside desperately hungry people, seeking anything. First response teams struggled to set up portable field clinics and hospitals. Even boats were used for this purpose, as these could travel from island to island as emergency first aid needs dictated. A field hospital was set up by the *Canadian Red Cross* next door to the darkened Ormoc District Hospital—the only public hospital that existed for a city of 190,000, prior to the storm. The Red Cross facility, staffed by a team of twenty-eight, was erected within forty-eight hours and immediately became a hub of activity.[56] Australia also deployed one of its portable field hospitals, marking the first time an Australian civilian response team ever conducted surgery in a field setting such as this. A team of thirty-seven treated fractured spines, those who had lost all sensation in their lower extremities, victims of skull fractures and many other types of extensive, penetrating injuries.

The ferocious wind field itself caused many injuries. Children contracted severe gastro-intestinal infections, and diarrhea, from drinking tainted water.[57] Telecommunication towers crumpled to the ground like toothpicks and the survivors' stories were absolutely gut wrenching. Nearly everyone in Tacloban lost one or more family members. The local agricultural industry was destroyed just before high harvest season. The winds snapped off almost every coconut palm, a major source of sustenance for so many. Coconuts, a main source of food, fiber, and charcoal, became airborne weaponry. One stretcher in the Canadian field hospital held a young man, Junile Bueno, whose lower back had been severely broken by a wind-projectile coconut, leaving him paralyzed from the waist down.[58]

Portable tent infirmaries provided triage, decontamination, outpatient treatment tent(s) and surgical services for casualties requiring immediate treatment and each contained an autoclave for equipment sterilization. The Humanity Road/Animals in Disaster NGO published an online directory of every NGO that had set up field operations within the strike zone.[59] This online resource was updated on a continuous, daily basis in the weeks after the storm. It provided revealing insights as to the behind-the-scenes efforts of many organizations because it listed every mobile medical unit in operation and the medical services provided at each site.[60] Amid the widespread destruction, many asked why a region so prone to intense storms could have suffered this much yet again:

> Take Tacloban, where thousands got to a big indoor stadium that was (previously) considered stormproof. The specially reinforced roof stayed on but people were killed instead by a 16-foot (5-meter) high surge of water which flooded the structure…the surge was like a tsunami. Nobody seems to have foreseen that it could do so much damage…the Asian Development Bank, for one, believes the severity of disaster events has been increasing because of rising sea and air temperatures. Sea levels in the region have been rising. For cities such as Manila, the capital of the Philippines, the risks are grave since the city is also sinking due to the extraction of groundwater, thereby increasing the risk of lethal flooding…the rickety, decentralized and often corrupt Philippine political system does not help either…local corruption takes its slice out of centrally allocated disaster aid funds. The question is whether Filipinos will accept the political way of doing things…or not.[61]

This begs the question, how can architecture for health more meaningfully contribute to the strengthening of existing healthcare facility networks, particularly in the aftermath of disaster?

Resilience and architecture

In 1973, C.S. (Buzz) Holling first defined resilience as 'the measure of an engineered system's ability to rebound to its operational integrity after having sustained sudden shock.'[62] That was more than forty years ago. In the context of rapid response, system breakdown occurs when a disaster response system is pushed beyond its accepted, normative, performative metrics.[63] *Resiliency,* at present, is trending strongly across a spectrum of disciplines, including macroeconomics, psychiatry, robotics, the health sciences, military tactical planning, global public health, the engineering disciplines, urban and regional planning, disaster mitigation and risk management science.[64] And yet it remains a murky, strangely underappreciated proposition in architecture.[65] From a review of published papers in the ecological and social sciences, researchers at the University of Melbourne recently assembled a list of a dozen different definitions for the term resilience, reporting descriptors ranging from coping, recovering, adapting, withstanding, to self-organizing.[66] Psychiatrists use the term to denote a patient's mental diversity, flexibility, and rebounding strength relative to one's personality type, and neuro-psychological disorder.[67] Engineers compute an eigenvalue—a mathematical construct for measuring the long-term probability of a particular event occurring or reoccurring, such as when the routine vibration of a bridge might lead to its collapse.[68] As such, an eigenvalue is a normative measure of resilience in the engineering sciences.[69] In 2012, the U.S. *National Academy of Sciences* released a lengthy report on disaster mitigation and resiliency, defining the latter as 'the ability to prepare and plan for, absorb, recover from, and more successfully adapt to future adverse events.'[70]

These are at once exciting and disturbing times. The inequitable distribution of global wealth, and the ramifications of climate change, call for new conceptualizations.[71] Problems must be approached as profound, systemic, complex, and interconnected, rather than as stand-alone phenomena, and interdisciplinary approaches have become essential if discourses are to be broadened.[72] Discourses centered on sustainability are related to, but distinct from, discourses centered on resilience. The two are not synonymous. They do complement one another and function interchangeably. Nonetheless, it is more than a simplistic yin and yang tension. Sustainability, broadly defined, centers on conservation and carbon neutral resources and technologies. Resilience, broadly defined, is not about conservation, or attempting to maintain something as it always was in the past. Neither is it about recapturing any current or lost 'normal' condition and in fact its adherents are highly skeptical of this as a goal if for no other reason than this is viewed as overly simplistic.[73] The Internet is an interconnected global structure. It maintains a relative degree of internal resiliency even though it outwardly appears to remain, at times, only marginally capable of doing so. When under threat, its redundancy capabilities kick in, swarming, enabling bounce-back.[74]

How can architecture anticipate such unexpected *externalities*? What can be learned from ecological systems in this regard? Marine ecosystems have succeeded at this since the Permian Period dating 250–300 million years ago. And tropical rainforests generate complicated self-regenerative transactions among their billions of constituent 'parts' despite countless disruptions and shocks to their ecosystems. Applying any lessons from ecologically resilient systems to be found in nature first requires that we accept that they indeed possess modularized interconnectivity—a network structure that allows it all to be held together by means of a deep, resonant redundancy. This requires an ability to support highly diverse structures across multiple scales, and to self-adapt and self-reorganize.[75] As Zolli argues:

> In disciplines as seemingly disconnected as economics, ecology, political science, cognitive science, and digital networking, scientists, policymakers, technologists, corporate leaders, and activists alike are asking the same basic questions: What causes one system to break down and another to rebound? How much change can a system absorb and still retain its integrity and purpose? What characteristics make a system adaptive to change? In an age of constant disruption, how do we build in better shock absorbers for ourselves, our communities, companies, economies, societies, and the planet?[76]

Precise definitions become complicated because different fields use the term in different ways. In engineering, as mentioned, resilience denotes the degree to which a structure such as a bridge can return to its baseline state after a sudden, disruptive event. In emergency response systems, it is about the speed with which critical infrastructure can be restored and humanitarian aid made available. In ecological science, it denotes an ecosystem's ability to keep from being irrevocably degraded. In psychology, it denotes the capacity of an individual to cope effectively with personal trauma. Zolli and Healy's definition builds on Holling's, and centers on the capacity of a system, enterprise, or a person to maintain its core purpose and integrity in the face of dramatically altered circumstances.[77]

Resiliency in architecture is a process of adapting to changed circumstances while continuing to meet and surpass traditional functions within a hyper-accelerated culture. A resilient work of architecture may be designed and manufactured with built-in, self-sensing mechanisms, to anticipate when an abrupt dislocation is about to occur that threatens its operability.[78] This can pinpoint when trouble lies ahead and the provision of onboard early warning technologies is but one such strategy to increase bounce-back.[79] These mechanisms may lie in dormancy for periods, then spring back into action, not unlike antibodies in the bloodstream fighting to restore a compromised human immune system.

Effective first response calls for *modularity* so that its constituent parts can be reconfigured as necessary.[80] One example of this is an inflatable structure with multiple modules so if one or more modules fail, others will pick up the slack, ensuring continued operations. Zolli and Healy recount Herb Simon, the polymath psychologist, political scientist, economist, and computer scientist who demonstrated the virtues of modularity by means of a parable about two watchmakers:

> Hora and Tempus were both craftsmen who built watches of equal complexity and beauty, comprising hundreds of parts. Yet Hora's business flourished, while Tempus's business failed. The reason? Hora built his watches modularly, fitting individual components into hierarchical assemblies that could be snapped together to complete the whole. Tempus, on the other hand, simply built his watches piece by piece until each was completed. In Simon's parable, the watchmakers are occasionally interrupted by a phone call with more orders for watches. What that happens, they must restart the task they were doing prior to the interruption. As such, Tempus must begin each watch over and over again, while much of Hora's prior work is preserved…if both watchmakers are interrupted just one percent of the time, Hora will complete nine watches

for every ten he tries to build. Tempus, on the other hand, will finish just forty-four watches for every one million…simplicity and interoperability enables the components of many resilient systems to *flock* or *swarm* like starlings when the time is right and to break into islands when under duress. These are the very features that make cloud computing possible—in which groups of linked, redundant servers swarm together, scaling up and down to complete a given task, then disband… not unlike bacteria (colonies).[81]

A resilient architecture, not unlike an economy, employs strategies for self-detecting unwanted intrusions and then minimizing the damage, even if this requires isolating the damaged areas.[82] The system must be able to continue to operate in a reduced state, if necessary, in the wake of any breach.[83] Architecture, for its part, can be surprisingly fragile and rife with indeterminism, whereas a resilient architecture, like life itself, will at times be messy, yet it requires that it (like us) remain strong.[84]

Portable architecture for health as prosthetic support

In medicine, a prosthesis, from the ancient Greek *prósthesis,* meaning 'addition, application, or attachment,' is an artificial device that replaces a missing body part severed through trauma, disease, amputation, or having never developed due to a congenital condition. This last cause was viewed as an act of retribution by the gods on an offending parent. Across the millennia, those with severe injuries either succumbed to their wounds or were disposed of right on the battlefield in the face of the inevitable. It is believed that amputations were performed in Neolithic times, from evidence in saws fabricated of stone and bone, and in amputated bone stumps found in unearthed skeletal remains. The first recorded instance of amputations and prosthetic replacement devices appears in the books of the Vedas, written in Sanskrit, in India. The oldest of the Vedas is the Rig-Veda, compiled between 3,500 and 1,000 B.C. It records that the leg of a Queen Vispla was amputated in battle. Afterwards, an iron leg was fitted to enable the Queen to walk and return to the battlefield. The ancient Egyptians also fabricated sophisticated prosthetic devices.[85]

The earliest account of an artificial leg in the West dates from about 300 B.C. based on artifacts unearthed in Capua, Italy, in 1858. This artifact was fabricated of bronze and iron, with a wooden core, and was worn as a below-knee device.[86] Hippocrates and Herodotus had written of this practice in the fifth century B.C. in Greece. The latter wrote the tale of Hegesistratus, a Greek diviner who severed his own foot to escape his Spartan captors and then replaced it with a wooden one, in 424 B.C.[87] During the Renaissance, prosthetic devices advanced significantly with the incorporation of iron, steel, copper, and wood. Functional prosthetics first appeared in the sixteenth century. The great French surgeon, Ambroise Pare, designed prostheses for both the upper and lower limbs, techniques perfected thorough multiple surgical trials. The invention of Morel's tourniquet in 1674 permitted the control of hemorrhage, and during the Napoleonic Wars this new procedure was perfected further.

With the introduction of anesthesia in 1846, followed by Lister's breakthrough in antisepsis in the late eighteenth century, further advancements in prosthetics occurred.[88] In the U.S. the Department of Veterans Affairs (DVA) led the way in technological breakthroughs after World War II, and this continued through the Vietnam War and up to the present day.[89] Currently, robotic, high tech prosthetics such as artificial limbs, smart wheelchairs, and person-building interfaces in furnishings, smart-walls and stairs, and sensing lighting systems are fabricated in lightweight carbon fiber and extremely durable plastics, including the use of 3D printing technology. Besides being far lighter and flexible, these products are being revolutionized by microprocessors that enable an individual to bounce back to an acceptable 'new normal.'

A transportable structure, when considered as a prosthetic device and not as a traditional stick-built/brick and mortar building, shares many qualities with prosthetic devices worn by humans. Both consist of offsite-built, pre-manufactured modular componentry. Both must be lightweight, pliable, modular, portable, malleable, adaptable to change in the face of sudden and at times, blunt impacts, and capable of returning to a pre-impacted (or approximated) state in the face of a disruptive event. Both receiving entities (whether a person or an installation site) must maintain reasonable functionality even if one or more modular components (other limbs, or sections/parts of a portable modular structure) become disrupted or go offline for any reason. Both must maintain fluidity with an ability to interdependently function within a larger system (the human body/the building within its broader site context) and finally, both must remain operational in diverse conditions and climates.

Lightweight, advanced prosthetic devices for humans are being developed in research laboratories in many places.[90] If only the same could be said for their architectural counterparts. A recent exhibit at the National Building Museum in Washington, D.C., 'Designing for Disaster,' attempted to reflect current thinking in architecture and planning in relation to the need for resilient planning and architectural design strategies. This exhibit was presented in four organizing themes: Earth, Air, Fire, and Water. A design competition was sponsored in conjunction with the exhibit (although only ten schemes were submitted) on the topic of designing a more resilient New York/New Jersey coastline. Inexplicably, these submittals were left out of the exhibit. The final section was a pantry equipped with emergency supplies such as plastic sheathing, duct tape, and sunblock lotion! This was a missed opportunity to address more substantial themes to say the least. It all came off as superficial while more profound aspects of life and death within disaster-stricken communities remained unaddressed and, strangest of all, only indirect reference was made to global climate change itself as a determinant.[91] Modularized portable structures for health cry out for inventive planning, programming, design, manufacture, materiality, packing, transiting, and assembly innovations. Architecture, as a discipline, lags in this regard.

Museum exhibits are one thing. But what of the salient, underlying forces that can yield a truly resilient, prosthetic architecture of first response? The success of any building, portable or otherwise, is ultimately to be judged by its connectivity with a place and its people, and significance within broader societal and environmental spheres. Here, connectivity denotes the building's role and function as a prosthetic device—*as a non-rooted, flexive, moveable intervention*—and the degree to which it can add something of significance that did not previously exist in a given place. Some of the myriad factors within this constellation of concern are illustrated in Figure 1.1. Here, six determinants are presented, each, with numerous associated fine-grain issues. Any or all of these fine-grain issues can and will bear on the success/failure of a prefab modular transportable for healthcare. Any or all can impact its efficacy as a prosthetic intervention. The six determinants are:

- *Socio-cultural*—Has the impacted population changed demographically since before the disaster event? Have individuals' population migratory patterns changed? What religions, religious cycles, and associated rituals are most prominent in the impacted population? What are the routine activities of daily living within the impacted population? In what ways has the overall quality of life been altered within the impacted population?
- *Political*—Are preexisting local land use and zoning regulations having a deleterious impact on the population's ability to return home to begin rebuilding (assuming they elect to return or are allowed by authorities to do so)? What is the role of the NGOs working in the impacted area? Does social unrest exist? Are there signs of social/political insurgency, and are certain individuals or lobby groups driving (or attempting to drive) the recovery? Hidden agendas? Is there reason to hold out hope the future will be better?
- *Economic*—Is the exchange of goods and services occurring satisfactorily? Are the supplies of food and other basic supplies meeting demand? Are basic supplies being distributed to the places most in need? Are local land values stable, diminishing in value, or increasing in value? How often are supplies arriving to the places most in need?
- *Climatic*—What are the local climatic conditions? What seasonal patterns will most likely impact the immediate area in the coming months? Is wind a particular problem at this location? If so, would another site be less prone to strong, potentially harmful wind gusts? Does this site receive adequate sunlight? Has the microclimate changed recently due to larger factors associated with global climate change? If so, how?
- *Geographical*—With regards to the natural ecosystem, what percentage is comprised of native, versus non-native animal and plant species? What soil types exist and are they sufficiently stable? Is the topography suitable for an installation? If in an earthquake zone, is the site being considered on or near a fault line? With regards to local hydrological conditions, are adequate water supplies available? Is local storm runoff/site drainage suitable and is standing water a health problem?
- *Ecological*—What is the ecological health of the local plant and animal species? Is there a significant amount of soil, air, or water pollution? How resilient are the plant and animal species in the aftermath of the disaster event? Are animal species interacting and co-existing? Has the number of species changed since before the event and is the level of diversity among these species the same as before the disaster event?

1.1 Transportable healthcare facility design determinants
Source: Adapted from 'Geographies of Change' diagram, source unknown, 2011

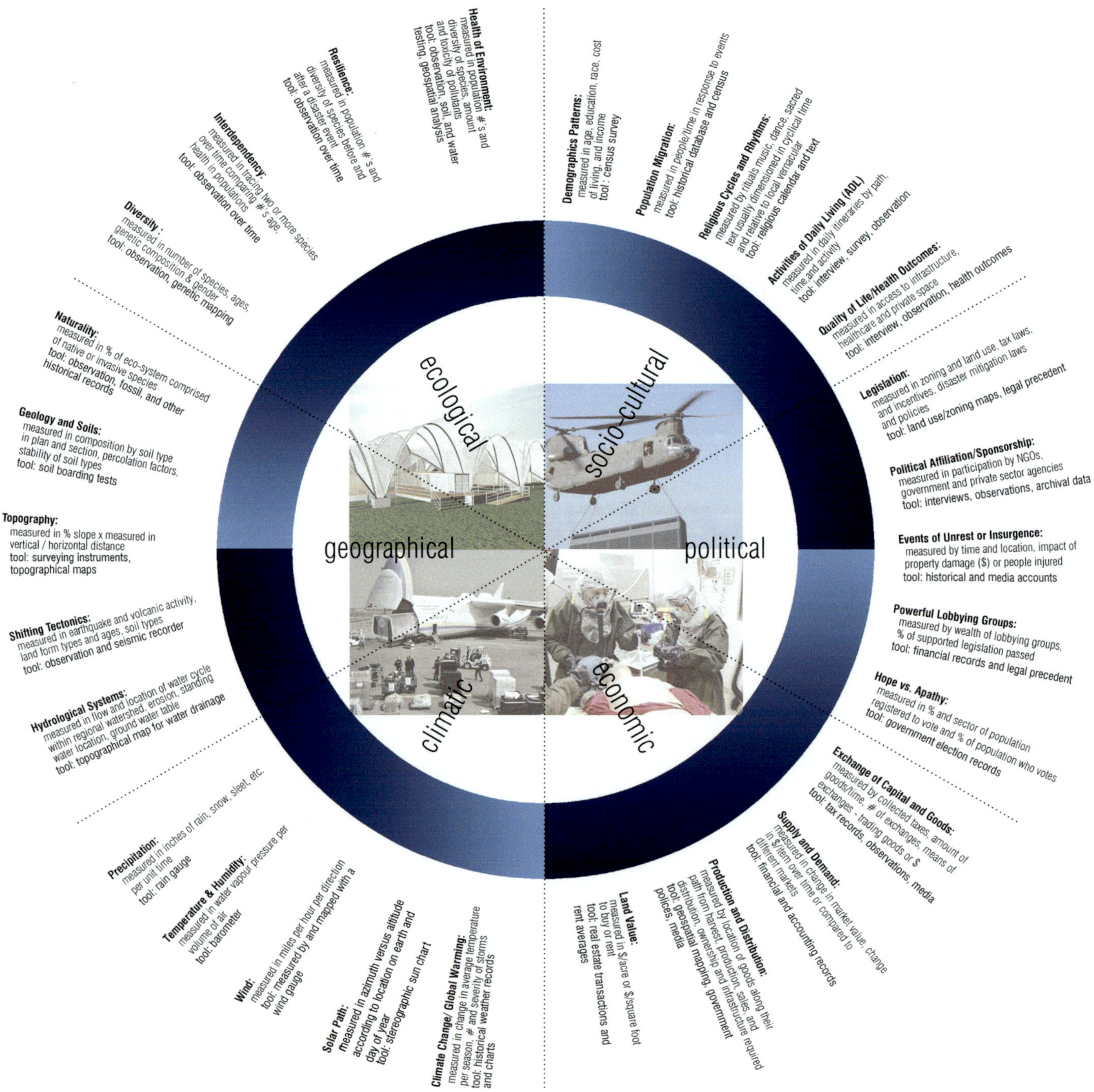

These six factors and the larger context they address constitute an evaluative nexus of concern for assessing any building, whether portable or permanent. It is something that others can build upon. But for this discussion, what about evaluating the performance of a portable building itself? Its success/failure remains next to impossible to know with any certainty without a set of performance metrics to assess its efficacy in the field. In other words, without such metrics any assessment of what has worked, and/or has not worked, remains guesswork. Evaluation tools exist for this purpose. Facility performance is measurable through the use of the *post occupancy evaluation* (POE) method. This method has been used by researchers and architects for decades but has rarely (if ever) been applied to transportable architecture for health. In fact, no peer-reviewed accounts of an empirical investigation of this type have been published. The POE methodology revolves around systematic appraisal, and is generally structured into four aspects of a structure's day-to-day performance. There are: (1) its patterns of everyday use by its occupants; (2) the assessment of its aesthetic attributes, its overall appearance, and its 'architectural significance' (admittedly itself a broad subject); (3) the level of environmental and technical support it provides its occupants, including thermal comfort, lighting, daylight, air quality, and the ability of occupants to control the immediate environment in these regards; and (4) the ability of the facility to be properly maintained and repaired, and its general upkeep.

The POE process can be conducted at varying degrees of specificity and depth. The basic levels of engagement include an indicative performance assessment, an investigative performance assessment, and the most in-depth level of analysis, a rigorous, diagnostic performance assessment. The indicative method is least rigorous, from a scientific standpoint, and the diagnostic method is the most scientifically precise. The former is qualitative, whereas the latter is empirical, quantitative, and (in theory) replicable, in other contexts.[92] Of course, in makeshift circumstances it may simply be impossible to conduct a facility performance assessment of any type. Here, an indicative POE may be all that is possible. Nevertheless, it can still be worth it to use even some parts of this methodology to judge the prosthetic amenity of an installation. Try to diagnose the facility itself, and solicit feedback from its occupants by means of interviews, surveys, photographs, videography, behavioral observation, and measurements of human thermal comfort. This will help in making future decisions about relocating a facility, expansion, contraction, or if it can accommodate, say, thirty added inpatient beds without a physical expansion. It will also be helpful in the design and manufacture of portable facilities in the future so the same wheel is not reinvented, repeatedly: mistakes made in one facility need not be replicated in twenty or fifty others. This is discussed further in Chapter 5, as is the importance of establishing an evidence-based approach to the design of prefab transportables for healthcare.

Challenges and opportunities

The *World Health Organization* (WHO) defines universal access to sickness prevention and primary healthcare as a basic human right.[93] In 2012, in the U.S. alone, according to the *Health Resources and Services Administration* (HRSA), there were an estimated 4,143 medically underserved communities throughout the nation. In addition, 5,830 communities were classified, geographically, as medical health professional shortage areas, and this included more than thirty-four million underserved individuals nationally. HRSA defines these areas as experiencing a shortage of primary medical care providers, and they may be rural, suburban, or urban communities.[94] Transportable facilities can address the health inequities referenced in these HRSA data, especially in communities geographically remote from urban medical centers. With access to healthcare a persistent problem in the Lower Nine, in New Orleans, ten years after Katrina, it remains a major reason why that community has been unable to rebound.[95] Why so? First, few local healthcare facilities are present. Second, poor public transit options exist. But the first of these barriers is perhaps most vexing, as the mindset of providers is such that only stationary brick and mortar clinics are viewed as acceptable.[96]

In South Carolina, as of 2014, more than 645,000 residents lacked access to sickness prevention medical care out of a statewide population of 4.6 million.[97] This state was designated a 'Health Professional Shortage Area' and its citizens remain highly underserved while only *five* mobile clinical units are out on the road to assist the state's medically underserved areas.[98] This, despite their numerous benefits. A mobile clinic can be driven out of harm's way, unlike a fixed-site facility. These and other portables for health are positioned to make the communities they serve more resilient. These offsite prefab 'facilities,' and prefab portable counterparts manufactured for temporary installations, are referred to here as *Redeployable Health Centers* (RHCs).

A *Redeployable Trauma Center* (RTC) differs from an RHC because it is designed and built for emergency medical care first and foremost. It is built for treating injuries sustained in a disaster, and for a more intensive level of care. A prefab modular RTC can be calibrated for expansion from a single module to as many as seventy-five units on a single site, and is adaptable to diverse climate and site conditions—from dense urban infill sites on city streets to remote rural regions. In terms of their design, tectonic attributes, and installation vocabularies, a range of prefab modular flat-pack systems, tent-based, containerized, and hybrid systems are available.[99] A third type of offsite prefab modular portable is the *Permanent Modular Installation* (PMI). This type of prefab healthcare facility can be completely built offsite and then transited to another site for permanent installation, or can consist of component parts built off site and then installed elsewhere in a conventionally built hospital or other type of healthcare environment.

These three types of portable buildings for health provide prosthetic support—whether as a component device plugged into a stationary healthcare facility, or as a freestanding structure.[100] To paraphrase Thomas Fisher, the underlying problem in architects' impotence in first response situations is due to *fracture-critical thinking*. He defines this as an unfortunate syndrome whereby society is now experiencing steep erosion in the quality of its critical infrastructural systems. Aged, obsolete bridges, civic structures, public transit systems, levee and seawall systems, public hospitals, and power grids are in need of repair and replacement. We are in a decades-long downward spiral due to public disinvestment in infrastructure, and this is having a concomitant effect of stymying the ability of the architect to take on a leadership role.[101] This is true to some extent although it is often too easy to blame others for our own shortcomings.

Certain hindrances perpetuate the status quo:

- *The engineers*—Transnational engineering firms dominate the disaster mitigation industry as the provider of first choice for offsite prefab modular structures. Their emphasis on bare bones functionality and logistical expediency continues to undermine the potential role of the timeless Vitruvian principles of commodity, firmness, and delight. In the U.S., the largest federal contracts (often no-bid contracts) are coveted by a small number of 'disaster capitalist' engineering firms.[102] These corporate disaster contractors dismiss *architecture*: 'We don't have time for architects (or architecture) because they are a needless cost item that just slows us down.' Engineering firms need to be incentivized to collaborate equitably with architects and industrial designers if the state of the art is to be advanced. These contractors' track record, to date, remains dismal, for the most part, anything but inspiring from an aesthetic standpoint. Of course they will shout back, 'This isn't about aesthetics.' But in point of fact it *can* be about function as much as aesthetics.
- *Educational preparation*—A Japanese architectural firm, Yasutaka Yoshimura Architects, right after the Tohuku catastrophe, developed a prototype container-shelter, the *Ex-Container Project*. It is for persons displaced by the 2011 disaster. It is modular, minimalist, and adaptable for use as health clinics. Their proportions are identical to intermodal ISO containers and they are stackable.[103] This type of thinking should be happening every day. The majority of architects, unfortunately, remain disengaged from disaster mitigation decision makers, and their contracted engineering firms. This has held the profession back, and from subsequently taking on a prominent role in what gets built and why. The university-level academic programs in architecture, for their part, continue to underperform in this regard.[104] Social engagement remains barely discernable on the radar screen, as most future architects still do not receive training in learning how to communicate with engineers and with organizations specializing in disaster mitigation.[105] Professional organizations such as the American Institute of Architects (AIA) and the Royal Institute of British Architects (RIBA) are only now awakening to the need for professional training on this. The professional schools' formal accrediting agencies, such as the National Architectural Accreditation Board (NAAB) in the U.S., for their part, remain behind the curve: interdisciplinary curricula are needed in resilience education. New curricula can bring together the health professions, the social sciences, disaster mitigation, and the disciplines of architecture, engineering, and industrial design.
- *Telescopic scaling*—Healthcare architecture suffers from a syndrome where its practitioners are unable to think beyond the

next commission. Added to this, firms that specialize in healthcare architecture do not communicate enough with one another for fear of giving away proprietary intellectual property. Many healthcare clients, for their part, continue to think of the architect as only capable of producing individual buildings. Even if this were acceptable in everyday professional practice, it is totally unacceptable in disaster response. Telescopic scaling requires being able to iteratively and reflectively scale up, or down, then back, when responding to something as complex as a disaster. This is the function of Figure 1.1 and the POE process, and both are equally important. A strong, well-directed individual/team must be able to do this, iteratively, and often within a matter of minutes. This is because decisions in these situations may have to be made very quickly. This is telescopic scaling.

In the following chapters the aforementioned *three types* of offsite-built, portable, prefabricated modular structures for health are explored much further:

- *Redeployable Health Centers* (RHC)—This type, typically for use in non-disaster situations, is an offsite-built vehicular mobile clinic, a portable but non-motorized healthcare facility, or hybrid. A RHC is positioned to play an important role in increasing a community's health status.
- *Redeployable Trauma Centers* (RTC)—This type is best suited to provide emergency and intensive care for victims of disaster. A pre-manufactured modular RTC is expandable from a single module to as many as seventy-five units and adaptable to diverse climatic and site conditions.
- *Permanent Modular Installations* (PMI)—These modular facilities are either complete freestanding installations built off site, or any internal component systems built off site and then transited to another site for permanent installation within a conventionally built healthcare facility.

The truest measure of human character is how one responds to adversity. First-response NGOs focus on the disaster event and its immediate aftermath—days, weeks, the first few months.[106] The WHO and the *United Nations*, through the *UN High Comissioner for Refugees* (UNHCR), will commit to staying many years if necessary.[107] The WHO, for its part, in 2012, did issue a report documenting more than fifty temporary field hospitals and mobile clinics it operated in eight quake-hit districts, including in Muzaffarabad, where the 400-bed Combined Military Hospital collapsed, killing over 200 patients inside, and a few recent UNHCR online publications include reports on facilities for Canadian-sponsored refugee resettlement programs.[108] But a physical facility itself is seldom if ever described in much detail. The UNHCR monthly journal *Refugees* contains many relevant articles and does, from time to time, include some descriptive information of this kind, usually about tent-based primary care clinics deployed to remote regions.[109] This situation needs to change. This barrage of technical reports, white papers, scholarly publications, and conferences needs to begin to focus more on the portable field infirmary as a vital support modality.[110]

Humanitarian aid organizations do a herculean job, even with minimally functional portable healthcare facilities. Opportunities await. *Médecins Sans Frontières* (MSF) is a French-founded, international NGO. Its headquarters is in Geneva, Switzerland. It was founded in 1971. It is well known for its efforts in war-torn regions and in places stricken with infectious disease.[111] Its origins were in the aftermath of the Biafra succession, founded by a group of French doctors and journalists committed to the belief that all people have a fundamental human right to medical care regardless of race, religion, or political affiliation. Furthermore, the needs of these people transcend national borders. This organization is now known in many places as *Doctors Without Borders* and private donations from individuals account for more than 80 percent of its funding. Governmental and private corporate sponsors provide the remaining support. In 2012 its annual budget was approximately $400 million. In 1999 it received the Nobel Peace Prize. In West Africa in the Ebola outbreak in 2014 this organization worked in seemingly impossible conditions. It set up its own tent infirmaries, and worked in those provided by the International Red Cross.[112] This organization has much knowledge to share on the role of the built environment in medical emergencies. Many facility-related lessons are to be learned from studying these clinics and hospitals so that in the future their facilities, as well as those operated by other NGOs, can be improved.

Architects, allied designers, engineers and others can learn from resilient people and especially from the victims of disaster. Their stories are both fascinating and instructive. Learn how they cope with severe dislocation, when the 'old normal' is no longer attainable. Learn from the NGOs who work in the disaster strike zones.[113] A discourse is needed between medical care providers and those who design and manufacture the facilities. Providers can learn a great deal from architects, industrial designers, and engineers, and vice versa. Seize the moment. The NGOs themselves are not immune to failure. The venerable WHO admitted its failure in miscalculating how fast Ebola was capable of traveling geographically.[114]

Note: on the matter of terminology, the terms *lift-pack* and *flat-pack* are used interchangeably in the following chapters. These terms refer to any portable structure that is shipped unassembled, and requires assembly by lifting up component parts from a flattened or otherwise compacted mode. All monetary references are in U.S. dollars.

CHAPTER 2

Transportables for health: a brief modern history

Portable structures for healthcare originate from two timeless dwelling types—the *tipi* and the *yurt*, both of which were lightweight, and able to be erected and disassembled by a few persons. Paleolithic North American tribes invented the tipi, and Sub-Saharan African tribesmen introduced independent refinements. A tipi could be relocated as the tribe followed migrating herds through tribal hunting lands. Conically shaped, with a framework of poles braced together at the top, sheathed in hand-sewn animal skins, a tipi could be erected quickly and then dragged by horse. Its conical configuration yielded unimpeded interior space and its rigid frame resisted strong gusts of wind. The 'infirmary' tipi provided sheltered space for the care of the sick and wounded. This shelter type would remain relatively unchanged for nearly 3,000 years.[1]

The *yurt* was a mainstay of the societies of the Central Steppes of Asia. Yurts were felt-sheathed frame tent structures favored by nomadic herders and they have been in widespread use for more than 2,000 years. Herodotus described felt-covered tents used by early nomads as early as 500 B.C. This type has evolved surprisingly little over the centuries from the time it was used by warriors in the Mongol invasion in the thirteenth century. The word 'yurt' is Turkic in origin and means 'site or space upon which a tent is put.' These lightweight portable structures have been referred to variously across the millennia as *boz uy* in Kyrgyz, *oey* in Turkman, and *ger* in Mongolian.[2]

A yurt's frame was traditionally a trellis wall with center poles extending from the crossing points at the top of the trellis to slots in the crown (roof). This trellised wall, with all joints fastened, allows its frame to swivel, with the structure elevated slightly above the ground, often positioned on stones or wood. Joints were made from rawhide segments and fastened to the wood poles. Its wall was shaped circularly to provide maximum structural support. The entire structure is secured by means of a tension band extending around the frame thereby restraining the roof's weight from pushing the trellis outward, yielding its ultimate rigid, circular form. The felt skins (initially sheepskins) draped over the structure kept out the elements. The center collar frame at the uppermost part of the roof often remained open for ventilation. These structures were lightweight and were, as in the case of the tipi, easily transited. Because the felt sheathing was separate from the structural frame, the yurt was adaptable seasonally to the changing elements simply by modifying the thickness of the sheathing, by adding or removing its layers of animal skins. Three to four people could erect a small yurt in less than two hours.[3] For transport, Bactrian camels or yaks, horses, and later, mule-drawn wagons, were the norm. Here too, its open interior space was well suited for the care of sick and injured tribal members.

As for transiting portable structures, horse and mule-drawn wagons and carriages date from Mesopotamia as early as 3000 B.C. Used for warfare by the Egyptians, near Easterners and Europeans, they were two-wheeled vehicles drawn by one or two horses. In the first century, Romans constructed suspension carriages using chains or leather straps, and in Ancient China the Zhou Dynasty used carriages for transportation although this practice virtually vanished, in time. By the Middle Ages, compartments fastened to a four-wheeled undercarriage came into widespread use.[4] A well-known example was the carriage outfitted for use by Napoleon throughout his military campaigns: it was an elaborate carriage-cum-portable structure. Later, traveling circus performers, medicine doctors, and gypsies of the nineteenth century perfected the use of the covered wagon as a performance space that could double as mobile living quarters. Usually made of wood, with four wheels and drawn by two horses, these mobile structures were practical and efficient, and did not have to be reassembled at every stop.[5]

Often, one mobile encampment structure was used as an *infirmary*—the place to take the sick and injured. In the nineteenth and twentieth centuries these advancements would spawn further advancements in field-based trauma medicine in times of war and this pattern continues to this day.[6] Their degree of resiliency is defined by an ability to tread lightly on the earth, portability, relatively low cost to build and maintain, reusability, and the capacity to 'bounce back' from an adverse event.[7] Against this backdrop, the following discussion is structured as three sections: (1) the evolution of portable, redeployable military field hospitals; (2) the evolution of motorized vehicular clinics for either military and civilian uses; and (3) the evolution of portable, reusable facilities for deployment in post-disaster strike zones.

Military transportables

> He who wishes to be a surgeon should go to war.
>
> Hippocrates[8]

An old adage goes, 'Necessity is the mother of invention.' In wartime this has been proven true, time and again. From the onset of recorded history, violent conflict between and within nations has shaped civilizations. Alexander the Great extended the influence of Ancient Greece throughout Asia Minor and far into India, with its hegemonistic culture. Islam, as an ancient religious and cultural force, proliferated throughout the Middle East, Northern Africa, and Southern Spain by means of near-continuous warfare across many generations.[9] In the case of the Romans, its armies were comprised of a large percentage of volunteers and slaves, and care of these wounded warriors was of little concern to the military hierarchy. A severely wounded 'marginal' soldier had scant prospects for survival. Over time, military commanders gradually came to appreciate the physicians who cared for the sick and wounded. This would lead to their acceptance of the battlefield military hospital.[10]

Hippocrates (460–370 B.C.) had come from the tradition of Greek natural philosophers and his writings can be found in more than sixty books.[11] He systematized medical care for various ailments in relation to seasonal determinants of health referred to as the *Four Humors*. This typology delineated the origins of what we today consider modern medical science, and he advocated for the autonomy of the physician.[12] He further asserted that war was the only proper training for a surgeon, with advancements in trauma care of necessity best developed during military conflict. Galen, born 130 A.D. in Pergamon, Turkey, was greatly influenced by the writings of Hippocrates and he acquired experience as a gladiatorial surgeon in the Pergamon military theatre in Asia Minor. His writings consist of more than 500 medical treatises and this essential body of work would bear on medical thought for much of the next 1,500 years.[13] Upon Galen's death, however, medical scientific inquiry virtually ceased for hundreds of years.[14]

Ambrose Paré (1510–1590) revolutionized the treatment of war wounds in tent field hospitals in the service of several French kings. Paré took note of the cleansing action of maggots when placed on wounds, and first used windlass traction for femoral fractures. He was the first to recognize spinal cord compression in vertebral fractures, leading to advancements in prosthetic limbs and braces.[15] Later, the innovations of John Hunter (1728–1793) influenced surgical thinking from the eighteenth century on through the period of colonial expansion by the major European powers in the seventeenth to nineteenth centuries.[16] Napoleon's Chief Surgeon, Dominique Jean Larry (1766–1842), personally performed over 200 amputations in a single twenty-four-hour period during the Russian campaign, and is noted for considering all aspects of trauma care, i.e. sanitation, food supplies, transport, training, and the layout and amenity of the portable tent field hospital.[17]

With an army of trained soldiers, and no longer merely consisting of slaves and marginalized social outcasts forced to fight, the Roman military had earlier been required to invest in its warriors' well-being.[18] New policies called for basic medical training to a handful of soldiers within each battalion. These medical specialists were precursors to modern-day combat medics; they treated wounds sustained in frontline combat at the battalion tent infirmary. The Romans had been the first to build a network of permanent military infirmaries (*valetudinariums*) complimented by their network of frontline tent infirmaries.[19]

Since the Empire was constantly conquering new lands, its military remained in a state of perpetual motion. Its network of stationary facilities, supported by portable tent-infirmaries, firmly established the Roman presence within a newly conquered territory. The fixed-site Roman valetudinarium evolved as a building type, as did the frontline tent infirmary.[20] The medical corps became renowned for its innovative procedures developed after the massive upheaval caused by the Roman Civil War, a fifteen-year conflict following Julius Caesar's assassination, in 44 B.C.[21] The newly anointed emperor, Augustus, formed an autonomous military medical corps:

> Before this, doctors had fairly low status. Augustus, realizing that they were key in an Empire and especially an army, gave all physicians that joined his new army medical corps dignified titles, land grants, and even special retirement benefits. For the next five hundred years, fueled by the motivations and opportunity for medical advancement supplied by the many battles, and supported by the powers that be, this group advanced the study and practice of medicine to a level not seen again until the late nineteenth century.[22]

Incentives for further specialization and scientific innovation led to new surgical instruments for the removal of projectiles such as arrowheads. Wounds were sanitized with strong wine to prevent infection. Greater understanding of blood circulation led to the development of tourniquets to help staunch the bleeding from severe wounds and the medical corps was now responsible for constructing latrines for all portable tent infirmaries as well as stationary hospitals.[23] Sedatives and painkillers were developed at this time, extracted from natural sources, i.e. morphine (opium poppies) and scopolamine (henbane), both remedies for pain management, soon to find their way into civilian life.

With the fall of Rome, the caring of sick and injured soldiers in the field waned in the West. Barbarian invaders destroyed most tangible evidence of prior Roman military medical advancements. Later, in the Byzantine Empire (324–1453), where aspects of Roman culture had continued to be revered, medical protocols still advanced little. The Dark Ages witnessed disastrous health outcomes across Europe, and the loss of Roman legion medical ingenuity during this period had a concomitantly adverse impact on both stationary and portable treatment facilities. Not until European armies initially contacted Islamic armies during the Crusades, when Charlemagne drove the Moors from Southern Spain, would the portable tent infirmary reappear as a distinct type.[24]

Meanwhile, in the Islamic world, early stationary hospitals were advanced. Nearly 200 years before the first permanent Islamic hospital, or *bimaristan*, was built in Damascus by the Ummayad Caliph Al-Walid, Muslim armies deployed mobile tent bimaristans. These portable infirmaries traveled with each army legion, a practice traceable to the era of the Prophet Muhammed.[25] These expressed the nomadic Bedouin way of life: encampments of lightweight, portable tents with the bimaristan tent no exception.[26] In time, these portable structures were enlarged and well-staffed:

> The idea of mobility dates from the time of the Prophet Muhammed (saws). During the Ghazwah Khandaq (the Battle of the Ditch) a separate tent was erected for the wounded. When Sa'id bin Mu'az was wounded and one of the blood vessels in his arm was injured, the Prophet ordered that he should be kept in the tent so that he could personally look after him. Later Caliphs and rulers developed and extended these 'MASH' units into true traveling dispensaries complete with doctors and pharmacists. Their mission was to meet the needs of outlying communities that were far from the major cities and permanent medical facilities. By the reign of the Seljuq Turkish Sultan Mohammed Saljuqi, the mobile hospital had become so extensive that its equipment needed forty camels to transport it.[27]

2.1 Makeshift field hospital conditions for the provision of emergency medical care, American Civil War, 1862

2.2 Open air 'hospital ward,' American Civil War, 1863

They often emulated attributes of permanent bimaristans, often located on hilltops or near water sources. Al Adoudi's permanent bimaristan was erected by Adoud al-Dawla bin Bawaih in Baghdad, adjacent to the River Deglah. By the twelfth and thirteenth centuries, non-portable Syrian and Egyptian permanent hospitals and their tent counterparts achieved sophistication, and endure as expressions of early Muslim civilization.[28] The permanent facilities attracted generous patronage, were elegant, spacious, and well equipped with libraries, laboratories, and elaborate pharmacies.[29]

Birthed by military conflict, Islam advanced medical knowledge whereas frontline battlefield medicine waned and nearly disappeared entirely in Western Europe during the Middle Ages. In time, lessons would be relearned from Ancient Rome and Greece but not until the early sixteenth century.[30] By the eighteenth century, portable field hospitals once again were deployed to the front in the West although armies lacked effective patient transport from the frontline and the injured soldier often died on the spot. Infirmaries were no more than crude tents, unsanitary, and rife with disease.[31] In the American Revolution in the late eighteenth century, a new wave of tent infirmaries would appear. With a fledging government and a newly established medical corps, Continental Army field infirmaries were low budget makeshift operations set up in barns and in forest clearings in the open outdoors.[32] After a battle, the nearest plantation house would be commandeered for ad hoc use as an infirmary, and the outbuildings were similarly adapted. The wartime physician has the opportunity to witness in a single day more than what one would otherwise witness in years of medical practice. The experience gained by medics on the battlefield during the American Revolutionary War, and later, in the War of 1812, would provide new impetus to the medical profession in the fledging United States of America. This knowledge soon found its way into civilian life.

American Civil War tent infirmaries (1861–1865)

Isambard Kingdom Brunel, a civil engineer, and Florence Nightingale, the founder of the modern nursing profession, would

2.3 Surgery performed in daylight at overcrowded tent field hospital, American Civil War, 1862

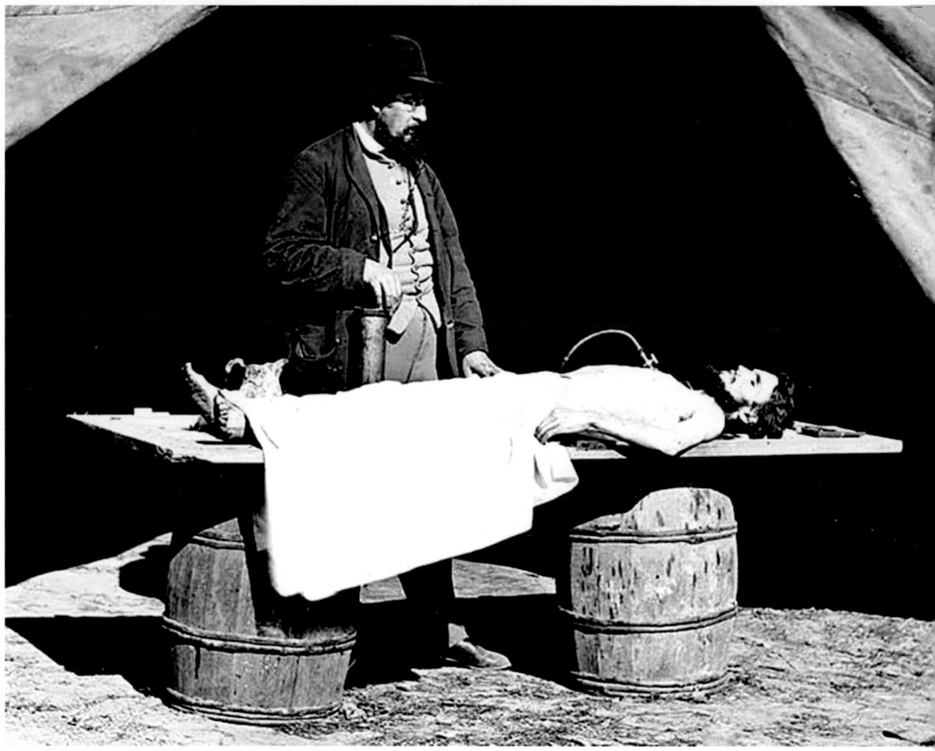

2.4 Natural light was conducive for outdoor surgery at this tent field hospital in the American Civil War, 1864

have an influence on frontline medicine in the American Civil War.[33] Brunel's prefabricated field hospital at Renkioi (see Chapter 3) was proven effective in the Crimean War a few years earlier although the preferred strategy in the American Civil War was for military field hospitals to still be set up ad hoc in adapted existing buildings (Figures 2.1 and 2.2).[34] Dr. Benjamin Rush noted, as did Nightingale, earlier, that casualties housed in open-air tents, barns, and haylofts recovered far more rapidly, with lower infection rates compared to soldiers kept in permanent, conventional hospitals; this, despite the bitter cold of winter and the intense heat and humidity of summer. He soon ordered that every patient be carried outdoors to take in fresh air and sunlight whenever possible.[35] From this, it was concluded that natural ventilation and direct sunlight were sources of substantive therapeutic benefit in the treatment of the sick, diseased, and injured—versus the typically stagnant air provided in a stationary hospital (Figures 2.3 and 2.4).

The grisly scene depicted in *Gone with the Wind* (1939) remains iconic in the history of film. It depicts a massive, ad-hoc, open ward outside from a church hastily adapted for use as a hospital. In the square, over a thousand wounded men lie exposed, dying.[36] In real life, the antebellum resort hotel at Point Clear, Alabama, now known as the Grand Hotel, was commandeered for use as a Confederate Army military hospital much the same way although when it became overcrowded its patients would be housed in crude tents in the grounds. In all, more than fifty Confederate military tent hospitals were set up between 1861 and 1865 in the South, of which some incorporated certain of Nightingale's provisos as set forth in her two recent books, *Notes on Hospitals* (1858) and *Notes on Nursing* (1859).[37] These infirmaries:

2.5 A set of surgeon's tools, including a saw for amputations, American Civil War, 1861–1865

> Varied in size according to the sick lists…Regulations allowed every regiment three 'hospital' tents, one 'Sibley' tent and one 'common' tent. The hospital tent was a white-walled tent, fifteen by fourteen feet, and high (peaked roof)… although men accustomed to more solid shelter did not always take kindly to tents.[38]

Infirmary tents usually housed eight beds. When too hot in summer, their sides were rolled up to ventilate heat gain and provide natural ventilation. With their flaps raised or lowered depending on the weather and time of day, some tents also served as surgical theatres.[39] The tents featured a large, attachable fly-over ridge cap, providing a plenum airspace to help keep the direct sun off the tent itself and to prevent excess heat gain within.[40] Field infirmaries also had tents dedicated as kitchens, living quarters for physicians, and barebones sleeping cots for the ambulance corps. The American writer Walt Whitman observed the following:

> I suppose you know that what we call 'hospital' here in the field…[it] is nothing but a collection of tents on the bare ground for a floor, rather hard accommodations for a sick man…they heat them here by digging a long trough in the ground under them, covering it over with old railroad iron and earth, and then building a fire at one end and letting it draw through and go out the other end, as both ends are open…this heats the ground through the middle of the 'hospital' quite well.[41]

Samuel H. Stout of the Army of Tennessee required his battalion infirmary tents be pitched ten feet apart, leaving twenty feet between rows. In addition to tents, rudimentary prefabricated metal sheds were sometimes erected for use as open wards. Kate Cumming, a well-known hospital civilian watchdog, advocated for patients to be housed in these tents because it was proven they indeed recovered far more quickly in the tents. Yet she found herself frequently at odds with the surgeons. They preferred the semi-permanent prefab sheds. Some of these temporary structures were 100 feet long by twelve feet in depth, with shingle roofs and open canvas sides, which could, similarly, be raised or lowered as the weather dictated. They were cheap, and able to be quickly assembled.[42]

Surgical procedures performed in these structures were crude by current standards (Figure 2.5). Worse, ammunition, especially bullets of the period, were not rifled to spin once they exited the barrel, as rounds do today. As a result there were no clean entry wounds. Because of this, the most common lifesaving measure was to amputate, often sending the patient into shock, or death would occur later due to complications from pneumonia or acquired infection. Worse, piles of amputated limbs would be stacked directly outside, this, in and of itself, a horrific, unhygienic practice.[43] Suffice to say, disease and infection were rampant. It became so large a problem that most officers soon objected to being treated in any type of field infirmary, tent or otherwise, due to the inhumane conditions. Other issues complicated matters, including highly erratic distribution lines for medical supplies that often required soldiers to walk twenty-five miles or more from a rail station supply depot to the nearest stationary or tent infirmary.[44] Casualty data from the American Civil War reveals that nearly two-thirds of the 620,000 total military deaths in the war resulted from non-battle incurred injuries, primarily from dysentery and typhoid.[45] Hygiene and sanitation was poor in the tents:

> Everything about the operation was septic. The surgeon operated in a blood and often pus-stained coat. He might hold his lancet in his mouth. If he dropped an instrument or sponge on the dirt, he merely picked it up, rinsed it in cold water, and continued. When loose pieces of bone and tissue had been removed, the wound would be packed with wet, unsterilized bandages. The bandages were to be kept wet with the patient kept quiet as possible, and given small but frequent doses of whisky, and possibly even quinine.[46]

From a surgical standpoint, suitable stationary buildings built as hospitals or adapted for use as such were most preferred. These were the 'buildings of opportunity' and were preferred over tents, which were perceived as more difficult to keep supplied and properly sanitized.[47] Regardless of the type of setting, permanent or a tent, wounds were examined and dressed although not antiseptically because few knew the importance of antisepsis. As a consequence, wounds suppurated, and so-called *laudable pus* was welcomed, indicating the patient had reached a critical milepost on the road to recovery. Surgeons did not sterilize their hands: this remained the main cause of cross-contamination of patients during and after surgeries. Careful hand washing and nail scrubbing simply rarely happened. Even with such unhygienic practices, tent-ward infirmary mortality rates were only around *30 percent* compared to those of stationary, 'permanent' hospitals of the period.[48]

World War I field hospitals (1914–1918)

During the American Civil War, U.S. Army ambulance corps were constituted to evacuate the sick and wounded from the battlefront.

2.6 A frontline triage station set up by the British Army, World War I, France

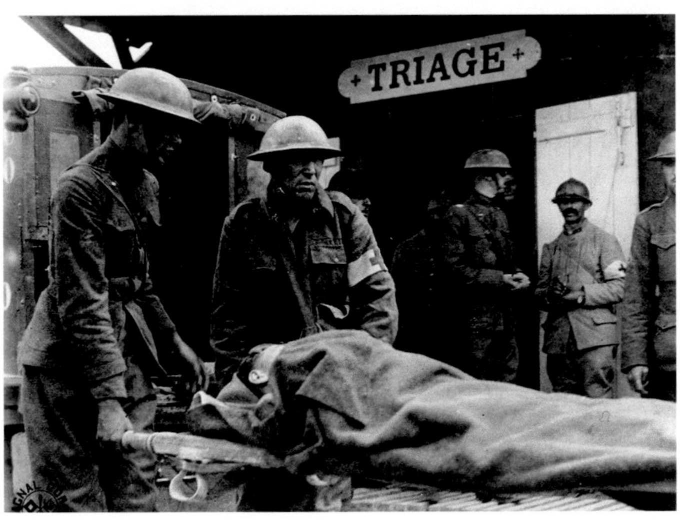

A three-tiered evacuation process consisted of: (1) a dressing first aid station at the edge of the battlefield to provide wound stabilization and tourniquets; (2) a field hospital in proximity to the battlefield where casualties were brought for triage and treatment, including surgery, post-surgical holding, and to prepare the patient for transport out from the frontlines; and (3) stationary rear-line hospitals where recovery continued, perhaps for months. But by 1914, the U.S. military medical command consisted of little more than scattered detachments of first aid stations embedded within battalion units. Ambulance companies evacuated casualties directly to stationary hospitals at the rear. The horrors of trench warfare in World War I would radically change all this.[49]

High rates of casualties, coupled with new, more severe types of injuries, required a new way of caring for the sick and wounded. Medical support was structured into echelons with the first echelon referred to as the 'Zone of the Advance' containing company first aid posts, battalion aid stations, dressing stations, and field hospitals.[50] The British Army and U.S. Army Medical Departments assigned each combat division an infirmary train supported by an ambulance unit, a tent field hospital, and a medical supply unit. After treatment at the tent field hospital, the wounded were transited to the second echelon of medical support, known as 'Lines of Communications.' This consisted of evacuation posts, base hospitals, and mobile surgical infirmaries. The third echelon, the 'Service of the Interior,' consisted of hospital care provided at 'Stateside Bases' on the U.S. mainland.[51]

In World War I, technological warfare resulted in injuries unfamiliar to surgeons. Recently introduced precision firearms included the machine gun and far-reaching artillery with unprecedented accuracy. More than twenty million were wounded and more than sixteen million died in this war.[52] Due to the severity of injuries sustained, roving combat medics were forced to move up further to the front lines, with dressing stations located in close proximity. Each rifle company was assigned two trained medics whose responsibility was to set up and operate the unit's dressing station. Dressing stations provided triage (Figure 2.6). The injured were stabilized here until an ambulance could provide transport to a tent infirmary, or the divisional railcar infirmary.

At these dressing stations, only procedures immediately required to save a life or render a soldier fit for transport were possible. Permanent dressings were possible only as time permitted and no operations whatsoever were performed under conditions so unfavorable. Above all, no one was held beyond the absolute minimum time necessary to secure transport out of harm's way. Conditions encountered in the field varied wildly. In some instances, an effective line of transport was in place but poor hospital accommodations prevailed, while at other times the opposite occurred. Often, the tent field infirmary was where the soldier's prospects of living or dying were decided. In this regard, World War I tent field infirmaries differed little from their predecessors in the American Civil War (Figure 2.7a–b). The use of adapted existing buildings, not unlike during the Civil War, continued to be the option of first choice compared to erecting a freestanding tent infirmary:

> Field hospitals should be easily seen and reached from front and rear (lines) and yet not be in the way of troops and trains. An ample supply of good water is necessary, and suitable (fixed-site) buildings are of great advantage. Such buildings should be utilized first, with only so much tentage put up as may be required.[53]

Tent hospitals in the field were to be expandable to maximize bed capacity (Figure 2.8). The pre- and post-operative tents had to be the most flexible (Figure 2.9). Each divisional infirmary and supply train provided support to four autonomous tent-based facilities, each set up six to eight miles from the frontline. Each of these installations had a normal condition capacity of 108 beds, expandable to 162, thereby providing a 432-bed (648-bed expanded) capability for a single combat division. In addition, each divisional section operated eight dispensaries for the provision of routine medical care for its troops and support personnel.[54] When a tent field hospital was fully activated it included the following functions: dispensary, kitchen, receiving and forwarding, slightly wounded, seriously wounded, operating room, and mortuary. By this time the preferred protocol was to station these portable installations at or very near the frontline, with a stationary hospital to the rear (Figure 2.10a–b). From the mobile triage station the injured were evacuated out. The overarching goal was to stabilize for transport to the rear and into the 'Lines of Communication' echelon of care. The World War I tent field hospital was in no way designed or intended to be a place of 'permanent care.' Instead, it was portable and anticipatory, poised to move about in response to the flow of combat activity within a theatre.[55]

2.7a–b Tentage, Evacuation Hospital No. 1, 1917 (top) and the Field Hospital of the 4th Division, Chateau de la Foret, 1918 (bottom) United States Army, World War I, France, 1918

World War II field hospitals (1938–1945)

World War II was the first truly world war.[56] With battles raging across Europe, Northern Africa, Asia, and the vast Pacific Ocean, tropical diseases posed unprecedented challenges to traditional methods for the provision of frontline emergency medical care and evacuation. Soldiers in the Pacific Theatre, in particular, were forced to cope with the worst of conditions. Their missions often consisted of wading through dense tropical jungles and swamps in search of hidden and highly bunkered Japanese outposts. Malaria, dysentery, yellow fever, and typhoid constantly threatened the well-being of allied soldiers to such an extent that at one point, the destructive effects of attacking tropical diseases seemed more of a threat than the threat posed by the actual enemy. By early 1943, the U.S. Army 32rd Infantry Division in New Guinea had more than 3,000 wounded soldiers in its tent field hospitals, many having been admitted due to contracting tropical diseases. At the peak of this epidemic, jungle fevers, manly malaria, peaked at 6,600 cases per 1,000 soldiers—on average, each and every soldier could expect to be admitted six times per year for treatment.[57]

2.8 Patient transporters delivering a wounded solider on a stretcher to a tent field hospital, World War I, France, 1917

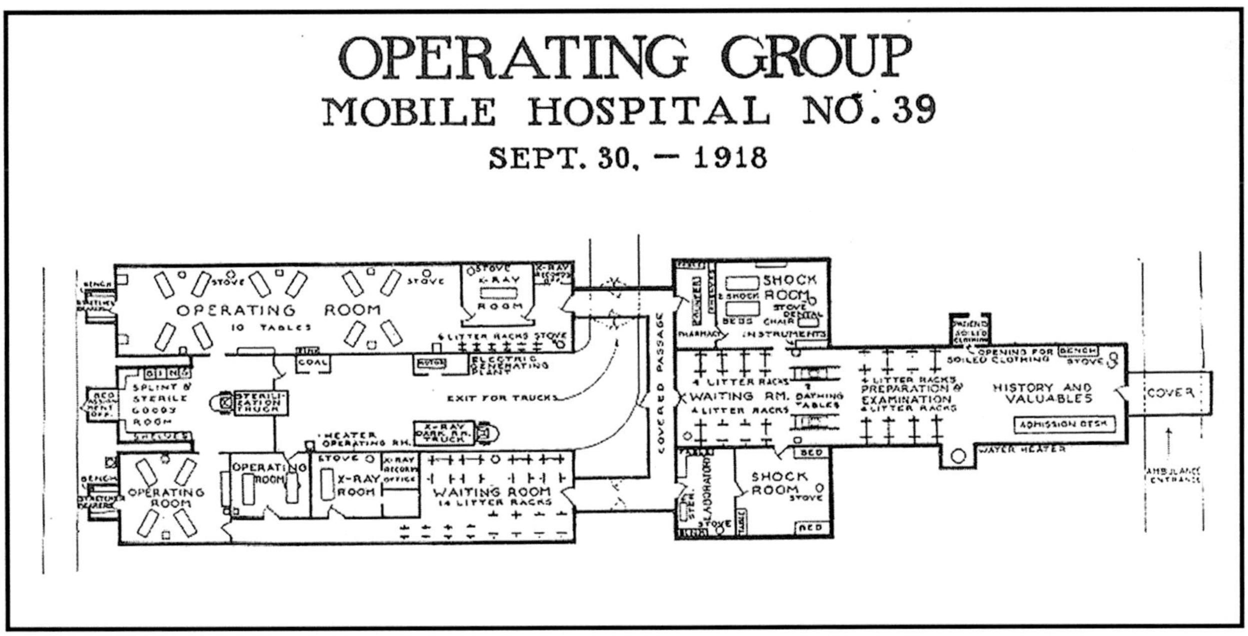

2.9 U.S. Army Mobile Hospital No. 39, World War I, France, 1918. Note the flanking 'Shock Rooms' identified in the plan. Compartmentalized interior spaces exhibit a high degree of specificity

Upon entering World War II, the U.S. Army had only *two* types of combat-deployable portable hospitals, the first being its *Evacuation Hospital* with a 400-bed capacity, fully mobile, and the capability to be split into two equal 200-bed facilities in separate locations. A second type, its *Station Hospital*, possessed a 750-bed capacity but was not particularly mobile and therefore was deployed as basically a stationary facility. In the early months, Evacuation and Station Hospitals had proved adequate in linear warfare contexts fought on fairly flat terrain, but as intense fighting spread to dense mountainous jungle settings it became a completely different story. Recognizing that these two facility types met neither the flexibility nor rapid response needs of the current conflict, a new type of portable field hospital was developed in 1942 with a 380-bed capacity. This configuration was capable of being broken down into platoons, running concurrently at three separate locations, and functioning at 100-bed capacity at each installation site.[58]

Along with the continuous battles fought against tropical diseases and the difficult terrain, allied forces were continually trying to adapt to an enemy which constantly altered the rules of engagement. Suffice to say, traversing a single mile though a newly cut dense jungle path (it would be hard to refer to these routes as

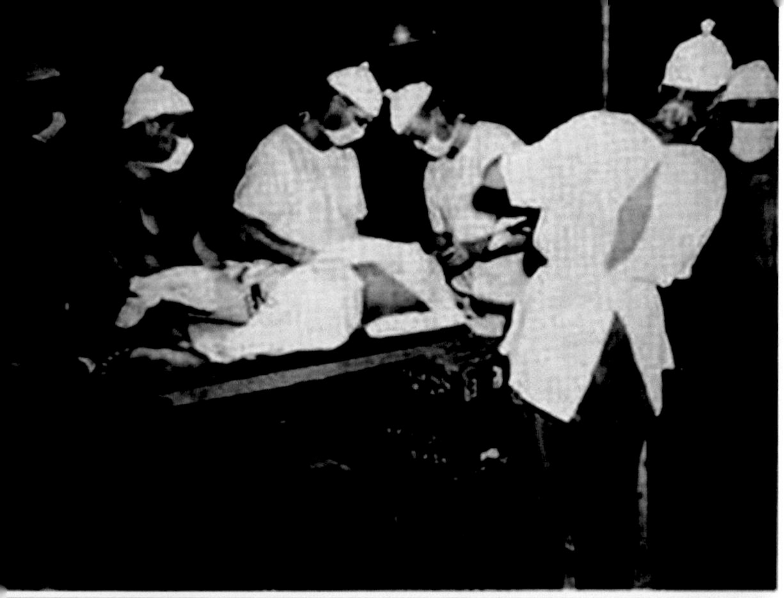

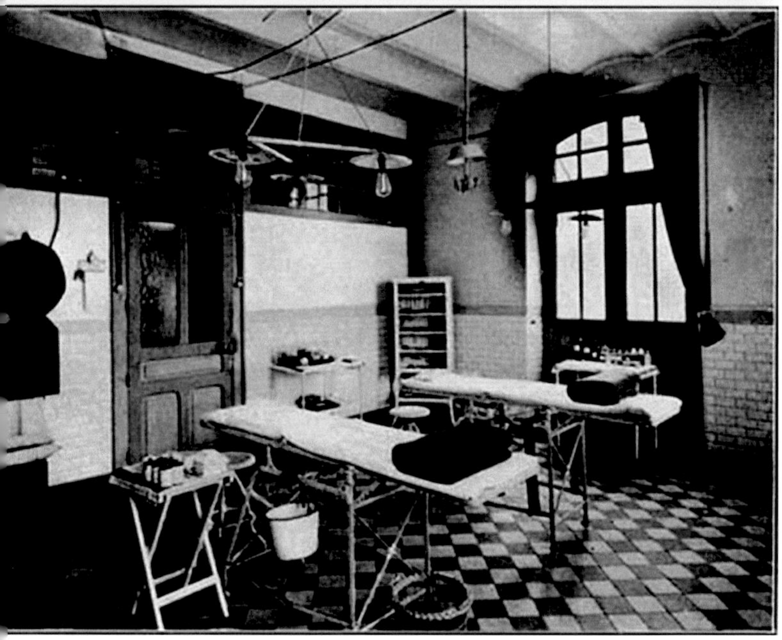

2.10a–b Operating room scene, 23rd Portable Surgical Hospital, U.S. Army, World War I, 1917 (top) and an interior of the surgical suite at its rear-line counterpart, Stationary Evacuation Hospital No. 2 at Baccarat, France, World War I, 1917 (bottom)

2.11a–b Precursor to the classic U.S. Army MASH unit, Pacific Theater, World War II, 1944 (top) and a trench being dug after an intense rainstorm, at Anzio, Italy, World War II, 1944. Trenches provided fortification, and prevented tent interiors from flooding during heavy rainstorms in allied forces' tent hospitals (bottom)

'roads') could take many days. While field hospitals generally were not a military target in the World War II European theatre, they became a prime target of the Japanese Army. Field hospitals and their personnel were put to the extreme test:

> Absolute lack of pity characterized the fighting. Breaking into an enemy hospital at Sanananda, allied soldiers slaughtered the patients, and the Japanese routinely bombed allied hospitals and shot medics while at work on the wounded. American casualties, knowing that snipers in the jungle would aim at the flickers of white that covered their wounds, soon tore the bandages off their wounds until the medics began to dye the bandages green.[59]

In the major combat theatres in the Pacific, such conditions caused field divisions to innovate to protect their portable tent field hospital from enemy attack. Often, this consisted of bunkering the facility down into the earth, protected with sandbags, and even adding wood slats across the top of the tent fabric, with camouflage foliage on top to conceal and fortify them structurally. Still others were deployed in low-lying areas, and were protected by the natural terrain (Figure 2.11a–b). The rough terrain in the Pacific theatre often hampered the ability to provide timely medical care to the wounded. Worse, the lack of roads and infrastructure presented a nightmarish proposition:

> The full range of the Army's conventional medical and emergency support could not be deployed....[because the] tent hospitals would remain many miles in the rear, and the divisional first aid stations were never intended to provide emergency life-saving surgery. With the Army's larger mobile hospitals unable to assume their traditional role in support of the frontline combat units, the chain of evacuation was interrupted at a critical point...many wounded soldiers would [and did] die from lack of [access to] life-saving surgery...or from the long and arduous evacuation trek along dense jungle trails from the frontal clearing stations to the nearest surgical unit.[60]

General MacArthur's chief surgeon in the Southwest Pacific Theatre, Dr. Percy J. Carroll, in 1942 developed a highly portable and mobile unit known as the *Portable Surgical Hospital* (PSH).[61]

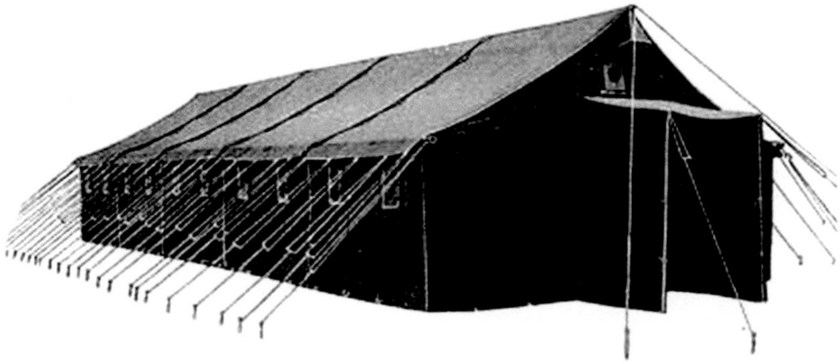

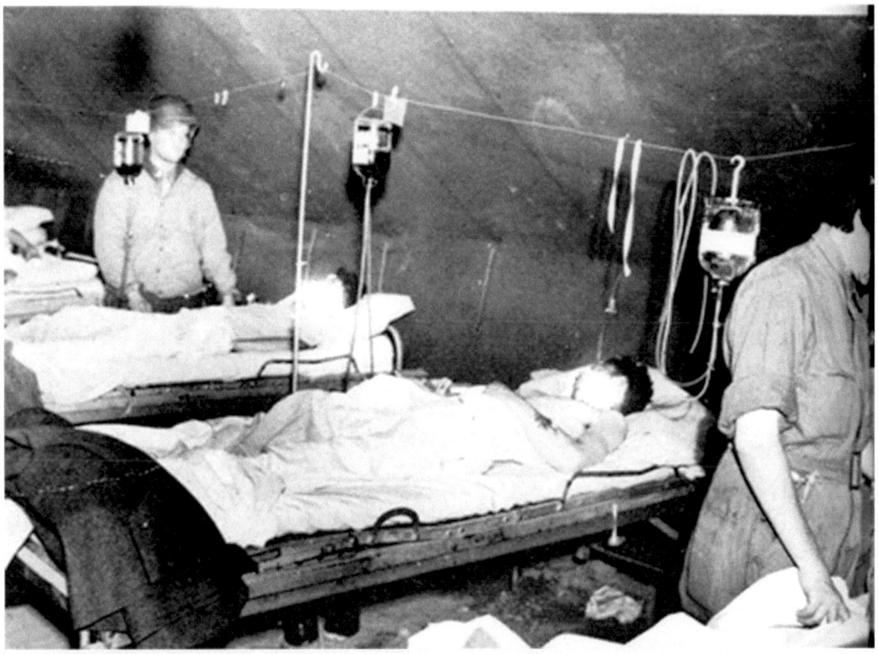

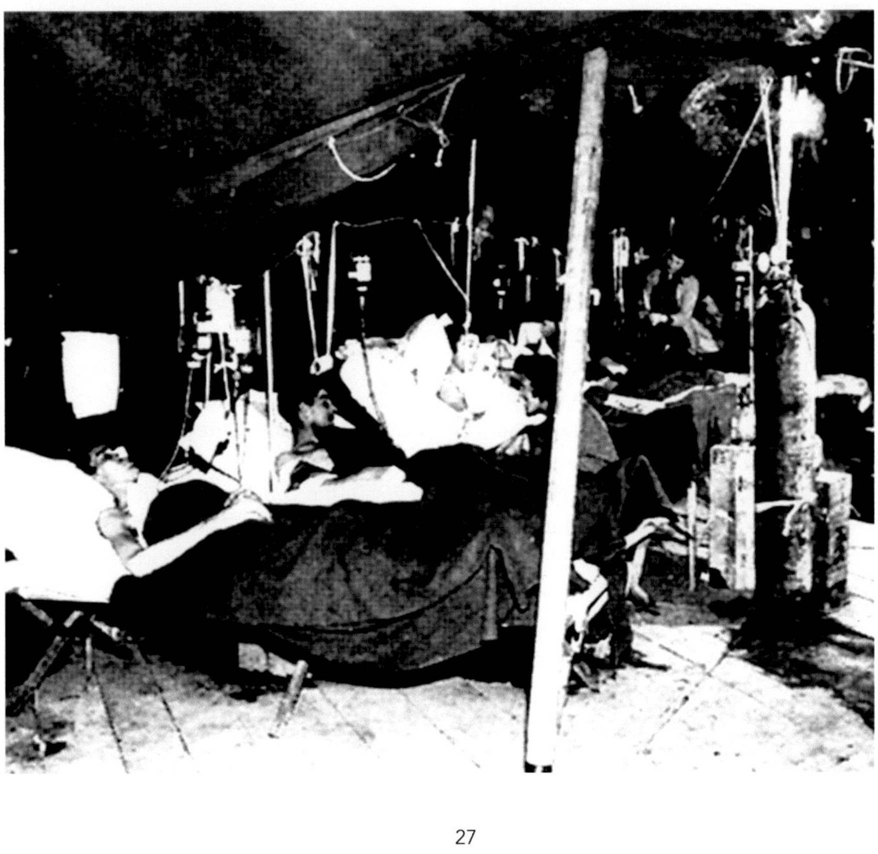

2.12a–c Inpatient tent-ward, U.S. Army Medical Corps, World War II, Philippines, 1944. Exterior view (top) and interior views (middle and bottom) depicting overcrowded conditions. Various life-support apparatus were suspended from tent 'ceilings'

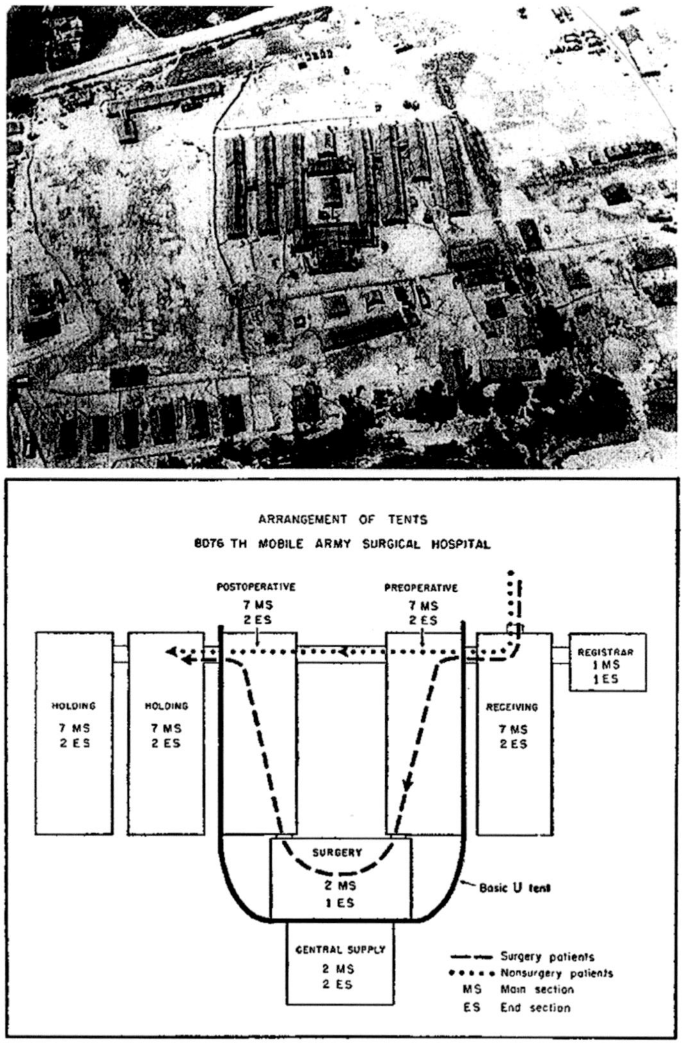

2.13a–b Aerial view (top) and tent-unit layout (bottom) of the 8076th MASH unit installation on the Korean Peninsula, U.S. Army, 1952. Patient-staff flow patterns differed for the treatment of surgical versus non-surgical patients

PSH units could provide the critically needed frontline emergency surgical support between the first aid clearing station and the mobile units to the rear. These portable installations would follow a division into battle and render life-saving treatment as close to the front as practicable. The problems of transiting were largely resolved because its necessary equipment could be carried by as few as twenty-nine men through the dense terrain.[62] The basic twenty-five-bed unit was designed to be self-sufficient and the soldiers stationed with it were trained to set it up and commission it relatively close to enemy lines (Figure 2.12a–c). Officers, alongside enlisted men, carried its gear down the jungle trails no wheeled, motorized vehicle could otherwise traverse, and they erected the main tents beneath lightweight cotton screening. The four officers and twenty-five enlisted soldiers assigned to the first prototype, the 3rd Portable, carried 1,250 pounds of equipment, including the twenty-five beds, in pack frames to the deployment site, pitching the tents only a few hundred yards from the nearest Japanese entrenchments. Bullets would clip the leaves from the branches and puncture holes in the tents, sometimes during transport, as the team was forced to manually transit, simultaneously, their personal gear with that of the field hospital.[63]

Troops in New Guinea were the first to be supported by a PSH.[64] As the only genuinely portable field hospital in the dense jungle, PSHs treated all types of patients with relative success, yet these structures came with their own problems. The 3rd Portable was not without its weaknesses: it lacked much of the equipment needed for definitive surgery, especially an anesthesia capability, due to manual, in-transit carrying weight limitations. Second, it had a limited bed capacity for holding post-op patients, especially abdominal cases, because MEDIVAC protocols often conflicted with in-place patient stabilization needs. Third, the experience levels of the assigned surgeons, especially after the first year, were minimal due to high attrition caused by heavy caseloads and grueling 24/7 work schedules. Fourth, logistical communications, equipment, and medications supply lines were sporadic.[65] Nearly always, the PSH required outside help from local sympathizers, pack animals, or locally procured vehicles for their redeployment to a different site. The advent of the 3rd PSH did succeed, notably, in providing the missing link in evacuation staging. The introduction of sulfa drugs, effective blood transfusion, and their staging as far forward as possible with acute care services onboard helped to significantly reduce the mortality rate in World War II field hospitals to as low as 3 percent.[66] Yet even with all their drawbacks, the PSH would provide the groundwork for all future U.S. Army military combat field hospitals such as the *Mobile Army Surgical Hospital* (MASH), and later, the *Combat Support Hospital* (CSH).

Military advancements: 1950 to the present

By 1950, the U.S. Army's mobile medical inventory consisted of an ungainly collection of six facility types: the Field Hospital, the Station Hospital, the General Hospital, the Evacuation Hospital, the Convalescent Hospital, and the Portable Surgical Hospital. Based on its experience with the 3rd Portable PSH in combat theatres in World War II, a new sixty-bed mobile army surgical hospital was commissioned. This new configuration was the Mobile Army Surgical Hospital, or *MASH*. It was to be the ultimate frontline surgical field hospital (Figure 2.13a–b): mobile, fully staffed with well-trained surgical and medical support personnel, equipped to provide definitive surgical and post-operative care for non-transportable patients. Each unit was organized into three distinct components: Headquarters, Professional Services (all patient care deliverables), and Administrative Services (housing all supply, mess, registrar, detachment service, and motor pool capabilities).[67]

MASH units

The MASH, as it quickly became known, was intended to bring lifesaving surgery closer to the critically wounded. Five MASH units were created on paper between 1948 and early 1950, but were not staffed or ready for combat when North Korea invaded South Korea on 25 June 1950. The MASH immediately replaced the PSH, and these two types of portable never co-existed in the same combat theatre. At the time, a new nomenclature was assigned: a mobile facility was either designated as CZ (mobile) or COMMZ (immobile).[68] In the latter category, the majority of facilities would be fixed-site. In the former category, portable structures were to be deployable in a matter of hours, with a variety of shell configurations and without any functional impediments, combined with an accelerated patient move-in timeline. By contrast, Station Hospitals and General Hospitals in the COMMZ class would require several weeks for full deployment as these permanent facilities were generally more complex, technical, and required larger staffs to stage and set up in the base command zone. Logistical operations were housed in semi-permanent support structures. Once established, these facilities were modifiable only by expanding their bed capacity and for this reason they were not to be relocated after initial set up, due to time and expense (unless strategic or tactical conditions were to suddenly alter).[69] Station Hospitals of this type were built on station posts and base camps, with bed capacities ranging from twenty-five to 900 beds on a single site. The last of the COMMZ hospitals that existed in the Army inventory as of 1950 was the General Hospital. General Hospitals were deployed in 1,000, 1,500 and 2,000-bed configurations with a full complement of logical support. The rule of thumb was any patient requiring additional treatment beyond 180 days would be relocated to a stationary General Hospital.[70]

By 1949 the U.S. Army's first five MASH units were ready for combat but basically sat idle except to provide routine medical care in garrisons at homeland bases. When the Korean conflict broke out in 1950, the first priority for these new portables was to deploy them to that Asian combat theatre. In July 1950, the 8th Army activated three provisional units and these proved highly mobile with some being moved once per week while still being capable of receiving high volumes of patients, including 608 in a single day for the 8076th MASH.[71] As the war wore on, new standards were established, while in downtime they were disassembled, loaded onto vehicles and were road-ready on six hours' notice. On arrival at a new deployment site, a unit could be (minimally) operational in as few as four hours.[72]

For a MASH, whenever the order was given to 'bug out' it had to be completely broken down, quickly, and its patients transported to a second (adjacent) unit. This disassembly/reassembly process occurred in two phases. First, in Phase I, the tents housing the registrar and receiving-and-holding were broken down. The laboratory, pharmacy, and admitting functions were moved over to the pre-operative ward. The broken-down tents were relocated with half of the personnel assigned to pre-op, post-op, surgical, and central supply, plus one receiving clerk. At the new location a new footprint was configured, consisting of pre-op, post-op, and surgical functions, including sterilization functions, and dressing stations. At this point, there are two parallel, functioning facilities, perhaps thirty or more miles apart. The hospital in the rear continues to admit patients until the forward installation is completed. When the advance unit begins to receive patients, the rear unit ceases all admissions. When all of its patients have been evacuated, the rear unit moves up and joins the advance hospital as Phase II of the redeployment. The remaining tents (Phase II) are then added to the basic footprint at the new site.[73]

The early prototypes incorporated the best features of their precursors in World War II. First conceived by Dr. Michael DeBakey, the MASH units saw extensive use in the Korean Conflict, with the final field unit decommissioned on 16 October 2006. It was then donated to the Pakistani Army for use in humanitarian missions. The early units embodied the most advancing thinking on portable hospitals.[74] These early units at times struggled to cope, however, with the extreme winters of the Korean Peninsula. This was made all the worse by the staggeringly high volumes of wounded who required treatment, and 1951–1952 was the coldest weather ever encountered in Korea with lows of 23–30 degrees below zero with heavy snow accumulations. Soldiers sometimes had to fight in little

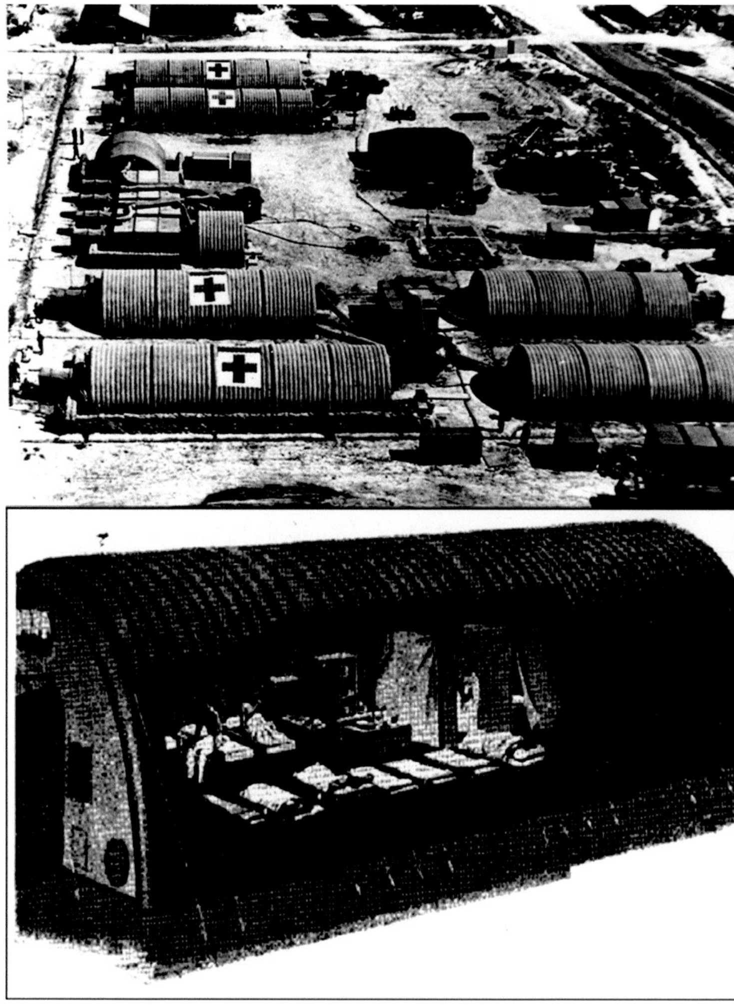

2.14a–b Aerial view of a typical pneumatic-supported inflatable inpatient ward (top), and a cutaway perspective of a typical inpatient ward (bottom), U.S. Army MUST portable field hospital, Fort Sam Houston, Texas, 1968

more than combat fatigues and field jackets. This resulted in thousands of cases of frostbite and many hundreds froze to death. In six days of admissions to the 8076th Army MASH unit in Kanuri, there were 1,836 total admits to the hospital and on a *single day* 608 were admitted.[75] There were only twelve medical officers and 120 enlisted men to staff this facility, and it lacked such amenities as blowers for heating units, and the entire facility was housed in tents. Routinely, thirteen or more patients were crammed into a single tent ward. The injured and frostbitten arrived in such massive numbers that patients overflowed into every conceivable nook and cranny. When ambulances arrived the medics would have to leave the wounded lying out in the snow on the open ground where, unfortunately, many froze to death even before they could be carried into the triage tent. However, being brought inside was no assurance against the freezing temperatures as the tents were so cold that patients even froze to death *inside*. With one's resistance already lowered significantly, there was no capacity for many to hang on. It was at this time that one of the most difficult decisions any medical officer ever has to make was made. The massive influx of casualties rendered it impossible for all to be cared for all at once. Tragically, the most seriously wounded were given morphine to prevent extreme pain, plus final rites, and then put outside to die. This then enabled the extremely pressed staff to tend to those who had at least a fighting chance of survival.[76]

By summer 1952, the rate of casualties had diminished somewhat and the MASH units were scaled back to 'normal' operational levels with a few being used as hemorrhagic fever hospitals in spring and summer and as frostbite and trench foot care facilities in winter. By the mid-1960s, the by-then vintage units were dropped from the Army's array of military medical portables and no further new units were manufactured. After 1963, a new type, the MUST system, would become the preferred, most mobile option. It would replace the MASH within the Army's portable medical facility armentarium.[77]

MUST hospitals

By the start of the Vietnam War (1965–1974), the tents that comprised the MASH units in Korea were supplanted by a pneumatic modular system known as MUST (Medical Unit, Self-Contained, Transportable). Its modules were inflatable and featured a double-walled fabric structural aperture (Figure 2.14a–b). Each inflated module could be configured as a twenty-bed ward with a surgical suite and laboratory, enabling the air-pressurized modules to be joined together forming a large, 400-bed hospital if so required (Figure 2.15).[78] The modules were arch-configured in section, inflated by one or more turbine engine power packs called *U-Packs*. The U-Packs supplied heated and cooled air, and compressed air for the structure so it could maintain its constant shape, and its power system was also a source of potable hot water. The logistical requirements were formidable, unfortunately. Fuel requirements alone were extraordinary. Every MUST field hospital required 2,400 gallons of aviation fuel each day, with some units requiring much more depending on the size and operational challenges encountered at the installation site. Each U-Pack consumed a minimum of thirty gallons of jet fuel per hour, often creating problems if supply lines were to become interrupted, as occurred often in the rough jungle terrain of the combat theatres in Vietnam. Worse, fragments from a single mortar attack could (and often did) deflate, i.e. completely collapse, major modular sections of the overall facility.[79] In a stoke of ingenuity, tires of nearby vehicles were melted down to patch the ensuing hole(s) so the module could be repaired, re-pressurized, and re-

2.15 Installation of the U.S. Army 43rd MUST portable inflatable hospital, in a hybrid installation with an aged PSH in Vietnam, 1968. By this time, hybrid facilities, consisting of inflatable modules and tents, were in side-by-side use

2.16 Aerial view, U.S. Army 93rd Evacuation Hospital, Long Binh, Vietnam, 1966. Units are configured in a cruciform pattern with four wings, yielding an open tented space at the center. This arrangement is remarkably similar to the cross-ward monastic hospitals during the Middle Ages in Northern Europe

2.17 Portable Field Hospital, Singapore, 1985. This facility is a hybrid container/tent installation. It borrows many features from American wartime precursors, principally the MUST/DEPMED facilities of the 1960s and early 1970s

commissioned; concrete pads were soon introduced so the modules would not sink down into or float along the surface of thick mud during the frequent, intense tropical downpours that would engulf the camp.[80]

The MUST prefab modular system was expandable from a basic twenty-bed configuration up to a 250-bed to even a 400-bed configuration. They did prove effective in providing relative protection from extreme temperature fluctuations. Additional design amenities included air conditioning, and a pre-packaged multi-purpose expandable hard-wall module measuring twelve feet in length by eight feet in height by seven feet in width. It weighed up to 10,000 pounds when fully packed for transport. Its fabric modules zipped together, each one inflated by means of the aforementioned U-Packs.[81] The inflatable modules housed patients, while the hard-walled containers housed essential functions such as the operating room, where precise environmental control was a necessity. The complexity of aligning and assembling a unit rendered them less agile then their MASH precursors. Instead of being operationalized on site within seventy-two hours, it usually took seven to nine days. In Vietnam, only 2.6 percent of the wounded who arrived at a surgical field hospital died, however, meaning that despite helicopter air evacuation, most deaths occurred on the battlefield before the injured ever made it to medical care.[82] With the emphasis now on leaner, faster-moving combat units, surgical teams were also being pressed ever farther forward toward the battlefront.

By 1968, hybrids composed of elements of MASH and MUST units were being deployed side by side in the Vietnam combat theatre (Figure 2.16). Unfortunately, as with its predecessor, this new type of field hospital had not been fully field-tested in a rough-terrain environment. Given the obvious problems with high fuel consumption, coupled with agility and chronic puncturing limitations, one Army medical surgeon concluded that the Army should just, 'Forget the MUST and start all over again once the [Vietnam] War is over.'[83]

DEPMEDS and TEMPER systems

After Vietnam, the U.S. Army Medical Department initiated the conversion of its fleet of fourteen MASH units. The military at this time was mandated by the United States Congress to create a standardized portable system that could be used across all four branches of the U.S. armed forces. The outmoded, problem-riddled MUST units and the remaining old-school MASH units from the Korean Conflict were replaced with yet another new type of portable hospital. The Deployable Medical System (DEPMEDS) would be designed as a high-tech, highly mobile, agile facility with all capabilities onboard and capable of treating virtually any type of wounded patient in any combat theatre, anywhere. The modular DEPMEDS system, for the first time, would allow for a high level of customization—a mission-specific field hospital tailored to local needs.[84] By 1980, the second-generation hybrid MUST/DEPMEDS system blended together the use of standard aluminum intermodal shipping containers (ISO) to house critical functions such as the laboratory, operating rooms, radiology, pharmacy, and the equipment sterilization unit (Figure 2.17). Their size was twenty feet long by eight feet high by eight feet wide. These rigid containers, each weighing close to 20,000 pounds when packed, were married with Tent, Expandable, Modular, Personnel (TEMPER) tents, housing the inpatient wards and all auxiliary functions of the hospital. Singapore developed a very similar version of this system, which showed the extent of its influence at the time.[85] In both the U.S. and the version developed in Singapore, passageways connect various hard-walled and tent-based modular components. Expansion could easily occur (Figure 2.18). But the DEPMED would soon fall victim to intense scrutiny for its deficiencies, mainly, high transport, erection, and repair costs.[86]

The medical equipment designed for DEPMEDS installations proved problematic. In design development, panels of experts had reviewed over 300 combat-related diagnoses and treatment regimens, with the central focus on the operating table, the patient bed, anesthesia equipment, and surgical carts.[87] Modifications continued

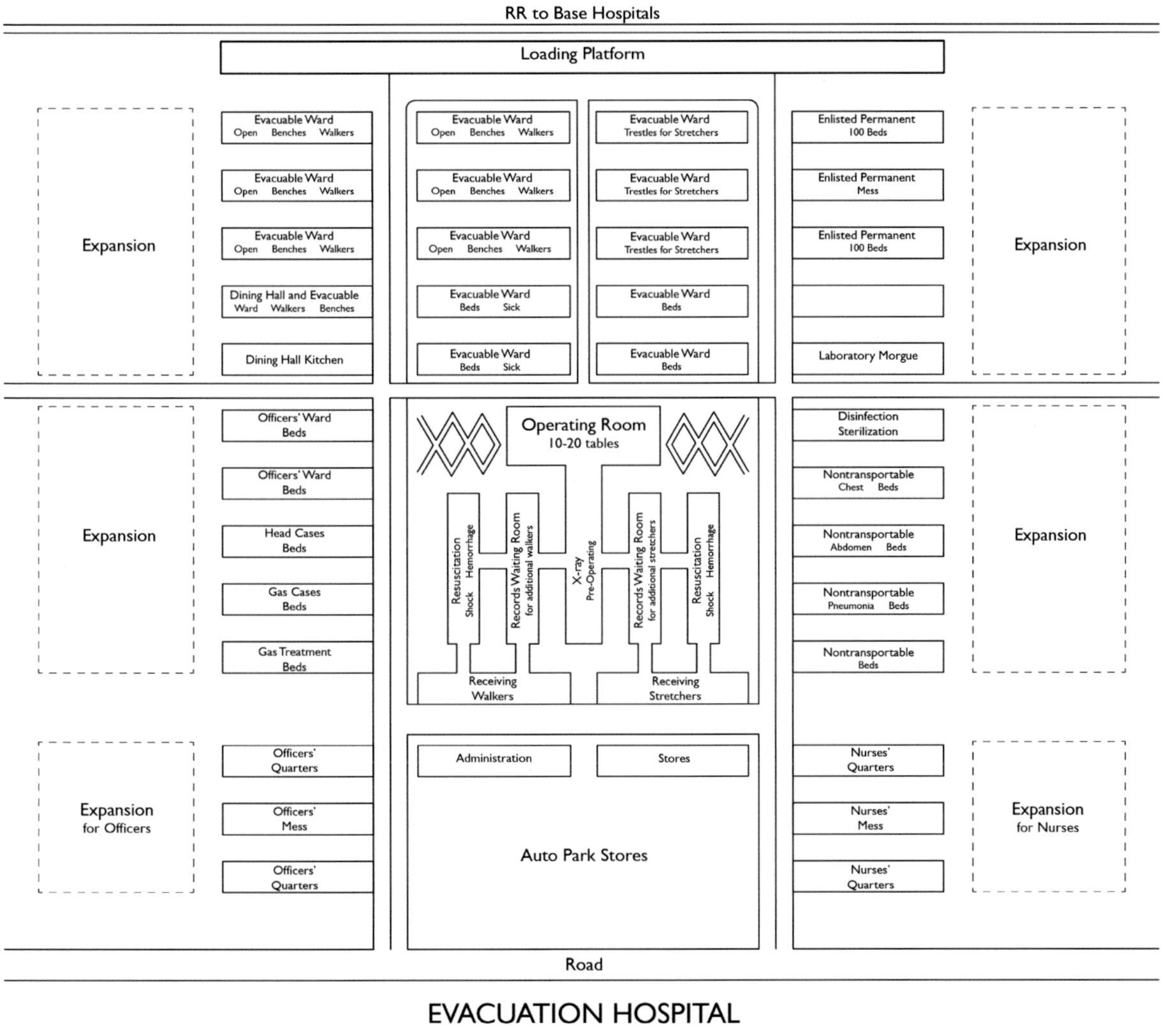

2.18 U.S. Army DEPMED/Combat Surgical Hospital (CSH) hybrid installation site plan drawing, 1984. Note the parcels set aside for future expansion

and by 1984, a hybrid DEPMED typology consisted of six facility types in a mix-and-match fashion including elements of the old MASH units, and a 500-bed Station Hospital.[88] As a reaction against this rather motley set of options, the first TEMPER hospitals were created. They were centered on a new ICU, post-operative ward, surgical unit, materials management, and dental care unit. Made of a magnesium alloy frame with canvas sheathing, each eight foot by twenty foot module had zip-down plastic window panels. Modules were in any of eight panel types, with three different door and five different window options, an inner 'wall' liner, and an insulated fabric floor.[89]

Combat Support Hospital (CSH)

By 1990, this typology had been further streamlined. In Operation Desert Storm (1990–1991), installations ranged from a sixteen-bed to a 256-bed configuration with the largest weighing more than 200,000 pounds (100 tons) in transport! Resiliency was attained by adding additional tent modules and a number of footprint options were possible (Figure 2.19a–b). The CSH differed from its numerous portable hospital precursors primarily in its larger size and its ease in accommodating the most sophisticated high tech medical equipment in the world at the time (Figure 2.20). With low American casualty rates in this combat theatre, the fixed-base camp CSH installation became the norm. The hybrid CSH/DEPMEDS (now housing from forty-four to 248 beds) hospitals garnered praise in the Persian Gulf combat theatre but their difficult deployment logistics—due to their relative immobility, sheer heaviness, and bulkiness—earned them a justified reputation as dependable facilities, once operational, but difficult as hell to get to a site and once there, hard to set up (Figure 2.21a–e).[90] A CSH was almost always stationed on an air base so medical evacuation (MEDIVAC) operations could more readily transport the injured to and from the combat zone. This way, the wounded could be quickly stabilized and then flown to a hospital elsewhere for further medical treatment (Figures 2.22 and 2.23).

In the Iraq War, the CSH served admirably:

> The hospital's primary mission is to provide fast, expert trauma treatment, over and over again: 'It's like a (fast food) restaurant,'

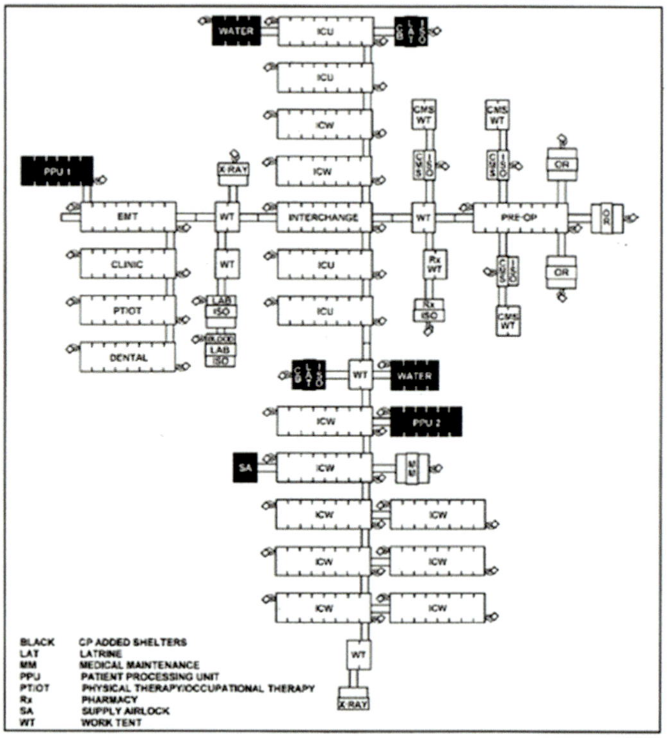

2.19a–b U.S. Army 248-bed Combat Surgical Hospital (CSH), aerial view (top) and site plan diagram (bottom), Operation Desert Storm, Iraq, 1991. Units were installed along a north-south axis with a single circulation spine

2.20 Unpacking the contents of an intermodal-shipping container containing a MASH unit during the Vietnam War, 1969

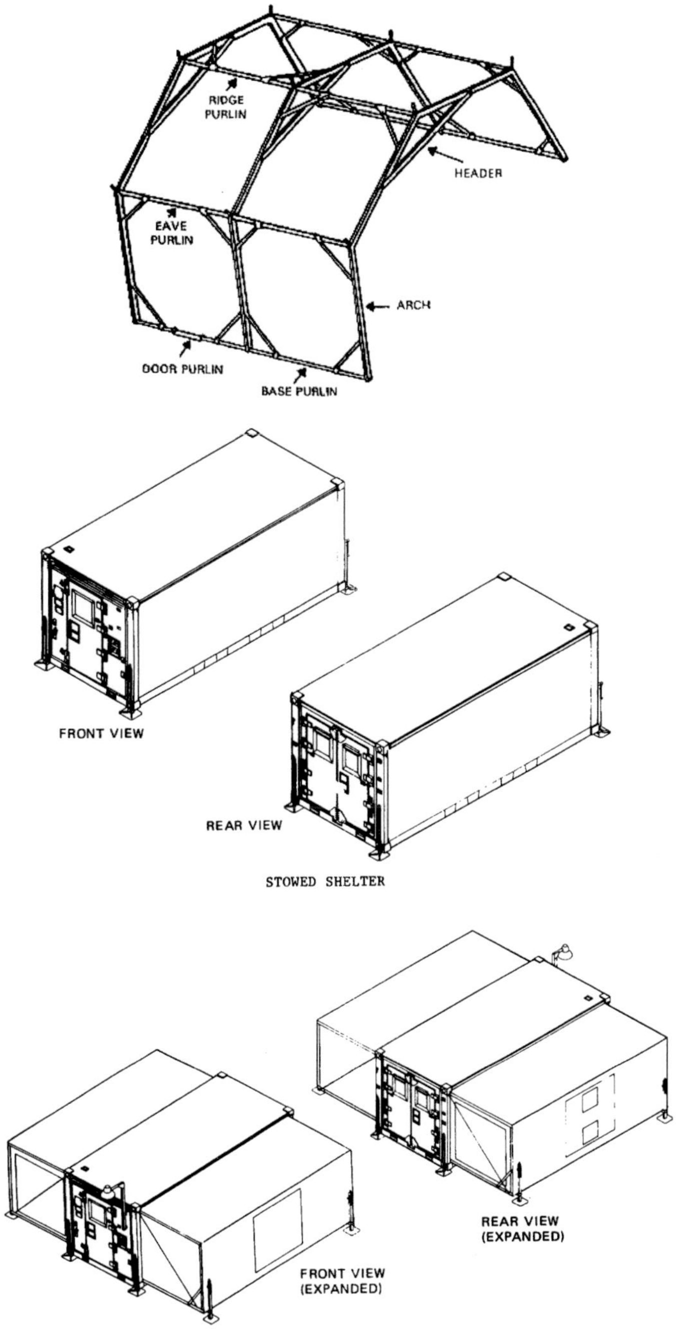

2.21 U.S. Army TEMPER module (top), and front and rear views of the tactical, expandable (ISO) units, stowed and ready for transport (middle), and the tactical, expandable (ISO) two side pop-out containerized modules, front and rear views, shown expanded (bottom), 1986

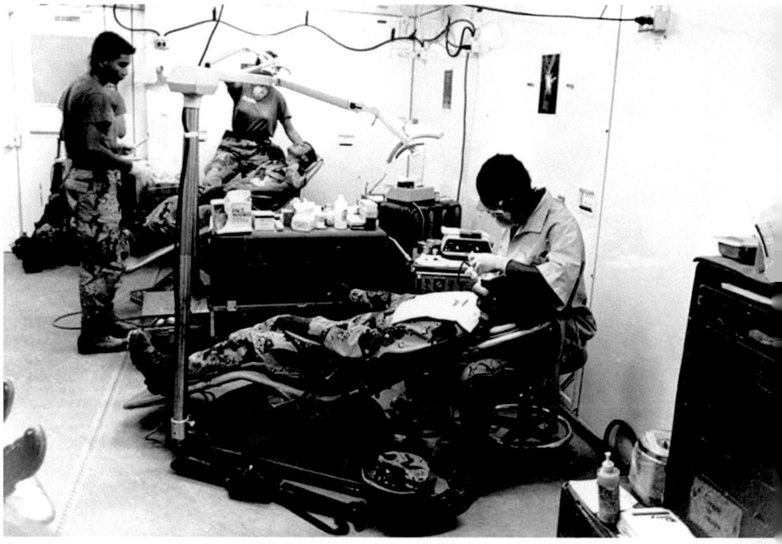

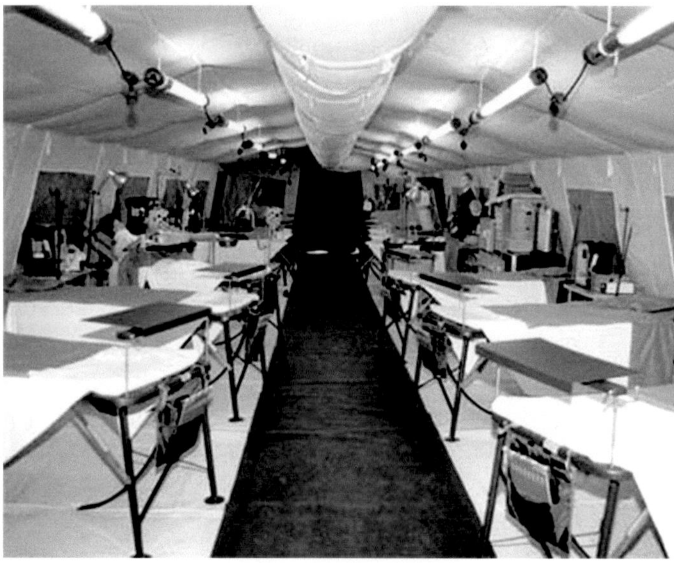

2.22 U.S. Army CSH containerized dental unit, Operation Desert Storm, Iraq, 1991

2.23 U.S. Army Operation Desert Storm, Iraq, postoperative tent, 1991. Note advancements in lighting, and air conditioning/heating system supply ducts that span the length of the ceiling of the tent

> said Capt. Laura Ricardo…'Get 'em in, get 'em out, get 'em in, get 'em out.' The rush to save lives begins with the sound of the helicopters bringing in the wounded, sometimes just fifteen minutes after they [soldiers] are hit. Once they're at the C.S.H., the pace doesn't slow. Troops might remain for only six hours, and are usually there no longer than forty-eight.[91]

The 248-bed configuration was singularly focused on patient stabilization prior to the patient's air evacuation to base hospitals in Germany and elsewhere. This was in large part attributable to the introduction, in 1995, of a far more lightweight alternative, requiring less than 1,000 square feet. This device was referred to as

2.24 U.S. Army infirmary train, Medical Department Hospital Ward Car 8906, World War II

the *Forward Surgical Team* (FST) surgical tent modules. There, surgeons performed operations of less than 2.5 hours duration. If necessary, two surgeries could be performed concurrently, side by side.[92] In all, nearly 37,000 soldiers were wounded in the Iraq War and in Afghanistan (as of the end of 2014) and the lives of an unprecedented 90 percent injured were saved.[93] By 2000, all of the old MASH units had been metamorphosed into CSH units with a modular capability, and this remains the global U.S. military field deployment standard to this day. Simultaneously, the major geopolitical conflicts of the twentieth century had given rise to an advanced understanding of metabolic care, fluid therapy, the treatment of hemorrhagic shock, the precise uses of antibiotics, resuscitation therapies, MEDIVAC helicopter transport, the electronic monitoring of patient vital signs, and sophisticated anesthetic procedures.[94]

Motorized military healthcare facilities

Trains

As previously discussed, infirmary trains were first used in Europe in World War I. These 'rolling hospitals' were designed and built by the British and were staged in combat theatres by British and allied forces (Figure 2.24) Eight types of rail cars were developed, each capable of rolling on a conventional rail line. A train consisted of a brake and infectious lying car, a staff car, kitchen and sick officer's car, one or more inpatient ward cars, one or more pharmacy cars, a kitchen and mess hall car, a ward and personnel administration car, and a brake and stores (supply) car (Figure 2.25a–b). These infirmaries could be quite lengthy, with more than fifty rail cars. This mode of transport provided advantages versus traversing the poor roads commonplace across the combat theatre.[95] By 1942, in World War II combat theatres, military infirmary railcar typology expanded somewhat, and now included a standardized kitchen/mess car and a two-tier (bunk) berth open ward rail car. World War II trains also included the, by now, standard complement of surgical, medical ward, a pharmacy car and a headquarters car (Figure 2.26 and Figure 2.27). These trains provided up to 256 beds in up to sixteen ward rail cars; each ward had eight double bunks housing sixteen patients. Two seats in the center aisle provided sitting space for ambulatory patients. Ward rail cars were equipped with sinks and medicine storage cabinets. Infirmary trains successfully evacuated thousands of combat casualties to base hospitals to the rear, and from there to outside the combat theatre.[96]

Amphibious infirmaries

For centuries, ships had been used as floating infirmaries, places where the sick and wounded were taken to from land-based battles, or from other ships within a seafaring armada. In battles at sea, military ships were commissioned and built as specialized infirmaries, as was the case in Napoleon's navy.[97] In the American Civil War, the USN *Hospital* floating steamship served communities for four years as it traveled up and down the Mississippi River

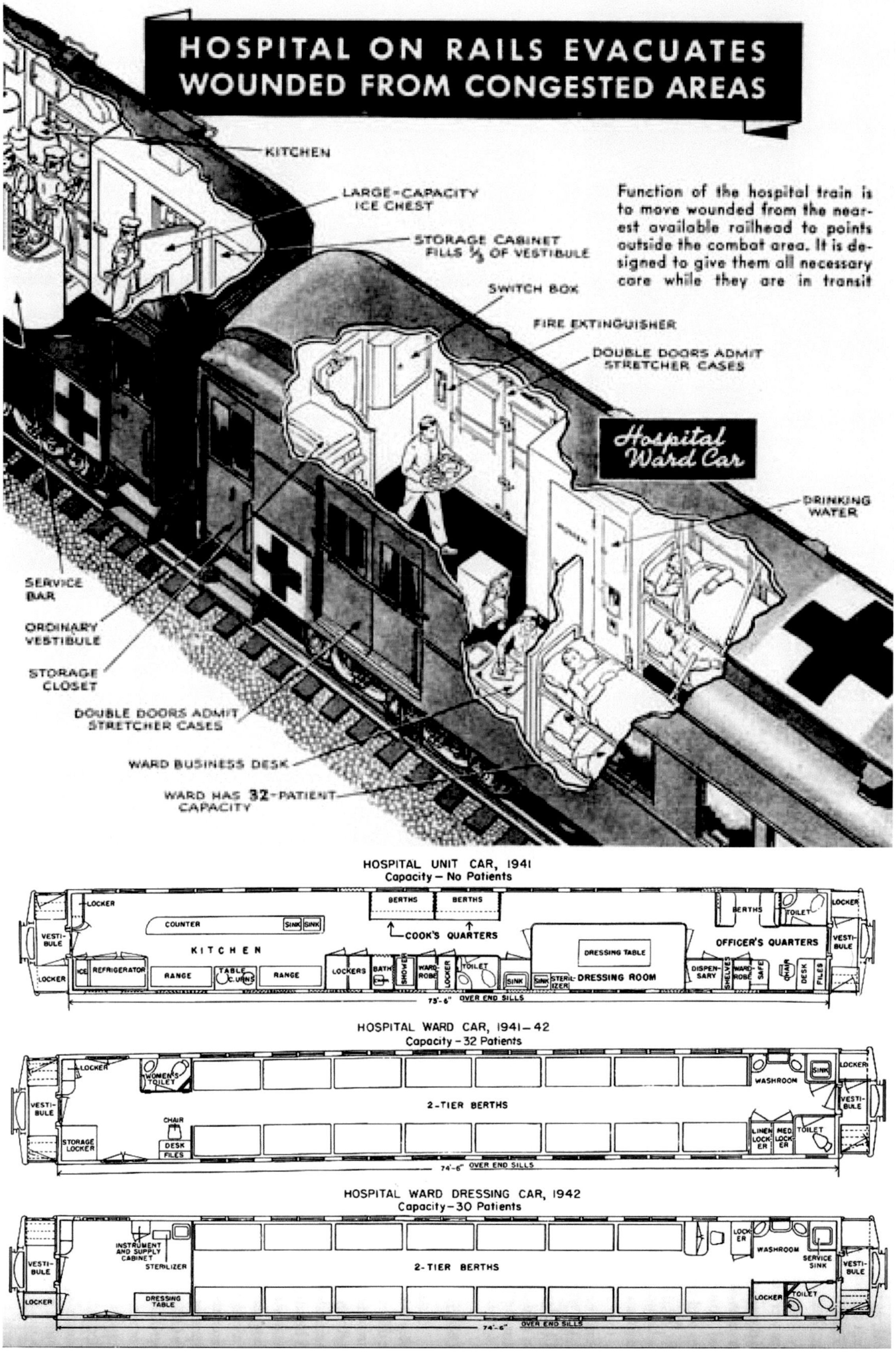

2.25a–b World War II 'Hospital on Rails,' 1941–1942, U.S. Army. Cutaway view depicts the interior (top), and the floor plan depicts a kitchen/officer's quarters car, a thirty-two-bed inpatient ward with two-tier births, and a thirty-two-bed postoperative ward, also with two-tier births (bottom)

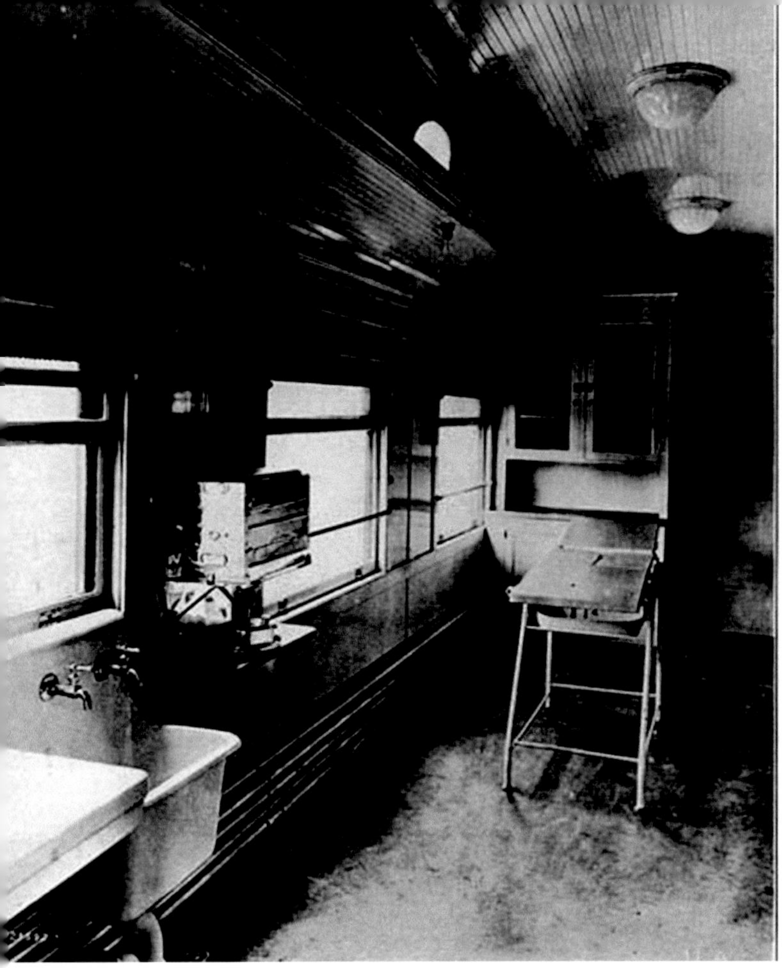

2.26 U.S. Army infirmary train, World War II, surgical car, 1944

2.27 U.S. Army infirmary train, World War II, postoperative railcar with 3-tier perimeter beds, 1944

(Figure 2.28a–b). This nautical hospital served ably throughout the war, providing care to more than 23,000 sick and wounded persons. It housed 450 beds and included a fully equipped surgical suite, open medical wards, kitchen/dining functions, and sleeping quarters for staff, including separate accommodations for nurses. Other types of infirmaries were created ad hoc from adapted agricultural and merchant marine vessels and barges; many included medical wards with minimal surgical capabilities. Typically, casualties were transported from land to ship by means of a narrow wooden gangplank.[98]

Trucks

Military transport vehicles were first used on a large scale in World War I. Field Hospital No. 353 of the 89th Division of the U.S. Army was deployed at Bernecourt, France, during the intense St. Mihiel Operation in 1915. This installation consisted of twenty tents, transported to and from the site in fourteen convoy trucks (Figure 2.29a–b). These trucks often traveled over unpaved roads, frequently close to enemy lines. As many as forty trucks would be deployed for a single tent hospital. Ambulances were first used in the American Civil War and these vehicles were nearly always horse drawn. In World War I and throughout World War II, motorized ambulances provided the critically important direct link with the portable field hospitals. Hybrid vehicles soon appeared, combining the amenity of a supply truck with a pop-up tent, and these were used as ad hoc triage and minor surgical procedure stations to stabilize the wounded (Figures 2.30a–b and 2.31a–b).[99]

Air transport

First authorized in 1926, the U.S. Army Air Squadron Corps was responsible during World War II for all Army aviation functions, notably its strategic bombing protocols, and by 1947 it had attained independence from its former parent service branch. At that time the squadron was rechristened the *United States Air Force* (USAF). By 1950, the chief role of its medical air evacuation squadrons was to furnish Army War Department leadership with guidance and logistical support on troop carrier and air transport deployment across and within evacuation zones, and oversight of all airborne MEDIVAC. It also provided basic in-flight medical care for the treatment of casualties. A USAF squadron consisted of four flights where each flight contained six identical teams of specialists, totaling twenty-four teams per squadron. Each aircraft was staffed with a medical corps officer, six nurses, and eight enlisted men. A triage team consisted of one registered nurse assisted by one enlisted trained specialist.[100]

First introduced during the Korean conflict in the early 1950s, the Bell helicopter proved to be an extraordinary invention in aiding in the rapid transport and treatment of the sick and injured. With the extremely high caseload of the MASH units taking their

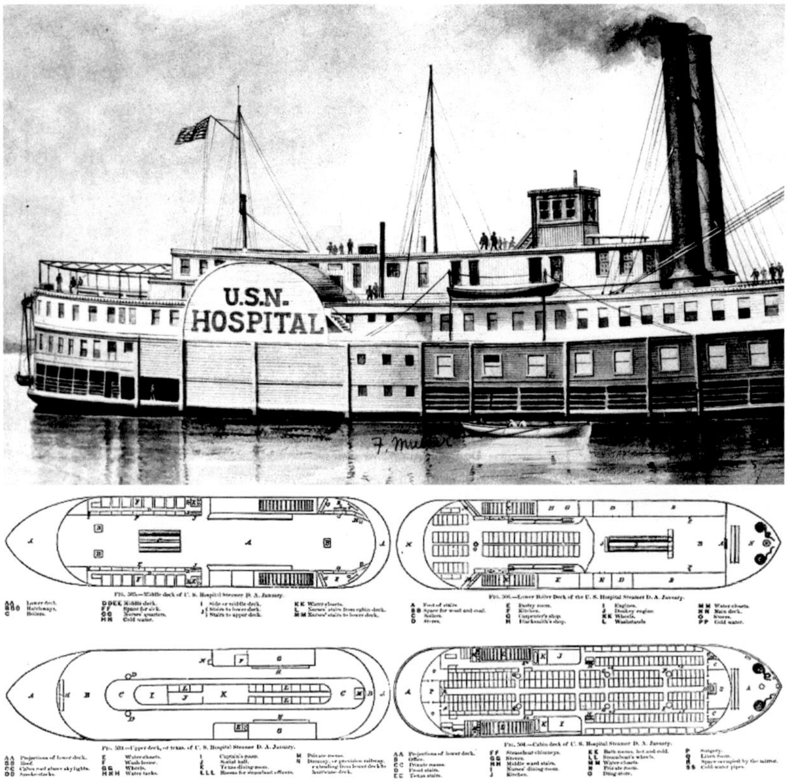

2.28a–b Exterior view, U.S. Navy (floating) Hospital, American Civil War, Mississippi River (top), and plans showing four lower decks (bottom), 1863. Note the dense placement of patient beds

2.29a–b Truck clinics stationed with U.S. Field Hospital, World War I, France, 1918 (top), and a World War I U.S. Army ambulance, France, 1918 (bottom)

2.30a–b Equipment sterilization truck stationed with the U.S. Army Mobile Field Hospital No. 20, World War I, France (left), and the sterilizing truck stationed with Mobile Field Hospital No.1, World War I, France, 1918 (right). Note the differences between the unit literally plugged into the side of a portable tent, versus the unit that remains autonomous

toll on medical personnel, and exacerbated further by excessive unit relocations, the receipt of battlefield casualties in the timeliest manner was of critical importance. Colonel Chauncey Dovell, the 8th U.S. Army Chief Surgeon, elected to experiment to explore their appropriate use in air evacuation operations. Soon thereafter, four helicopters were assigned to each MASH field unit to enhance the field hospital resupply chain, and facilitate patient delivery to a base hospital to the rear. As the conflict wore on, the decision was made at high command to initiate MEDIVAC of the most severely injured straight to Japan for further treatment and convalescence. The Bell helicopter had, by then, proven indispensable as it was significantly faster and provided a smoother ride than any ground ambulance. Without helicopters, seriously wounded patients would have otherwise required up to three weeks of additional post-operative care at the MASH to reach a recuperative stage where one could tolerate the seventy mile or more journey over rough terrain on the most feeble of back roads to a base hospital. The helicopter therefore proved highly effective in reducing patient trauma and would have a transformative effect on frontline healthcare from that moment on; this more than compensated for the increased travel distances involved in air flights within combat theatres.[101] Intensive surgical procedures need no longer occur at the MASH if patient stabilization could be accomplished with greater efficacy by means of MEDIVAC. The patient could now be transported from the front lines for more definitive care elsewhere more expeditiously than ever before in history.[102]

2.31a–b Setting up the tent over a mobile surgical truck in Tunisia, North Africa, World War II, 1944 (top), and a diagram depicting its full deployment over the truck (bottom). The tent is tethered by cables to the ground and to the truck cab, at numerous locations

Transportables: civilian precursors

Meanwhile, in the civilian sector, 'modern', offsite-built, prefabricated, portable tent hospitals were being explored. One such effort was the portable hospital first shown publicly in Denmark in 1882. It borrowed from ancient tents and yurts.[103] This structure was unveiled at the International Health Exhibition, held in Copenhagen that year. This prototype was a Danish invention. At the time, it attracted wide public interest, interest from local health commissions, and from private sector entrepreneurs:

> These hospitals are made in several sizes, from a one-roomed cottage upwards, and besides hospital use, may be devoted to a variety of purposes. They were invented and patented a few years since by Captain Doecker, of Denmark, and have been very generally patronized on the Continent... an examination will show them to be constructed of the simplest and lightest materials compatible with a due regard for strength. The walls and roofs are composed of a series of panels or frames, either connected by hinges for readily folding up, or when put together, secured by hooks and eyes; while the flooring is set out in sections ready for laying on the joists, the projecting ends of the latter serving as bearing for the walls. No foundation or digging for pegs or uprights is required, it merely being required to choose a level spot, when the hospital of small size can be erected without skilled labor in a few minutes, and the larger ones in a proportionately short space of time, also without skilled labor...They stand perfectly firm, and will resist any gale. The outer sides of the frames mentioned as forming the walls, etc., are covered with canvas, and upon that is glued a layer of felt. This excellent non-conductor prevents the external air from affecting the interior, which is thereby kept cool in summer and warm in winter. Sir Robert Rawlinson, in a recent lecture upon the 'Hygiene of War,' said: 'This invention seems particularly suitable for portable hospitals and tents during warfare...as their weight...[is] only about half that of wooden huts...These constructions may be most fully ventilated...To my belief, the Doecker hospital huts are the most perfect portable structures ever invented for the purposes intended. The price is low, compared with anything else of the kind before the public, as it is said that the cost of these portable hospitals is hardly one-fifth of that of ordinary brick huts, a fact which, combined with their other important features, should lead to their extensive adoption in this country [the U.K.]'.[104]

Doecker's 'hospital hut' was portrayed as state of the art although it never caught on as intended. This was likely due to widely held biases against portable buildings on the part of the general public. Class-based prejudices prevailed and these structures were castigated as being best suited for the underclasses. At this time, portable structures for human occupancy of any type were negatively associated with roving gypsy colonies, as were the vehicles they traveled in from one camp to another—and the camps and their inhabitants endured severe social stigmatization. They were marginalized. Portable tent infirmaries, while admired for their proven tactical amenity in times of war, nonetheless were still considered to be wholly inappropriate, insubstantial, and unreliable for everyday use in civilian settings because of their being unhygienic.[105]

In the 1837 book *The Origin and History of Missions*, Thomas Smith had described numerous missions recently undertaken, including one trip to Constantinople (present-day Istanbul) consisting of the establishment of a medical aid station, physician, four missionaries, three female assistants, and five native assistants. The focus had been on aiding destroyed hospitals in numerous towns that had been burned to the ground.[106] Twenty-five years later, the *International Red Cross* came into being, at the initiative of Henry Dunant, who had aided casualties at the Battle of Solferino (1859). Afterwards he strenuously lobbied political leaders to take proactive, universal action to protect future war victims everywhere. His two goals were a treaty that would oblige armies to care for all wartime casualties and, in peacetime, the creation of national societies, globally, charged with aiding and working alongside military medical services in the aftermath of disaster. His vision was published in *Un Souvenir de Solferino*, and subsequently the Public Welfare Committee in his hometown of Geneva, Switzerland took him up and this became the predecessor to the current *International Committee of the Red Cross* (ICRC), which first met in Geneva in 1863.[107] Its first field operation was in 1864 in the war between Germany and Denmark, where ICRC 'delegates' were sent in to provide assistance, with the ICRC functioning as a neutral humanitarian aid organization. The initial Geneva Convention

2.32 American Red Cross World War II Donuts Commissary Truck, England. The American public would not view this as an acceptable method for the delivery of healthcare in civilian contexts until the polio and TB scares of the 1950s

protocols were in time expanded to include humanitarian aid operations globally, and Dunant would receive the first Nobel Peace Prize, awarded to him in 1901.[108]

This new paradigm for frontline humanitarian aid would soon be put to the test in the United States. In the devastating San Francisco earthquake of 1906, dozens of horrific fires consumed the city for several days and more than 3,000 people died as 80 percent of the city was destroyed. In the quake's immediate aftermath, 4,000 U.S. Army troops were deployed to establish civil order, but this force was quickly withdrawn as the city itself attempted to assume responsibility for this fledging disaster relief effort. Before evacuating, the U.S. Army had constructed 5,610 small temporary wooden 'relief houses' to accommodate 20,000 displaced persons, and these dwellings were clustered into eleven camps. The exteriors of these structures were painted in drab olive paint. The U.S. Congress appropriated $2.5 million for disaster relief aid, and President Theodore Roosevelt requested the *American Red Cross* to lead the effort to provide post-disaster housing assistance, food, and healthcare services. A few days later, the first Red Cross medical tents and open-air soup kitchens were set in the city through the support of an additional sum of $8.5 million in donated private sector funds.[109]

In time, in the civilian sector, the nomadic, one-off 'gypsy-like' horse drawn wagon-tent clinics of the late nineteenth century would evolve into 'modern' motorized clinics-on-wheels. Prior to the invention of the telegraph machine, the telephone, and the construction of railroads, weeks were often required to send information, often by horseback. This would be transformed by the invention of the internal combustion engine. Concurrently, missionaries, religious-based or otherwise, were increasingly dispensing post-disaster humanitarian aid. A missionary, by definition, was an individual dispatched on a focused journey, a sojourn made possible through charitable sponsorships based on the reputation of the group he or she represented. Religious charitable sponsoring organizations predominated. Missions were carried out in any city, territory, or foreign country in need, premised on the assumption aid recipients were already in poor shape and lacking in even the most basic of day-to-day necessities.

Later, during World War II in the U.K., the *American Red Cross* operated mobile food trucks in London and in a number of European cities, and on European allied forces military bases. These 'Donut Trucks' dispensed free coffee and donuts to military personnel (Figure 2.32).[110] The Red Cross provided the lion's share of first response post-disaster aid from the 1930s through the early 1980s, following hurricanes, tornadoes, floods, earthquakes, and severe droughts. The Red Cross continues to work closely with federally dispatched military units in disaster zones within the United States and the U.S. military assists as well, when called upon, often through its *U.S. Army National Guard.*[111]

Government to the rescue

A tacit agreement, or compact, exists between the military and civilian sectors of the U.S. government whereby the military is to be called in, in the event of an extreme national emergency on U.S. soil. Meanwhile, politicians at all levels of government are in a never-ending quest to find less costly alternatives as post-disaster reconstruction budgets soar to astronomical levels. In 1984, the U.S. Department of Health and Human Services (HHS), Department of Veteran Affairs (DVA), and the Department of Defense (DOD) established the *National Disaster Medical System* (NDMS).[112] The NDMS is a section of the HHS given the authority for managing the

2.33 Delivery of thirty-six Medical Coaches, Inc. (now Medcoach) mobile vehicular clinics, Havana, Cuba, 1949

federal government's medical response in any major medical emergency. This arrangement grew out of recommendations prepared by the 'Emergency Mobilization Preparedness Board' established by then-President Ronald Reagan in 1981. The main function of the NDMS has been to establish a single, integrated response capability in the event of mass casualties in a domestic disaster, or overseas conventional war.

This program's tripartite core functions are, first, a centrally coordinated *Medical Response Function*—involving NDMS response teams for field-assessing local medical needs, equipment and supply needs, victim identification, mortuary services, and veterinary services, on site. The first response team structure sounds byzantine, even comical, with respect to the penchant for acronyms: DMATs (Disaster Medical Assistance Teams), DMORTs (Disaster Medical Operational Response Teams), and DVATs (Disaster Veterinary Assistance Teams). The NDMS central command's second core function consists of *Patient Evacuation Protocols*—involving all communications, transportation, and the NDMS medical regulating system activated to evacuate patients from the mobilization center (ground zero in the disaster zone) to reception facilities elsewhere (emergency shelters) where victims receive more definitive medical care. These various teams communicate regarding all evacuation information at the federal, state, and local levels. The third core function is the *Definitive Medical Care Function*—when a victim is admitted to an NDMS-sanctioned portable infirmary, or a stationary hospital, with injuries/illnesses sustained in a public health emergency.[113]

In 2003, the NDMS was transferred to the U.S. *Department of Homeland Security*, and then into the *Federal Emergency Management Agency* (FEMA). In 2005, this system was put to the extreme test for the first time in Hurricane Katrina, with mixed results. As discussed in Chapter 1, the federal response to Katrina was needlessly delayed because of a failed federal response.[114] As currently structured, the NDMS arm of FEMA is responsible for all pre-disaster preparations, and post-disaster response, including on-the-ground team composition, management, training, and communication systems. By 2014, with more than 100 mobile units deployed across the nation, and over 9,000 medical personnel on alert, the NDMS and FEMA collectively announced they now had the requisite financial resources, organizational structure, and equipment to get the job done right, unlike during Katrina in 2005.[115]

Mobile vehicular clinics

By the 1920s, in developed nations, international medical assistance following a disaster had begun to shift from mission work to more government-sponsored disaster relief operations. In the U.S., an extensive railway network, and a growing network of intra-city paved roads made it possible to transport supplies and personnel far more expediently than before. Automobiles led to more efficient evacuations and the first mobile clinics were commissioned in the years following World War II. The civilian counterpart to the vehicular military clinic was now used for polio and tuberculosis screening, vaccinations, and mental health counseling.[116] By 1950, the recreational vehicle (RV) industry was expanding, and it received the first commissions to construct mobile vehicular clinics for civilian use. These units were adapted from the standard recreational camper configurations first sold back in the 1930s, and specifically, the iconic *Airstream* recreational camper. The largest order ever for mobile medical clinics occurred when a U.S. company, Medical Coaches, Inc. (now Medcoach) delivered thirty-six vehicular units to the government of Cuba in Havana, in 1949 (Figure 2.33). Ian Smith designed these units. They housed amenities previously found only in stationary hospitals. The coaches were equipped with air conditioning.

2.34a–c By the 1950s, Medcoach was building mobile clinics for many parts of the world, including South America, Latin America, and Africa

Medcoach, in the coming years would construct more than 20,000 custom-designed mobile medical units and sell them in more than 100 countries and throughout North America. After Smith's death in 1976, his son continued the legacy, assuming the role of President of the company.[117] In the 1950s, cities and towns throughout the U.S. and other developed nations sought to procure their own mobile polio screening and TB unit. By the 1960s, mobile clinics were integrated into community contexts as part of an expanded palette of local and statewide public health services, i.e. cancer screening, kidney dialysis, and as 'Bloodmobiles.' Early adopters of the products manufactured by Medical Coaches (and soon, its competitors) included the Republic of Congo in 1950, the Ministry of Health in India in 1961, and numerous developing nations' health ministries in the decades since (Figure 2.34a–c).

In 1987, the *Children's Health Fund* deployed its first mobile clinic in New York City, dedicated to the poor and homeless. Other units served migrant farmers in California, Florida, South Carolina, and other places with high percentages of migrant farmworkers. In migrant farm contexts, the patients often lack English language skills and health insurance. In addition, these clinics remained open beyond the normal hours of operations, and often late into the night, to be there for field workers coming back after a long day in the fields. These units were stationed in parking lots, anywhere they could.[118] This generation of mobile clinics traveled with an ever-expanding array of medical testing and health screening equipment.[119] In 1991, Medcoach built the first mobile magnetic resonance imaging (MRI), in conjunction with Miller Medical Systems and Siemens Medical. Soon, traveling clinics were a common sight at suburban shopping malls across the U.S. More than 200 mobile mammography units were on the road by 2000, with most domiciled at medical centers, where they are also called upon for backup support. This is because hospitals often rely on their mobile clinic during hospital renovation and expansion projects. Some mobile clinics are co-owned by more than one medical center, sharing the cost burden of the equipment purchase.[120]

The growing demand for vehicular clinics became an industry subsector. By 2000, four major U.S. manufacturers had emerged: MOEX, Medical Coaches (which later merged with MOEX), Winnebago, and Perspective Enterprise. The typical unit was now widely accepted for use for community health education, and included immunization vaccines, nutritional education, and primary care in addition to diagnostic imaging capabilities (Figures 2.35 and 2.36). Units were manufactured thirty-five to forty feet in length, equipped with sophisticated wireless 'curbside computational' capabilities considered to be the mobile equivalent to hospital bedside computerization. The interior compartments allowed for multiple floor plan options for a client to select from. The two basic plan types were the side-corridor unit and the

2.35 By the 1990s, mobile units were being purchased by hundreds of hospitals and public health agencies in many parts of the world. This unit features a pop-out extension, and a large electric-powered canopy-awning

2.36 The interiors of mobile truck-clinics are complex, with an array of diagnostic testing machinery, and multiple treatment bays

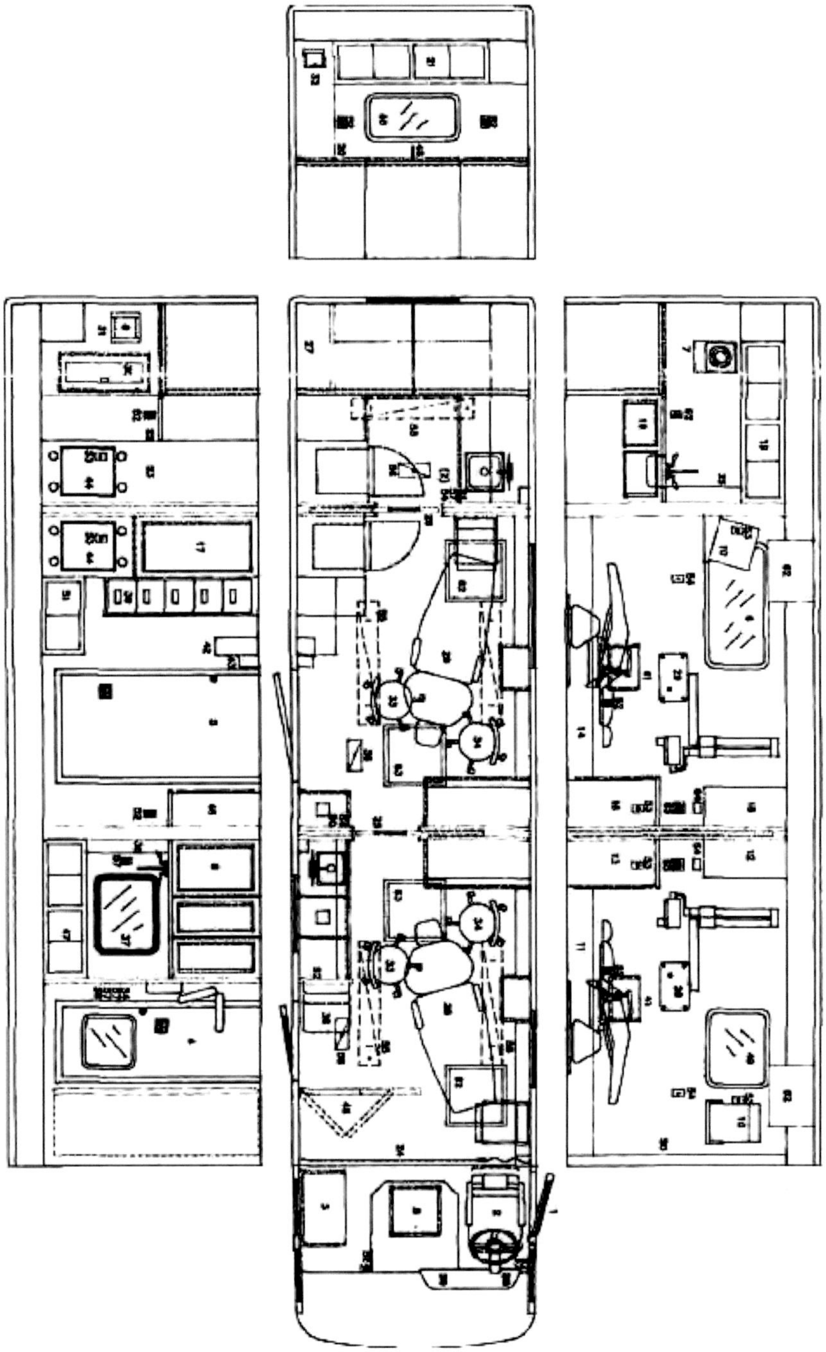

Key:
1. driver's door
2. driver's seat
3. storage
4. entry/exit door with: 20" x 20" fixed glass window
5. wheelchair door with deadbolt lock
6. 48" x 24" fixed glass window
7. exhaust vent with extension
8. motor cover table (fixed height)
9. sink cabinet with adjustable shelves
10. (2) wall shelf with TV/VCR
11. water line chase
12. double overhead cabinet with locking sliding doors
13. work counter
14. water line chase
15. double overhead cabinet
16. work counter
17. closet with coat rod/refrigerator cabinet
18. stainless steel countertop/sink
19. overhead cabinet
20. stainless steel countertop
21. overhead cabinet
22. stainless steel countertop
23. refrigerator cabinet with vent
24. cab separation curtain
25. pocket door with 12" x 12" leaded glass
26. pocket door with 12" x 12" Plexiglas®
27. electric wall
28. (2) dental chair
29. (2) intra-oral X-ray
30. 125A 120V/240V breaker panel
31. cam switch
32. 12V fuse panel
33. (2) doctor's stool
34. (2) assistant's stool
35. vent stack/water line chase
36. jump seat
37. 30" x 24" emergency exit window
38. vent stack/water line chase
39. 5 drawer file cabinet
40. 36" x 18" fixed window
41. (2) fold-down writing surface
42. wheelchair lift control box
43. wheelchair lift manual release
44. (2) 1.8 cubic foot refrigerator
45. bi-fold leaded wall
46. countertop with hinged cover
47. overhead cabinet
48. 4" high Plexiglas divider
49. 30" x 24" fixed window
50. a/c line chase
51. overhead cabinet

1-54. (9) 110V duplex receptacle
55. (5) 48" fluorescent light fixture
1-58. (3) 12V fluorescent light fixture/switch
59. 12V auxiliary power outlet
60-61. surface mount X-ray control (front X-ray)
62-63. (2) "HEPA-Care" filtration system
64. (2) computer prewire (CAT-5 cable)
65. (2) 110V quadplex receptacle

2.37 Mobile truck clinic owned by San Jacinto Methodist Hospital, Texas, 2014

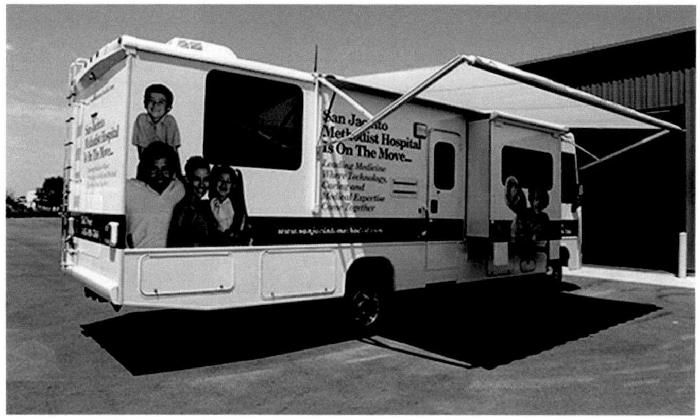

2.38 Mobile radiology units provide cancer screening and related services. Manufacturers customize the basic chassis and interior compartment to suit client requirements.

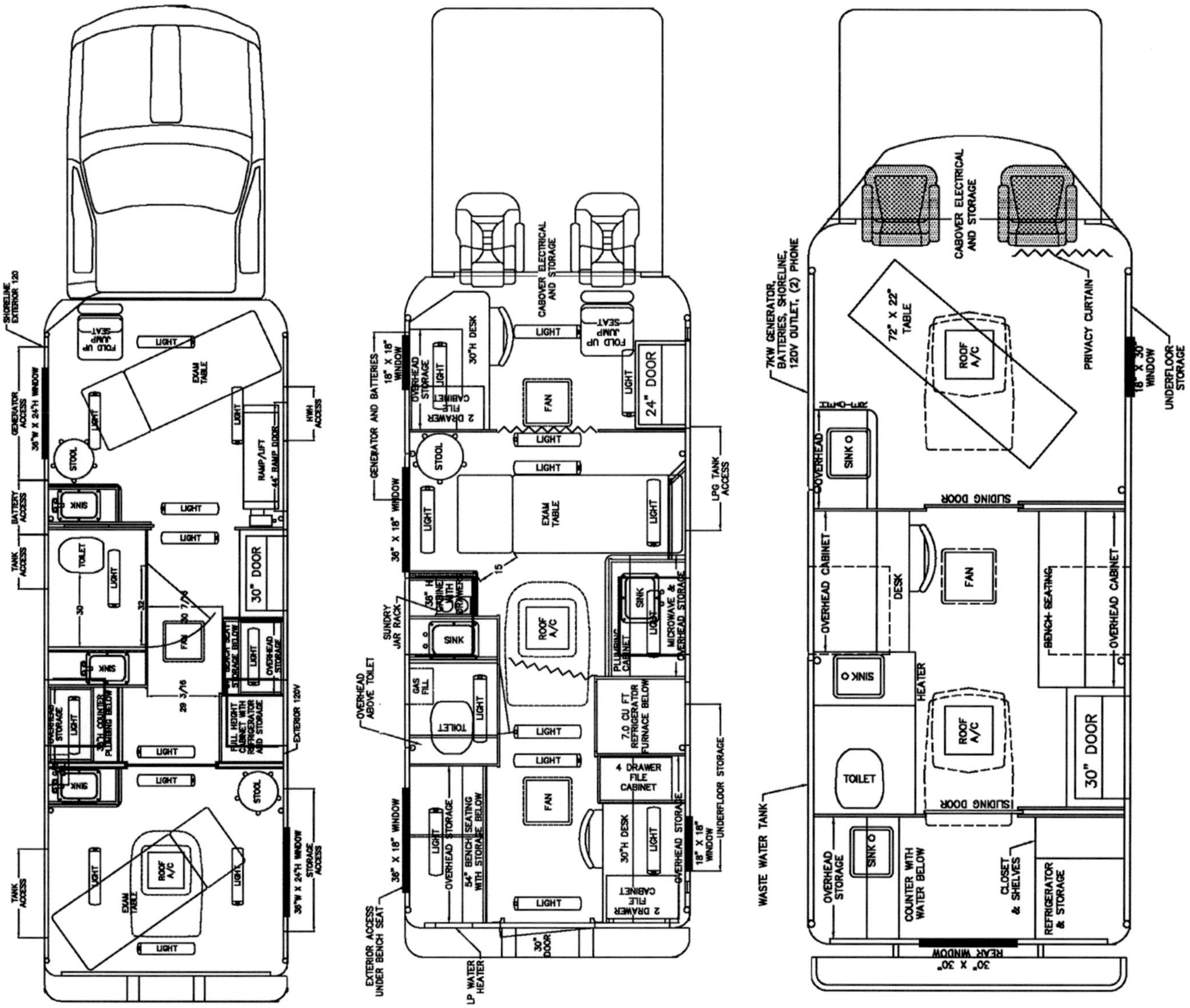

center-corridor unit. Automakers, including General Motors and Ford, provided the basic undercarriage, engine, and transmission. The interior of the clinic was made to order at the factory.[121]

The mobile clinic was adapted, essentially, from a vehicle built for recreational purposes (Figures 2.37 and 2.38). In the 2000–2010 period, Medcoach introduced the first mobile high definition PET/CT scanner linear accelerator. In 2008, this manufacturer built its first mobile brachytherapy unit, a non-radioactive radiation treatment unit for cancer patients. By 2015, the company had built more than 300 mobile MRI vehicular clinics.[122]

This new generation of vehicular clinics was owned and operated by government, local medical centers, and humanitarian NGOs. Another recent example was the Carolinas MED-1, built for rapid response in the field wherever and whenever local, stationary, hospital resources become unavailable. It was designed and manufactured in the wake of the growing number of terrorist and public health casualty events globally, such as the terrorist attack in the Tokyo subway in 1995, the proliferation of bio-infectious agents such as SARS, anthrax, and periodic pandemic bird flu outbreaks. It can respond to infectious diseases such as the virulent Ebola virus, functioning as a quarantine unit.[123] Hospital surge demand can be relieved and Carolinas MED-1 has an onboard decontamination unit that can be set up virtually anywhere.[124] In 2005, the Carolinas MED-1 was deployed for the first time to the Mississippi Gulf Coast and New Orleans in the aftermath of Hurricane Katrina.[125] At the forty-five-day mark, this medical unit had cared for more than 7,500 disaster victims, and saved many lives.[126]

Summary

One of the best-known examples of prefab modularity was the Crystal Palace, built in Hyde Park, London for the Great Exhibition of 1851. Designed by Joseph Paxton and commissioned in a period of two weeks, it was composed of lightweight, inexpensive materials, i.e. iron, wood and glass. The construction period lasted two months, and principally consisted of assembling offsite-built components. At the exhibition's conclusion the structure was disassembled and relocated to another location.[127] Four years later, as previously mentioned, Isambard Kingdom Brunel's prefabricated hospital would be erected in Renkioi, Turkey, in the Crimean War. This would become known as the first modern, offsite-built prefab hospital. Later, an offshoot, the Quonset hut was mass-manufactured as a cheap way to provide efficient, yet spartan accommodations; Quonsets are discussed further in the following chapter.[128]

During the 1970s, prefab modularity began to appear on a noticeable scale in hospitals. But change has come slowly. In 2009, the U.S. *National Research Council* issued a report calling for greater use of offsite manufacturing as an opportunity to improve the nation's competitiveness in the global construction market.[129] In 2010, the Seattle office of Perkins + Will partnered with Whitley Manufacturing to produce two offsite-built outpatient oncology clinics. Two resultant facilities, the outpatient clinic in Edmonds, Washington (see Chapter 3) and a second outpatient clinic, in Ballard, Washington, were offsite-built and then transported to their permanent sites for installation and final assembly (see Chapter 6). Swedish-Ballard would be among the first offsite-built prefab healthcare facilities to receive Leadership in Energy and Environmental Design (LEED) certification (2013). All 180 inpatient rooms at the Miami Valley Heart and Orthopedic Center, in Dayton, Ohio (2010), designed by the Columbus office of NBBJ, were built off site using *Building Information Modeling* (BIM) software (see Chapter 6).

Much of this was made possible by advances in transportation technology. In 1955, the intermodal shipping container (ISO) was invented by Malcolm P. McLean. McLean was a trucking executive in North Carolina who had purchased a steamship company with the goal of transiting clip-on, removable, truck-size trailer modules with their cargo inside, remaining fully intact. To him, this strategy was far more expedient—enabling, for example, a single container to be lifted up from a vehicle directly onto a ship without first having to unload it. Soon, this innovation would be referred to as *intermodalism*. A container with its cargo inside could now be networked using different modes of transit and distributed through a coordinated chain of ships, trucks, and trains, a process to revolutionize existing logistical models and eventually transforming international trade.[130] In a similar vein, the experimental work of the New York City-based firm LOT-EK has been recognized for pushing the boundaries of the standard shipping container although, to date, this firm has not built any buildings specifically for healthcare. Other architects have done so, however. One example, the recent, modestly scaled 'Clinic in a Can' installation, houses patient intake/interview, consult, and examination bays, plus radiology equipment, a surgery bay, and support spaces, in three adapted intermodal containers. These modules are deployed as three wings around a semi-enclosed courtyard (Figures 2.39 and 2.40). Each module is forty feet in length, relatively easy to install, and can be relocated or reconfigured if, for instance, additional units are added.[131] The recent 'Mobile AIDS Relief Clinic for Sub Saharan Africa OUTREACH' design competition was held to stimulate designers' inventive applications of tents, containers, and hybrid combinations thereof. It was sponsored by the U.S.-based NGO *Architecture for Humanity*.[132] A significant percentage of the 530 submittals featured variations on the basic intermodal shipping container.[133] Two other recent additions to this line of inquiry were the

2.39 'Clinic in a Can' installation in Haiti, 2010. In the future, this and similar low-tech containerized solutions will likely be viewed as seminal to in the evolution of twenty-first-century disaster mitigation architecture

2.40 'Clinic in a Can' installation, illustrating two floor plan options, one housing a surgical unit (left), and a second configuration housing preventive/ wellness care, non-surgical procedures, and dental care (right), 2014

'Containers to Clinics' (C2C) women's health clinics built for post-earthquake Haiti, in 2010, and the colorful, informally composed, mixed-use *Contertainer* clinic and community center in Batu, East Jawa, Indonesia, designed by dpavilion Architects (see Chapter 6). Architects in many parts of the world are now exploring the possibilities of the adapted intermodal shipping container, and especially its DIY (do it yourself) advantages.

In these accelerated times, it is worthwhile to pause to take cognizance of quintessential, landmark events in the history and development of prefab modular architecture for health. For this reason, a timeline-chronology on the subject is presented. It can be instructive to view events against a backdrop of parallel events/ periods in architectural history, and in society at large (Figure 2.41). One cannot not know history if one is to act cogently, in the present and the future.[134] Military conflicts have consistently provided the stage, as prime drivers of technical advancements in portable medical facilities. Over the course of history, the military field hospital has evolved from minimalist yurt and tent structures to sophisticated offsite-built prefabricated systems, and their affordances endure. The record indicates that offsite-built structures and componentry have, over time, exhibited numerous advantages over traditionally built healthcare facilities including: (1) comparative advantages in re-configurability; (2) the advantage of modularity without necessarily compromising customization options; (3) physical lightness; (4) lower construction cost compared to a comparable, conventionally-built building; (5), a higher level of quality control attained in factory-controlled conditions compared to most traditional construction sites; (6) a shorter project construction timeline; and (7) the option of redeployment to another site. Significant breakthroughs in this timeline/chronology have been framed by two epochs—the Industrial Revolution, including the twentieth century innovations of Buckminster Fuller,

2.41 Timeline of key events and developments in the modern history of portable prefabricated architecture for health, and some prognostications for the future

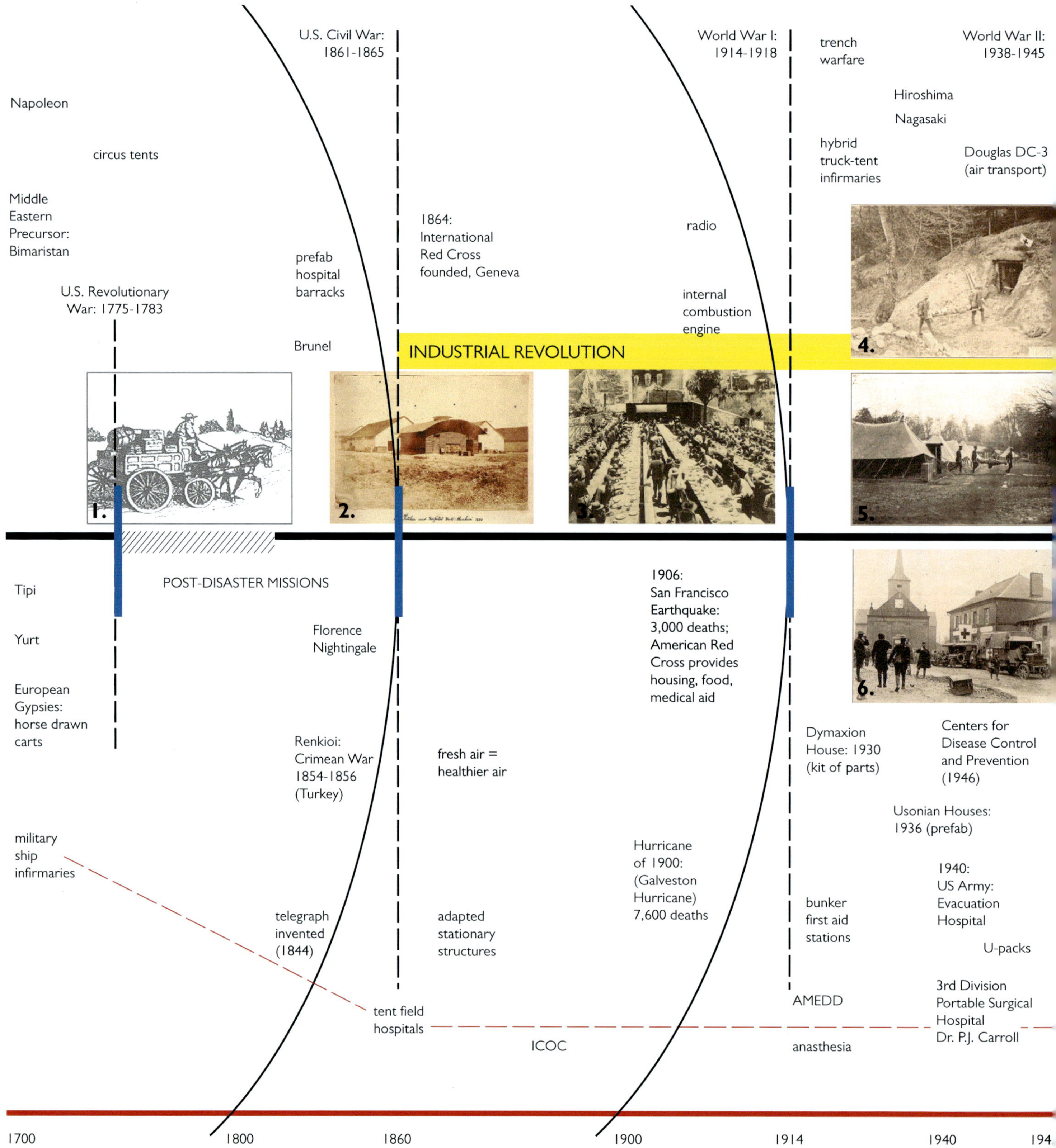

Vietnam War: 1954-1975

Cold War: 1947-1991

helicopter MEDIVAC

churches, barns, resorts, mansions adapted to makeshift hospitals

Korean War: 1950-1953

M.U.S.T.

NASA

1969: first moonwalk

1979: FEMA established

LOT-EK

Prefabricated/ Modularized (P/M)

social media

9/11

2005: Hurricane Katrina: 1,858 US deaths

drought

transformer RTC / RHC

WATER WARS

unforeseen pandemics

INFORMATION REVOLUTION

7.

Bristol Freighter

bloodmobiles

1984: US National Disaster Medical System (NDMS)

9.

11.

1943: church-cum-infirmary, Philippines

1949: Medical Coach, Inc. delivers 36 mobile vehicular units to Cuba

8.

10.

iDAPT/CEAL (Toronto Rehab)

Ebola pandemic

digital divide

solar powered transportables

global sea level rise/ innundated coastal zones

television

M.A.S.H.

WHO Founded: 1948

nuclear weapons

1955: ISO Intermodal shipping container invented

ARCHIGRAM

Combat Support Hospital (CSH)

TEMPER

DEPMEDS

prefab stationary hospital

INTERNET

bioterrorism

Gulf War: 1990-1991

MEDCOACH

iPad

tsunami

Iraq/Afghanistan Wars: 2003-2012

Carolina MED-1

app-mania

SMART_SYSTEMS

e-health/ m-health

virtual medicine

robotics

1950 1960 1970 1990 2000 2050

including his Dymaxion House (1930),[135] and the work of Frank Lloyd Wright, and his Usonian houses of the 1930s,[136] and the Information Revolution, signifying the advent of ubiquitous, mobile, personal computation and its profound ramifications in contemporary culture and society.[137] Within this timeline/chronology, numerous 'waves' therefore become identifiable and these events tend to be bracketed by major military conflicts.

Acts of war, as recounted in this chapter have, more than anything else, fueled innovations in prefab modularity and in portable healthcare facilities over the past century and a half. Wartime advances in transportation have also indelibly shaped this landscape. The helicopter has profoundly impacted the technological evolution of the portable field hospital. Without the ability to rapidly MEDIVAC casualties out from the front lines in combat theaters to base hospitals at the rear, the degree of acceptance of the field hospital as a viable healthcare setting would likely have never occurred. In the Iraq War, the portable field hospital was the proving ground for the introduction of new pharmaceuticals, medication therapies, treatment protocols, and even the design of combat gear worn by soldiers.[138] The portable military field hospital was transformed from a place of extremely poor sanitation and hygiene into one of cleanliness, and these developments have been transferred to the realm of the portable civilian field infirmary. Instead of the injured facing near-certain amputation, or likely death, due to the occurrence of rampant infection, the portable field hospital evolved into a place where even severe head trauma wounds can be treated with neurosurgery and other advanced procedures.[139]

Those who dismiss portable healthcare facilities assume these structures must, of necessity, be excessively utilitarian—even ugly—in their appearances and therefore remain immune, aesthetically disconnected from the core Vitruvian precepts of *commodity, firmness and delight*.[140] From this point on in the twenty-first century, projecting outward to 2050, myriad opportunities exist to explore many new building technologies, and these include the ability of these structures and their componentry to be *intelligent*, that is, to possess the ability to self-sense their own well-being, or 'architectural health' status. The level of information provided by (and about) the facility, in and of itself, will immeasurably aid because individuals are already challenged, just doing the best they can on a day-to-day basis. Albeit, drab, monotonous installations lack in aesthetics. This misses, however, the unprecedented opportunity to pursue and attain architectural design excellence in this emerging area. This is examined further in the following chapters.

Offsite

CHAPTER 3

> Honor and respect the mateline. Maximize the factory, minimize the field.
>
> SHoP Architects, 2012.[1]

The modern offsite-built prefab hospital originated in 1854, soon after Britain entered the Crimean War, in reaction to the decrepit Turkish Selimiye Barracks, at Scutari. This facility had been adapted for use as the sole British Army Hospital at the battlefront. There, casualties after admittance became extremely high, as the hospitalized patients contracted cholera, dysentery, typhoid and malaria due to poor sanitary conditions. After witnessing this unfolding disaster firsthand, Florence Nightingale wrote to *The Times of London* requesting for the government to provide a rapid response. The British government was taken aback by the revelations of the inhumane conditions at Scutari—including the potable water supply running through the carcass of a dead horse. Nightingale, for her part, stayed on, supervising its transformation and becoming world-renowned as a result of her tireless work and many important contributions. Meanwhile, in February 1855, Isambard Kingdom Brunel was invited by the Permanent Under Secretary at the War Office, Sir Benjamin Hawes (the husband of Isambard's sister) to produce a prefabricated hospital able to be quickly built off site and transported by ship to an installation site in the Crimea. Brunel designed a unit ward housing fifty patients, ninety feet long by forty wide and divided into two side-by-side open wards. This building envelope responded well to the necessities of hygiene, sanitation, natural ventilation, site drainage dictates, and the need for temperature control—all in keeping with Nightingale's findings independently drawn from her prior and concurrent work. These open wards were to be integrated into a 1,000-bed configuration, based on up to three long rows of ward *modules* totaling sixty in number. Brunel did not specify a definitive site plan but did insist that these modules be assembled and connected together on site by English workers, for quality control purposes. He left this task to the site engineer, John Brunton, who decided to arrange the initial installation of modules on two sides of three long, double-loaded circulation spines. Brunton exploited the site's topographical amenity by drawing freshwater from an uphill stream down through the hospital site; these ditches drained directly out to the sea. The pairing of back-to-back ward modules would not, however, have met with Nightingale's approval because half of the beds in a given ward were placed up against the

3.1 Brunel's revolutionary prefabricated hospital built at Renkioi, Turkey in 1855

windowless corridor-spine wall, too far from the outer windowed perimeter wall.[2] Dr. Edmund Alexander Parkes traveled to Turkey to select a site and oversee operations. Parkes selected Renkioi on the Asiatic bank of the Dardanelles near the fabled city of Troy. It was 500 miles away, then a three or four-day journey from the Crimea. Importantly, it lay outside the malaria zone in which the stricken Scutari barracks infirmary was located. Parkes remained on site at Renkioi until the end of the war in 1856. Modules took six days to design and manufacture. Price & Co. built them on the grounds of a railway yard in England and the first shipment left Southampton Docks in January 1855 and the hospital's last shipment of component kit-of-parts reached Renkioi in May 1855. By July, the entire Phase I facility was assembled and ready to admit its first 300 patients, and by December reached full capacity of 1,000 patient beds.

The hospital was to have been expanded to 2,000 beds but hostilities ceased before that would occur. After the fall of Sevastopol, it was shuttered in July 1856 and then sold off to the Ottoman Empire in September 1856. It was then disassembled and relocated elsewhere. But even for its short lifespan, it was an immense achievement (Figure 3.1). Of the approximately 1,300 patients admitted, only fifty deaths occurred there. Meanwhile, at Scutari, the death rate was as high as ten times that number. Civilian physicians ran the hospital at Renkioi as opposed to military officers, with complete command of its daily operation. For the U.K. this practice would become standardized after this war. Dr. Parkes, its Medical Superintendent, became the first Professor of Hygiene at the new Army Medical School, ensuring that 'the prevention of disease and the promotion of health' would henceforth be the highest priority of the British Army Medical Services. Today almost nothing survives of the Renkioi hospital, although tourists regularly visit its site. While in use for only eighteen months, the injury and disease mortality rate fell from 42 percent to only 3.5 percent.[3] There is no record of Brunel and Nightingale having ever directly met face to face although Nightingale would later refer to this hospital as 'those magnificent huts.' All major offsite-built prefabricated components, including timber frame trusses, had been built and shipped from a distant factory in the U.K.

For many years after this, a general disinterest in prefabrication yielded few developments for healthcare uses. After World War I, hospital superintendents and their architects gradually came to appreciate how certain fixed components such as nurse's stations, interior window assemblies, tube-based transport systems for intra-departmental communications, modular inpatient rooms and bathrooms, headwalls, and transport systems for supplies might be more efficiently and cheaply built off site, shipped, and then permanently installed elsewhere.[4] The allied forces in World War II,

3.2a–c Component parts of a prefab modular Quonset structure, circa 1930s

for their part, were forced to relearn the virtues of Brunel's hospital at Renkioi and they erected offsite-built prefab barrel-vaulted *Quonset huts* and other types of open wards in grid layouts, not unlike the site plan at Renkioi. Quonsets were soon in widespread use. Many hundreds of these offsite-built steel modules were built on combat theater base hospital sites because they: (1) met stringent sanitation and hygiene requirements; (2) provided unobstructed interior spaces; (3) presented a somewhat positive interior ambiance; (4) met tough structural and durability standards; and (5) met natural daylight and natural ventilation requirements (Figure 3.2a–c).

The construction industry is the largest single global economic sector. Prefab modularity is a rapidly growing segment within this industry and healthcare is but one subsector. The planet's growing affordable housing crisis represents perhaps the most pressing need for resource-efficient, off-the-shelf, less labor-intensive solutions that simultaneously allow meaningful design options for their inhabitants.[5] Prefabrication denotes the manufacture of a part, component, or larger modular assembly off site in a workshop or factory.[6] The aim is to improve design quality, achieve greater consistency, eliminate excess building materials, and save money and time. Recent advancements in prefab Structural Insulated Panel Systems (SIPs), pre-structured framing systems, and CAD/CAM laminated timber framing assemblies with sustainably harvested wood structural components are but three facets of this movement attracting favorable attention as modern-day equivalents to ancient precursors discussed in the previous chapter.[7]

X-Prefab

Building types other than healthcare appear to have received the bulk of designers' and engineering attention in the past decade. For instance, the race is on to construct the world's tallest prefabricated building although recent efforts have run into obstacles. In the city of Changsha, Hunan, in South-Central China, Sky City, a planned 202-floor building, was designed to be built of prefab modular units constructed on site in the unrealistically short period of a mere ninety days. Its builders were forced to halt site preparation in 2013 after government regulators required numerous last minute building permit approvals. This mad rush to stack prefab modules high into the sky is not exactly new. More than forty years ago, the Nakagin Capsule Tower was built in the Shimbashi District of Tokyo. Designed by Kisho Kurokawa, a mixed-use prefab modular tower (1970–1972), it stands today as a rare built example of the Japanese Metabolist movement in the 1960s and early 1970s. It was composed of 140 concrete pod 'living capsules,' each a 300 square foot prefab unit and stacked fifteen levels atop one another in a seemingly random zigzag pattern.[8] As of 2012, only thirty modules remained in use as apartments, with the other capsules languishing in ignominy as storage bins, or simply abandoned.[9] North America's tallest modular prefab tower, at thirty-two levels, is the $4.9 billion B2 BKYLN, at the Barclays Center redevelopment site in Brooklyn, New York.[10] Plagued with problems from the outset, including strong opposition from local construction unions, this project was halted in August 2014. The

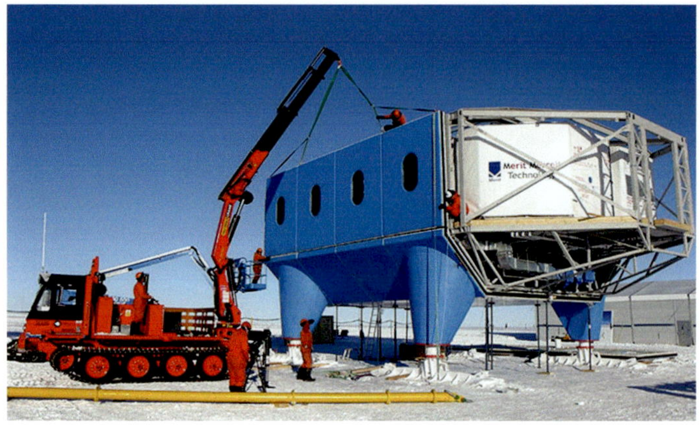

3.3 Exterior, Halley VI Antarctic Research Station, Antarctica, 2013, Hugh Broughton Architects

developer, Greenland Forest City Ratner Partners, and the construction manager, Skanska USA Building Inc., sued one another for cost overruns and innumerable delays. Only ten floors had been completed. The developer has ruled out any further modular prefab buildings at the Brooklyn site.[11]

Meanwhile, diverse other types of non-healthcare, offsite-built prefab *X-Prefab* structures include emergency housing for post-disaster strike zones and extreme climates. These systems are transited by air, sea, rail, and truck, and include the hexagonal tent system manufactured by Western Shelter Systems, which allows for interconnectivity between modules, yielding an all-weather installation. A typical installation consists of a mix of 18-wheeler trucks and white fabric tent modules. The trailers house support functions including kitchens and personal hygiene amenities. A complete facility, in transport, requires only one-fourth the shipping footprint compared to when fully deployed.[12]

STAR-TIDES manufactures a number of modular prefab housing systems, including a flat-pack system for rapid deployment. These are used as first responder housing, security stations, dormitories, emergency operations centers, and military uses, and as staging points for disaster relief organizations.[13] A module is erectable in fifteen minutes with four people, and dozens of units can be installed in an encampment in a single day by fewer than fifty workers. These structures provide ample fodder for critics of prefab, however, for their small windows and spartan aesthetic although they do feature heating and air conditioning, and sit atop low piers. STAR-TIDES' MOHAB (Inflatable Mobile Habitat) features a rectangular 'hub' at the center of the site, surrounded by as many as 100 pneumatic dwellings, interconnected by means of an inflatable double-loaded circulation spine. As many as six double-loaded 'dwelling wings' can be connected. Their exterior skin is a twenty centimeter thick fabric shell with an outer layer of ultraviolet-resistant, PVC-coated fabric and an inner layer of weatherproof thermoplastic polyurethane. Each inflated module measures 6 meters in length by 2.38 meters in width by 3.4 meters in height. The walls, when inflated, are twenty centimeters thick and each structure houses up to three double bunk beds and a corresponding number of storage lockers.[14] The *Ex-Container* (2011), by the Tokyo-based firm Yasutaka Yoshimura Architects, was designed in response to the 2011 Tohoku earthquake and tsunami. Standard thirty-foot long ISO shipping containers are stripped to their bare structural frame and repurposed as emergency housing modules. Each container is re/pre-manufactured off site with pristine all-white panels, wood paneled interiors, skylights, residential fixtures, and full-height glass with sliding doors and an open-air balcony at one end. More than 500 (at this writing) have been deployed in the disaster strike zone.[15]

Extreme X-Prefab was the subject of a 2005 design competition sponsored by the British Antarctic Survey that included a healthcare modular component within a larger building footprint.[16] The competition brief called for an offsite-built prefab monitoring station for the Brunt Ice Shelf in Antarctica. The built scheme, by Hugh Broughton Architects, together with the engineering firm AECOM, is the Halley VI Antarctic Research Station (2005–2013). The design challenge was to create laboratory and living accommodations capable of withstanding extreme cold weather, situated above multiple waves of voluminous snowfall, and able to be relocated (as if on very large skis) inland periodically to avoid risk of being stranded on an iceberg, if and when an ice shelf should break apart (Figure 3.3). A crew of up to fifteen spends eight months onboard including 105 days of total darkness. Module facades are in sky blue (research and sleeping quarters), and deep red (the large central module housing the 'social hub'). A highly durable fiberglass panelized system (GRP)—a material commonly used in high speed train and airplane manufacturing—was developed for exterior cladding as it can withstand low temperatures, is lightweight, and relatively easy to handle. Modules were formed by pouring resin into large formwork through very narrow tubes, with the panels affixed by means of formidable rubber gaskets. Many challenges were encountered during the transit and facility erection stages. The largest prefab panels measured 10.4 meters by 3.3 meters, and some operational problems have been encountered since its completion and occupancy.[17]

Twentieth century prefab—a dubious legacy

With twenty-first century prefabricated architecture, there are many, many lessons to be gleaned from the past. Dating from the early nineteenth century, the British Empire sought to further its colonization ambitions by developing prefabricated houses, churches, commercial buildings and ornate government structures

3.4 Dymaxion House prototype, Buckminster Fuller, 1930

made of wood and cast iron, for shipment to Australia, India, and other distant points.[18] By the early twentieth century, elaborate prefab commercial storefront facades and ornate interior embellishments yielded commercial success for numerous U.S. and European manufacturers. These offsite-built products showed up in corner pharmacies, banks, restaurants, and elsewhere.[19] In the 1930s, Sears, Roebuck and Company began to sell 'turnkey' prefabricated single-family residences with everything prepackaged for shipment to virtually anywhere. Thousands of these kits were sold.[20]

At this same time, renowned modernists who were pioneers of the International Style and other streams of modernism, desired to incorporate the virtues of mass production in their work although these efforts garnered little critical respect or widespread popularity. Most such efforts in time were abandoned for lack of political support, capital investment, or sheer disinterest.[21] Le Corbusier was a staunch advocate for mass-producing his worker housing prototypes, his 'machines for living.' This work included the Citrohan House (1920–1930)—a project clearly inspired by early automobile production assembly lines. However, the consensus among historians today is that he was mainly interested at the time in setting up onsite mass production lines, and not necessarily offsite manufacturing sites.[22] Nonetheless, Corbu's book *Aircraft* (1935) unabashedly and somewhat quixotically extolled the virtues of factory-built artifacts in everyday life.[23]

The period between World War I and World War II was one of tremendous conceptual innovation. Centered in Europe, these efforts manifest in a diverse set of prefab initiatives from Buckminster Fuller, Le Corbusier, Walter Gropius, Hannes Meyer, and others. After World War II broke out, most factories had switched over to strictly military production and California would emerge in the U.S. as the epicenter of much creative work in architectural prefabrication.[24] Charles and Ray Eames produced highly compelling work from the late 1940s in their case study program of experimental houses commissioned by, and published in, *Arts and Architecture* magazine (under the 'patronage' of John Entenza).[25] By the early 1950s, offsite prefabrication thinking was advancing rapidly with the expressed goal of getting mass-produced housing to expanding mass markets as quickly as possible.[26]

Walter Gropius had long been a champion of offsite prefabrication,[27] and Buckminster Fuller's stainless steel Dymaxion House prototype in 1930 was hailed as a pioneering breakthrough in prefabrication, not unlike the era's concurrent advances in jet airliner design (Figure 3.4).[28] Architects' utopian visions were also driven by political agendas ranging from Marxist to social democratic. Frank Lloyd Wright's Usonian houses of the 1930s and early 1940s sought to extend the scope of prefab modularity into the American middle class suburban landscape.[29] And the Lustron experiments in the late 1940s stand as a singularly bold effort to produce higher quality housing for the suburban postwar masses.[30] All would fail for one reason or another.

Two experiments of that era are particularly germane to the current groundswell of interest in prefab architecture for health. The first was by Walter Gropius, working with Konrad Wachsmann. The second experiment was the large-scale middle class housing developments built by Joseph Eichler in the 1950s through early 1970s in Northern California.[31] Gropius and his colleagues had worked together at the Bauhaus in Weimar, Germany until it was shuttered by Hitler in 1933. There, they had developed prototypes for panelized prefab houses. After World War II ended in 1945, Gropius' team sought to pursue a larger initiative in the U.S. in collaboration with the General Motors Corporation, in a venture called the *General Panel Corporation*. Some upfront seed capital was invested in this venture by the U.S. government. A large plant was built in California but everything soon went bankrupt, with little to show for the energy, time, and resources invested.[32]

In the case of Eichler, his work met with somewhat broader acceptance. Eichler had vetted many of California's most talented young modern architects and commissioned them to develop replicable, high-quality house prototypes reflective of the then in-vogue 'California Lifestyle'—based on openness, transparency, connectivity with the landscape, and adaptability to their inhabitants' daily needs and larger social aspirations. His was not to be a factory-centric approach, but rather a lower tech approach, relying on the availability of inexpensive skilled carpenters and 2 × 4 inch-based wood-framed panelized components. This differed from Gropius' vision of a massive offsite factory with a high production capacity.[33] Eichler believed in the power of the relationship between building and landscape, and in the owner's ability to have a role in the design process.[34] From these two excursions in prefab modularity it would appear that, today, the right combination of end user design options, system flexibility, and advanced factory production techniques just may strike a chord with the healthcare industry.

In the book *Refabricating Architecture*, Stephen Kieran and James Timberlake make a compelling case for prefabrication in twenty-first-century architecture.[35] They assert that throughout recorded history, handcraft, i.e. craftsmanship, was the fundamental means to fabricate an artifact, whether large or small. The designer of a product was often one and the same with its maker in an age when thinking and making were inextricably interwoven, and indigenous vernacular traditions were the pure expression of this relationship. Craftsmanship was the wellspring of all manufactured commodities. Today, machines have supplanted the function of handcraft. Many pioneering architects of the twentieth century, nevertheless, pursued a brand of utopianism implicit in machine-based production and these failed experiments serve collectively, today, as a cautionary tale of idealism overrun by a host of counterintuitive forces. These forces undermined, subverted, and ultimately drowned out any salient populist marketing message. As the construction industry consolidated in the 1960s and 1970s, various national organizations in the U.S., including the American Plywood Association and the National Association of Homebuilders, made repeated lukewarm efforts to spark innovation in prefab, particularly with respect to emergent just-in-time manufacturing platforms and in 'mass customization.' Perhaps the time is right to try yet again but in a new way. It is precisely this need to synthesize prefab, mass customization, and the therapeutic affordances of landscape that *right now* can be of such timely impact in offsite-built prefabricated healthcare architecture.[36]

Modernism sought to find salient ways to translate the consistency, replicability, and cost efficiencies of industrialization to certain longstanding traditions and types, and achieved little success:

> When Le Corbusier praised grain silos and factories because their pure form had been shaped by the economic rules of mass production, he came down in favor of [the] engineers. They are the unselfconscious makers...the producers of modern form. For Le Corbusier, engineers, unlike architects, are not guided by preconceptions about appearance. Instead, they possess a single-minded focus on purpose and economy. Poetic mass, surface, and plan result from the filters of economics and process through which their projects must

pass…[he] saw great promise in the production of architecture by machines, particularly in housing where it offered a way to fulfill a social housing agenda…Great architecture is today equated with art. Commodity today is generally seen as anti-art, the stuff of commerce. Commodity, most believe, is the creed of the philistine. It is possible, however, to see commodity instead as the crucible of art itself and to recognize the process engineer…as the high priest of this new art. It is not the engineer as a designer of artifacts that we applaud, but rather as a designer of processes that show the way forward in art…This reality is completely contrary to the artistic and contractual structure of much current architecture, which [reduces] architects into mere stylists.[37]

For Corbu, the prevailing political and socio-economic agendas were to be revolutionized within a New Epoch whereby the mass production of dwellings for the worker classes were to assume a central role.[38] To Kieran and Timberlake, writing today, a simple and yet, in their words, 'seemingly ineluctable' equation has continued to hinder progress: *Q(uality) x S(cope) = C(ost) x T(ime)*. They argue against this prevailing paradigm in mainstream architecture—whereby quality and scope is directly correlated with the cost and time to execute a project, regardless of how long it takes to finish it—as a fiction. They assert, on the contrary, that while the vast majority of architects still cling to this obsolescent assumption, other industries such as the automotive, shipbuilding, and aerospace industries have refused to do so. In those industries, the process engineer 'lives to obliterate the equilibrium of this law.' In these industries, in sharp contrast to how most buildings are built today, the industrial engineer functions as the prime force, a change agent who pushes beyond the 'obsolete gravitational fields' of cost and time, within a new paradigm: *Q(uality) x S(cope) > C(ost) x T(ime)*:

Why is this restatement [of] the old equilibrium between art and expenditure possible in other industries that also make complex artifacts? It is too easy to dismiss these examples [cars, ships, and planes] as having no relevance for architecture, which is [traditionally] fixed to the ground and custom crafted in the field rather than factory produced… lessons [to be] learned are not about outward form, style, or appearance. They are about processes and materials developed…that have overturned the ancient equilibrium between the expenditure of resources and acquisition of benefits…the process of making is no longer entirely linear… integration, not segregation…producers [now can] engage in design, and designers engage in production [which] becomes part of the design process by working with assemblers from the outset; designers picture how things are made, sequences of assembly, and joining systems. Material scientists are drawn into direct conversation and problem solving with product engineers and even with designers. The intelligence of all [four core] discipline [clusters] is used as a collective source of inspiration and constraint.[39]

The global manufacture of automobiles is currently dominated by integrated production platforms, with each platform composed of hundreds of constituent parts provided by as many as hundreds of parts suppliers. This requires the methodical disassembly of the artifact that is to be mass-produced and then its reassembly by means of the articulation of a number of its major *chunks,* or modular sections. It is a process of absolutely and totally reconstituting the artifact. It is about breaking down and then rebuilding the manufacturing *process* itself and in so doing 'perfecting' the desired final product. This approach does not occur in most conventional architecture today, healthcare or otherwise. The final automobile today becomes whole only at the very end of a long assembly process. Along the assembly line, various modular sections are plugged in with each module containing its own constellation of autonomous internal parts. In this industry, design and production teams are formed at the outset to design and procure each independent module. Each one is preassembled off site with every part, down to every screw, defined and controlled by a 3D process template that details all functions and installation procedures. Pretesting occurs iteratively and quality control 'gates' exist at key stages, requiring certification before production can advance to the next stage. This results in high quality control, more customization options, less production time, and a lower final cost of the product. Each autonomous module arrives at the final assembly plant complete and ready to be attached quickly to the vehicle, thereby drastically reducing the overall time-to-market for the complete car. Each outsourced supplier focuses on perfecting how its own module (or multiple modules) will fit precisely within the total vehicle.[40]

Why can't this approach work with architecture for health? But perhaps I am jumping a bit ahead with regards to the main thesis here:

> *Architects (and Architecture) can no longer afford to ignore the societal benefits of offsite prefabrication in light of the urgent needs of an increasingly crowded, resource-depleted planet now experiencing the profound effects of climate change.*

A major impediment to change remains the building construction industry itself. Change is considered too expensive, time consuming, and risky. And the U.S. government, for its part, still does not really support prefabrication at this scale.[41] In Japan, by contrast, its federal government adopted prefab modularity in the 1950s as the fastest way to rebuild its destroyed housing stock after the carpet-bombing raids in World War II.[42] And the modernists' fundamental problem, argue Kieran and Timberlake, was the lack of mass appeal of their 'high design' prefab housing prototypes.[43] They argue that at the present time modular construction no longer need be a 'slave to mass production, repetition, and sameness' and that even the term *offsite* itself is now becoming fashionable in more design spheres. They assert that 80–90 percent of the production of a 'custom' structure is buildable off site and that mass repetition is no longer a necessity.[44]

By contrast, a conventional building is conceived and executed strikingly differently because it is constructed iteratively in the field, and if its various parts do not fit properly they have to be replaced or somehow modified. This is a wasteful process of hit and miss. In offsite manufacturing, feedback is continually provided to the architectural and engineering (A/E) team and to the construction management (CM) team. Shop drawings come far earlier in the process and trial and error is virtually eradicated. The conventional method of field-fitting everything is the opposite of what happens in offsite manufacturing, because everything must be pre-fitted, and troubleshooting typically occurs far too late in the building process. With Building Information Modeling (BIM) especially, logistical parameters are ascertained at the outset of design visualization in a virtual environment where pre-engineering calculations can be performed simultaneously. As a result, in-the-field problems encountered are by comparison minimal, or virtually non-existent.

The emergence of BIM has greatly advanced the case for offsite prefabrication in healthcare architecture, which is a highly complex proposition, as compared to most other building types, because it enables visualization of the final outcome *a priori*. All components and modularized assemblies are solid-modeled in 3D with additional benefits to be accrued as identified through concurrent cost and schedule modeling. All this is integrated with design from the project's outset and continues uninterrupted through to the project's completion and occupancy. This can exponentially improve communications among all key players in the building design and delivery process from top to bottom and from start to finish. It is now possible, therefore, to virtually *see* and walk through a hospital prior to its construction. Perhaps the greatest breakthrough made possible through BIM and similar building modeling packages is the possibility to now be able to rapidly explore and perfect new, unorthodox materiality palettes and formal geometric vocabularies in healthcare architecture.[45] By comparison, the rate of inculcation of new materials and formal compositional strategies in healthcare and other types of architecture across the centuries was slow and laborious:

> Stone, clay, masonry, wood, and thatch came first. Many centuries later, concrete was invented. Still later, metals were added, first as reinforcements and fasteners. Glass came into use as a building material about a thousand years ago, and the use of iron as a structural element is a nineteenth-century phenomenon. The rate at which new materials were invented and applied to architecture escalated dramatically during the twentieth century, especially after WWII…[and yet this] pales in comparison to the exponential explosion of new materials in the last quarter century…beyond lies a world of purposeful form yet to be explored.[46]

Offsite-built prefab healthcare facilities for permanent sites

In the 1960s and 1970s, experiments in offsite-built prefab modular healthcare facilities for installation on permanent sites occurred although most of these yielded no more success than the previously mentioned mid-twentieth-century forays into post-World War II mass-produced prefab housing. Perhaps the most noteworthy of these failed experiments was the utopian *Automedic Hospital*. The Automedic was envisioned as a fixed-site prefab inpatient care facility. Developed by Dr. Hugh C. Maguire of Montgomery, Alabama, it would garner a combination of scorn, derision, and praise from both within and outside of the American healthcare industry. A forty-bed prototype was built off site and was marketed to rural communities as a permanent-site, low-cost alternative to costly brick and mortar hospital expansions. It was equipped with a radiology suite, furnishings, and all surgical instrumentation. It could be in business sixty days from the onset of site preparation. Its cost in 1965 was $760,000. The first Automedic prototype was installed next to a hospital in Montgomery. A second prototype, installed at the New York State fair in 1964, was intended to showcase its innovativeness. To the public it looked like some sort of spaceship or flying saucer. This was attributable to its circular shape, a low, one-level profile, and its panelized stainless steel exterior cladding. Its entire interior floor plan was radial and a continuous corridor connected all spaces including the inpatient rooms, which were a mixture of private, semi-private, and one four-bed open ward. The prototypes were marketed as featuring state-of-the art heating, ventilation and air conditioning (HVAC) systems. But it would be an uphill battle from the outset:

> The Automedic Hospital faced several serious hurdles from the start. First, it was expensive. In 1965, the cost was about $19,000 per bed, and this figure was higher in extreme climates or where local fire codes required automated smoke detectors, sprinkler systems, smoke barriers, or fire-rated doors. Finally, the hospital did not meet Hill-Burton eligibility standards for federal construction funding. In addition, many potential customers regarded it to be best used as a special care unit for burn victims, pediatric care, or cardiac care—not as a general care facility for the suburbs or rural communities, as its creators had envisioned…[its] origins could be traced back to the portable Dymaxion House…and the Airstream trailer…the creators' optimism was never allowed to be tested on a wide-scale basis. A number of units were purchased by existing hospitals for use as temporary expansion quarters (during renovation to an adjacent main hospital), or as overflow for chronically overcrowded nursing units. But, to the frustration of its creators, [its] potential…to be exported to developing countries or used by the U.S. military, were never to be realized. The unit was conceived as a utopian, mass produced, affordable medical-care machine—innovative, efficient, yet radically different—but its creator was to become the butt of jokes.[47]

Similar experiments in prefab for healthcare at this time included a 1966 initiative to build and ship, over a five-year period, forty-two prefab infirmaries and outpatient clinics from Britain to the Ministry of Health in the State of Amazonas in South America. A consortium of two British entities, the Oxford Architects Partnership and Mariani and Associates, working with the International Professional Consortium for Health Services and the Brazilian government, designed these prefab modular units. In 1971, this region had a population of one million, with a ratio of 60,000 persons per physician and only one hospital bed per 5,000 persons and these were among the lowest ratios in the world at the time. The first installation had been in Manaus (1968). By 1975, this situation had changed dramatically, with one physician per 12,000 persons and one hospital bed for every 1,500 persons. This ingenious plan was premised on five basic prefab 'model types' ranging from a thirty-bed infirmary to a public health station for immunizations and disease prevention education.[48]

Another initiative, designed by the architectural firm Cashion-Horie, of Pomona, California, resulted in the installation of only three (of what had been envisioned as fifty or more) offsite-built outpatient clinics, and were built by Designed Facilities Corporation, of El Monte, California. This company had had no prior experience with offsite prefab for healthcare. The three clinics were transited and installed on permanent sites in the Watts Section of Los Angeles, in West Oakland, California, and in Mound Bayou, Mississippi. On the other hand, another firm, Marshall Erdman and Associates, of Madison, Wisconsin, had success with this same strategy to such an extent that by 1970 it had already designed and installed more than a thousand partially (hybrid) prefab medical facilities in the U.S. These facilities were highly standardized, and perfunctory at best.[49] In Japan, recently, Sankyo Frontier, Ltd., a leader in prefab healthcare facilities, has leveraged its nationwide sales network to provide prefab modular healthcare facilities of many types for permanent sites in co-sponsorship with the Japan Prefabricated Construction Suppliers and Manufacturers

Association. In a dental clinic offsite-built by Sankyo in Tokyo (2010), a small, residentially scaled prefab modular facility features adjoining prefab exterior decks, and wheelchair access ramps. All plumbing, electrical, and HVAC support is located beneath the module. The interiors of these modulars are, in comparison to their 1960s and 1970s precursors, strikingly attractive, inviting in scale, materials, and overall aesthetic appearance (Figure 3.5a–b). In an outpatient primary care clinic, also designed and manufactured by Sankyo, near Sendai (2010), various modules' proportions can be clearly 'read' in its façade, and all interior spaces appear to be constructed similar to that of a conventionally built permanent site clinic, except it all happened off site. Sankyo's modules for healthcare are exclusively manufactured in highly controlled factory environments.[50]

The Japanese and the British are among the global leaders in recent healthcare prefab modularity for permanent sites. The Bristol, England Royal Infirmary Redevelopment Project (2010–2014) featured many modular assemblies manufactured off site, including all patient room headwall components, ICU 'vitals columns,' entire surgical suite installations, and the facility's modularized diagnostic imaging suites.[51] Hospitals in the U.K. and elsewhere are now being constructed with every inpatient room equipped with a prefab headwall system with all medical gases and electrical support housed within sleek, attractive, panelized headwall modules. The currently in-vogue *acuity adaptable* inpatient room concept is ideally suited to this approach because the same patient headwall module allows for it to be used equally effectively as an ICU room module. Both vertical and horizontal surface-mount headwalls can easily be plugged into HVAC and electrical system modules. With their built-in natural wood finished cabinetry, they appear rather elegant and add to the room's overall ambiance.

A related module, the freestanding, full height 'vitals column,' is generally of two types, fixed or rotating. These are installed permanently to both the floor and ceiling, thereby freeing up the patient headwall. Because the vitals column swivels, this allows the nurse to be able to stand in a single spot while adjusting flow meters, suction regulators, infusion pumps, and related accruements. The nurse need not walk behind the column, or to both sides of the patient's bed, as it rotates on its own to the desired position. As with a wall-mounted headwall apparatus, all medical gases and electrical outlets are housed within these one

3.5a–b Prefab modular dental clinic, Tokyo, Japan, 2010

foot by one foot devices. Ceiling-mounted patient lift modules are also being widely adopted in hospitals and in long-term care facilities for the aged. They have been proven to significantly reduce the number of workplace injuries sustained by nurses and other care providers.[52] Wall-mounted as well as freestanding modular computer workstations are now in widespread use, as are bedside lighting extender 'arms,' convertible furnishings for overnight use by patients' families, and plug-in personal hygiene modules.[53]

Experiments with offsite-built bathroom/shower modules have occurred since the 1980s. Eggrock Modular Solutions has become a leading North American manufacturer, including an order for 500 bathroom modules for the Royal Jubilee Hospital in Victoria, British Columbia (2009).[54] In keeping with Kieran and Timberlake's persuasive prodding, its products emulate supply chain metrics borrowed from the automotive and aeronautics industries. Using prebuilt, outsourced components, its modular bathrooms draw together eight different construction trades, coordinated not unlike an automotive assembly line. This includes all pre-installed wall, ceiling and floor finishes, lighting, electrical componentry, and mirrors, even the hairdryers. At the factory, moisture resistant wallboard is installed on a steel frame structure, and all steel

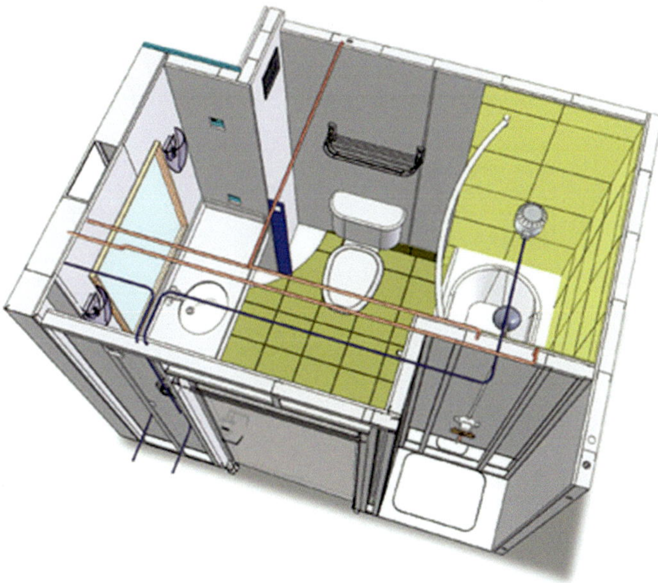

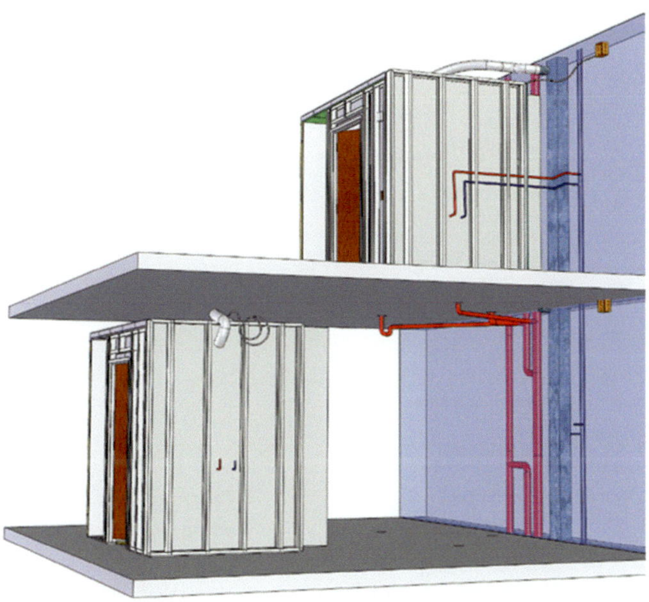

3.6a–c Eggrock Modular Solutions bath/shower pod, Royal Jubilee Hospital, Victoria, British Columbia, 2009

structural blocking for showerheads, tub spouts, and wall-mounted accessories are installed. Upon arrival at the permanent installation site, only a few hours are required to connect each pod to the building's HVAC, plumbing, and electrical systems. Every mateline is pre-engineered, and all major building code inspections are conducted at the factory (Figure 3.6a–c).

Manufacturers of prefab bathroom modules claim their products result in virtually no change orders because all specifications are agreed to up front for a guaranteed price, less waste is sent to landfills, site theft is non-existent because the pods are wrapped, locked, and secured, and the construction trades are better coordinated. Eggrock (since 2010 a subsidiary of Innovative Modular Pre-Fabrication LLC) extolls the virtues of offsite construction:

> A bathroom is an oversized appliance, not unlike a dishwasher…just as a builder would never consider building a dishwasher on the construction site, we believe that someday (all) builders will feel the same way about bathrooms.[55]

Units are installed from the top floor down so plumbers can easily access all piping from below. Ground floor units are hooked up to 'boxed out' plumbing feedlines similar to traditionally built bathrooms. Each module has a coiled electrical line connected to the nearest junction box. Plumbing connections consist of hot and cold lines and all waste lines are easily attachable to risers. Installation drawings are provided of all pipefitting locations to ensure properly aligned matelines. Virtually every unused scrap of material is recycled, and site trash removal to local landfills is reduced by ten cubic yards per unit versus a traditional, onsite-built bathroom—a benefit with enormous implications for the completed building's LEED certification.

Swedish/Edmonds Medical Oncology Clinic

Swedish Health Network, the largest non-profit healthcare provider in the greater Seattle area, opened a prefab modular outpatient clinic on its Edmonds Campus, near Seattle, Washington, in 2013. This 17,000 square foot facility was designed by the Seattle office of Perkins+Will, with offsite components built by Whitley

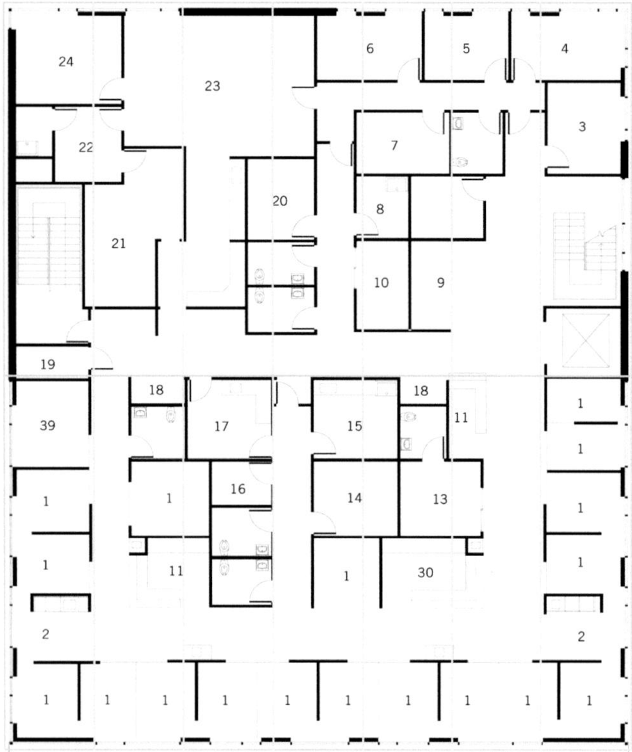

Level 2

Key:
1 Soiled
2 Clean
3 Exam
4 Office
5 Nurse
6 I.T.
7 Work
8 Reception
9 Waiting
10 Scale
11 Med. Prep
12 Janitor's Closet
13 Blood Draw
14 Lab
15 Break Room

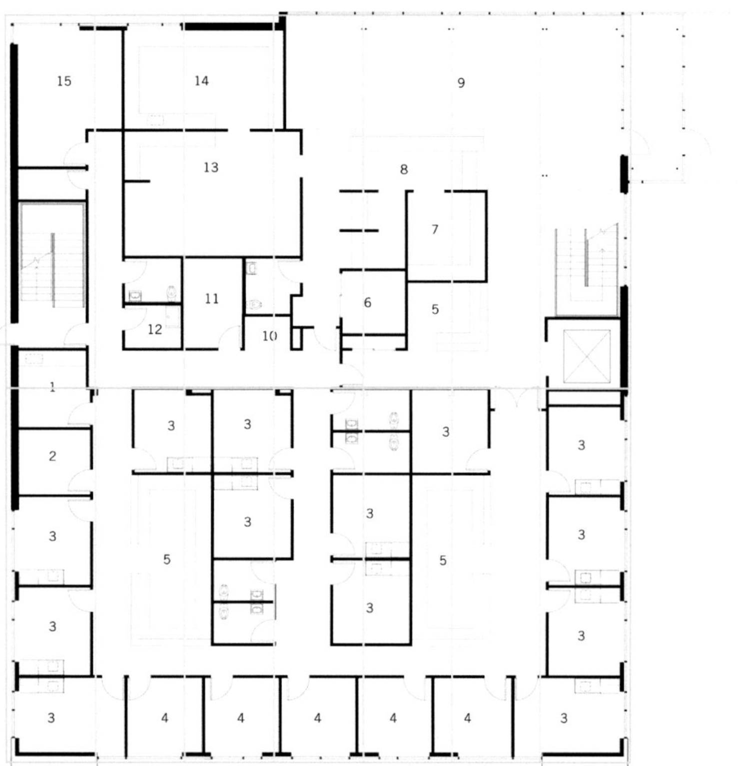

Level 1

Key:
1 Infusion
2 Nourishment
3 Financial
4 Research Office
5 Site Manager
6 Hotelling
7 Pharmacy Storage
8 Janitor's Closet
9 Sub Waiting
10 I.T.
11 Nurse / Greet
12 Scale
13 Isolation Room
14 Clean
15 Solid Waste
16 Storage
17 Med. Prep
18 Scale
19 Gurney
20 Soiled Holding
21 Chemotherapy Work Room
22 Ante Room
23 Pharmacy
24 Unit Manager Office

3.7a–c Swedish Edmonds Medical Oncology Clinic, Edmonds, Washington, Perkins+Will. Floor plans and exterior view of modules awaiting shipment to installation site, 2012

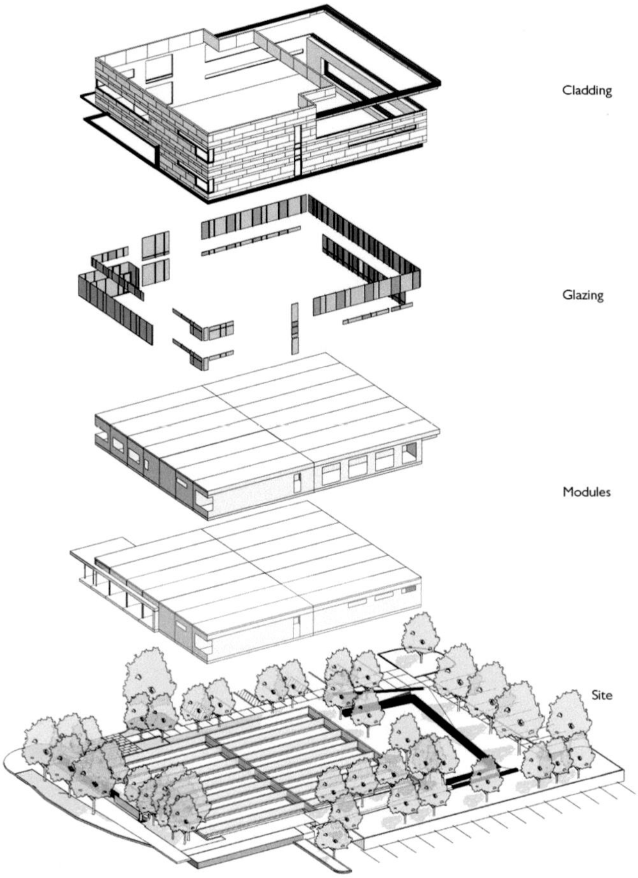

3.8 Swedish Edmonds Medical Oncology Clinics, Perkins+Will. Blow-apart axonometric view, 2012

3.9a–b Swedish Edmonds, Perkins+Will. Construction sequence, 2012

3.10a–b Swedish Edmonds, Perkins+Will. Construction sequence, 2012 (continued)

Manufacturing, in conjunction with RAD Technology Medical Systems. Skanska USA was responsible for site development. Prefab was chosen due to the client's need for an accelerated construction timetable. The first level houses the main waiting room, registration and the clinic's oncology diagnostic and treatment rooms. A second level houses twenty infusion (chemotherapy) stations, a pharmacy, and various support functions (Figure 3.7a–c). The assembly process involved a total of twenty-nine offsite-built modular units, placed side by side horizontally and stacked atop one another. Onsite assembly was accomplished in just two days (Figure 3.8). The building features low-e glazing and a cement-like rain screen exterior cladding system. The clinic accommodates up to 175 outpatient visits daily, most of whom reside throughout the Seattle north metro area.[56] A series of construction photos illustrate the onsite delivery and assembly process from site preparation, offsite module fabrication, transiting, the assembly of offsite with site-built components and the facility's completion (Figures 3.9a–b and 3.10a–b).

Miami Valley Hospital Heart and Orthopedic Center

Premier Health Partners, a joint venture, built its 500,000 square foot, twelve-level addition to Miami Valley Hospital in Dayton, Ohio (2010–2012) in half the time it would have taken conventionally. This was the first hospital construction project in the U.S. to make use of prefabrication of all major mechanical, electrical, headwall, bathroom, and plumbing components (see Chapter 6).[57] At Miami Valley, multi-trade coordination occurred from the outset, with contractors and subcontractors working side by side in the same warehouse space, a facility located a few miles from the construction site. For this hospital client, this arrangement was unique because larger subassemblies than usual were to be manufactured off site. Transiting of these larger modules was made possible mainly due to the close proximity of the factory to the construction site. In a unique arrangement, multiple subcontractors worked concurrently at the offsite plant. A half dozen trades worked together in this same space. Cross-trade collaboration in the manufacture of prefabricated building modules on a hospital project had seldom if ever occurred before to this extent in the U.S. healthcare industry.

In most hospitals, in plan, an A/B A/B 'mirrored' pattern occurs in the layout of the inpatient rooms. This results in walking down a hospital corridor and looking into two rooms at once, seeing the patient bed headwalls sharing the common wall between the two rooms. By contrast, Miami Valley featured same-handed rooms, where every bed had the same orientation and the headwalls were therefore not mirrored. This early planning decision to adopt *same handedness* was driven by the staff's desire for clinical standardization, to reduce nursing and ancillary staff injuries, and to reduce the occurrence of medical errors. This decision was noteworthy because prefab was, to the A/E team, not to be seen as an end in and of itself, nor to merely streamline the construction timetable. It was viewed as a *both/and* design opportunity, originating from the client's nursing care model, a model that was to be applied identically to all 178 inpatient rooms in the facility. Prefabrication therefore aptly extended the client's vision as well as that of the A/E team and it was viewed as an appropriate strategy relative to the shared aims of all key stakeholders in the final outcome.

NBBJ soon learned, however, that neither the winning bidder nor its subcontractors were very clear on exactly how to bid a job that called for offsite prefab. It had submitted a bid that was basically cost-neutral, meaning that the Miami Valley facility could have been built conventionally, or otherwise, for the same guaranteed maximum price (GMP) and on the same construction timeline. It knew it could realize some savings through prefab, but was equally concerned with the increased risk associated with

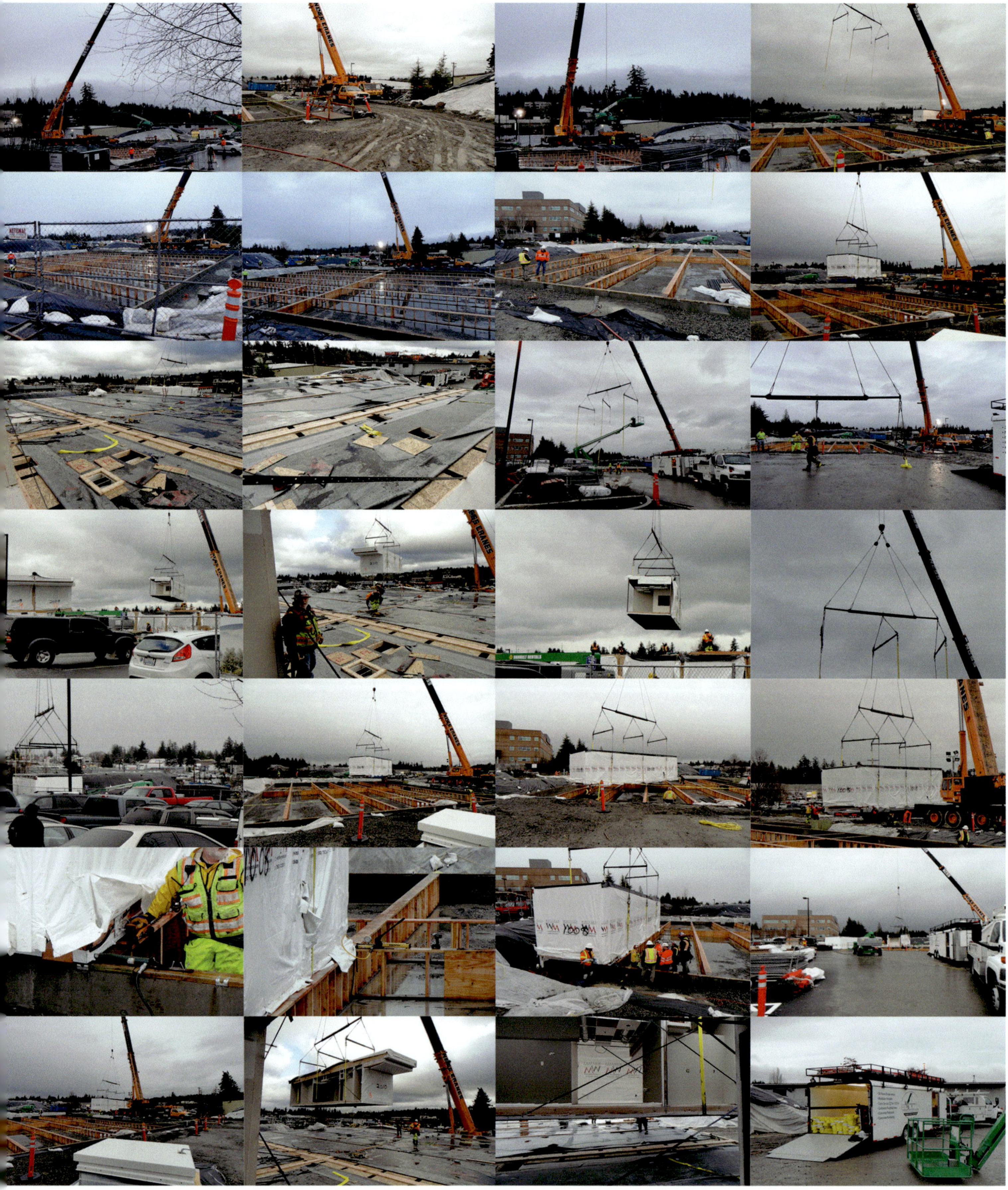

MEDICAL ONCOLOGY
SWEDISH CANCER INSTITUTE
21632
FIRE LANE
Open House
NO PARKING FIRE LANE

something it hadn't before been forced to consider in a bid, at least to this extent and as a result, it was unsure as to how best to proceed, and therefore submitted both a conventional and a prefab-centric base bid, in effect, neutralizing the submitted GMP. This measure was seen by the lead contractor as the best way to take account of any attendant work stoppages, scheduling issues, cost overruns, or other unforeseen problems that may be encountered down the road.

The 178 patient rooms and 120 mechanical/electrical/plumbing (MEP) racks at Miami Valley were built by a core team of eighteen workers in one shop by means of cross working, training, and partnering, interwoven across five assembly lines. These eighteen workers maintained a high level of productivity, regardless of the weather outside, working more efficiently than would have been achievable on an outdoors job site. For example, a typical plumber's installation quota in a conventional build is approximately 200 lineal feet of pipe per day. By contrast, the plumbers working on this project in the warehouse were able to install 600 lineal feet of pipe per day. Also, in a conventional build, workers often spend an inordinate amount of time every day looking for materials and the right tools for a particular task: 'Is that drill bit stored in the job box down on the third floor, or the second floor?' Things are always being moved about, becoming lost or misplaced. Excessive wait times are often incurred at the elevator lift to get materials and assemblies up and down the building frame, a matter compounded by workers who have to constantly go up and down ladders and the elevator lift looking around for parts and tools. However, in this case, everything was concentrated in one place in the plant and organized along an assembly line for each line of racks being fabricated. Because of this, wasted time was wrung out of the production schedule. This measure alone yielded time and cost savings of up to 300 percent at some points in the manufacturing sequence, versus a traditional build for an inpatient hospital tower of this size.

Additionally, a higher level of worker safety was achieved in the Miami Valley project. A variable air flow valve (VAV) box device, for example, is a ventilation flow rate control box that is mounted above the ceiling plane. In a conventional build, each VAV box is installed individually, requiring one-at-a-time fine-tuning, with workers going up and down ladders repeatedly to coordinate the installation of each and every VAV device. Off site, much of this labor is avoided. Moreover, from an ergonomic perspective, simply being able to work on a single horizontal manufacturing floor was far more efficient than always traversing ladders, resulting in a safer work environment. BIM modeling played a key role in standardizing this design and manufacturing process, as it allowed for a more precise just-in-time ordering of materials, tighter matelines, and higher overall quality control. This also resulted in less waste in the form of cutoff scraps, less waste in the dumpster, and less waste taken to the landfill.

As mentioned, weather did not have any opportunity to wreak havoc with the offsite construction schedule due to 'off days.' It was easier to find and test for leaks indoors, and far less dust is generated off site, versus on site. This resulted in plumbing and related componentry that was cleaner to begin with, and produced at a higher overall quality. As for building code compliance, inspections and commissioning was made more expedient because equipment testing did not need to occur exclusively on site. The completed modules were left unsealed in the factory, prior to their transit, in order for each to be technically classified as 'open' construction rather than 'closed' construction. Inspectors visited both the warehouse and the outdoors job site and therefore were able to readily inspect everything both in its pre-installed and its installed state at the permanent construction site. This made for effective communications and comparatively few complications. Each bath/shower module's interior walls were sheetrocked, but their exterior walls were left unfinished until site delivery so that the final inspection could occur on site. Otherwise, at the factory, closed prefab modular construction may have triggered myriad code issues with Underwriters Laboratory (UL) and delays in securing component classifications and assembly approvals. A hospital is a highly systems-intensive environment, with complex arrays of devices and conduits crisscrossing, snaking around one another within restrictive plenum spaces above the ceiling. In a conventional build, even when all is going smoothly, various trades compete for elbowroom and are forced to work around one another, often, in tight space conditions. When the schedule slips, even by a week or so, the coordinated sequencing of the subcontractor trades on the site can become discombobulated.

At Miami Valley, the offsite-built prefabricated modules were BIM-choreographed from the outset. In future renovations this client will as a result realize time and cost savings because initial project design coordination yielded additional maneuvering space in the ceiling plenum rack than would otherwise have been attainable. Because it is prudent to design the finished ceiling plane to ensure access panels at two points within a given zone, prefab modularity can recapture some of the full height access benefits of the old walk-through plenums from the heyday of the (now-dead) interstitial floor movement of the 1970s and 1980s. The type of modules and servicing access points at Miami Valley are the twenty-first-century equivalent of what was once known as full-floor interstitialism. These spaces do allow for humans to move within the plenum rack, but a main advantage is their provision of direct access from below, continuously if need be. A prefab MEP rack installation (as is discussed below) is a feasible strategy in older, historic buildings with tight floor-to-floor heights. Healthcare clients continue to demand flexibility, but virtually no client at this time is willing to pay the premium up-front cost for a full-height interstitial floor. That era is over because it inflates the overall volume of the building envelope, adding to the expansiveness of its exterior cladding and thereby increasing total project cost by as much as 40 percent.

At Miami Valley, first, two existing buildings had to be demolished. These structures sat right in the middle of the footprint of the new inpatient tower. The challenge was to remove these two buildings while maintaining a mission-critical elevated corridor that connected one side of the hospital campus with the other. The new facility would eventually house the new equivalent to this corridor, but during construction, a temporary bypass was required to be built to maintain continuous circulation access through the campus while the new tower was being built. This was initially assumed to be an expensive device that would only be used temporarily. The challenge was that demolition would have to be delayed until this conduit bridge was constructed and it was going to need to be robust structurally because critical care patients were to be transported on a 24/7 basis on stretchers. Plus it had to be heated and cooled with humidity control, and basically as robust as permanent construction. If a conventional build, it was estimated this conduit would cost $2 million to build—for a structure that itself would later be demolished. The only thing temporary about it was that it was to be essentially thrown away on the day the new facility opened (see Chapter 6).

Instead, a prefabricated bypass bridge was purchased "off the shelf". While still in the prefabrication mindset, the A/E team searched widely for a suitable solution. Was there an existing product that could be purchased and used temporarily and then possibly reused elsewhere? Skanska suggested the purchase of a prefabricated airport jetway that could serve as the temporary bridge connector at Miami Valley. A unit was purchased from a manufacturer that builds jetways for airports around the world. The vendor chosen indicated it would be able to meet the client's requirements but added it had never been asked to adapt its products for anything like this. The vendor responded very quickly, for half the price of a conventional build. Instead of $2 million, this prefab elevated connector cost $1 million. And as predicted, later it was dismantled for reuse elsewhere. Serendipity. This jetway-cum-bridge was installed in a mere three days. Less than two weeks later, demolition of the two existing campus buildings was complete.

Ohio Health Methodist—Riverside

The Neuroscience Institute at Ohio Health Methodist Hospital (2012–2014), in Columbus, Ohio, by NBBJ Columbus, is a 224-bed inpatient facility with eight neurological surgical suites, three open-heart operating suites, two stereotactic radiosurgery vaults, three radiology laboratories, and thirty diagnostic and treatment rooms (Figure 3.11a–b). Its 'parti' revolves around a large atrium garden that transmits natural daylight into every patient room, and inpatient room accommodations are provided for family members. NBBJ partnered with the CM, Whiting-Turner, in a design-build, with the CM co-located in NBBJ's office. Once again, BIM was implemented.[58] A noteworthy feature at Riverside, relative to prefab modularity, is its curvilinear footprint. A continuously curving sixteen-foot wide corridor zone runs throughout the entire inpatient floor, partially extending into spaces to either side. As opposed to the case at Miami Valley, the contractor planned from the bid stage for prefab to be the core driver of the project, and had the foresight to rent ample warehouse space in Columbus early on, as this allowed for wider than normal radial modules to be fabricated there. Two assembly lines were laid out initially although eventually six lines would operate at the warehouse. By building curvilinear modular 'chunks,' matelines and component specs were met for each subsystem within the HVAC/MEP racks, together with the

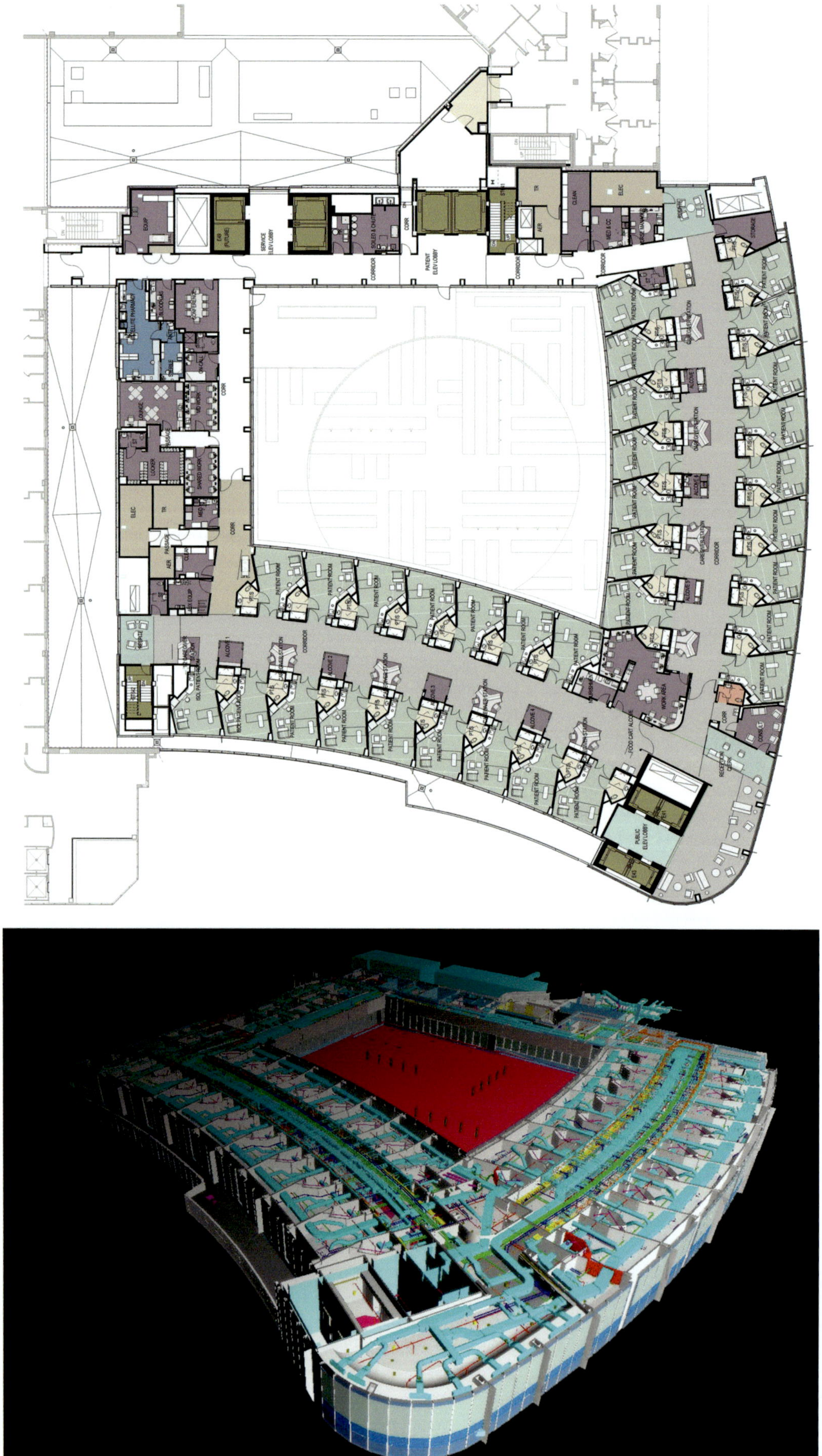

3.11a–b Ohio Health Methodist—Riverside, floor plan and BIM-generated rendering, NBBJ, 2012

graduated inflection occurring from one segment of the curved rack component to the next. This greatly reduced the number of trips back and forth, transiting time, and the cost of labor. By using prefab the CM saved more than 2,000 man-hours per floor, and when multiplied over seven floors it saved an estimated $2–3 million in total project cost. At Riverside, offsite prefabrication was built into the base bid from the very beginning and this, as mentioned, was the major difference from Miami Valley. At Riverside, scheduling, phasing, trade coordination, and the budget were entirely premised on this. The workflow from project outset to completion therefore occurred fluidly without any significant interruptions or unforeseen problems.

The prefab strategy at Riverside used BIM logistics analysis to optimize assembly procedures, warehouse storage methods, the estimation of each module's duration at the warehouse prior to just-in-time transiting, and the means of transit. These metrics were indexed to the construction schedule simultaneously occurring at the permanent construction site. The project's overall scheduling fluidity stemmed from the superstructure itself, whose structural design precluded the need for massive beams crossing over the top of the racks that would otherwise have restricted the ability to horizontally slide the modules in on the various floors. This also ensured a clear, unobstructed gap between the bulkheads on each side, and the floor and ceiling slabs below and above. Each module was built on a caster-pallet and pre-fitted for the forklift truck. Upon arrival at the site it could be lifted from the flatbed truck and then incrementally 'craned' into the skeletal frame. This type of 'rolling' assembly line had previously proved successful in the Miami Valley project.

The contractor and CM set up shop at the NBBJ Columbus office, working side by side with the A/E team. As a design-build project, NBBJ teamed with Whiting-Turner Construction for two years. Rather than work independently elsewhere, everyone was working together, and this contributed significantly to a collaborative work spirit. Everybody was on the same office floor of the building and all project consultants were able to share the same 'war room' (Figure 3.12a–d). Most firms only show two or three different conceptual designs when meeting with a client. With the use of BIM combined with the close proximity of the contractor and CM, thirty different concepts were quickly generated, yet only three were brought to the client for direct input and review. Also, a large-scale model was built for use in the office, allowing the entire A/E and CM team to conduct numerous invaluable 'stand-up' meetings beside this model. In the case of the landscape design of the site's rain garden, the civil and mechanical engineers, and everyone, saw exactly the way water was to fill the garden and this added much clarity to everyone's comprehension and appreciation of the initial design intent and functionality of this site feature.

At Miami Valley, there had been three prefabricated modules: the MEP infrastructural racks, the inpatient rooms and headwalls, and the connecting jetway bridge. At Riverside, there were nine, revolving around the operating room ceiling module, the ceiling subsystem module, and the examination room module. By late 2014, NBBJ Columbus was working on its third prefab-driven hospital—a renovation, this time. To a hospital, shutting down an inpatient wing for an entire year to renovate it is almost always expensive and extremely inconvenient for everyone involved. Every service has to be temporarily relocated and this is often very difficult, with commissioning requirements and patient safety regulations such as the *Health Insurance Portability and Accountability Act of 1996* (HIPAA) in the U.S.[59] With prefab now being used more in U.S. healthcare facility renovation projects, modular components can be constructed off site then installed in the existing envelope, significantly reducing the downtime and the hospital's need to search out temporary accommodations for every displaced department. Componentry can snap together and be reconfigured in response to rapidly changing needs. It will not be uncommon to reconfigure entire floors by simply bringing in a crew overnight on *one night*, armed with basically just a set of Allen wrenches and an array of smart-system partitions, fixtures, and equipment with various plug-and-play assemblage options. This is the future of prefab modularity in hospital renovation projects (Figure 3.13a–c).

In the U.S., the *Affordable Care Act of 2010* is leading to many changes in the way that hospitals build and how they are managed.[60] Many healthcare providers, particularly in densely populated urban areas, will outgrow their existing buildings more quickly than before as more citizens acquire health insurance. This will cause premature facility obsolescence for the clients that NBBJ, Perkins+Will, and other healthcare design A/E firms work with. Clinging to traditional methods in facility renovation is a lose-lose proposition in terms of time lost, i.e. downtime, because the client is unable to generate the lost revenue. Moreover, one square foot

3.12a–d Ohio Health Methodist—Riverside, offsite factory views and installation sequence of prefab modules, NBBJ, 2013

of renovation in a hospital generates 150 pounds of construction debris sent to a local landfill. By embracing prefab modularity the client will discard far less and be able to adapt to change far more readily. In the future, new construction and renovation projects will be more expeditious, flexible, and of a higher overall quality. BIM, for its part, is facilitating an unprecedented synthesis of internal building systems, landscape design, and site planning as a single process.[61] An inventory spreadsheet is generated for every single module and its component parts. This level of efficiency is what routinely occurs in the automotive, aeronautical, and shipbuilding industries.[62] Hyper-visualization of the entire design, manufacturing, and construction process is the future. As for the logistics of construction, in the case of Miami Valley, eighteen workers worked on multiple shifts across five offsite assembly platforms versus an estimated seventy-five or more workers otherwise required to finish the job, a workforce that is typically limited to working during daylight hours.[63]

The future—prefab modularity and health

In architecture for health, new ideas are adopted in incremental fits and starts by the mainstream profession. Clients are certainly not generally known as being ardent early adopters. Innovation, because of this, often begins in small-scale projects and with the cost of housing skyrocketing in many urban centers, recent

3.13a–c Ohio Health Methodist—Riverside campus, bath/shower pods installation, NBBJ, 2013

affordable housing strategies based on the use of offsite prefab modularity are something that should be taken into serious consideration by healthcare organizations at this time. On this point, in New York City, a design competition in 2011 focused on the provision of mid-rise, affordable housing and the winning submittal, by nARCHITECTS, was a ten-floor fifty-five-unit prefab modular rental micro-apartment building for the city's Kip's Bay neighborhood in Brooklyn.[64] Another small-scale example with crossover potential is the eight-foot deep by twenty-foot long solar-powered, foldout *Resto Muvbox* (2008), in Montreal, by Daniel Noiseux. This *pop-up restaurant* is a recycled ISO shipping container that can unfold in a few minutes, metamorphosing into a gourmet diner with a seating capacity of twenty-eight.[65]

Prefab may involve a healthcare client overcoming its fear of the unknown.[66] As previously mentioned, Japan and the U.K. are global leaders in fostering offsite prefabrication in the healthcare sector. The U.K. government-based universal healthcare provider, the National Health Service (NHS) has built warehouses just outside the border of towns where a new hospital is to be built, and similar practices are rather common in Japan.[67] There and elsewhere, architects continue to test the possibilities of prefab modularity in offbeat, at times bizarre micro-dwellings and commercial structures that have strong potential for adaption to healthcare purposes and especially in the arena of small-scale prefab outpatient clinics. One such example, the *m-ch* (micro-compact home), by Richard Horden (2005) of Horden Cherry Lee Architects, London, is a durable compact dwelling for one or two people, in a 2.66m by 1.98m cube; it weighs 2.2 tons and can be adapted to diverse site contexts.[68] Another precedent, the *Push Button House* (2012), by Adam Kalkin, is an ISO-container house that begins life as a generic shipping container, until a button is pushed and it turns into a house. It robotic walls unfold to reveal a fully functional dwelling complete with built-in minimalist furnishings. The prototype was unveiled at Art Basel in Miami Beach in 2012.[69] The time is right for small-scale prefab prototypes such as these to be experimented with in relation to healthcare.

Another recent precedent, the *Sauna Box*, is a half-size variant on the generic ISO container; it was designed for use in cold weather regions by the Canadian design studio *Castor Canadensis*. It is a weatherized, transportable unit that requires little site preparation, with a wood-fired stove, and photovoltaic panels on the roof. Each unit can be custom-fitted to suit its inhabitants' needs. Its outer skin is clad in Corten steel and it is saltwater-resistant, making this module appear both utilitarian and sculptural at once, and its standard shipping container doors extend its overall industrial aesthetic.[70] The experimental *Das Park Hotel* in Berne, Austria (2013) consists of three large-diameter concrete sewerage drainpipes, adapted for use as a 'hotel room,' with each fitted with a wood-fabricated platform bed, a mural on one end of the concrete pipe, and a circular window wall/door on the other end of this transformed utilitarian pipe. These pipes are aligned in rows, and each module features a circular skylight.[71] Another, the *FiNCUBE* dwelling (2010) by Werner Aisslinger and Josef Innerhofer of Berlin, is a poetic essay in flat-pack modularity, fabricated in wood and glass. It is a 500 square foot home that sits on a concrete (or steel) pad and its capsular, lozenge-like parti' is essentially a pristine glass box, partially obscured by a lightweight, latticed horizontal sunscreen.[72] Suffice to say, it would be hoped that these and similar experiments in prefab might attract the creativity of healthcare architects and their clients, in the face of the massive challenges ahead.[73]

In 2012, the U.S. engineering and consulting firm FMI released its landmark white paper, 'Modularization and Prefabrication—Role Development and Evolution.' In it, a study for the National Institute of Standards and Technology is reported on the state of prefab modularization and how it can improve productivity across the U.S. construction industry in the next two decades. Among the findings, offsite prefab saves up to 50 percent of construction scheduling time, cuts project costs, significantly reduces landfill waste, and results in higher quality control from start to finish.[74] Case in point: in 2011, a 225mph tornado killed more than 150 people and destroyed 7,000 homes in Joplin, Missouri, including the local 700,000-plus square foot community hospital, St. John's Mercy. A modular replacement hospital was designed by Aspen Street Architects and built off site by Walden Structures. The new St. John's Mercy is a 150,000 square foot, two-level acute care modular prefab hospital. Installation began on site in November 2011, with the arrival of the first of its 224 modules. Completion and occupancy of this replacement facility occurred *prior* to the one-year anniversary of the Joplin tornado—an otherwise impossible timetable compared to a conventionally built acute care hospital.[75]

When NBBJ worked with Skanska on the Miami Valley project, Skanska was able to apply its considerable knowledge of prefab, acquired in working with hospitals in the U.K. In the U.K., the builder may take on full financial responsibility for funding the project upfront, building it, and then operating it for a time. Skanska has worked on more than $1 billion in healthcare sector work in the U.K. to date and all of it has incorporated prefab. They have tremendous traction with prefab in other countries as well. Australia and New Zealand are both making strides in prefab hospitals and outpatient clinics. Unfortunately, union resistance remains a key impediment to prefab in the U.S., along with (not coincidentally) politically reactive public sector clients who remain resistant to change. Also, why is it that industrial designers are so far ahead of the curve on all this as compared to architects? Is it because architects are still not trained to think systemically? Is it because architects are trained (by default) to view mass production as the enemy of design creativity and originality? Industrial designers, it is true, are educated radically differently: they value the virtues of offsite prefab.[76] Advances in the exciting crossover potential between architecture to industrial design are yielding experimental facades such as the *Pixel Building,* in Melbourne, Australia (2010–2012), designed by Dylan Brady of Melbourne's *Studio 505*.[77] With large works of sculpture now being made by means of 3D printing, it is now possible to model complex, concave, convex compositions previously unrealizable without a reliance on highly labor-intensive traditional construction methods used for centuries.[78] A simple cube can now be fabricated in about the same time as it takes to fabricate a highly complex, biomorphic-shaped structure, and in far less time than if handcrafted.[79]

In addition, in too many places local building codes continue to have an inhibiting effect on the potential of offsite prefab. The *Automedic Clinic* of the 1960s was doomed from the start for this very reason.[80] Animosities between local building code officials, construction trades, and advocates of offsite prefab make it hard to overcome this so-called fear of the unknown. Wherever local labor costs remain low, the testing and refinement of new assemblies, materiality palettes and the like is frequently stymied for this reason.[81] If it is axiomatic that small-scale buildings are where innovation most often gesticulates in healthcare, in the U.S., the vast majority of permanent site prefab modular buildings built to date have been less than 25,000 square feet and no more than two levels in height. This may portend what is to come.[82]

The road ahead, regardless, poses these (among other) challenges:

1. *Full-platform building prefabrication*—Will this result in the same blandness in healthcare architecture that came to characterize the U.S. mobile home industry? The design (aesthetic) narrative must be about more than just 'stacking boxes.'
2. *Ecological advantages*—Advances in prefab modularity can guide further advances in ecological sustainability. The main threat to this is fervent anti-prefab sentiment from contractors, labor unions, and other denialists.
3. *Research and development investment*—Research and development funding is essential. Multinational contractor cartels will monopolize global prefab building markets, stifling architectural innovation, unless inventive partnering occurs.
4. *The pitfalls of globalization*—Prefab modularity must be locally rooted in environmental, climatic, socio-cultural, economic, and political realities. Prefab plants are needed nearer to markets because colonialist policies can be disastrous.

In Chapter 1, a typology of prefab modular architecture for health was presented. This consisted of *Redeployable Trauma Centers* (RTCs), *Redeployable Health Centers* (RHCs), and *Permanent Modular Installations* (PMIs). The present chapter has addressed this third facility type, the PMI. Recent advancements were reviewed on the design, manufacture, and construction of modular buildings and modular componentry built off site, for transport to a permanent site for assembly and completion. Modular buildings of this type can be either turnkey, or a series of modules assembled together into a unified whole at the permanent construction site. At the conclusion of Chapter 2, three challenges to the further creative and aesthetic development of prefab modularity in healthcare architecture were cited. These center on the dominance of the engineer because it is he or she who, at present, tends to control offsite prefab at the scale of a building. Second, improved architectural education is needed on the design possibilities of prefab in healthcare, and beyond. Third, telescopic scaling skill sets are needed so the architect will think and act in the broadest sense so that his or her creative design contributions will make more sense in the larger scheme of things. This will involve confronting a vexing, ever-present dilemma—determining the appropriate percentage of building construction to occur off site, versus on site. In the following chapters this issue is examined in greater detail.

PART 2

Design

Pop-up clinics

CHAPTER 4

Humans have picked up and moved structures from place to place since the earliest Neolithic settlements. Then, as now, entire 'communities' are set up then disassembled for transport elsewhere.[1] For thousands of years, annual religious traditions have given rise to impermanent settlements whose very existence is fleeting, even ephemeral. The largest human gathering of this type in the world occurs in India. Upwards of a million pilgrims gather where the Ganges and Yamuna rivers meet with a third, mythical river. The fifty-five-day long festival of *Kumbh Mela* takes place every three years. Officials estimated that the 2013 iteration of the massive festival was the largest gathering ever in history. As many as 100 million persons passed through this temporary—or *pop-up*—urban aggregation. It became a virtual city.[2] Spatially, it covered an area approximately one half the size of the city of Athens, and it was the world's largest religious gathering:

> Visitors take turns dashing into the river to wash away karmic sins. The ritual 'Royal Bath' was timed to match an auspicious planetary alignment, when believers say spiritual energy flows to earth. 'I wash away all my sins from this life and before,' said a wandering ascetic Swami Shankranand Saraswati, 77, shivering naked in the cold. He said he gave up a career as a senior civil servant forty years ago to become a holy man, travelled on foot for decades and ate only nuts and fruit. The festival has its roots in a Hindu tradition that says the god Vishnu wrested from demons a golden pot containing the nectar of immortality. In a 12-day fight for possession, four drops fell to earth, in the cities of Allahabad, Haridwar, Ujjain and Nasik. Every three years a Kumbh Mela is held at one of these spots, with the festival at Allahabad the holiest of them all.[3]

More than 2,000 years old, this festival is a meeting point for the Hindu *sadhus*, some of whom live in forests or in Himalayan caves and who belong to dozens of inter-related congregations. These sects have their own administrations and elect leaders, but are also known for violent clashes periodically with one another. The festival is growing in size with each iteration due to improved roads, a rising middle class that wishes to preserve its ancient religious traditions, and the advent of advanced communications such as mobile phones and Wi-Fi Internet that has connected once-remote places with one another to a degree unlike anything ever before imaginable. Now, smartphone apps guide pilgrims around the site and provide updates on key resources including food, shelter, and sanitation.

Pilgrims travel to this *pop-up city* by their own means. Upon arrival, they must completely fend for themselves for their sustenance. The sadhus catch up with longtime social contacts, make new friends and business contacts, and discuss scripture—just as has been happening for centuries within this temporary urban community. The local infrastructure provided by the state of Uttar Pradesh consisted of 35,000 toilets, 340 miles (550 kilometers) of potable water pipes, and ninety-five miles (155 kilometers) of temporary roads leading to and from the riverbank site. In 2013, the massive event attracted global attention, tragically, when a stampede killed many hundreds of pilgrims. This provided additional evidence to those who worry the event has grown to an unsustainable size, twelve million, by some estimates.[4] As the sheer size of this recurring event has ballooned, the problem of providing temporary healthcare facilities on site has become exponentially more challenging to national and local government public health agencies in India. Key questions are now, 'What types of facilities will best serve the needs of the masses of pilgrims who converge on the site?' 'Should the primary focus be on disease prevention, or the treatment of after-the-fact acute illness?' and 'Where are the best installation sites for portable, or *instantaneous*, healthcare facilities?'

The Kumbh Mela has grown to the point where it, along with a growing number of other types of pop-up cities, including alternative music extravaganzas such as the annual Burning Man festival in the American Southwest, requires reexamination—and in particular in relation to the notion of community, place and human wellness in the twenty-first century. In an age of instant gratification, we immerse ourselves in a burgeoning sea of digital media. This transformative technology has increased in sophistication to the point where real-time human experience has become unable to match its virtual counterpart, as in the case of the pseudo-paganistic Burning Man festival.[5] Burning Man's historical precursors include immense Hindu pilgrimages such as Kumbh Mela.

These events are microcosms of larger trends that are becoming worrisome from the standpoint of the inability of public and private sector agencies to provide sustainable healthcare support where the need may be temporary and yet acute, over the course of a weekend, month, or even year and beyond. The ability to support healthcare needs in these nomadic contexts can become unsustainable regardless of whether the event is a voluntary one, such as a religious pilgrimage or music festival, or due to a disaster or other type of involuntary yet transformative event. A joint World Health Organization and UN-HABITAT report published in 2010 called for the unmasking of such involuntary, burgeoning 'hidden cities' worldwide, characterized by chronic and growing health inequalities, at this turning point in global population growth. For the first time ever, the majority of the world's population is living in cities, and this population continues to expand. In terms of statistics, in 1990 fewer than half lived in urban areas.[6] By 2010, more than half lived in cities, and by 2050 this proportion will swell to seven out of every ten persons. The number of urban dwellers continues to swell by nearly sixty million *every year*. This demographic shift from rural to urban life has far reaching consequences with profound impacts on squatter settlements and related pop-up aggregations. The inhabitants of these 'instant places' nearly always have little or no control over their own destiny, are nearly always desperately poor, and beholden to the mercy and compassion of others.[7]

The core thesis of this chapter is that an offsite-built, prefabricated modular pop-up clinic, a *Redeployable Health Center* (RHC), is a viable intervention in medically underserved communities. A modular pop-up can enhance a community's overall resiliency because it can be brought in on short notice, be set up and begin operations relatively quickly and this thereby makes it possible for local residents to receive healthcare services that they may not have otherwise received or had access to, and in the event of a disaster, this same process is equally appropriate in caring for the medically underserved. In the case of displaced residents after a disaster, the presence of this type of clinic can help to attract residents back home to rebuild their homes, places of worship, and community. Autonomous RHCs are architectural prosthetic devices because they address:

- *The dual threats of global climate change and population growth*—Many disaster strike zones experience difficult population rebounding due to the continued consequences of sea level rise, and weather events with unprecedented adverse outcomes. Effective architectural responses must be able to absorb impacts and bounce back—as life and death outcomes may hang in the balance.

- *A lack of local health facility options*—In the U.S. alone, thousands of abandoned buildings dot the everyday vernacular landscapes of inner urban neighborhoods, suburbia, and rural communities. Often, these buildings remain viable for reuse as healthcare resources on a temporary basis as local needs dictate, serving as adjuncts to existing hospitals and outpatient health centers.

Health inequities in the everyday built landscape

Health inequality is a crisis of increasing magnitude with each passing day, with the effects of climate change and the unequal distribution of wealth now further magnifying health disparities worldwide. Health disparities have existed in the built environment across the millennia and this is nothing new, of course. But they are becoming more acute and at a larger population scale than ever before in poor communities, places most susceptible to sudden, involuntary, dramatic, disruptive change.[8] A growing area of qualitative research centers on the systematic study of the everyday ordinary settings and landscapes that we encounter in our day-to-day lives. This area of inquiry has opened up a broad bandwidth of pertinent work to the present discussion, ranging from the origins of post-World War II suburbia, the history of the automobile and sprawl in both developing and in advanced developed societies, the type and influence of ubiquitous commercial roadside vernacular building types, and patterns of discrimination by race, gender, sexual orientation, and socio-economic class. Paul Groth defines cultural landscape studies as the interaction of people and place, of the relationship between a social group and its buildings and places, from the high-style cathedral to the corporate office tower to the depression-era Hooverville hut, a farmer's barbed-wire fence, to an abandoned post-war drive-in theater. It is about the history of how people use (and disuse) everyday space and buildings, rooms, streets, fields, yards, to establish their personal identity and a place's larger cultural identity. This knowledge of and appreciation for the value of otherwise overlooked, dismissed, ordinary environments can foster a deeper cultural understanding and lessen the urban and environmental dangers resulting from people who cannot or are unable to see and interpret their immediate surroundings.[9]

Architecture is but one manifestation within multiple, contiguous, polymorphic cultural landscapes. A portrait of a given building or building type can be delineated across multiple site contexts and the systematic documentation of these yields patterns. The day-to-day patterns that define a people and their community symbolize what is most important to them, and about them. The documentation of this information can amount to a complex rue of archival and synchronous information that is often ethnographic in nature. These data are obtainable through surveys, interviews, and incisive visual documentation. In general, data are frequently acquired through research methods developed in the social sciences. Multifaceted assemblages of data, appropriate to the people and places documented, have been at the heart and soul of the most fascinating work published to date in this field; a critical discourse continues to evolve, increasingly sophisticated in its methodologies and reach. Cultural geographers, literary theorists, biologists, art historians, historians, social theorists, anthropologists, landscape architects, and architects have all made insightful contributions.[10] This author studied the pre-disaster and post-Hurricane Katrina conditions in New Orleans through this methodological lens.[11] Instantaneous, voluntary, pop-up cities, disaster zones, and disadvantaged neighborhoods are suited to contemporary *temporary* healthcare installations in the everyday ordinary landscape, and both can benefit immensely from incisive architectural prosthetic support.[12]

Architecture, both as a profession and academic discipline has, for the most part, overlooked the merits of cultural landscape analysis. One outcome is that the architecture of the ordinary everyday milieu continues to evade serious attention.[13] And yet these places are all around us. They represent a continuum from serious to the superficial. Instantaneous voluntary pop-up cities appear across the United States during 'tailgating' in conjunction with collegiate sporting events. Pop-up 'tailgate cities' are created on football Saturdays, and on the day of National Football League (NFL) games.[14] Thousands of rabid fans flock to these staging sites even though they exist for a mere few hours. Such events pop up in ordinary open grassy fields and in sprawling asphalt parking lots. Ardent fans drive their Winnebagos from near and far to set up camp the night before along with their barbecue grills, tents, flat screens, and folding chairs.[15]

The landscape of everyday places and buildings calls for thoughtful reappraisal, beyond the bombastic overtones of a pop-up sporting event. A building type of particular relevance to the core thesis of this chapter is the storefront pop-up. The United States and a growing number of developed countries are currently plagued by many underperforming or shuttered shopping malls and forlorn roadside strip centers.[16] The decades leading up to the near-global financial meltdown of 2008 were characterized by the construction of tens of thousands of these places: countless poorly built fast-food franchises representing an array of banal commercial and institutional typologies. The Internet site *deadmalls.com* cleverly documents the plight of malls that fell victim to economic hard times, shifting demographic trends, and consumers' changing aesthetic tastes. Thousands of these places are struggling to survive. After having lost their anchor department stores, the smaller stores, one by one, begin to disappear. One solution to this phenomenon is for retailers to take advantage of the high vacancy rates in fading malls and strip centers by installing temporary pop-up stores. These pop-ups have been experimented with with considerable success. It is a win-win because it is an opportunity for the retailer to set up shop for only a period of weeks or a few months without a long-term commitment. The mall owner benefits from the injection of increased foot traffic these pop-ups attract to an otherwise empty storefront.[17]

This trend, *pop-up retail*, first gained notice in 2004. The premise is that if new products can come and go, why can't the stores that display them do the same? This is precisely what more and more retailers have begun to do, in one-time galleria mall and strip mall spaces where a chic boutique might spring up for a short period and then disappear, to a mobile store/unit that can roam throughout a cityscape and beyond, seeking out its clientele. By 2015, temporary retail establishments appeared globally with increasing frequency. An app, *Storefront*, aimed to become the *Airbnb* of pop-up merchandising. It launched in Chicago in 2014 as a means to help connect retailers, designers, and artists attracted to pop-up spaces with short-term leases.[18] Sometimes a retailer's pop-up appears spontaneously, unannounced. This is done to seize the moment and quickly draw crowds in, then it immediately vanishes, morphing into something else, somewhere else. It is a technique that theaters and the venerable *Cirque du Soleil* has perfected over a period of decades with their pop-up tent installations set up in cities for a short duration. It is even occurring with small-scale urban pop-up museums.[19] Descriptive terms increasingly associated with pop-up retailing include *massclusivity* and *planned spontaneity*.[20]

Examples of instantaneous pop-up retail installations include the airline *Song's* pop-up in Manhattan, open for only nine weeks in 2003. This store featured samples from Song's in-flight menu plus travel gear and even airline tickets. That same year, the North American discount retailer, *Target*, opened a temporary 1,500 square foot store in Rockefeller Center to celebrate its new women's clothing line, 'Mizrahi'.[21] Target also staged a pop-up outlet on a barge on the Hudson River during that Christmas season. An exclusive retail concept store, Vacant, opened stores for one month only in major cities including New York, London, Tokyo, Shanghai, Paris, Berlin, Stockholm and Los Angeles. It showcased a range of one-off, limited edition items from established brands and emerging designers. Its new pop-up storefront locations are announced by email and Twitter, fueling a 'here now, gone tomorrow' *zeitgeist*.[22] High-end pop-up boutiques and restaurants have become common in many parts of the world.[23] But this trend also provides the unprecedented opportunity to rethink everyday ordinary dying shopping malls, faded roadside commercial strips, and fading suburbs.[24] Traditional brick and mortar retailers are now threatened with, in the words of Jeff Jordan, 'economic destruction,' by their more advantaged online competition. The e-commerce revolution, combined with the overbuilding of malls across the United States in the period 1980–2008, seriously dampened the value of brick and mortar real estate.[25] The severe recession of 2008 triggered a malaise that persists in many segments of the U.S. retail industry:

> Most real estate professionals understand that profound changes are afoot…The Wall Street Journal reports: 'Green Street Advisor, an analysis firm that tracks REITs [Real Estate Investment Trusts], has forecast that 10 percent of the roughly 1,000 large malls in the U.S. will fail within the next ten years (by 2022) and be converted into something with far less retail…many mall CEOs predict the attrition rate will be higher.' Daniel Hurwitz, president and CEO of DDR observes, 'I don't think we're overbuilt, I think we're under-demolished.'…Unfortunately for mall owners; the content on deadmalls.com is about to expand substantially. There are just too many malls in America.[26]

It isn't just commercial malls that are prime candidates for reinvention. With shifts in demographics, population levels, and economic fortunes at the local level, many older religious and educational facilities are being downsized, closed, and abandoned. This has resulted in a wave of shuttered gymnasiums and other large-span open spaces very well suited for a pop-up health clinic installation. These strip center storefronts, theaters, auto dealerships, warehouses, enclosed malls, branch banks, churches, and their gymnasiums, all offer new possibilities for conversion to new uses to make their communities more resilient in the face of change.

Pop-up clinics: case studies

Access to healthcare is critical to the well-being of any community. In the U.S., a network of local, state, and federal health agencies endeavor to coordinate efforts to serve a diverse and growing population of 323.5 million. According to the U.S. Census Bureau, in 2012 there were forty-eight million persons (15.4 percent of the population) without health insurance.[27] Historically, the majority of these persons have lived their entire lives in medically underserved places. These individuals and the communities they live in frequently suffer from insufficient access to outpatient health clinics and insufficient access to inpatient services at local hospitals.[28]

This lack of access to proper diagnosis and treatment for illness, disease prevention education, and wellness care often forces these persons, who are often poor, to travel excessive distances to reach a healthcare provider. Because needed care is put off, sometimes for many years, more intensive healthcare must be sought, at a point later in the illness cycle after a person's condition has worsened significantly. Hospital care at this point is much more costly and is nearly always the result of the patient's condition not having been attended to properly (if at all) at a preventable stage.[29] Late-stage illness diagnosis and treatment often requires emergency room care. Worse, many patients and families, lacking a means of transport such as a private family car, or good, reliable rail transport, by default, may fall entirely out of the healthcare equation and opt to not seek any sort of care at all even when the stricken individual's condition has become terminal.[30]

Beside this, the phenomenon known as *food deserts* is on the rise; this condition persists wherever local options for purchasing fresh food are scarce to nonexistent. Grocery chains have been fleeing U.S. inner city neighborhoods for two generations. What's left? A small army of unhealthy stores with low nutrition offerings is all that remains—establishments specializing in high fat foods and sugar-filled beverages. As discussed in Chapter 1, in New Orleans' Lower Ninth Ward there are still no 'healthy' grocery stores ten years after Hurricane Katrina. The closest is a Wal-Mart in Chalmette, more than 2.5 miles away and beyond walking distance.[31] An urban food desert is also highly likely to be medically underserved. As for non-urban areas, in the U.S. more than two-thirds of all outpatient clinics for the medically underserved are currently located in rural communities, far from urban centers. As in the case of their urban counterparts, the physical condition and quality of this national network is extremely uneven.[32] The dilemma facing local care providers—especially in the not-for-profit governmental sector—is either too few facilities whatsoever or too many poor quality facilities.[33] Healthcare facility in-access among the medically underserved in the U.S. is reaching a crisis stage.[34] A physician or nurse may be forced to work in a poorly planned and poorly maintained freestanding outpatient clinic for decades.[35]

The U.S. Congress created the federal *Medicaid* program in 1965 to serve the needs of Americans lacking private health insurance.[36] In 2010, United States Congress passed the federal *Affordable Care Act of 2010* (ACA) that, for the first time, provided healthcare insurance coverage to as many as thirty-one million uninsured Americans (of the forty-eight million total who remain uninsured). With the ACA's full implementation still on the horizon, concerns grew over a fear that previously uninsured patients would overwhelm the aforementioned network of community outpatient health centers and stand-alone hospitals.[37] With the prospect of millions of previously uninsured patients now entering the healthcare system the poorest quality facilities may reach breakdown stage, i.e. overcrowding, building envelope failures, a near-total lack of patient confidentiality. Hundreds if not thousands of other facilities will limp along, particularly those in the heart of economically disadvantaged communities.[38]

With or without an adequate financial reinvestment in the nations' healthcare infrastructure, there will undoubtedly be a significant need for hundreds of new, temporary pop-up installations across the U.S. in the coming years. This need will exist across the everyday ordinary landscape, for their use in everyday routine 'good times' and for their use in highly disruptive 'bad times' following a disaster event. A pop-up installation can replace or serve as supplemental support to an existing overburdened, aging, permanent clinic. A situation persists where, unfortunately, no national database on the status of this physical inventory is available at this time although the need for such an inventory and national knowledge repository is greater than ever before.[39] In keeping with the need for the architect to be able to telescopically scale one's interpretation of and response to larger discourses, the following section consists of architectural prototypes to fortify and extend the quality of freestanding outpatient health clinics. In so doing the architect is able to address the primacy of engineering leadership in prefab modularity at this time. In addition the education of the architect is that much furthered on this subject, as the research reported below comes from the academy, not the profession (see Chapter 1). The aim of the discussion, which follows, is to examine the potential of offsite-built, prefab modularity in everyday ordinary contexts and in post-disaster contexts.

New Orleans and Charleston—medically at-risk communities

The inhabitants of New Orleans, Louisiana and Charleston, South Carolina have been geographically vulnerable for nearly 300 years. These two historic American cities grew as the result of the shipping trade and strategic military interests. In the twenty-first century their tourist economies now predominate. Now, also, both are facing increasingly adverse consequences due to the ramifications of global climate change. Both places are surrounded by large bodies of water, both are situated slightly above, or below sea level, both experience land subsidence, both are densely developed, and both metro areas are subject to repetitive tidal surge flooding. In New Orleans' case, parts of the city lie as much as twelve feet below sea level.[40] In both places, a parade of technologically advanced civil works projects have been built since the 1800s to improve drainage, with varying degrees of success. As mentioned in Chapter 1, in the case of New Orleans, oil and gas exploration canals dredged through the swamps have decimated its vast former protective network of buffering wetlands. The Gulf of Mexico coastline, less than sixty miles from the Central Business District and the historic Vieux Carré, is indisputably receding.[41]

In the case of Charleston, this city was settled at the tip of a peninsula that juts out at the confluence of two rivers, the Ashley River and the Cooper River. The crown of this narrow peninsula is at most ten feet above sea level and only a seawall at its southernmost edge buffers it from the tidal surges. There are no protective levees anywhere else on the peninsula or in the nearby low-lying suburban and coastal areas. The surrounding suburban region was all originally wetlands; many of these areas have been developed while some sections are mandated as protected open space. Both cities across the generations opted to sprawl out over their adjoining wetlands as their boundaries were gradually expanded due to population growth and suburbanization. A recent study of the Charleston peninsula metro area, conducted by a team of architectural students at Clemson University working under the direction of Professor Robert Miller, focused on the impact of rising sea level on storm surge flooding in a major hurricane. Charleston last sustained a direct hit from a hurricane in Hurricane Hugo in 1993, resulting in eleven deaths. It is yet to experience a disaster of the magnitude of Katrina. The team's findings were sobering.[42]

These two historic cities are in need of technically sophisticated and yet socially compassionate enhancement from the standpoint of making them more resilient in the face of the threat of flooding. But change comes slow. Bureaucracies need to be awakened because in a surprising number of coastal municipalities the existence of climate change still remains disputed.[43] The mounting evidence has led climatologists, geographers, urbanists, civil engineers, and housing experts to view Hurricane Katrina, Typhoon Haiyan and Superstorm Sandy as harbingers of the new normal in coastal zones.[44] Making matters worse, coastal cities such as New Orleans and Charleston face severe pre-storm evacuation obstacles because only a few major roads lead out of the metro area. In the case of Katrina this had a major impact on the length and complexity of the evacuation; to some extent it suppressed the number of people able to do so while others simply gave up trying. As a consequence, the death toll spiraled. Few places remain to seek refuge when 125,000 residences are destroyed or severely damaged.[45] Beyond any underlying psychological explanations that may or may not have triggered a personal decision whether to stay or leave, this disaster epitomized the consequences of lacking the monetary means to evacuate or a vehicle in which to do so.[46] As discussed earlier, for those left behind and for those who sought to return, this debacle reverberated throughout American society and raised concern internationally on the need for the presence of better emergency housing and medical care.[47]

While New Orleans and Charleston share much in common such as geography, major seaports, and tourism, both harbor sizeable, medically at-risk urban populations, and the governments of the states they are located in need to do more. Louisiana refuses to join the federal ACA program.[48] An editorial appearing in New Orleans' daily newspaper, *The Times-Picayune*, concluded it is in the state's best interest to join this program.[49] In South Carolina, the situation is just as challenging for the medically uninsured/underserved.[50] South Carolina currently ranks forty-eighth nationally (out of fifty states) in the health status of its residents.[51] The question arises, what can architects, working in consort with health planners and direct care providers, do to build greater resiliency into the healthcare equation? What can be done to improve access to healthcare in the aftermath of disaster as well as in ordinary, everyday, underserved contexts? In response, a team of Clemson University graduate students in the Graduate Option in Architecture + Health (Team 699), led by this author, traveled to New Orleans and to Charleston in the Spring of 2013.[52] It would be a two-phase sequence of activity with Phase I (research) followed by Phase II (design).

At the start of the research phase, a post-occupancy evaluation (a performance assessment metric discussed earlier) was conducted in the largest pop-up clinic ever set up in a vacant shopping mall in the U.S., or possibly anywhere else. It opened three months after Katrina in December 2005 in the former, by then vacant, Lord & Taylor department store in New Orleans' downtown core. This store was a major anchor of a large enclosed mall, the New Orleans Center, built in the late 1980s. This dead mall is located next door to the immense domed sports stadium that sustained heavy damage in the hurricane (now known as the Mercedes Benz Superdome). This pop-up clinic totaled 18,000 square feet and occupied the entire footprint of this two-level former department store. Interviews were conducted with administrative staff, direct caregivers, and with patients (see Interview 1 in the Appendix). With its eighteen-foot ceilings, its single pair central escalators that were always breaking down due to a high, high volume of use by staff and patients, and a total lack of privacy throughout, it was a real challenge to operate this clinic on daily basis. The game plan, initially right after the disaster, was for this pop-up to remain open for only three years at most—in reality, it would remain open for ten years, until relocated to the newly constructed LSU Health Sciences Center in the summer of 2015, five blocks away.

This pop-up clinic provided inspiration to take this idea a step further and explore the amenity of other types of buildings suitable to host a pop-up clinic installation. More than thirty potential host buildings/sites were studied in the two cities. In both places, the research-based design team canvased numerous neighborhoods, documenting existing buildings suitable in terms of their location, condition, infrastructure, i.e. public transit and roads, crime and safety, and the degree to which they were 'known' within their surrounding neighborhood. Behavioral observation, photos, site mapping, and floor plans were produced on each candidate. Data collected on the set of pop-up sites selected for further analysis included focused interviews with local residents, extensive photographic documentation, and the production of a set of base maps of each selected installation site. These base maps documented land-use patterns, roadway accessibility, walking–cycling amenities, and the propensity for flooding, architectural landmarks, and urban anomalies. Photographs and base maps for six host-building sites are presented below. A room key accompanies the first of the six host structures and this key applies equally to the entire set of six (referred to as *Host Structures 1–6*).

Next, two templates for offsite-built, prefabricated modular clinic designs were produced by the research-based design team, for testing in the six hosts in New Orleans and Charleston. These templates are referred to as *Pop-Up System A* and *Pop-Up System B*. Prototype A is shown installed in Host Structures 1 through 3 (HS-1 through HS-3), and Prototype B is shown installed in Host Structures 4 through 6 (HS-4 through HS-6):

> *Pop-Up System A*—This rectilinear, container-like prototype is a lift-pack system, based on a two foot by four foot platform, featuring translucent structural panels and diagonal structural reinforcing struts. It was designed by a team led by George Hughes and Valerie Or (Team 699). The system was inspired by the automotive industry's use

of standardized modular componentry in the manufacture of its products, whereby major elements of a module are designed as autonomous 'chunks' and then assembled together with other modules in a process that allows for a degree of customization of a final, mass-produced product (see Chapter 3). Individual modules, for instance, can be manufactured with or without a compartmentalized ceiling grid. This grid can be left open as an option, depending on the availability and condition of the host structure's environmental control system. Alternatively, individual modules can be powered by the system's own onboard environmental control system. Light fixtures are mounted to this overhead grid. Modules are fabricated to be lightweight, flexible, adaptable to various ambient light conditions, and to provide secure entry-access portals. All electrical raceways are housed beneath the floor plane and run through plug-in panelized walls. The system can be reshaped, in plan, as dictated by the configurability limitations posed by the footprint of the host structure. Wall panel-mounted LED lighting provides additional lighting in the interior. Each module has lightweight, lockable, sliding pocket doors, and modules can be elevated up to one foot above the base floor surface to accommodate uneven floor surfaces. A wheelchair access ramp can be attached at a module's entry portal. Wall panels are fabricated in light hues, with accent panels able to be fabricated in virtually any color, thereby allowing for further customization of the final product. Furnishings and storage cabinets clip on to interior wall panels and are able to be repositioned and a number of design options are possible with respect to the system's interior room components. The water supply is fabricated in flexible tubing and handwashing sinks can be added/subtracted based on user requirements. System A is depicted (below), and is 'tested' in Host Structures 1–3 (HS-1–3):

1 Church of Christ, Charleston

The Church of Christ is located on King Street on the Charleston peninsula in the district bounded by Interstate 26 (I-26) to the north. It is a low to moderate-income residential neighborhood built in the late nineteenth and early twentieth century, bisected by the Mid-Town East–West expressway that connects to the suburb of Mount Pleasant to the east and the suburban Ashley area to the west. A Baptist congregation constructed this church in the late nineteenth century. The chapel's altar is at the center of its symmetrical plan, with a wing to either side used for related congregational functions. Its advantages as an installation site include its centrality, its walkable and bikeable location, its revered status as a social and architectural landmark within Charleston's venerable African-American community, its direct access to major roads leading into and from the city, and its location on a bus transit route (Figures 4.1 and 4.2a–b).

In Host Structure 1 (HS-1), the system is deployed across three main spatial zones. The main entry to the Church serves as the public entrance and from there the patient proceeds to sign in (1) then proceeds to the main waiting area, seating is provided in a retained section of church pews (2). Patients then proceed to one of the four intake/interview alcoves (I1–4). The chapel facility itself is otherwise unaltered by the modular installation. The side zone to the right of the main waiting area houses six examination rooms (E1–6) and six behavioral health consult rooms (C1–6). The laboratory (3) is housed between the main waiting room and the core clinic spaces, To the left side of the core sign-in and waiting/intake zone are various clinical support functions, including the pharmacy (13), staff offices, a conference room (5, 12, 20), the staff kitchen and staff respite room (21), and a TB/STD exam room (26) for diagnostic assessment and treatment (Figures 4.3 to 4.6a–c).

2 Chase Bank, New Orleans

This branch location of the Chase Bank is located on Harrison Avenue in the Lakeview Section of New Orleans, a neighborhood that experienced severe flooding in Katrina, having taken on twelve feet of toxic floodwater in 2005. Many residential, commercial, and religious structures sustained severe damage in the area. Hundreds of ruined homes had to be demolished and the rebuilt businesses, schools, and residences in the immediate vicinity of this bank are symbols of the intense resilience of local residents to fight back to reclaim their neighborhood (and city) in the face of seemingly insurmountable odds. Many new businesses have opened in the past decade, and the street and surrounding neighborhood are now vibrant and symbolize a determined spirit to rebound. Many tear down lots remain, however, and these vacant parcels are a stark reminder of just how severe the damage was. Ten years after the disaster, many homeowners still had not rebuilt because they had relocated permanently elsewhere, or because they simply could not afford to rebuild. This branch bank's amenity as a host structure centers on it being elevated an entire level up from the street, allowing for a parking area and access drive below. The bank itself did not flood or sustain significant related damage. This structure was selected for its elevated main level, its centrality in the active, rebuilding, Lakeview district of the city, and for its appropriateness as a central location for a health clinic that can also double as a station point for disaster aid services, such as a Red Cross or FEMA assistance center that could be set up in the shaded, open-air, street-level space on the site in the event of another disaster (Figures 4.7 and 4.8a–c).

In this host structure (HS-2), the ground level interior spaces would house behavioral health consultation services (C5–7), patient and staff restrooms, and an immunization suite (17). A ground level location is convenient for patients in need of vaccinations, including tetanus, because they can be administrated both indoors and outdoors on the busiest days while patients are protected from the elements. This precludes the need for patients to walk upstairs (or via elevator) to the second level of the clinic. The main/upper level of the installation houses the sign-in station (1), main waiting area (2), and clerical/intake zones (I1–4, 4–5) in direct proximity to the stairway/elevator area. The clinical core is comprised of the examination rooms (E1–6), subwaiting area (2) and laboratory (3). Behavioral health consult rooms (C1–4) are located directly across, and support functions are aligned along the outer perimeter edge of the building envelope opposite the examination rooms and clerical/intake zone. The layout is spacious and its perimeter circulation promotes patient wayfinding. If additional exam room capacity is required, this host structure could easily accommodate through the elimination of the outer perimeter corridor and by reconfiguring the exam room and converting the staff intake/clerical cores into semi-private clusters with an internal (inboard) corridor (Figures 4.3 to 4.6a–c).

3 Charter Math and Science, Charleston

This school gymnasium, located on King Street, was built in the 1920s and is part of a grade 6–12 school campus that serves 480 students. The campus is situated in the heart of the Charleston peninsula. In 2007, Charter Math and Science received a $650,000 grant to guide and support its transition out of the Charleston public school system into a quasi-private run Charter Academy. The advantages of this installation site center on the gym's unobstructed clear span space allowing for multiple footprint re-configurations and staff-patient flow options, and its location on a corner site as this allows direct access for equipment and supplies vis-à-vis a side entry, its location on a major bus transit route, and adjacent open space on the campus that, in a post-disaster scenario, can be pressed into service as a disaster aid station point for the Red Cross, FEMA, or other assistance. The campus is a civic landmark within the immediate neighborhood and the city (Figures 4.9 and 4.10a–b).

In this host structure (HS-3), the installation is configured as a single symmetrical 'block' of modules with a perimeter racetrack circulation and a center aisle that creates two equivalent zones to either side—a decision made to take maximum advantage of the interior's openness due to the absence of structural columns. The public entrance is from King Street, and the patient immediately enters into the sign-in and main waiting area. The intake/interview and clerical zone is housed in the left hand block (I1–4 and 6) as is the subwaiting area and the exam room core (E1–8). The laboratory (3), health education conference room (20), volunteers' office (24), and general clinic support spaces (18, 25) are in close proximity to the examination rooms. The eighteen foot ceiling height in this space allows for an optional mezzanine. The mezzanine level can be used for the storage of supplies by FEMA and/or the American Red Cross to provide an extra measure of resiliency. The modular system's interlocking, interchangeable components allow for re-configurability as needs evolve in time (Figures 4.3 to 4.6a–c).

Sammy's
CORNER STORE
SUNNYSIDE AVE
RUTLEDGE

4.1 Urban Fabric Analysis 1

4.2a–b Church of Christ, Charleston, exterior and plan

Key:

C1-C4	behavioral health consultation*	13	medications
E1-E6	examination room*	14	subwaiting
I1-I4	patient intake*	15	nutrition
1	patient sign-in	16	director
2	waiting area	17	immunizations
3	laboratory	18	physicians
4	medications	19	biohazardous waste
5	office	20	health education/ conference
6	clerical: work zone	21	staff kitchen
7	medical records	22	housekeeping/janitor
8	staff restroom	23	storeroom
9	men's restroom	24	volunteers
10	women's restroom	25	nursing
11	patient restroom	26	TB/STD
12	environmental health		

* The number of rooms varies across the following six case study sites as a function of its installation site footprint.

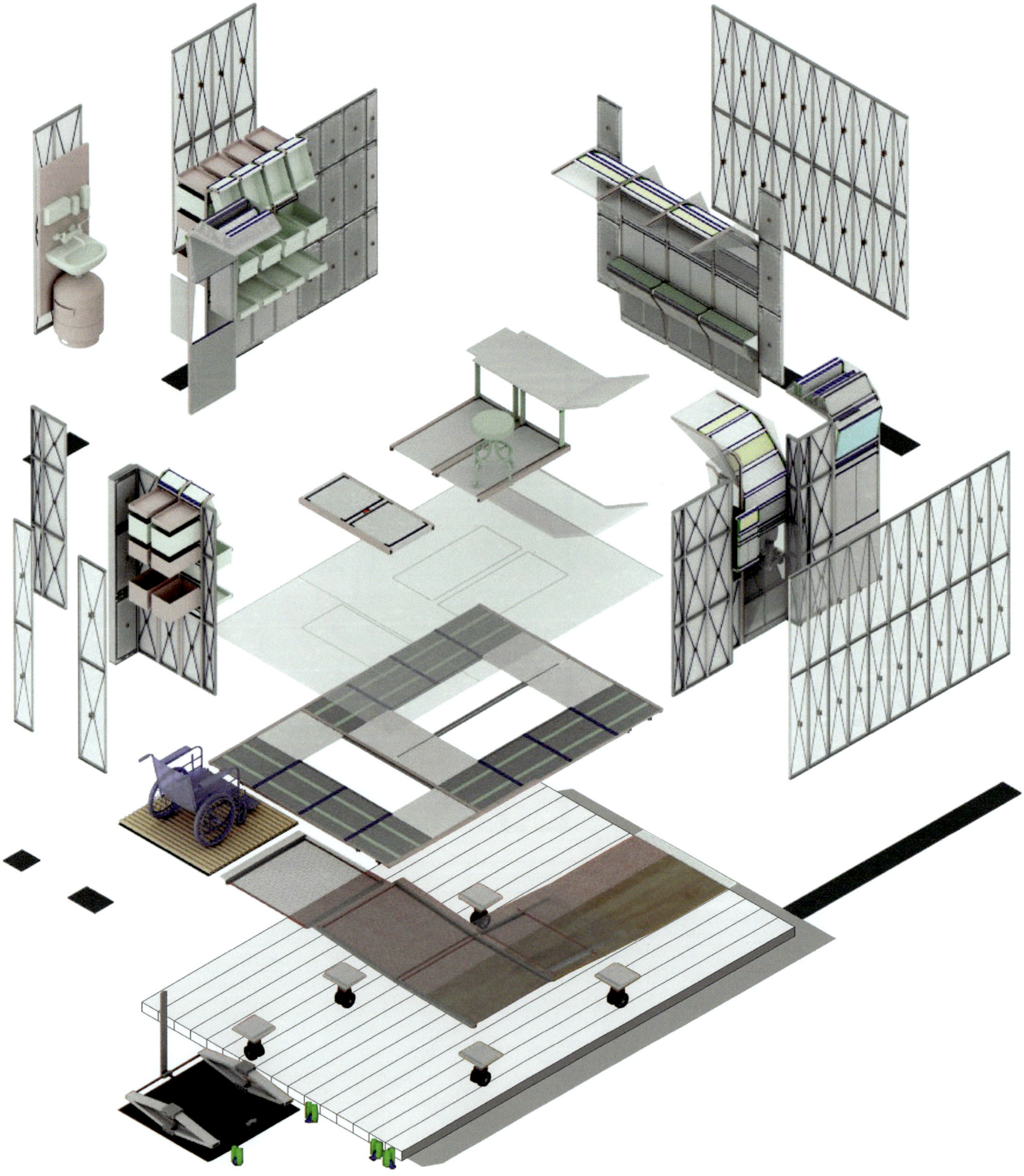

4.3 Blow-apart axonometric of typical exam room module

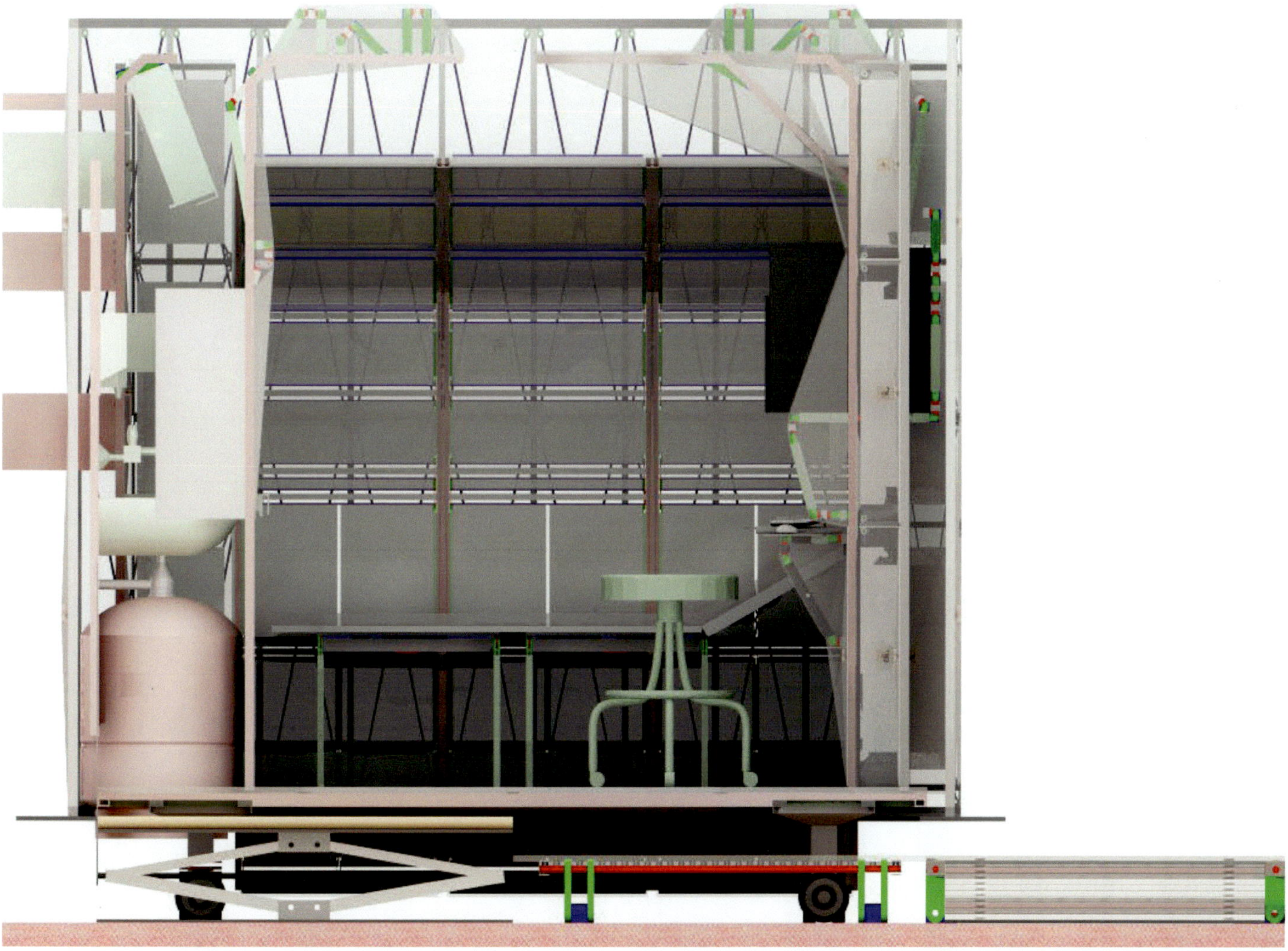

4.4 Section, typical exam room module

4.5a–c Interior views of pop-up installation: interior pathways, and consult room

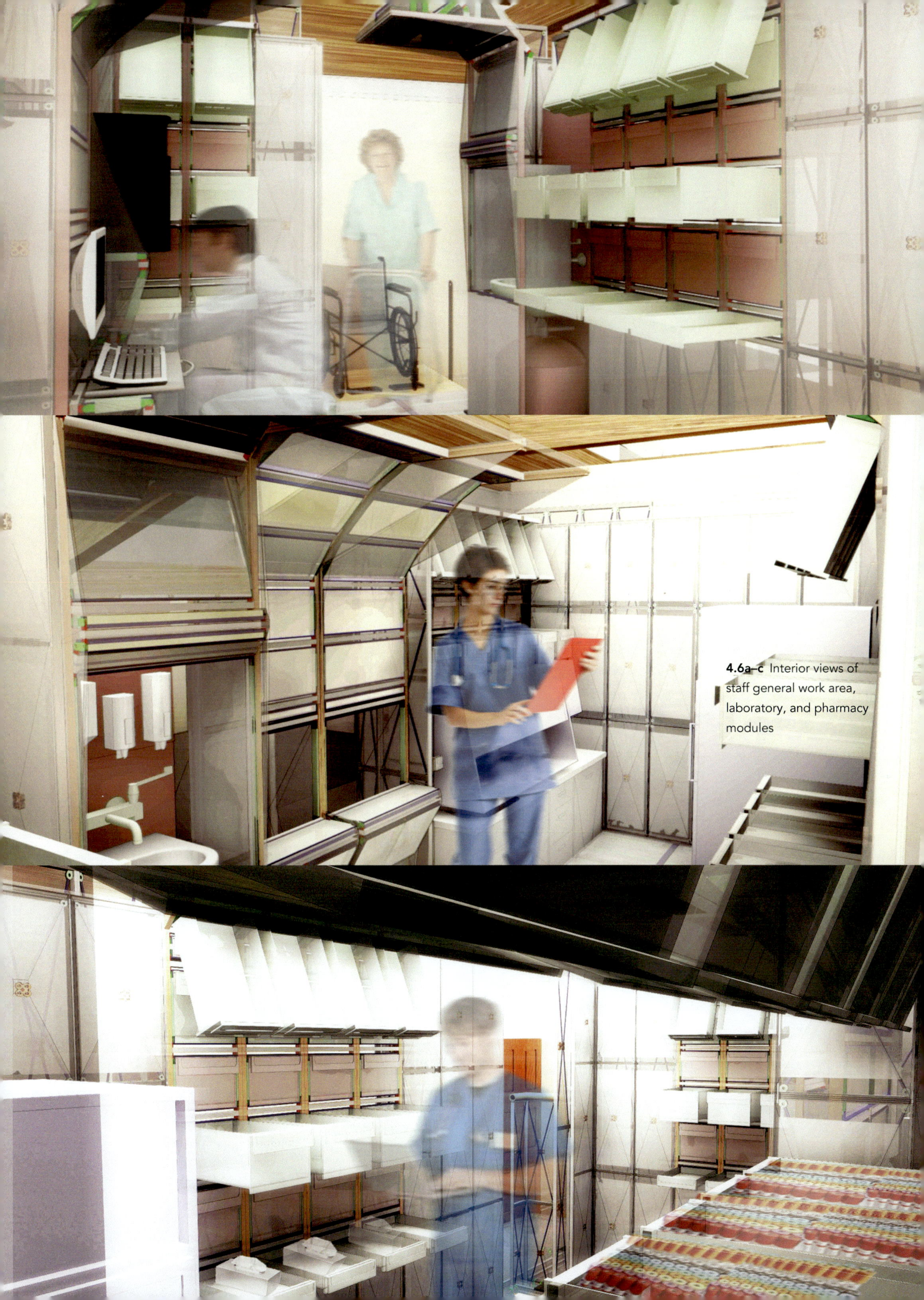

4.6a–c Interior views of staff general work area, laboratory, and pharmacy modules

WHITNEY BANK
The Velvet Cactus

4.7 Urban Fabric Analysis 2

4.8a–c Chase Bank, New Orleans, exterior and plan

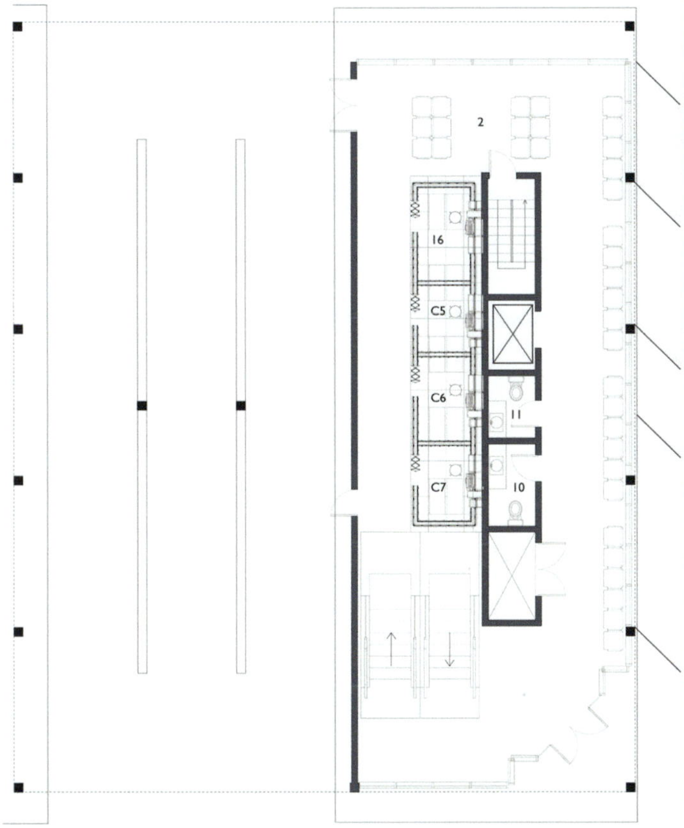

LEVEL 1

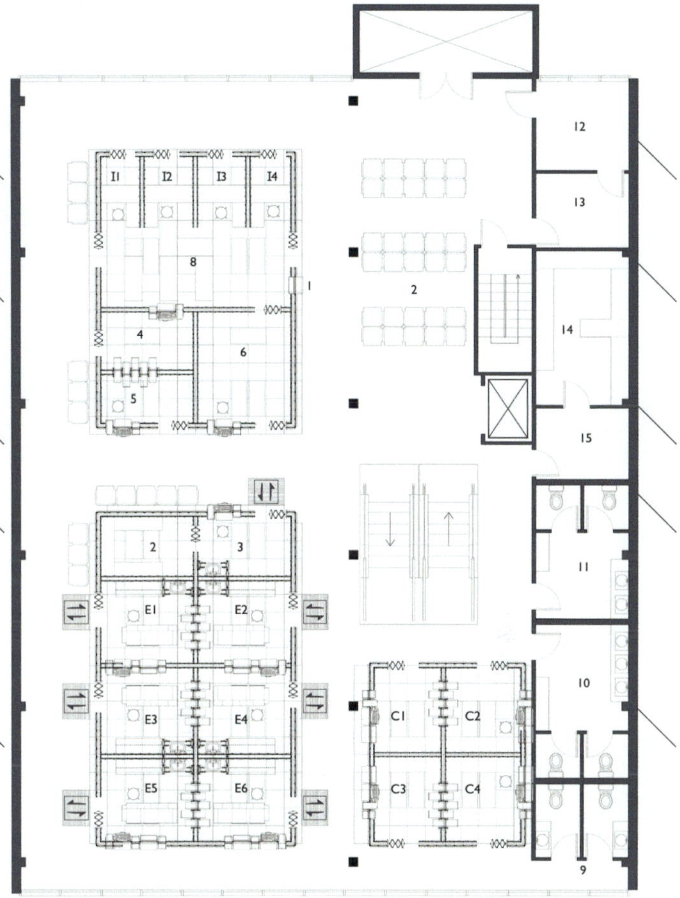

LEVEL 2

PALACE
The Fabulous ELLEN BRIGHT Hall
FAMILY DOLLAR
GREAT WALL Express
TAKE-OUT
722-8080
FOOD LION

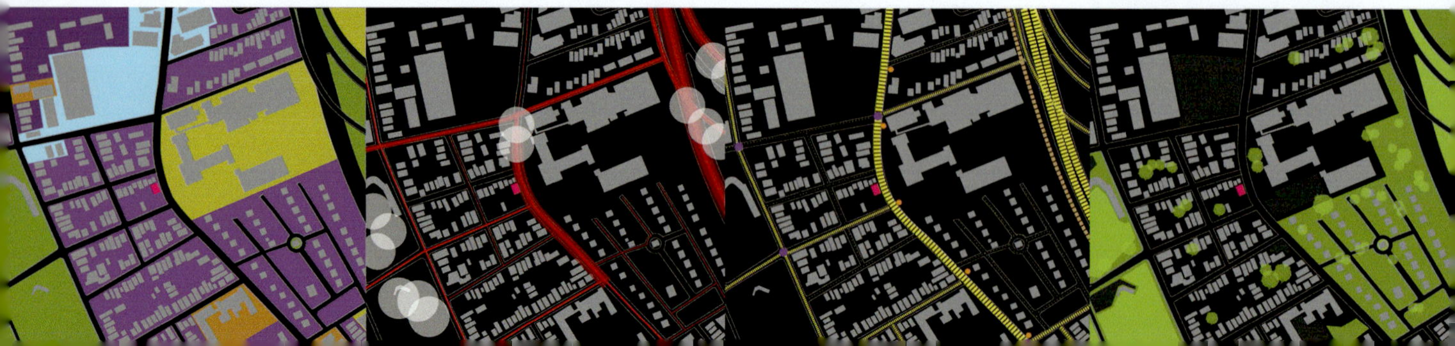

4.9 Urban Fabric Analysis 3

4.10a–b Charter Math and Science Academy, Charleston, exterior and plan

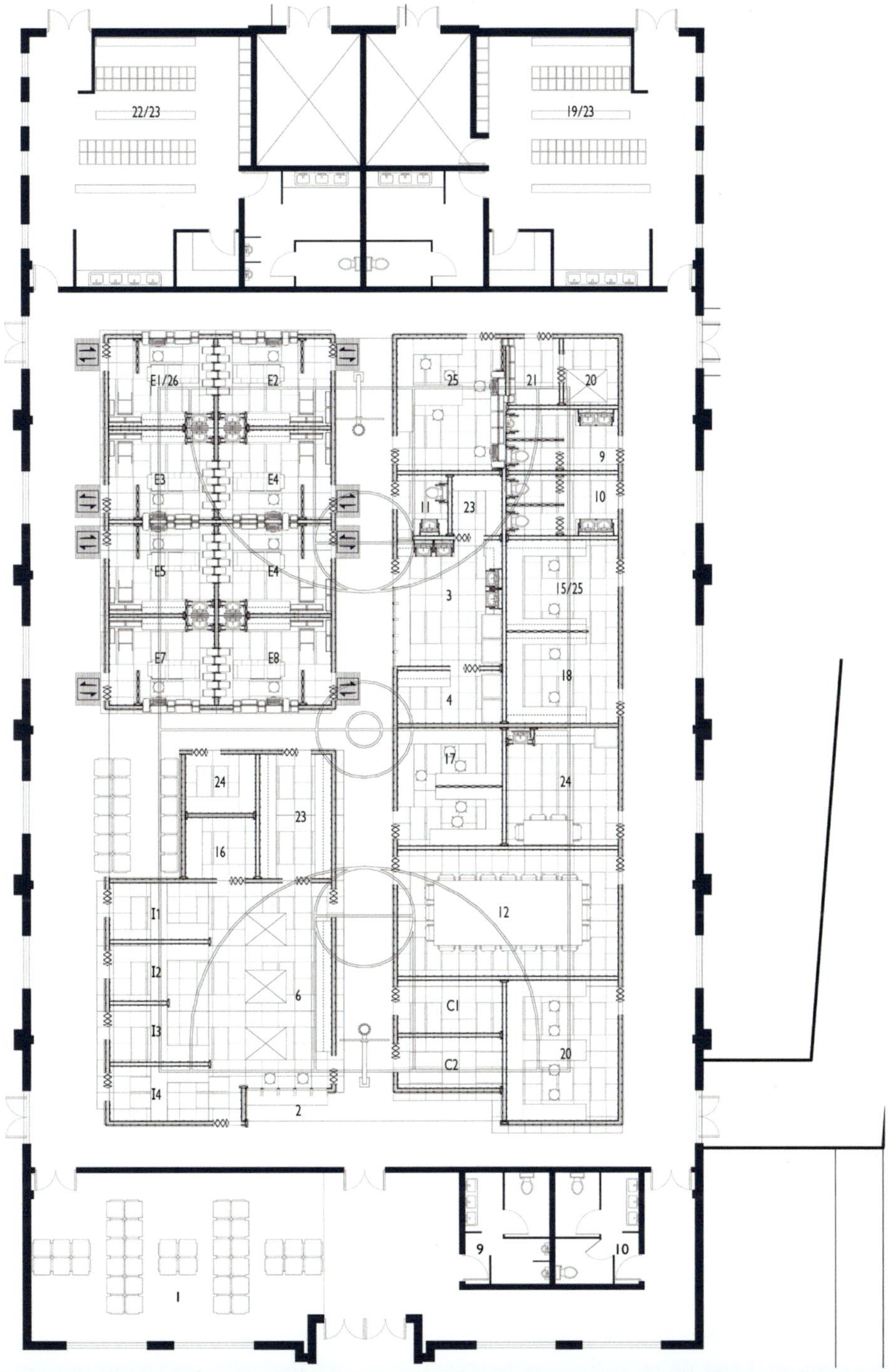

Pop-Up System B—The aesthetic appearance of most outpatient health clinics is uninspiring, largely due to their monotony and sheer institutionalism. Examination rooms are painted in drab colors, furnishings are spartan and uncomfortable, and they are frequently too small for anyone other than the caregiver and the patient to occupy at the same time—conditions tantamount to sensory deprivation and a claustrophobic experience. In response, System B is a lift-pack system featuring a wrap-around LED panel display that enables its wall surfaces to become a vibrant, ever-changing blank canvas for the display of sampled visual content. The intent is to directly challenge the status quo in outpatient clinic settings by creating a stimulating, memorable experience for the patient and visitor. This strategy is rooted in the full-height wall murals, and colorful directional graphics and wayfinding aids, commissioned for hospitals and various types of specialty clinics in the past decade. Similarly, imagery depicted on this system's interior and exterior wall panels can be diverse, anything from seascapes to forest and mountain scenes to urban scenes and beyond and it is this changeable narrative that can result in a memorable visual experience. This system was designed by the team of Yanwen Xiao and Kimberly Bandy (Team 699). Modules sit on the floor plane although adjustable feet are able to equalize or 'smooth out' uneven floor conditions. Interiors feature wrap-around data displays to display health education information, and can be used for telemedicine conferencing. Furnishings are clip-on and adaptable and able to be repositioned. Modules can be added or subtracted and the water supply here is also of flexible tubing, with additive/subtractive plumbing fixtures. LED technology is embedded within the wall panels. As mentioned, sampled content can range from naturescapes to urban scenes, to even portraits of people in the local community. The projection of photo portraits is inspired by a much larger, civic-scaled artwork—the Crown Fountain at Chicago's Millennium Park, by Jauma Plensa (2004), a twenty-foot tall sculpture that captures the city's multiculturalism, projecting larger than life portraits of Chicagoans. System B is 'tested' in Host Structures 4 through 6 (HS-4–6):

4 Riverwalk Marketplace, New Orleans

The Mississippi River riverfront has been at the center of the city's shipping industry and its commerce since the early eighteenth century although it had fallen into disrepair by the mid-twentieth century. The decision was made to hold the 1984 World's Fair in New Orleans along the downtown riverfront in the warehouse district, a decision made to help revive this downtrodden area through the stimulation of new development. The World's Fair encompassed ninety acres along the riverfront and many historic industrial buildings were converted for use as pavilions during the exposition. This event has fueled the neighborhood's continued renaissance over the past three decades. One structure, the Riverwalk Shopping Mall, a structure built for the fair, was afterward adapted into an enclosed shopping mall. The mall hugs the waterfront along its nearly three-block long site. On two levels, dozens of boutiques and national chain stores line a main level in a double loaded configuration along a single circulation spine. At the midsection of its linear, narrow footprint, it rises to a second level where a transitional element houses an open staircase and set of escalators, functioning as a transitional 'bridge' between two major sections of the mall. A food court is located at the far (upriver) end of the mall and with an adjoining outdoor promenade, allowing for dramatic up-close views of large passenger and merchant ships—in a city where tall earthen levees restrict the ability to directly see the river. Mostly tourists and conventioneers frequent the mall, although it lost most of its tenants in Katrina's aftermath and sat fallow until it reopened in 2014 as an urban outlet mall (Figures 4.11 and 4.12a–b).

This host structure's (HS-4) openness presents numerous installation options. Four clusters of modules surround the open atrium at the mall's midsection. An elevator and two sets of stairs are also in close proximity. This space receives abundant natural daylight and is spacious, with high ceilings and full-height windows on the riverside of the building that afford full views of the Mississippi. Modules are placed clockwise around the atrium without impeding the space's existing circulation paths. The sign-in station is located across from the escalator; behind this is the open workspace for clerical personnel (6) and the patient intake/interview stations (I1–4) while on the opposite side of this cluster there are two consult rooms (C3–4), the Director's Office (16) and a workspace for volunteers (24). The cluster of modules to the left house an immunization room (17), the TB/STD diagnosis and treatment room (26), and the environmental health program area (12). A third grouping of modules houses eight examination rooms (E1–8), and a fourth houses a laboratory (3/13), and related clinical support spaces (C1–2). Two existing open areas are repurposed as waiting areas with seating positioned to allow patients to look out towards the river (2, 14). Each clinic module has a fixed ceiling/lighting grid with internalized environmental control, in response to human comfort and security requirements (Figures 4.13 and 4.14a–b).

5 Handelman's Furniture Store, New Orleans

Handelman's was once a prominent furniture store, built in the late 1920s on Dryades Street (now Orthea Castle Haley Boulevard) in New Orleans' historic Central City neighborhood. This three-level building has been a prominent local landmark for seventy-five years, standing the test of time while the surrounding area fell into severe decline in the mid-1960s, when it began to suffer from suburban white flight. This street and the surrounding neighborhood was once the epicenter of the city's Jewish population, its schools and its synagogues. In the Jim Crow era, it was the only Caucasian-dominated neighborhood where African-Americans were allowed to shop. This historic building has stood vacant for most of the past thirty years (Figures 4.15 and 4.16a–b).

Host Structure 5 (HS-5), as viewed from the street, displays the tattered remnants of the grandeur of the former furniture store, with its expansive street level commercial storefront, and large bay windows on the two upper floors. The second and third levels are also unutilized at present, and are well suited for use as private loft residences, or as administrative offices for a healthcare organization and/or disaster relief organization. At the street level the interior is unobstructed save for a column grid of heavy cypress timber. The flooring on the upper levels is constructed of thick cypress planks. The public entrance is off O.C. Haley Boulevard and the patient directly encounters the sign-in station as he or she enters the clinic (1), and its adjacent clerical staff work zone located directly behind the sign-in station (6), with the patient intake/interview stations located along one side within this zone (I1–3) and adjoining the main waiting area (2). The staff is able to view directly into the waiting area, via full-height glass windows and doors. This area also houses three consultation rooms (C1–3), the environmental health program area (12), an office for volunteers (24), and the staff kitchen and respite room (21). The cluster of rooms to the rear-left houses eight examination rooms (E1–8), an adjacent subwaiting area (14), with a third cluster housing nursing support spaces (25), a conference room (20), and general clinic support. The existing core, located behind the open staircase at the center, houses restrooms and additional nursing support workspaces, and supply storage (8, 25). Modules are dispersed around the existing wood column grid, which acts as an organizing aperture, establishing spatiality, scale, and rhythm. In this installation scenario, some modules require closed-grid ceilings while others have a column situated within. The outer surfaces of the modules, with their LED-generated visual displays, provide accentuation to the natural, roughhewn timber columns, read as 'trees' amid a simulated natural landscape (Figures 4.13 and 4.14a–b).

6 Folly Theatre, New Orleans

Built as Philip Foto's Folly in 1915 on Opelousas Street, the former Folly Movie Theater is located in Algiers Point on New Orleans' West Bank, across the Mississippi River from the central business district. This theater was a prominent civic landmark in the Algiers Point neighborhood until it was shuttered in the mid-1990s. A local Pentecostal congregation recently purchased it and it currently serves as a church and community center. In bygone days it presented live vaudeville stage shows and, later, first run feature films, musical concerts, and live theater. Its theatrical era ended years ago although this grand old theater has been well preserved. It presented itself as a viable host structure due to its central location, its long, open interior structural spans unrestricted by columns, its corner location including direct side door access for equipment and supplies, its location across from a public transit stop, and its close, walkable proximity to residential areas (Figures 4.17 and 4.18a–b).

Host Structure 6 (HS-6) is defined by three clusters of modules, its 'racetrack' circulation pattern, and the main theater's large single volume. Clinic support functions are housed in modules located at the front and rear of the host structure. The entrance

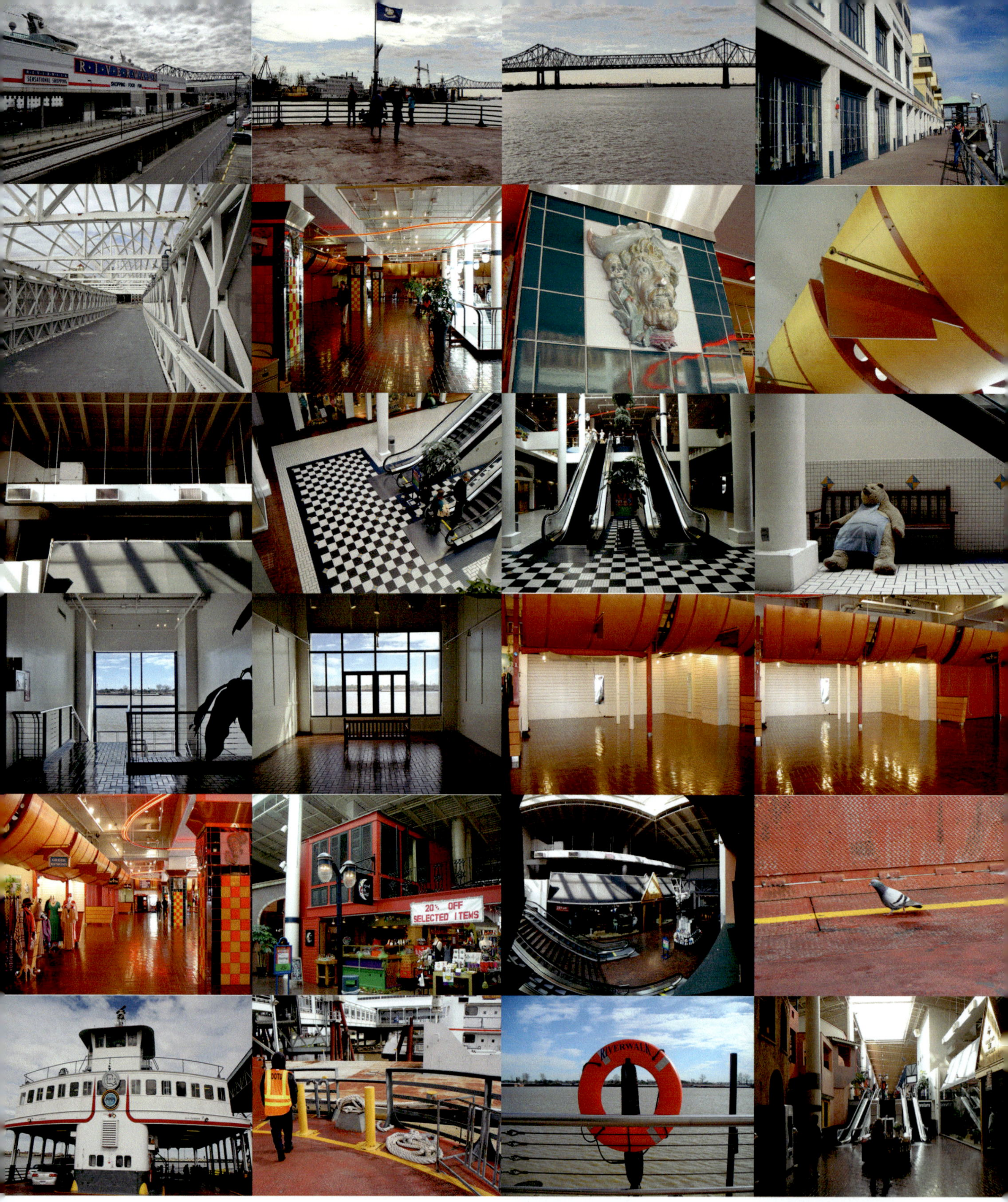
SENSATIONAL SHOPPING
20% OFF
SELECTED ITEMS
RIVERWALK

4.11 Urban Fabric Analysis 4

4.12a–b Riverwalk Marketplace, New Orleans, interior view and plan

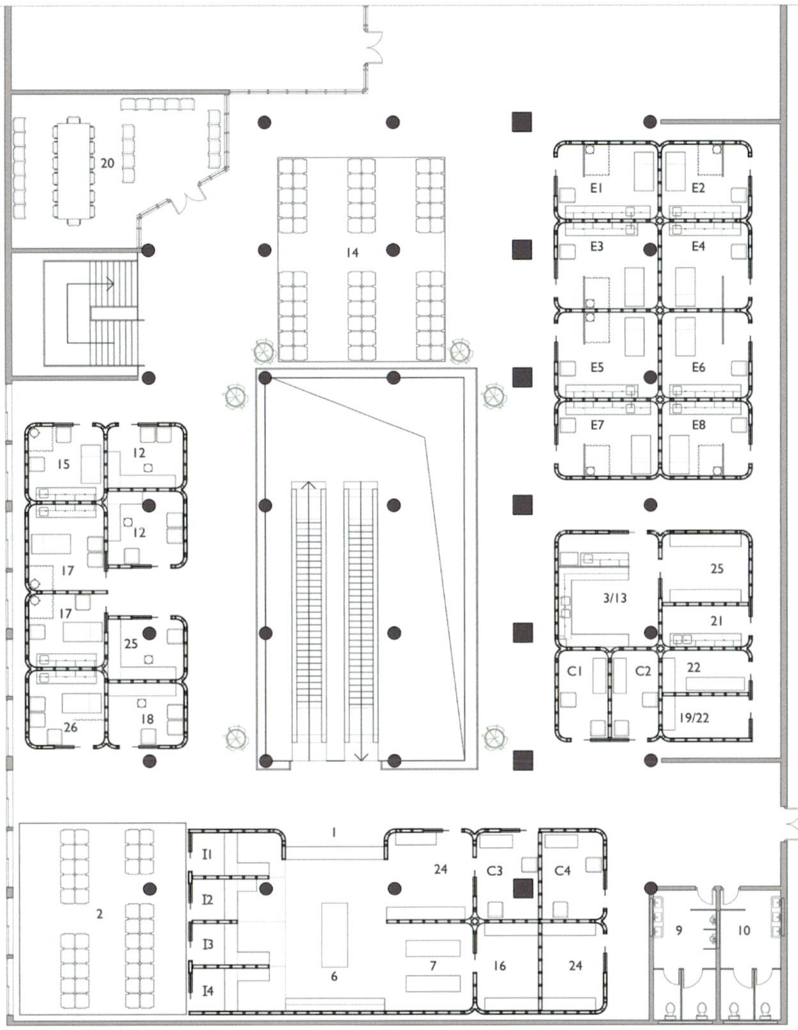

lobby leads to the main waiting 'room' (2) and the patient sign-in station (2), then to the clerical work zone (6) and the patient intake stations (I1–4). The modular cluster (to the left) contains eight examination rooms (E1–8) and the subwaiting area (14), while a second modular cluster houses additional support functions including the laboratory (3) and the pharmacy (13). Each module's ceiling plane is left as an open grid so occupants can appreciate an ornately painted mural high above in this former movie palace (Figure 4.13 and 4.14a–b).

Architectural attributes shared by the two pop-up prototypes include their: (1) *flexibility*—these systems are able to be expanded or reduced in number, and their footprint reconfigured, relative to the limitations of the host structure and its immediate site environs; (2) *lightness*—this denotes a spatially transparent, open ambiance without compromising patient (and staff) privacy or personal security; (3) *modular autonomy*—individual modules are structurally and functionally autonomous so that if one part of the system should experience functional problems then the other modules can continue to function until repairs are performed; (4) *resiliency*—these installations' prosthetic resiliency covaries with the host structure's infrastructure. This includes its HVAC and electrical systems, although the modular installation brings its own support to function in tandem with the host's systems, or it can be self-reliant, if needed; and (5) *transparency*—views are provided to the outdoors and every reasonable effort is made to locate waiting areas in portions of the host building that provide natural daylight, meaningful views to the outdoors, and natural ventilation.

Twelve additional pop-up clinic installation sites in Charleston and New Orleans are presented in Appendix 1.

Redeployable health centers and community empowerment

Places such as New Orleans and Charleston are prime candidates for architectural interventions to aid the medically underserved.[53] Existing community outpatient clinics will benefit from this type of *hardening*. Resiliency is thereby increased. Prefabricated, modular, redeployable pop-ups are one way this can be accomplished.[54] In the U.S., the resources have recently been put in place to make this happen, in the form of the aforementioned ACA legislation.[55] It is important to not overlook how the ACA's laudable goal of increasing the public's access to healthcare can be met while at the same time bringing new life to worthy vacant and temporarily available buildings in the core of historic cities, and elsewhere. Julia Christensen, in her 2008 book *Big Box Reuse,* documented the plight of vacant commercial buildings across the U.S. and the many ways they can be resuscitated through adaptive use.[56] Her book contains dozens of relevant case studies. As for the due diligence aspect of selecting and evaluating a candidate building for this type of repurposing, the *post occupancy evaluation* (POE) is a well-proven method to assess the suitability of any currently vacant building as a host structure.[57] Suffice to say, it can be in the best interest of a healthcare provider organization to invest in the POE process as a means to acquire the data needed to make more informed decisions.[58] Second, the community-based research described in this chapter needs to happen more frequently within the academy.[59] This will require a shift in thinking. At present, most evidence-based research in architecture and health remains centered on inpatient care settings, i.e. hospitals, although this emphasis overlooks equally important challenges at this time.[60] The disciplinary specialty of architecture and health is not alone in needing to rethink its position and place within the larger scheme of things. Sociologists have begun the process of acknowledging that their current sociological notions of sustainability can no longer account for the complexity, indeterminacy, and pace of unfolding societal events.

Debra Davidson writes:

> Instead of restricting our efforts to hunting for the *Sustainability Grail*...there is tremendous benefit in evaluating social systems characterized by conditions clearly at the other end of the spectrum, in the form of extreme environmental scarcity, catastrophic events, and the wide swath of grey zone in between. There are compelling epistemological reasons to do so...climate change looms as potentially the most foreboding of stressors confronting society since the Industrial Revolution, manifesting in multiple economic, environmental and health crises at the regional and global scale.[61]

4.13 The exterior wall surfaces of the core module are interchangeable. This pop-up installation depicts a Louisiana cypress swamp

4.14a–b Structural anatomy of an exam/procedure room module (left), and a laboratory module (right)

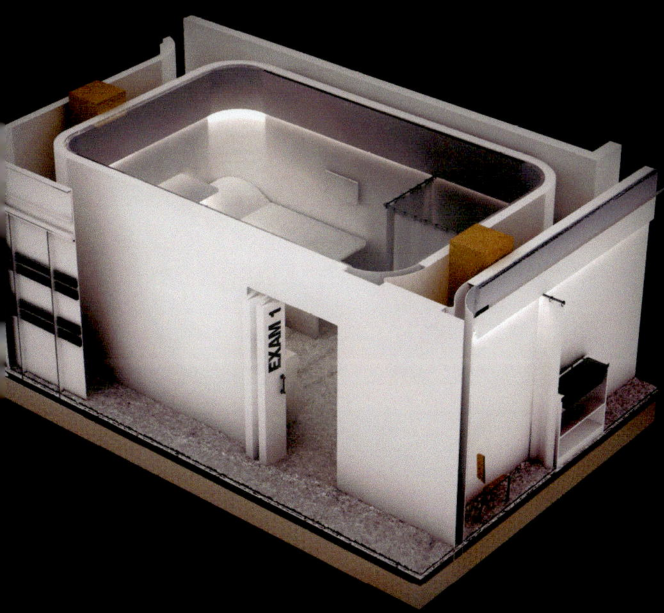

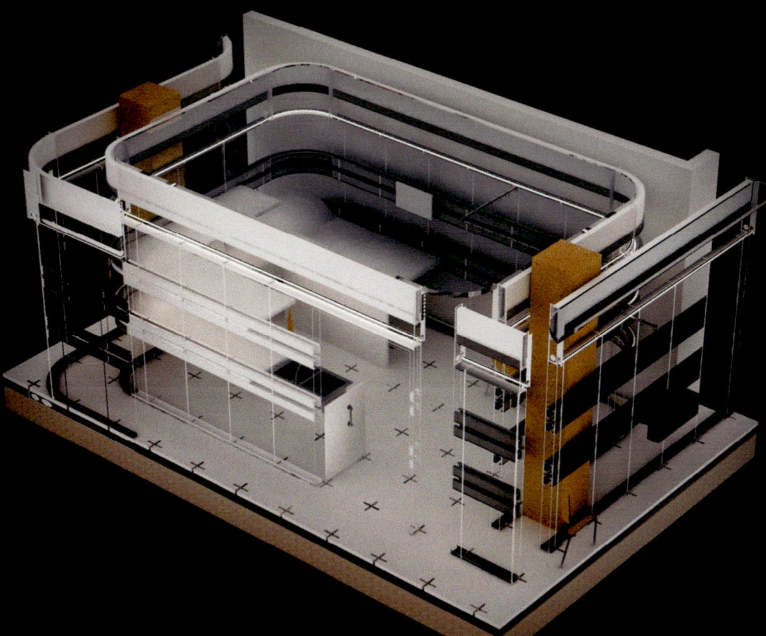

Harry's
BOXING GYM
Harry's

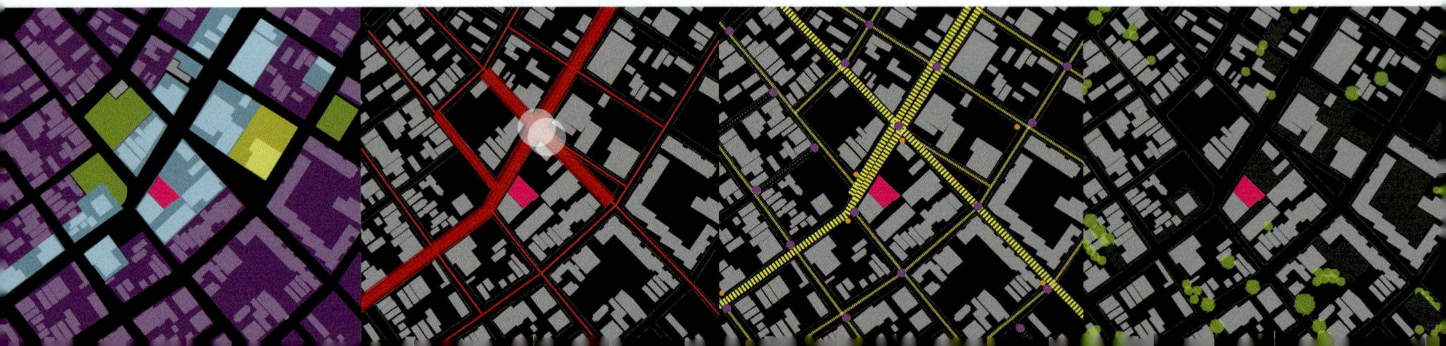

4.15 Urban Fabric Analysis 5

4.16a–b Handelman's Furniture Store, New Orleans, exterior and plan

GULF
Rita's
Home of The
Mohawk
Hunters
DELCAZAL
PLAYGROUND

4.17 Urban Fabric Analysis 6

4.18a–b Folly Theater, New Orleans, exterior and plan

Sociologists and other social scientists are now refocusing on how the coalescence and bundling together of social capital occurs in a local community and how it copes with the unprecedented environmental challenges it faces. At the grassroots level, the situation is clearly in flux.[62] Being able to see new critical thresholds, referred to as 'tipping points,' together with the design professional's ability to telescopically scale the issues at hand—the ability to see the forest from the trees—will be at the forefront. Davidson uses the term *multiscaling* to define the types of feedback-response mechanisms that are now needed in order to address complex issues at multiple scales, arguing that archaic, normative systems must be shed, transmogrified, and redefined.[63] Healthcare architecture, at the grassroots level, can be at the forefront of this redirection of social capital.[64] Housing, healthcare, education, transportation, and a host of other urban social support systems in medically at-risk communities call for a reappraisal in everyday contexts *and* in the aftermath of disaster. For the architectural profession, and for the schools of architecture, it is an ethical issue as much as anything. The challenge is rooted in how the profession wishes to perceive itself as much as how it wishes to be perceived by society in this century.[65] Choosing a suitable host building for a *Redeployable Health Center* (RHC) such as the modular pop-up clinics discussed above, or a *Redeployable Trauma Center* (RTC), can be a painstaking process fraught with deliberation, indifference, NIMBYism, setbacks, budget issues, and so on.[66] Because of all this, thoughtful, deliberative planning and analysis will result from the most salient issues having been fleshed out *a priori* in the form of guidelines that can serve as baseline parameters to question, and build upon.[67] This is the focus of the following chapter.

CHAPTER 5

Planning and design considerations for transportable healthcare

A transportable structure for healthcare is a complex and often contradictory building type. It is a system of subsystems, withstanding the rigors of being built in one location and then assembled permanently at another, or being able to be disassembled and reassembled—perhaps many times during its lifespan. This is something a conventional brick and mortar building is not designed to do. A permanent building is not *designed* to be moved. Sometimes, of course, it becomes necessary for a permanent building, such as an historic schoolhouse, to be moved to a new site, or when a structure must be relocated to make way for a highway-widening project. But this is usually the option of last resort. The challenge for the designer and manufacturer of a modular transportable structure for health is to achieve aesthetic legitimacy without compromising functional performance or adaptability. It is about visual appearance, physical lightness, spatial dexterity, compactness and operational performance, often, in unknown site contexts. Optimally, a transportable structure for health possesses these capabilities:

- Adapts to local healthcare needs and local physical environment determinants.
- Contributes to saving lives, and the alleviation of health inequities in medically underserved communities globally.
- Is an ecologically sensitive intervention that treads lightly on the earth's finite non-renewable resources.
- Achieves resiliency in rapid response contexts insofar as the structure is able to withstand systemic shock, and 'bounce-back.'
- Attains compliance with local construction and regulatory life safety codes and standards.
- Provides a care setting that fosters partnerships with allied healthcare provider organizations.
- Functions as a prosthetic device in human health promotion in everyday and post-disaster contexts.

The compendium of planning and design principles presented below represents an attempt to give architectural expression to aesthetic, functional, cultural, and symbolic issues as they relate to site selection, environmental sustainability, architectural resiliency, and the importance of local acceptance in places where the structure is deployed. Architects, allied designers, and collaborating engineers are advised to approach the provision of portable architecture for health in professional practice with an attitude of openness, compassion, and empathy. Three types of support—instrumental, aesthetic, and symbolic—are addressed below. This compendium addresses form, function, and aesthetics as fundamental to human physical and psychological health and well-being, and environmental health.[1] The eighty planning and design considerations are as follows:

1 **Site and context:**
   Stereotypes
   Rapid recognition
   Networking
   Staffing
   Sustainability
   Adaptability
2 **Transiting and commissioning:**
   Rail-based infirmaries
   Airborne infirmaries
   Telemedicine
   Closepacking and lightness
   Docking and portals
   Deployment team
   Vehicular infirmaries
   Emergency Operations Center (EOC)
   AIRVAC/MEDIVAC
   Helipads
   Power generation
   Refrigeration
   Phased installation
   Commissioning
3 **Arrival and semi-public spaces:**
   Patient intake
   Triage stations
   Decontamination
   Inboard decon units
   Waiting areas
   Streamline circulation
   Wayfinding
   Safe corners and intersections
   Bereavement
4 **Diagnostic and treatment functions:**
   Facility-acquired infection
   Pre-operative units
   Surgical units
   Post-operative units
   Module adjacencies
   Pharmaceuticals
   Dietary support
   Diagnostic imaging
   Personal hygiene
   Exam and procedure rooms
   Infectious disease installations
   Infectious disease ICUs
   Laboratories
   Patient confidentiality
   Prospect-refuge amenities
   Positive distractions
5 **Pop-up clinics:**
   Historic buildings
   Evaluating a host structure
   Preparing a host structure
   Strategic partnering
   Phased installations
   Patient intake (pop-ups)
   Expandable components
   Repurpose vacant buildings
   Modular ceilings (pop-ups)
6 **Facility tectonics:**
   Virtues of low-tech
   Environmental control
   Biomorphic vocabularies
   Lightweight pneumatics
   Weatherization
   Vaulted tents
   Ridge tents
   Panelized systems
   Modular ceilings
   Expandable modules
   Doors/thresholds/vestibules
   Modular flooring
   Intelligent building systems
   3D-printing technology
   3D-printed components
7 **Administration/total environment:**
   Strategic partnering (Part II)

Evidence-based research and design
Resilience and facility management
Mockups and simulations
Staff accommodations (Part II)
Equipment and supplies
Security systems
Sound attenuation
Lean and portables
Offsite manufacturing
Selecting an offsite manufacturer

These planning and design considerations are discussed in relation to three types of installations. As defined in Chapter 1, these are:

- *Redeployable Health Centers* (RHC)—This facility type, typically for use in non-disaster situations, is a pre-manufactured offsite-built vehicular mobile clinic, a portable but non-motorized healthcare facility, or a hybrid. An RHC is well positioned to increase a community's health status.
- *Redeployable Trauma Centers* (RTC)—This facility type is best suited to provide emergency and intensive care for victims of disaster. A pre-manufactured modular RTC is expandable from a single module to as many as seventy-five units on a single site and is adaptable to diverse climatic and site conditions.
- *Permanent Modular Installations* (PMI)—These modular facilities for healthcare are either complete freestanding installations built off site, or internal component systems built off site, then transited to another site for permanent installation within a conventional construction.

Prefabricated modularity (PM) refers to all three installation types. Healthcare provider organizations represent different types, as short-term disaster response programs differ significantly from longer-term humanitarian aid programs. Yet they share overarching aims and philosophies: the former is geared to function most effectively in a first response mode whereas the latter type of organization is geared to function across a longer timeframe in the same place. First-response non-governmental organizations (NGOs) focus on the disaster event and its immediate aftermath—days, weeks, the first few months—whereas the *World Health Organization* (WHO) and the *United Nations* (UNHCR) are strongly committed to staying in a city or region for years if necessary. These planning and design considerations are for use by architects, industrial designers, urban and regional planners, engineers, humanitarian assistance agencies, governmental health agencies and direct care providers, including physicians, nurses, onsite technical support personnel, philanthropic foundations, grassroots community organizations, health policy specialists, global disaster relief organizations, and by researchers across a spectrum of disciplines. Themes and issues presented here, along with the eighteen case studies presented in the following chapter (Chapter 6), together, become an interwoven narrative.

1 Site and context

Stereotypes

Portable structures for healthcare are dismissed by some as being: (1) logistically inefficient and too costly to build and operate; (2) unable to satisfy local life safety building codes and regulations; (3) susceptible to structural failure due to their temporal nature; (4) unable to meet human comfort levels on a consistent basis; and (5) strictly utilitarian in their visual appearance with little creative maneuvering room with regards to aesthetics or associated functionality. The organization *Architecture for Humanity* recently put a spotlight on advancing the state of the art on the role of transportable structures for health in global disaster response. Its 2003 international design competition, a 'Mobile HIV/AIDS Clinic for Sub-Saharan Africa,' generated wide interest. Some entries were more pragmatic than others, but most entries were innovative in some way.[2] Prefab modularity was explored in nearly every submittal.[3] This competition represents a turning point of sorts, and published literature remains sparse, although a significant literature exists in Japan (in Japanese).[4] Investments in research and development can lead to design and manufacturing breakthroughs, and negative stereotypes will persist until additional systematic inquiries are funded, and more structures of this type are built and shown to be useful in the field. This includes performance assessments carried out in real-time/space. These structures are of four types: pneumatic fabric-based systems, flat-pack modular systems, containerized systems, and hybrids combining elements of the previous three. Hybrids can be side-by-side pop-out modules (pneumatic or otherwise), and systems representing a mix of soft-walled tents and shipping containers protected by a canvas roof system above. Some side-by-side hybrids are containers connected to modules assembled from flat-pack panels comprising flooring, wall, ceilings, etc. (see Chapter 6). The challenge for the architect, industrial designer, interiors specialist, structural engineer, and industrial engineer is to determine the best design, manufacturing, and assembly strategy relative to prespecified performance requirements.

Rapid recognition

In post-disaster contexts it is critical that a freestanding installation be easily identified whether in a rural landscape or a dense urban environment. Individuals on foot, ambulances, search and rescue boats and MEDIVAC aircraft approaching the facility need to be able to locate it from some distance. Whether approaching by foot, vehicle, ship or air, its legibility and visibility are paramount on a 24/7 basis. Recognition is achievable by means of an exterior color scheme with signifying markers clearly discernable vis-à-vis color-coded logos and a recognizable insignia such as the blood-red insignia cross of the *International Red Cross* (Red Crescent). An installation's exterior (and interior) color palette may at first seem to be of secondary concern, and yet color, when combined with compositional form and the size of the overall installation, communicates a great deal. An all-white facility with a large red cross on its roof and sidewalls may not be enough in some places. Signification and legibility can be enhanced using design strategies premised on contrasting fields so that some modules, such as the triage tent, are more prominently identifiable, or by varying the materials of construction of this module to set it visually apart. A dark purple logo set against an olive-colored backfield will be difficult to see at night where every tent is otherwise identical. Logos and graphics set against a contrasting color field, combined with more than one type of modular component within the overall system, are recommended. In addition, its exterior appearance may inadvertently conjure negative associations in the eyes of a local population or local host government for any number of reasons, i.e. conjuring superstitions, or inappropriate cultural stereotypes. Learn what has worked in the past and improve upon these precedents.[5] Appropriate color palettes and formal compositions, aesthetically interesting yet readily comprehended, are preferable versus a confusing, inadvertently controversial palette or logo. A disaster is neither the time nor place for confounding, inscrutable facility messaging. Unambiguous 'coding' creates a clear, focused, architectural image and identity for the installation and clearly communicates its mission and purpose (Figure 5.1).

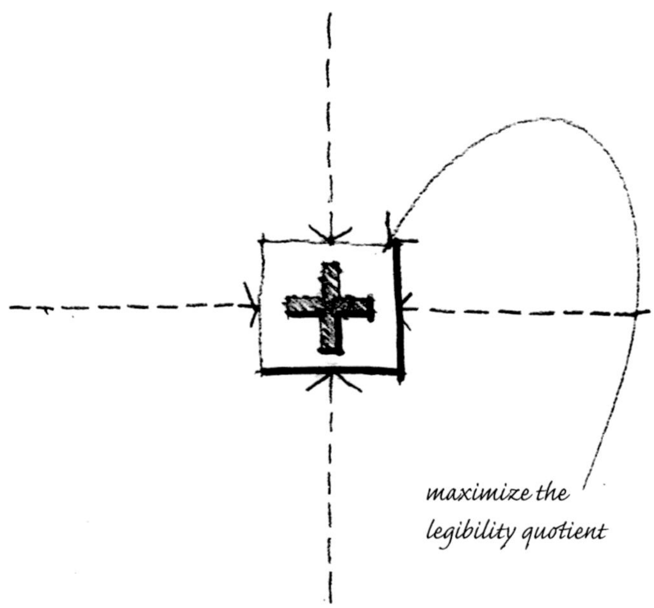

5.1 Design for rapid recognition, day or night

Networking

Some RTCs serve as mothership installations with satellites networked, tethered, to them in some way. This tethering can be physical, or figurative. Outlying sites' day-to-day operations depend on the support provided by the core RTC installation, and vice versa. Satellite RTCs are structurally freestanding installations whose primary purpose is to take patients in initially and then refer them to the larger installation for additional treatment. These plug-in satellites serve as midpoints in a continuum of emergency medicine, providing initial emergency first aid, and serve as station points for the transport of patients to a main installation that may be many miles away. The satellite must be nimble and equipped to decontaminate victims quickly, if necessary. Create a hub and spoke system where the main or lead RTC field infirmary is geographically near to its associated network of satellites. A second scenario is for this first point of contact facility to be at the front line of a disaster with the main or lead RTC to the rear and a permanent hospital option for longer-term treatment located outside the disaster strike zone. In 1999, in Turkey, in that nation's most densely populated regional industrial center, two massive earthquakes struck less than three months apart. Together, more than 17,100 persons died, with more than 300,000 homes damaged or destroyed. The Turkish Red Crescent Society, working in consort with the British government and the Danish Red Cross, set up six RTCs with one functioning as the lead and the five others as support-feeder facilities. Casualties were transported from destroyed villages first to one of the satellite field infirmaries, which were set up midway between the towns most impacted. These mobile infirmaries took in casualties and provided immediate treatment, and casualties needing further care were taken first to the main RTC, and later, if necessary, to one of a half dozen stationary hospitals in urban areas beyond the hardest hit area.[6]

Staffing

Physicians and nurses may travel considerable distances to a disaster strike zone and, upon arriving, find very few amenities for them. The need for amenities, i.e. overnight accommodations for caregivers, is very important. Michael Daniel, a designer at Frog Design in Austin, Texas, has developed *Reaction Housing*, offsite-built prefab shelters deployable in extreme contexts, shipped flat-packed, stored at a central warehouse, and manufactured for intermodal transport. Upon arrival, a team of four can unload and erect a unit without complex tools or machinery. Each unit arrives at its installation site furnished. The units themselves cost less than $5,000 each, are reusable, and can be adapted to occupants' needs in terms of internal furnishings and equipment. This is but one example of a sensible alternative to the one-time amenity of the disastrous $65,000 FEMA trailer, of which 95,000 were deployed to the U.S. Gulf Coast in the aftermath of Hurricanes Katrina and Rita in 2005—about 5 percent of which housed emergency medical and disaster mitigation staff personnel. These trailers were often set up in isolated areas with foreboding wire fences around encampments of as many as seventy-five on a single parking lot or grassy field. Better ways to house staff first responders are needed and a Reaction Housing unit, while smaller, can sleep up to four and can be set up as an integral part of an RTC installation. With many units, they can be arranged in semi-circles, grids, or clusters, thereby yielding semi-private exterior space. Individual units are connectible to an existing power source or a self-powered climate control system. The units look like large sugar cubes, equipped with personal hygiene devices, a small kitchen, sleeping-living space, solar panels, a rainwater catchment device, and a potable water reservoir.[7] As units are raised up a foot or more above the ground, provide universal access ramps for a percentage of units (Figure 5.2). Disaster relief organizations will often go to lengths to provide proper housing to sustain staff morale and a higher rate of staff retention.

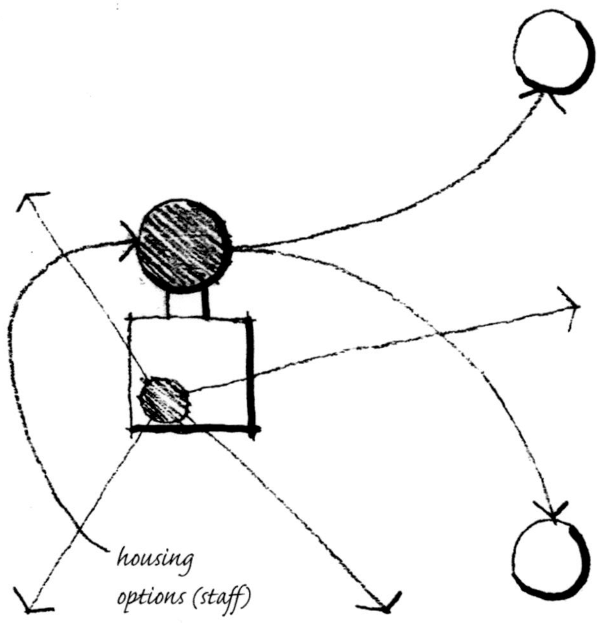

5.2 Provide overnight accommodations for staff personnel

Sustainability

A portable structure for health is intrinsically sustainable due to the way it is designed and manufactured for use in a new place at a later time. The aim is to conserve material resources similar to how an automobile is designed and efficiently manufactured to generate the minimal amount of material waste and to be used in many different places at different times across its life. By contrast, conventional healthcare facilities, from project inception to design to construction to commissioning and occupancy, take far longer and are by definition less *green* because they eschew the principles and affordances of prefab modularity (see Chapter 3). The mobile clinics of the 1950s provide the blueprint for twenty-first-century transportables for health because they were conceived and produced this way. A coach module was constructed atop a modified motor home chassis borrowed from manufacturers' product lines of commercial recreational vehicles. Chassis and coach modules were built separately and then assembled, entirely in the factory. From the early 1950s on they have served as portable immunization, blood donor, polio, and tuberculosis clinics. A recent expression of sustainability in a portable facility is the two-part mobile system comprised of an eighteen-wheeler trailer module pulled by a standard truck cab. The *Carolinas MED-1* is a sustainable, hybrid RTC/RHC that serves as a rolling hospital infirmary for the provision of acuity-adaptive care, that is, a level of care that can be intensified as needed (see Chapter 2). Strive to eliminate known toxic building materials, and make use of recycled materials, harness solar energy for its day-to-day operations, and seek to reduce dependency on the earth's finite resources.[8] New ideas often originate in the academy: a prototype developed by the New Institute of Technology School of Architecture and Design, the *SodaBIB* (Bottle Interface Bracket) transforms empty bottles of water into a carbon neutral, rigid palette form that can be used as a structurally insulated panel (SIP)-like wall panel system—this lightweight, weather-resistant membrane is well-suited for use in portable structures for healthcare.[9]

Adaptability

A work of architecture can be transformative. A transformer toy is analogous, in the way it can evolve from one physical state to another and then back.[10] In nature, changeable, adaptable forms abound. The term *arthropod* describes the large nests of potter wasps, colonies of industrious insects that gather muddy soil together and then transform this material into remarkable spherical containers to house their progeny. Strangely enough, these wasps top off their spheres with a symmetrical neck that looks much like that on a human-made pot in a design that is aesthetically fascinating.[11] In the same way, a building can operate in one state and then transform itself into another, thereby changing from one operative condition to a second or third (or more). The classic 1972 book *Arthropods: New Design Futures*, by Jim Burns, is filled with alternative environments designed in the late 1960s through early 1970s.[12] Many examples in this book were exhibit installations intended as fleeting, momentary, sharing a sense of elusiveness and temporality. They were un-rooted, in a traditional sense (Figure 5.3). A recent design competition, the *Zombie Safe House Competition*, was held in 2011 and one entrant in this offbeat competition, Austin Fleming, of Texas, won the competition's 'Gold Shovel Award.' His 'Vagabond Mobile Safe House' was a backpack-worn, spring-activated structure fabricated of 'ribs' and deployed by a ripcord. This ripcord activates counterweighted loads evenly dispersed throughout the module, providing its structural rigidity. Anchor bolts prevent unwanted structural distortion while the module is activated. From the exterior the module resembles an armadillo resting on the ground. The module stands four feet high, is eight feet long, and is a horror film-like deep reddish-blue metallic color. It can house three persons. In its adapted state a periscope air intake device provides filtered oxygen for inhabitants nestled within. The unit can be transformed spontaneously using an iPhone application, is mass-producible, and sold relatively cheaply. It can be set up quickly and manufactured with minimal material waste.[13]

5.3 Anticipate myriad installation sites, including a football stadium

2 Transiting and commissioning

Rail-based infirmaries

Emergency healthcare in a disaster strike zone requires a rapid response in highly fluid conditions. This is nothing new. In the American Civil War (1861–1865), military and commandeered civilian railcars transported patients to and from the front lines, such as the open-ward railcar infirmaries that transported casualties to and from the Mower Hospital in Philadelphia. When the train pulled into the depot the wounded were taken off and brought into the barracks hospital.[14] During World War I, infirmary trains were similarly deployed to the Western Front; the British Royal Army Medical Corps transited over 100,000 battle casualties from Flanders in one month in 1914 alone.[15] The means of patient transport is critical to any military unit or system's efficacy in the field of combat and the same holds in civilian contexts. Dutch Health, a private sector manufacturer, recently developed a railcar hospital outfitted with high tech medical equipment and a wide array of related amenities. This train is equipped with specially designed air-conditioned coaches, a hospital-equivalent surgical theater, industrial-grade autoclaves, a changing room, sterilization room, patient wards containing up to eight beds each, on-board power generators, a pantry/dining car, morgue railcar, a storeroom for medical provisions, a classroom car, and lodging cars for medical staff and administrators. This RTC was built to provide diagnostic, medical and surgical treatment to patients in remote communities who otherwise would lack access to any permanent fixed-site hospital or any other medical facility. It is deployable to regions impacted by natural or human-made disasters as long as local rail lines remain operable. Ideally, hospital trains such as this example in The Netherlands are staffed and operated by full-time personnel who also work in regional fixed-site medical centers and are on-call for whenever or wherever they may be needed in the field.[16]

Airborne infirmaries

ORBIS International is an NGO dedicated to the prevention of blindness and treatment of blinding eye diseases in developing countries. Since 1982, it has helped to train more than 300,000 eye care specialists and provided medical and optical care to more than 18.8 million people in ninety-two countries.[17] This NGO is well known for its *Flying Eye Hospital*—a portable ophthalmic hospital and teaching facility located aboard a DC-10 jet aircraft. A team of volunteer pilots transports this flying clinic to diverse locales to teach eyesight-saving skills and to treat patients.[18] In addition to its flying RHC, ORBIS operates hospital-based programs in several countries where it collaborates with local care providers. Its 'Cyber-Sight' program uses the Internet to network with coordinated global teams of ophthalmologists. This organization was a founding partner, along with the WHO, of 'Vision 2020: The Right to Sight,' a global initiative whose aim is to eradicate contracted blindness by 2020. The ORBIS MD-10-30F aircraft recently replaced the old DC-10, and it features a more sophisticated modular hospital suite—the first aircraft-cum-clinic with an operating suite for laser treatment, an equipment sterilization bay, post-surgical recovery bay, and also a 48-seat classroom.[19] The ORBIS transportable eye infirmary is a rapid response facility, functioning as a supplemental prosthetic device to comparable land-based facilities.[20] ORBIS is not alone: in 2014, a Royal Danish Air Force transport plane was adapted and re-commissioned for use as a MEDIVAC flying infectious disease isolation ward for Ebola victims transported for hospitalized treatment outside the 'hot zone;' this facility is staffed by a physician, nurse, and four to six medics who accompany each patient en route. This team wears impervious suits, protective hoods, vinyl boots, and communicates via two-way radios. These airborne facilities have significant take-off and landing needs, however, and therefore usually require a conventional airport runway. The location of the airport from where victims are located can be problematic, but can be overcome with effective ground transport.[21]

Telemedicine

International disaster relief is often a low-tech proposition, with the relief effort in the first days after an event chaotic and random. The local power grid will be down and may be down for weeks if not longer and telecommunications systems may be working sporadically at best. One way to avoid this randomness is for the RTC or RHC installation to have its own 'onboard' satellite dish and power source to re-establish essential global telecommunications. Telemedicine consists of the use of digital technologies in medical care. A remotely located RTC in a disaster strike zone can be linked via synchronous satellite communications, i.e. videoconferencing. Satellite-based GPS-guided systems linked the U.S. Army Combat Surgical Hospitals (CSH) facilities in Iraq and Afghanistan with hospital ships situated offshore in international waters, and with U.S. Army military base hospitals in Europe. It is standard procedure in twenty-first-century combat theaters to use telemedicine in support of front-line medical personnel. Installations operated by the *International Red Cross, Doctors Without Borders*, and another disaster relief agencies use satellite telecommunications. In the age of the smartphone, mobile technologies are further reshaping this landscape. Smartphone apps have quickly become invaluable tools in the aftermath of disaster. Body-worn micro-devices and their apps can now self-monitor a person's health status and are also being used for the self-diagnoses of infectious diseases, including Ebola, and apps are capable of making the facility itself 'smarter.' One such app, *Canary*, can survey and monitor a facility's well-being through a combination of high definition video cameras, motion detectors, and fire-detection sensors. Another, *Smart_things*, can detect a roof leak by means of a nano-moisture sensor in conjunction with a smartphone application. Another app, *August*, can lock and unlock doors (particularly useful in inventory control of pharmaceuticals and other supplies requiring highly secure logistics). Philips Corporation has patented a *smart-light* device that can change colors and illumination levels, controllable by means of an app. The app can activate a simulated sunrise or sunset in a portable infirmary's patient ward, for instance.[22] Without a telemedicine hookup, critical procedures are hindered, performed the old-school way such as in the Philippines after Typhoon Haiyan when the power grid went down for months in some places and telecommunications were sporadic (Figure 5.4).

Closepacking and lightness

Buckminster Fuller investigated timeless geometries and their closepacking amenities, drawing from Plato's writings dating from 400 B.C. Later, Euclid described the five platonic bodies, regular polyhedral forms with identical sides: the tetrahedron, octahedron, icosahedron, hexahedron cube, and the dodecahedron. The packing together of these polyhedral permutations in dense grids is known as *closepacking* (Figure 5.5). These fundamental geometries have been extensively investigated in mathematics in their solid as well as fluid states.[23] Platonic systems are applicable to flat-pack panelized, containerized, and tent-based systems, and in hybrid combinations thereof. The combination of a system's closepacked properties and its mass determine its lightness quotient in transit, premised

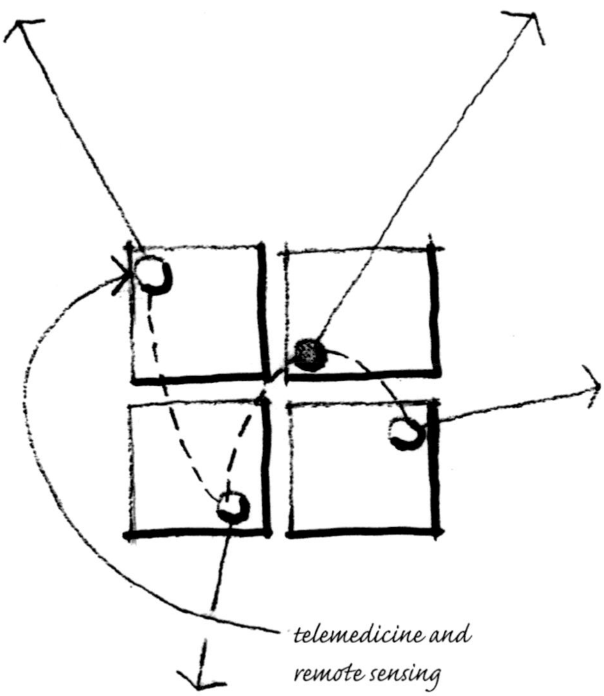

5.4 Telemedicine capabilities extend the outward 'reach' of the facility

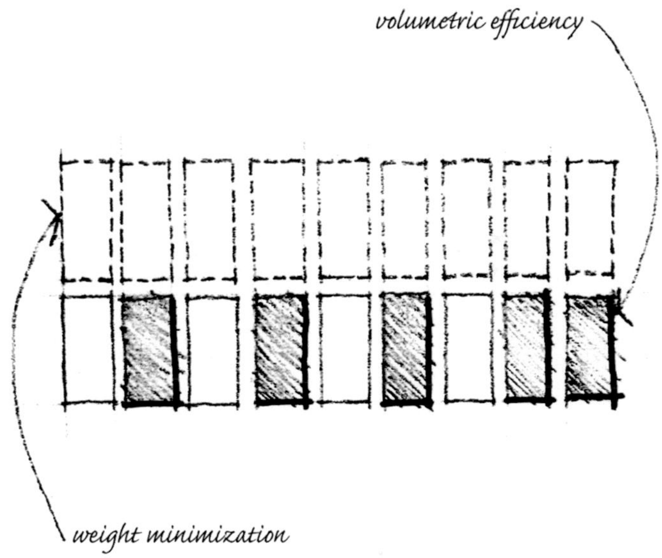

5.5 Employ closepacking to maximize volume and weight efficiencies in transit

on the degree to which it makes maximum use of the minimal physical space while en route to its point of destination. Achieving a 1:1 correlation between these two factors is, in theory and in practice, something to be aimed for on the part of the architect (Figure 5.6). For example, a tetrahedron-based, containerized RTC system can be shipped on a vessel in tightly stacked rows. Or, if the system is a flat-pack, the containers it is shipped in should maximize its closepacked quotient and because of this a prefab modular RTC or RHC shipped in either mode must strive to maximize both its physical *lightness* and its *mass*. The permanent site healthcare architecture equivalency, maximum lightness by means of minimal mass, is evident in Herzog and de Meuron's REHAB Basel (2000–2002), in Basel, Switzerland.[24] As for portable clinics, the European firm *4of7 Architecture's* competition submittal for a mobile pediatric clinic for a site in Rwanda made extensive use of densely closepacked geometries and the repetitive use of a flat-pack hexagonal corrugated steel panel system. Modules are tightly packed together both in transit and when the facility is assembled and fully operational. With each module, its structural frame is first erected, then its infill panels are attached. Up to fifty modules can be clustered around a single outdoor courtyard. This one-level scheme and the firm's intriguing accompanying video on its home page website shows this system being erected sequentially in an unfolding pattern of closepacked, tightly interlocked geometries.[25]

Docking and portals

Medical centers located in disaster zones and military combat theaters are prone to going offline—just when most needed to be operational. In the aftermath of Hurricane Katrina, all but two of New Orleans's twelve hospitals went down completely; the same occurred at most of the area's nursing homes. In the case of Baptist Memorial Medical Center, uptown, dozens of patients died in the days following the flood as the hospital's infrastructure totally

5.6 Intermodal shipping containers en route to their destination

failed in 95-degree heat (see Chapter 1). Here, an RTC could have been set up on its large parking deck roof, docked, and plugged directly into the hospital. The backup generation support alone from the RTC would have saved lives. Similarly, the Israeli government recently commissioned an RTC installable in a parking deck of a medical center in Tel Aviv in the event a hospital there goes offline. There, the RTC is installed and power is then restored to the hospital. These shared capabilities represent a win-win for both hospital and the RTC in the delivery of emergency trauma care. Shared capability can be extended to the entire facility and its equipment. Particularly in disaster-prone regions, design and build land-based healthcare facilities to allow for RTCs to directly dock to an interactive plug-in portal. Correspondently, design and manufacture the RTC to be able to achieve high connectivity in this manner. In the Iraq War, the U.S. military sought, wherever possible precisely this type of docking situation with its portable hospitals. The search was always on for local stationary hospitals that would be able to accommodate a military RTC (CSH, in U.S. Army parlance) facility to be set up close by in immediate proximity. The portable installation would be set up on the same site next to the hospital, and this made it far easier to transport patients, personnel and supplies back and forth between the two. Together, the two become a single entity, with one's capabilities complemented by the other's (see Interview 3 in Appendix 2 for a more detailed discussion).

Deployment team

No portable structure for health is viable without a team of well-trained physicians, nurses, lab technicians, medical assistants, logistics specialists, and administrative team. A care provider's aim is for this team to be ready. Readiness requires adequate funding to be able to conduct periodic training exercises and simulated drills with emergency management officials to develop and pretest various first-response scenarios. The organization may have stockpiled caches of medical supplies staged at sites across a region. The goal of simulated training exercises is to improve the mobilization effort including the tracking of medical equipment, the RTC or RHC, the tracking of victims, and how to maximize first responders' abilities and performance. In the field, selecting a suitable installation site must be done quickly and much can go wrong. Time is of the essence. Any delays in deployment will impede relief efforts. A number of NGOs publish guidelines on this and on how to effectively deploy first response teams to the field. One excellent example is a report published by the WHO in association with the *Pan American Health Organization* (PAHO), 'WHO-PAHO Guidelines for the Use of Foreign Field Hospitals in the Aftermath of Sudden-Impact Disasters.'[26] Site selection, facility deployment, and its commissioning begins with due diligence. A site must be safe and not onerously difficult to reach. USAID is a U.S. governmental relief organization that provides global aid in the aftermath of disaster. Its *Universal Assessment Checklist* is extensive and was developed to ensure first responders adhere to the essential aspects of a relief operation. This metric requires assessing displaced victims' health status, the availability of food supplies, the status of local water and sanitation systems, local transportation, the presence of any viable remaining buildings, the status of search and rescue relief operations, and the probability of a displaced population to be able to return home, and when. Strangely, no questions in this checklist address any aspect of the facility itself, or its performance.[27]

Vehicular infirmaries

The mobile *bus clinic* manufactured by Johnson Mobile Medical Solutions features six kidney dialysis stations, aligned in a row. The main compartment houses storage cabinets for medications and supplies, a fold-down desk and second storage closet, and a unisex restroom. This type of uni-modular mobile clinic has the advantage of the diagnostic and treatment zone being completely autonomous from the driver's area while both still being able to share the same overall interior compartment (Figure 5.7). A recent example of a two-part modular configuration is the aforementioned *Carolinas MED-1* facility that served admirably in New Orleans in the aftermath of Katrina. This mobile unit consists of two fifty-three-foot tractor-trailers, each pulled by a conventional eighteen-wheeler truck cab. The trailer module has pop-out pods that expand the interior work zone of each trailer to approximately 1,000 square feet. The pods house a two-bed shock resuscitation and surgical unit, with two other pods comprising a 120-bed emergency care unit. An exterior canvas tent, supported by aluminum struts, extends the treatment zone. This open-air space is protected from the elements with large fans and a ceiling-mounted heating system. In the critical care bay, hemodynamic and cardiac monitors provide blood pressure monitoring, pulse oximetry, end-tidal capnometry, electrocardiography equipment, continuous ST-segment analysis, and arterial, central venous, and catheter monitoring. One bed in its ICU is dedicated for adult patients, the other for pediatric patients. The interiors of the two trailer modules house eight general care treatment bays, including seven inpatient beds, a dental suite, and an ear/nose/throat (ENT) treatment bay. Medical supplies are stored in cabinets throughout, and gowns and linens are stored in cabinets at each bed location. Four portable cardiac monitors and defibrillators are onboard.[28] The pop-out sides are stabilized by means of hydraulic 'legs' extending to the ground. The U.S. Department of Homeland Security provided funding for Carolinas MED-1 (see Chapter 2).

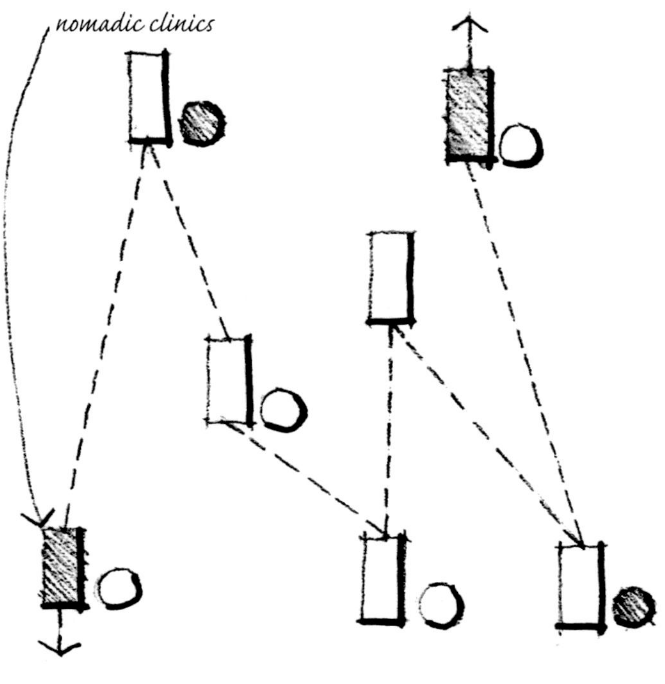

5.7 Mobile vehicular plug-in units extend the space capacity of an existing hospital

Emergency Operations Center (EOC)

In the aftermath of Katrina in 2005, the State of Louisiana built a permanent site statewide EOC facility in Baton Rouge, whose construction was federally funded by FEMA. Local governments in disaster-prone areas across the U.S. are building similarly funded, permanent site *hardening* facilities to attain a greater degree of resiliency in anticipation of, and coping with, the aftermath of disaster. The nature of global disasters also calls for portable structures that can be deployed, especially to remote regions far from urban centers. A number of manufacturers provide portable offsite-built prefab emergency command support center units expressly for this purpose. Some are for permanent sites and others, mostly containerized units, are portable and redeployable. These prefab units are built for rapid commissioning in the field. Some are equipped with pop-out side modules enabling the interior work zone to double in size. Modules are typically fifteen feet or twenty feet in length by eight to ten feet wide and the units sit directly on the ground, or on steel piers, such as the Emergency Operations Center (EOC) built by Nordic Shelter AS (Norway). Some organizations have purchased many such units. This enables expanded, further-specialized EOC operations. The bright red Nordic Shelter unit is visible from afar to assist airborne flights' rapid location of the installation. Modules are self-sufficient and carry onboard their own HVAC and electrical support, audiovisual/

IT equipment, alarm/security systems, and protective EOC air filtration systems.[29] This portable, containerized command center is compatible with an RTC or RHC and benefits are accruable by installing them side by side, or on sites near to one another. The city of Philadelphia purchased a portable system it calls the 'EOC in a box.' This mission control center is equipped with telecommunications capabilities, emergency power generation, all equipment and furnishings, and a tactical operations room and was funded by a grant by the U.S. Department of Homeland Security.[30] The community of Santa Paula, California owns a similar mobile EOC that is deployable anywhere as needed.[31]

AIRVAC/MEDIVAC

In the days following Katrina in 2005, Blackwater, a private sector defense contractor based in Virginia, dispatched an SA-330 Puma helicopter to assist in evacuating medically-sensitive disaster victims from the flood zone out to rear-line regional medical centers. And the U.S. Coast Guard at one point had more than 10 percent of its entire personnel stationed along the Gulf Coast to assist in the recovery effort. Countless missions were conducted in its bright orange and white helicopters with the U.S. Coast Guard insignia on their sides. By the second day after the flood, 137 victims had been rescued from ruined urban neighborhoods and by the third day Coast Guard helicopters had rescued 1,259 more stranded survivors from rooftops. By then, fourteen additional units had arrived to assist in search and rescue, along with additional Coast Guard units deployed from Houston and Corpus Christi, Texas. By the end of that first week this squadron completed a total of 2,859 emergency rescues.[32] Victims of disasters and casualties of war are often transported to a field-based RTC or permanent site hospital via airborne emergency medical evacuation, widely known as AIRVAC, or MEDIVAC. This is a process that may take anywhere from a half-hour to up to many hours and everything depends on hierarchically layered, complex, unpredictable and ever-changing logistical factors. In 2012, this author conducted a systematic assessment of the FEMA-built Statewide Emergency Medical Shelter, in Alexandria Louisiana. The post occupancy evaluation (POE) was commissioned by the State of Louisiana Department of Health and Hospitals and was focused on retrofit measures to enhance this 30,000 square foot facility's performance in the event of a future medical emergency evacuation. Built after Katrina in 2008 with FEMA federal funds, this permanent site shelter was erected to house medically sensitive patients of all ages who require evacuation from the coastal zone to the south. Among the findings, the shelter's helipad was built too close in proximity to the facility and the propellers' wind field can be extremely strong—forceful enough to knock an adult down to the ground. Whenever a helicopter lands or takes off, the wind field intensity is such that nearby windows in the shelter structure are sometimes completely blown out.

Helipads

Earthquakes occur with frequency in the highlands bordering India and Pakistan. One recent disaster was the 2005 Kashmir earthquake that killed 79,000 people, resulting in more than $5 billion in damage. A majority of the quake's fatalities occurred in a remote part of Pakistan, and poor access to this mountainous and landlocked region complicated the relief efforts of multiple international disaster relief agencies. To counter this dilemma, regional and international aid organizations ingeniously set up twenty-four emergency helipads across the mountainous, hard-to-access Kashmir region. The 'air ambulances' provided by the Pakistani government were used extensively during this search and rescue operation.[33] In remote locations, especially, any site selected for the installation of an RTC or similar emergency aid structure needs to be large enough to accommodate helicopters coming and going on a frequent basis. This is especially so in the first days and weeks following a disaster event. A helipad is an important amenity in the case of larger RTC facilities because they will undoubtedly have a larger bed capacity and this means a higher number of victims will be arriving and departing on a 24/7 basis. The sheer volume of casualties being transited in and out will be significant. In urban settings, by contrast, it may be preferable to set up the mobile facility in a wide roadway median or on a sufficiently wide city street with a grassy median, because these settings can be used as a helicopter landing zone as well. In the case of rural, remote sites, on the other hand, due to rough, uneven terrain, it may be necessary to lay down a temporary airfield matting device. These soft pad surfaces are used as temporary helipads, taxiways, parking aprons,

5.8a–b Emergency electrical generation is a portable healthcare facility's lifeline

and access roads for military and disaster relief operations. They cause minimal disruption to the environmental ecosystem and they can also protect the equipment from getting stuck by sinking into wet soil or poor quality dry soil. These portable helipad mattings can be stretched out to help smooth out the ground surface relatively quickly. The *MegaDeck* airfield-matting device bears a compressive load strength of up to 600psi, in ideal soil conditions. The manufacturer recommends use of a soil stabilizer compound to provide additional helipad stabilization in less-than-ideal site conditions such as those mentioned above.[34]

Power generation

Without proper electrical support—lighting for critical tasks and refrigeration for time-sensitive pharmaceuticals—it is extremely challenging to provide effective emergency medical care in a remote location, a location perhaps hundreds of miles from the nearest population center. A portable facility must be able to be deployed to the installation site, assembled, commissioned and fully running in the shortest possible time. Its emergency power generation and interior lighting systems must be durable, able to withstand extreme temperature conditions, and rough, in-transit routes. They must be properly positioned next to the structure to function without undue difficulty and adapt to changing needs on an around-the-clock basis (Figure 5.8a–b). They must be repairable and the tools to do so must be readily available. In many cases, a second unit is brought in from the start in case the lead unit goes down for some reason. The backup unit is an insurance policy because the presence of reliable emergency power generation has life and death ramifications for the patient in surgery, the technician performing a lab test, or the nurse who needs to quickly triage a patient's wound. The lights have to remain on, and any interruptions in power can potentially trigger adverse consequences. Power generation is therefore integral to the success of on-site operations. Fuel-powered backup generation remains the industry standard, with the fuel brought in and stored on site. When it becomes necessary for relief operations to continue beyond sixty days, explore longer-term power source options. Solar-powered generators can be coordinated in tandem with fuel-based units, with either or both systems connected to a conventional power grid until such time when it comes back online. It is prudent to designate only one zone for continuous power even if the rest of the facility remains dark, not unlike a high-rise hotel keeping its egress routes illuminated in a building blackout. As an alternative, roof-mounted solar panels can be affixed atop RTCs and RHCs to power the lighting system, diagnostic and treatment spaces including surgical suites, exam rooms, and medical supply and pharmaceutical refrigeration units. Manufacturers are responding by beginning to market solar panels that are connectible to conventional fuel-powered units. The *Portable Solar Generator* (PSG4) system produced by Solarline Corporation is suitable for disaster relief operations as it can operate completely off grid.[35]

Refrigeration

A portable healthcare facility cannot function without a high quality, dependable, durable refrigeration system on a 24/7 basis. Thermally insulated carry-on units and large ISO containers are required to provide refrigeration for the storage of temperature-sensitive lab specimens and medical supplies. Perishable supplies and pharmaceuticals must be kept in safe storage for days, often

5.9 U.S. Army CSH installation, airport tarmac, Iraq, 2010

under extreme weather conditions. Safe Global Corporation manufactures mobile modules for the biomedical sciences, disaster relief organizations, and the military. Its refrigeration units are suitable for air transport and hold product approvals from both the U.S. Federal Aviation Administration (FAA) and the European Aviation Safety Agency (EASA). Continuous thermal control is provided by means of compressors. These devices are an alternative to the comparatively high cost and transport challenges associated with the age-old method of having to transport dry ice over long distances. More than 10,000 units of *AcuTemp*, this company's carry-on mobile refrigeration device, have been purchased for use in post-disaster settings. After Typhoon Haiyan in 2013, hundreds of these devices were deployed to the Philippines for use in RTCs and for the storage of laboratory samples, vaccines, pharmaceuticals, and all temperature/date-sensitive perishables. International relief agencies use these portable, hand-held 'passive insulated' devices because they are lightweight and powered either by a full-size generator, or batteries. Mid-size units fit onto a forklift palette.[36] For vaccine storage, the typical individual refrigeration unit is a twelve volt DC, fifteen foot, three inch high efficiency unit, proven particularly effective in the field for the storage of vaccines. Dietary services also require refrigeration support on a 24/7 basis. The *Japan Ground Self-Defense Force* (JGSDF) in 2013 unveiled a series of state-of-the-art mobile refrigeration devices for use in post-disaster strike zones. Its refrigeration and associated water treatment equipment includes a mobile field kitchen, a water filtration system capable of treating seventy metric tons of fresh water or thirty tons of seawater in a single day, a laundry unit, and a portable bathing/shower module. The mobile field kitchen is capable of preparing meals for 200 people in forty-five minutes' cooking time, an outcome made possible by a modular refrigeration/freezer unit reduced to one-fourth the size of the JGSDF's earlier standard version. It includes a feed water pump and a 1,000-liter potable water storage tank.[37]

Phased installation

The U.S. Army *Military Health System's* (MHS) network of CSHs are staged as three different deployment packages: forty beds, eighty beds, and 120 beds. The MHS protocol is to begin with the smallest configuration and then ramp up bed capacity if and when the need to do so becomes essential. In domestic post-disaster locations, the forty-bed facility type continues to serve adequately. This configuration has been deployed numerous times in military theatres during the Iraq War and the Afghanistan War. In certain situations, large configurations were deployed in these combat zones in a phased manner. Regardless of the bed capacity, considerable training is required to set up and operate a CSH. A two-week field-based training program is required, accompanied by classroom training. Six combat-ready MHS portable hospitals are prepositioned at this writing on three U.S. bases, and two bases overseas. These instillation footprints must allow for expansion if/when the need arises. Personnel are trained to phase installations whereby a small facility is set up on the base with training provided on how to expand it without shutting down or disrupting the flow of patient care within the core facility, while it is being doubled or tripled in size. In corresponding civilian contexts, a professionally licensed contractor may set up the portable infirmary, whether tented, containerized, or a hybrid system. Critical steps in the planning process are similar, and include, ideally, prior experience and a proven track record in past installations, the ability to troubleshoot potential problems and glitches, and the knowledge to set up the initial configuration to allow for its future expansion if needed. In operations where a facility is to be in service for a period of six months or more, it is prudent to have a thirty-day, sixty-day, ninety-day (and beyond) contingency plan. Initial installations require site preparation, including locating the helipad (if required on site), a staging area for storage of empty shipping containers, and the positioning of power generation units so as not to require relocation during subsequent expansion(s). Whether in military or civilian contexts, proper due diligence is necessary as this guides initial bed capacity and allotment, and internal circulation layout. In some situations the Phase II section is erected at the same time as Phase I, and this space is left unoccupied shell space, just as in a permanent building, in anticipation of future need (Figure 5.9).

Commissioning

The commissioning of an offsite-built redeployable structure is in many ways similar to conventionally built buildings. But in certain ways it is quite different. Commissioning consists of verifying, in new construction, by means of inspections and testing, the structure's entire mechanical, plumbing, electrical, fire/life safety, building envelope, interior, lighting, wastewater, and building security subsystems to determine if they fully comply with the owner's requirements, the architectural and engineering (A/E) team, the offsite manufacturer(s) and onsite construction manager (CM). The owner's performance criteria are translated into extensive checklists that guide all code inspections, and guide the review of all steps undertaken from the beginning of project to its final completion. It ensures a project is completed in accord with parameters agreed to by all contractually binding parties.[38] In the case of a portable, commissioning also requires reviewing assembly and subassembly processes along the way while the pop-up and its component systems are being built and installed in the factory. Code inspections are conducted at the factory prior to the shipment of the final product. The commissioning agent, ideally, is a third party, independent from the client and the prime contractor/manufacturer. This individual or team is responsible for performing all final inspections of a transportable. At the factory, the completed structure is assembled in a parking lot or field, or a nearby site such as a school, as agreed to by all parties—this is its *local deployment*. Here, everything is tested and inspected—and final *pre-commissioning* occurs at this time. The staff that will use the facility in the field, in disaster situations, or otherwise, may participate in this process. In the case of a pop-up clinic, for instance, the structure's modules and onboard equipment may leave the factory at substantial completion stage. The commissioning process here would be in two phases, with Phase I consisting of the pre-commission part occurring for that portion of the substantially completed structure that arrives at the test-site host structure. Final commissioning is next. The Phase II final commissioning occurs when installation is completed *inside* the test-site host; this is its 100 percent completion stage. This two-step process ensures the entire structure can be successfully transported, and is able to function successfully after its final assembly is completed inside a field deployment site. In some cases, the client may require that this process is repeated off site—then deployed to a different site for formal commissioning.

3 Arrival and semi-public spaces

Patient intake

A healthcare facility without an identifiable public entrance is a torso without a head. If it is too hard to locate the entrance, critical time is lost in getting a disaster victim into triage. In triage, confidentiality and privacy are in extremely short supply as it is. The sign-in station may just be a folding table and a few chairs, outside. Small-scale clinics may not have enough space indoors for any triage or intake activities. In more commodious conditions, triage and intake may occur in a more structured room setting, perhaps indoors. There, victims are interviewed individually in semi-private, partitioned interview stations affording at least a modicum of privacy. Triage stations are often makeshift—in some cases, however, it may be possible to set up one station for AIRVAC/MEDIVAC use and a second for persons arriving by foot or vehicle. It is recommended that the patient intake tent/canopy is expandable if the need exists to accommodate many victims at once, and to provide shelter from the elements. This area may be subdivided into more than one consult alcove, if space permits. In interior conditions, triage and associated patient interview/intake may be located adjoining circulation paths and public areas, i.e. patient consultation and examination rooms, near the main waiting area. Provide a series of informal spaces for interpersonal communication to occur between caregiver, patient, and family versus the barn-like waiting areas of many hospitals. Provide a few seats at the end of an interior corridor, for use in consultation, perhaps located next to the clinical treatment zone. Where feasible, provide natural ventilation and daylight in these in-between spaces. Small, decentralized niches such as these can provide momentary respite from the surrounding intensity and can help to take pressure off of the public zone, i.e. main entrance, waiting areas, and patient interview/intake stations. The use of color-coded floors or walls can help to distinguish these spaces from adjoining spaces (Figure 5.10).

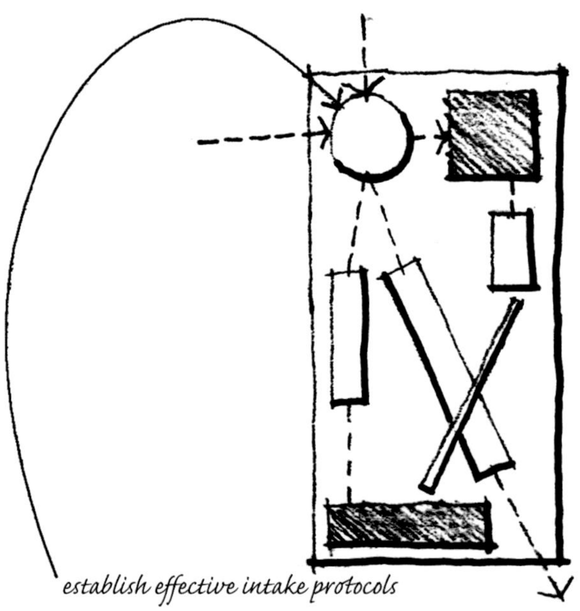

5.10 Streamline patient intake/interview processes to avoid unnecessary delays

Triage stations

Triage is the initial evaluation of the severity of a person's injuries, and involves determining the priority of who shall be attended to first.[39] It is the initial point of contact between patient and caregiver. The term 'triage' comes from the French verb *trier*, meaning to separate, sift, or select.[40] The term has its origins in the Napoleonic Wars and it was used further in World War I by French doctors treating the wounded at aid stations along the battlefront. Casualties were divided into one of three categories: those who were likely to live regardless of what care they received, those who were likely to die regardless of what care they received, and those for whom immediate care might make a positive difference in a life-saving outcome. These broad categories are still used by Emergency Medical Services (EMS) teams. Resources are seldom sufficient for all victims who need to be treated immediately, and time is of the essence. It may be impossible to set up any more than a single folding table and a few chairs and to position them in the open air or inside a tent. Triage stations must be easily seen as one approaches the installation. Chaotic conditions may necessitate multiple triage stations. In the aftermath of the chemical plant explosion in Waggeman, Louisiana in 2009, dozens of victims were triaged on site outdoors, then transported to nearby hospitals for further treatment. In the aftermath of the 9/11 World Trade Center terrorist attack in New York City in 2001, casualties were treated on open-air loading docks and in parking lots near the scene. In the case of the Boston Marathon terrorism bombing in 2013, a first aid tent, fortunately, had been pre-stationed at the finish line in close proximity to the site of the explosion. This greatly facilitated the rapid triaging of casualties. The RTC must rapidly triage incoming victims and to provide a staging area large enough to accommodate victims' families. This may call for an outdoor triage station in addition to a corresponding indoor station. The outdoor component should be large enough to accommodate as many as 200 incoming victims within a short timeframe. In extreme situations, patients may be simply marked with colored flagging tape or marker pens. The five categories are, from most severe: Black/Expectant (near death), Red/Immediate (immediate surgery required), Yellow/Observation (condition stable at moment), Green/Wait (walking wounded) and White (able to be dismissed). Preprinted cards for this purpose are known as a triage tag. Triage stations should be properly equipped with appropriate medical supplies, with the option of a decontamination unit set up in close proximity to the triage station.

Decontamination

Decontamination (decon, or decontam) is the process of cleansing an object, substance, or living organism to remove foreign contaminants or hazardous materials, including chemicals, radioactive substances, and infectious disease agents (Figure

5.12 Modular, portable decontamination unit with individual shower bays

5.11).[41] Decontamination prevents the spread of various life-threatening microorganisms. It is standard practice in surgery, forensics, veterinary science and the environmental sciences to eradicate life-threatening chemical agents by physical means such as chemical neutralization, or detoxification. Decontamination of the human skin is the primary focus, and the treatment of eyes and any bodily wounds must be expeditiously performed. Casualty decontamination refers to acutely exposed accident victims in the aftermath of a human-induced event, or a natural disaster.[42] A ten-shower stall installation is considered a mid-size unit. Modules are manufactured in single- or double-door configurations and are usually installed directly on the ground. Freestanding, fabric-sheathed decontamination modules often require only a few persons to deploy and often have easily repairable components. They are fabricated of impact-resistant materials, and pneumatic (air inflated) units remain structurally stable for up to forty-eight hours without requiring re-inflation.[43] One product for this purpose, the *DRASH* module, contains eight stalls with its own self-supplied fresh and wastewater system, and a common washbasin and small changing area (Figure 5.12). An eight-stall module is eight feet by sixteen feet in plan. It is manufactured in tan, or green, and is mildew resistant. Modules feature their own onboard water heater, plumbing system, sinks, benches and small common area, light fixtures, bladders for fresh water supply and wastewater removal, a containment berm, and a slightly raised floor. Water is supplied by thirty-five-foot long heavy-duty hoses, connected to a primary water source. Each stall has a showerhead and a rigid-wall containment berm sidewall eight feet in height. An automated pump controls the water flow rate. Note: the water heating system at minimum should be a 425,000 BTU/twenty-eight gallons per minute, self-heating, thermostatically controlled system, with a ten-gallon onboard fuel tank with drain plug. Fuels to power a decontamination unit include diesel, kerosene, and home heating oil. A built-in anti-scald protection device with in-line GFI protection should be provided onboard and the power generator should at minimum be a 1/5 hp, 120V, 60hz, single-phase burner motor with a solid state, non-flame system igniter.[44]

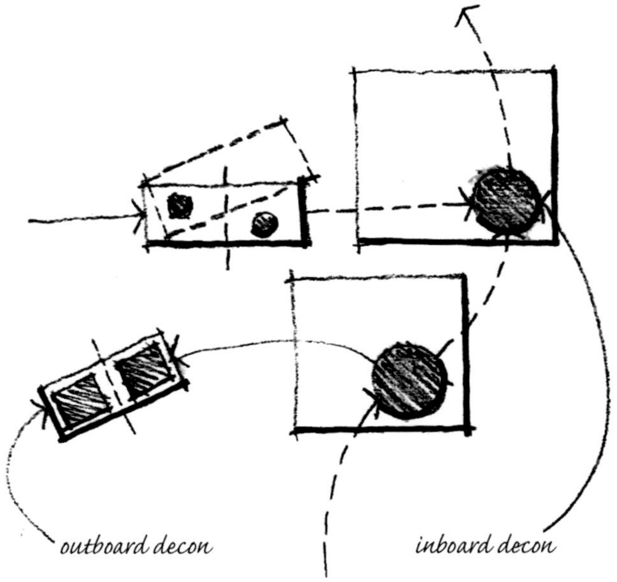

5.11 Decontamination units can either be freestanding (outboard) or housed within a core platform (inboard)

Inboard decon units

Inboard decontamination units are, similarly, for victims of human-induced accidents and natural disasters where casualties are in immediate need of treatment. This unit type is integral to the facility, and is therefore not freestanding. Inboard units' shower stalls and various support spaces are compartmentalized, somewhat different from those of a freestanding unit (see above). Accident victims pass through a cleansing station after having been exposed to a hazardous and/or life-threatening chemical agent.[45] Inboard decon modules are shipped to the site as part of a larger portable field hospital. The unit is delivered either as a prefab module, or as a flat-pack system (Figure 5.13). Flat-packs require assembly on site. A pressure is maintained at a lower (negative) level compared to the exterior atmosphere, and is High-Efficiency Particulate Arrestance (HEPA)-filtered before being exhausted outside. Shower wastewater is also filtered to remove particulate matter prior to offsite disposal. Inboard decon units can be of two types: an open-air tent with natural ventilation, or a panelized system with natural ventilation or with artificially provided ventilation. An inboard decon unit in a mid-sized RTC installation

5.13 Communal decontamination shower module interior

should provide ten three-part (shower/clean shower/changing) sub-compartments. Requirements for an inboard unit include a changing room, and hot and cold water feed lines color-coded with quick release fittings arranged to not allow for crossover of the hot and cold water supply into other parts of the RTC. As with outboard units, each stall has its own showerhead, and on/off taps for hot and cold water are to be commercial grade. At a minimum, a 125-liter electric hot water system with a 2400-watt electric heater, minimum, is required. A pressure-reducing valve on the tank inlet is mounted on its own trolley, and wastewater is collected in a single pump/filter tank assembly, independent from the RTC's other water supply system.[46] In larger emergencies, freestanding decontamination units can be installed on site nearby. Consider providing space within the mainframe chassis for inboard decon but in a way that allows this space to be broken down or used for another function. This space could then be converted into a second waiting area, additional exam rooms, or an office for volunteers, for instance.

RTCs—The waiting areas may at worst be a makeshift space outdoors. If interior space exists, provide seating for as many as fifty patients, assuming that some overflow will still occur during peak utilization times/days. Suffice to say, the preferable arrangement is to provide both interior and adjunctive sheltered waiting outdoors. Many facilities provide a tent or awning with insect net screening for the waiting area. This allows for flexibility if additional chairs need to be added.

PMIs—Here, the conditions of a conventional brick and mortar healthcare facility can be replicated. Panelized and containerized prefab systems are frequently installed directly on a concrete pad. This was the case with the *Contertainer,* where the waiting room is housed in an onsite-built portion of the building (see Chapter 6). Once a decision is made to go with prefab modular, give careful consideration to the waiting room(s), their size, configuration, finishes, adjacency to the main public entrance and to the triage, decontamination, and intake zone. Provide accessible wheelchair ramps and associated navigational aids for wayfinding.

Waiting areas

No single, ideal, waiting room layout is applicable to all types of portable structures for healthcare. With regards to an RHC for use as a primary care clinic, with pop-ups, the host itself provides space for the waiting 'room.' The New Orleans and Charleston hosts selected for installations provide adequate space, including a repurposed vacant church, former furniture store, former movie theater, and school gymnasiums (see Chapter 4). Albeit repurposed spaces, even those with bare concrete floors, may seem less than ideal, this strategy makes it possible to not have to build, and transit, these additional prefab modular components. The first C2C containerized clinic deployed to Haiti in 2010 featured a canvas canopy attached to one of the containers. This outdoor waiting area has a wood deck, benches, and is integral to the overall installation. The clinic's interior waiting area is quite small, however, as it allows no more than a few patients in it at any one time (see Chapter 6).

Streamline circulation

Every part of a portable structure for health must provide maximum functional support. In post-World War II hospitals, the long monotonous corridors often were confusing and extremely difficult to navigate due to their windowless, circuitous paths, and their poor lighting. Ridiculous striped lines were necessary on the floors just so one could get about: the yellow line goes to admitting, the red line goes to the ICU, and so on. Today, naturally day-lit, single- and double-loaded corridors that adjoin courtyards and green space are highly desirable amenities in the hospital environment. First and foremost, in an RTC or RHC the vast majority of interior space will be needed for patient intake/interview, diagnosis and treatment, and the general clinical zones. It would be excessive to provide multiple interior circulation paths within an RTC or RHC facility, i.e. front of the house/back of the house corridors, as in a conventional permanent site hospital. This will only obfuscate the flow of people and supplies in emergencies. On the other hand, too few corridors will result in insanely restrictive bottlenecks. Easily negotiated, clear, and appropriately wide interior circulation paths are obviously preferable for these reasons. The navigability of a crowded hallway can be enhanced through the use of color, natural daylighting, windows, and skylights and the absence or at least minimization of overtly 'blind' corridor intersections. An alternate strategy is for some of these circulation paths to be placed on the exterior of the mainframe platform to function in tandem with one or more corridors located within the interior of the facility's platform. Since physical weight is a factor in the structure's portability while in transit, it's preferable that fewer but wider corridors are designed in lieu of more numerous, yet narrower corridors. This will result in fewer shipping containers needed as perhaps 10–15 percent of the total gross interior space of the main platform 'chassis' can be eliminated (see discussion of Lean in this context). Minimize the interior gross floor area devoted to circulation without sacrificing the internal movement of people, equipment, or supplies. Eschew circulation paths that bisect or cut through quiet zones. Route the circulation around quiet zones, buffered from noisy public areas (Figure 5.14).[47]

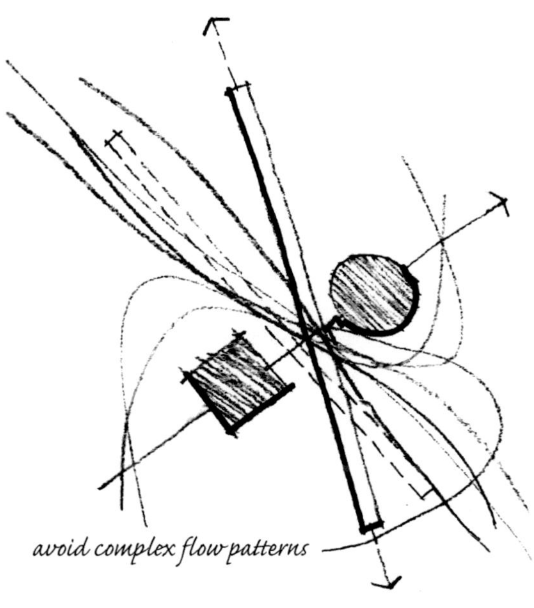

5.14 Too many corridors are as problematic as too few corridors, resulting in bottlenecks

Wayfinding

A large medical center can seem overwhelming when one is forced to search in the dead of night for the emergency room entrance. In an emergency everything seems to happen so fast, making this all the more exasperating. When approaching the installation, make sure signage is clear, unambiguous, and communicates the equivalent of 'Emergency Hospital!' The instantly recognizable bright red cross of the *International Red Cross* immediately signifies this humanitarian organization's presence. Other disaster aid organizations have their own iconic signage. Do not rely solely on a single freestanding sign as it alone may be inadequate, is subject to being damaged or destroyed, and will likely be difficult to see from any distance. When approaching by air, make sure one or more large signs are clearly and securely affixed to the roof of the facility. Redundant cueing is an effective means to *code* the facility, both indoors and out, from a wayfinding perspective, whether approaching by air, land, or water. In poorly designed conditions, the sign-in/waiting room areas are indistinguishable from one another. Spatial features quickly meld into one another becoming a blur. Conditions such as these can trigger environmental stress in persons regardless of one's age, gender, or cultural background. It is unsettling to abruptly 'fall into' a trauma care facility with so little information provided about how to proceed, unless well-sequenced navigational aids, redundant cueing, and an effective directional graphics system is provided. This information will help to reduce occupants' stress while reducing needless decision making at corridor intersections and in bottlenecked conditions. Redundant cueing incorporates multiple interpretable cues into a space. These can include a floor pattern that is coordinated with the design of the walls and even the ceilings. Or, where directional signage is placed above, overhead, as well as next to each room in a way where one cue reinforces the other. This builds wayfinding amenity into the interior environment. Transparency and openness can achieve this, especially in public zones. Avoid the archaic painted stripes on the floor and long, narrow, dreary circulation routes that require everyone and everything to travel up and down the same path all the time. Provide views to the outside at key intervals and in patient treatment areas with natural daylight and views.

Safe corners and intersections

In any healthcare facility, the presence of sharp, right-angled corners where circulation paths intersect can be a cause of accidents. Children running down a corridor, or playing hide and seek in places where they should not, can result in injuries caused by running into or falling onto hard-edged corners along corridors and at the corridor intersections. The same happens with hard-edged corners on furniture, and with equipment such as medical supply carts. Staff personnel, for their part, routinely transport medical and clerical supplies throughout and they deserve clear sightlines to see around blind spots in order to avoid run-ins. It is children, however, who are particularly prone to personal injury caused by running into this same supply cart. Provide doors at thresholds between zones, from public to quiet, to control accidents, and keep children out of places they do not need to be in unless accompanied by a parent, sibling, or guardian. The doors between these zones can be problematic, in their own right. This is because a young child will invariably run headfirst into an all-glass door. Instead, provide only those doors absolutely needed, with the uppermost portion of each door manufactured with see-through glass, and its lower half fitted, perhaps, with obscured glass. This will provide required functional separation in a way whereby a child can discern the lower, obscured panel from the upper, see-through vision panel. Design the corners of room modules to be rounded, wherever feasible. This will provide additional amenity, reduce accidents, and make the facility more navigable at pathway intersections (see Chapter 4). Waiting rooms, intake cares, classrooms, procedure rooms, examination rooms, and transitional spaces are well suited for softened corners, especially when located along highly trafficked circulation paths within a RTC or RHC (Figure 5.15).

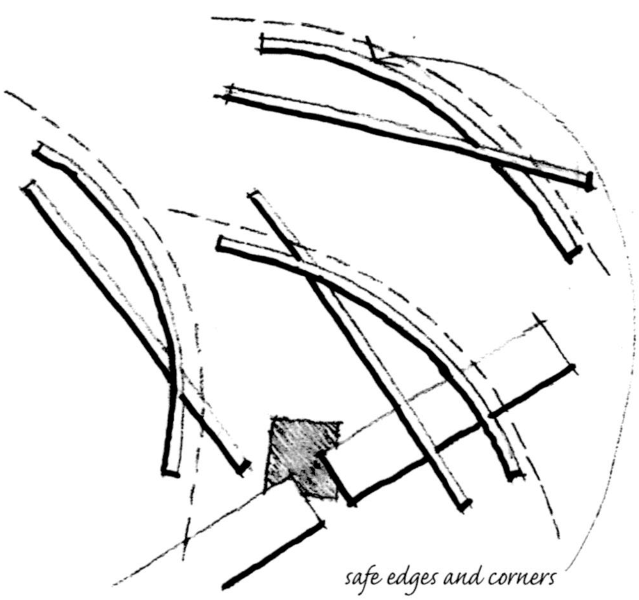

5.15 Eschew hard-sharp edges on modules as these can cause needless accidents

Bereavement

In the aftermath of Typhoon Haiyan in the Philippines in 2013, a middle-aged man who suffered a broken leg did not receive any sort of medical treatment for a week even though he arrived at the hospital a mere one day after the storm passed. As a result, he developed a life-threatening infection. His leg was amputated. Even as he lay desperately ill in his bed, he was unable to be seen by his surviving family members due to the hospital's extremely overcrowded conditions (see Chapter 1). He soon died. Many victims died in hospital due to hospital-acquired infections. Sadly, afterwards, his body had to be taken outside for his surviving family members just to see it.[48] It is understandable why the experience of death and bereavement remains so under-discussed in emergencies and in disasters. There is so much going on at once—*everything* seems upside down. Regardless, a hospital corridor, or worse, being forced outdoors, is unacceptable for grieving the loss of a friend or loved one. Attitudes toward death, dying, and bereavement differ as a function of cultural norms and traditions, but this is not a valid excuse in and of itself.[49] Often, a makeshift tent is set up on the RTC site, or nearby somewhere, for receiving and processing the deceased. Although the facility itself may be overcrowded, if it is open at all, having a place—anyplace—to experience, share, and express one's personal grief is of great importance. Within the RTC's hierarchy of public-to-private spaces, this place can be located outdoors, in a tent, or indoors in a room with its own door, with visual privacy. Just provide *something*. It is unnatural to deny this. Most installations have little room for prayer or meditation. Yet in a time of crisis, being able to think and reflect, can ameliorate stress, and help one to maintain some degree of dignity. Provide a space for spiritual respite, a quiet zone away from the hubbub, with subdued lighting, floor mats, and privacy screening. With respect to morgues, locate them at the rear of the site, farthest from the public entrance.

4 Diagnostic and treatment functions

Facility-acquired infection

From a logistical standpoint, much can go wrong in setting up a portable field hospital—parts of the structure don't arrive on time, the wrong power generator arrives, shortages of critically needed pharmaceuticals, a roof leaks, causing rainwater penetration, a tent that partially collapsed earlier in the day, and so on. From the moment it opens, the RTC or RHC must be a source of hope, trust, and confidence, not mistrust, uncertainty, or misery. Things will go wrong. It is the work of the entire planning and design team, including the engineer and the manufacturers, to ensure the facility itself does not cause harm in any way to its inhabitants. This begins with the physical setting in preventing unhealthful conditions. Surfaces and equipment must be easily re-sanitized because hospital-acquired infections, including nosocomial infections, are a leading cause of death in hospitals. A portable may inadvertently contribute to facility-acquired illnesses by means of three transmission pathways—the indoor air, human contact with contaminated surfaces and equipment, and contaminated water. In the U.S., the Centers for Disease Control and Prevention's (CDC) healthcare-associated infection (HAI) annual prevalence survey provides a national estimate of the overall problem of HAIs in conventional U.S. hospitals. In 2011, this survey found that that on any given day, about one in twenty-five hospital patients acquires at least one facility-associated infection. There were an estimated 722,000 HAIs in U.S. acute care hospitals in 2011. About 75,000 hospital patients with HAIs died during their hospitalizations that year in the U.S. and more than half of all HAIs occurred outside of the ICU setting.[50] The cost of treating patients who acquire these infections is estimated at $5 billion each year. Many are drug resistant and difficult to treat or entirely eradicate. Patients are particularly vulnerable when immunocompromised or otherwise become vulnerable due to age, medical/surgical complications, or collateral illnesses.[51] It may be that while receiving treatment for a broken arm one is exposed to something far worse. While at the RTC or RHC the patient could be exposed to an MRSA infection or an airborne contagion. The institutional transmission of virulent airborne infections such as TB remains a problem as well, especially in settings where negative pressure isolation rooms are unavailable. Naturally ventilated portable hospitals are widely praised for this feature.[52] In hospital emergency trauma centers in the U.S., a recent trend has been toward higher acuity rates among admitted patients, an occurrence generally attributable to the aging of American society. In a post-disaster setting, by contrast, victims are of all ages. Evidence-based design research literature on this subject in conventional hospitals suggests the physical setting is a potential contributor to a host of hospital-acquired illnesses (2008).[53] No empirical studies, to date, however, have been reported on this issue with respect to portable hospitals. To paraphrase Florence Nightingale, *a redeployable healthcare environment shall do no harm.*

Pre-operative units

Containerized units are often preferred for pre-operative care because they provide a more predictable, technically elaborate setting, compared to tents. These units are typically housed in a single ISO container equipped with a single door and perhaps windows on both the front and rear walls, with double doors on the front wall to allow connectivity with tent modules to one side and to the operating theatre on the other. One or both walls may be specified with window sunscreens and with the ability to be completely concealed from the exterior side. These units usually contain one double sink, a disinfectant distributor, one paper towel distributor, a water heater, one mobile table, two mobile tables for storing tools and medical equipment for patient preparation, two wheelchairs, a nursing/physician workstation, one or more modular storage units for supplies, a full size refrigerator, trash receptacles, two carts for hazardous medical waste, and a storage room for two (or more) medical gas cylinders. The preparation (scrub) compartment in pre-operative modules is subdivided into an entry zone and a staff cleanup and clothes change zone. A connecting door to the adjacent surgical unit module is electronically controlled. The onboard shower-prep area houses two stainless steel sinks, soap dispensers, disinfectant and towel dispensers, boiler unit, benches and chairs, storage cabinets for clean scrubs and miscellaneous medical items, x-ray aprons, clothing storage, trash receptacles, linen hampers, a backup air conditioning/heating unit, and germicidal lamps. A large water system bladder module houses the potable water supply and wastewater collection equipment. This equipment includes a potable water tank, a freshwater submersible pump, expansion tank for purified water, pipe heating, sensor controllers and couplings for connectivity to water dispersal apparatus, and a toolkit for routine maintenance and repairs. Potable water is supplied by the fresh water reservoir comprised of a leveling valve and pump although the tank itself is typically not pressurized. The water supply system must withstand temperatures of -20 degrees C (heated) to 49 degrees C with easily assembled plumbing components. This system should be protected from external contaminants, allowing for rapid drainage and re-sanitization following procedures.[54] Make every provision during design and manufacturing to ensure the pre-operative unit is re-sanitizable with minimum difficulty. This applies to all walls, floors, and equipment.

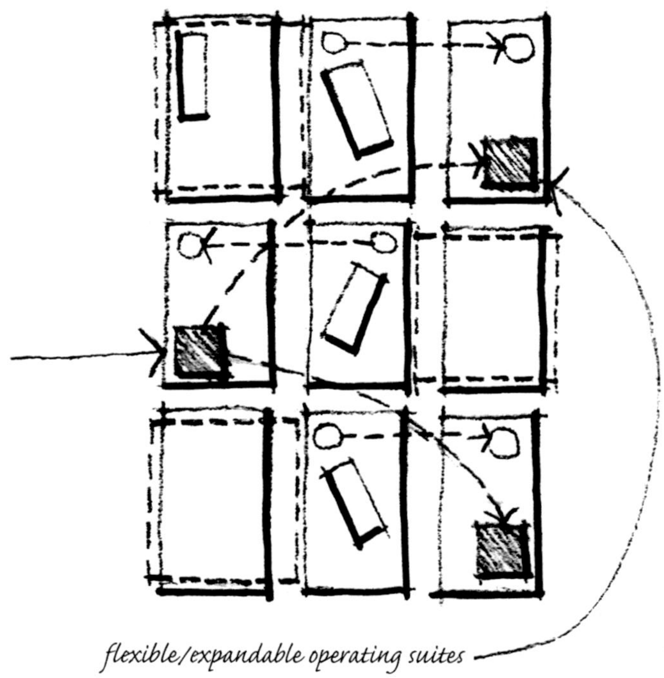

5.16 Pop-out surgical modules provide additional space and greater internal use options

Surgical units

The containerized RTC manufactured by AGER Industries consists of six individual modules that are linked together to form a single contiguous mobile surgical unit. This installation is a mix of hard and soft-walled units designed for simplified deployment while allowing for significant flexibility as needs evolve in the field (Figure 5.16). The system consists of a surgical/operating theater module housed in two ISO containers, one pre-operative container, one medical staff prep container, one power generation container, one utility container providing water and waste management, three inflatable patient bed ward tents (each 7 meters by 5 meters by 2.5 meters), one inflatable ward tent for staff support (5 meters by 5 meters by 2.5 meters) and three inflatable ward tents for related diagnostic and treatment (each 17 meters by 8 meters by 4 meters). The operating suite/unit is windowless, here, but the overall volume is expandable using the pop-out sections. Leveling jacks allow for accurate positioning of the six units and each one is equipped with distribution systems for medical oxygen, compressed air, and nitrous oxide. The maximum weight for a single (loaded) container does not exceed 12,000 kilograms. The approximate internal size of two interconnected modules at full deployment is 5800mm (length) by 4650mm (width) by 2000mm (height). One container is fitted with a double door in front and a single door to the side and the door dimensions are 1000mm by 1900mm or 1200mm by 1900mm (width by height). Doors must be airtight and electronically operable with a ninety-degree opening radius. The lighting apparatus and surgical procedure table is situated at the center of this module, with support equipment and storage units in close proximity. The procedure table specified in the AGER Industries system is the Braun Type 22.6015B Operating

Table. The Braun Encore 1750 3 Gas System anesthesia and ventilation machine is also specified. In addition, a germicidal ultraviolet lamp is provided, as are portable operating lamps that meet the following minimum performance specifications: lightness and portability, and a polygon reflector A-Class heat isolation glass with true color temperature at 4300K. It is a dual control system operated by means of infrared remote control, and a control panel on the cupola with an adjustable illumination level from 0–100 percent. The cupola's design includes a spare bulb housed in it and a system alarm that beeps once per minute and can be muted with a key; this is a memory function that reinstates the illumination level by means of the backup bulb. Also included is a detachable lamp handle that can be re-sterilized.[55] Once again, make every provision during design and manufacturing to ensure the total surgical unit is re-sanitizable with minimum difficulty. This applies to all walls, floors, and equipment.

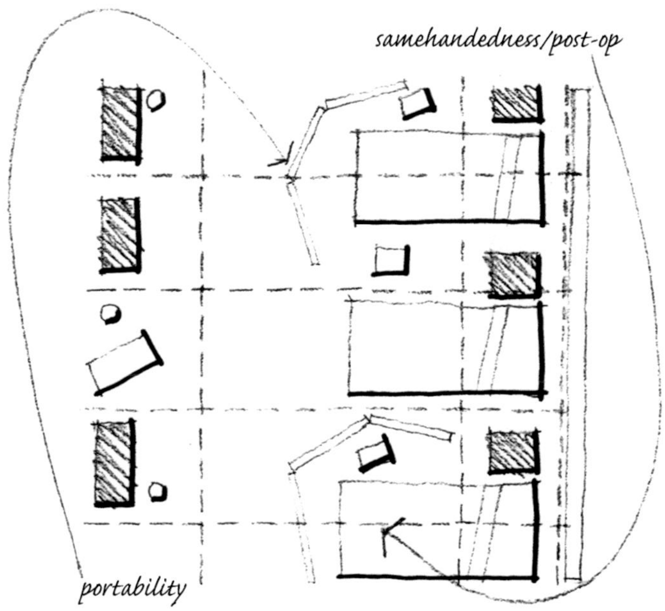

5.17 *Same-handed* inpatient beds may be preferable, in theory, but impracticable in ad hoc conditions in the field

Post-operative units

RTCs and conventional hospitals are not the same. In fixed-site, all-private room hospitals, recent evidence-based research suggests the importance, from a care delivery and nursing standpoint, of positioning every bed in the medical/surgical unit with a *same-handed* orientation. That is, with the patient's same side, be it the patient's left side, or the patient's right side, always closest to the door connecting to the hallway, in every room. This is seen as an improvement over the old, mirrored, back-to-back bed placement (with a shared headwall) so prevalent in medical-surgical units of the post-World War II era.[56] But in an open ward, the beds are usually arrayed along the two outer walls and this does allow, in theory at least, the caregiver to be able to access every bed from the same side if he or she so chooses. Granted, a same-handed bed orientation in an RTC open ward requires all medical gases, electrical outlets, and related equipment to be located on the same side of the bed. Here, however, the 'headwall' may be no more than the tent's fabric inner liner. This may therefore not always be a practical option in the often unpredictable, unforgiving world of a portable healthcare environment if for no other reason than *same-handedness* may require additional space, even additional wards (Figure 5.17). Also, there are often other things to worry about of a potentially larger magnitude such as, for instance, when a pneumatic ward module inexplicably begins to depressurize. Structure-based issues, in other words, can take precedent and this is (usually) not an issue in a conventional hospital. The brick and mortar building is there as it was built, period. With a tent, wind resistance is a high priority and it is recommended, for instance, a unit is able to withstand winds of a minimum 100 kilometers per hour, and, for snow loads, to withstand 15 kilograms per square meter. The module must be lightweight—generally not to exceed 775 kilograms for a unit with an interior usable area of 150 square meters. Exterior fabric sheathing material is at minimum a polyvinyl-coated fabric (1100Dtex) that is highly fire-resistant, and fungus/mold-resistant. These modules' inner liner insulation material is, ideally, cotton, and the floor tiles at minimum, polyvinyl, set in a flooring grid system or a fabric membrane surface anchored to the floor and to the tent. The standard kit-of-parts for maintenance is to also include, at a minimum, anchoring pegs and hammers, manual pump(s), a fabric repair kit, and a detailed technical manual to ensure proper use and maintenance. The prototype field hospital manufactured by AGAR Industries specifies three tent module sizes: large (145 square meters), medium (42 square meters), and small (28 square meters). However, there are exceptions: the isolation wards in the U.S. Army's CSH installations now feature *samehanded* beds (see Case Study 7 in Chapter 6).

Module adjacencies

The positioning of the pre-operative, surgical, and post-operative units is one of the most important factors in the overall success of an RTC. If these component parts are poorly located in relation to one another, a lot can go wrong. It can be miserable to have to cope with cramped and overcrowded quarters in the immediate aftermath of a disaster event. It is not recommended, for instance, for a nurse to have to go outdoors in the rain while on shift unless absolutely necessary to retrieve supplies. The highly skilled physicians, nurses, lab technicians, and logistics specialists who run an RTC must constantly adapt within an atmosphere characterized by unpredictability and sometimes abrupt change. Improvisation is a normative condition, as one often must scurry about elsewhere to locate equipment, supplies, medications, and other essentials otherwise taken for granted in a 'normal' brick and mortar hospital workplace. In an RTC, staffing, logistical support systems, and administrative policies will require continual reassessment on an ad hoc basis to ensure that core zones within the installation, as a system, are working well in terms of their spatial interrelationships. This consists of their physical proximity and orientation to one another, and their degree of interconnectedness. The facility should be assessed continuously to make sure that this is occurring. Position core modules in such a manner that vestibular connections are secure and are weatherproof. This will aid workers who spend their shifts within the core clinical zone.[57] Interconnectedness is dependent upon adjacencies. Some footprints achieve this more than others. SAAB, the Swedish auto manufacturer, recently unveiled (not unlike a new car model) a 'turnkey' RTC it refers to as the portable *Medical Care Solution* (MCS). It is an entirely tent-based RTC that houses triage, major surgery, dentistry, radiology, ICU capability, and inpatient wards. This system maximizes the amenity of the installation footprint.[58] A completely containerized system may feature accordion-like elements between modules, with the modules positioned in a tightly clustered grid. In hybrids, a mixture of tents and containers are set in an orthogonal pattern on the site, similarly connected by fabric vestibules (see Case Studies 3 and 7 in Chapter 6). As for non-orthogonal installations, the *QuickSpace 72* system (see Case Study 5 in Chapter 6) is configured as a pinwheel with a central circulation zone at the center of its five 'fingers.'

Pharmaceuticals

Medications must be stored in secure, containerized bins, in a high-security space yet in a manner that simultaneously facilitates their efficient retrieval and distribution. The threat of break-ins and theft is real in post-disaster strike zones. Security is critical. In fixed-site hospitals, recent research indicates that automated medication dispensing systems such as mobile adaptions of the *Pixis Med Station* can greatly aid in nurse and pharmacist productivity by simplifying workflow patterns and medication distribution times.[59] This has been found to reduce medication wait times, protects against unwanted diversions, can improve data archiving, and result in improved inventory control. A bar-coded system for inventory and storage, dosing, distribution, and dosing container retrieval is recommended. Much improvisation occurs in the field, so it is therefore critical that the medications storage and distribution systems allow for flexibility to a certain extent with regards to the space provided for staff to prepare dosages, and a staging area for their distribution. Borrow as many best practices as possible from well-run comparable systems in brick and mortar hospitals. Field conditions in an RTC or RHC will often be far from perfect—there will, for instance, be little opportunity to incorporate robotic pharmaceutical distribution devices—yet the storage, security, and distribution methodology expressed in the aforementioned *Pixis Med Station* can serve as a model. Because medications will arrive in high-impact plastic modular cases they can immediately be placed in a closepacked arrangement inside a storage module inside the facility. It is not recommended that any dosage prep or dispensing functions be housed in an open unsecured tent, as tents are only minimally securable compared to a hard-walled, containerized module. Wherever possible, provide all medications/pharmacy storage, prep, and distribution functions in a single module within the most highly secure zone on the site. Locate this module next to operating theater modules and pre-operative and post-operative units (Figure 5.18).

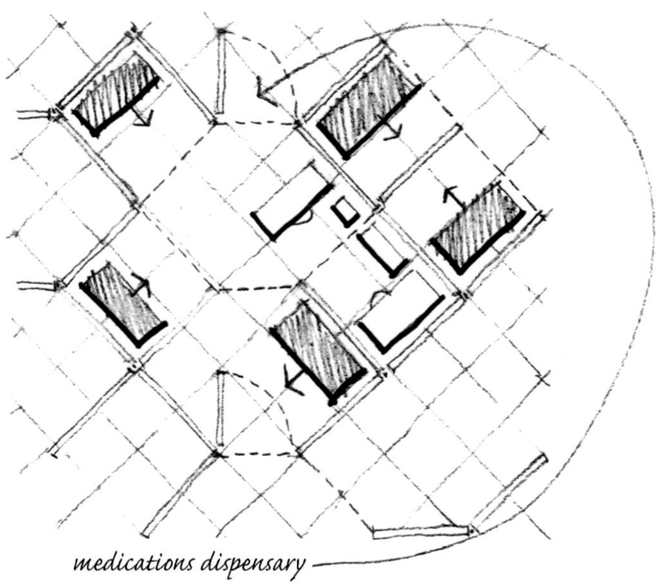

5.18 Pharmaceuticals need to be stored in and dispensed from a secure module

Dietary support

When a local or regional power grid gets knocked out, the local food supply is among the first things to experience breakdown. Few grocery, drug stores, or retail food establishments are resilient enough to withstand a lengthy blackout. Backup generators are costly to purchase and operate over extended periods. Even where backup generation is available, a food establishment's inventory must be sold or given away quickly before its perishables spoil because an outbreak of salmonella can become a secondary disaster in itself, compounding the effects of the first. In the aftermath of Hurricane Alicia in Houston in 1984, *Good Company*, a local Texas 'B-B-Q Shrine' on Kirby Drive, set up an emergency generator the day after, and within one hour customers were lined up around the block. The owners would otherwise have lost tens of thousands of dollars' worth of inventory. But not every situation is like this. Most locally impacted populations within the first week will begin to experience severely diminished food options. The RTC needs to be independent in this regard, when this is possible. In emergencies in the U.S., the U.S. Army and FEMA will bring food into the disaster zone and these supplies are dispensed from numerous makeshift distribution centers, including to medical personnel. In 2009, a catastrophic earthquake destroyed much of the Sumatran city of Pedang, killing many hundreds. Two days later, an Australian private sector corporation provided prefab modular emergency housing and a mobile kitchen, for the staff of the Australian Army's RTC that was deployed to the disaster site. The kitchen was housed in a tent connected to adjoining containerized modules within the installation. This consisted of all-stainless steel full-size freezers, food prep islands, and a dishwasher unit with drying rack, wire rack shelving, all cooking utensils, and large fans to ensure proper natural ventilation. All equipment was securable by means of lock-down wheels.[60] In Port Fouchon, Louisiana, a large white kitchen/dining 'mess hall' tent was erected next to the prefab modular floating dormitory brought in to house many hundreds of migrant oil cleanup workers in the days and weeks after the Gulf of Mexico BP platform explosion in 2010.

Diagnostic imaging

The diagnostic imaging unit must be durable, compact, portable, and quickly serviceable on site because this equipment is technologically precise and can be extremely sensitive to sudden disruptions. The precise calibration, climate control, and security requirements of this equipment requires it is housed in a highly controlled area within the facility. This area must provide protection from excessive temperatures and humidity levels, be away from direct sunlight and excessively noisy areas, be provided with a uniform lighting level, and provide for maximum patient privacy during tests. In most hospitals, the diagnostic imaging suite is relatively unadorned aesthetically, and affords scant sensory amenity for patients or for the direct care providers who staff this department. Recent trends in hospital-based and outpatient diagnostic imaging units have led to aesthetic improvements. These include the use of simulated scenes of nature and simulated natural daylight provided in the form of *faux* windows and skylights, i.e. surrogate windows affording a 'view' of nature via rear-projection. Nature surrogation can now be seen in thousands of diagnostic imaging departments and it has improved their ambiance. Also, calming, soothing, colors can reduce a patient's anxiety and stress level while undergoing tests of this kind as some patients experience claustrophobia while inside a CT scan device. In an RTC, many patients may require diagnostic testing in a very short timeframe and for this reason a separate imaging module is recommended, connected via electric (or manual) doors to adjoining pre-operative and diagnostic and treatment zones. Manufacturers market products, including lightweight, compact digital radiology equipment such as that marketed by Amadeo. Its *M-DR System* and its *Leonardo DR Mini* suitcase are Wi-Fi-powered devices that can be dropped in by parachute and are housed in rugged, shockproof containers. These devices feature a touchscreen and full visual monitor, and are connected to a cloud-based system for accessing/archiving imagery and associated data via the Internet. The benefits of cloud archiving include up-down network scaling and data access, and global connectivity via satellite GPS networks. Another small-scale, portable product, the *dicomPACS DX-R* unit, displays x-ray images on a flat-LED panel display. Its benefits include flexibility, durability, and global IT interfacing.[61]

Personal hygiene

The personal hygiene needs of occupants within an RTC or RHC are multiple and can be deceptively complex. First, staff and patients require restrooms strategically located and fully accessible to persons with physical limitations. The units need to be easily identified whether inboard or outboard. Freestanding modules, apart from the main facility, are frequently used in conjunction with tents; in disaster relief operations. Also, it can often be faster to get a modular bathroom/shower unit shipped to a site, if it is freestanding. If these amenities are located inboard, provide two (or more) patient restrooms adjacent to the main public entrance near the check-in station and main waiting room. Option: designate restrooms as unisex, but if so, also do this in the diagnostic, treatment, and other zones throughout the facility. In spaces of this type, those used by patients, provide an infant changing table. This device may be affixed to a wall and pulled down, or provided as a built-in table or countertop. Provide compartmentalized commode-W/C stalls in bathrooms, and similarly, provide multiple compartmentalized showers. Sinks and urinals are not compartmentalized. Staff will have separate shower accommodations but if their shower room/module is to be communal, it must be out of visual sight of any patients, or others. Whether located indoors or outside, lightweight, waterproof fabric membrane partitions are suitable (depending on the ambient outdoor temperature). Staff personnel often prefer their showering and gowning functions to be housed in a separate zone adjacent to their sleeping quarters yet near to their personal locker, but this may not always be practicable because staff and patient personal hygiene spaces may not be able to be seperate from one another. This is where things can get complicated because, instead, it may be less costly and require shorter, less extensive hoses and plumbing apparatus if the water supply system is centralized, meaning that the staff and patients' personal hygiene spaces may need to be located back to back.

Exam and procedure rooms

Triage, the decontamination unit, surgical unit, clinical support, laboratory, pharmacy, patient wards, and the examination/procedure rooms are indispensable. Following triage, the examination is the point at which a determination is made as to the best course of treatment relative to the type/severity of injury. Important decisions are made as to the best medical care options available on site. The exam/procedure rooms are, ideally, located near the heart of the clinical zone while near to the waiting room, the diagnostic testing unit, laboratory, and medications dispensary, and yet not distant from pre-operative, surgical, and post-operative units. The door to the exam/procedure rooms should not compromise patient privacy or confidentiality. Provide floor and wall surfaces, and equipment and furnishings that can be kept sanitized in order to eliminate any possibility of facility-acquired infection (see above). Provide a gowning alcove within the exam/

5.19 Removing deceased Ebola victims from their homes in Sierra Leone, 2014

procedure room, with a bench, pull curtain, and an examination table, a sink, and work counter with cabinets below and above. The workspace drop-down counter should be large enough for a laptop. Provide space for two chairs. The recommended room size is eighty to ninety square feet for each exam/procedure room, although one or two such rooms may need to be slightly larger (100–110 square feet per room). For example, six exam/procedure rooms of one size and two somewhat larger exam/procedure rooms may be positioned along the same corridor in a single cluster. In some situations, it may be preferable for all eight rooms to be identical in size so any (or all) rooms can become *acuity adaptable*—able to be used in a step-up manner in accord with the intensity of the care required. As for furnishings, select a lightweight exam/procedure table. Equipment and furnishings should be plugged into the walls of the module. Provide clip-on cabinets for medical supplies. A pair of side-by-side rooms should be reconfigurable into a single space by removing shared wall partitions.

Infectious disease installations

Ebola, previously known as the Ebola hemorrhagic fever, is rare and deadly, caused by contracting infection from one of the five Ebola virus strains. The disease was first discovered in 1976 near the Ebola River in what is now the Democratic Republic of Congo. Since, small-scale outbreaks have occurred sporadically in West Africa. The natural reservoir host of the Ebola virus remains unknown. However, on the basis of evidence and the nature of similar viruses, researchers believe this virus is animal-borne and that bats are the most likely host species. Four of its five virus strains occur in an animal host native to Africa. The Ebola pandemic in West Africa presents a continued public health threat. As of January 2015, more than 6,500 victims had died, and the general public had difficulty grasping the gravity of the global public health threat (Figure 5.19).[62] This disease was the subject of the 1995 film *Outbreak*. It depicted a rural town in the Northwest U.S. overtaken by the disease; this film attempted to realistically depict the use of containerized isolation ICU units.[63] RTCs dedicated for this purpose becomes, in effect, quarantine hospitals. Ebola is a vicious disease that completely overtakes the human immune system with great rapidity, its victims dying within weeks after first contracting the infection. The dire shortage of hospital beds to treat Ebola victims in Monrovia, Liberia in the fall of 2014 became so severe that ambulances would pick up persons raging with the symptoms, sometimes drive them aimlessly for hours, then drop them back at their home because nowhere were there available beds to take them for treatment. The odds of surviving Ebola at home, without intravenous hydration, are slim to none. Health workers complained they could not throw down mattresses on the floor fast enough in

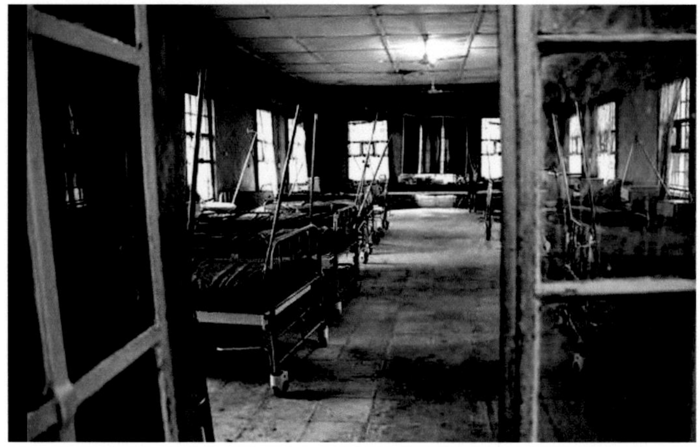

5.20 Abandoned Kenema District Hospital, Sierra Leone, 2014

the hospitals and makeshift clinics that were set up, and numerous hospitals in the region themselves were abandoned for fear that *they* too had become infection-spreading agents (Figure 5.20). Some organizations, including *Médecins Sans Frontières* (MSF)—Doctors Without Borders—asked European nations and the United States for disaster medical aid as the disease spread from country to country. A WHO-run clinic opened in what was a former dental office and it became severely overcrowded the day it opened. Meanwhile, across town, workers at a Doctors Without Borders clinic assembled a 400-bed tent infirmary in the mud and rain. Required equipment for this type of intensive care facility includes hundreds of head-to-toe protective suits for the caregivers, at least 25,000 liters of water, and 2,500 gallons of bleach—on hand every day.[64] The British set up a semi-permanent eighty-bed RTC at Kerry Town, in Sierra Leone. Completed in just eight weeks, six more tent clinics would be built, bringing the total capacity to 700 beds. British funding was provided for burial teams as well as for the establishment of nearly 100 walk-in treatment stations in towns and villages.[65]

Infectious disease ICUs

The WHO stipulates that an Ebola infectious disease quarantine unit—a facility entirely devoted to Ebola—should admit no more than 200 patients at any one time. This maximum capacity requires a staff of 300–600 highly trained specialists. Five stages of diagnosis and treatment govern care in an Ebola RTC field hospital (Figure 5.21a–b): (1) *Triage area*—Patients with symptoms indicative of an Ebola infection are examined in an open-air tent by medical workers wearing highly protective clothing. (2) *Low-probability holding ward*—Persons who might not have Ebola are held here for hours (or days) until tests reveal whether they are victims. (3) *High-probability ward*—If the medical staff suspects the individual has contracted the disease, the individual is cared for in this tent until final test results are in. (4) *Ebola ward*—Confirmed cases are treated here. Because no cure yet exists, the medical staff can provide only palliative (comfort and pain-relieving) care which, in some cases, can increase one's chances of survival. (5) *Morgue*—In some towns, as many as 75 percent of all contracted cases die. Bodies are stored temporarily in a morgue tent until proper burial can take place locally. All medical waste is incinerated a short distance from the field hospital. Two fences surround the entire installation.

Four more tents provide additional essential functions: (6) *Main entrance tent*—Patients with clear signs of an Ebola infection are taken straight to the Ebola ward without passing through triage. (7) *Dressing room tent*—Medical staff entering the clinic don protective equipment, consisting of a dressing gown, apron, respirator, surgical cap, goggles, vinyl boots and two pairs of gloves. Clinical staff work in pairs of two, checking one another's suits for any small tears or openings. (8) *Undressing room tent*—Workers here undress very slowly and carefully to prevent self-infection, washing hands after removing each item of protective clothing. Some equipment can be reused after sterilization, most items must be incinerated immediately. (9) *Recovered patient exit tent*—Recovered patients take an antiseptic shower, put on clean street clothes and pass through multiple decontamination basins before departing. No longer infectious, these individuals now carry antibodies against reacquiring the virus for as many as ten years.[66]

In reality, variations of this protocol exist but every treatment center must adhere to minimum WHO standards. Some encampments are housed entirely in tents, while others are housed in offsite-built prefab modules shipped in and then commissioned on site in conjunction with the tent-wards. Every RTC brought into the afflicted region for Ebola victims, to date, has been some sort of prefab system, whether containerized, tent-based, or a hybrid. Humanitarian NGOs took the lead early on in the portable facility procurement process.

Laboratories

When *Doctors Without Borders* established the first of its three 100-bed Stage 1-RTCs in Haiti in 2010, it brought in two surgical units, a recovery area, an intensive care unit, a trauma care unit, and physical rehabilitation services. This totaled forty-five tons of equipment and was supplied by logistics centers in Europe and Central America. The RTC was assembled in three days on a continuous twenty-four-hour basis. The hospital had to be shipped first to the Dominican Republic and then trucked overland to Port-au-Prince. Its equipment included plastic flooring, tents, air conditioners, generators, communications equipment and beds, as well as surgical equipment,

5.21a–c World Health Organization recommended layout for an Ebola infirmary in West Africa, 2014

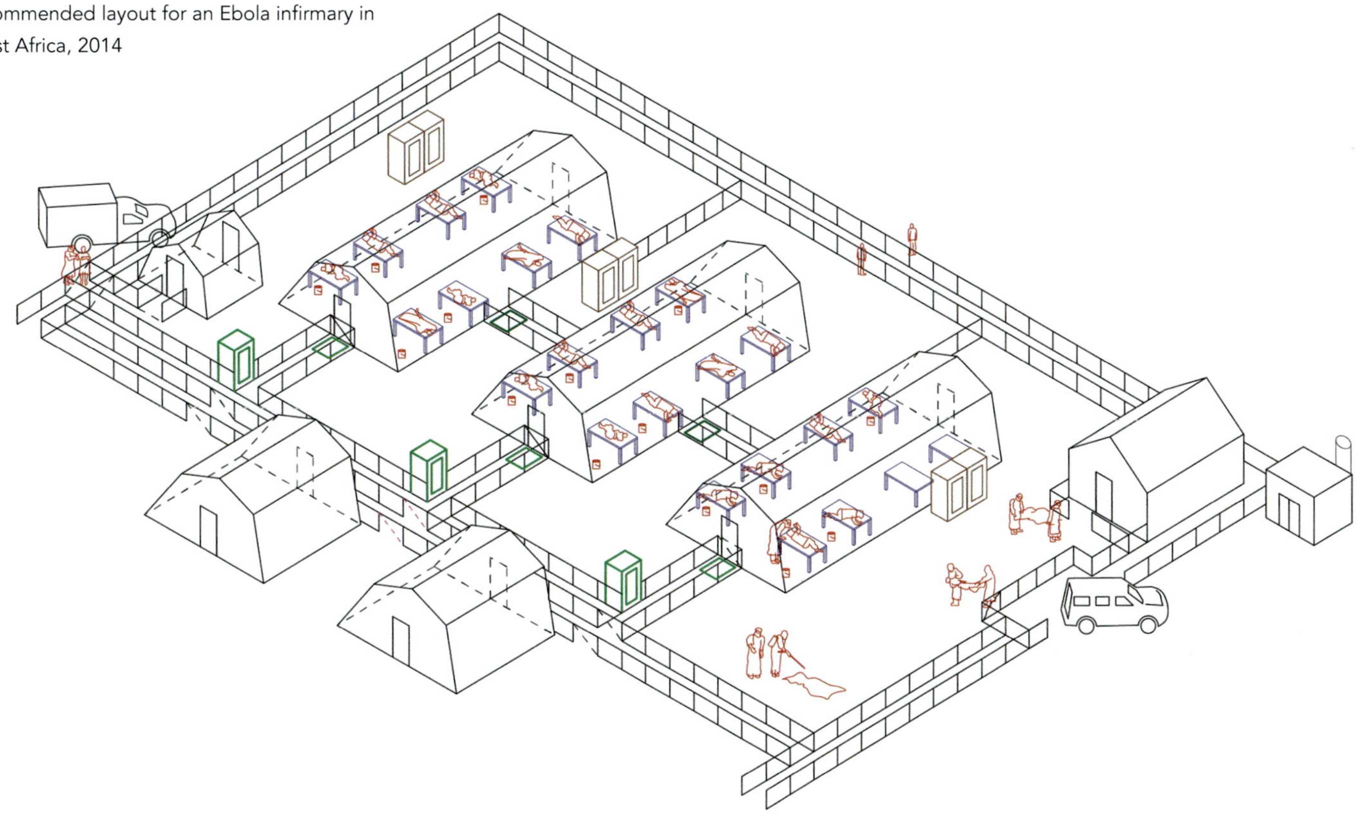

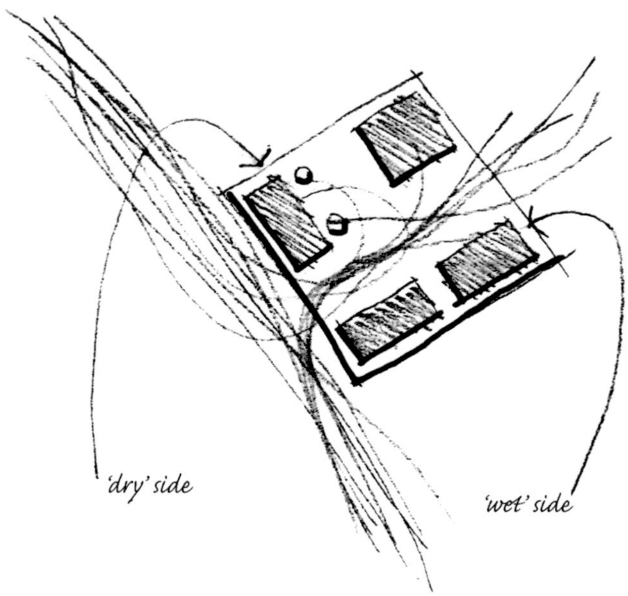

5.22 Create a compact laboratory with compartmentalized workstations, refrigeration unit(s), and secure storage for medical supplies

diagnostic machines, laboratory test equipment, and pharmaceuticals. Pneumatic pumps inflated the tents and when fully inflated a 'plug and play' system commenced whereby EKG machines, autoclaves for equipment sterilization, defibrillators, and the lab equipment was set up, including a blood bank. Thirty physicians and support personnel staffed this facility working on eight-hour and twelve-hour staggered shifts. During a twenty-four-hour period, eighty to one hundred medical personal were on duty to treat the many hundreds of patients in need. Medical supplies were refreshed weekly by a central pharmacy established locally, brought in by sea.[67] The lab had a 'wet' side and a general 'dry' test-workspace side. Two full-size refrigerators were for specimens and supplies, compartmentalized stainless steel and high impact plastic sinks, one workstation on each side of the lab, and a toilet/sink compartment. Provide proper ventilation and lighting. The DMAT team dispatched from Australia in the aftermath of the Asian Tsunami in December 2004 reported that its strong laboratory logistics team was paramount in that operation's overall success.[68] Many RTC laboratories are housed in securable tents. In the case of a module, its features and equipment may require some reworking, i.e. the location and type of doors and whether sliding or hinged. Include one or more one foot by one foot stainless steel pass-through portals for staff to transfer paperwork, patient specimens, and other items from nurse to lab tech without having to walk down a corridor to and from the laboratory. Containerized ISO modules generally work well as RTC labs and if additional capacity is needed an additional module can be added (Figure 5.22).

Patient confidentiality

Nurses and physicians often say that, in an emergency, privacy is the last thing on anyone's mind. There are many more urgent matters to attend to and in a life or death situation anything goes, basically. But this need not imply that privacy is dismissible, or of no consequence. *Personal Health Information* (PHI) consists of any identifying information about an individual obtained in oral or recorded form, if that information relates directly to the physical or mental health of the individual. This includes information on the health history of an individual's family, or significant others. It relates to the anticipation of care to be provided to an individual in an organized, systematic manner; it relates to payments made or the eligibility for care with respect to an individual; it relates to the extraction from an individual of any body part or bodily fluid; it pertains to the identity of an individual's legal decision maker, if not him or herself. For the caregiver, all ethical obligations are to be complied with, and especially those that establish and preserve the highest degree of patient–caregiver trust. The patient's PHI must remain confidential because maintaining this is fundamental to being able to provide a high standard of patient care. Patients who trust their private information will remain so are more likely to provide the caregiver with accurate and full disclosure and this will, in theory, result in better treatment.[69] Highly trafficked circulation zones in an RTC or RHC are usually in and near the main entrance and the intake/interview and waiting areas. In a double-loaded corridor layout, for instance, it is not preferable from the patient's perspective for passersby to be able to see directly in, or by looking directly across the hall. It is recommended that doors be staggered because, otherwise, patient confidentiality will be diminished. Sometimes this may be unavoidable, such as the physician who

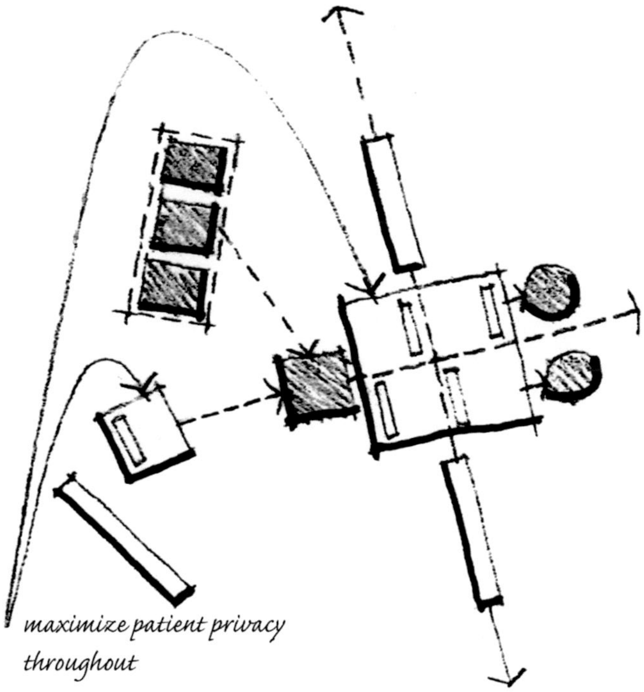

5.23 Respect the needs and wishes of patients and their families

prefers moving as expediently as possible from one examination room to the next through interconnected doors that are always kept open. Second, the location of the exam/procedure table is important as this equally relates to patient privacy. Consideration of these issues will result in a more compassionate healthcare environment (Figure 5.23).

Prospect-refuge amenities

Staff burnout is a major concern in humanitarian relief operations. A 'normal' tour of duty may be for three months, then a nurse or physician returns home. Reinforcements are brought in and the pattern repeats itself. On a day-to-day basis, however, things can get difficult when one is so far from home and away from friends and

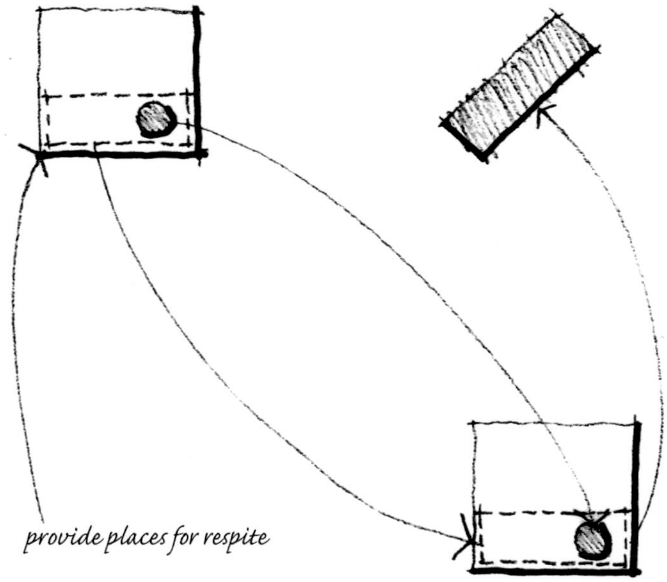

5.24 Provide a place to briefly get away from a chaotic work environment

family. Sometimes one just needs to get away for a moment, away from a chaotic, unpredictable work setting where things seem so discombobulated. This is particularly so in tight, overcrowded work settings with few if any 'relief valves' to depressurize the work atmosphere. An overcrowded or otherwise stressful work environment serves no one's best interests—neither caregiver, nor patient. An exam room too cramped with equipment with little room to maneuver is a source of dissatisfaction for a nurse or physician. He or she makes the best of a difficult situation. With every square foot in a portable structure for healthcare at a premium due to so many limiting factors, it stands to reason pressure can be considerable during programming and schematic design for the system designer to pack as much into as small an area as possible—where 'X number of modules *must* support X number of procedures each day.' Prospect-refuge theory speaks to the value of providing the caregiver with options to 'get away' without physically getting away completely. This is important in any healthcare environment, whether in an ICU, adult psychiatric hospital or a hospice.[70] *Prospect,* here, denotes being with others while engaged cooperatively in carrying out one's daily responsibilities, whereas *refuge* denotes the need at some times to disengage—to extract oneself from the work setting to 'restore' or recharge. This can simply consist of gazing out a window for a short time, going to a staff break area/kitchen, or a patio behind a screened wall. Or this may require going to a separate tent that houses a staff break room/kitchen. This also pertains to an RHC located in an urban neighborhood where its mission is to care for the medically underserved. Strive to design one or more of such spaces for the caregiver on site, as this can result in less staff fatigue and burnout (Figure 5.24).

Positive distractions

Most container modules adapted for use as RTCs and RHCs are windowless. Their windowlessness is striking and is tantamount to sensory deprivation. Such conditions can be stressful. Worse, the standard ISO container can be claustrophobic. Humanize these containers by creating visual connectivity with the external world. Views to outside, and interior wall murals, have become integral to many hospitals; murals are one way to bring the exterior world indoors in otherwise windowless spaces. A long tradition includes the large-scale health-themed mural created by Gordon Cullen for the main lobby of the Finsbury Health Centre, in London (1936–1938).[71] Here, with art, the health center's mission was celebrated. Art can be used as a spatial orientation device to enhance wayfinding. Second, artworks can create an 'event space,' transforming a drab wall or corridor into something memorable. In the U.S., Robin C. Hanson is a leader in the incorporation of murals as positive distractions in hospitals and specialty outpatient clinics. Her installations are found at key intersections of corridors and in various rooms throughout. These photomurals depict iconic natural scenes such as waterfalls, forests, and bodies of water (Figures 5.25 and 5.26). Scenes are sampled for their intrinsic therapeutic affordances and are often colorful, vibrant, and serve as directional/navigational aids (see Chapter 4). Exam, consult rooms, waiting areas, labs, and other staff work zones can be made more interesting in this way.

5.25 Nature surrogates afford visual and cognitive respite

5.26 Install surrogate representations of nature in places where they can provide the maximum therapeutic amenity

Naturescape installations have been in use in hospitals for decades—why not creatively experiment with them in a portable healthcare structure?

5 Pop-up clinics

Historic buildings

Vacant warehouses, churches, theaters, commercial storefronts, schools, and gymnasiums await new lives as potential hosts for pop-up clinics. In historic landmark districts located in coastal cities vulnerable to rising seas due to global climate change, cities that include San Francisco, London, Tokyo, New York, New Orleans, Singapore, and Miami, opportunities await to adapt historic, endangered buildings to healthcare uses both for normal everyday use, and for use in the aftermath of disaster. In everyday situations, a host can provide existing physical space that would otherwise be so difficult to secure, and after a disaster, a host structure may need only minimal repairs to be suitable. As part of the work of local EOCs, it would be prudent for these organizations to generate a list of buildings potentially available in their area for this purpose. Either way, it is recommended that due diligence guide this process *a priori* with regards to any building being considered as a host. Comparative due diligence should guide the process; assess multiple candidates for their suitability. In emergencies, be open-minded to unconventional solutions because sometimes serendipity will occur. It just may be that that old movie theater, school gym, or warehouse may in fact work out even though at first sight it may appear hopeless. Persevere, and if it is available, the owner just might be willing to provide favorable lease (or purchase) terms. If the infrastructural start-up costs to be incurred are minimal, and if it already has operational plumbing, HVAC and electrical systems, it just might work out—but any final decision should be based on the recommendation of a consulting architect (Figure 5.27). Keep in mind that it may seem a bizarre fit at first. However, don't force-fit an installation into an obviously incompatible host—be cautious, deliberate, yet open-minded. Interview persons knowledgeable with the immediate neighborhood who are familiar with the structure; seek out persons who know its strengths as well as limitations with regards to the potential for its temporary adaptation into an outpatient health clinic. Conduct a SWOT analysis—strengths, weaknesses, opportunities and threats—with respect to any potential host structure. To date, a key precedent is the vacant Lord & Taylor department store in downtown New Orleans that was converted into an 18,000 square foot pop-up clinic right after Hurricane Katrina in 2005 (see Chapter 4). Prior, in that situation, numerous potential hosts were comparatively studied within a very short time frame.[72]

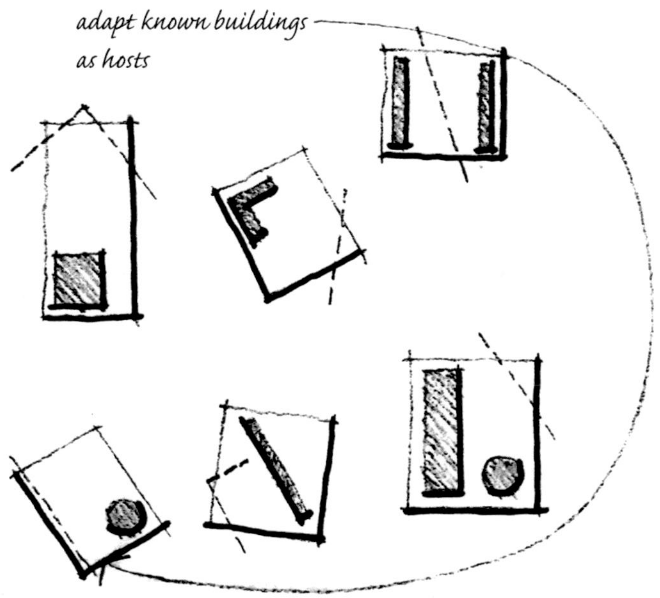

5.27 Assess diverse types of existing buildings as host structures for pop-up clinics

Evaluating a host structure

When multiple host structures are in consideration for a pop-up clinic, it is prudent, as mentioned, to comparatively weigh the options before jumping into anything prematurely. *Tissue sampling* consists of a process whereby the host structure, its immediate environs, and its neighborhood/urban context are comparatively documented, with the host candidate geographically situated at the heart of any urban contextual tissue to be sampled. Documentation should consist, at a minimum, of photographs and the production of a series of base maps that document land uses, parking availability, natural and landscape features, existing utilities, and the condition of adjoining buildings and any open space. If, say, six host candidates are to be assessed, this compare/contrast process constitutes due diligence. It is recommended an architect compile this information. Additional maps can be prepared of hosts' urban fabric contexts, such as neighborhood landmarks and anomalies in the spirit of Lynch's classic book *Image of the City*.[73] Examples of memorable buildings and places in a local area may include a large commercial billboard that teeters atop a small red frame house, or an unsightly cellphone transmission tower—in short, anything that sticks out as unusual or unexpected but is memorable for some reason. Base maps should document all existing healthcare facilities in the study area, inpatient and outpatient, and all primary and secondary streets, local census tract statistics, pertinent *Geographic Information Systems* (GIS) data, and environmental concerns such as whether the site is a brownfield or greyfield site.[74] Document any public gathering places that have a tendency to attract loitering or any unsavory activities, and document all building setbacks, height restrictions, bike lane availability, transit links, sidewalks and pedestrian paths such as through a nearby park. Also record experiential data such as sources of undue noise, odors, smoke, and other environmental pollutants (see Chapter 4). This mapping process will yield a visual and quantitative profile of the host's neighborhood and the broader urban fabric.[75] As mentioned above, a host candidate may seem at first an odd fit but may in fact turn out to be excellent—this will depend on the willingness of the stakeholders to keep an open mind and a willingness to take a calculated risk.

Preparing a host structure

Once a host structure has been selected, it probably will need some degree of retrofitting, including its air conditioning, heating, plumbing, lighting, security, and electrical systems. Some modifications to one or more of these building systems will likely be necessary for the host to meet minimum code requirements for occupancy. In some situations, a waiver of a local zoning classification may be required. These issues can hold a project up for weeks if not months. It can be exasperating if a client discovers the need for costly retrofitting after the lease has been signed, or the building has been purchased. During due diligence, therefore, assess the host for anything that must be done to ensure it will support the modular installation. Make the most of what is already there. The advantages of this strategy include cost savings and less prep time required from project start to move-in day. Submitting a set of contractual drawings to city hall for plan and code review can be an exasperating process in and of itself. After Katrina in 2005, the Building Permit Section at New Orleans City Hall was overwhelmed with plan review submittals as thousands of citizens began the arduous process of repairs needed so they could return home. Soon, the office was three months behind but even in normal times, code and plan review can be a lengthy process. Regarding any host, the following systems must be carefully assessed for their condition, age, and operability: HVAC and electrical capacity, plumbing and water supply, natural gas, sewerage capacity, any existing security system, live load-bearing capacities, and the structural integrity of the physical envelope and its foundation. Also, it may be necessary to replace some existing windows or doors, repair a roof damaged in the disaster, and to weatherproof the masonry to repair cracks and other things that can lead to worse problems later. One advantage of a pop-up, ideally, is its ability to be relatively self-reliant. But at the same time it is best to strive for a 50/50 balance or better, where the host provides the majority of systems support, i.e. the electricity and plumbing/sewerage. The modular installation will bring onboard its own plumbing tie-ins and HVAC system because, for one, the pop-up will require many more sinks than the host probably has, and second, this higher number of sinks will place a burden on the existing drainage/sewerage capacity. Strive to achieve balance. If need be, ductwork, electrical cables, and water lines can be brought into the host from equipment set up outside the building, using umbilical links feeding into the building envelope. Another example of a 50/50 balance would be the use of the host's ceiling light fixtures together with the installation's onboard lighting system.

Strategic partnering

A pop-up clinic need not be financed or operated solely by any single healthcare organization, whether its lead sponsor is in the public or the private sector. If the intent is for it to operate as one site within a larger network, with staff personnel moving from location to location, a partnership can be beneficial to all parties.

Perhaps a local for-profit urban medical center wishes to partner with an international NGO, i.e. a private foundation whose focus is healthcare. This can make it possible for the medical center to reestablish its footprint in the community relatively quickly while its main campus is being repaired or rebuilt such as in the event a tidal surge inundates the medical center's first floor, for instance, with the repairs projected to require a year or longer to complete. A pop-up installation is ideally positioned to provide a continuous flow of services to medically underserved patient populations who would otherwise be cut off from medical care. In this way, primary care and urgent care services can continue uninterrupted, including immunizations, prenatal and well baby examinations, nutritional counseling, diagnosis and treatment of mental illness, prosthetic fitting and outpatient rehabilitation services, screening and treatment for TB and HIV/AIDS, pre-cancer screening, and minor surgical procedures. After a disaster, being able to maintain continuity of care makes it more possible for a displaced population to return home. The other commonly used strategy is for the external NGO, such as Doctors Without Borders, to come in and set up its own clinics independent of any local healthcare provider. Whether in post-disaster or routine everyday contexts, the pop-up can function as an effective prosthetic device, reinforcing and extending the reach of available services in the local community. Beforehand, as previously discussed, identify and secure the financing, leasing or purchase of the host and complete all zoning, plan review, and code approval steps, and retrofit the host as required. Identify any partner organizations, determine the administrative hierarchy, and develop a sustainable staffing (or co-staffing) plan. Perhaps the local medical center, after seeing how a first local pop-up succeeds, will opt to set up two or three more in the metro area while the infrastructure of its main campus is being repaired. The Memorial Hospital System in Tampa, Florida has taken steps to ensure the relative continuity of its services in this way by establishing partnerships with numerous local providers, in anticipation of future need.[76]

Phased installations

A high percentage of permanent site hospitals and clinics are planned for phased expansion on their sites. This expansion might happen over a period of many years, involving the demolition of existing structures. Expansion may occur in an existing parking lot; regardless, this process requires gathering together many types of data. These data, presumably, will lead to sound decisions and actions while simultaneously yielding a master plan with multiple contingencies and optional courses of action. One of these contingencies is being able to project the level of patient utilization of the pop-up installation on opening day, a month later, six months, a year later, and so on. This process calls for deliberate, structured due diligence because without this everything is reduced to guesswork. Its physical size, staffing, equipment, and day-to-day scheduling will depend on this information. The repurposing of a host structure requires knowing beforehand its minimum capacity as well as its maximum capacity. In situations where uncertainty prevails on this point, it is recommended that a host be selected that allows for additional modules to be installed at a later time, perhaps in a two-phase strategy. In Phase I, core modules are installed allowing, say, for a maximum capacity of eight examination rooms. In Phase II, six additional exam room modules and a larger lab module are installed. When growth needs outstrip a host's available physical space, it will in all likelihood be necessary to install all-weather modules, outdoors (because pop-ups are typically not designed for all-weather conditions). These units can be installed on the same site right next to the host structure if space permits. Containers have many advantages in this scenario because they are adaptable and can work off the same power generation source. Containers are in wide use as dwellings, schools, dormitories, clinics, emergency shelters, libraries, and police substations. In 2003, the firm *HyBrid Architecture* coined the term *cargotecture* and it captures containers' broad adaptability. These units can be slotted into narrow sites by means of a crane, shipped to remote sites, and stacked vertically. This last option can be appropriate for the provision of onsite temporary accommodations for staff personnel. In June of 2010, *Hospitals of Hope* deployed two of its containerized 'Clinics in a Can' to Haiti in partnership with *Heart to Heart International*.[77] In November of that same year, *Containers 2 Clinics* commissioned its first of three containerized women's health clinics, and installed it next to the Grace Children's Hospital, in Port-au-Prince (see Chapter 6).

Patient intake (pop-ups)

In permanent site hospitals and clinics, widely accepted space planning templates exist for the layout of patient sign-in, interview, and waiting areas. Best practices in this regard are widely emulated within the healthcare industry. In the U.S., minimum standards for the provision of patient confidentiality within these parts of a facility are governed by the *Health Insurance Portability and Accountability Act of 1996* (HIPAA).[78] This legislation applies to both permanent site, and portable, redeployable healthcare facilities on U.S. soil. But in the chaotic conditions of a portable field hospital, in reality, minimum standards for patient confidentiality are very difficult to put in place or adhere to. But this does not justify throwing aside any consideration of, or provisions for, patient privacy and confidentiality with respect to one's sensitive medical information. One or more intake/interview stations may be set up, ad hoc, side-by-side along a circulation path, allowing for multiple, interview/intake sessions to occur at once. The number of such stations should be correlated with the type of the facility and its bed capacity, if inpatient care is to be provided on site. Align these intake/interview stations directly across from a main waiting area while not far from the main public entrance. The door or threshold at each station should be, if an actual door, made of 'vision' Plexiglas or another type of light-emitting inset panel. Swing doors will require too much space and can cause run-in accidents in highly trafficked areas. Instead, provide a sliding pocket door, if feasible, or a simple side-pull accordion door that when fully pulled shut will afford an acceptable level of visual and acoustical separation. As for the desktop work surface within each station, allow for this surface to be either snapped in, a drop-down, or a clip-on device, placed between the station's two sidewalls. On the backside (staff side) of this space, the staff person should have open, direct access to a shared work zone without having to pass through a door or curtain. In the intake/interview station, provide space for two chairs on the patient side and for a single chair on the station's inner side, for the staff person. The dimensions of each station should be no less than five feet wide by eight feet deep. A ten-foot depth is most preferable. Within this space, do not install any type of separating Plexiglas window between the patient and the corresponding staff person. These stations may be equipped with either an open, or dropped ceiling grid with infill panels, depending on the ceiling height of the host structure, and any security requirements pre-specified for the overall installation.

Expandable components

Pop-up modules must function autonomously, as a self-contained entity, yet plug into a larger modular platform. As one part of a larger system, every unit must be designed and manufactured to withstand being pushed to its limit in order for it to contribute maximally to the success of the total installation. A given module must double or even sometimes triple function in this regard, i.e. a wall panel will provide visual privacy while also housing electrical conduit, plumbing lines, and/or an operable sliding window, as well as a drop down bench or work surface. In some situations a module will also be expandable outward or upward within, or as an extension of, its larger system. Total system X by Y by Z coordinate integration is essential, multi-dimensionally, and with respect to each module's onboard componentry—its wall panels, flooring, ceilings, lighting, plug-in/clip-on storage bins, horizontal work surfaces, drop-down/pullout seating devices, privacy sliding or accordion doors, and so on. It is a precise kit-of-parts. When assembled in its base condition, a system's constituent modules, collectively, become, in effect, a *machine for health*. In the experimental Architecture+Health studio at Clemson University in 2013, a prototype diagnostic/treatment room module developed by George Hughes featured expandable componentry, within a base configuration/footprint. This footprint can accommodate equipment within it such as a meds dispensary (Figure 5.28). The ability of certain inner parts of this module to become larger, expanding, either outward or upward in physical size requires a ceiling that can be removed, or can itself become a pop-up device. A host structure may impose certain limits on the ability for this to occur, however, due to a low ceiling height or other limitations. Vertical/horizontal expansion of this type may be possible, nevertheless, at the next deployment site. As discussed earlier, horizontal expansion needs may call for additional containerized units to be added to the installation site, outdoors, in proximity to the host structure. A pop-up should be expandable by means of this and other types of modular and aggregate platform components. One example of a containerized unit that expresses

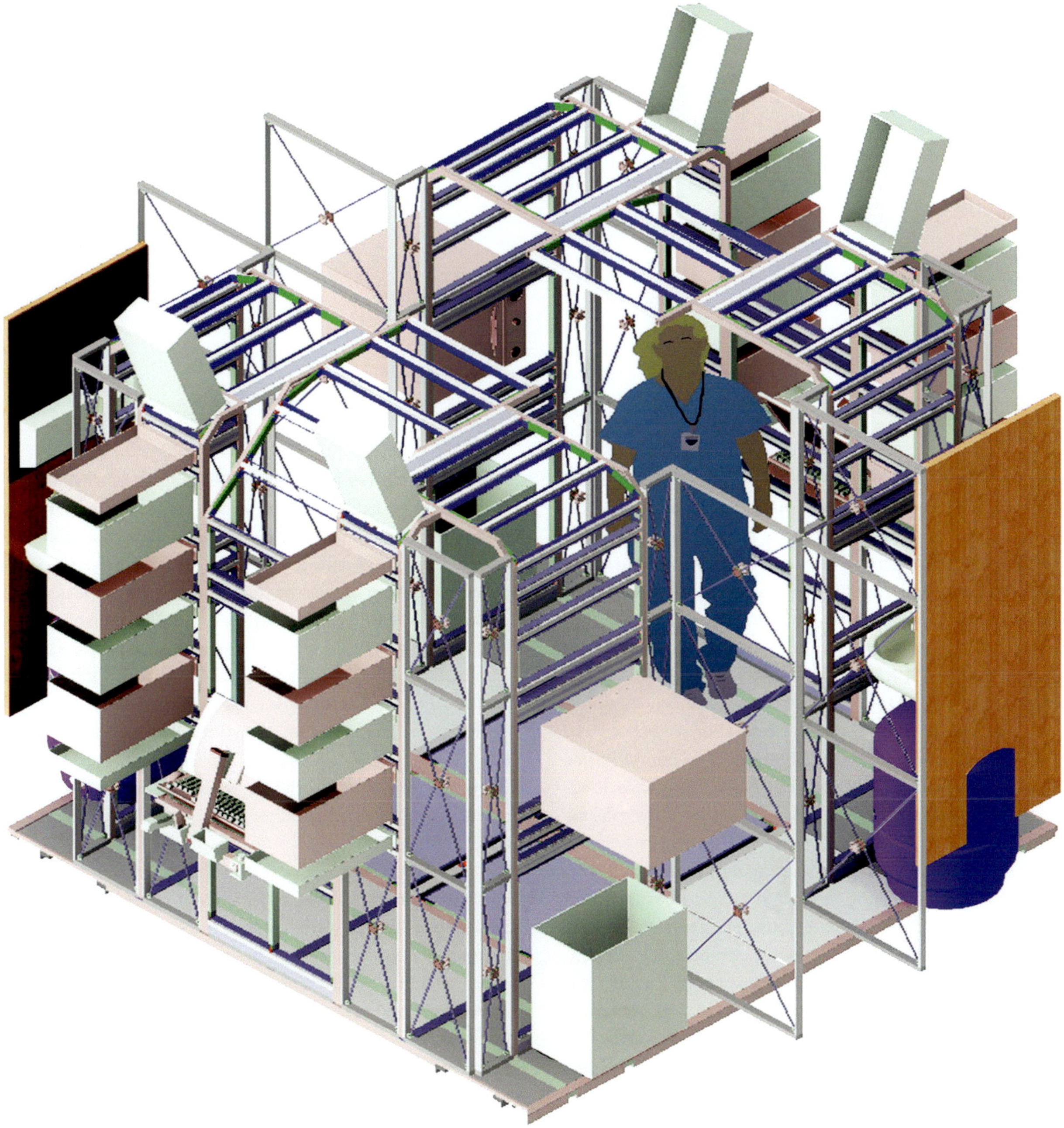

5.28 A pop-up pharmacy module with a lightweight shelving-rack system

this type of expandability is the *RxBox* prototype developed at Rensselaer Polytechnic Institute, in upstate New York. This unit features a pop-up solar screen device mounted three feet above the roof of the container (Figure 5.29).[79]

Repurpose vacant buildings

An abandoned Sears's department store, or a vacant, castoff Wal-Mart, J.C. Penny's, Circuit City, or Best Buy electronics store all hold tremendous potential for repurposing as a pop-up host structure.[80] Since the typical, abandoned mass retail big-box store carcass is BIG—50,000+ square feet in size, and with so many out there, new uses are called for. These immense building envelopes

5.29 Clip-on sunscreen device atop the RxBox prototype, Rensselaer Polytechnic Institute, New York State, 2012

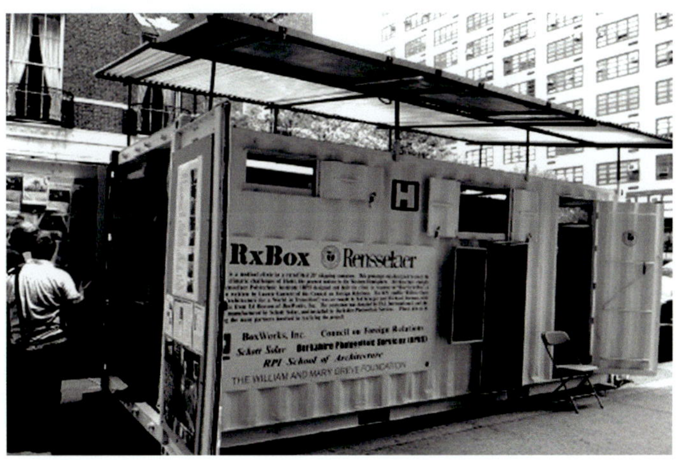

will otherwise just continue to sit idle, blighting their communities. Bring together a variety of health-related stores and medical services. A patient coming to one of these repurposed buildings can have his or her prescriptions after a clinic appointment. An effective mixture of services might include a pharmacy, outpatient physical rehabilitation medicine, a podiatry clinic, a wellness/fitness center, a mobility assistance aid store, and an ophthalmologist's office. It may be necessary to amend existing zoning laws to allow for this to happen. But this strategy can help to improve medically underserved populations' access to healthcare in everyday situations, and/or resuscitate communities impacted by disaster. Some of the occupants of a repurposed big-box host may be permanent tenants, while others perhaps may be on site on a temporary basis. Either way, this arrangement can provide the local community with a broader range of goods and services accessible within walking, biking, or a short car trip than would otherwise be the case. Conduct due diligence and adopt best practices from elsewhere in identifying and adapting vacant big-box carcasses located along public transit routes. In St. Bernard Parish, Louisiana, after Hurricane Katrina in 2005, the sole local Wal-Mart in the parish was flooded with ten feet of floodwater and sat abandoned for five years before it was eventually gutted and re-commissioned as a Wal-Mart once again. Instead, this carcass could have been repurposed to aid in the disaster relief and it would have been a win-win for the general public and for Wal-Mart's international PR machine. Wal-Mart did, reluctantly, agree, six months after the flood, to allow the St. Bernard Health Center to set up its operations in four prefab modular FEMA travel trailers on one corner of the vast Wal-Mart parking lot.[81] This clinic functioned there for three years, and it was a success by nearly any measure. Nonetheless, a major opportunity was missed to house a modular pop-up within the footprint of the big box months (if not years) sooner.

Modular ceilings (pop-ups)

A pop-up should be designed and built to fit into diverse host structures whose ceilings will vary from a minimum height of twelve feet to twenty-five feet or more. Examples of low-ceiling buildings include office buildings and older storefront commercial spaces. Building types with ceilings suitably high to qualify as a host structure include auditoriums, gyms, warehouses, banks, larger commercial spaces such as the vacant shells of mass merchandising outlets, or even a shopping mall food court (see Chapter 4). As mentioned earlier, in New Orleans, the Louisiana State University/Health Sciences Center's (LSU/HSC) pop-up clinic in New Orleans was set up weeks after Hurricane Katrina in 2005 in a vacant Lord & Taylor department store. It eventually grew to a size of 18,000 square feet, filling the abandoned department store. Its ceilings were too high, unfortunately, and did not provide an adequate measure of security for either staff personnel or for the patients. In a POE conducted by this author, with the Clemson University Team 899 in 2013, it was learned that that the majority of staff persons who had worked at this clinic since it opened cited its chronically poor acoustics as one of the most unnerving and chronically unmanageable aspects of their entire experience. Not a single room partition wall within this pop-up installation was equipped with a dropped (secondary) ceiling. This caused a pervasive lack of patient confidentiality because people could readily look into virtually any partition from the floor level above due to the large central atrium. This type of host may have been far more suitable if the pop-up modules had come equipped with their own independent ceiling grid system. Therefore, design each pop-up module, and the larger system of which it is a part, with the option for built-in, fixed ceiling panels set within a uniform grid. Panels can be installed, initially, and then removed later if for some reason it is decided it would be better to modify the ceiling system so that the grid is open, in some, but not all parts of the installation. Or, the ceiling grid may be from the outset left open entirely; this option can be the best of both worlds, especially in the case of a sufficiently low ceiling, because a grid left open allows the host's lighting to bathe interior spaces of the pop-up. Also, being able to look upward can create a greater sense of spaciousness. Maintain human scale without compromising privacy or security requirements, and if loss of privacy or excessive noise is expected to be a problem, specify a fixed ceiling inset panel with its own lighting system.

6 Facility tectonics

Virtues of low-tech

Sustainable materiality has become a catchphrase in architecture. It denotes the use of ecologically sensitive building materials in both old and new ways. Designers, for their part, are currently experimenting with a wide array of strategies to achieve this. Japanese architect Shigeru Ban has designed experimental structures using ecologically sensitive materials, including cardboard tubes, and has applied his approach to temporary disaster housing for places as geographically and culturally diverse as Haiti, Rwanda, and Japan.[82] Most people view cardboard tubes as fit for nothing more than the recycle bin, yet his research has led to new possibilities in paper-fabricated emergency shelters. Others are experimenting with bamboo as a structural material in emergency housing, using center pole and/or support beam technical applications. This consists of interdependency within a unified structural system. A shelter of this type can be erected with a minimum of poles. One such system, the *Reciproboo* shelter, utilizes a four-pole configuration whose nucleus is a simple square frame—this provides a basis for the addition of sidewalls and a roof. The poles are laid together in an overlapping fashion, based on the square. Twine is used to bundle the poles together and then the frame is elevated and held aloft by two poles, and anchored to the ground using cable or rope. Fabric tarp or plastic sheathing is then applied to the framework for shade and protection from the elements. The basic kit-of-parts includes seven poles, a tarpaulin, twine and rope, with everything configured in a modular fashion to yield a strong shelter form. Each unit provides 220 square feet of interior usable space and can be assembled for under $100. Its designers are at present in the process of sharing this low-tech modular design solution with a number of international NGO disaster aid agencies and recently conducted a workshop in Nepal using green bamboo poles as structural elements. This very basic, low-tech solution, to date, however, has not been fully tested in an actual disaster strike zone.[83] Regardless, it is a promising example of a low-tech approach to affordable post-disaster sheltering, designed and produced in a DIY spirit. From this standpoint, the classic *yurt* structural form, perhaps the oldest modular form of all, warrants a twenty-first-century low-tech reappraisal in transportation for health (see Chapter 2).

Environmental control

Containerized and tent-based modular systems have precise HVAC requirements for the provision of mechanically conditioned air and, alternatively, the provision of natural ventilation, and many design strategies are possible. One product provided with the AGAR Industries Mobile Field Hospital, in its portable units, is the Dantherm ACM-18. This off-the-shelf environmental control unit can be part of an interconnected modular system.[84] More than 5,000 of these units are currently in active service with North Atlantic Treaty Organization (NATO) forces and this system has proven to be cost-effective in the field. The ACM-18 is a self-contained HVAC unit that transits compactly, has fully interchangeable components, and requires minimum staging and space requirements. All components are coded with a standardized NATO Stock Number (NSN) as this allows for rapid integration into standard logistical and deployment supply chains. The NATO-NSN, for example, is NSN No. 4120-22616-8876, consisting of one ACM-18 with 5.6kW cooling, 16kW heating capacity, with a soft starter-ignition system. The ACM-18 was developed to provide air conditioning in temporary, transportable buildings and shelters. It is a compact, lightweight HVAC unit fabricated in aluminum with a rigid steel frame, and designed to be located outdoors with fresh air intake and exhaust soft ducting connecting the unit to its 'assigned' container(s) or tent module(s). This unit is suited for RTC and RHC installations where a high air filtration rate is required, as it features a dual filtration system driven by a cooling circuit and two large fans. The evaporator unit features a radial fan, which draws warm internal air into the module through the chiller to produce cooled air. The condenser unit contains two coils and a large axial blower-fan to exhaust used air from the interior directly to the outside atmosphere and the unit's heating coil provides warm air to the interior. It is recommended that a mock-up installation is erected (see below) so that this and perhaps two or three other comparable HVAC systems can be comparatively pretested for their performance in a controlled setting over a period of time and in a variety of (perhaps simulated) weather conditions. It is arguable that natural ventilation is often preferred over mechanical HVAC systems in these care settings. To transmit fresh air to the interior, however, it is important to have the option to zip open a window. Some physicians will argue that fresh air is critical, but view amenity irrelevant, in a post-disaster situation, arguing, 'The role of natural ventilation, and not view, in emergency medicine is the only thing that matters!' In practice, a mix of natural and artificial systems is effective.

Biomorphic vocabularies

There is no rule that requires a transportable healthcare facility to be singularly rectilinear, assiduously *box-like*. Buckminster Fuller's curvilinear geodesic dome and its myriad permutations over the past sixty years have proven their resiliency, durability, and cross-cultural acceptability (Figure 5.30). The geodesic dome, the tensegrity geometries associated with it and with other closepacked tessellations, afford a fascinating alternative—to the relentless rectilinearity of the vast majority of emergency housing and other modular building systems for rapid deployment at this time. One example is *World Shelters*, an NGO based in California that produces a line of geodesic domes called the *U-Dome 100* and *U-Dome 200* for use as emergency post-disaster housing. Relevant to healthcare applications, this unit is sixteen feet in diameter by twelve feet in height. Wall panels are fabricated in recycled, flame-retardant, corrugated polypropylene, five millimeters thick and are precision die-cut into five shapes, and include pre-punched holes for connecting bolts. The panels are built for a five-year lifespan. No independent interior structural frame is necessary: panel flaps double as support struts able to withstand high wind, driving rain, and are assembled with simple tools. An aborted, 3,000 square foot proposal for Haiti in 2010 was to have consisted of a triage/trauma center, a mobile surgical suite, and thirty patient beds, to be staffed by the NGO *Project HOPE*. It would have consisted of two, forty-four-foot diameter domes with room compartments inside. Its galvanized steel frame and panels can be hand-assembled, have windows, are equipped with roof vent fans, and are (partially) solar-powered.[85] Another product, the *Weaved Disaster Shelter*, by Jordanian/Canadian designer Abeer Seikaly, fuses the indigenous vernacular of the desert with a generic domed structure principally of structural fabric. Its beige modular walls are fabricated in plastic and reflect solar gain, with an onboard water filtration system, and it generates its own heat and electricity. Its walls, in section, have an interstitial space for the provision of natural ventilation. From the exterior these domes appear as large hand-woven baskets, a design inspired by nomadic tribal huts.[86] The water bladder is another biomorphic-shaped, prefab modular product for the storage and retrieval of water in hot, arid regions, and in disaster strike zones. Produced by Structure-Flex and distributed by *Oxfam*, an international NGO, many bladder modules arrived in Haiti after the earthquake. Oxfam has been using prefab bladders such as this for over twenty years. Resembling huge yellow pillows, they are compact in transit, lightweight, and relatively easy to set up and use.[87] On a far larger scale, the floating, circular infirmary proposed by Clay Philips (2012/CU A+H) is deployable in either a modular or flat-pack mode, and is expandable in height. It is an additive system, with modules stackable on top of one another (Figure 5.31).

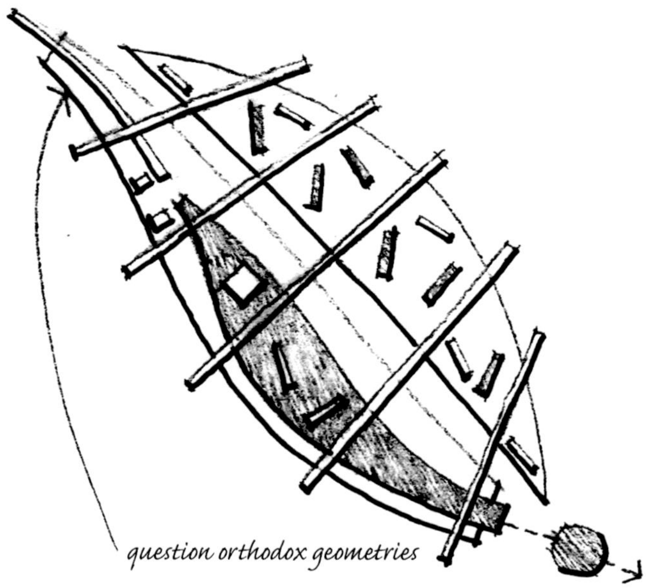

5.30 Explore curvilinear prefab systems as an alternative to relentless orthogonality

Lightweight pneumatics

This portable type begins as a flattened fabric membrane that is shipped in flat-pack mode to an installation site, and then inflated

5.31 A floating prefab modular hospital reminiscent of the utopian schemes of the 1960s put forth by Todd Wheeler, and Archigram

into a fully inhabitable structure. In assembly, its membrane wall panels can be inflated in an hour compared to the laborious task of shipping pre-built modular units to an installation site and then having to complete the rest of it part by part. The advantage of pneumatic systems centers is their compactness prior to and during transport. Upon inflation, membrane sectional panels are connected to one another and to HVAC, plumbing and electrical systems. In Texas in 2010, a joint initiative of Presbyterian-Harris Methodist and Arlington Memorial Medical Centers yielded a pneumatic trauma center known as the *Field Surge Program*. The Office of Emergency Management of Texas Health Resources (THR) partly funded it and wholly operates it. This RTC consists of two forty-bed patient care wards: one unit was privately funded and built, and a second unit is co-owned by THR and the City of Arlington, Texas. Together, this system cost $1.2 million. The two forty-bed Isolation Unit/ICUs each contain 2,000 square feet of floor space, a self-contained electrical system, including a power generator, HVAC and electrical system, germicidal air filtration device with negative pressure, fluorescent lighting, triage stations, eighteen acuity adaptable patient beds, and twelve ICU beds. The system is transited to a site in two, thirty-two-foot climate controlled semi-trailers. Each inflatable unit is fabricated in hybrid fiber-polymer material, with a Velcro inner liner membrane, and stabilized by a system of interior and exterior tension cables. It can be erected by four to six persons and with two hand-held pneumatic (leaf) blowers in approximately twenty minutes. Its fabric walls are perpendicular to the floor plane, and its ceiling is semi-vaulted. Insulated, coil-like ductwork provides five tons of HVAC support inside. Once inflated, the air is self-monitored by a pressurized valve device, and each pneumatic arc-supported strut/column has a dedicated pressurized relief valve (the power generator is a 37.5kw trailer mount unit with 53g fuel cell). After this is activated, its hardened doors are zipped into place. The unit can tether from its air-filled support columns, or from staked tension cables.[88] As for onboard medical equipment, mobile oxygen and medical gases are stationed at each patient bed and one *Dinamap* portable unit is provided for every ten beds. If negative pressure is required for any patient requiring isolation, a clear plastic screen is affixed by a Velcro strip to the floor, and to nearby air-supported columns.

Weatherization

The success of any portable building depends on its ability to provide (more than) adequate protection from the elements. While this may sound obvious, it is a difficult challenge. There are so many moving parts. A modular system will consist of many hundreds of component parts and these must fit tightly together to provide air-locked, waterproofed interior conditions. A transportable is a system of systems, beginning with its flooring, walls, ceiling, and roof systems. In a fully containerized system a relatively high level of weatherproofing, i.e. climate control, is pre-manufactured into the unit and especially in the case of containerized units. On the other hand, with an entirely flat-pack system the probability is greater that some assembly tolerances will be exceeded because there are so many more moving parts that require proper, precise assembly, and in a certain order. Small, weatherized single-purpose rapid response shelters are being deployed in the aftermath of human-induced and natural disasters. One example is the *Tornado Shelter*, a system specifically built for deployment in the region commonly referred to as tornado alley in the midsection of the U.S.[89] This prefab modular shelter is an aboveground module that is erected on a flat site, prior to tornado season. It is one level in height and its low profile deflects intense horizontal windfields. It features a lateral bracing system, and the module itself functions as a 'suction cup,' resisting updraft wind currents that typically can reach 150

5.32 Ebola infirmary tent-wards in construction in Uganda, 2014

miles per hour and beyond in an F5 tornado. This bracing system enables the 40,000 pound steel module to cling to the earth and in effect increase its resistive weight capacity to 115,000 psi as it takes a direct hit. The design takes advantage of the changing barometric wind pressures when high wind forces suddenly strike against it. As for housing, the FLOAT house designed by Morphosis in New Orleans' Lower Ninth Ward was also inspired by weather, and water in particular. It can self-sustain its power needs, surviving by rising, boat-like, as the floodwaters rise in a disaster event. Its chassis (pier foundation) elevates gradually as the water rises, while the superstructure (vessel) remains intact, fully weatherized.[90]

Vaulted tents

Tent structures for healthcare have been in use for more than a thousand years. They have proven their worth in wartime, peacetime, in disaster mitigation missions, and are often preferred over containerized structures. They are viewed as flexible, light in weight, offering ease of assembly with their flat-pack kit-of-parts, they can be naturally ventilated, and they are connectable to mechanical systems to provide heating and air conditioning. Tents continue to be the preferred shelter option within the non-military disaster relief community, and manufacturers in countries worldwide vie for market share. Tent-based systems are particularly favored at this time by numerous prominent international humanitarian disaster relief agencies. Manufacturers such as Alaska Medical Shelter Systems produce barrel-vaulted tent systems for military and civilian use. Their products are indicative of current thinking. Evenly spaced ribbed steel tubing at eight-foot or ten-foot intervals structurally support their tents, with each module twenty feet in width by sixty feet in length. This system is available in sand (beige) and in olive (dark green). Numerous units can be interconnected by means of snap-together, weatherized vestibules. A fabric membrane floor is provided and HVAC and electrical systems are powered by a generator (one unit per tent), with flexible duct tubing. Lift pack systems such as this are recommended where the deployment period is to be of a relatively short duration. This current generation of tents in some ways harkens back (both in section, and in their size) to the classic corrugated steel Quonset huts of World War II. The Quonset is a prefabricated, barrel-vaulted (in cross section) permanent site structure, with its single, curving uniform radius reaching to the ground on both sides. The World War II variant was based on the *Nissen hut* developed by the British military during World War I. The name *Quonset* comes from the place where they were first manufactured in the U.S., at Quonset Point, at the Naval Construction Battalion Center in Davisville, Rhode Island. In 1941 the U.S. Navy commissioned an all-purpose, lightweight building that could be shipped anywhere and assembled without skilled labor. Its standard dimensions (in plan) were sixteen feet by thirty-six feet, twenty feet by forty feet, and forty feet by one hundred feet. These highly adaptable structures became barracks, latrines, offices, medical facilities, including quarantine (isolation) wards, base family housing units, repair shops, schools, and bakeries. Between 150,000 and 170,000 Quonsets were manufactured during World War II. After the war, they were sold as surplus to the general public. Some units remain in use on military bases and elsewhere worldwide.[91] The current generation of barrel-vaulted, soft-walled tent structures is most often used either freestanding (see Chapter 6) or in the case of longer deployment periods, in cold climates, as part of a hybrid system.

Ridge tents

This is another venerable type of tent, with origins in Neolithic *tipi* structures. Ridge tents are characterized by a roof peak, or ridgeline, in section, resulting from the placement of the highest vertical support brace(s) at the center, in a linear row, or in a circular or rectangular volume, when fully upright. Shorter, vertical bracings support ridge tent sidewalls (Figure 5.32). Openings are typically located at the two (short) edges. The manufacturer DRASH produces the *J Series* of large-scale military tents. These provide 1,250 square feet of interior space for multiple applications ranging from maintenance facilities to logistical support to mobile medical triage and treatment centers. They can be purchased either in pneumatic or manual configurations. The erection time for this tent is under forty minutes, and is achieved with the assistance of a low-pressure air blower and bladder that comes with its assembly kit. This system is transported flat-pack in a trailer, towed by a truck with a towing capacity greater than 6,000 pounds. The tent units are positioned over an inflatable air bladder plenum. Set up and take down is accomplished using the air blower connected to the bladder. No manual lifting or extensive assembly process is required. This system is also offered on a hydraulic container platform with the ability to fit on a forklift pallet and complies with U.S. military requirements for its modular soft-walled tent systems. Each unit is shipped to its installation site with a titanium structural frame, fabric sheathing and fabric flooring, storage trailer, and forklift truck, the aforementioned blower and bladder unit with flexible HVAC ductwork, a ladder and a sledge hammer, two vestibule entranceways with built-in screen doors, zipper-screen windows with vinyl insets, light fixtures and electrical wiring kit, ground stakes, and low and high wind stabilizer cables. These units are operable in temperatures ranging from -50 degrees Fahrenheit to +131 degrees Fahrenheit (-45.5 degrees Celsius to 55 degrees Celsius).[92]

Panelized systems

Most portable structures for health feature some percentage of hard-walled componentry. Some systems are entirely hard-walled, whereas others are a mixture of hard walls with soft wall 'panels' made of fabric sheathing fastened and stabilized within the structural grid-frame. Usually, a mixture of both types is desired in situations where, for example, an inboard decontamination unit/ shower requires soft wall panels while the remainder of the facility requires rigid panels. The blending of these two types is preferred, here, as this can more fully support a more expansive range of functions. Hard panel systems require rigid connections at their uppermost and lowermost connecting points to avoid panel distortion, bowing, creasing, or rippling. In the case of a hard-wall flat-pack system where the platform grid flooring is to be installed first, followed by the walls, and then roof, it is instructive to provide rigid, weatherized fasteners that are relatively easy to install and connect. This can be achieved with steel L-clips, U-clips, or turnbuckles, where one device is slotted into, hooked, clipped, or tightened, in conjunction with holes or clips affixed to the panel, with a universal wrench used to achieve rigidity. Polyurethane and other types of plastic fasteners are not recommended for these applications. Instead, use lightweight alloys as these will prove more durable in repeated take down and set up operations. A recently introduced panelized system, the *Quick Space 72H* emergency shelter, features lightweight, rigid, modular walls designed to interlock, with many configuration options (see Chapter 6). One panel slips behind another panel and then is fastened with a combination clip/pin device. The outer panel has clips that allow the inner panel to plug into it from behind.[93] The portable infirmary prototype designed by Julie Randolph (2013/CU A+H) makes use of a rigid, panelized wall system that is designed for installation on flat, open sites such as in the tornado alley region of the U.S. midsection (Figure 5.33a–c). This offsite prefab flat-pack system is constructed of hard wall panels, with a modular floor and ceiling system, an A/B interlocking organizational pattern, in plan.

Modular ceilings

In a healthcare facility, whether conventionally built on a permanent site, or portable, the differentiation of interior ceiling heights, and ceiling typology, depends on the function of individual rooms as well as their larger spatial context. The type of light fixtures, and their quantity, must be coordinated with the multiplicity of functions occurring within. Too often, the ceiling *and* room lighting are both

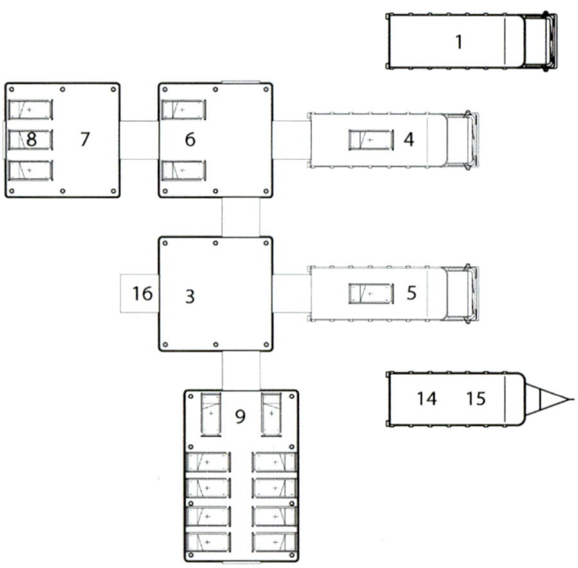

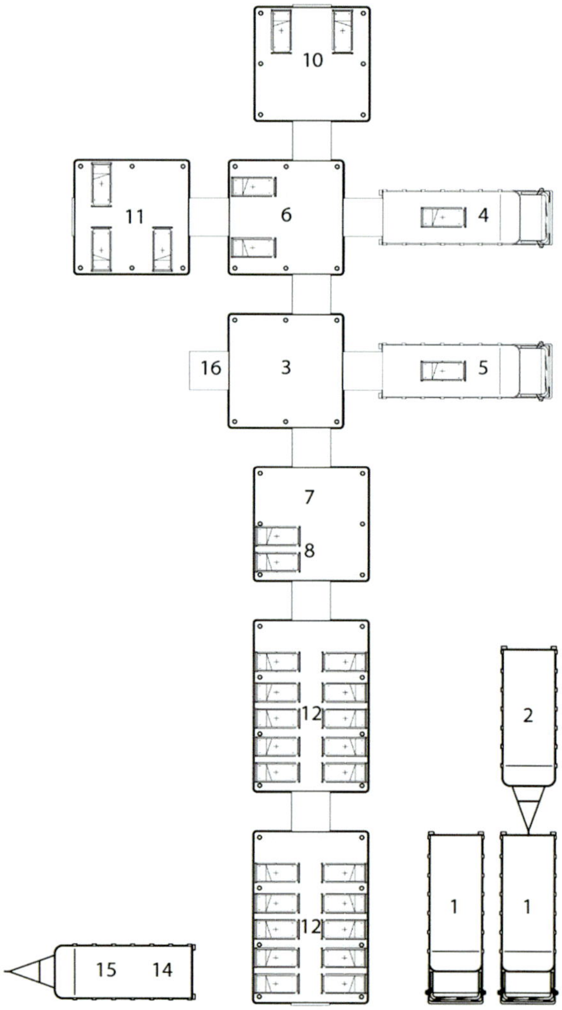

Key:

1 truck (transport mode)
2 trailer
3 registration/waiting area
4 diagnostic and treatment
5 radiology/laboratory
6 pre-operating
7 medical supplies
8 isolation area
9 post-procedure
10 triage/emergency
11 ICU
12 inpatient ward
13 generator
14 showers
15 water closets
16 arrival/entry

5.33a–c Prototype modular infirmary for deployment in 'tornado alley' in the United States' midsection, with multiple footprint configurations

inadequate and this likely resulted from inattention during design. A poorly designed ceiling will often result in poor lighting quality, making a space appear drab and featureless. In an RTC or RHC, rooms have specific ceiling requirements, while the overall max ceiling height remains constant. This is good, because in a containerized or hybrid system, it is important to not compromise the containers' closepacking virtues—as this is their prime advantage in transit. Too many different container shapes and sizes would be confusing and counterproductive. Regardless, varied ceiling conditions, some open-grid, others closed-grid, can make interiors more visually interesting while allowing individual rooms to be more attuned to their individual functions. It is an opportunity to inject color and materials to soften and transform an otherwise spartan aesthetic. The ceiling plane thereby becomes a device unto itself, or *palette*, for the infusion of visual content that can therapeutically enhance the occupant's experience—achieved through representations of a sky, for example. In tent-based RTCs and in hybrid tent-container systems, an overarching umbrella tent can provide a sense of enclosure while shielding ultraviolet rays. In other cases, an open grid ceiling is preferred, depending on whether HVAC support is required and if the module is to be weatherized. Light fixtures are affixed to this open (dropped) grid in order to provide task lighting while not precluding its spatiality where the patient is able to look up and see into a larger volume, made visible by means of an open grid. Equipment storerooms, of course, do not need this level of design expression. The security issues associated with ceiling and lighting design center on some components remaining operable even if other parts of the installation lose power (Figure 5.34).

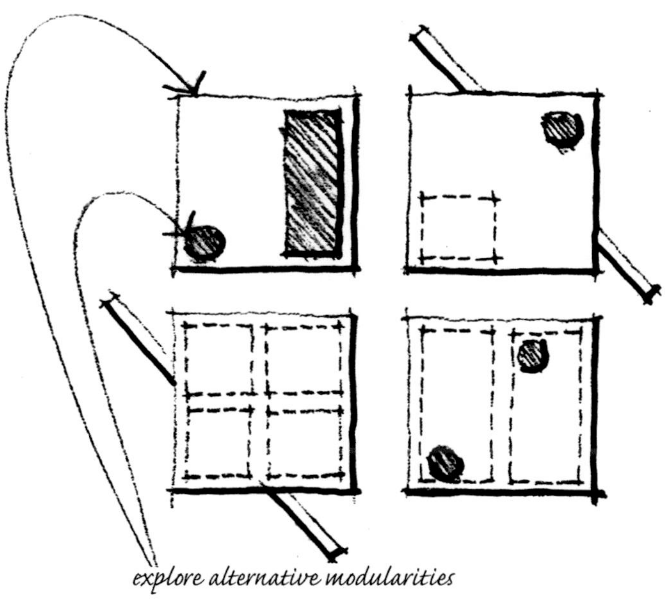

5.34 Modular components are assembled into larger 'chunks' whether in a fixed-site facility or in a redeployable facility

Expandable modules

There are generally two types of containerized expandable modules in use at this time in portable, non-vehicular, installations: mobile diagnostic imaging modules, and surgical suite modules. The basic 'chassis' is a standard ISO container. Expandable modules are typically governed by the dimensions of the basic ISO unit (prior to its expansion): eight to ten feet wide by nine to ten feet in height by twenty or thirty feet in length. Various manufacturers offer combinations of modules, a blend of mobility, functionality, and customization. One manufacturer, Johnson Medical Health Care Facilities, produces a mobile field hospital unit. Johnson built its first such expandable modular unit in 1998, as the first manufacturer to do so. Its early units were deployed to the site of the largest public hospital in Kuala Lumpur, Malaysia where it was docked/plugged into an existing medical facility. These units host mobile operating theaters, ICUs, CCUs, cardiac catheter labs, and X-ray equipment. A hospital can rent or purchase an expandable module as a means to continue to provide services uninterrupted, with minimal disruption to workflow or to patients' care needs (see Chapter 6). In so doing, patients can receive a level of care comparable to that in a conventional hospital setting. Several units are linked together to form an entire department and modules can be configured to allow for docking, as mentioned, into an existing facility. Johnson Medical's modules are widely used in hospital renovation and expansion projects. As for vehicular, truck-transited, expandable clinics-on-wheels, the most common type of expandable facility in use, units are usually not proportioned to be compatible with standard ISO container sizes. Major surgical procedures can be performed in this type of expandable (see earlier discussion in this chapter and in Chapters 2, 3, and 6). These feature pop-out sides, each approximately eight feet in width, not dissimilar from the pop-out modules of Johnson's expandables. Manufacturers such as Johnson work closely with their clients to meet precise ergonomic requirements for all onboard equipment, and its placement.

Doors/thresholds/vestibules

Conventional swing doors make little sense in a portable healthcare facility. First, they take up entirely too much space because they open either into the room, taking up essential space better used for other things, or they open outward, often directly onto a highly trafficked corridor. Second, their sheer mass renders them heavy and difficult to operate. Instead, where feasible, provide lightweight doors—lightweight sliding pocket doors constructed of aluminum or another lightweight alloy. Explore malleable doors made of plastic, high-durability fabric doors, and entry vestibule assemblies. These should be able to be opened and closed readily. In Japan, the Kokura Rehabilitation Hospital, in Kyushu Prefecture, by the firm Yasui Masahiro and Associates, Tokyo (2001) employed sliding pocket doors at the entrance to every inpatient room as well as at entrances to therapy treatment areas.[94] A second strategy consists of screening. Many existing portable field hospitals extensively utilize side-pull canvas curtains and screening devices mounted on a track, affixed to a transom rod. This type of 'door' is more difficult to secure and lock in some instances, yet can be designed to be lightweight and comparatively easier to transport, plus, they can compactly store in containers en route to deployment. Full-height screening that is pulled from one side can be color-coded to denote a room's specialized function. For instance, the door-threshold to an immunization tent or container can be differentiated from the nearby exam/consultation rooms. Color-coding can also be used throughout to designate non-patient care work zones from patient treatment spaces. Pull screens are not recommended as 'doors' to rooms that require a high level of privacy or security, as was the case in the ad hoc 30,000 square foot *pop-up* clinic set up in New Orleans by the LSU Health Sciences Center in the aftermath of Katrina. Set up in an abandoned department store, here, rigid, lockable pocket doors would have been far more suitable. Instead, pull curtains were installed that, in most instances, did not meet minimum-security requirements (see Chapter 4). After a period of a few months, lockable accordion side-pull doors, fabricated of a more substantive material, were installed to replace the flimsy curtains, and this resulted in additional privacy and fewer off-hour break-ins (Figure 5.35).

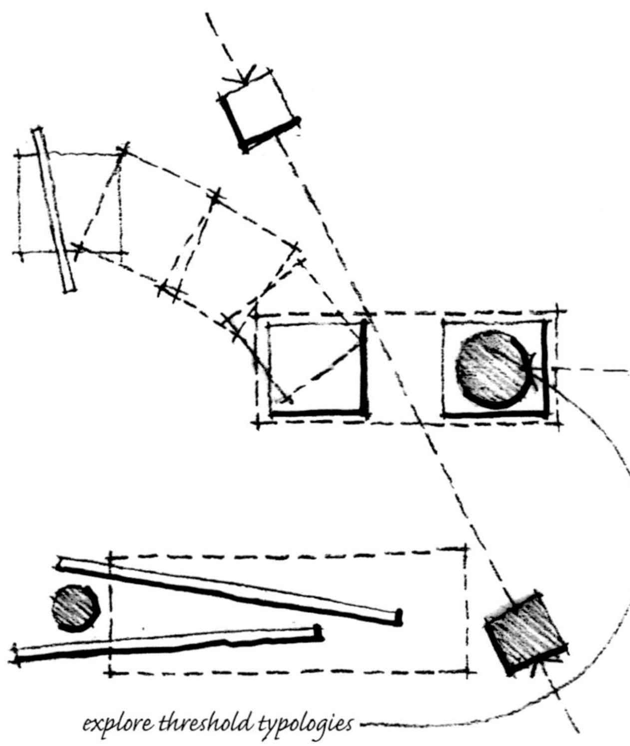

5.35 Avoid conventional swing-out doors as these are dangerous and take up too much space

Modular flooring

Conventional soft-walled tent systems for healthcare installations are nearly always equipped with a soft membrane floor. This surface is integral to the module, and is staked out and laid down prior to anything else. Because of this, its careful and precise positioning is essential. Soft flooring surfaces lie directly on the ground and therefore are very different from platform grid flooring, which is elevated above the ground plane and supported by telescopic or hydraulic legs with webbed footings. In the case of a raised modular floor, its floor grid/plane functions as a datum upon which the entire structural assembly depends. The type and quality of the ground surface upon which a facility is erected is therefore critical to the success of the structure. In a *pop-up* RHC, for instance, the floor surface of an otherwise worthy host structure may be too uneven, discontinuous, or insubstantial. Surface variations such as abrupt shifts from a concrete slab to tile to carpet within the same immediate area may be too extreme. In such conditions it is disadvantageous to install a pre-engineered modular system that sits directly on such a random (not to mention unsanitary) ground plane. In these situations, provide a raised, structurally autonomous modular floor grid with all electrical raceways built in, in support of wall panels, then easily plugged into the modular floor grid. As discussed below, the floor grid system should possess the capability to self-sense when its allowable live load has been exceeded on any part of the floor surface, so it can early warn before a system failure occurs. This type of digitally driven, computerized flooring system therefore becomes, in effect, an *active* rather than passive building subsystem. In 2012, IBM obtained a U.S. patent for a modularized flooring system of this type, a touch- and movement-sensitive system able to detect and categorize different types of movement occurring upon it. The floor surface can 'recognize' when a person is standing upon it, taking cognizance of varying live load weights and shapes of objects and people. Most interestingly, it is able to self-sense between a rolling wheelchair versus a person standing, using an assistive walking device such as a cane.[95]

Intelligent building systems

We are on the threshold of exciting advances in the design and manufacture of *intelligent* portable structures for healthcare, breakthroughs made possible by new building technologies. It has become possible to design and fabricate self-sensing *smart* modules and their componentry, including wall panels, flooring and ceiling systems, lighting, and security systems. Environmental control systems can, for instance, self-regulate indoor thermal heat gain levels. Before, a component failure could occur suddenly, causing unfortunate consequences in day-to-day operations because it was impossible to detect its eminent failure. In the worst cases, this inability to know what was about to happen resulted in unfortunate accidents, even personal injury. Anything can happen when one or more structural connections fails, when a panel ruptures, a ceiling grid comes ajar, when all the lights suddenly go out, when a pocket door falls off its track, or when intersecting wall panels become disconnected—to name but a few things that can go wrong. These failures may occur due to weather conditions such as a strong gust of wind, a sudden hailstorm or heavy downpour, or poor soil conditions beneath the structure as a result of subsidence or poor drainage. Self-sensing systems and components will warn with precision and with self-correcting capabilities, precluding the need to completely shut down the entire facility to fix one module.[96] The degree of onboard resiliency will be stunning in this regard. The RTC or RHC independently will, in other words, be smart enough to sense its own well-being and possess the self-sensing ability to know, for instance, if the temperature and humidly levels are adequate on the north side of the platform in the hot midday sun. If an electrical circuit has malfunctioned, its onboard computers will trace the source, or detect which floor panels have become weakened and on the verge of failure because the maximum recommended floor load was exceeded. It will detect which light fixture is damaged due to water infiltration from a leak in the roof overhead, and roof abnormalities will be detectable before they occur. Laser cutting CNC technology is a related technology with many applications in offsite-built healthcare facilities that can make the system far more intelligent. Digital design technologies offer amazing possibilities for portable healthcare facilities. These methods will result in the generation of less waste and residual materials than current subtractive processes such as milling or cutting.

3D printing technology

This process starts with the designer drawing an object in 3D using modeling software, which is then exported to a printer using a software file format, then the 3D printer creates the finished object, layer by layer. Various methods of 3D printing exist, but all use a digitally controlled arm that moves around the print bed, layering materials such as powder or plastic onto the binding agent (such as glue or heat) to create a shape. It is 'built up' on the print bed. There is no 'assembly' required in the traditional sense but there is always a post-production process, which must be done by hand to remove excess powder or residual material, and this step allows the desired final object to emerge. The more detailed the model, the longer the process takes. Leftover materials are removed and some can then be reused in the next 3D model. This process, *stereo lithography* (SLA) therefore typically uses a laser to draw an object in a vat of liquid resin in order to print the final object. *Fused deposition modeling* (FDM), or fused filament fabrication, works much like a giant 3D cake-icing machine, but with plastic. The print head uses melted plastic, which then solidifies to create a 'slice' of an object once it leaves the extrusion nozzle; subsequent 'slices' render the complete object (Figure 5.36). *Selective laser sintering* (SLS) is similar to SLA although, here, powder is fused together by the laser, replacing the bed of liquid resin. SLS allows for printing with myriad types of powdered materials, including ceramics, nylon, silver and steel. *Objet (PolyJet)* works in theory much like a conventional inkjet printer, traversing across a platform printing extremely fine layers of resin instead of ink. An enormous benefit in using 3D printing technology is that every object can be different, design studies are reproducible relatively quickly, and can achieve great geometric complexity. Since 2009 when the first 3D printer kits were commercially sold, they have continued to come down in cost. In Denmark, an entire single family home was 3D-printed in 2012 by the Danish architects Fredrik Agdrup and Nicholas Bjorndal and their firm *Eentileen*. This was completed with a laptop, a printer and 820 sheets of plywood. They constructed a 125 square meter (1,325 square foot) dwelling in four weeks. The immense appeal of all this in post-disaster architecture lies in its adaptability to diverse building types and sites.[97] Designers and manufacturers are collaborating to create an entirely new generation of products: *MakerBot* pioneered a low-cost, easy to use, desk-top 3D printer with a customization option; it is one of many start-up companies, with others manufacturing 3D-printed human organs and a host of previously unrealizable prosthetic devices.[98]

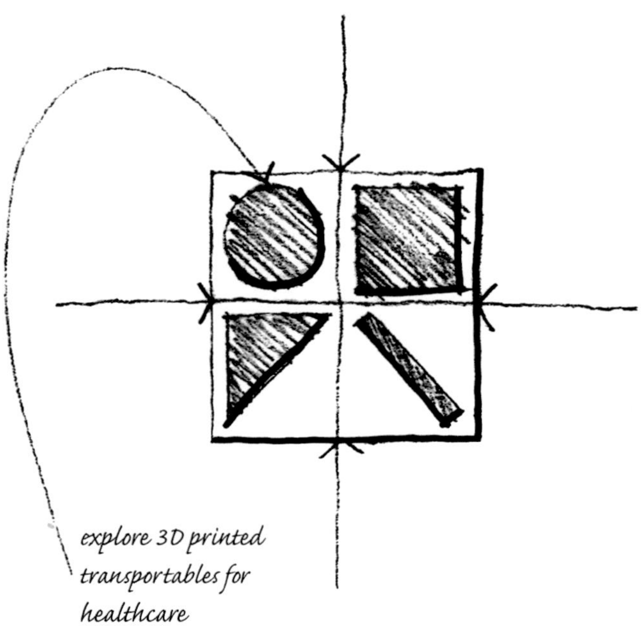

5.36 Weigh the advantages and disadvantages of emerging fabrication methodss

3D-printed components

This technology can offer an innovative way of making components for prefab permanent site buildings, and prefab portable structures for healthcare. The 'printing' takes place with minimal human intervention. However, a high level of designer input is required during the digital design process in order to develop the required 3D software model, during the post-production clean-up phase of the object, and the removal of any temporary support structure built to support the object during its printing. This is before the actual manual assembly of componentry can begin. A key challenge, at present, is that modules or components produced may be difficult to practically reuse after one deployment. Materiality is therefore also important to consider from the outset in relation to any outdoor installation environment where an artifact is to be installed. Depending on the material used, 3D-printed components may be difficult to repair if damaged in the field. The fabrication of building components and small structures is occurring, in some laboratories, using room-size printers, printing up to two square meters per hour, and even in the printing of objects for anticipated structures to be transported to the moon. As mentioned above, successful medical applications are now attainable in the mass customisation of human organs and prosthetic devices—bioprinting—the 'printing' of structurally and functionally accurate human organs and tissue. In terms of disaster relief, there is the obvious problem of moving delicate, cumbersome 3D printers along with binding agents and materials to remote sites (although materials could perhaps be sourced locally). An example of design experimentation with this technology is the *KamerMaker* (Dutch for 'room maker'), a movable 3D printer that prints large components from bio-plastics with a high degree of detail and variability. *KamerMaker* is capable of transforming recycled waste plastics into furniture, sailboats, and other items of up to 500 cubic feet.[99] Its creators, at Amsterdam-based *DUS Architecture*, envision large-scale 3D printers on site in disaster-stricken communities to quickly manufacture temporary emergency housing made from discarded plastics or any material that can melt and then re-harden. However, one challenge remaining is that, in the case of componentry this large in size, and with a sufficiently high degree of detail, each print can at present take hours (even days) to print.[100] In a 2012 TED talk, Behrokh Khoshnevis demonstrated the potential of this construction method with a full-scale concrete structure built with a 3D printer that was transported to the installation site.[101] It will be up to the ingenuity of architects, structural engineers, and industrial designers to experiment to determine whether it is more effective to transport 3D printing apparatus to the disaster site, versus continuing to build componentry off site in a factory perhaps thousands of miles away, and face the logistical challenges of shipping prefab-produced products long distances.

7 Administration/total environment

Strategic partnering (Part II)

The financial and logistical challenges involved in designing, manufacturing, deploying, assembling, and commissioning a portable healthcare facility are many, but they pale in comparison to the challenges associated with its day-to-day operation. For this reason, the ability to establish partnerships between a government sponsor, working collaboratively with an NGO, can be mutually beneficial and a win-win for all parties. The *Containers2Clinics* (C2C) NGO in Haiti commissioned and owns its three installations. This organization works in tandem with local public general hospitals. Or, a governmental agency will purchase a portable structure and then hand its day-to-day operations over to Doctors Without Borders, or the International Red Cross. The Israeli government owns the facility it shipped to Haiti after the 2010 earthquake, and operated it, collaboratively, with local medical aid providers. It is surprising how many North American medical centers located in at-risk coastal communities still do not have in place contingencies for what to do in the event of a local disaster event. One such case, until very recently, was the Medical Center of South Carolina (MUSC), located in Charleston, South Carolina. The MUSC campus is built on a floodplain on the west side of the Charleston peninsula and it periodically floods during heavy rainstorms. A hurricane-force wind field could easily push a massive wall of tidal surge across its entire campus. In such an event, MUSC would experience major infrastructural and operational breakdowns, with core capabilities shuttered by having been knocked completely offline. Because the staff would be required to remain on call, they could have to return as soon as the storm passes and the floodwaters recede. One or more RTCs or RHCs, owned by MUSC, or U.S. Army CSH facility would, ideally, beforehand, be waiting in the wings for deployment in Charleston or on the MUSC campus, and could be installed at the medical center right next to its emergency department/trauma care unit. The facilities, one portable, one permanent site, could work side by side, thereby significantly increasing the capacity to provide care for hurricane victims and the displaced. Drawing upon the strengths of each, a more robust rapid response is achievable than had either MUSC, or a locally run RTC, opted to go solo.

Evidence-based research and design

The evidence-based research and design (E-BR+D) movement is premised on three basic assumptions: (1) patients should be able to devote their full energies to healing and to full recovery without having to cope with an unsupportive or counter therapeutic physical environment; (2) healthcare providers should be able to perform their routine daily duties without becoming ill themselves, or being injured at work due to an unsupportive physical environment; and (3) facilities with a limited life span or whose operations generate excessive biomedical waste, may cause adverse health conditions.[102] The fundamental aim of E-BR+D in hospital and related permanent site clinical settings is to minimize the healthcare setting as a contributor in any adverse medical event experienced by any patient, anywhere.[103] Recently, a parallel focus has emerged, in a host of professions beyond the design professions and the health sciences, including engineering, the aeronautical industry, the military sector, and industrial design. Accordingly, levels of E-BR+D professional engagement have been articulated for the benefit of architectural practitioners. The four upwardly rigorous levels of involvement are: *Level 1* practitioners keep up with current best practices and pursue their work on a daily basis within a reflective professional practice attitude and outlook. Here, one's work is measured against benchmark metrics drawn from published projects published in peer-reviewed journals. *Level 2* practitioners read the research literature and interpret and incorporate findings in their work on a rigorous basis. *Level 3* practitioners, in addition to following the empirical literature and the professional glossies, develop their own hypotheses and then test them out in the course of their professional work or in the context of a design competition submittal, then report their findings in peer-reviewed forums including various conferences, and professional, peer-reviewed journals. Detailed performance criteria are developed at the outset of a project and the built outcome is assessed against these criteria. At this level of engagement, practitioners acquire and always update their understanding of basic research methods and seek out consultants and continuing education opportunities to advance their knowledge of relevant theory and its applications in their work. *Level 4* practitioners are, for lack of a better term, scholar-practitioners, who closely follow the peer-reviewed empirical literature, hypothesize the outcomes of their design decisions *a priori*, measure outcomes, and report the results of this systematic process at conferences and in peer-reviewed publications. These individuals and firms subject their work to the highest standards of rigor and scrutiny by their peers.[104]

Resilience and facility management

In the U.S., the *Leadership in Energy Efficient Environmental Design* program, or what has become widely known as LEED, is a widely accepted rating/certification system initiated and operated by the *United States Green Building Council* (USGBC). This program, significantly, does not (yet) address prefab portable structures for health within the rubric of its current rating system. While portable buildings are not yet part of its manifold of concern, however, offsite-built permanent modular installations (PMIs) *are* currently within the parameters of the LEED program. The LEED program, for its part, it should be stated, has been an overall success in its focus on permanent site buildings and neighborhoods, prefab and otherwise. Unfortunately, due to the scant attention still generally devoted to healthcare building types other than permanent site buildings, it remains impossible to rate a portable, redeployable structure with regards to the degree to which it will be environmentally *green* in its day-to-day use, and/or sufficiently hardened in response to a sudden, adverse event. This needs to change. There will come, in the near future, a point in time when a LEED-type rating system will be needed for portable, redeployable buildings for healthcare. This will occur when more examples come into use, because only then will the time, expense, and effort required in a new certification program that reaches out to these structures be monetarily justified. Nonetheless, with or without codification, a portable building for health must achieve more than sustainability—it must be *resilient*. This implies two things. First, the necessity to demonstrate the portable's physical integrity, the *greenness* of its design, its manufacture, in-transit protocols, material palette, the onsite assembly process, and its power generation system. Second, the redeployable structure should be able to withstand a physical setback and then capably surmount, to overcome, to bounce back after an adverse event. This performance standard must be the responsibility of the A/E team, all consultants, the manufacturer, and the individual or team assigned oversight of its daily operations in the field. A portable healthcare facility, whether an RTC, or a RHC, be it a modular pop-up, a fully containerized clinic, or a vehicular mobile clinic, should be philosophically guided (and continuously assessed) by means of sustainable, resilient, facility management principles, theories, and practices.

Mockups and simulations

Mockups and simulations of various rooms and their equipment can help in identifying strengths, weaknesses, and opportunities for improvement in the design, function, and manufacture of a prefab modular system. It is a long-standing tradition within healthcare A/E firms, an important step, because the client may require the A/E team build one or more full-scale replicas of a part (or multiple parts) of the facility during the schematic design phase. Unfortunately, no statistics exist on the number of mockups and room simulations constructed annually, nor are statistics complied on the specific *types* of rooms or their componentry. Since neither frequency- nor type-based data are available, it becomes difficult to say with any certainty which types of spaces are most likely to be simulated in this manner, although frequently simulated room types include waiting rooms, exam rooms, laboratories, surgical suites, preoperative and post-operative units, patient rooms, ICUs, NICUs and other intensive care settings, emergency/trauma care departments, and staff workstations. The inpatient room/ward, for many reasons, would probably be at or near the top of any such list. The patient room and its larger context, the medical–surgical unit, has been at the center of the mock up/simulation equation for a long time and for many reasons: it remains at center stage for experimenting with new care philosophies, aesthetic vocabularies, and technologies. The 'mocking up' of these spaces has occurred over the past half-century in a process often a lot like this: the client provides some space on its campus—perhaps in a warehouse or in unoccupied shell space—to function as staging area for constructing and testing out a preliminary design, or a room or series of rooms. Staff and patients then 'use it' and rate its functionality, aesthetics, and overall amenity. Often, multiple iterations are constructed in this way, with each iteration based on the previous round of user feedback. If this process works relatively well with respect to permanent site facilities, it stands to reason it would work well with a prefab portable structure. For this reason, it is recommended the mock up/simulation method explored in the design and construction of transportables be for health. It can be a cost-effective way to test and iteratively retest the amenity and appropriateness of a design's aesthetics, materiality, and modular assemblies (Figure 5.37).

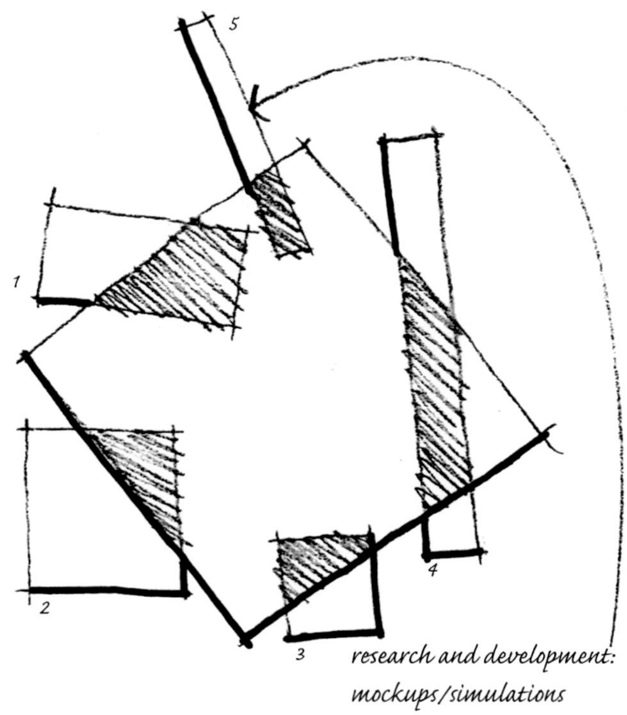

5.37 Build 'test' modules that can be assessed by the direct caregivers who will work in them out in the field

Staff accommodations

The nurse who volunteers to work in a portable field hospital or clinic in the aftermath of disaster knows he or she is about to be pressed to the limit. His or her skill sets and personal abilities will be challenged, daily. He or she will work long shifts, constantly be in need of supplies including basic necessities such as food and patient medications, and will be required to simultaneously perform the duties of many different caregivers, often simultaneously. These challenges include serving as nurse, chaplain, psychological councilor, logistics coordinator and local ambassador, to cite but a few roles he or she will likely be called upon to fill. It is hard, challenging work and because of this it is prudent to provide these individuals with as many amenities as possible and to build into the physical care setting as much logistical support as possible. Having a comfortable bed of one's own is one such amenity—a place to bathe, or obtain respite, if momentarily, from the rigors of one's duties. The provision of a staff break room, and commodious sleeping quarters, is greatly appreciated by staff personnel—some of whom have traveled thousands of miles from home. They will value a small kitchen and a place to eat without being in the center of a chaotic whirlpool of activity. In addition, as mentioned earlier, an outdoor getaway, yet near, can serve as a refuge. As for workspaces, provide a central zone with workstations and a large table at the center. Provide a mixture of private and semi-private alcoves for staff consultations with patients, and with one another. Reduce staff travel distances within core clinical work zones. Between-room connections, such as between a lab and an adjoining nursing staff workroom, will save unnecessary walking through a busy public area. Anything to save unnecessary steps and trips from here to there is appreciated, and will result in a less chaotic work environment. Cluster these staff workspaces together in a way to make work feel less tedious and tiring, without compromising patient care. Boston-based *Partners in Health* (PIH) has been working in Haiti since the 2010 earthquake. This NGO trains nurses to work in district hospitals and rural clinics in a nation that has extreme great difficulty rebuilding. It emphasizes the importance of being able to make the most with what one has to work with.[105]

Equipment and supplies

Provide multiple storage options in support of the diverse operations of a portable healthcare facility. Granted, it can be difficult to predict equipment and supply needs on a day-to-day basis. At best, one often has to guestimate because anything more precise is next to impossible. One thing is certain: when a shipment arrives there must be a safe, accessible place to put it. If food supplies, these parcels may be subject to theft and pilfering by local gangs. Providing adequate storage space can become highly problematic. Storage is generally of three types:

- *Type 1*—High security bins for the storage of medical supplies, and especially pharmaceuticals. These bins are manufactured of extremely durable polymers, lightweight yet able to withstand a gunshot inflicted from a range of within twenty feet. Provide lockable wheels that can be permanently affixed and cannot be removed, not unlike a 'dolly' so that the unit can be placed directly on a floor surface and the various bins can be chain-locked together, if necessary. Provide shelving in the interior work zone, with security straps to keep supply parcels stationary and these parcels should be chain-locked as well.
- *Type 2*—Provide personnel storage units or securable wall-mounted lockers, installed so they cannot be moved. One alternative, in the overnight staff accommodations area, would be to provide wall-mounted storage lockers or bins able to hold the personal possessions of staff personnel and to allow for rapid retrieval of personal clothing items, day or night. A separate storage bin or locker can contain uniforms and other items required while the staff member is on shift. These lockers are ideally housed in or directly adjacent to the staff shower/bath area.
- *Type 3*—Many patients will arrive with few, if any, personal belongings; they may be carrying only a suitcase or knapsack. There must be a safe place to store these personal artifacts, in a place accessible to the patients and their family members. If space allows, provide a separate small locker for each patient, adjacent to the ward, approximately one foot wide by one foot in depth by two to three feet in height. This will allow for clothing and a few personal artifacts during a patient's stay for observation and treatment. Every storage unit or locker is to be secured with a conventional lock-key, especially in the event of a disruption to the electrical power system. Provide modular storage devices that are easy to wipe down and disinfect, as these devices can become carriers of highly contagious stactyracus viruses and related MRSA microorganisms (Figure 5.38).

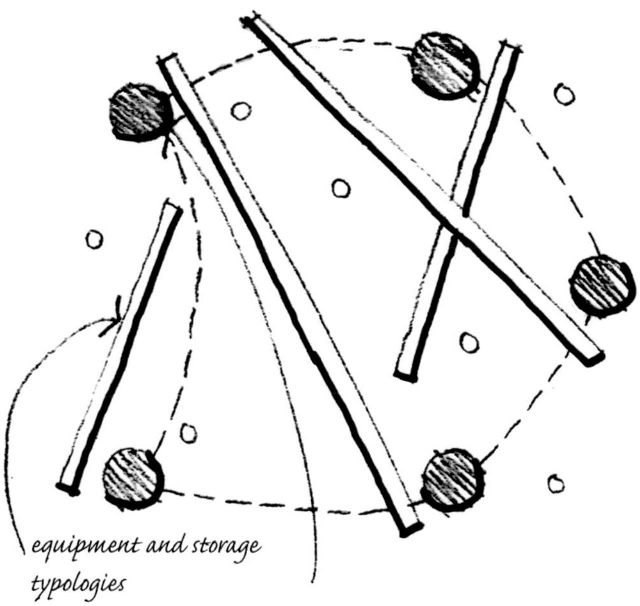

5.38 Provide flexible storage space for use by staff, patients, and other occupants

Security systems

Chaos rules in the intense aftermath of disaster. As soon as an installation site is selected, secure it. In the aftermath of the Haitian earthquake in 2010, some portable structures in Port-au-Prince initially deemed acceptable as *International Red Cross* trauma aid station sites had to be relocated because it was learned that the landowner had not granted permission, nor had been 'acceptably compensated' (bribed) beforehand. But time does not wait in these situations. As soon as the facility arrives at the dock or the airstrip, is transited to the installation site, and assembled and commissioned, there may already be a long line of patients at triage. Compounding matters, personal safety may be minimal until law and order can be re-established within the local jurisdiction. Victims may have sustained significant emotional and physical trauma, perhaps having witnessed the loss of a loved one. In such stressful situations it is critical for the diagnostic and treatment environment and its immediate environs to be perceived as safe harbor. The threat of being violated via theft or bodily harm may exist in the surrounding community but this atmosphere of unlawfulness cannot be tolerated on the immediate site. If it does, this will fundamentally disrupt the quality and flow of care and subsequently will have a deleterious impact on the well-being of staff personnel as well as patients and any accompanying family members. Consider the erection of stationary security buffers between any surrounding streets, the main entry, and semi-private and private zones accessing the site and provide some measure of physical separation from the larger, more uncertain, realm beyond. Similarly, inside, every zone within the facility must be securable and pose no threat to its occupants. Miniature, high-tech surveillance cameras can be built into key module panels and ceilings. Also, in uncertain situations, security guards should be posted on a 24/7 basis, without creating a fortress-like atmosphere. An effective security system establishes and reinforces the presence of order, will improve the quality of life for its occupants, and communicate that this place is literally a *port in the storm*—part of the solution, not the problem.

Sound attenuation

The noise levels within a busy emergency department can be cacophonous, rising during peak activity periods. People and supplies constantly coming and going, overcrowded waiting rooms, crying infants—all can be sources of cognitive stress for the staff and others. There are ways to mask unwanted sounds that are difficult to control. Ambient soundscaping is a method proven effective in certain healthcare environments, i.e. sensory immersion rooms in a hospice environment, and as a method to mask unwanted sounds in preoperative, surgical, and post-operative areas. This type of positive auditory stimulus consists of adding a sound source that blends seamlessly into the background. This masking out of otherwise intrusive sounds can help to alleviate tedium and, as mentioned, stress. The aim, from a psychological perspective, is to counter environmentally-induced sources of stress. Developed in the late 1970s, ambient soundscaping arose from the emerging synthesizer-driven popular music idioms, and Brian Eno is widely regarded as one of the idiom's founders. Ambient soundscaping is conceptual, experimental, atmospheric, and unobtrusive. But it is *not* muzak. They are not the same.[106] Ambient music crosses over multiple idioms and its sonic imagery can evoke spaciousness, openness, and tranquility. Its precursors are both ancient and high tech: a simple bamboo flute or synthesized electronica.[107] Its function is to induce relaxation, contemplation, inspiration, and peaceful, expansive moods.[108] Sounds can be sculpted, evocative of specific imagery, and tailored to mask noises generated from nearby highly trafficked rooms and corridors. In selecting a host structure for a pop-up clinic, for example, the structure's acoustical properties will at first glance probably be of little or no priority in assessing its merits. Acoustics, and noise, however, can soon emerge as a negative factor from the moment anyone enters the building. Particularly in industrial buildings, such as warehouses with high ceilings, the host's interior proportions and its hard surfaces may become an echo chamber, causing sounds to bounce off of the ceilings, walls, and other hard surfaces and even sounds emanating from the floor have a tendency to billow upward, contributing to the din (Figure 5.39).

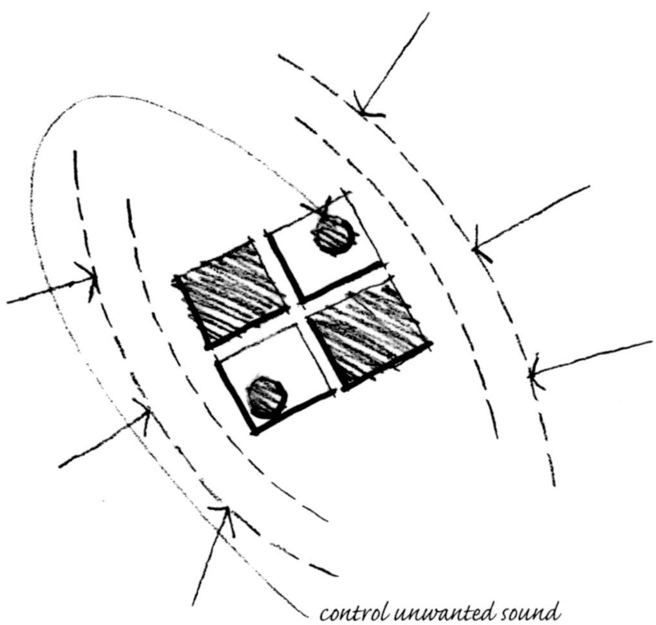

5.39 Excessive noise is a significant source of cognitive dissonance and stress in care settings

Lean and portables

In North America, the *Lean* movement has gained remarkable traction since 2000. Its objective is to root out waste and save time in hospitals and allied healthcare facilities. The problem, as most often stated by its adherents, is that there is inefficiency and far too much waste in day-to-day facility operations. Lean is heavily adapted from Toyota's production system, and its originator, Taiichi Ohno.[109] Lean is both a philosophy and a methodology whose aim is to produce the highest quality 'product' in the shortest amount of time, at the lowest possible cost, by eliminating the 'seven wastes.' It aims to foster a culture that encourages all employees to continually look for further efficiencies and greater productivity. The seven wastes (with corollaries to a portable health facility indicated in parenthesis) are: overproduction (facility overcapacity), wasted time (a caregiving team needlessly waiting for supplies and support services), inefficient product transport causing needless delays (transport snafus), excess processing time and steps (dysfunctional logistics), lax inventory control (lack of supplies, redundant or poor quality equipment, lack of inventory control), unnecessary physical movement (excessive staff and patient travel distances and awkward flow), and defective outcomes (lactogenic illness, facility-acquired infections, medical errors). Lean requires, first and foremost, the deconstruction of an organization's operations flowchart and its procedures, then its reconstruction and re-standardization with the aim of attaining repeatable, stable, methods and metrics that can consistently yield a more predictable, reliable outcome. The second fundamental aim, as mentioned, is to establish a workplace culture whereby the staff is continually looking for new ways to question itself, new ways to streamline.[110] Other examples of pertinent goals in a portable healthcare facility might include: reducing bed prep time, streamlining patient intake/interviews and patient discharge, and creating a workplan to comprehensively monitor and sustain further improvements in facility operations. In a post-disaster strike zone, the attainment of a high degree of operational precision may sound oxymoronic in the face of having to get by each day with minimal staffing, minimal supplies, and so on. However, if the Lean philosophy and methodology can save even a single life, it is worth investigating, in extreme situational contexts.

Offsite manufacturing

It can be daunting to seek out a manufacturer for a portable healthcare facility. The U.S.-based *Modular Building Institute* (MBI), based in Charlottesville, Virginia, is an international, non-profit trade association serving the prefab modular construction industry. Founded in 1983, membership consists of prefab manufacturers, contractors, and dealers in two distinct sectors of the industry—permanent modular construction (PMC) and relocatable buildings (RB). Most MBI members are North American-based although members are also based in Australia, Azerbaijan, Chile, Poland, the Russian Federation, South Africa, Turkey, Argentina, Hong Kong, Finland, India, Mexico, Mongolia, Peru, Puerto Rico, Taiwan, and the U.K. Associate members in the MBI are companies that supply building components, services, and financing, internationally. This organization is perhaps the most well-known clearinghouse for best practices and innovations in North America. It champions the advantages of offsite-built buildings, as they cause less site disturbances, greater flexibility, enhanced adaptive use options, generate less material waste during construction, and yield improved indoor air quality levels within a highly controlled manufacturing environment (from a worker air quality health standpoint) as well as in the completed, inhabited building. The MBI states this approach can be faster to produce and install by up to 50 percent compared to conventional onsite construction. Weather delays are virtually eliminated, and prefab modular assemblies are code-inspected at the plant. Also, the MBI claims this approach is safer because factory controlled conditions result in fewer accidents compared to conventional outdoor construction. Prefab modular is pre-engineered with Building Information Modeling (BIM) software, and the finished building—whether a portable or permanent site structure—can be virtually indistinguishable in quality and appearance from its conventionally built counterpart.[111] In the U.S., members of the MBI include manufacturers that provide in-house engineering and design services for healthcare projects, in-plant construction and turnkey warranties, code compliance, and compliance with U.S. Occupational Safety and Health Administration (OSHA) workplace standards. These manufacturers' prefab modular buildings include rural and urban health centers, acute care facilities, pharmacies and labs, physical therapy and rehabilitation centers, and diagnostic imaging centers.[112] The number of American prefab modular manufacturers with experience in healthcare has grown since 2000.[113] Similarly, in Canada, manufacturers have grown more numerous, including Modspace Corporation, with its twelve factories located across the country.[114] Most recently, in-plant code compliance and product testing as part of the commissioning process has become a marketing and public relations focus for many of these manufacturers.[115]

Selecting an offsite manufacturer

Compared to the brick and mortar construction industry, offsite prefab modular construction, in most parts of the world, remains in its infancy. It may be a challenge to find a fabricator with the right experience and mindset or a source whose factory capacity and work team is equipped to build a portable, redeployable, or permanent installation healthcare structure. But: this is not to say that a given manufacturer would necessarily, on principle, be disqualified from the outset from entering this growing segment of the global construction industry. More participants are needed if future demand is to be met. The leadership and membership of the MBI is starting to get onboard (but the MBI still archaically refers to portable structures as 'reusable' facilities). It now advocates with, and on behalf of, the North American architectural profession. In PMIs there is only one site so everything is geared for one location. Obviously, in the case of an RTC or RHC it is more of a challenge because a product is being designed and built for *unknown* site circumstances. Because of this, it is important that the client, architect, and the builder contractually establish project parameters from project start to turnkey occupancy (and often beyond in the case of redeployables). In the case of an RTC or RHC, the client may be asked to sign-off on certain preconditions of a product warranty in order to receive full protection. Alibaba.com is one website that functions as a clearinghouse for this, and has connections to prefab building suppliers based in Mainland China, South Africa, India, the United Arab Emirates, Argentina, Australia, Canada, and Denmark.[116] Another useful information source is ThomasNet.com. Its homepage lists manufacturers of mobile medical coaches as well as many types of offsite-built portables.[117] Other experienced manufacturers include Weatherhaven, with factories in Australia, Canada, South Africa, and South America,[118] and the lightweight transportable clinics manufactured by Forts

Fold-Out shelters, whose main factory is in Florida.[119] The current generation of university students can also help to blaze new trails. Students at Arizona State University repurposed a standard ISO container into a portable clinic for deployment to Kenya. Their *G3Box* was the focus of a non-profit (U.S. 401c corporation) created in 2013. Through the website, IndieGoGo.com, they quickly met their $17,650 goal, indicative of the widespread interest in all this (Figure 5.40).[120]

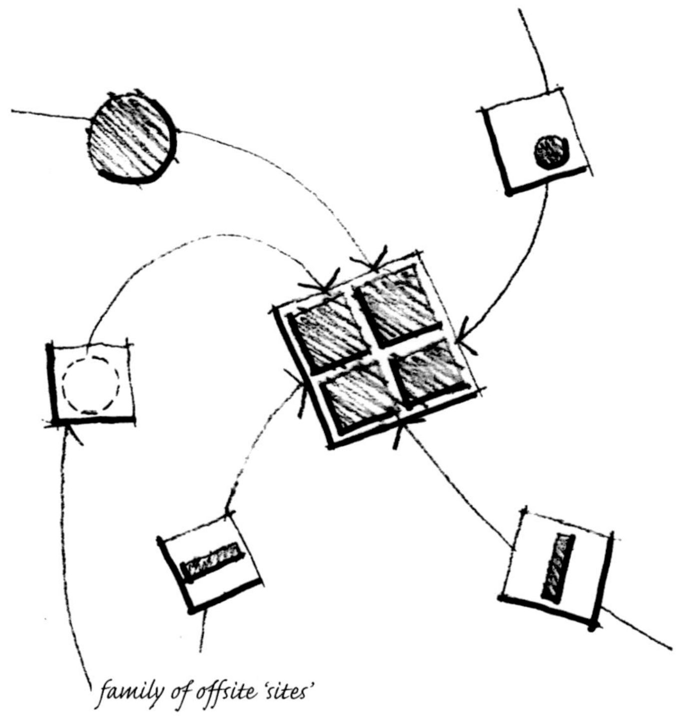

5.40 Source components from suppliers based on proven methods in the automotive and in other industries

PART 3

Case studies

Case studies 1–18

CHAPTER 6

The projects

Modular and containerized systems

1 Women's Health Clinic, Port-au-Prince, Haiti:
STANTEC/STACK Design

2 Mobile Field Hospital System 3:1, Germany:
Zeppelin Mobile Systems (ZMS), GmbH, Germany

3 Contertainer, Batu, East Jawa, Indonesia:
dpavilion Architects, Surabaya, Indonesia

Panelized and tent-based systems

4 Mobile Field Hospital, USA:
BLU-MED Response Systems/Alaska Structures

5 QS72 Clinic, Japan:
Quickspace, Ltd.

6 Portable Isolation Containment System (PICS), Canada:
Design Shelter, Inc.

7 Combat Army Support Hospital (CSH), USA:
U.S. Army Corps of Engineers

Vehicular and guided systems

8 AMoHS, USA:
Advanced Mobile Hospital Systems Inc.

9 Mobile Field Hospital, Morocco:
Hord Coplan Macht Architects/Engineers, Baltimore, Maryland + Spevco/MONARCH Corporation

10 Mobile Airship HIV Clinic (prototype), Sub-Saharan Africa:
JAG Design

11 Toronto Rehab CEAL/iDAPT Centre, Canada:
Murphy Hilgers Architects/Aecon Group, Inc./Toronto Rehabilitation Institute

Prefab hospitals and clinics

12 Puyo General Hospital, Puyo, Ecuador:
PmMt Arquitectura, Ecuador

13 Swedish Medical Oncology Clinic, Ballard, Washington, USA:
Perkins+Will, Seattle, Washington

14 Miami Valley Heart and Orthopedic Center, Dayton, Ohio, USA:
NBBJ, Columbus, Ohio

RTC prognostications

15 Raptor Prototype, USA:
Gregory Swindon, CU/A+H

16 SmartPOD Prototype, USA:
George Hughes, CU/A+H

17 Seagull Prototype, USA:
Ryan Ramsey, CU/A+H

18 RDoC Pop-up Pavilion-Clinic, San Francisco, USA:
Perkins+Will, San Francisco/Michael Bardin with Degenkolb Engineers, Mazzetti Engineering, San Francisco

Eighteen case studies are presented in this chapter. Collectively, they represent a cross section of portable architecture for health. Public sector portable structures frequently originate in military organizations, whereas private sector portables tend to originate from not-for-profit NGOs. A prefab modular building for a permanent installation site can originate in either. The eighteen projects represent acute care hospitals, a research institute, emergency trauma care facilities, mobile vehicular clinics, and primary care facilities. Each case study was selected based on pre-specified criteria. First, it must be a completed building, or if unbuilt, a proposal that can be developed further to become a built project. In a few cases, a project selected for inclusion awaits construction funding. Second, the case study must be innovative in some way. Third, each case study must exhibit design excellence in terms of its formal attributes, materiality, tectonics, constructability, and functionality. Fourth, each case study must be capable of exhibiting rapid response amenity—rapid connectivity—in terms of expeditiously getting it to where it needs to be and then once there, being able to be readily assembled and opened in a timely manner. In terms of the definitions presented in Chapter 1, a given case study is either a *Redeployable Health Center* (RHC), a *Redeployable Trauma Center* (RTC), or a *Permanent Modular Installation* (PMI). Beyond this, each case study represents one of five basic variants:

- *Vehicular-based nomadics*—Prefab modular mobile clinics and infirmaries are built on a generic truck chassis with the interior compartment built separately, then assembled onto the chassis, followed by final assembly. A second type is a two-part system, where a truck cab pulls a module housing the medical component, with the two components built independently.
- *Tent and pneumatic systems*—The tent is the father of all portable structures for healthcare. Tents are lightweight, versatile, and cross-culturally adaptable to occupant needs, topographically challenging terrain, and diverse climates. Tents have evolved significantly in recent years, including the emergence of modular pneumatic systems.
- *Containerized systems*—Variations on the ubiquitous intermodal-shipping container is a preferred choice for many healthcare provider organizations because these modular units possess structural strength and resiliency. Containerized systems perform well in densely closepacked conditions while in transit. Systems for healthcare applications are typically custom-built.
- *Flat-pack and pop-up systems*—These portable structures for health consist of prefab modular kit-of-parts assemblies shipped inside perhaps thirty to forty standard intermodal containers, or a similar, custom-built container. The structure's components are removed, assembled, and often, in-transit containers are stored on site and remain available for ancillary uses.
- *Hybrid systems*—These systems consist of *composite facilities*, a synthesis of mobile vehicular units and tents, or containers combined with either conventional tents or pneumatic tents.

Hybrid systems provide advantages including greater aesthetic freedom, and an ability to effectively distribute functions between the 'hard' and 'soft' zones of the installation.

At the scale of site deployment

A portable structure for health is usually designed and built for an unknown site. Permanent site installations, on the other hand, are built for one and only one site. In the case of portables, the selection of an installation site is governed by multiple determinants. A system may arrive at a site with its own site prep equipment, perhaps consisting of earthmoving devices and forklifts. Flat sites are most advantageous and these include football pitches, rooftop parking decks, sufficiently wide streets, paved parking lots, parkland, and open fields. It is often preferable to tether the installation to a local hospital, such as in the case of the BLU-MED facility deployed to the site of the destroyed St. Joseph's hospital in Joplin, Missouri after the catastrophic F-5 tornado in 2012.

At the scale of an individual module

Prefabricated, factory-assembled modules, and prefab modular flat-pack systems, are two widely used facility configurations. Flat-packs attain their volumetric modularity and structural integrity on site. Containerized units may or may not require assembly at the installation site. Each module is autonomous yet integral to its larger modular platform when fully assembled. All connections must fit well, and prove watertight. The personnel who erect and operate the installation need to be suitably trained in order to make the highest and best use of the completed structure, and in the case of vehicles, to ensure they are properly deployed.

At the scale of a room

If it is true that everything begins with the module, then its performance and functionality will determine the overall success of the installation. All interior spaces, their equipment and furnishings, as well as the facility's larger, intangible, ambient qualities, must focus on maximizing the patient care experience. In programming, design, and in manufacture, person–environment interdependencies need to be identified at the outset of the planning process in order to achieve the maximum degree of fit—in terms of rooms, their sizes, and interior amenities along with spatial orientation, ambiance, adjoining internal circulation, and natural daylight and ventilation.

In terms of sustainability and resilience

The movement towards carbon neutrality and resiliency in architecture for health is slowly advancing, although forward progress tends to occur in fits and starts. Metrics are needed to calculate the greenness of a portable structure and to be able to comparatively assess different design and manufacturing options with regards to performance criteria centered on sustainability (ecological attributes) and resilience (bounce-back attributes). Life-cycle energy costs, mechanical, electrical and plumbing systems (MEP) equipment, furnishings, maintenance factors, and the anticipated rate of facility obsolescence can all be quantified. In time, energy self-sufficiency must become the baseline standard with the ability to bring to the site onboard, hybrid power sources just as with a hybrid automobile—to enable a seamless transfer between multiple energy sources, i.e. from fossil fuel to electrical grid, or from photovoltaic cells to wind power, and back in order to extend the installation's maximum *range*.

Defining a portable building is not a straightforward task because it becomes entangled with defining a work of *architecture* versus the construction of a *building*. If a portable structure aims to express, in built form, its creators' creative ambitions, then it must be considered as *architecture*. It should be the ambition of all who appreciate and understand the nature of temporal architecture to be able to draw the distinction between a transportable building and *transportable architecture*. In the case of the latter, the case must be made for its broader relevance and importance in the shaping of the present and future built environment. Moveable structures are often prematurely dismissed, overlooked, considered too pragmatic and nothing more. This line of reasoning assumes they cannot also aspire to be poetic. These eighteen case studies are all *buildings*, including the prognostications presented near the end of the chapter, but many aspire to be much more. It is left up to the reader to ascertain which ones are already (or possess the potential to become) genuine works of *architecture*.

1 Women's Health Clinic, Haiti

ARCHITECT: STANTEC/STACK Design
ENGINEER: Allied Container Systems (Manufacturer)
CLIENT/SPONSOR: Containers2Clinics (C2C), Oakbrook, Illinois
TYPE OF CARE: Outpatient primary care (RHC)
NUMBER OF BEDS: N/A
FEATURED MATERIALS: ISO containers
METHOD OF ASSEMBLY: Modular/onsite construction
SITE CONTEXT: Rural
DEPLOYMENT (MIN/MAX): 3,000 square feet
COMPLETED: 2010

Context/site

In January of 2010, the catastrophic earthquake of magnitude 7.0 that struck Haiti, approximately twenty-five miles from the capital of Port-au-Prince, displaced three million people. The death toll ranged from 160,000 to the Haitian government's own estimate of 220,000. The region's hospitals and clinics were either severely damaged or destroyed entirely. Early relief efforts were stymied by impenetrable political red tape, an inability to achieve coordination among myriad, competing, global humanitarian assistance organizations, and a lack of local governmental planning or guidance of any sort. Port-au-Prince's morgues were overwhelmed with tens of thousands of bodies, and mass graves had to be dug. After the first wave of disaster response faded, the focus turned to the absence of adequate housing, food, proper sanitation, and medical care (see Chapter 1).[1]

Containers2Clinics (C2C) is a non-profit, charitable NGO based in the Chicago metro area that aims to improve the health of women and thereby improve global access to healthcare in medically underserved communities in the developing world. It aims to achieve this through the use of prefab modular portable clinics (see Interview 2 in the Appendix). Affiliations established with local healthcare providers enables C2C to supplement locally available healthcare services in situations where the existing facilities are either non-functioning, or overwhelmed, due to an exceedingly high demand for care, i.e. child and maternal healthcare, immunizations, nutritional health education, reproductive health, and perinatal and gynecological care. C2C clinics provide much-needed additional capacity that enables an existing local provider to extend its reach outward into places that would otherwise not have any access whatsoever to healthcare services. C2C works with architectural design teams to provide containerized outpatient women's health clinics in support of local humanitarian aid needs. Local healthcare personnel staff these clinics, working alongside volunteers from beyond Haiti.

The generic intermodal shipping container, in this scenario, provided a blank canvas, as a durable and readily transportable platform and one that could be modified and customized to provide natural ventilation and daylight. With the organization's aim to establish and then strengthen access to rural healthcare by providing additional facility capacity, C2C opened its first clinic at Grace Children's Hospital, in Port-au-Prince, Haiti, four months after the earthquake. By 2014, three C2C clinics were up and running and more than 20,000 patients had received treatment. The first clinic was designed as a joint venture between Anshen + Allen, in consort with Stack Design Build. Allied Container Systems manufactured the first prototype.

Building/unit

The design challenge was to develop a standardized outpatient care platform that could be transported by ship to locales not only in Haiti but globally and then transited on land over difficult terrain to remote communities. Its customized containers, culled from an estimated inventory of twenty million castoffs worldwide, were adapted to provide appropriate functional space, space for the storage of medical equipment and supplies, ventilation/natural cooling capabilities, personal hygiene, and a requisite level of security. Two eight foot by twenty foot containers were modified according to the

6.1.1 C2C Women's Health Clinic, Port-au-Prince, Haiti, at night

6.1.2 Intermodal containers modified to include windows, doors, minimal HVAC/MEP support, and medical equipment

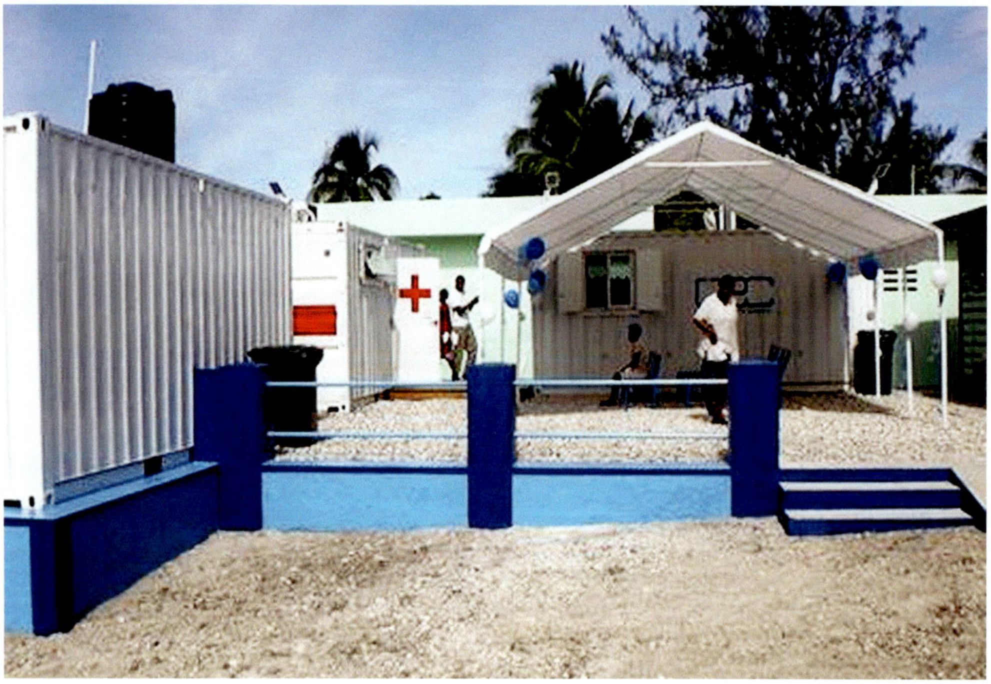

6.1.3 A canopy shades an outdoor waiting area. Container-modules typically require a flat site and because of this, this installation site was raised and leveled

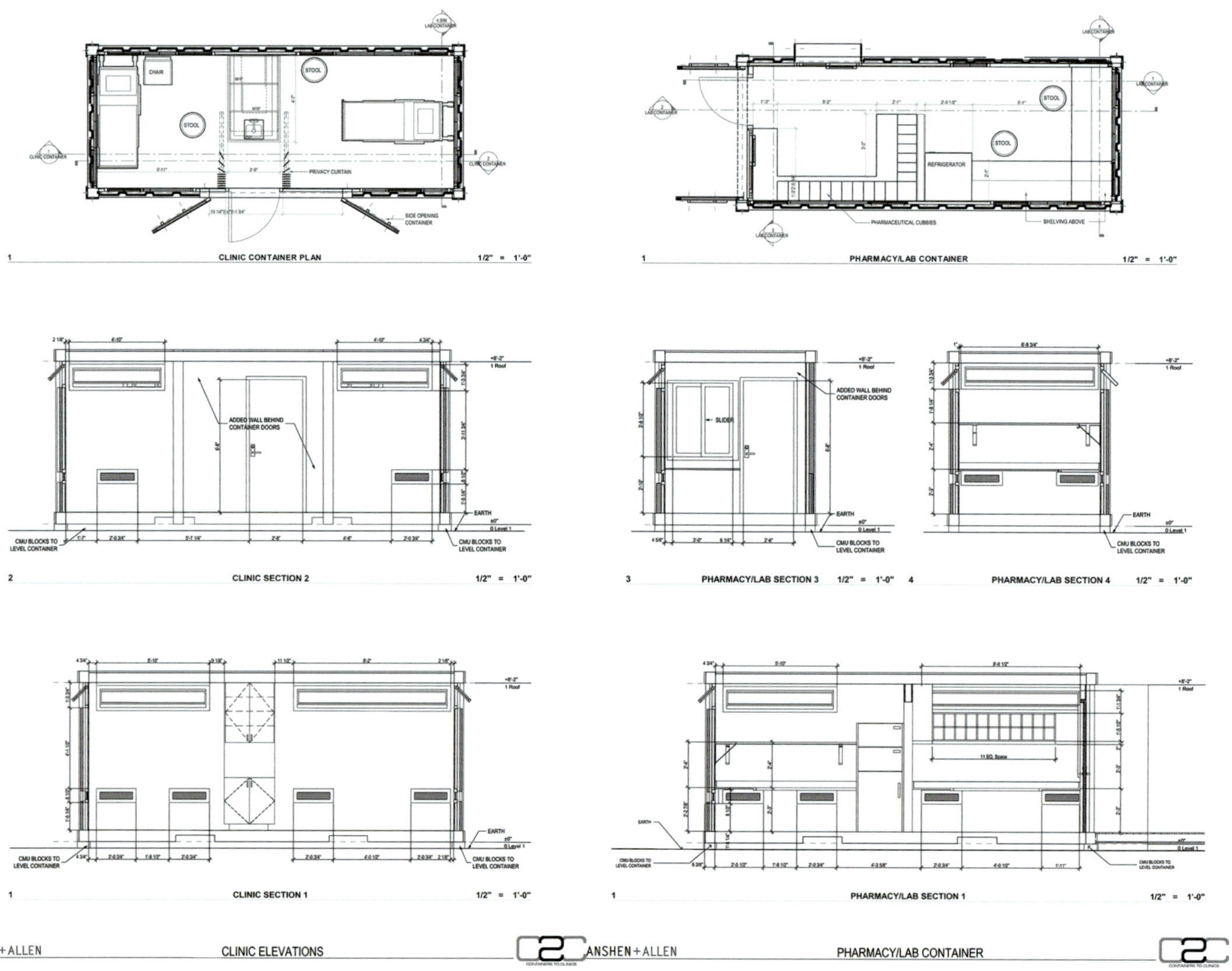

6.1.4a–f Working drawings indicate the modifications to transform generic ISO containers into something much more

6.1.5a–f Renderings of a two-module C2C installation highlight an umbrella-like solar screen

6.1.6 Cutaway view of a two-bed module, with a small nursing work/ supply core situated in between. A pair of accordion panels provides functional separation and a modicum of privacy

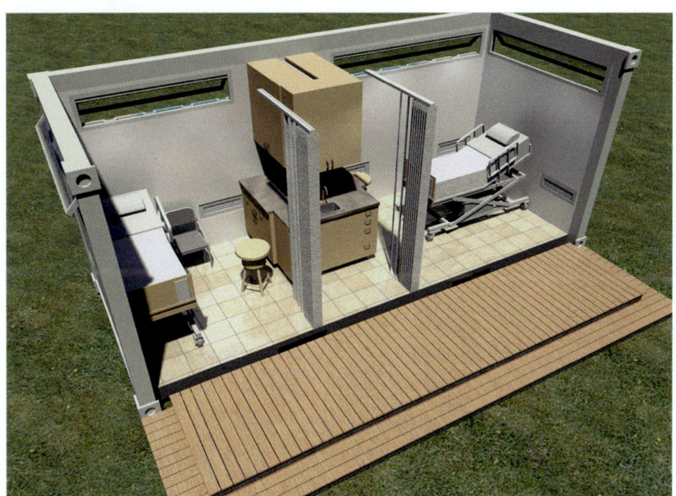

6.1.7 Blow-apart axonometric view of a module

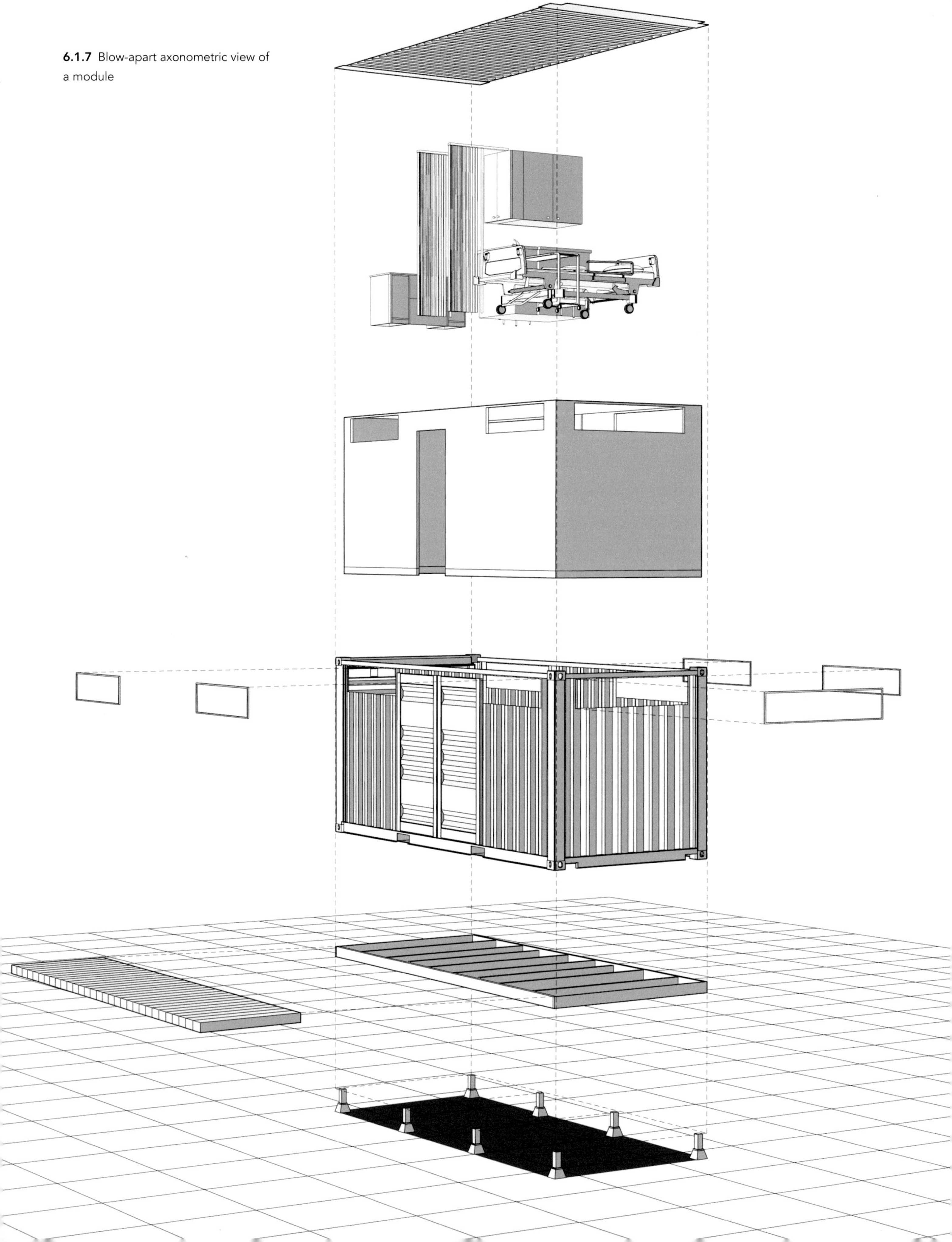

client's, and patients', needs. The project brief consisted of these two containers housing a fully equipped examination/consultation room, a diagnostic imaging lab, pharmacy/medications storeroom, a small break area for staff, and a removable partition wall with an interlocking door, for use in lockdown security situations.

The redesigned containers were painted in heat-reflective paint, and were equipped with solar-powered fans and photovoltaic-powered light fixtures (Figures 6.1.1 to 6.1.4a–f). The modules were interconnected by means of a wood platform that serves as an open-air waiting room, protected by a canvas tent, with seating provided. The modules are sited in an L-configuration, and are expandable with the addition of a third or fourth container, as needed, creating a courtyard at the center.[2] To C2C, the most appealing aspects of the adaptation of modified shipping containers remains their strength, durability, portability, and reliability in installations of varying size and complexity at diverse sites both in Haiti and elsewhere worldwide. This organization has plans to expand its outreach activities in the service of medically disenfranchised populations (Figures 6.1.5a–f to 6.1.7).

2 Mobile Field Hospital System 3:1, Germany

ENGINEERS: Zeppelin Mobile Systems (ZMS), GmbH, Germany
CLIENT/SPONSOR: United Nations
TYPE OF CARE: Step-up acuity-adaptable unit (RTC)
NUMBER OF BEDS: Variable
FEATURED MATERIALS: Steel, fabric, polyurethane
METHOD OF ASSEMBLY: Containerized
SITE CONTEXT: Variable
DEPLOYMENT (MIN/MAX): 250/600+ square feet
COMPLETED: 2009

Context/site

Zeppelin Mobile Systems (ZMS), of Germany, manufactures mobile field hospitals for military and civilian organizations that have been purchased by organizations in Norway, Sweden, Estonia, Germany, and elsewhere. The ZMS System 3:1 depicted here was built for the United Nations' international relief program. The ZMS System 3:1 meets the minimum design and equipment standards of the *International Red Cross*. At first, it may appear rather generic, but in fact it is a customized, high-tech variation on the standard intermodal ISO container. The base module is a 20-foot long container that can expand horizontally outward on either side by means of pop-out components, one on each side of the base module. This system is earthquake-resistant and has proven to be highly resilient in diverse site and climatic contexts. The expanded module is well suited for installation on relatively flat, unobstructed sites and in situations where many units can be connected together in tight, orthogonal grids. The modules sit slightly above the ground plane, supported by one-foot high adjustable leg/stabilizers in order to ensure a level floor surface, and to ensure structural stability. Flexible, accordion-like connectors link the modules together and large gasket connectors ensure a fully weatherized internal circulation system. These strong yet flexible connectors ensure a safe, sanitized/sterile work environment. The accordion connectors are approximately six feet in length, although some minor tolerances are acceptable, i.e. built into the modules, and connecting parts, due to soil conditions that can vary from site to site. Installation options range from one to as many as fifty units on a single site and the weatherized internal circulation network allows many options to provide a higher percentage of intensive medical care, for instance, by setting up many similar units in close proximity to one another (Figures 6.2.1 and 6.2.2).

Building/unit

When deployed in dense groupings, the field hospital has the capacity to house a relatively large pre-operative, surgical, and post-operative section. In the post-operative bays, patients await MEDIVAC transport for more intensive care, if needed, at a stationary base hospital. The surgical units consist of a core module with its pair of pop-out hard-walled extenders, tripling the floor area of the core. Its sides pull out horizontally not unlike dresser drawers. Modules are specially equipped to house the field hospital's tactical medical command unit, and the inpatient modules each contain twelve beds, as well as nursing and technical

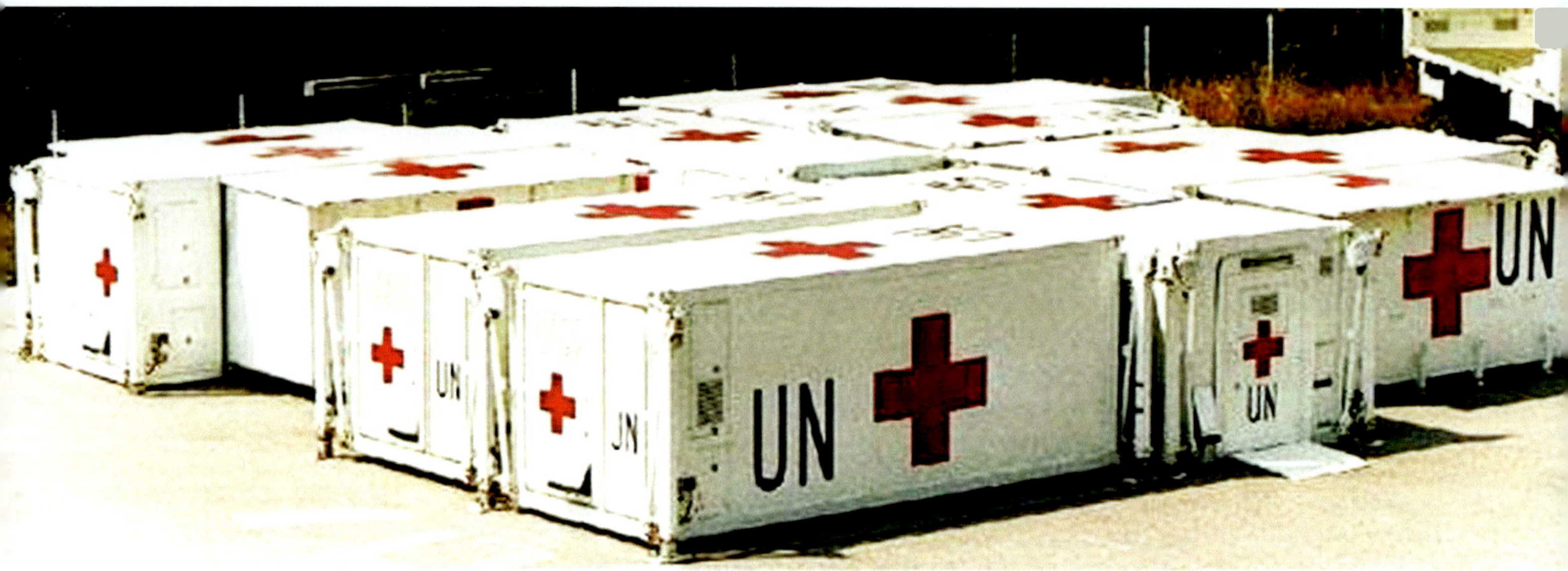

6.2.1 Mobile Field Hospital System 3:1, Germany. Units are densely clustered to maximize functional relationships and minimize staff walking distances

6.2.2 Accordion-like vestibular connectors facilitate weather tight passageways between modules

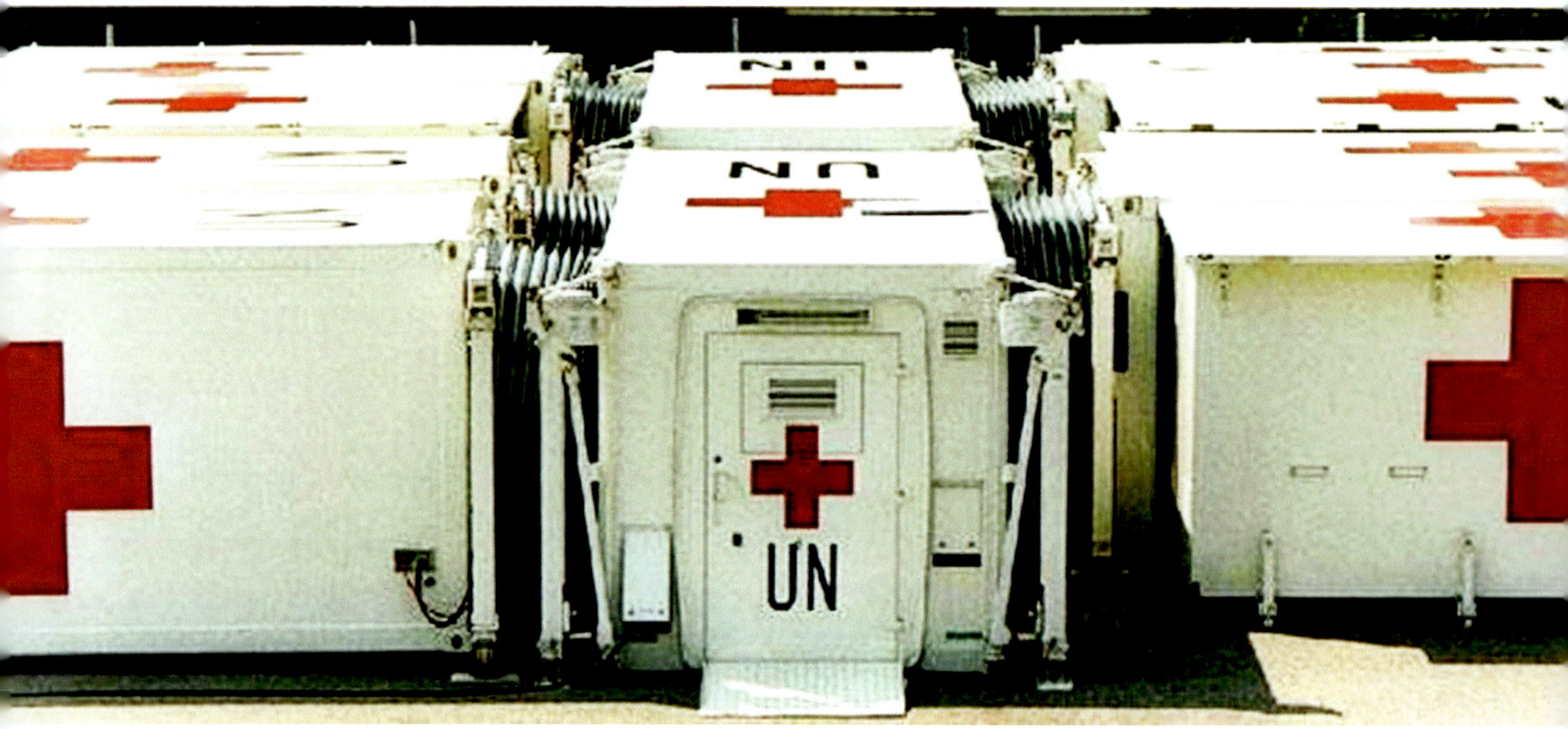

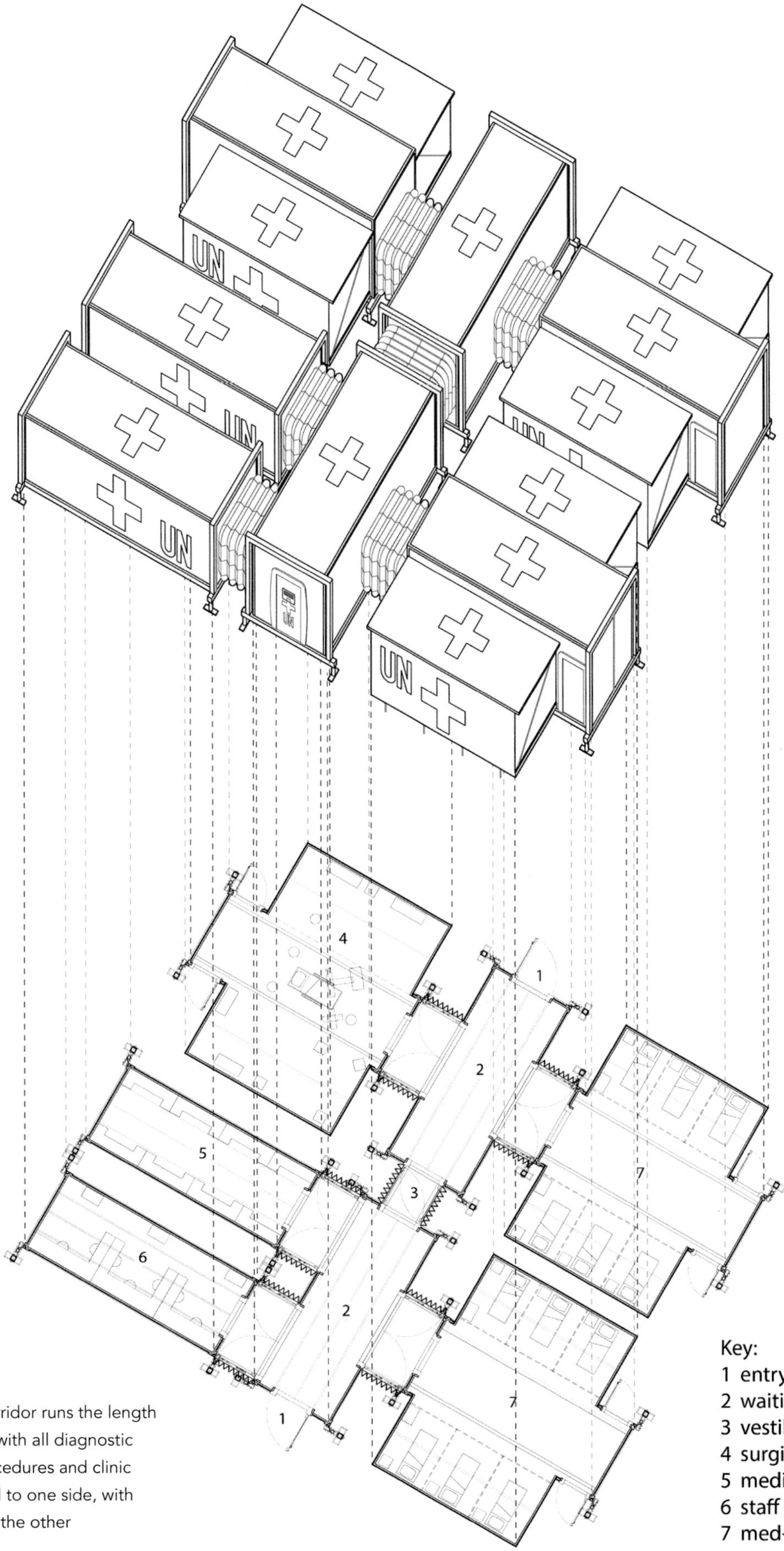

Key:
1 entry
2 waiting/triage
3 vestibule/connector
4 surgical suite
5 medication/storeroom
6 staff support/consultation
7 med-surgical units

6.2.3 A central corridor runs the length of the installation, with all diagnostic and treatment procedures and clinic support centralized to one side, with inpatient wards on the other

6.2.4 Modules feature dual pop-out extensions, tripling interior usable space. Sidewalls lift up to become roofs and diagonal struts provide structural stability

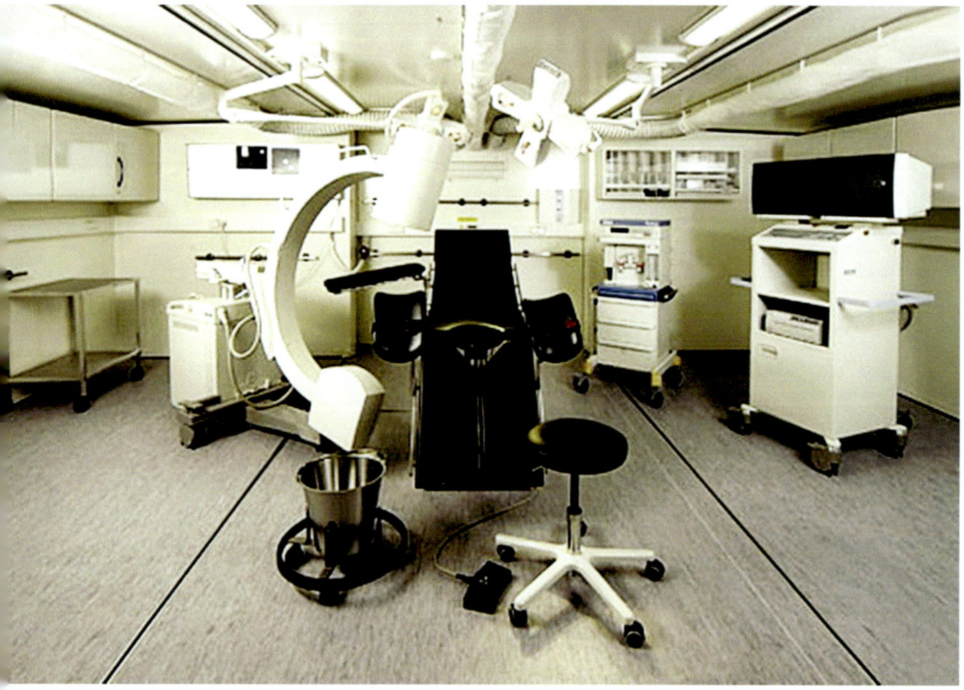

6.2.5 Interior of a module as fully expanded. All medical equipment is shipped with the system and must be compact, durable, and lightweight

support. The installation is equipped with chemical and biological filtration systems, an integrated diesel generator, advanced air filtration system, heating and cooling systems, a dehumidifier unit, a lighting system, and full telecommunications. Compressed air, oxygen, anesthesia gases, and potable water are provided. The installation can operate entirely off-grid in remote sites that lack functioning utilities, ensuring operations will not be interrupted (Figures 6.2.3 to 6.2.5).

A power generator module is designed specifically for the ZMS System 3:1, with additional modules for storage of equipment and supplies. Pre-operative staging and post-operative observation quarters house services ranging from basic surgery on extremities, to shock treatment, neurosurgery, burn treatment and skin grafts, and other major surgical procedures. In addition, ear, nose, and throat, dentistry, urology and gynecology, and laboratory services are provided, i.e. from food chemistry, to microbiology. In large installations, dietary support modules house kitchen and dining areas. This system can be deployed on the top deck of a naval vessel. It thereby becomes a nautical hospital. This system has been built to comply with maritime safety standards, and is certified by international maritime insurance carriers. Here, as on land, the system can be set up and modified as needs evolve to accommodate diverse medical requirements, from primary care, general medical and dental care, laboratory and radiology diagnostic services, surgery, and post-operative treatment. Nautical deployments allow, as do installations on land, for acuity adaptability. This has proven to be a cost-effective means to extend a vessel's capabilities. Whether at sea or on land, the system is adaptable, with tools provided in the onboard kit-of-parts, including if a module needs to be replaced or repositioned. These operations are performed using deck-mounted highboy cranes. Modules are transited to vessels by conventional modes of transport, or can be airlifted in by helicopter (Figure 6.2.6).

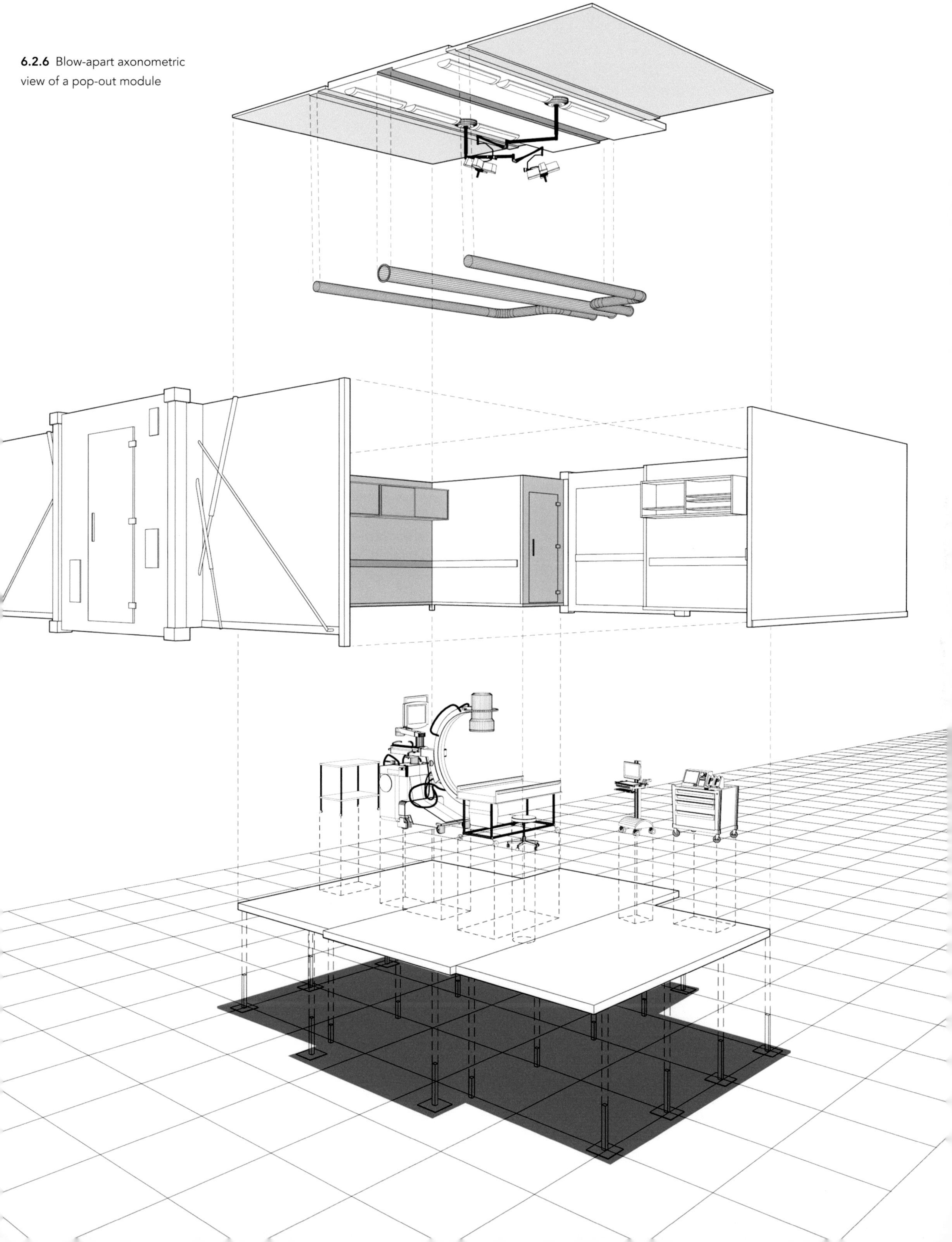

6.2.6 Blow-apart axonometric view of a pop-out module

3 Contertainer, Batu, East Jawa, Indonesia

ARCHITECT: dpavilion Architects, Surabaya, Indonesia
ENGINEER: Junaedi Masil and Associates, Surjo, Indonesia
CLIENT/SPONSOR: East Jawa Ministry of Public Works, Indonesia
TYPE OF CARE: Outpatient care/public library (PMI)
NUMBER OF BEDS: N/A
FEATURED MATERIALS: ISO containers/glass/steel
METHOD OF ASSEMBLY: Modular/onsite construction
SITE CONTEXT: Rural
INSTALLATION: 9,500 square feet
COMPLETED: 2009

Context/site

LOT-EK, the New York City architectural firm founded in 1993, was among the first to seriously rethink the generic intermodal ISO container, in its built projects, publications, and gallery exhibitions. Its philosophy has centered on a process it refers to as *up-cycling*—reexamining ready-made, low-tech, ordinary disposables and transforming them into inhabitable architecture. In claiming, reinterpreting, and reassembling the ubiquitous shipping container, the firm's aim has been to explore the ISO's latent possibilities. Many firms have been inspired by the work of LOT-EK, including the Indonesian firm dpavilion Architects, who were commissioned to design a mixed-use building loosely in the spirit of LOT-EK, and Japan's Team Zoo. Team Zoo is widely known for its multi-programmatic, or trans-programmatic, buildings including its Kazura Clinic (1980–1982) in Chiba, Japan, a biomorphic-shaped building that combined a pediatric clinic with a day hospital and a physician's residence—all within an unconventional building envelope (Figures 6.3.1 and 6.3.2).[3]

LOT-EK's recent art school project, the 'APAP Open School,' in Anyang, Korea (2012) is composed of bright yellow containers lifted up on pilotis with one container jutting upward at a skewed angle above the roofline of this datum-like 'box.'[4] The *Contertainer* is reminiscent of this project, an amalgam of two concepts: container and entertainer. It is located in Batu, a rural but rapidly urbanizing new town and former tribal village, a place that retains vestiges of its deep agricultural heritage. This facility is essentially a public, civic structure, housing a branch library and a primary care clinic. Both are free to the citizens of the local community. The Contertainer is a mixed-use structure, and in contrast to the aforementioned Team Zoo project, is not a single volume but an expressive assemblage of multiple volumes choreographed in a kinetic, even frenetic manner. Its inventiveness lies in its unconventionality, questioning the ISO container and in the process shattering its blandness. Similarly, Team Zoo's trans-programmatic building functioned as a tour de force in its use of playful, intersecting, undulating forms, although far, far heavier in appearance, as it was executed in a very different material palette—cast-in-place concrete. dpavilion's structure, by contrast, is composed of eight recycled containers that branch out from a vertical circulation/structural core. The prefab modules are lifted up above the ground plane on stilts, and are painted in bold primaries with each color-coded to a different internal function. In the case of the library, the blue container houses popular literature, the red houses books on science and technology and the yellow one houses the women's literature collection and a reading room. The green container houses the main lobby and arrival area, with the red container extending above an outdoor terrace with tables and chairs for reading.[5]

Building/unit

The clinic is housed on the ground level next to a ramp that threads its way upward to levels two and three above, where the library is located. The containers are cantilevered, with some modules appearing to be suspended rather precariously. The effect is one where the overall composition remains more intriguing than the sum of its parts (the containers, in this case). The plinth that houses the clinic functions as a tree trunk with various container-cum-branches extending upward and outward, seemingly randomly. Large cutouts break the otherwise windowless containers; they also provide a modicum of shade, although this seems somewhat gestural at best and would appear to have little effect in abating any actual heat gain that would undoubtedly build up in the interior. The red module on the uppermost level cantilevers above the circular outdoor reading room deck that itself contains a cutout

6.3.1 Contertainer, Batu, East Jawa, Indonesia. This iconic, mixed-use structure is a landmark in the local community

connecting it back to the ground level. A transparent, internalized circulation 'box,' sheathed in glass, becomes a beacon at night. Forms are playfully juxtaposed against one another and yet, collectively, do not compete.

The outpatient health clinic, as mentioned, is housed in the base of the structure, and its waiting room features full-height windows. This part of the building appears anchored, in contrast to the weightless, more acrobatically composed library module above. It is a place that establishes a strong civic presence by means of a bold formal vocabulary and playful use of color (Figures 6.3.3 and 6.3.4a–c). The Contertainer is in keeping with architects' increasing efforts to transcend the limitations of ISO container-themed, small-scale residential and commercial retail commissions and applying their attributes to civic aims and ambitions. In Vancouver, British Columbia, the Downtown Eastside Social Housing Project is another such example of this increasing ambitiousness. It consists of twelve recycled containers that form the basis of a three-level, twelve-unit residential complex for formerly homeless women. It is Canada's first recycled shipping container-based project of its type. The intent is for its residents to stabilize their personal lives and get back into the mainstream of everyday life. The local community, both in the case of the Contertainer and in the case of the Eastside Social Housing Project, view their prefab containerized buildings with pride (Figures 6.3.5 and 6.3.6).[6]

6.3.2 An animated juxtaposition of reworked intermodal containers in bright colors, punctuated by a transparent container-like element housing circulation

6.3.3 Formal attributes of the containers are carefully exploited, with units cantilevered, jutting out at oblique angles

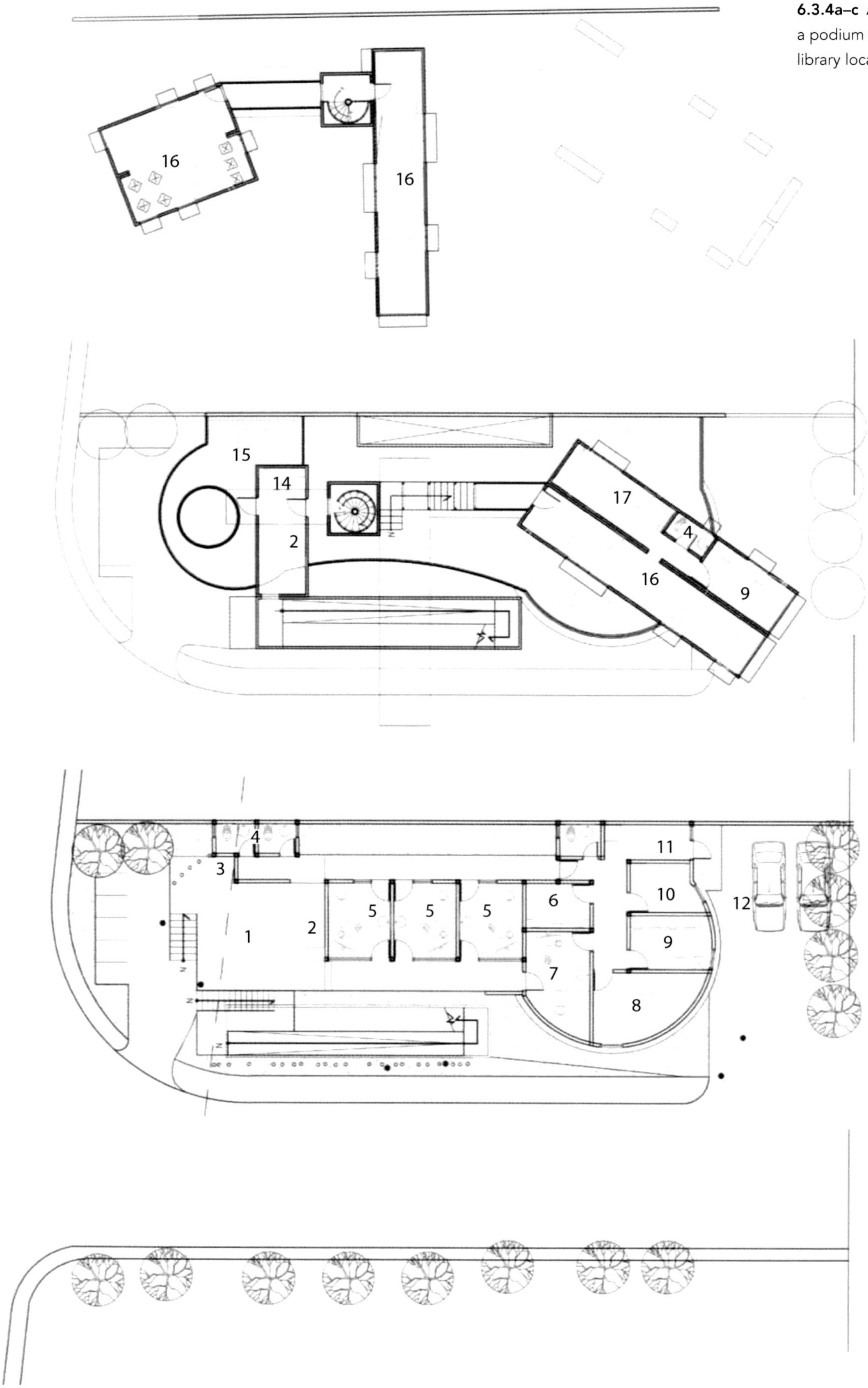

6.3.4a–c A health center is housed in a podium at ground level, with a library located on the two levels above

Key:
1 waiting room
2 reception
3 security
4 toilet
5 dentist room
6 potion room
7 radiology
8 meeting room
9 back office
10 restroom
11 pantry
12 car parking
13 motorcycle parking
14 locker
15 open space
16 reading room
17 collection room

6.3.5 The transparent circulation 'container' extends from the podium to the library above

6.3.6 Reception desk and waiting area with skylight cutout shown at left

4 Mobile Field Hospital, USA

ARCHITECT/ENGINEER: BLU-MED Response Systems/Alaska Structures
CLIENT/SPONSOR: Missouri Disaster Medical Assistance Team (DMAT)
TYPE OF CARE: Trauma care/stabilization center (RTC)
NUMBER OF BEDS: 10–200
FEATURED MATERIALS: Aluminum/fabric membrane
METHOD OF ASSEMBLY: Flat-pack
SITE CONTEXT: Variable
DEPLOYMENT (MIN/MAX): 1,500/30,000+ square feet
COMPLETED: 2009

Context/site

Considered the deadliest tornado in the U.S. since record keeping began in 1950, an EF-5 with 200 miles per hour winds killed more than 130 persons and injured more than 900 in Missouri in 2011. About one-third of the town of Joplin was left in total ruins, with 7,000 homes destroyed, including the total loss of the seven-level St. John's Mercy Hospital, one of the community's two major hospitals. Within hours after the storm passed, the Missouri Disaster Medical Assistance Team (DMAT) responded. Three days later services were restored on the St. John's campus by means of the deployment and commissioning of DMAT's 8,000 square foot mobile field hospital. This facility, manufactured by BLU-MED, had been deployed at Branson, Missouri some months earlier and that flat-pack facility was packed up and transported within four hours to Joplin. A sixty-bed facility configuration was erected within fifteen hours by the combined efforts of the Missouri National Guard, Missouri DMAT, and BLU-MED's disaster response consultants. The facility is designed to withstand 100 miles per hour winds and is built for a ten-year lifespan. This installation remained in place until the stationary hospital was rebuilt and reopened.[7]

BLU-MED worked closely with Alaska Structures. Alaska Structures designs, engineers, and constructs prefab modular fabric membrane tent systems for extreme environments. Since its founding in 1975, more than 50,000 units have been deployed to more than fifty nations around the world. This includes more than 30,000 throughout Alaska, and 15,000 units in Afghanistan and Iraq. It is a full service system consisting of flat-pack tents for use as mobile emergency rooms, operating suites, trauma centers, emergency operations centers (EOCs), with portable hospital surge capacity to aid stationary hospitals during emergencies, a decontamination unit, patient isolation wards, and a freestanding outpatient clinic. As is the case with similar flat-pack systems based on prevailing tent technology, the system is additive. As few as one or two units can be deployed, up to as many as forty or more (Figures 6.4.1 and 6.4.2). The manufacturer provides numerous options in this regard, with each configuration provided with equipment needed for first response deployment in disaster strike zones. Individual units can be fitted for specialized equipment, supplies, and logistical support such as infectious disease isolation units (Figure 6.4.3a–d).

Building/unit

This system can be expanded up to a 200-bed capacity with 30,000 square feet of occupied floor area, and operational in twenty-four hours from the time of arrival at the installation site. Support systems include waste disposal, food services, fuel supply, and potable water/wastewater systems. Individual modules are eighteen feet wide by thirty-five feet long by twelve feet high and appear in section as Quonset huts not unlike the classic ones used in World War II (see Chapters 3 and 5). Their curved roofs are sheathed in bright red and white fabric, and the two ends of each unit are sheathed in bright blue fabric. End walls of the modules feature fabric zipper/airlock fabric door panels and entry vestibules. A team of ten to twenty workers can erect a module's curved aluminum structural tubing, after the overall footprint of the total installation has been ascertained and each module has been carefully staked. The intent of the bold exterior color scheme of this non-military transportable for health is for the installation to be readily spotted from a distance by land, sea, or air.

In plan, the tent-modules are straightforward, featuring a central spine for internal circulation and the movement of equipment and supplies. In a thirty-bed installation (shown in partial deployment mode here) the main entrance is flanked by a surgical suite, triage

6.4.1 BLU-MED Mobile Field Hospital, deployed in the earthquake strike zone in Haiti in 2010

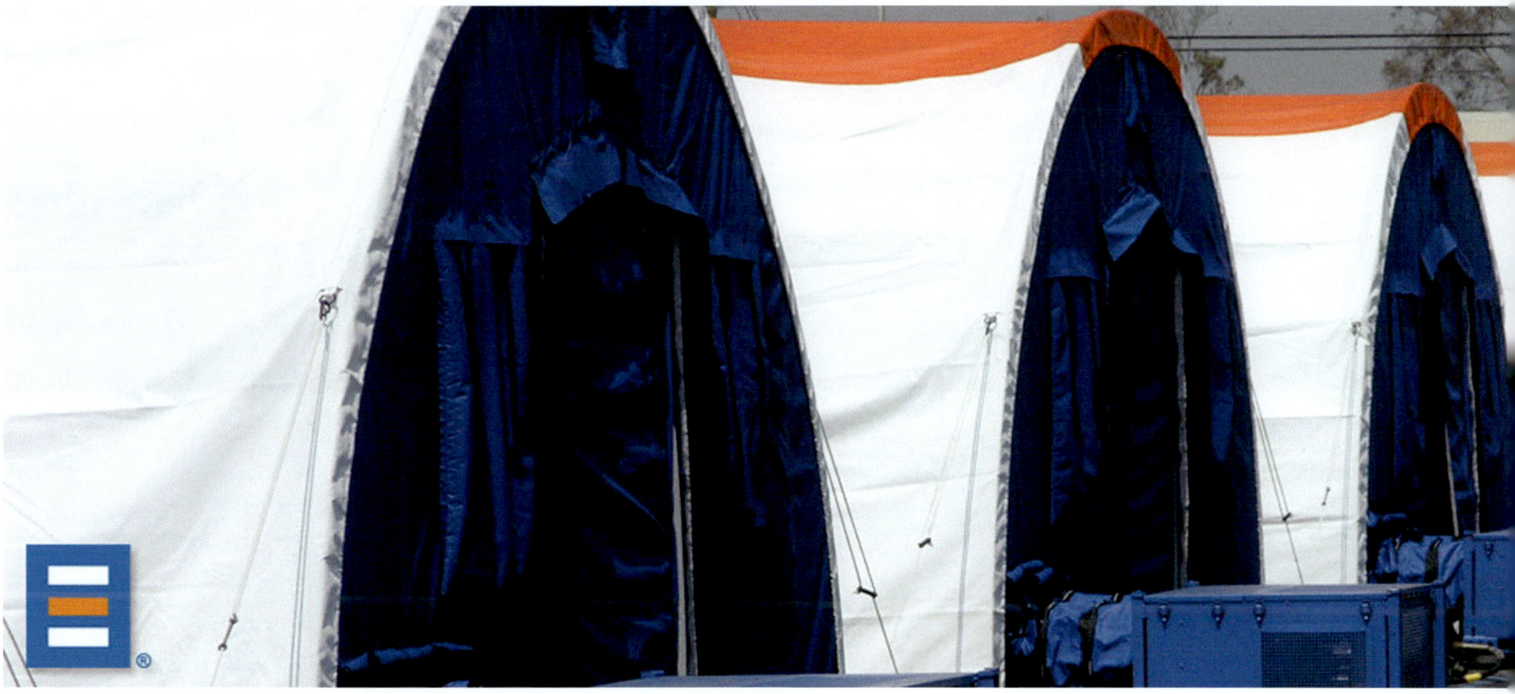

6.4.2 Tents are barrel-vaulted and sheathed in multi-membrane fabric. Entrance thresholds are zipper and snap-activated and each module has an HVAC unit and pneumatic compressor

6.4.3a–d Modules can be assembled in three hours or less. The bright red stripe on the roof enhances identification from afar for MEDIVAC purposes, and to facilitate food/supply airdrops

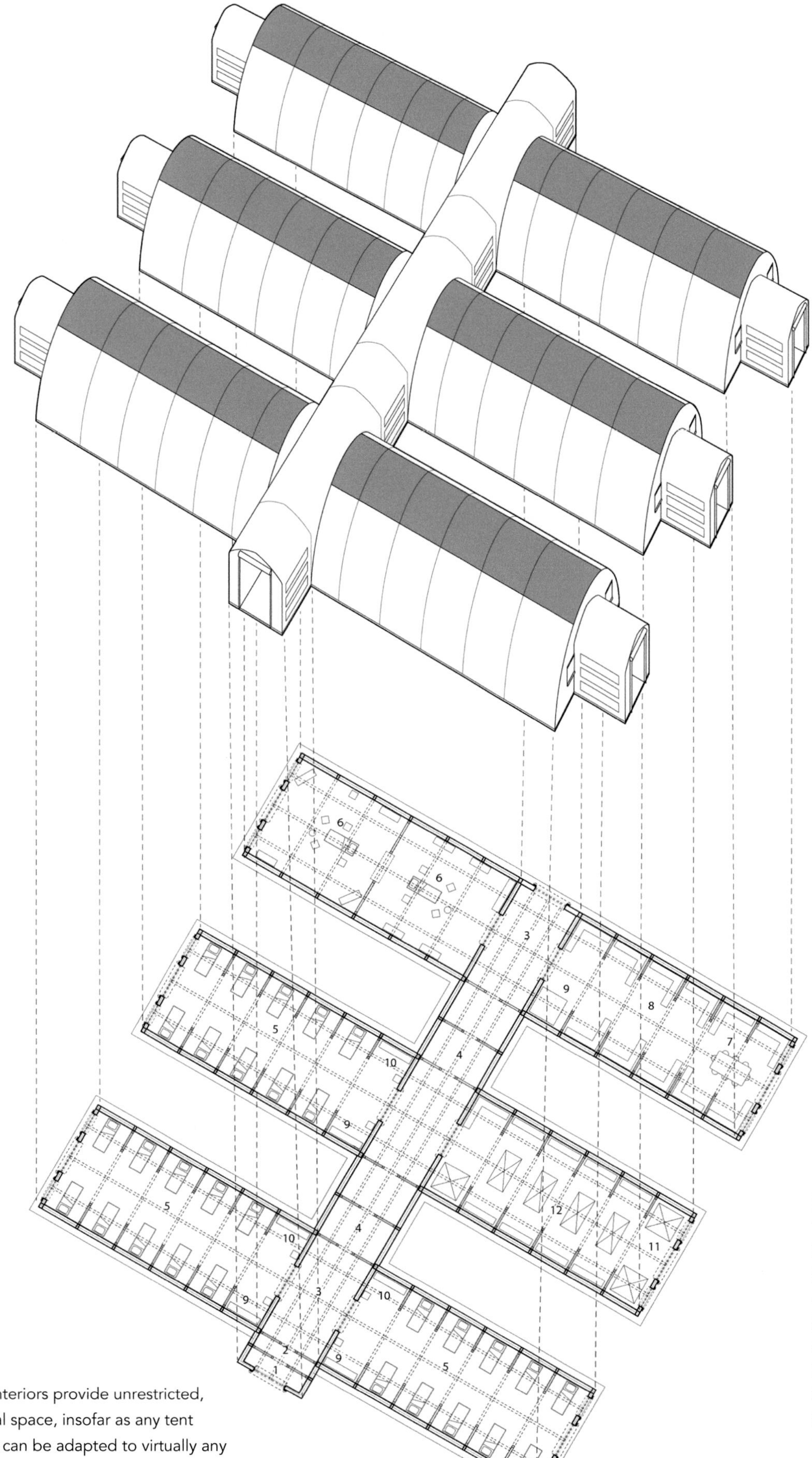

6.4.4 Interiors provide unrestricted, universal space, insofar as any tent module can be adapted to virtually any function. This installation depicts patient wards, housing, and a surgical unit

Key:
1 arrival
2 vestibule
3 waiting
4 consultation
5 med/surgical units
6 surgical suite
7 conference/nursing
8 exam/triage
9 nursing/observation
10 supplies
11 medications
12 supplies/storeroom

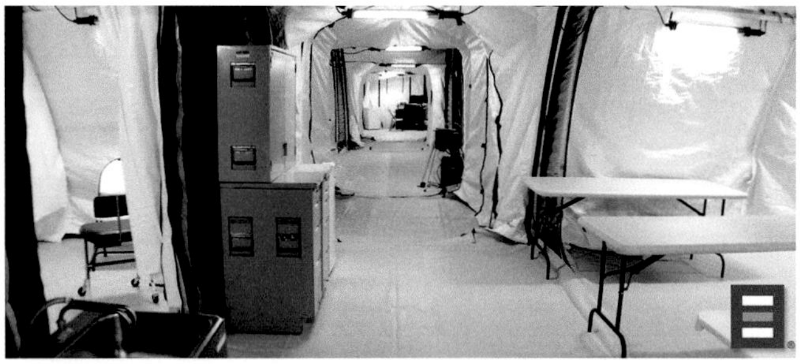

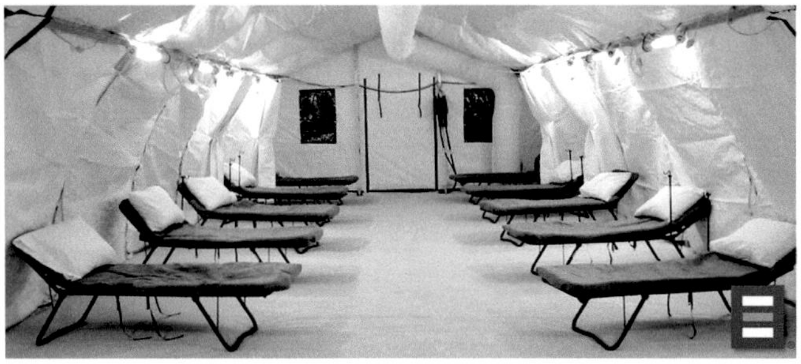
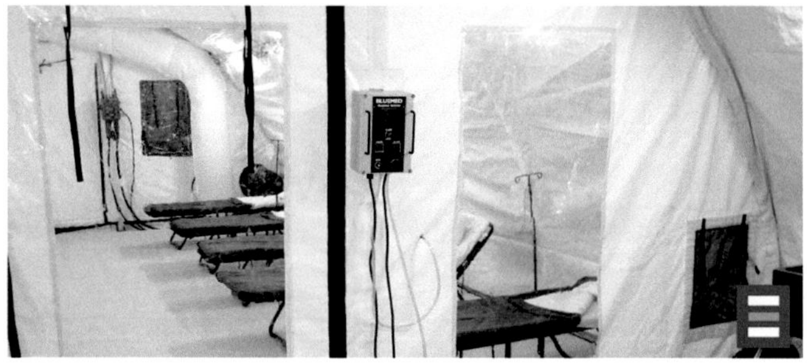
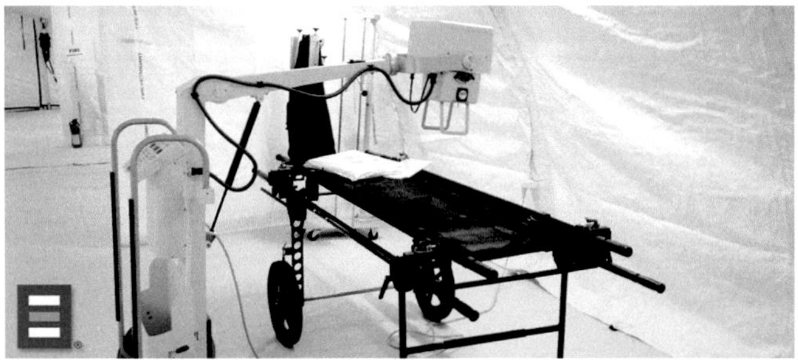
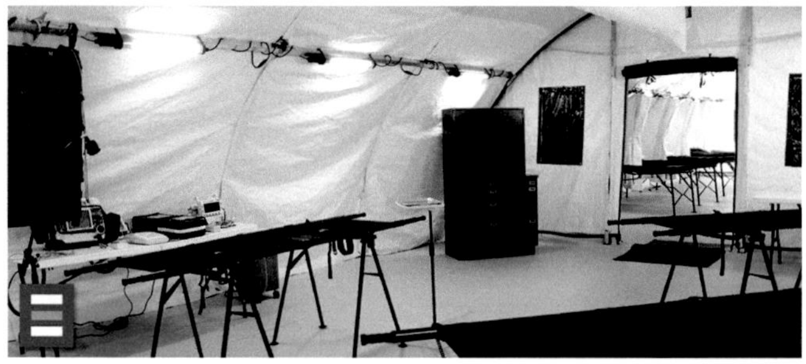
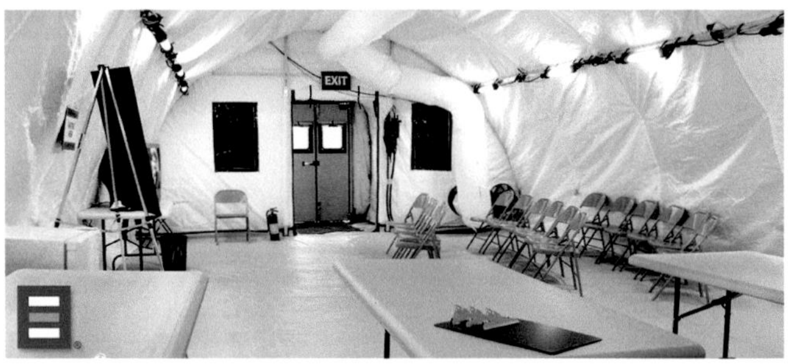
EXIT

Response Systems
www.blu-med.com

6.4.5a–l Modules are equipped with an inner fabric liner in compliance with CDC and WHO standards for infectious disease isolation units, and roll-down fabric entry thresholds

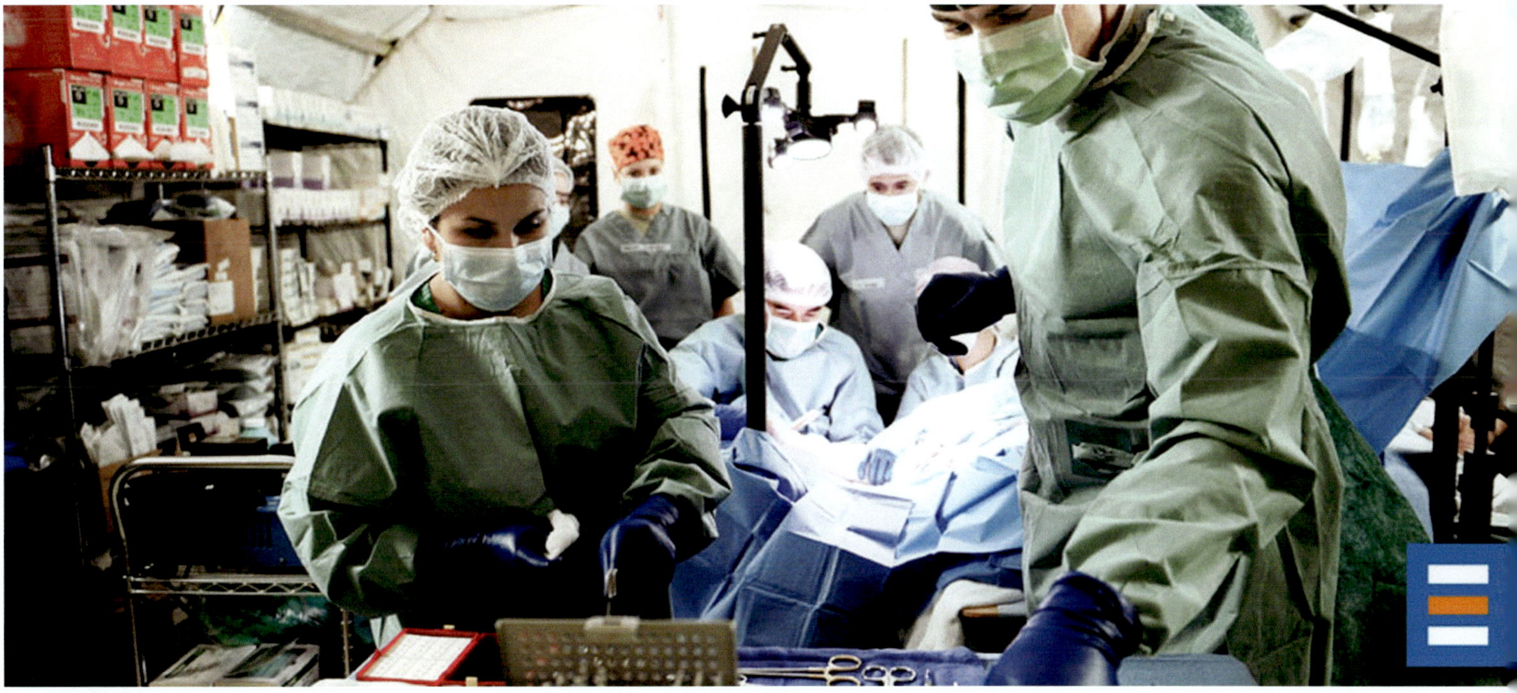

6.4.6 The surgical unit houses essential equipment. Note the portable adjustable surgical lamp at center

station, and nursing support functions (Figure 6.4.4). Typically, eighteen-wheelers are used to transport this field hospital in intermodal containers, with all system components, including beds, all diagnostic and treatment equipment, HVAC system, and power generators. The interiors are spartan, and they feature bands of fluorescent lights strung along the long sidewalls of each tent module. The operating suite is comparable to many stationary community hospitals, and contains the requisite amenities for basic life-saving surgeries (Figure 6.4.5a–l). The entry vestibules to the surgical tent and other tents are equipped with multiple doors (two) to provide an airlock, and a window, and are sheathed in blue fabric. These components feature stripes on their sidewalls. The aesthetic possibilities of this system-type remain yet to be fully explored, although its functionality in pressing circumstances has been proven repeatedly (Figures 6.4.6 and 6.4.7).

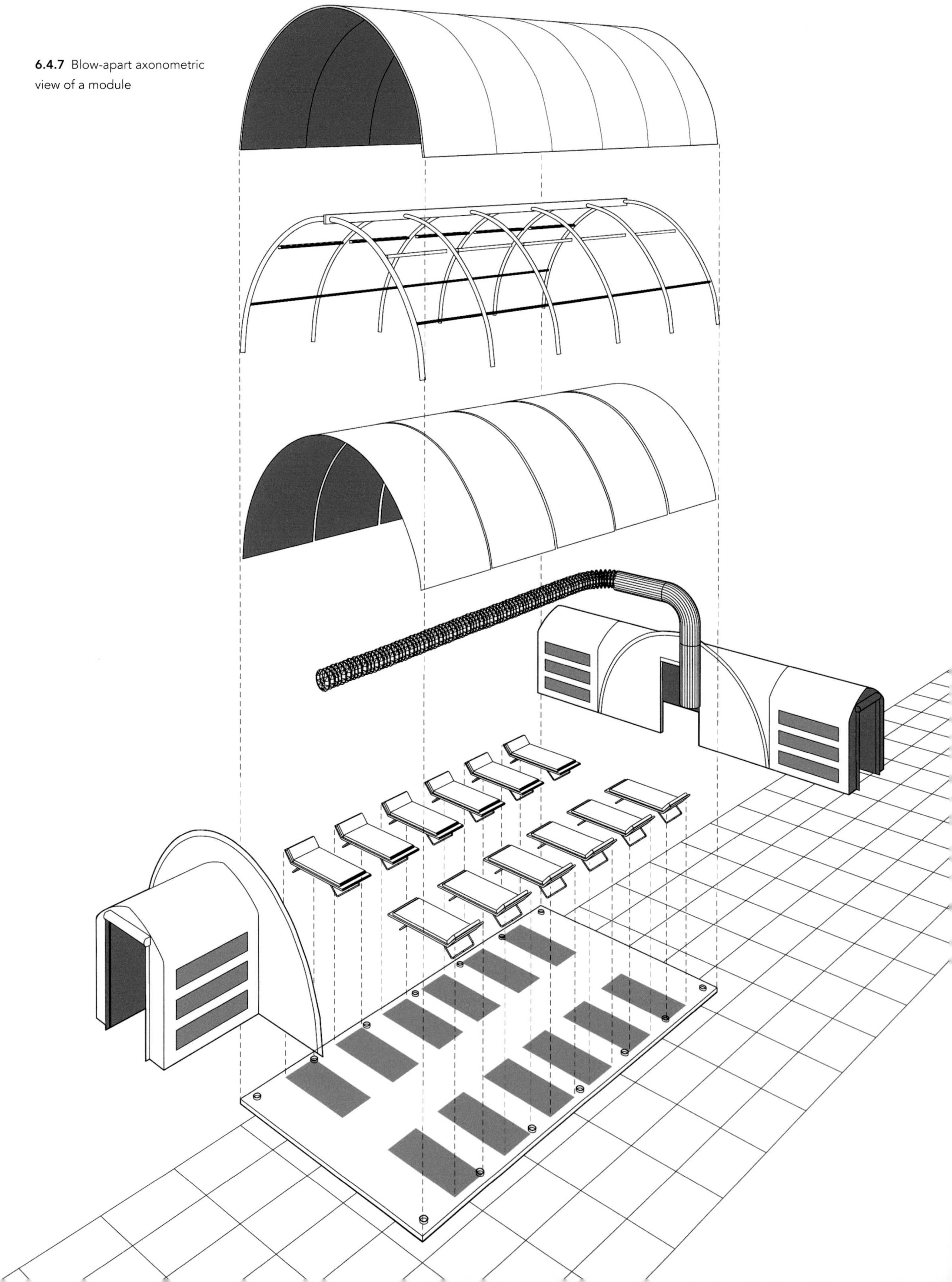

6.4.7 Blow-apart axonometric view of a module

5 QS72 Clinic, Japan

ARCHITECT/ENGINEER: Quickspace, Ltd./Daiichi Kensetsu Corp., Japan
CLIENT/SPONSOR: Japan Red Cross Society
TYPE OF CARE: Post-disaster trauma care/housing (RHC/RTC)
NUMBER OF BEDS: N/A (outpatient)
FEATURED MATERIALS: Polypropylene panels/aluminum
METHOD OF ASSEMBLY: Flat-pack
SITE CONTEXT: Variable
DEPLOYMENT (MIN/MAX): 225+ square feet
COMPLETED: 2010

Context/site

The Tohoku earthquake and tsunami of 2011 was a magnitude 9.0 undersea mega thrust earthquake off the coast of Japan, with its epicenter approximately forty-three miles east of the Oshika Peninsula. It was the most powerful earthquake ever recorded off Japan's coast, and the fifth most powerful in the world since modern record keeping began in 1900. This massive earthquake event triggered tsunami waves that peaked at 133 feet in Iwate Prefecture.[8] In the Sendai region, it travelled six miles inland. As of February 2014, a National Police Agency report in Japan confirmed 15,889 deaths, more than 6,000 injured, with more than 2,000 still missing.[9] Nearly 400,000 buildings were either destroyed, or partially collapsed. Approximately 4.4 million households in northeastern Japan were left without electricity and 1.5 million without water. Architects were at a near total loss as to how best to begin to provide disaster aid and shelter assistance. The situation in Japan, in this regard, differed little from the situation in much of the world when these types of events occur, with architects literally unable to function in a first response capacity to any type of major disaster. In the aftermath of this devastating event, Japan received offers of assistance from 116 nations and twenty-eight international NGOs. As of March 2012, donations to areas affected by the disaster totaled $520 billion and 930,000 victims had received some type of humanitarian assistance.[10] Architects, industrial designers, and engineers in Japan immediately began to develop prototypes for rapid deployment in the aftermath of future disasters. One such system for rapid deployment was the *Quickspace 72* (QS72), a portable system designed and developed by Quickspace, Ltd. (Figures 6.5.1a–e and 6.5.2a–f).

Building/unit

The QS72 prefab system is comprised of several different module types (Figures 6.5.3 and 6.5.4a–c). It is based on the precepts of closepacking theory and origami. Its architectural vocabulary expresses lightness, adaptability to diverse sites, interchangeability of its constituent parts, and a low-tech DIY aesthetic. The system is designed and manufactured for emergency shelter and/or use as an RHC or RTC installation. The lightness and compact size of this flat-pack system allows for relatively easy transiting via a small flatbed truck. Panel and ceiling components are fabricated of rigid polypropylene plastic panels with high thermal insulation properties. The intent is for these system components to be recycled after having reached their useful life span after multiple deployments—estimated to be five years. It is a foldout kit-of-parts that opens upward and outward horizontally from its in-transit mode, and is specifically designed for transport in generic intermodal shipping containers. By combining a number of units together in various permutations, diverse, interesting patterns are attainable.

The system is based on a combination of accordion-like and panelized elements plugged into one another, rectilinearly, and hexagonally (Figure 6.5.5). Multiple patterns and assembles can be composed out of five basic panel types. Each composite panel is approximately fifteen feet in length by nine feet in height by three inches in thickness. Assembly starts with these panels, and the next step is to arrange them in the desired footprint, then lock them together with clips and anchor pins. Then the roof is attached and locked into place. Each rigid panel has two small windows, one on each end, with a lift-up latch. The principles of origami are indeed in evidence when the system is fully built. Under the sponsorship of the *Japan Red Cross Society*, 100 units were deployed to the impacted disaster zone after the 2011 earthquake and tsunami (Figure 6.5.6a–b). On the site of the destroyed Ishinomaki Red Cross Hospital, the system was deployed for use for two months as a temporary clinic, and as an EOC staffed by

6.5.1a–e QS72 Portable Field Clinic, Japan. The images on the left depict a demonstration installation while those on the right are renderings of module footprint options

volunteer medical personnel from outside the region. The director of the hospital found the QS72 units quite helpful, and recommended that this system become standard equipment in future post-disaster contexts. Additional units, in fact, were available at the time but were unable to be distributed as quickly as needed to the strike zone, due to cumbersome governmental red tape.[11]

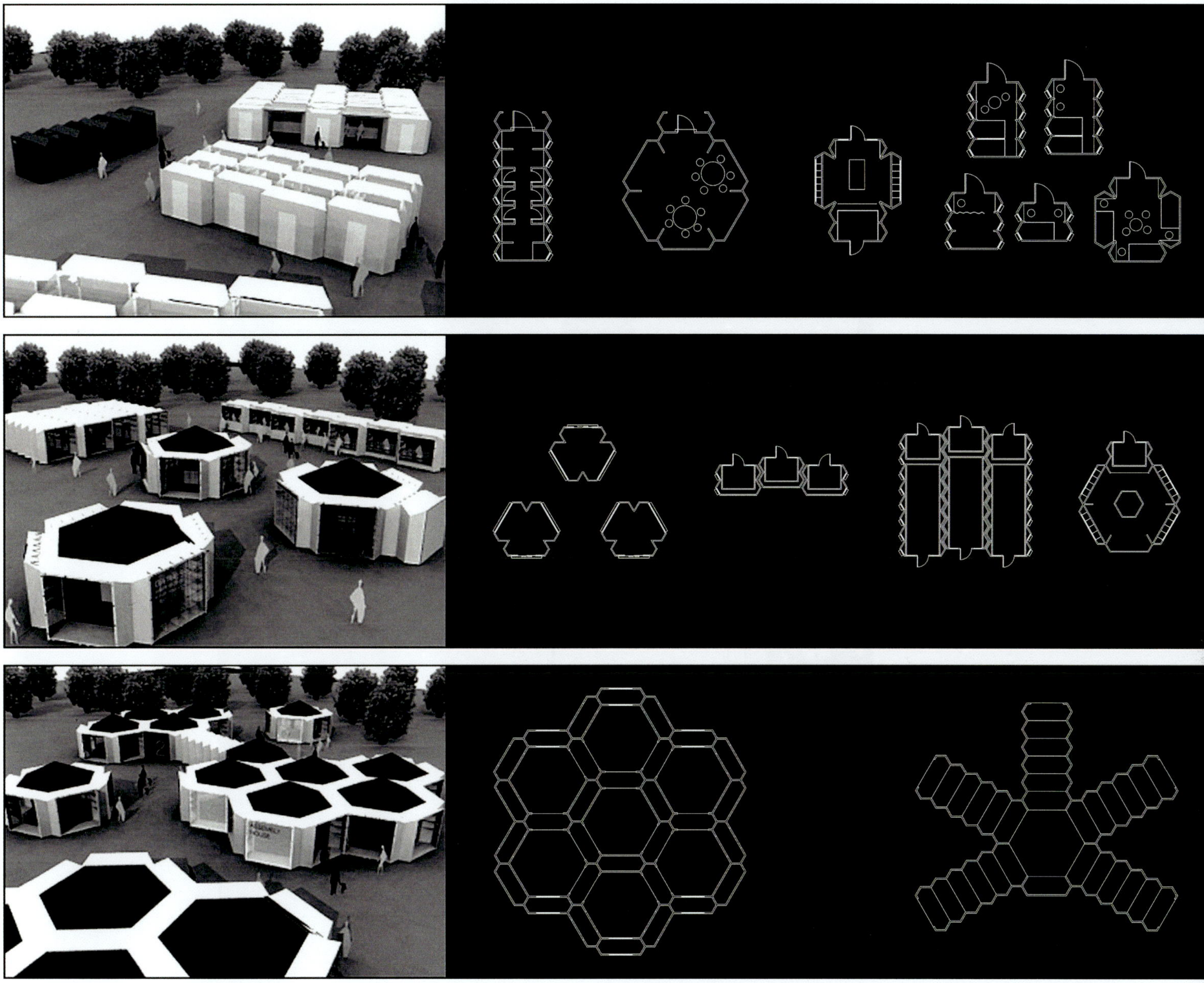

6.5.2a–f The QS72 family of geometries stems from the hexagon, a generative device in both regularized and compressed spatial conditions

6.5.3 A regularized hexagonal module installed outdoors, with a fabric membrane floor surface

6.5.4a–c Wall and roof panels achieve maximum compressive strength while maximizing lightness and the ability to be easily locked together

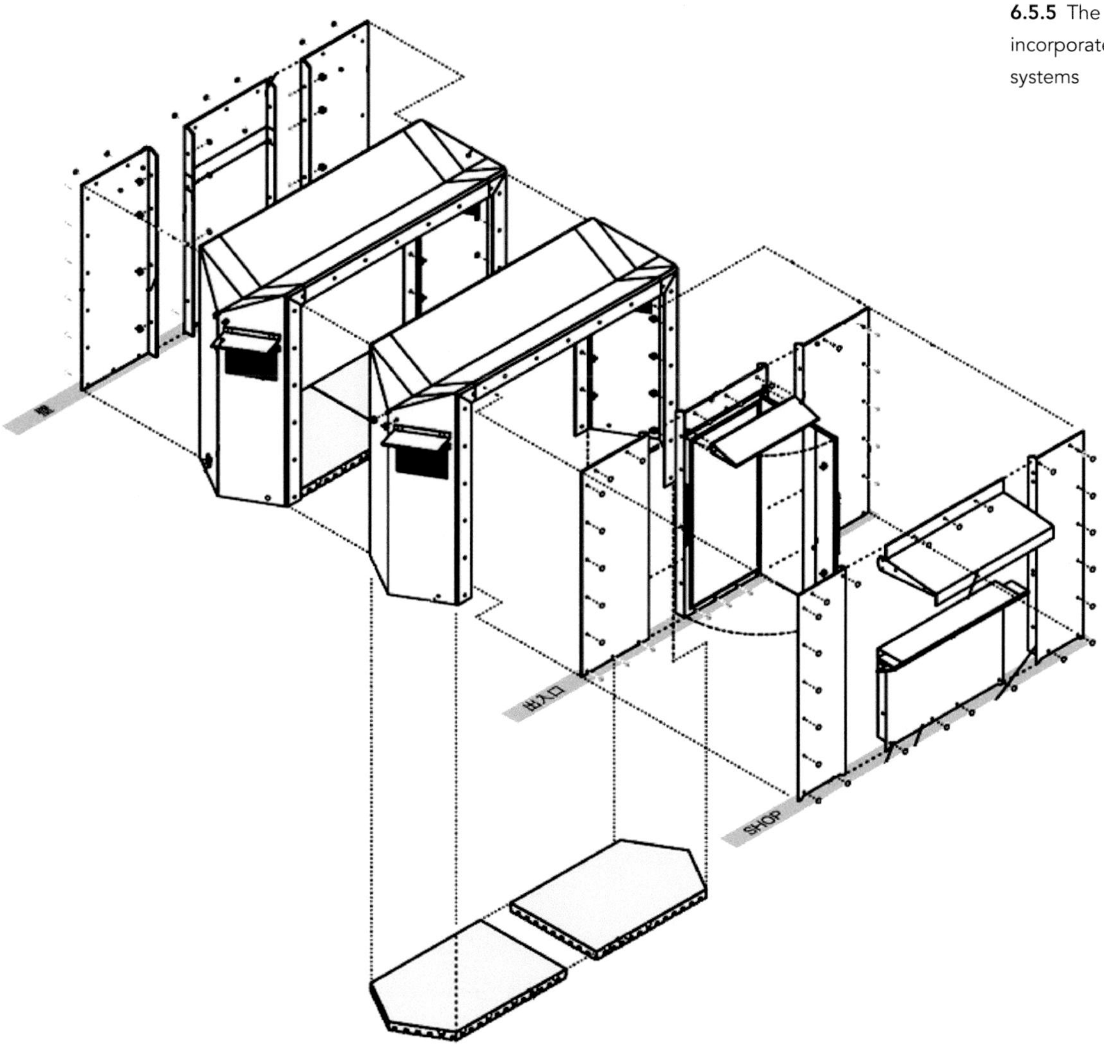

6.5.5 The QS72 provides the option to incorporate conventional HVAC/MEP systems

6.5.6a–b Hexagonal modules plug into one another in a hub-and-spoke network

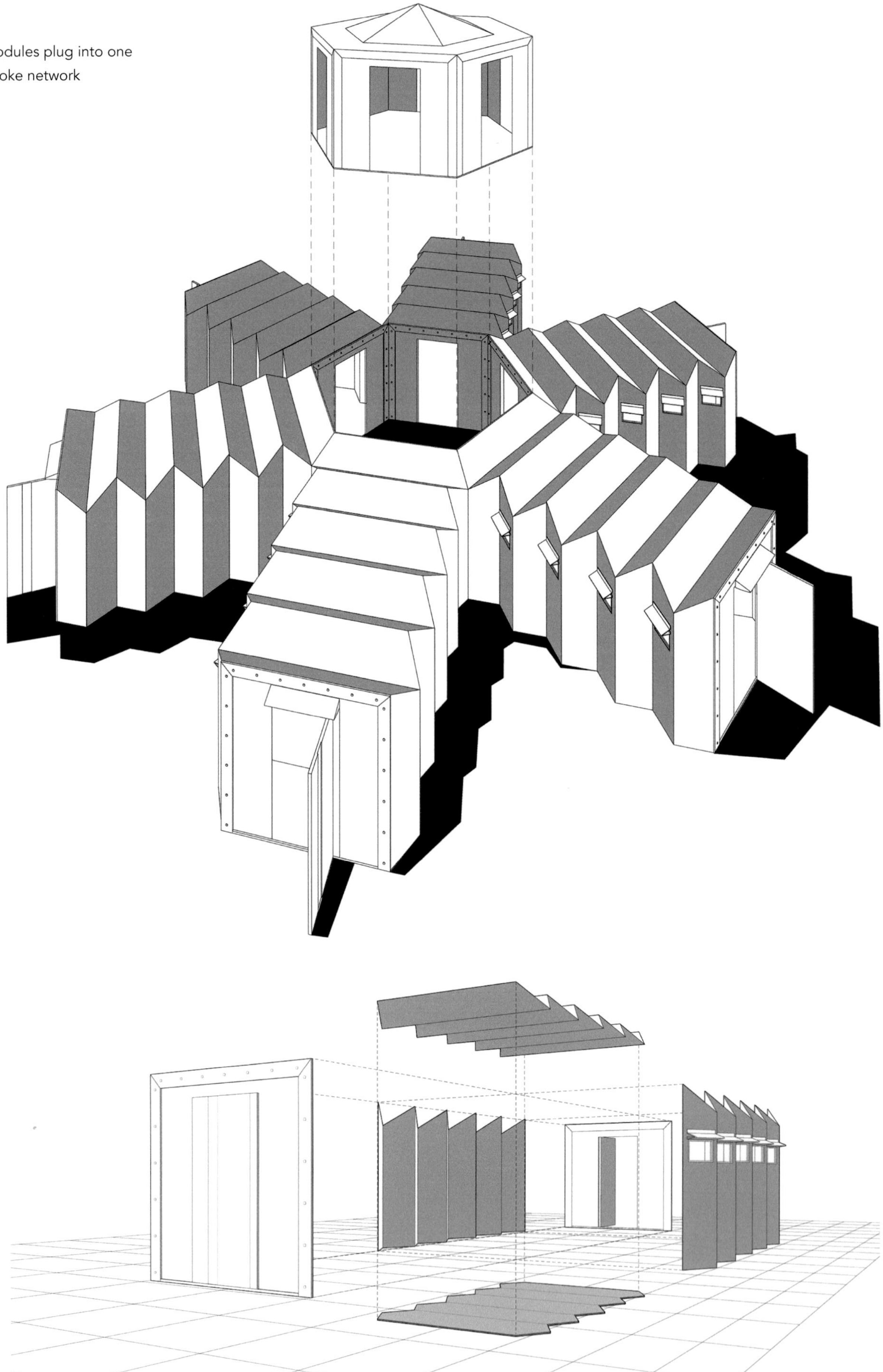

6 Portable Isolation Containment System (PICS), Canada

ARCHITECT/ENGINEER: Design Shelter, Inc.
CLIENT/SPONSOR: Capital Health Authority, Edmonton and Area, Canada
TYPE OF CARE: Outpatient (RHC/RTC)
NUMBER OF BEDS: 10–100
FEATURED MATERIALS: Fabric membrane/aluminum
METHOD OF ASSEMBLY: Flat-pack
SITE CONTEXT: Variable
DEPLOYMENT (MIN/MAX): 1,500/25,000 square feet
COMPLETED: 2008

Context/site

Design Shelter, Inc. (DSI) is a Mississauga, Ontario-based manufacturer of portable emergency shelters and accessories. It specializes in providing transportable trauma care facilities to emergency management teams in North America and beyond. Its prefab modular tent-based systems have been deployed in response to health emergencies in post-disaster strike zones, including floods, tornadoes, droughts, and earthquakes. Its installations are geared for use by bioterrorism and anti-terrorism first responder medical teams. One such installation, the *Portable Isolation Containment System* (PICS), in Edmonton, Alberta, provides, at the present time, primary care services to the greater Edmonton area. Its main mission, however, is to be on 24/7 call for rapid deployment in the event of a local or regional disaster event. DSI partnered with FailSafe Air Safety Systems in the development of the PICS. PICS is a stand-alone portable system designed to be used to complement a stationary hospital's exceeded surge-demand capacity and for the isolation of victims of highly infectious microbial public health outbreaks such as TB, SARS, Avian flu, and Bird flu, and the Ebola virus. It is equipped with a decontamination unit for mitigating the effects of bioterrorism, such as an anthrax or smallpox outbreak (Figures 6.6.1 and 6.6.2).

DSI designed PICS as a stand-alone isolation unit, as needed, up to a ten-bed inpatient open ward configuration. Multiples of this ten-bed unit are connectible, thereby expanding the facility's capacity by up to 100 beds. Tents can be easily connected with airlock vestibular passageways (Figure 6.6.3a–l). Its HVAC system utilizes state-of-the-art HEPA filtration with optional HEGA filtration, as well as standard duel-directed UV light fixtures. This system is able to produce ozone for tent and equipment decontamination functions following an infectious disease outbreak. Heat is provided by 20kW of forced air electric heat and cooling utilizing a three-ton air conditioner unit (per tent module), with an optional five-ton unit available for installations located in extreme climates. This system is fully expandable and adaptable to diverse site contexts and occupant needs, including in support of routine services such as primary care, with the ability to be ratcheted up in acuity adaptability in the event of a full-scale public health pandemic or related emergency.

Building/unit

Each tent is designed for either negative (isolation) pressure mode or positive pressure environment. Each unit is nineteen feet in width by thirty-five feet in length, and outfitted with double-width doors at each end, and thermal insulated vinyl flooring, a wiring harness kit, fluorescent light system, and integrated physician/nurse workstations with Wi-Fi telecommunications. The ambient environment within the tents can be naturally ventilated, and yet conditioned for maximum efficiency. This is seen as a core advantage compared to the weight and bulkiness of hard-walled, containerized field hospitals (Figure 6.6.4a–j). In the case of the PICS that is owned and operated by Edmonton's Capital Health Authority and Area, it was installed on the campus of the Walter Mackenzie Medical Center. It is tethered to its adjacent, stationary hospital by means of a connecting passageway. Two tents are set up on this site, with full HVAC support. Its narrow site footprint precluded additional tent-units on site that are also owned by this agency; these additional units are available for larger installations throughout the region. The site prep and erection of the units takes one day, by a team of five or six trained individuals. The tents' structural framework is erected partially on the ground and the canvas sheathing is applied, then stabilizing poles are added beneath, thereby enabling the unit to be lifted to its full height. The internal membrane liner is then snapped into place.

6.6.1 The Portable Isolation Containment System (PICS) is shown installed in Edmonton, Alberta, Canada

In plan, the simplicity of this system is self-evident, with octagons of two types constituting the core installation: an elongated octagonal unit, and a non-elongated/regular octagonal unit. These are connected by means of the vestibular connectors. The structural system consists of aluminum tubular struts. The configuration illustrated here is a freestanding installation with two entry points and four wings—housing administration and staff support, a triage station, examination stations, and two inpatient infectious disease isolation bays. Interior spaces are bright, airy, and equipped with state-of-the-art diagnostic and treatment equipment, allowing for the provision of a high level of medical care. The PICS has been purchased for use by numerous municipalities in Canada, and by numerous agencies elsewhere including the *World Health Organization* (WHO), the *National Emergency Management Agency* (NEMA) of Trinidad and Tobago, and the *Organization of American States* (OAS) for use in diverse everyday contexts, and post-disaster contexts (Figure 6.6.5).

6.6.2 This system emanates from an octagon in plan, expressed at the intersection of circulation elements, and in elongated form as patient care and general support modules

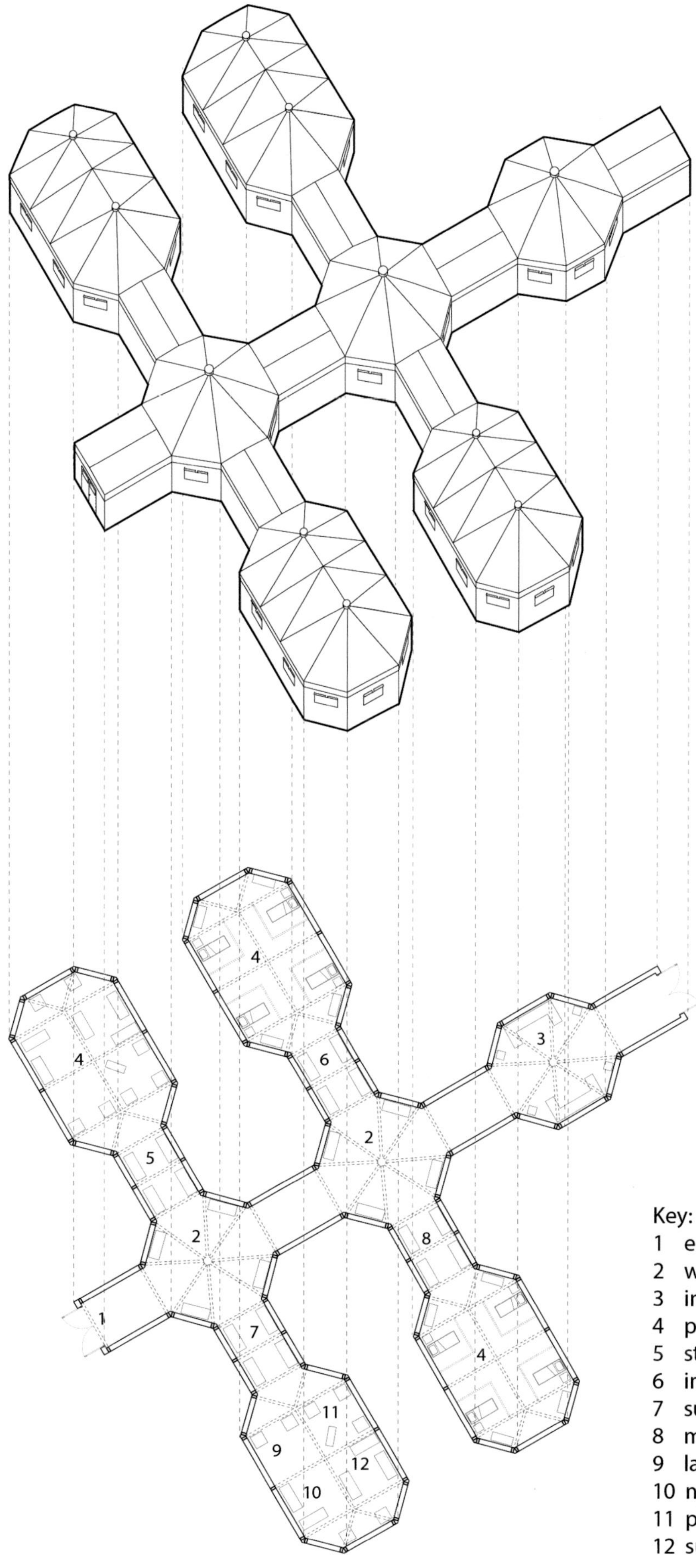

Key:

1 entry
2 waiting
3 intake/triage
4 patient assessment
5 staff/counseling
6 immunization
7 supplies
8 medications
9 laboratory
10 nursing staff support
11 physicians support
12 supplies

6.6.3a–l Modules are relatively easy to assemble, and based on conventional tent technology

6.6.4a–j Interiors feature multi-layered fabric membranes for ceilings and floors, and each module has its own HVAC system

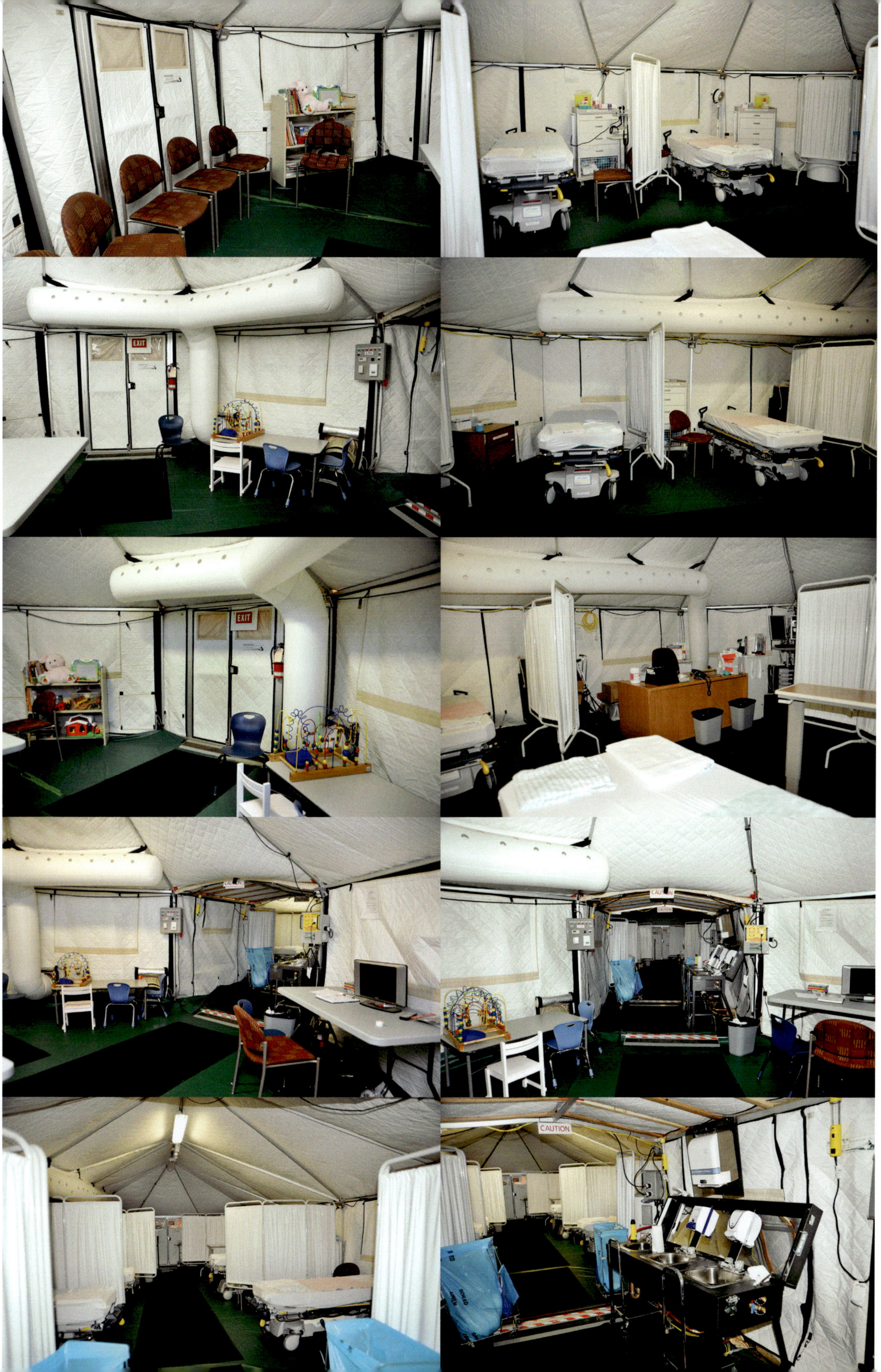
EXIT
EXIT
CAUTION

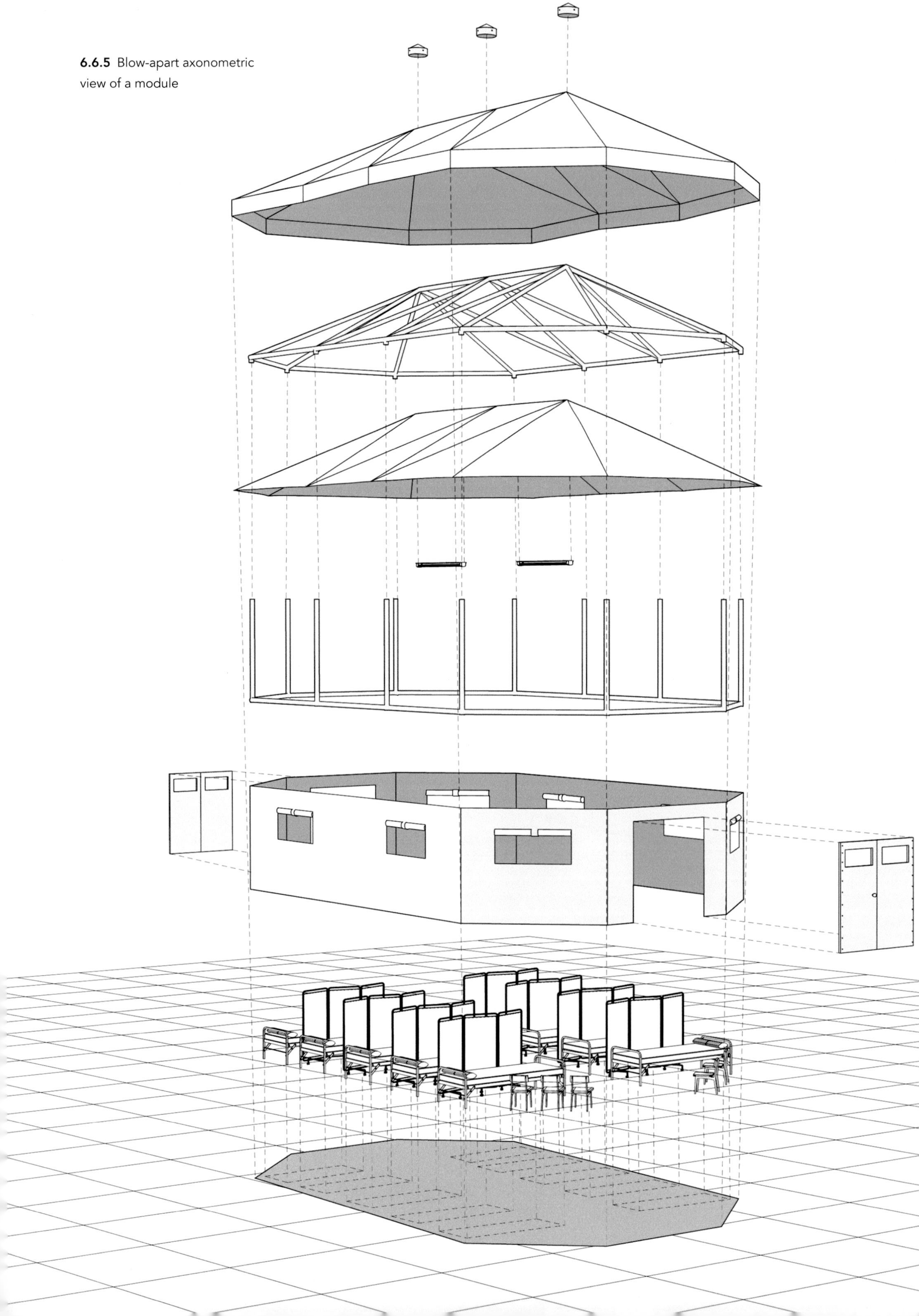

6.6.5 Blow-apart axonometric view of a module

7 Combat Army Support Hospital (CSH), USA

ARCHITECT/ENGINEER: U.S. Army Corps of Engineers
CLIENT/SPONSOR: Department of Defense (DOD), Washington, D.C.
TYPE OF CARE: Inpatient/outpatient (RTC)
NUMBER OF BEDS: 120–1,000
FEATURED MATERIALS: Containers/modular tents
METHOD OF ASSEMBLY: Modules/flat-pack
SITE CONTEXT: Variable
DEPLOYMENT (MIN/MAX): 3,000/54,000 square feet
COMPLETED: 1991

Context/site

The Deployable Medical Systems (DEPMEDS) field hospital was developed as a result of the U.S. Congress's concern with military cost overruns. This system has since become widely known as the *Combat Surgical Hospital* (CSH). When the *Defense Medical Standardization Board* was established in the early 1980s, it was assigned oversight of the development of a portable, redeployable, prefab modularized structure. This oversight body henceforth guided the various branches of the U.S. military in the standardization of their various field hospitals. The first 'test' of the new DEPMEDS prototype occurred at Fort Hood, Texas, where the 21st Evacuation Hospital performed an in-service exercise from August to December of 1984. In February 1988, the 8th Evacuation Hospital, at Fort Ord, California, was dispatched to Fort Liggett, California, and there, a 400-bed DEPMEDS was erected, and eighty-five surgeons and dozens of additional support personnel conducted a field test of it. This installation became the first formal DEPMEDS field hospital, and became the centerpiece of the U.S. Army's *Force Modernization Medical Force 2000* master plan. This became the standard metric for all portable field hospitals in the U.S. military, and functions in this capacity to this day (see Interview 3 in the Appendix).

In January 1989, the first international humanitarian deployment took place, in Honduras (Figure 10.7.1). It occurred in support of a local road-building initiative. Soon thereafter, it was deployed to Europe, for prepositioning in anticipation of a potential emergency there. A large portion of this installation was then transported to Iraq in 1991 in support of *Operation Desert Storm*. Since then, this system has been deployed in every U.S. military theatre. In addition to military deployments in Iraq and in Afghanistan, a humanitarian deployment of a scaled-down DEPMED occurred in the aftermath of Katrina in 2005.

Building/unit

The DEPMED is air-transportable and assembled on site. Critical care modules are housed in a customized variant of a generic ISO container, housing laboratories, radiology, pharmacy, a surgical equipment sterilization unit, and the operating suite. Auxiliary functions are housed in TEMPER units (tent, expandable, modular, personnel) tents as well as in a handful of adjacent mobile vans. DEPMEDS modules are linked together with weatherized vestibules, connecting all support areas, including a central laboratory and tent modules housing a total (in full deployment) of 1,000 inpatient beds in wards (Figures 6.7.2 and 6.7.3). The DEPMED is thereby linked with TEMPER tent modules according to each deployment mission's specific needs—whether humanitarian, or combat-based (Figure 6.7.4). The site for an installation must be firm and relatively flat, whether on soil or on a paved surface, to allow for modules and tents to be positioned in such manner as to allow for direct, strong connections between the individual modules, such as between a radiology module and its adjoining support areas. The requirement of a flat site often requires significant engineering reworking to flatten it, to dispel any irregularities and maximize the site's drainage. This may entail stripping away the topsoil: a necessary trade off in order to avoid difficult, muddy conditions during rainstorms. Therefore, due diligence must be devoted to this from the outset of the site selection process. Brown and grey water sewerage must be fully drained away from the immediate environs (Figure 6.7.5a–d).

A DEPMEDS installation is designed and installed to function autonomously, with fully self-sufficient environmental control on a 24/7 basis—not dissimilar from a submerged submarine's ability to remain fully operational far below the ocean surface for weeks (and longer) at a time. This is achieved by means of M28-CPE (Collective

Protection Equipment) for the installation's power, waste management and sewerage treatment equipment, in order to extended its operations for a 72-hour mission and beyond, in a highly air-contaminated environment. This, in response to a bioterrorist attack, perhaps caused by nerve gas or anthrax (Figure 6.7.6a–f). In addition to the state-of-the-art HVAC system, the M28-CPE system includes high velocity fans able to filter out contaminated air. In bioterrorist attack scenarios, every person must be decontaminated prior to entering the facility. Each individual is held in an airlock shower/prep unit while all contaminants are purged. The first operational field-test of this system occurred in 1997, at Fort Carson, Colorado. A staff of more than 400 persons successfully performed advanced medical procedures while encapsulated in a DEPMED continuously for three days; subsequently, this same DEPMED would acquire actual field-testing in a combat zone soon thereafter, in Iraq (Figure 6.7.7).[12]

6.7.1 A variant of the Combat Army Support Hospital (CSH) with its exterior earth tones blending into its site context

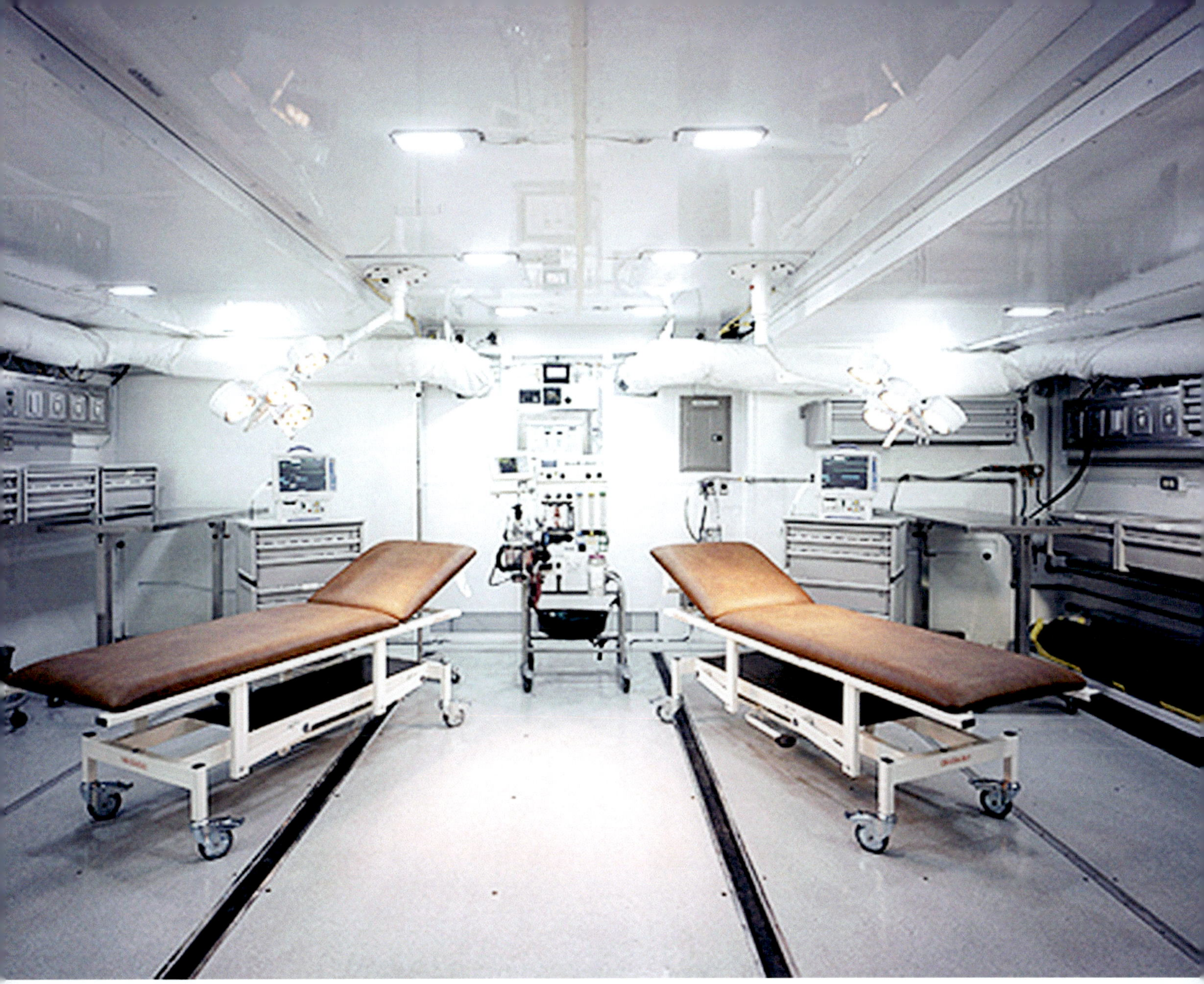

6.7.2 Interiors of modules feature dual pop-out extensions housing state-of-the-art surgical equipment

6.7.3 The core CSH and its variants provide multiple installation footprint options in response to a given site's determinants

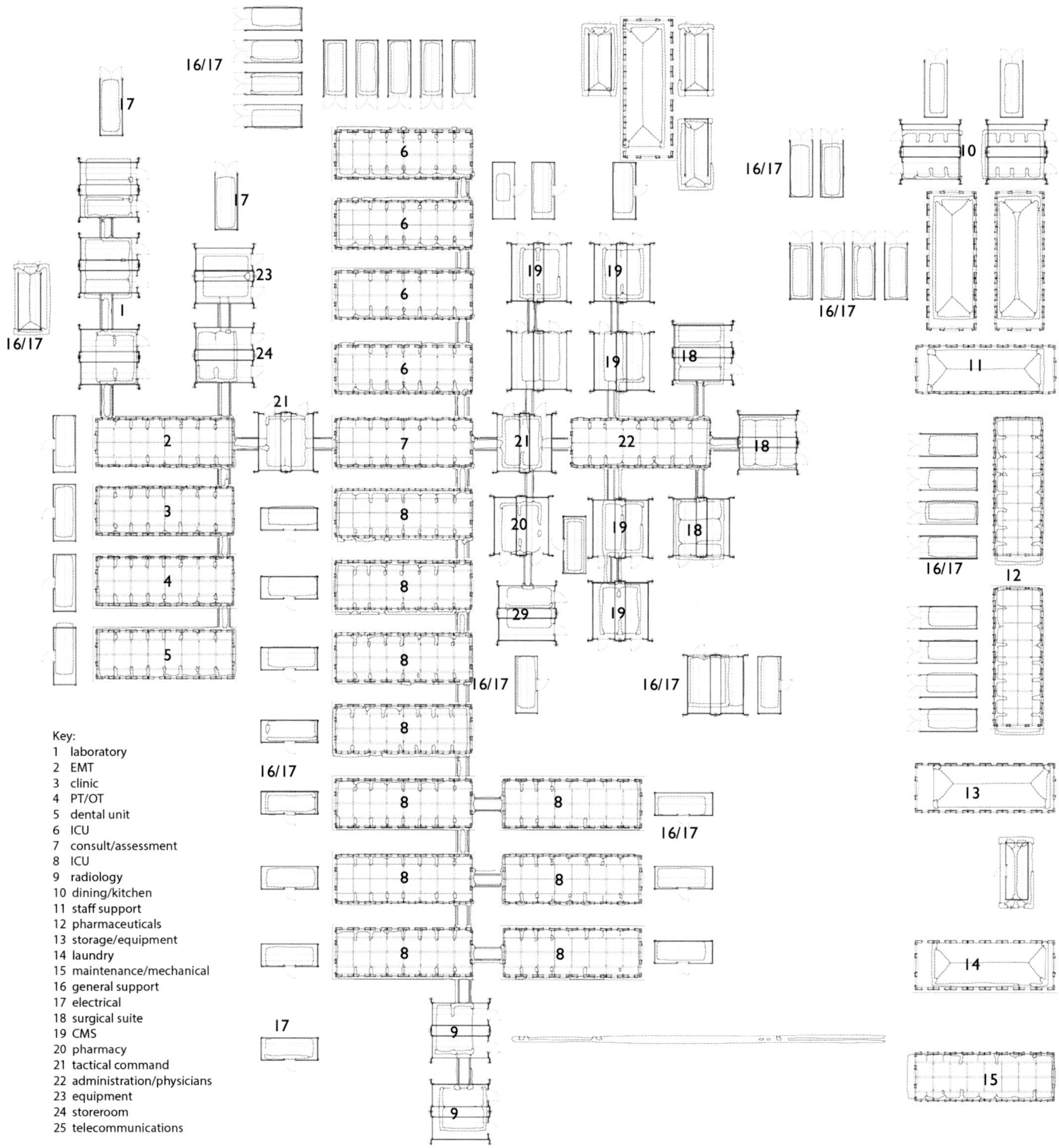

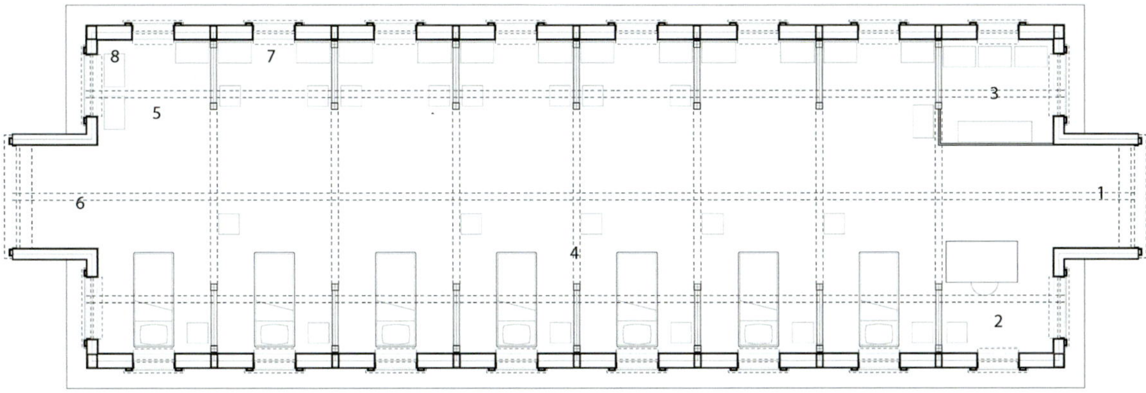

Key:
1 entry
2 nursing station
3 equipment/medical records/meds
4 inpatient beds
5 waiting
6 emergency exit
7 physician/consult
8 clean/soiled utilities

6.7.4 Pre-operative tent modules house seven beds, as shown here, and can accommodate up to fourteen beds

6.7.5a–d The CSH system arrives at an installation site with its own trucks, with all supplies and equipment packed in intermodal containers

6.7.6a–f Interiors are assembled with floor and wall fabric membranes, and ribbon-like lighting, and each module has its own HVAC unit. The image at lower left is of the training center where this facility is currently stationed

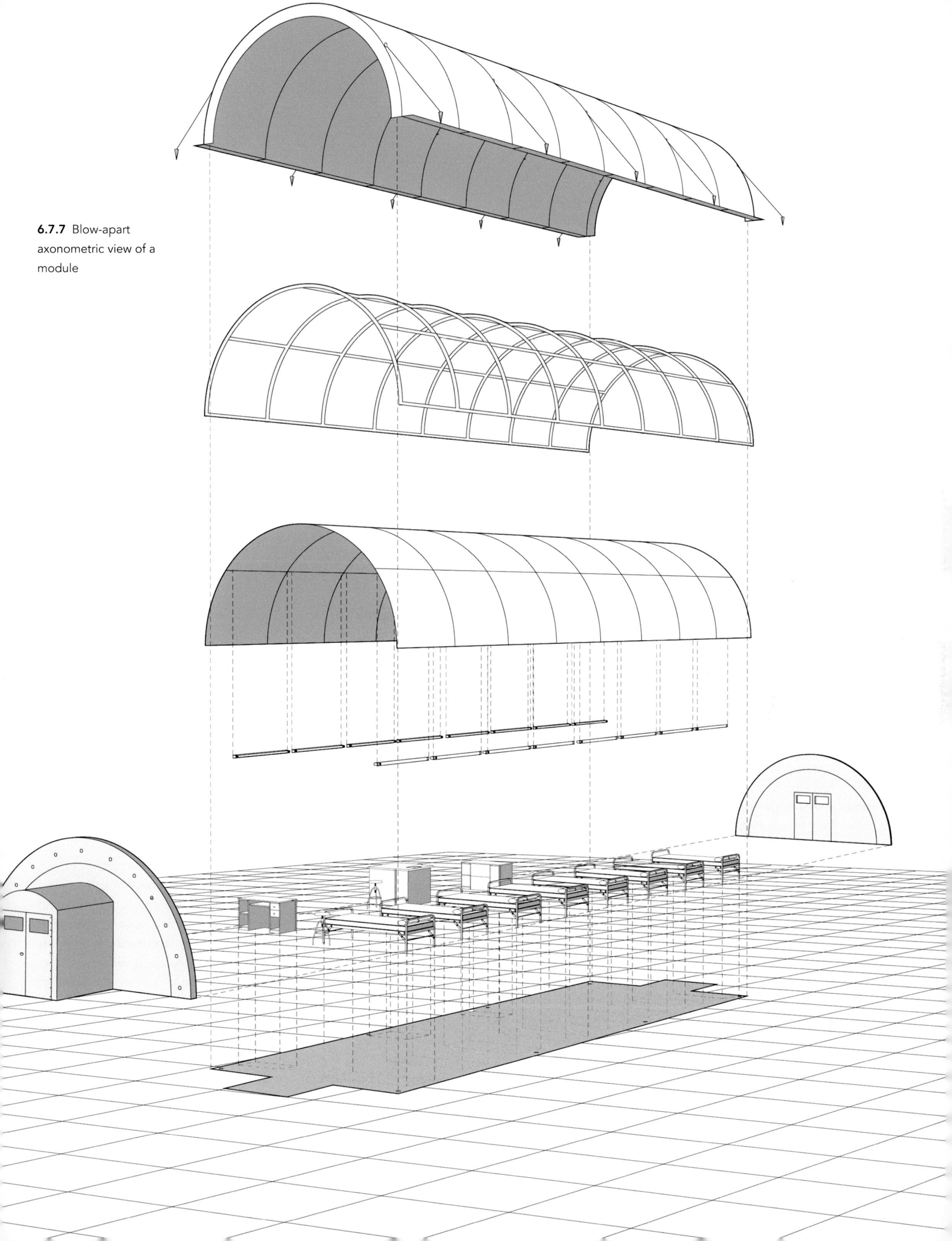

6.7.7 Blow-apart axonometric view of a module

8 AMoHS, USA

ARCHITECT/ENGINEER: Advanced Mobile Hospital Systems, Inc.
CLIENT/SPONSOR: State University of New York, Stony Brook, USA
TYPE OF CARE: Vehicular trauma/surgical unit (RHC)
NUMBER OF BEDS: 10+
FEATURED MATERIALS: Steel/lightweight alloys
METHOD OF ASSEMBLY: Modular/plug-in
SITE CONTEXT: Variable
DEPLOYMENT (MIN/MAX): 2,500/10,500 square feet
COMPLETED: 2009

Context/site

First manufactured in 2009, the *AMoHS* is a portable field hospital for civilian use including governmental agencies, hospitals, multi-campus medical centers, and humanitarian NGOs. The AMoHS platform is able to grow or contract in accord with clients' requirements. It is a two-part system, with a semi-trailer cab, and a clinical module. This differs from the 'medical bus,' or 'medical truck' platforms typically manufactured in one of four lengths: a thirty-two foot (ten meter) rugged truck chassis, with a single exam room, a forty foot (12.2 meter) truck chassis, with two to three exam rooms, a fifty-three foot (sixteen meter) triple expandable 1000 square foot (ninety-three square meter) trailer, and a sixty foot (18.2 meter) double expandable pop-up configuration (Figure 6.8.1a–d). These platforms and the two-part AMoHS can be deployed as a single unit or in multiples, where they can be physically connected to a stationary hospital, or can function independently. The system exceeds the minimum construction and performance standards set by the U.S. Joint Commission for the Accreditation of Healthcare Organizations (JCAHO). In the Ebola outbreak in 2014, this, and other manufacturers focused more of their marketing to governmental health ministries and NGO humanitarian aid organizations. The AMoHS can be transited anywhere worldwide via airlift or ship, and is well suited for use as an infectious disease isolation unit (Figure 6.8.2a–b).[13]

Vehicular health clinics possess one key advantage over all other types of transportable health facilities: they can be *driven* into a disaster zone, reaching their destination in twenty-four hours or less. They are proven in meeting the needs of human victims of disaster, but are also proven in meeting the needs of animal species victimized by adverse, traumatic events. Too often, the emergency care needs of animals are overlooked. In the U.S., *People for the Ethical Treatment of Animals* (PETA) initiated its Mobile Clinics Division (MCD). These vehicular clinics treat victimized animals across the U.S. with an onboard staff consisting of a licensed veterinarian, veterinary assistant, staff technician, and tech assistant who checks in and registers each animal. Its three mobile units currently operating in the state of Virginia are on the road an average of six days per week crisscrossing the state. Since their purchase in 2001, PETA's mobile clinics in Virginia have treated hundreds of thousands of mistreated dogs and cats (Figure 6.8.3a–e).[14]

Building/unit

The AMoHS installation depicted here consists of modules connected by vestibular airlocks. Positive airflow is maintained in multi-unit installations and the onboard HVAC system makes it possible to not have to leave the installation itself to obtain supplies and the like (Figure 6.8.4). Each unit has full IT/teleconferencing support and can physically dock with a stationary medical facility. If a given client requires additional capacity, numerous units can be installed in a grid pattern on a site. AMoHS surgical units are customizable to suit clients' specialized requirements. A key feature of this system is that it functions to, literally, extend a stationary hospital's usable space, providing backup support over an extended time period. It can replicate essential functions of its stationary counterpart, including surgical services when, for instance, four additional AMoHS surgical units are required (Figure 6.8.5). Each AMoHS unit is outfitted with MEP/HVAC and medical gases. Each operating suite is seventeen feet by twenty-two feet and the HVAC system provides twenty-five air exchanges per hour. This unit can be equipped with more than one anesthesia station. Biohazardous waste is handled the same as in a conventional hospital. Onboard nurses' stations, pre-operative, and post-operative bays are fully equipped. The unit computer server is housed in a loft compartment. The AMoHS units stationed at Stony Brook in New York State are docked to the adjacent stationary hospital, and are able to be reconfigured if and when additional workspace or patient care capacity is required. Similarly, the units' airlock vestibules can be relocated or multiplied, as needed (Figures 6.8.6 and 6.8.7).

6.8.1a–d The Advanced Mobile Hospital System (AMoHS) is an autonomous vehicular clinic able to be plugged into a stationary medical facility

6.8.2a–b Truck units feature a center door entry, yielding two interior compartments of equivalent size. This configuration depicts two exam/procedure bays

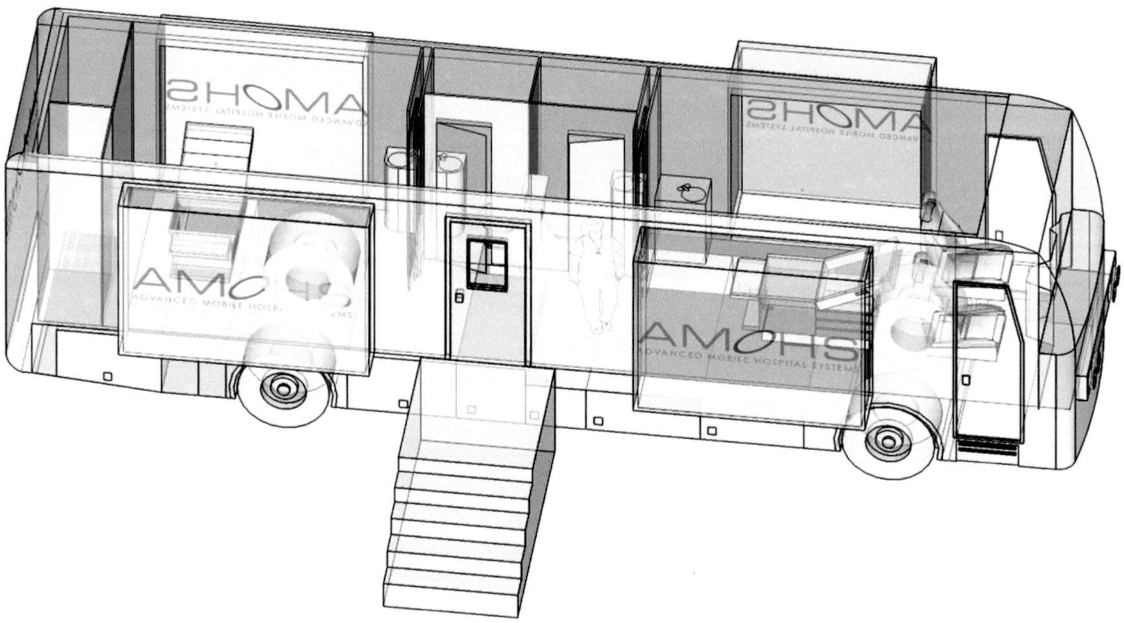

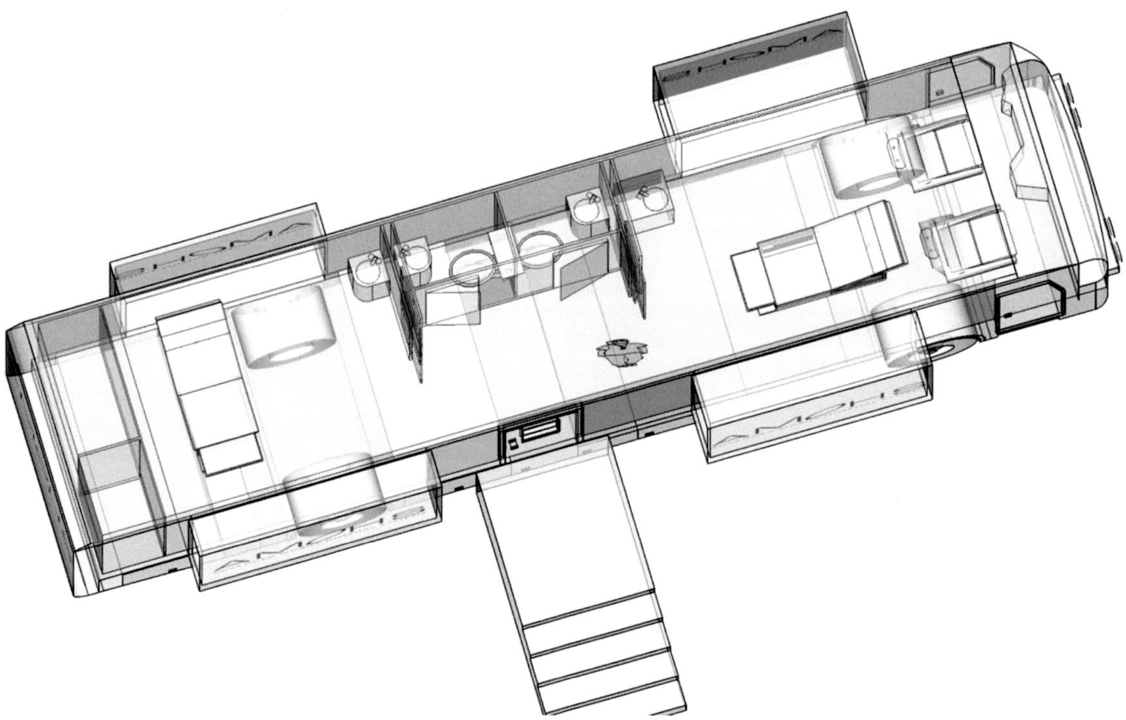

Surgical Examination

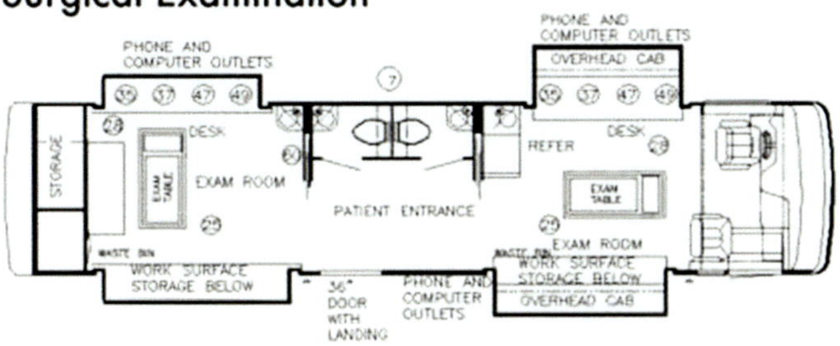

Laboratory Unit

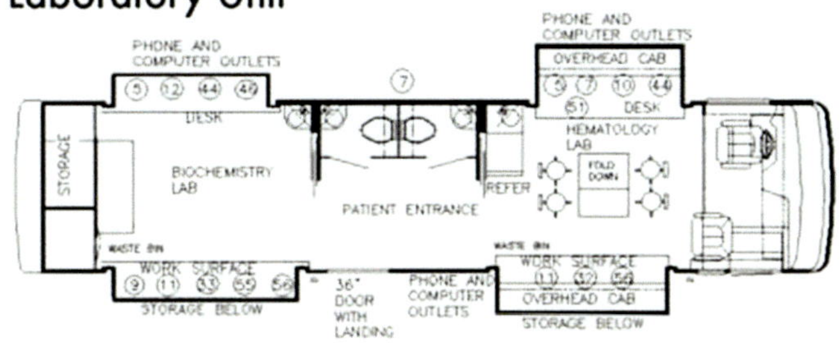

Internal Medicine

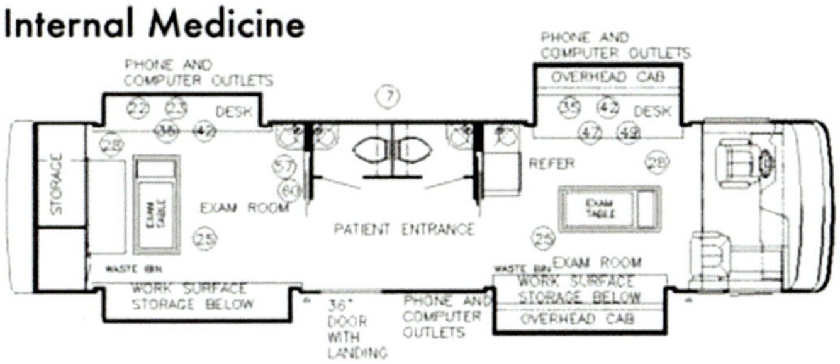

Dental Examination

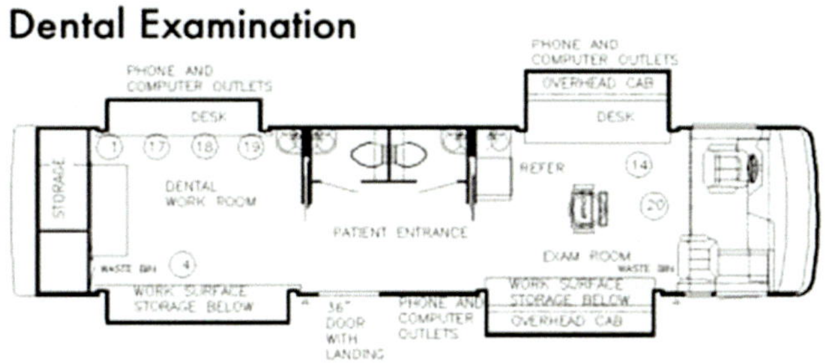

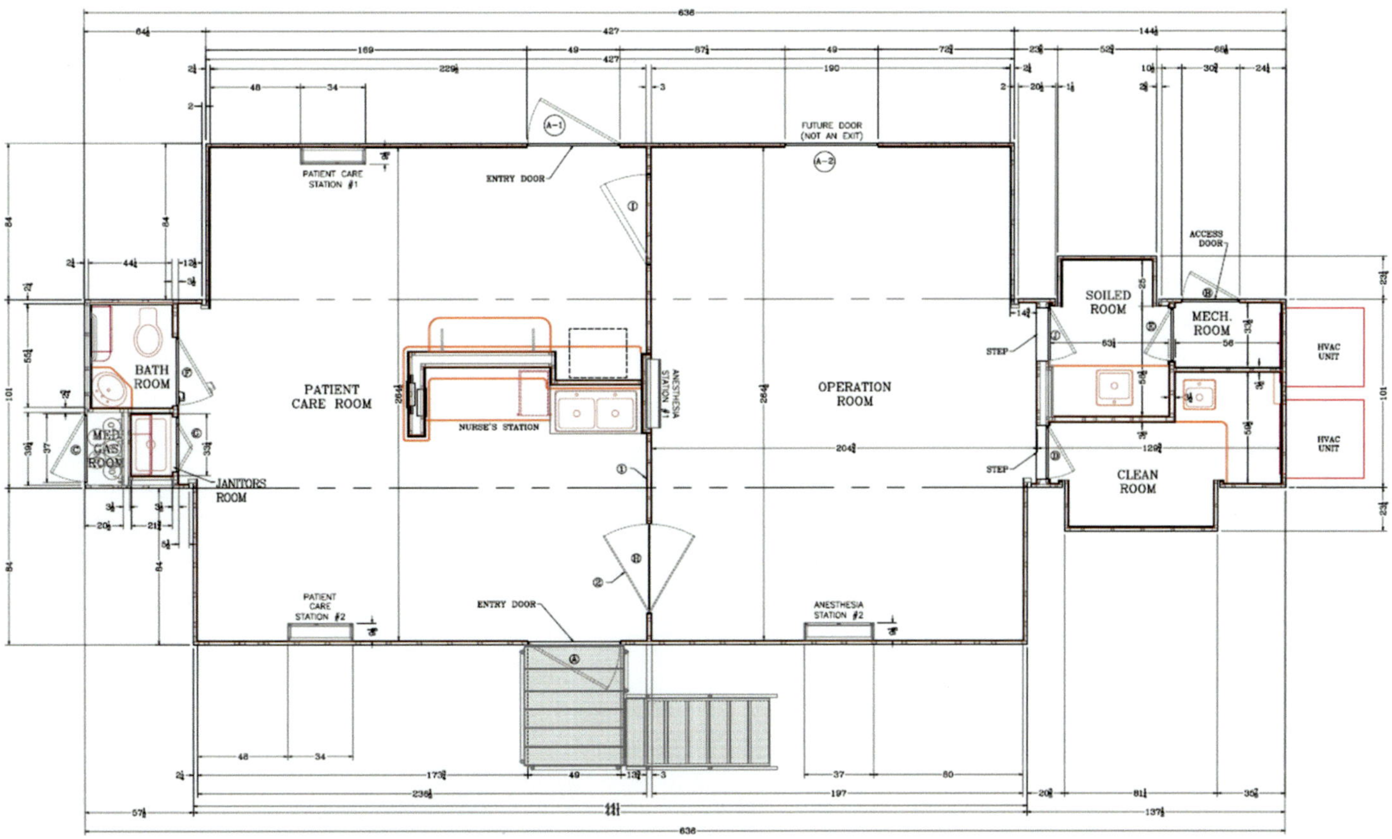

6.8.3a–e Four distinct pop-out variants, surgical, laboratory, internal medicine, and dental examination, triple the amount of interior occupied space beyond the core module

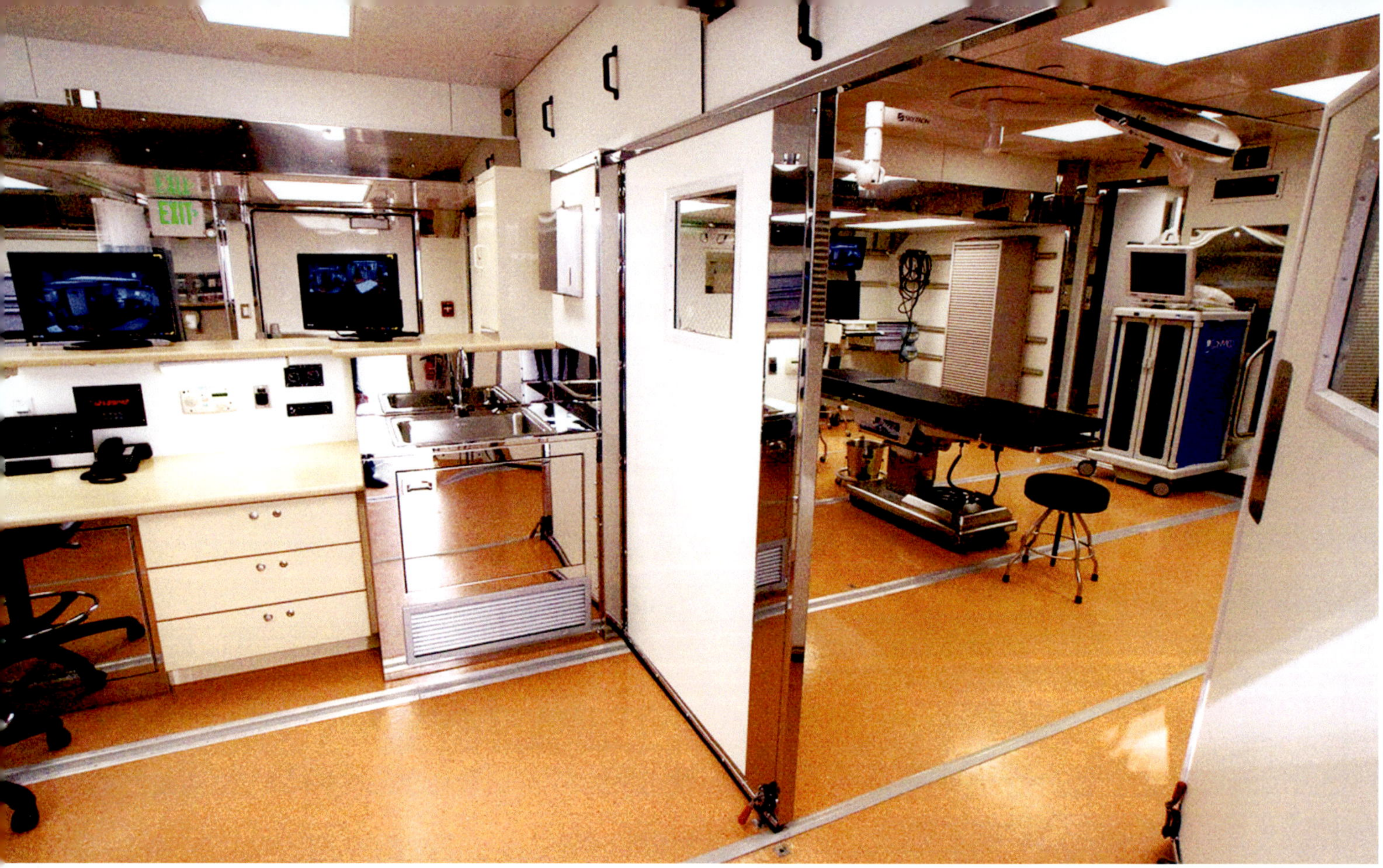

6.8.4 Interior spaces appear strikingly like those of a conventional hospital

6.8.5 Interior equipment is comparable to that in a conventional hospital

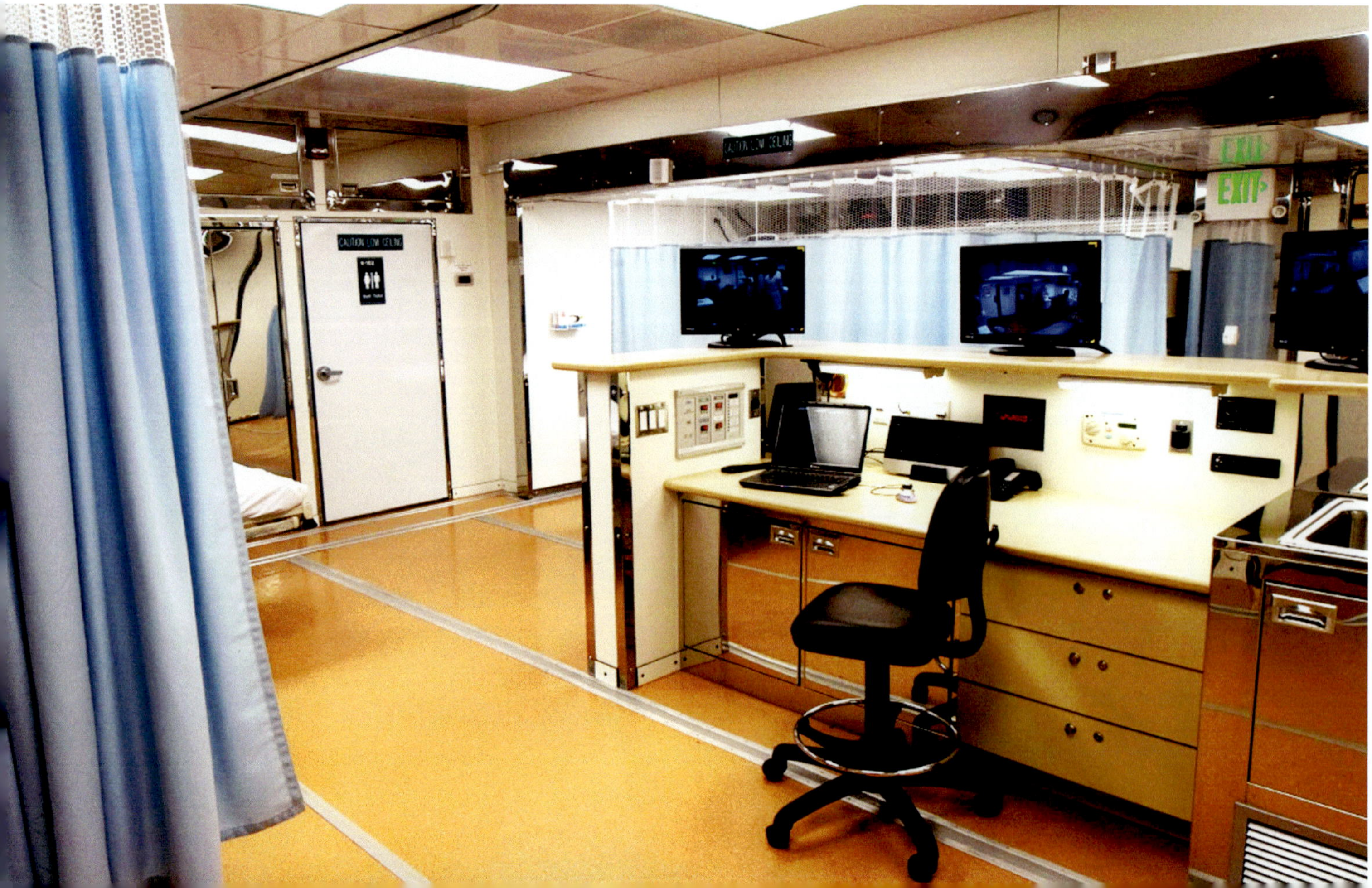

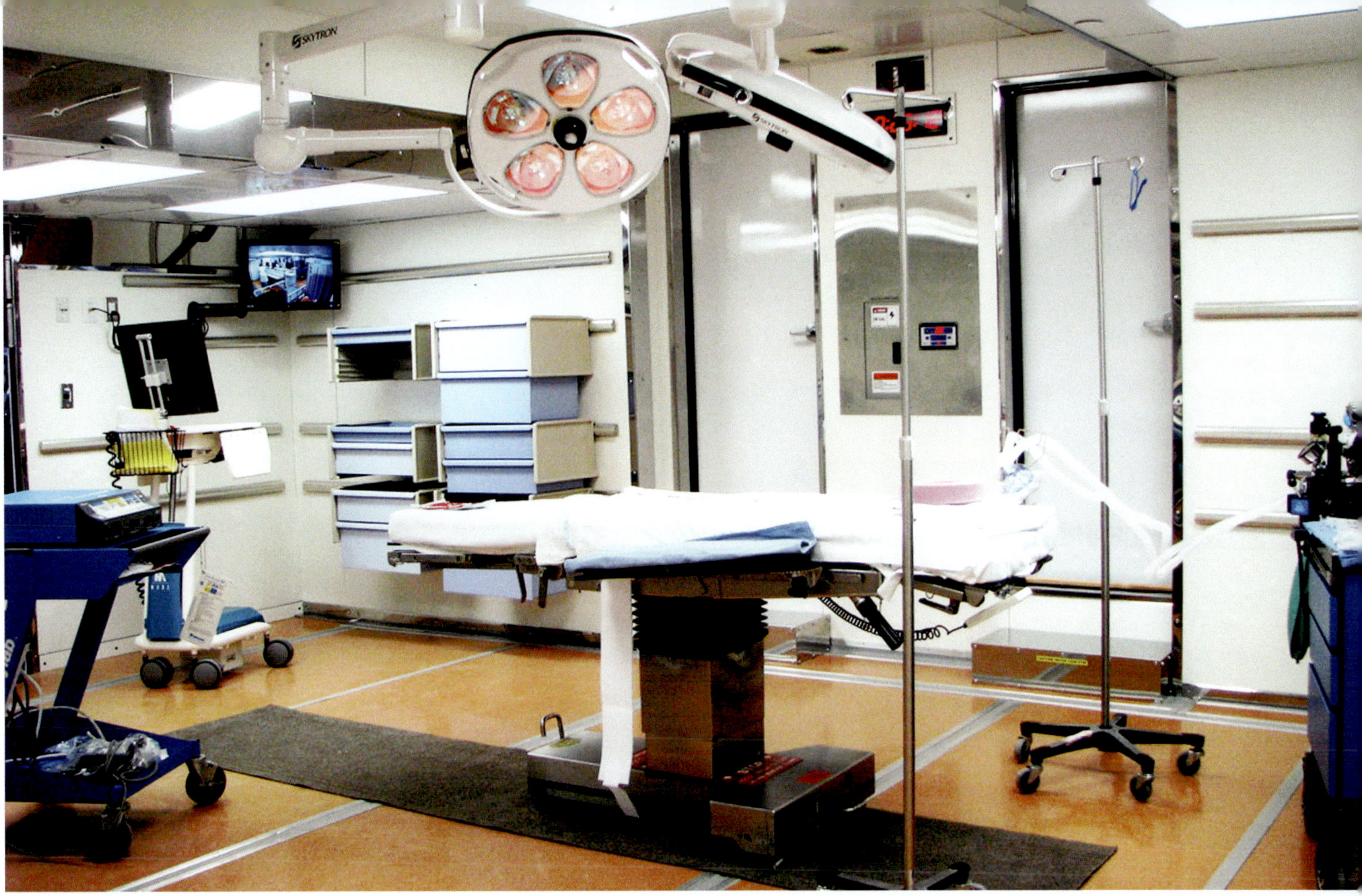

6.8.6 Equipment is transported inside of the vehicle in lock-down mode, but when unattached can be moved about as needed

6.8.7 Patient beds are virtually identical to those in a conventional hospital

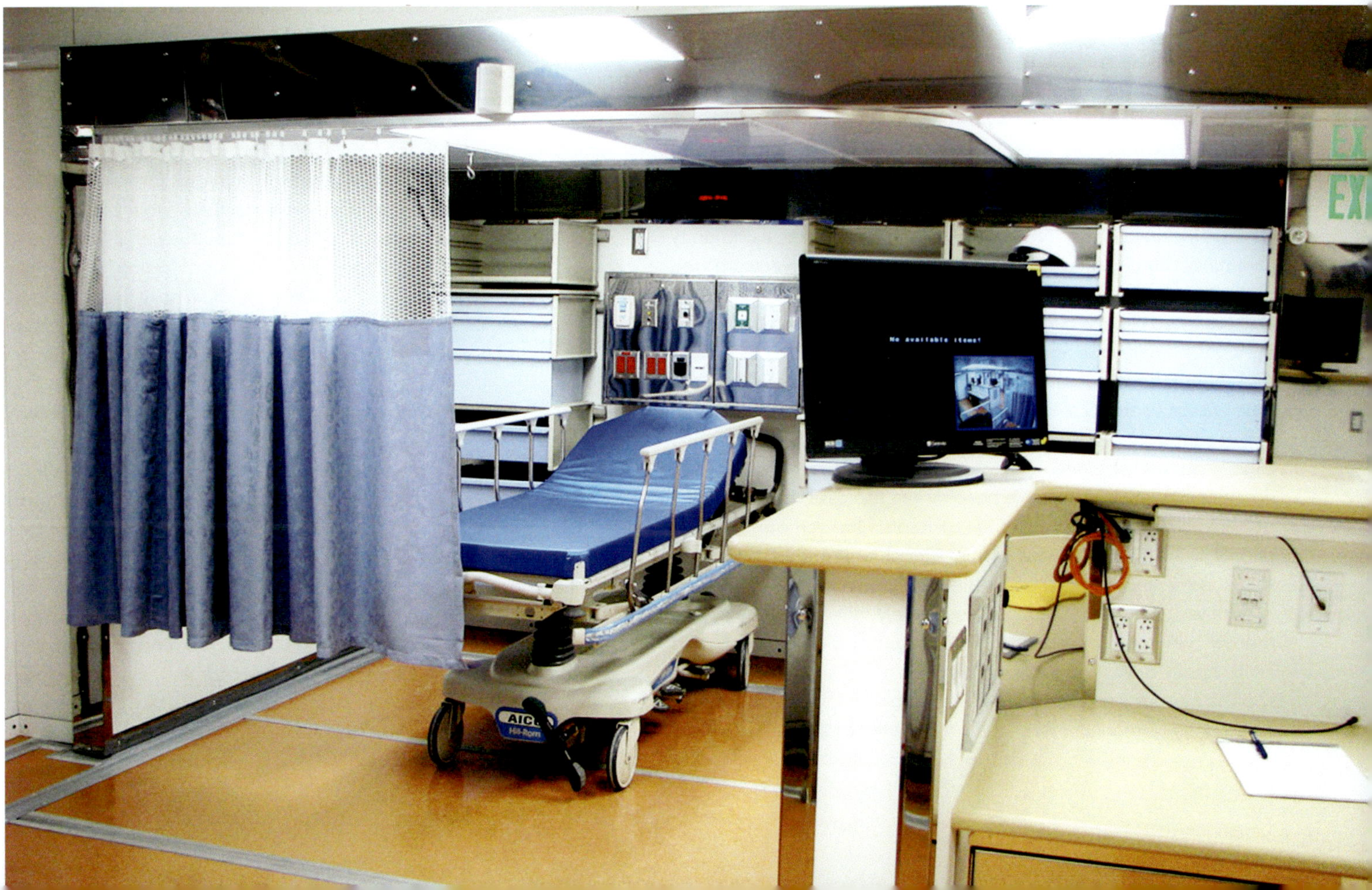

9 Mobile Field Hospital, Morocco

ARCHITECT/ENGINEER: Hord Coplan Macht, Baltimore, Maryland, with Spevco/MONARCH Corporation
CLIENT/SPONSOR: Ministry of Health, Morocco
TYPE OF CARE: Primary and acute care (RHC/RTC)
NUMBER OF BEDS: 48
FEATURED MATERIALS: Steel/tensile-fabric
METHOD OF ASSEMBLY: Modular/plug-in
SITE CONTEXT: Variable
DEPLOYMENT (MIN/MAX): 3,385/55,000 square feet
COMPLETED: 2010 (proposed)

Context/site

As discussed in Chapter 2, vehicular-based mobile health clinics have been in use since World War I, providing a lifeline, for triage, and first aid treatment of casualties on the battlefront. They made possible the rapid transport over roads of the injured to behind-the-lines base hospitals. In civilian contexts, their use has continued to this day and they are proliferating at this time. Local and international organizations in the U.S. now operate mobile vehicular clinics, including the NGO *Ministries of Health*, community hospitals, humanitarian-focused NGOs, and University-based tertiary medical centers. One such university medical center-owned and operated clinic is docked at the University of Arizona. This unit provides primary care and is capable of traveling to remote locales throughout the Arizona desert, serving communities with otherwise little access to medical care, and aiding persons who lack private transportation (see Interview 4 in the Appendix). This vehicular clinic possesses telemedicine capabilities, establishing a synchronous link with its base hospital—in this case, the University of Arizona Medical Center in Tucson. Its remote, mobile telemedicine services focus on nutritional health education, and retinal screenings for diabetic patients who are uninsured and risk blindness if left untreated.[15] Unfortunately, the vast majority of mobile vehicular clinics remain, in general, minimalist and aesthetically drab. In the spirit of developing an aesthetically more sophisticated response, MONARCH Corporation teamed with an established American A/E firm to produce a prototype for presentation at the Arab Health Congress, an event held in Dubai, United Emirates in 2010. The renderings produced for this event depict a prototype installed in a desert context in Morocco (Figures 6.9.1 and 6.9.2).

Building/unit

The installation depicted here consists of fifty-eight semi-trailer vehicle units configured as a self-sufficient forty-eight-bed field hospital. The modular clinic units house virtually all aspects of a stationary hospital—from waiting areas, triage, admit, to surgical suites with four operating bays, patient wards, isolation units, a maternity unit, a physical rehabilitation unit, a pharmacy, and laboratories. This installation represents one vision of how advanced medical care can be transported to distant, climatically extreme, medically underserved places, urban or otherwise (Figures 6.9.3 and 6.9.4). Various units are dedicated for specialized types of care, i.e. women's reproductive health clinic. Multiple units can be installed on the same site, and then remobilized to another a week later, and so on, then return to the base unit. This re-docking at a base unit allows for its restocking, equipment sterilization, and any maintenance work that may be required. The 'base hospital' provides a mixture of inpatient and outpatient care. The plugging-in and unplugging of various specialized nomadic units, working off of a base field hospital platform, allows for the installation to exert a far broader offsite reach, thereby extending geographically the scope of care to the region.

Other modules can be outfitted as an MRI Imaging/Radiology Unit, for CT/mammography scanning, with an onboard nurses' station and a patient waiting area. Others can be equipped for primary care, including immunizations and child and maternal health, with still others equipped as nomadic emergency care units. Here, the unit template developed by the architects houses two trauma care treatment bays, eight urgent care beds, with an umbilical link to an ambulance bay that in turn connects with an existing stationary hospital and in so doing extends that facility's capacity. Another scenario envisioned is for an installation to be equipped and staffed as an institution affiliated with a local university medical center. Here, the goal would be to field-

6.9.1 The mobile field hospital variant presented here was developed for the Morocco Ministry of Health

educate future physicians and allied healthcare professionals for work in medically underserved communities (Figures 6.9.5 and 6.9.6).

The field hospital illustrated here is estimated to be able to be disassembled, relocated to a new site, and re-commissioned in fourteen days or less. In full deployment, it would total 55,000 square feet, and include the following functions: entry lobby, waiting, patient reception/registration, and intake (3,015 square feet), on-call suite comprised of male/female shower units, on-call rooms and physician's lounge (5,025 square feet), dining, kitchen, serving area (4,020 square feet), optional exterior patio for dining, emergency unit (5,000 square feet), pharmacy (1,000 square feet), administration (2,000 square feet), laboratory/phlebotomy (2,000 square feet), ICU suite consisting of eight beds (3,015 square feet), imaging suite consisting of MRI, CT/radiology diagnostic apparatus (5000 square feet), surgical suite consisting of four operating rooms, four preoperative beds and four postoperative recovery beds (7,000 square feet), material management/central sterile unit (3,845 square feet), ambulance entry bay (725 square feet), an isolation corridor (1245 square feet), and general circulation (2,330 square feet), in a total of fifty double expandable modular units plus seven accordion-like vestibule connectors. As per the specifications of proposed manufacturer U.S. Monarch Systems, each unit would be eight feet in width by fifty-two feet in length with a shipping volume of 3,385 cubic feet. In its pop-out expanded mode it would be twenty-two feet in width by fifty-two feet in length with an expanded occupied space volume of 7,480 cubic feet.[16] One important addition to this system (not depicted here) would be the inclusion of roof-mounted or independent freestanding (ground-sited) photovoltaic panels.[17]

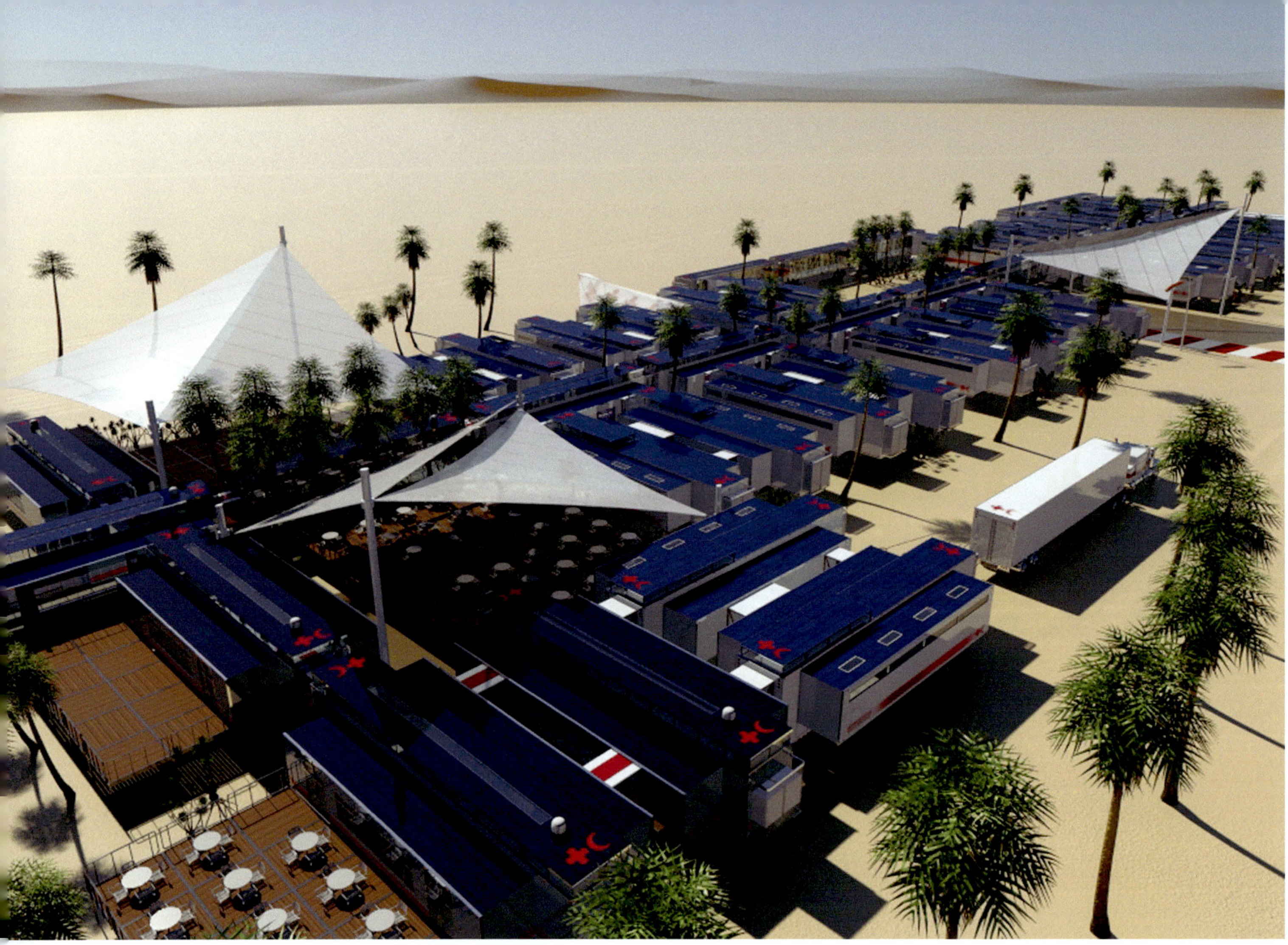

6.9.2 In full-scale installation mode this vehicular, truck-based system becomes a nomadic hospital

6.9.3 Vehicles can be arranged in clusters to create courtyards, with shade screens providing protection from the sun and desert sandstorms

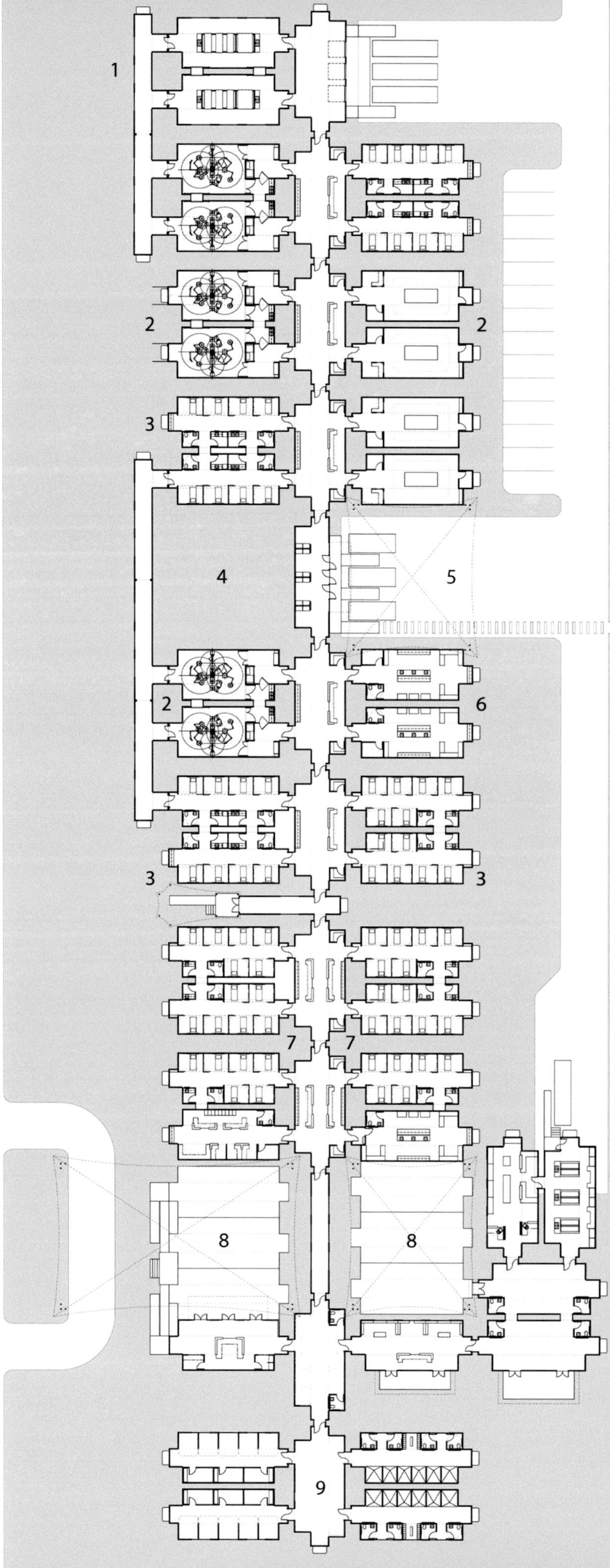

6.9.4 The installation shown here features a central circulation spine with various units flanking it in a double loaded configuration

Key:
1 materials management
2 surgical suites
3 post-op
4 courtyard
5 emergency
6 staff/administration
7 inpatient units
8 food services/dining
9 staff dormitory/support
10 helipad

6.9.5 An outdoor dining courtyard is shielded by a large sunscreen

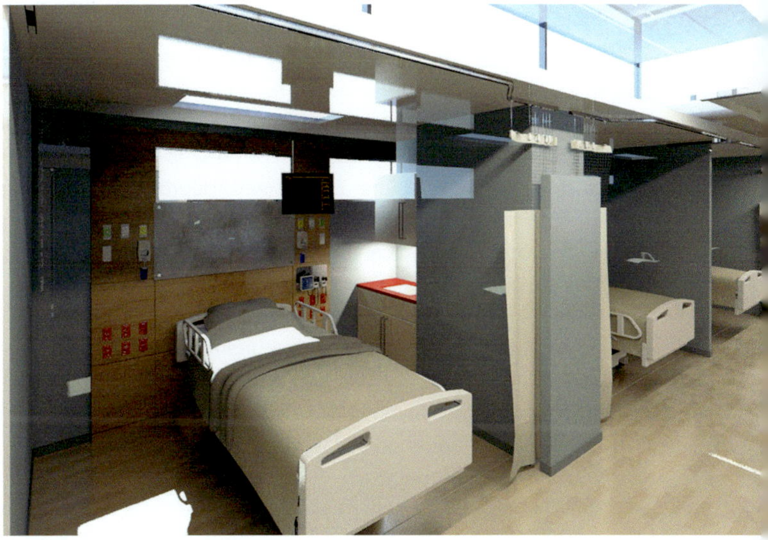

6.9.6 Inpatient units have equipment and furnishings comparable to those in a conventional hospital. Each patient bed zone has its own sink, storage, privacy panel, and natural daylight

10 Mobile Airship HIV Clinic (prototype), Sub-Saharan Africa

ARCHITECT/ENGINEER: JAG Design, San Francisco
CLIENT/SPONSOR: Architecture for Humanity
TYPE OF CARE: HIV/AIDS diagnostic-treatment (RHC)
NUMBER OF BEDS: N/A (outpatient)
FEATURED MATERIALS: Fabric membrane/lightweight alloys
METHOD OF ASSEMBLY: Flat-pack/pneumatic
SITE CONTEXT: Variable
DEPLOYMENT (MIN/MAX): 1,500 square feet
COMPLETED: 2004 (proposal)

Context/site

Lightweight modern airships continue to fascinate. A blimp is a non-rigid airship, an airship without a continuous structural framework, a continuously rigid outer skin, or a keel. Unlike a rigid airship, i.e. a Zeppelin, it relies on pressurized gas to provide its upward lift (helium rather than hydrogen) within the envelope and it relies on the strength of this activated envelope to maintain structural integrity. Pneumatic airships are generally assumed to date from 1915, with their origin in the U.K. during World War I when the British experimented with lighter-than-air aircraft. The initial British non-rigid aircraft was called an *A-limp*. Soon thereafter, a second version called the *B-limp* was deemed to be more successful.[18] Horace Short, already well known for his wry coining of new, descriptive, technical terms, named it the 'Blimp', adding, "What else would you call it?'[19]

The HIV/AIDS airship and clinic prototype is conceived to function as an iconic symbol of global health organizations' need for broader reach in the diagnosis and treatment of this disease in remote regions of Sub-Saharan Africa. This prototype was an entry in a 2004 design competition initiated by *Architecture for Humanity*, a multinational NGO founded in 1999 (Figures 6.10.1 to 6.10.4a–b). It capitalizes on modern helium airship technological advances of recent decades. The windows are operable in the cabin so parcels can be dropped to the ground below. The airship itself becomes a communications medium, a blank canvas for projecting health-related text-messaging. With a sustainable cruising speed of 50 miles per hour the airship is unrestricted, able to access difficult terrain across extended travel distances compared to land-based vehicles—especially where conventional roads simply do not exist. The flight endurance record for an airship of this type is eleven days, having flown from Massachusetts to Europe, Africa, and back to the U.S. without once refueling or landing (Figure 6.10.5a–k).

Airships have captured the imagination of millions in times of war and peace. Every continent currently maintains landing facilities accessible to airships of this type and size. Its propulsion system is relatively simple to operate and maintain, basically the equivalent to a 600hp diesel engine. Portable mooring masts can be operationalized to provide a secure landing pad, and the airship rotates around this mast much like a weathervane, capable of withstanding hurricane-force winds of up to 150 miles per hour. Its payload capacity is up to 160 tons and its self-stabilizing capability allows its clinic module to remain operational and online via satellite telecommunications while the airship is aloft.

Building/unit

Why not adapt these airships into flying clinics? Why not design and build portable, lightweight airships with ground-based triage, decontamination, and even emergency surgical capabilities? An airship clinic can be a symbol of hope, assisting in humanitarian aid efforts throughout the world in the aftermath of drought, famine, hurricanes, typhoons, earthquakes, and times of war. Places otherwise inaccessible and with poor roads, with no nearby rail lines or large airports, can be accessed, places such as the Australian outback and remote parts of Sub-Saharan Africa (Figure 6.10.6a–d). As for its onboard payload, a cable-secured bladder is able to house the cargo lifting equipment, and fore and aft bladders contain ballast to stabilize the airship during lifting/hoisting procedures.

This type of airship is able to hover slightly above its landing surface and under the right conditions still possess near-vertical operational capabilities, particularly if it is equipped with vector-stabilizing engines (Figure 6.10.7). In such conditions it is possible to pick up a payload (clinic pod) and in turn land it on the ground again elsewhere. When disengaged from the cockpit the clinic

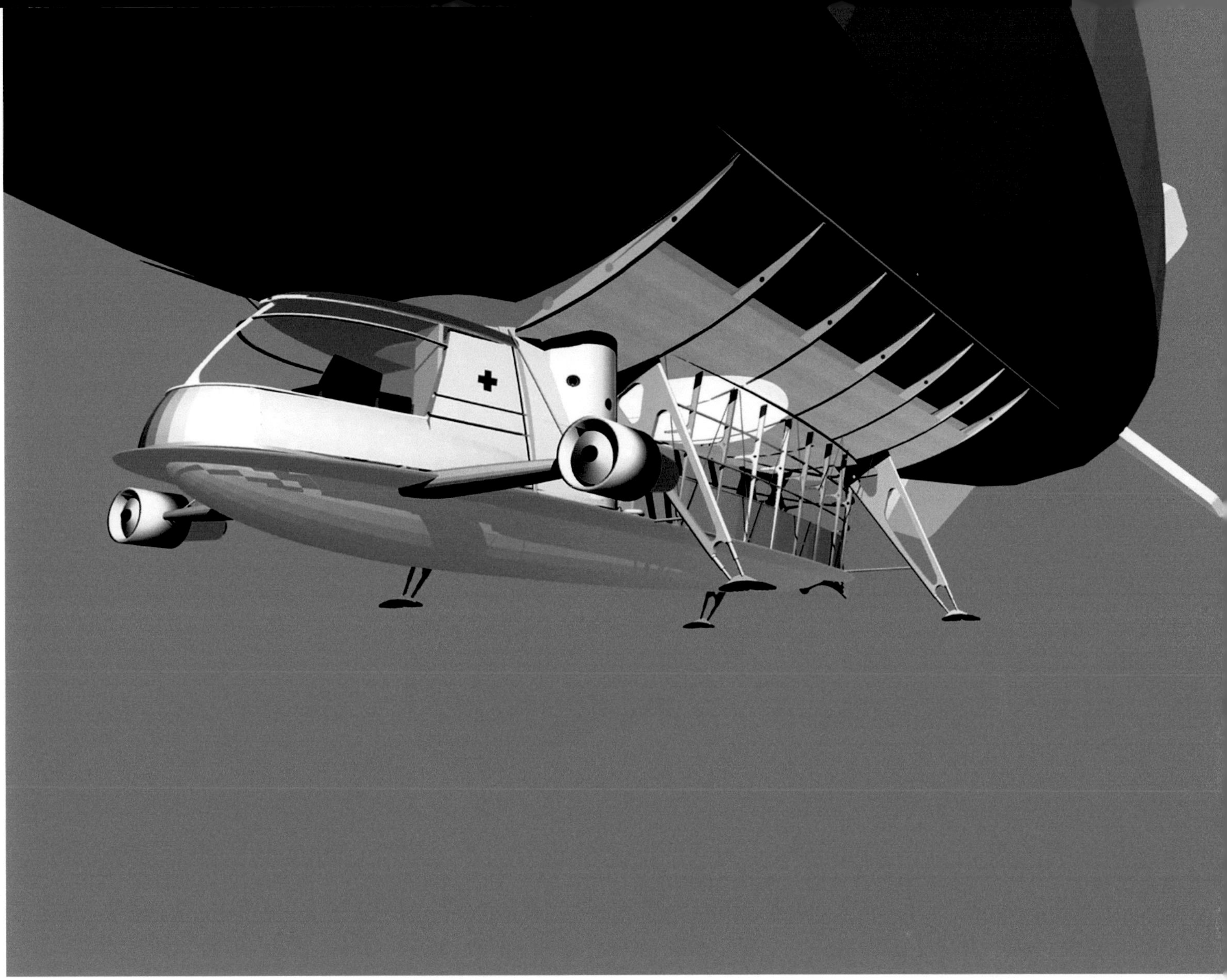

6.10.1 Mobile airship HIV clinic prototype for Sub-Saharan Africa

component is approximately fifty-five feet by fourteen feet and is a self-contained facility equipped with foldout sleeping bunks for the staff, and storage bins for supplies, pharmaceuticals, exam/procedure tables, potable water, and waste holding bins. Once on the ground, adjustable feet and legs level the clinic, and tension cables coiled at the outriggers of the roof are utilized to tether the airship to the ground. Tarps can be strung along these tension cables to provide tented (shaded) areas for use as classrooms, or diagnosis and treatment 'rooms.' Showers, bathroom compartments, and interior and exterior scrub sinks are in the onboard pod. A motorcycle with a stretcher sidecar is depicted mounted to the rear of the clinic pod, to provide a local ground transport option to transport patients too weak to venture to the clinic on their own, and for general staff use, locally.[20]

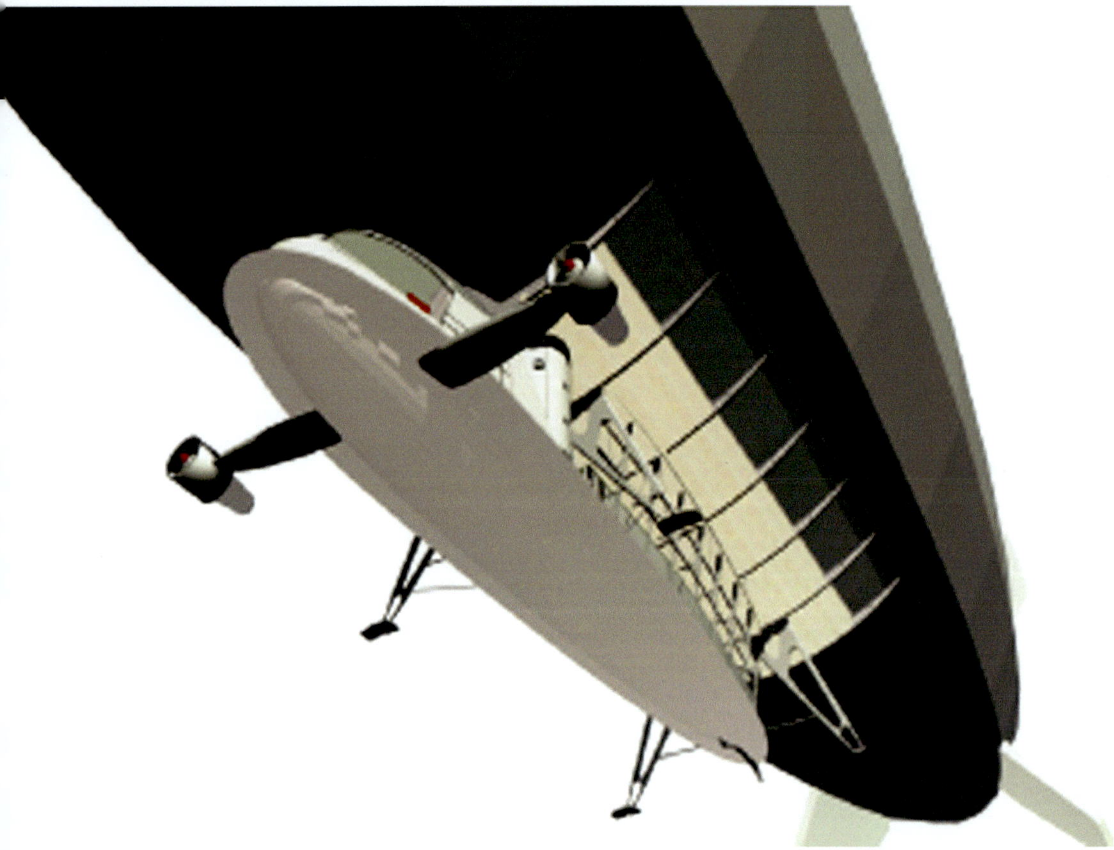

6.10.2 This lightweight airship-clinic is deployable virtually anywhere with suitable landing conditions

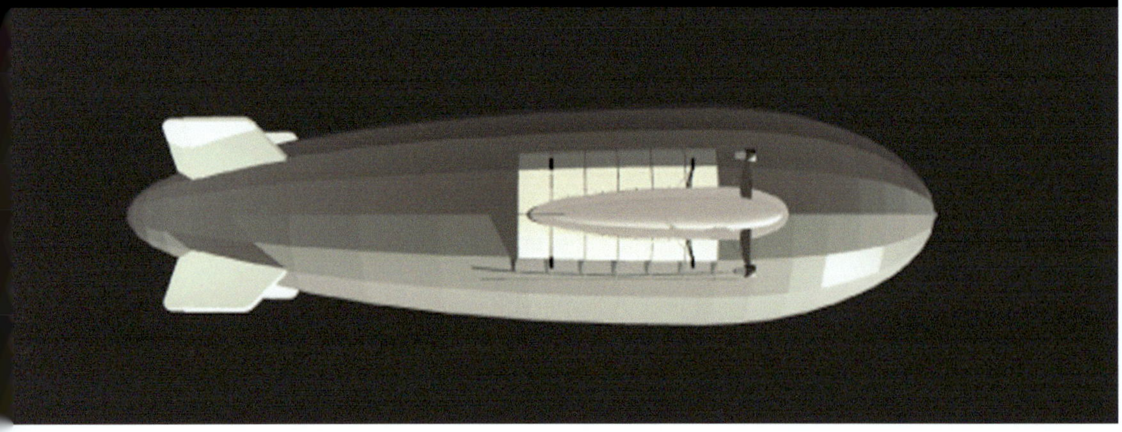

6.10.3a–b A clinic-pod module is nested beneath the superstructure, shown affixed at the airship's midsection

6.10.4a–b A more detailed view reveals the clinic-pod as an autonomous structure. Upon landing, feet stabilize it, allowing for its disengagement from the airship.

6.10.5a–k Upon disengagement, the structure becomes freestanding and the airship can return later to retrieve it—a critical feature in situations where the airship itself is unable to land

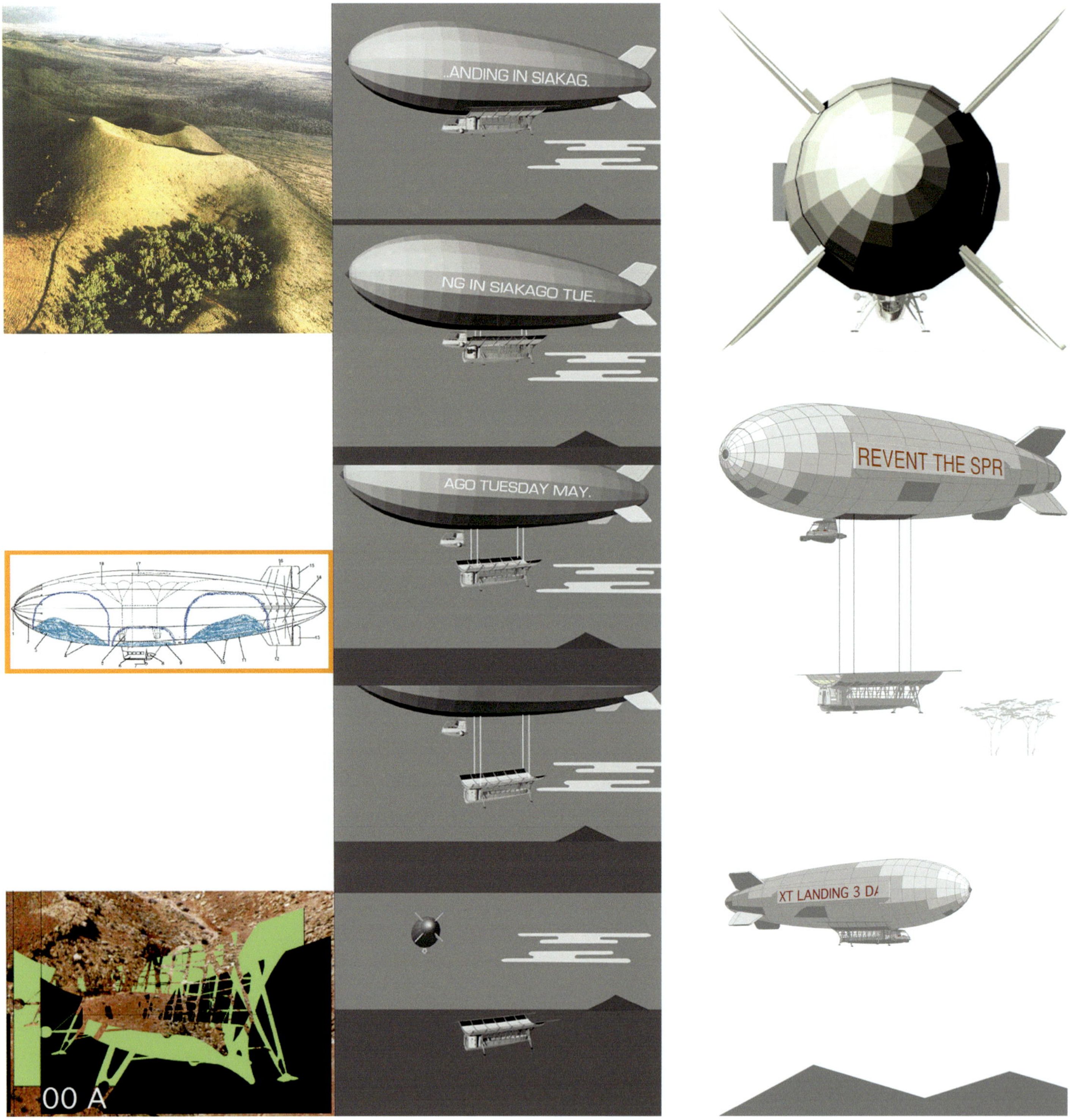

6.10.6a–d When in its disengaged mode the clinic-pod becomes an intriguing structure in its own right

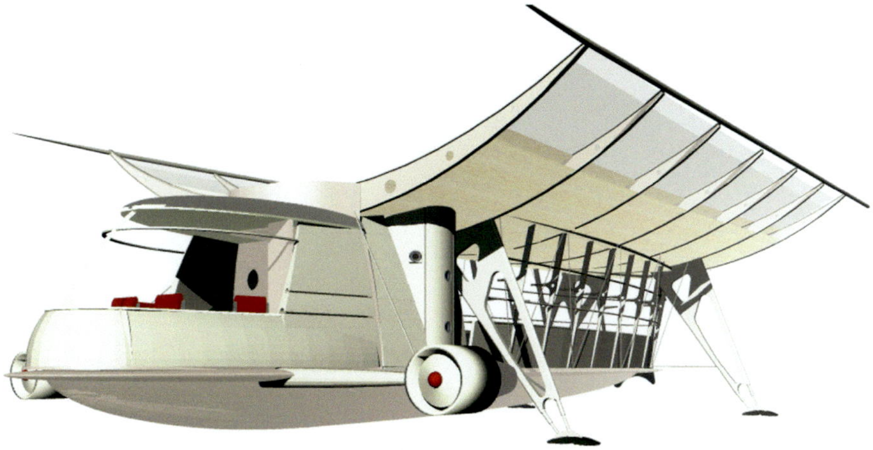

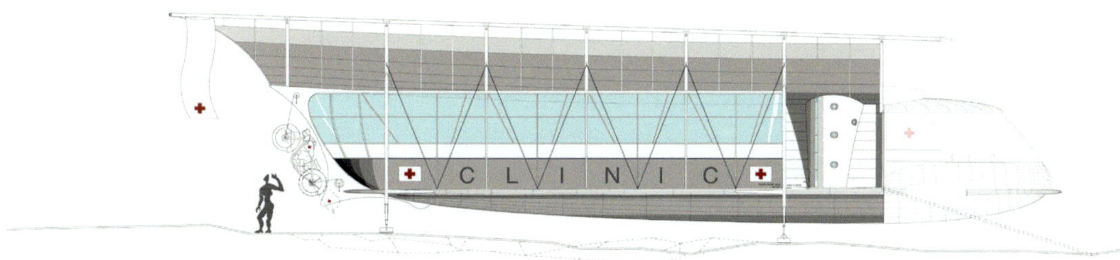

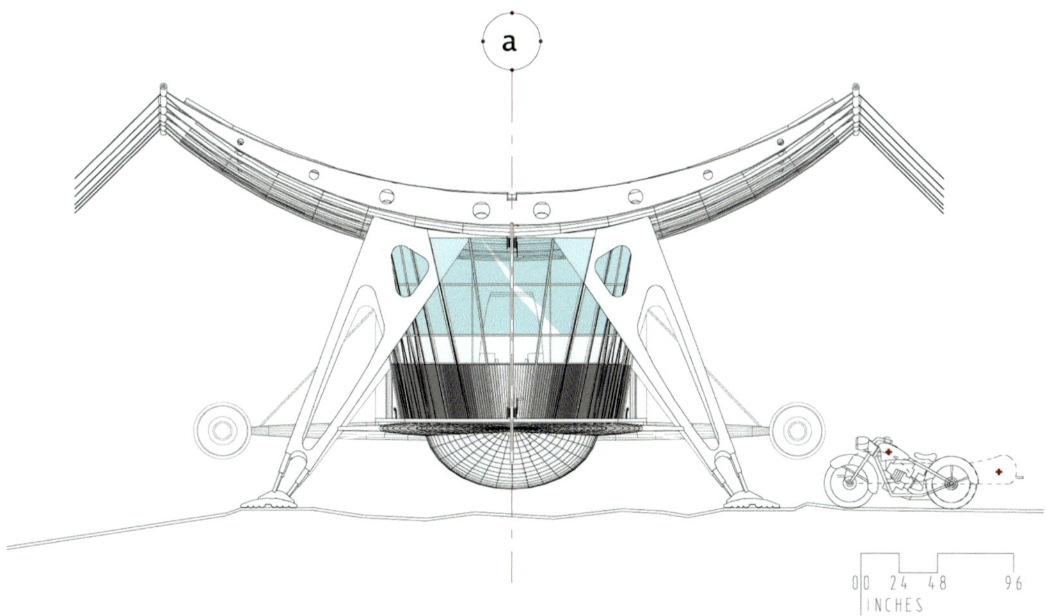

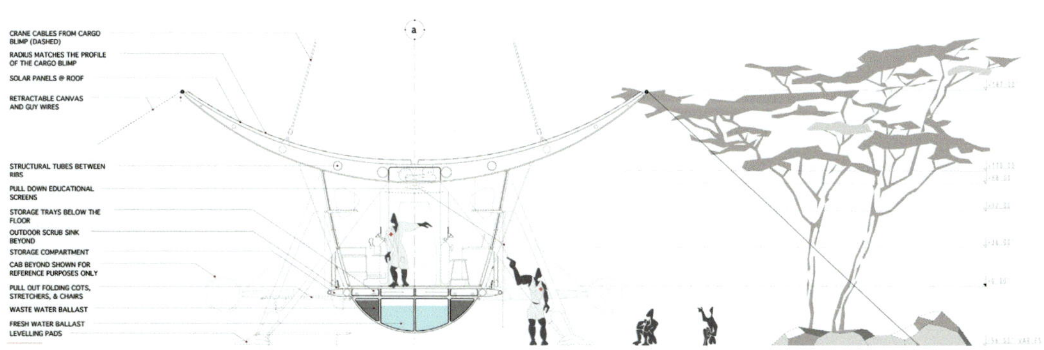

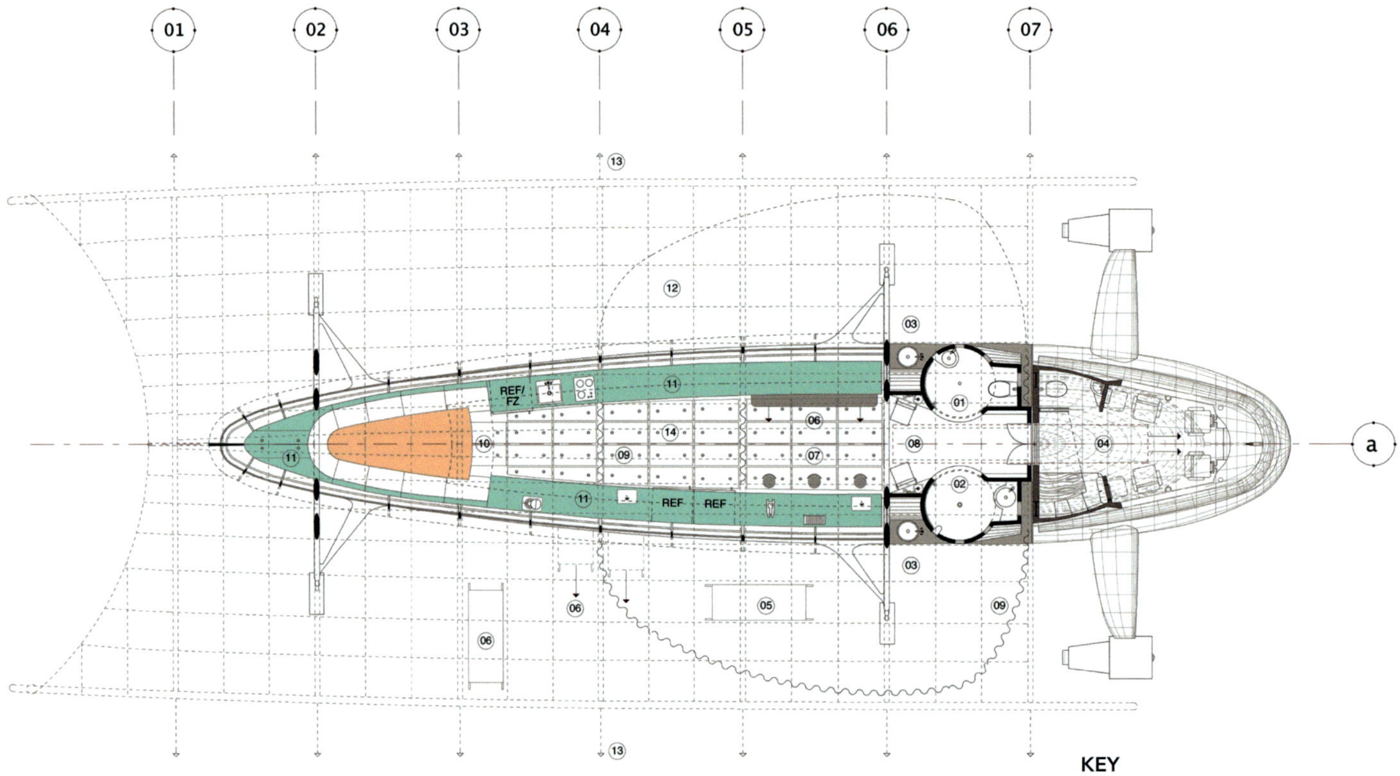

KEY

1 bathroom
2 shower
3 outdoor scrub sink
4 cockpit (reference)
5 open air clinic
6 pull-out cots and chairs
7 research/testing
8 indoor clinic area
9 privacy screens
10 staff area
11 storage compartments
12 open air classroom
13 guy wires and sunshade
14 floor hatches

6.10.7 On-board functions are proportioned and arranged to maximize the number of primary care medical services able to be provided

11 Toronto Rehab CEAL/iDAPT Centre, Canada

ARCHITECT/ENGINEER: Murphy Hilgers Architects/Aecon Group, Inc./Toronto Rehabilitation Institute/Sunjoo Advani
CLIENT/SPONSOR: Toronto Rehabilitation Institute-UHN/Province of Ontario/Canadian Federal Government
TYPE OF CARE: Rehabilitation (PMI)
NUMBER OF BEDS: 420
FEATURED MATERIALS: Stainless steel/polymers
METHOD OF ASSEMBLY: Modular/onsite construction
SITE CONTEXT: Inpatient research hospital
INSTALLATION: 65,000 square feet
COMPLETED: 2012

Context/site

The Toronto Rehabilitation Institute, part of the University Health Network (UHN), owns and operates the $36 million, 65,000 square foot *iDAPT* (Intelligent Design for Adaptation, Participation and Technology). iDAPT is one of the world's most technologically advanced rehabilitation research centers. Its eighty-five researchers and more than 200 graduate and post-doctoral students focus on three core areas: injury prevention, restoration of functional autonomy/quality of life after a disabling injury or illness, and assistive living devices to support people in the home and in the everyday environment. Interdisciplinary teams of scientists and students are drawn together from across the spectrum of biomedical and clinical disciplines. They work collaboratively to develop and test new methods, technologies, products, and treatments in physical medicine and rehabilitation.[21] The CEAL Centre is the subterranean research laboratory located beneath Toronto Rehab's University Centre and is, in many ways, the focal point within iDAPT. CEAL features the world's first hydraulic motion simulator, uniquely combining motion, visual, and aural simulation techniques in a virtual built environment lab context. More than 21,000 persons in the province of Ontario visit an emergency room each winter due to slips and falls on ice and snow. Research occurs at iDAPT in the areas of fall-reduction through eradication of accident-causing preconditions, advances in building codes, in next-generation mobility assistance devices, the design of accident-reducing devices for residential settings, and new devices to reduce hospital-acquired infection rates during inpatient rehabilitation (Figure 6.11.1a–d).[22]

Building/unit

The CEAL/iDAPT motion simulator is located four levels below street level. Inside this prefab module, the mercury level can be modified to dip down to -10 degrees Celsius, with howling winds whipping up snow in swirling circles. The main testing room that houses this moveable device is within a three-level volume that reaches upwards of eighty feet from the floor. Three levels above the simulator, in a mission control room, researchers monitor and control all aspects of the experiments. Inside the simulator, an elderly woman, secured in a body harness inside, attempts to walk across an icy floor and then climb up an icy set of stairs. The motion simulator tilts the pod about twenty degrees, intentionally throwing her off balance. This structure, dubbed the *WinterLab* module is, in effect, a massive robotic apparatus (Figure 6.11.2a–c). Its stainless steel exterior features a brightly colored mural of Toronto's skyline at sunset. The module is perched atop a moveable, flexible armature capable of tilting and shaking on demand. Researchers studying rehabilitation patients' propensity for falls inside the simulator document an individual's every move. This modular pod is one of thirteen research laboratories at Toronto Rehab, where researchers discover how accessibility issues in natural and built environments can be better negotiated.[23]

CEAL includes this NASA-like hydraulic motion simulator together with its three interchangeable, modular configurations for experiments: *WinterLab*, *StairLab*, and *StreetLab* (Figure 6.11.4a–c). The basic modular device is a test-bed with a portable platform supported by large telescopic legs, which in turn support variously themed 'payloads.' The three different moveable lab modules, each measuring six by six meters, are repositioned and rotated via a ceiling-mounted track high above the testing floor. Research subjects are fitted with motion-tracking systems that record eye movements, heart rate, skin temperature, electrical brainwaves, and muscle movements during tests. The aim is to hyper-simulate, that is, to take everyday real-world conditions and place a more

6.11.1a–d The CEAL/iDAPT simulator module at Toronto Rehabilitation Hospital, shown shaking in the midst of an experiment

6.11.2a–c The interior of the *StreetLab* simulator module at the CEAL/iDAPT Centre. Experiments on urban navigability and safety are conducted with patients undergoing physical therapy and rehabilitation

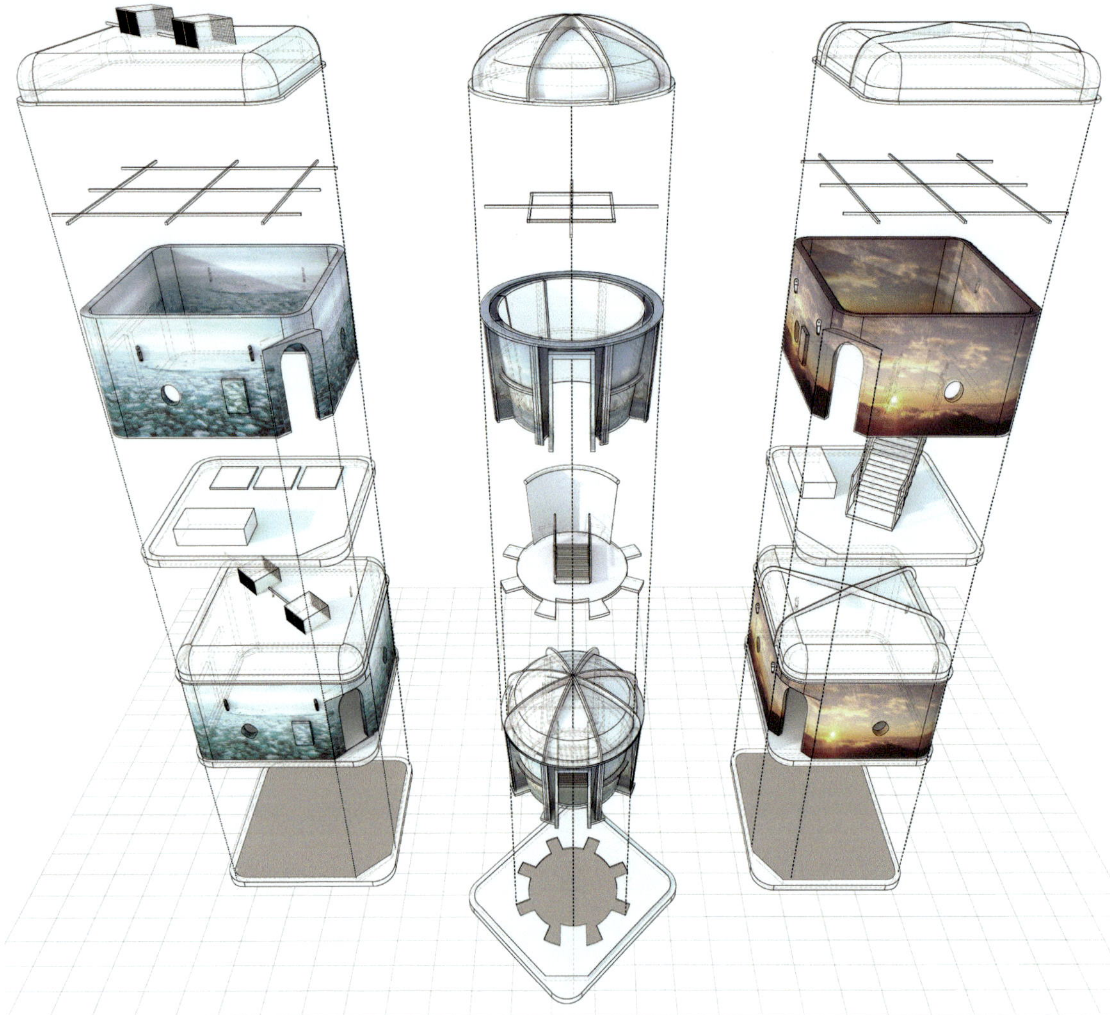

6.11.3a–c Three motion simulator modules are depicted—*WinterLab, StairLab* and *StreetLab* (left to right)

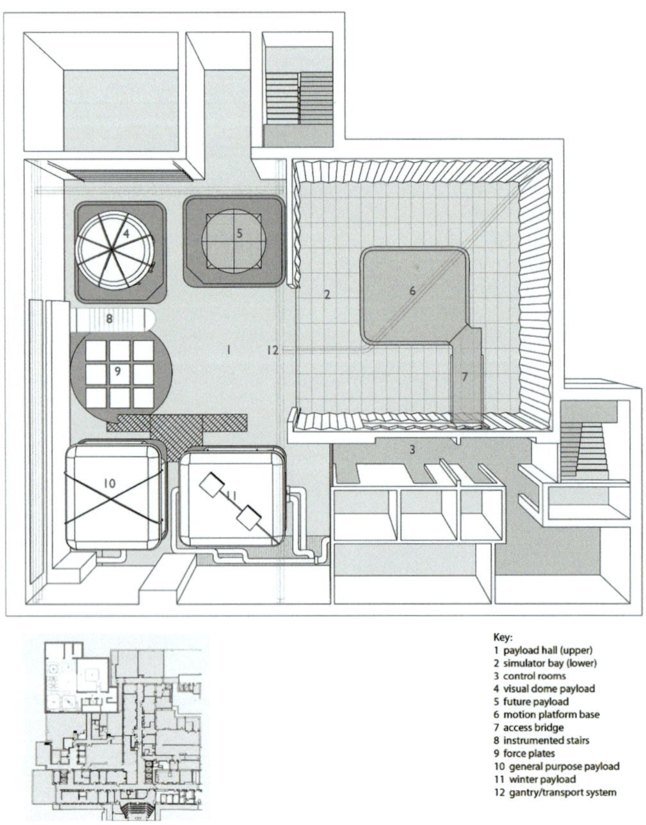

6.11.4a–b Plan of the interior of the CEAL/iDAPT Centre. The laboratory occupies a four-level high space at Toronto Rehab in downtown Toronto

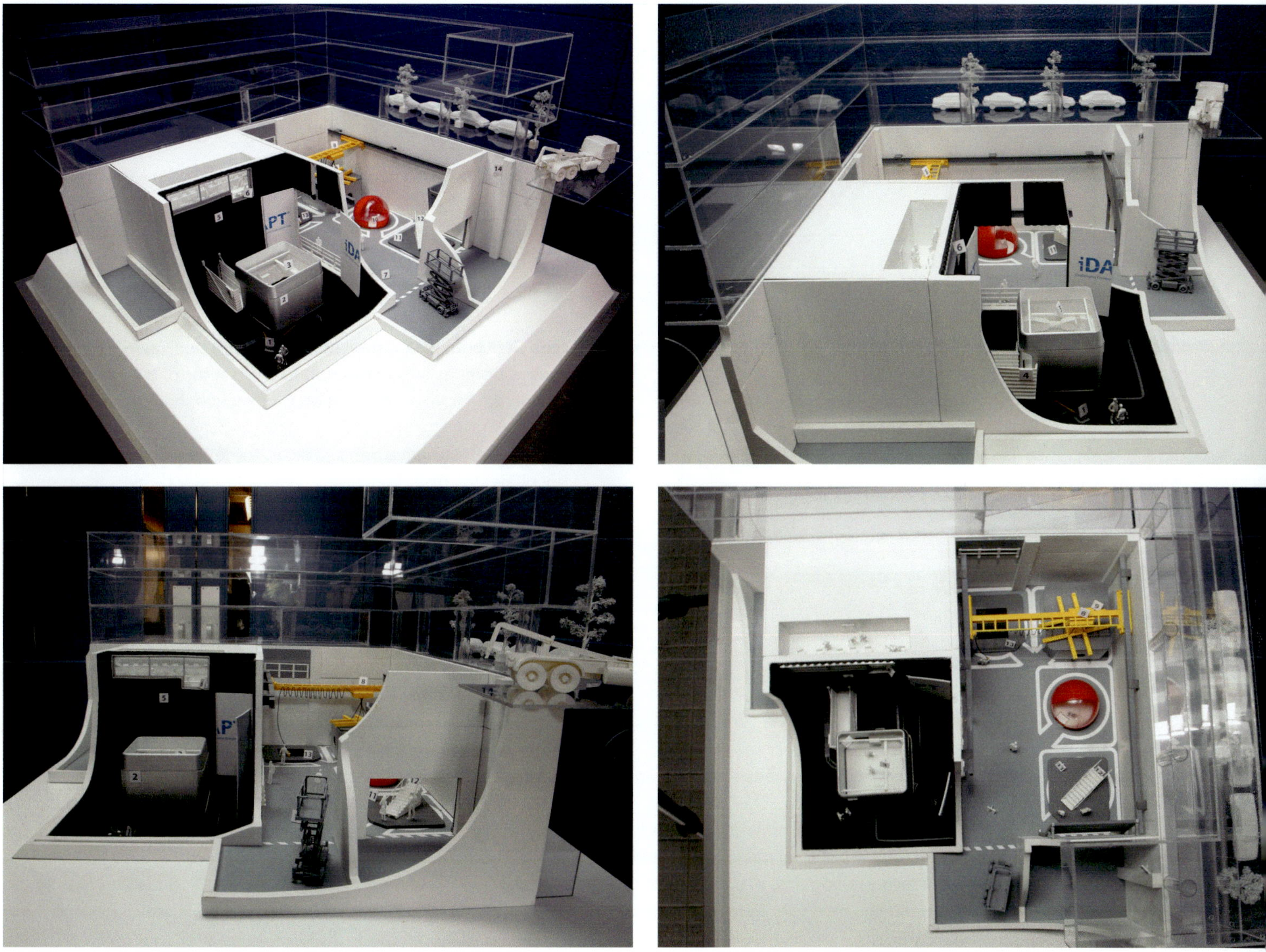

6.11.5a–d Model of the CEAL/iDAPT Centre, illustrating the center's warehouse-like 'shell space' re-configurability as needs dictate

scrutinized focus on their ramifications for an individual experiencing physical and/or sensory losses (Figure 6.11.3a–b).

In the *StairLab* configuration, a staircase is activated on cue, causing a person to stumble or fall. Sensors embedded in the stairs and handrails continuously collect data to aid researchers in learning more about what causes falls. The *StreetLab* simulator configuration recreates an intersection in Toronto's downtown core, and consists of 3D streetscapes projected onto the screen, accompanied by a realistic urban soundscape. Its payload features a 180-degree field-of-view visual projection screen combined with treadmill interface and a wheelchair simulator. Its display system is a *virtual reality dome* where subjects can walk, virtually, through downtown Toronto while being challenged by traffic clogged intersections and various obstacles and obstructions (Figure 6.11.4a–c). This system was designed and calibrated in Canada by *domeprojection.com*. This firm developed the projection system for the dome, making it possible for research subjects to negotiate, for example, a jagged, irregularly surfaced sidewalk while attempting to cope with the simultaneous rattling sound and motion of a passing virtual streetcar (Figure 6.11.5a–d).

12 Puyo General Hospital, Puyo, Ecuador

ARCHITECT/ENGINEER: PmMt Architectura, Ecuador
CLIENT/SPONSOR: Makiber, SA/Salud Ecuador, Ministry of Health
TYPE OF CARE: Inpatient (PMI)
NUMBER OF BEDS: 125
FEATURED MATERIALS: Steel/Plexiglas
METHOD OF ASSEMBLY: Flat-pack/onsite construction
SITE CONTEXT: Rural
INSTALLATION: 160,000 square feet
COMPLETED: 2012

Context/site

The Hospital de Puyo is a bold architectural response to a dilemma that affects many countries in Latin America. The challenge in Ecuador essentially called for a hospital to be built and opened in record time—less than one year from the start of design to opening day. This was achieved without relinquishing design or construction quality or any diminished internal medical planning, overall functionality, campus site planning, or landscaping. Prefab modularity was adopted at the outset as this approach was viewed as most appropriate in terms of maintaining quality control throughout the manufacture, construction, commissioning, and start-up of the hospital's day-to-day operations. This hospital features a significant percentage of prefabricated components, combined with a percentage of onsite conventional construction. This project would not have happened without a significant commitment on the part of the client, the A/E team, the local manufacturing industry, and the support of a local, medically underserved community (Figure 6.12.1).

In Latin America and elsewhere, momentum is increasing to commission the design and manufacture of offsite prefab hospitals. The Libyan government, through United Libyan Holdings, in 2014, issued a Request for Proposals (RFP) to design and construct thirty-three prefabricated public hospitals variously classified as general hospitals, with a subset of these designated as specialty hospitals to be built across Libya in sixty-bed and 120-bed capacities. Additionally, new private hospitals and clinics are currently in planning, each affiliated with a healthcare institution located outside Libya. The national ministry of health aims to guide the redevelopment and expansion of this sector of the economy as a means to improve the nation's collective health status (Figure 6.12.2).[24]

In India, one physician's mission to deliver low-cost community hospitals to disenfranchised populations led him to modular prefabrication. Dr. Devi Shetty is the founder of the Narayana Hrudayalaya 'health city' in Bengaluru. There, open-heart surgery is performed on a high-volume basis, and in so doing reduces medical costs significantly. In India, approximately 40 percent of the population must either borrow money or sell private assets to pay for hospitalization. In response, a 300-bed offsite prefab heart specialty hospital recently opened in the city of Mysore. It was completed in less than six months for $4 million. In India, this same hospital would have cost nearly $30 million and have required three years to erect if using traditional construction methods.[25] A second hospital, the CSM Hospital, at Gandhinagar, Bellary (2014) is another recent prefab hospital in India. This thirty-six-bed acute care facility was designed and built by *Speed 4 Prefab Solutions Pvt., Ltd*, based in Mumbai. It is modest in size, at 2,500 square feet and two levels in height. It houses an ICU and a surgical suite, an NICU, labor and delivery room, and its adjacent diagnostic wing houses radiology and ECG equipment, a waiting room, administrative suite, and a dayroom.[26]

Building/unit

These built projects are in many ways akin to the 125-bed hospital in Puyo, Ecuador. The facility serves a population of 85,000 and was built in the province of Pastaz (Figure 6.12.3). It includes a hemodialysis center, a long-term care unit, internal medicine obstetrics/gynecology services, a neurology unit, and two ICUs. The hospital's footprint is an orthogonal grid. Within this grid, by means of addition/subtraction, a pattern emerges of mass/void in a consistent A/B A/B rhythm. The superordinate planning grid informs all internal circulation by means of numerous, repetitively proportioned elements—each rectilinear—with outdoor courtyards interspersed in between, providing natural ventilation and daylight to their adjoining interiors. Without these, an excessively dense, centralized footprint would have resulted. A total of ten landscaped,

6.12.1 Puyo General Hospital, in Puyo, Ecuador, filled a void in the local healthcare landscape—a large canopy at the main entrance establishes an inviting image

open-air courtyards contribute to its overall openness, human scale, and ambiance (Figures 6.12.4 and 6.12.5). On one far side of the footprint, there are five exterior courtyards and on the opposing side, four similar, exterior spaces. The main arrival pavilion is spacious with its vaulted ceiling reaching upward, drawing natural daylight within.

The prefab parts of the hospital were manufactured with componentry assembled both at the factory and at the construction site. Modules arrived at the site in flat-pack mode and were then erected on top of a monolithic concrete foundation. The result was a series of small-scale, individualized buildings with conventional infill construction. These modules were connected to one another, to the central circulation network, and then to the centralized support functions of the hospital. The overall composition's constituent 'base' structures are minimally articulated, and feature simple shed roofs. Their profile, individually and collectively, in a way references a streetscape of private residences. These buildings-within-a-building are sheathed in steel panels, in light colors, and with translucent panels of tempered glass, vertically ribbed, thereby obscuring direct view into interior spaces from the outside. In this way, natural daylight is transmitted into the interior without sacrificing patient privacy (Figure 6.12.6). The hospital campus was master planned with future expansion in mind as demand dictates, and funding allows. In all, this hospital made effective use of a core module of replicable size and complexity, and then it was repeated, additively, to great overall effect. The landscaped courtyards in between the modular structures provide counterpoint. And in this regard its design and construction strategy is not dissimilar from Brunel's U.K.-built field hospital, assembled at Renkioi, Turkey in 1855 (see Chapter 3).

6.12.2 Offsite prefab of a replicated module facilitated a faster construction timeline compared to traditional construction methods

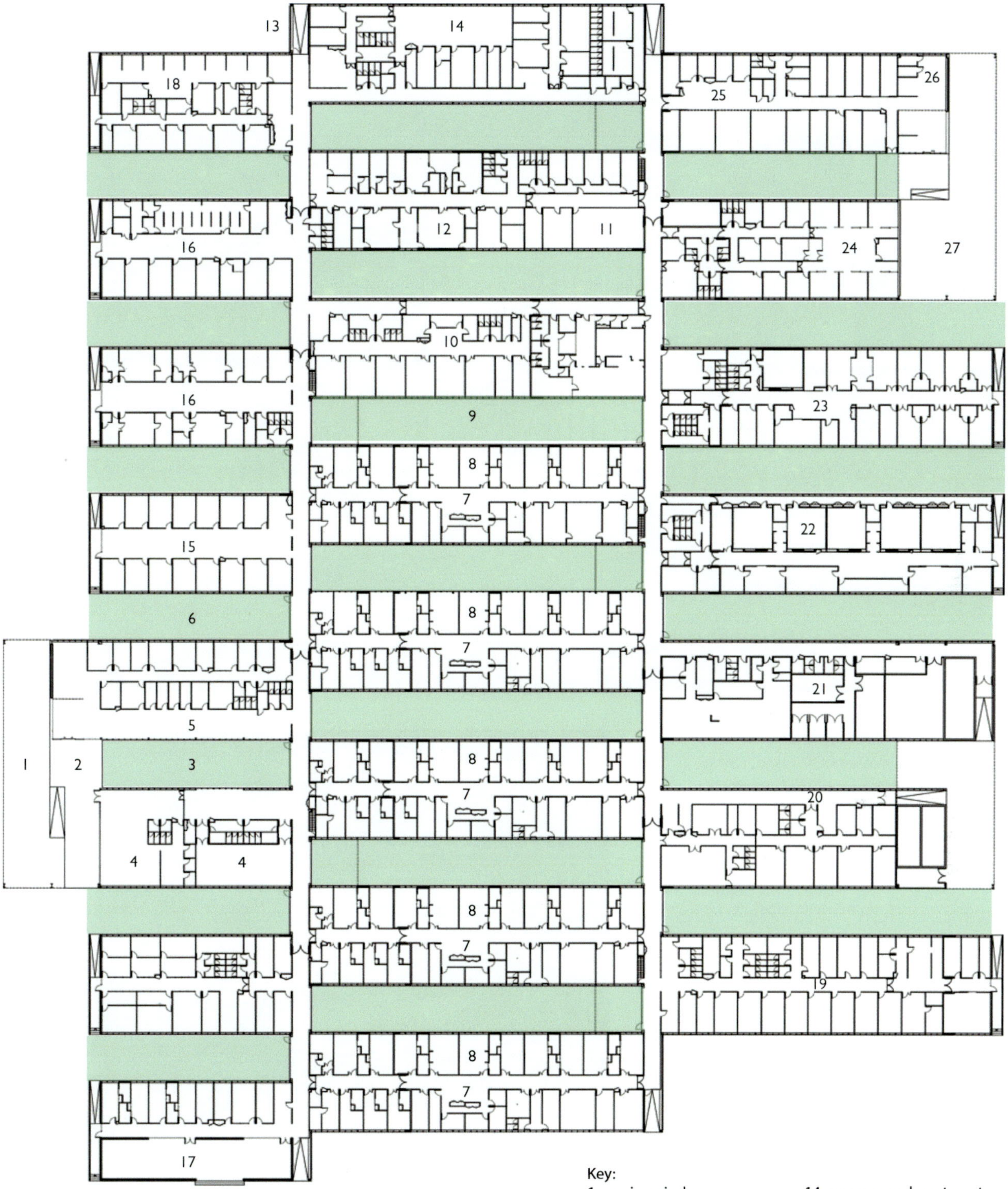

Key:

1 main arrival canopy
2 lobby/foyer
3 children's exterior play space/garden
4 administration
5 admissions/records
6 landscaped courtyard
7 nursing station
8 inpatient rooms
9 courtyard/garden exterior
10 post-surgical unit
11 NICU
12 ICU
13 emergency entrance
14 emergency department
15 counseling/physicians
16 behavioral health
17 materials management
18 outpatient surgery
19 psychiatric unit
20 pediatric health unit
21 central supply/pharmacy
22 surgical suites/support
23 isolation unit/support
24 CCU/nursing support
25 physicians/administration
26 shipping/receiving/morgue
27 ambulance staging

6.12.3 The replicated modules are arrayed in an A/B mass/void pattern, a strategy that yielded multiple open-air courtyards

6.12.4 The scale and shape of the prefab modular 'buildings' establishes a quasi-residential image, further accentuated by green lawns and courtyards situated in between the structures

6.12.5 Courtyards provide natural ventilation, views, and daylight—the opportunity to obtain direct contact with nature

6.12.6 Public circulation arteries throughout the hospital enhance occupants' wayfinding and establish spatial transparency—openness

13 Swedish Medical Oncology Clinic, Ballard, Washington, USA

ARCHITECT/ENGINEER: Perkins+Will, Seattle, and RAD Technology Medical
CLIENT/SPONSOR: Swedish Hospital Network/Swedish Cancer Institute (SCI)
TYPE OF CARE: Oncology (PMI)
NUMBER OF BEDS: N/A (outpatient)
FEATURED MATERIALS: Steel
METHOD OF ASSEMBLY: Modular/onsite construction
SITE CONTEXT: Suburban
INSTALLATION: 3,900 square feet
COMPLETED: 2014

Context/site

Swedish Medical Center had reached maximum capacity on its campus in North Seattle, and its outpatient cancer treatment facility at that site was in immediate need of relocation in the shortest possible timeframe. The aim was to cause minimal disruption to services. In response, a patented, offsite-built prefab radiotherapy treatment vault and clinic unit, by *RAD Technology Medical Systems* (RAD) was erected in the parking lot of Swedish Medical's Ballard hospital campus. RAD is a design-build manufacturer of prefab modular clinics and componentry for interim or permanent installations, marketed as saving construction time, and thereby accelerating revenue streams. RAD makes extensive use of offsite manufacturing processes and assemblies.

The Swedish Ballard clinic was completed in four months from the date of groundbreaking, to the installation of its equipment. Final inspections and commissioning required an additional thirty days (Figures 6.13.1 and 6.13.2). It is estimated that offsite prefab resulted in a 50 percent reduction in the project's total construction time, while yielding a facility in compliance with U.S. Green Building Council LEED Silver certification. The Swedish-Ballard facility is home to the first radiation treatment unit of its kind in the Seattle metro area. The building envelope consists of prefab modules for the radiotherapy and chemotherapy vaults, and for exam rooms and administrative/support areas. Prefab components were constructed in a plant nearby and trucked to the installation site.

The clinic's scale, massing, and exterior material palette complement the existing medical center campus and its immediate site environs, including an adjacent residential neighborhood (Figures 6.13.3 and 6.13.4).

Building/unit

The client's goal and that of the design team was to create an inviting, residentially scaled clinic. In addition, the facility was to look 'permanent', not temporary. The 'parti' is one level, characterized by a low component (at the main entrance) and a taller component (in the diagnostic and treatment area). The radiotherapy vault is the larger element and it is sheathed in a copper-hued aluminum panel system. A steel and wood canopy, and sidewalk, lead to the main entrance, the sign-in counter and the main waiting area. In all, there are four modules; these consist of an inner vault, its sheathing/encasement, the examination rooms, and administration. A twelve foot by sixty foot module comprising the core of the parti' was of necessity conventionally (non-prefab) built. All major componentry and finish materials, however, on the main modular components were built off site, i.e. MEP and lighting systems, and then transited to the construction site for final assembly (Figure 6.13.5).

The footprint was kept below 4,000 square feet so as to not require lengthy review processes at the local or state levels. This facility was, by and large, portable, and hence, was legally considered an item of 'equipment.' Because of this there was no requirement to define it as a conventional building, i.e. as a traditional, capital investment line item. This designation provided for many degrees of freedom from the client's standpoint, in contrast to conventional construction, where otherwise, in stationary new construction or in renovations, this would have been a fixed capital asset. The site was changed midstream. Despite this, offsite prefab work continued uninterrupted. The exterior landscaping, and the interior spaces, are human-scaled. The exterior cladding attempts to break the scale down to relate to the neighborhood. The clinic's interior spaces have laminate hardwood flooring, contributing to a residentialist ambiance (Figures 6.13.6 and 6.13.7). Rapidly designed and built outpatient facilities such as this will be needed in greater numbers to meet the increasing healthcare demands of an aging U.S. population.

6.13.1 Swedish Medical Oncology Clinic, in Ballard, Washington is a mostly offsite-built outpatient clinic in the Seattle metro area

6.13.2 The building massing consists of two sections, one housing diagnostic imaging equipment, and a smaller element housing support

6.13.3 In plan and in section, the imaging vault dominates the composition

Key:

1-2 exam room	10 office
3 office	11 dosimetry
4 waiting	12 EVS/storage
5 reception	13 hallway
6 registration	14 control
7 nurse station	15 server
8 sub-waiting	16 electrical/mechanical
9 gowning	17 vault

6.13.4 An arrival canopy extends outward, establishing an inviting entry sequence

6.13.5 Landscaping and spatial transparency in the public areas create a human scale

6.13.6 Exterior cladding consists of interlocking panels affixed to a prefab mainframe

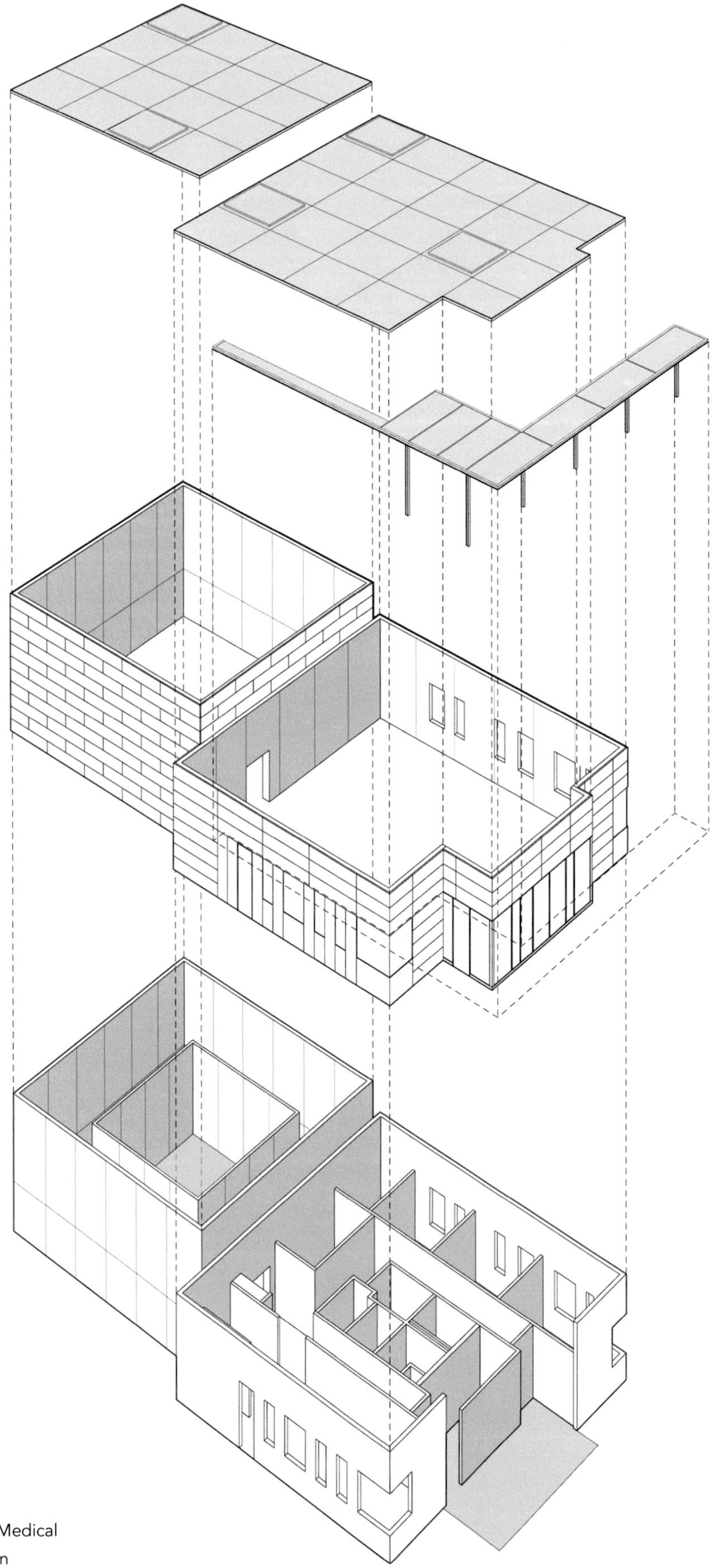

6.13.7 Axonometric view, Swedish Medical Oncology Clinic, Ballard, Washington

14 Miami Valley Heart and Orthopedic Center, Dayton, Ohio, USA

ARCHITECT/ENGINEER: NBBJ, Columbus, Ohio
CLIENT/SPONSOR: Miami Valley Heart and Orthopedic Center
TYPE OF CARE: Inpatient (PMI)
NUMBER OF BEDS: 178
FEATURED MATERIALS: Steel/polymers
METHOD OF ASSEMBLY: Modular
SITE CONTEXT: Urban
INSTALLATION: 500,000 square feet
COMPLETED: 2013

Context/site

The Miami Valley Heart and Orthopedic Center is a twelve-level facility, housing seven floors of acuity adaptable inpatient rooms. The facility master plan drew from best practices in offsite prefab manufacturing and the adoption of offsite construction methods shortened the construction schedule by two months. This resulted in a lower unit cost ($309 per square foot).The site strategy entailed hollowing out a parcel within the older existing campus, accomplished by removing two existing buildings, with the new building inserted into the combined footprint of the two demolished structures. It consists of a podium housing diagnostic and treatment functions, with an inpatient tower above. A courtyard at the center of the campus would need to continue to have a park-like ambiance, with its waterfall, trees, gardens and pedestrian paths. This landscaped space would function as a counterpoint to the height and straightforwardness of the patient tower. As for its design, floor-to-ceiling windows throughout the bed tower afford full views and all inpatient rooms, all overhead MEP racks, the inpatient toilet modules, and the headwall/footwall components were designed using Building Information Modeling (BIM). This componentry was manufactured off site, then transported to the construction site for installation in a conventionally built super-structural frame (Figure 6.14.1).

The use of BIM on this project contributed to fewer weather-related delays and contingencies, and made possible tighter componentry tolerances, less site-generated material waste, resulted in no worker injuries and lower labor costs, and yielded a faster total project turnaround time.[27] Each inpatient room is acuity adaptable, able to support low-acuity cases up to cardiac ICU patients, and as medical care services evolve over time, the patient floor templates can be modified (Figure 6.14.2). This was the first hospital designed by NBBJ with this amount of prefab, and it was done in partnership with Skanska Corporation, who provided construction management services. The use of offsite prefab reduced local landfill debris by nearly 80 percent. This resulted in a more energy-efficient building envelope than mandated by current local building codes, and a 60 percent reduction in the building's energy operational costs was attained versus a comparable, conventionally-built facility. The completed building received LEED Silver certification, the largest hospital in Ohio to do so, to date (Figure 6.14.3).

Building/unit

Miami Valley is the first mainstream hospital project in the U.S. to make such extensive use of offsite prefab. By contrast, numerous mainstream healthcare facilities have been constructed in Europe in the past decade in this way. Offsite prefab techniques developed in Europe were borrowed for incorporation at Miami Valley. The fabrication warehouse was off site, yet located just a few miles from the job site in Dayton, Ohio. In the typical prefab healthcare facility project, a manufacturer usually specializes in only one type of component, i.e. the toilet modules, or the prefab wall system, such as what the firm DIRTT often does. The NBBJ approach in the case of Miami Valley differed in that the temporary rented warehouse space housed all of the construction MEP trades together and these subcontractors worked side by side on numerous modular components and assemblies. This warehouse was not meant to become a permanent factory, only to serve as temporary shell space for the duration of the project.

The floor plan in the bed tower is replicated from floor to floor, and subdivided into three wings, with each wing housing twelve bedrooms (Figure 6.14.4a–b). To Skanska, the challenge was that the patient room itself was about 280 square feet and the toilet compartment added another eighty square feet. This would have resulted in too large an object to transit, lift, and slide into place. A

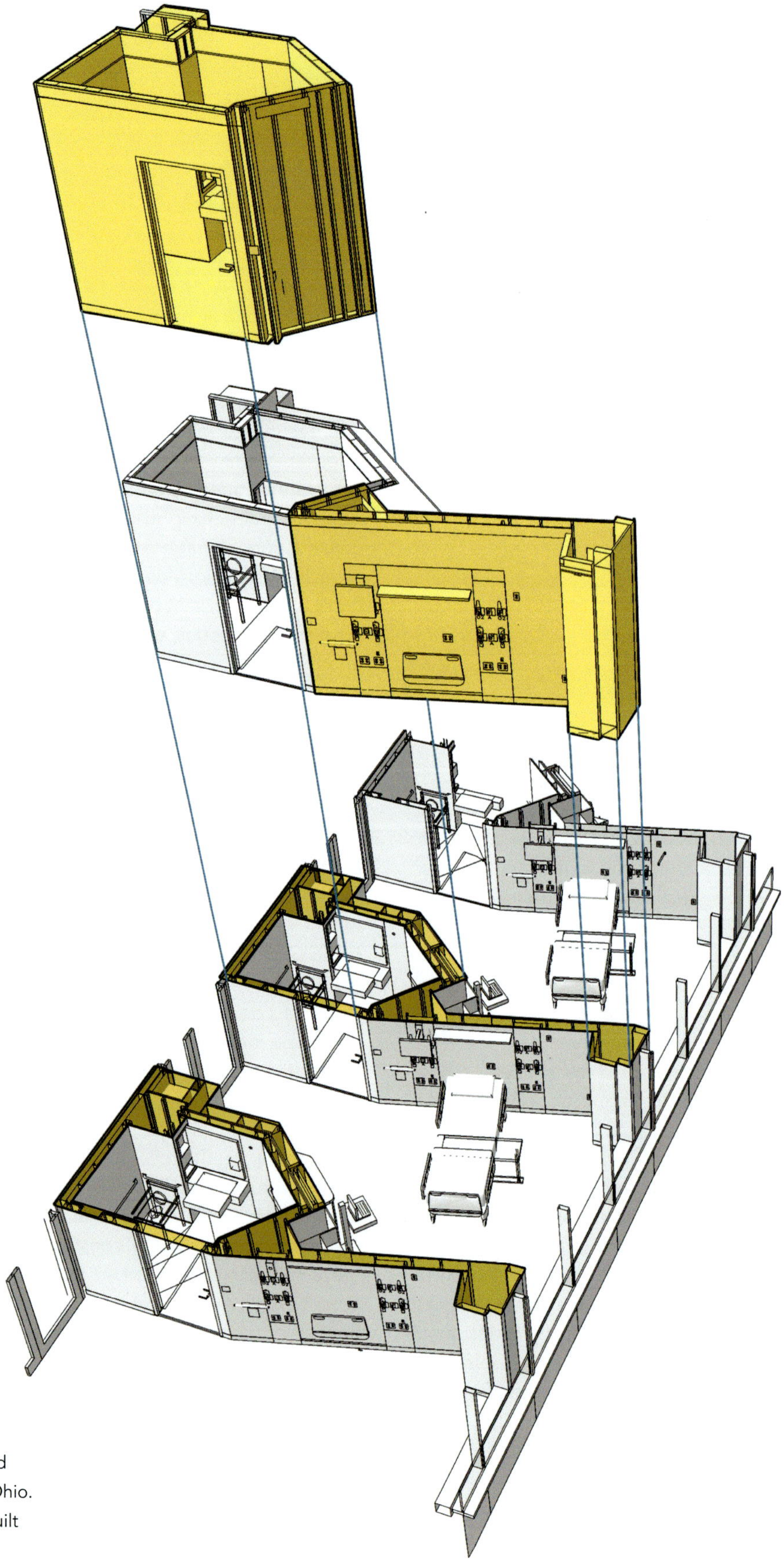

6.14.1 Miami Valley Heart and Orthopedic Center, Dayton, Ohio. Axonometric view of offsite-built modular componentry

6.14.2 Exterior view of main arrival zone and canopy at Miami Valley with the bed tower rising above a platform support base

6.14.3 View at night looking into public areas in the patient bed tower at Miami Valley Heart and Orthopedic Center

6.14.4a–b Typical patient floor indicating (in yellow) inpatient room prefab elements (top) and the prefab building system MEP modular 'raceway' (bottom)

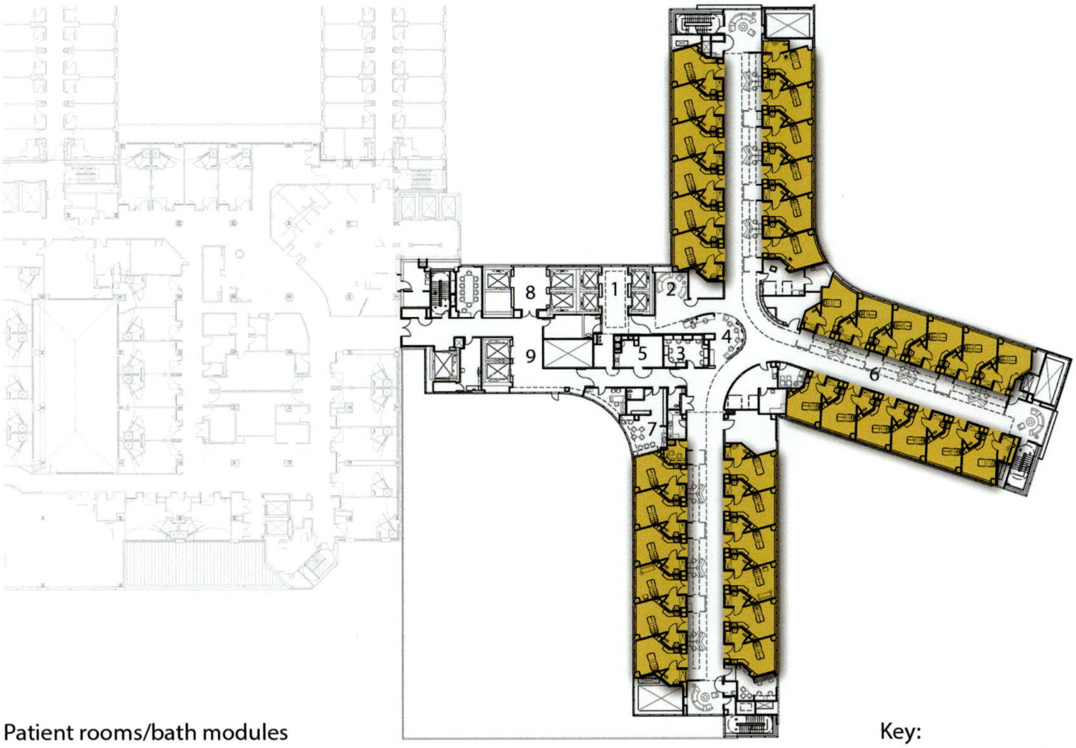

Patient rooms/bath modules

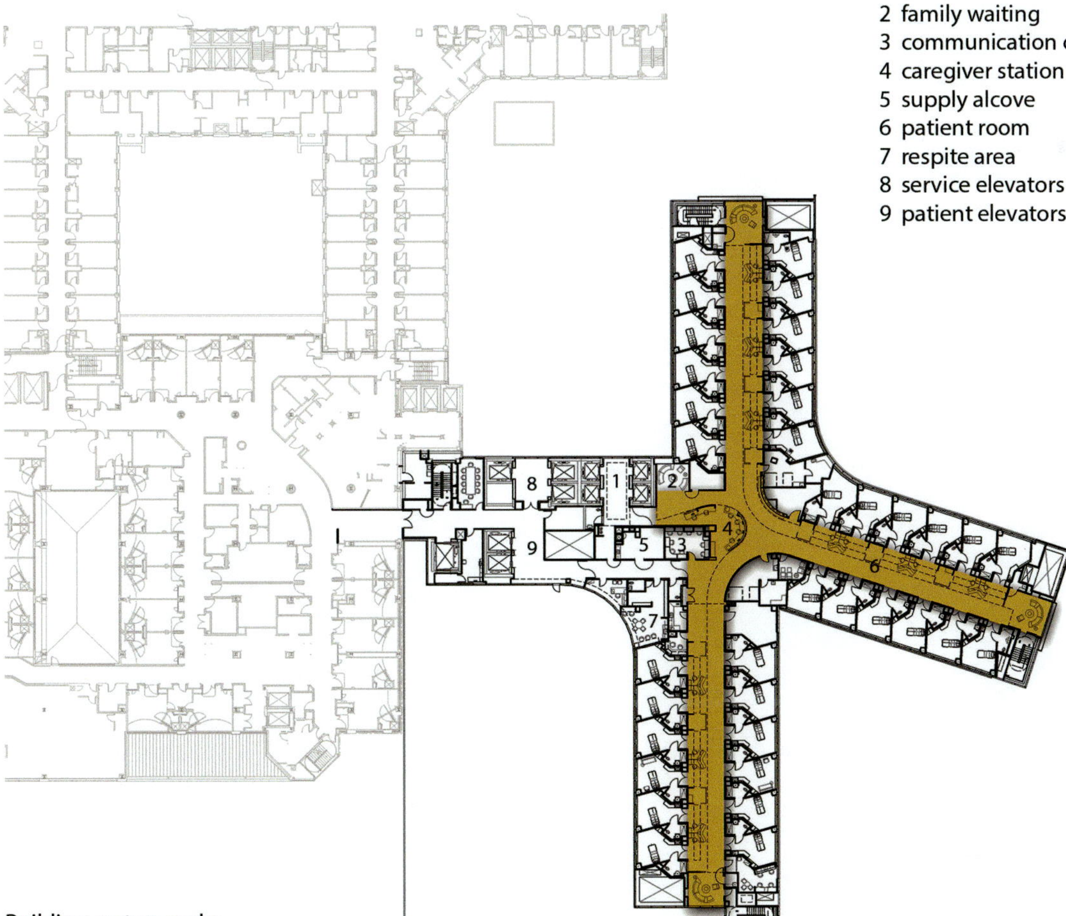

Building system racks

Key:
1 visitor elevators
2 family waiting
3 communication center
4 caregiver station
5 supply alcove
6 patient room
7 respite area
8 service elevators
9 patient elevators and transport

6.14.5a–b
BIM-generated perspective views of prefab components installed on inpatient floors at Miami Valley

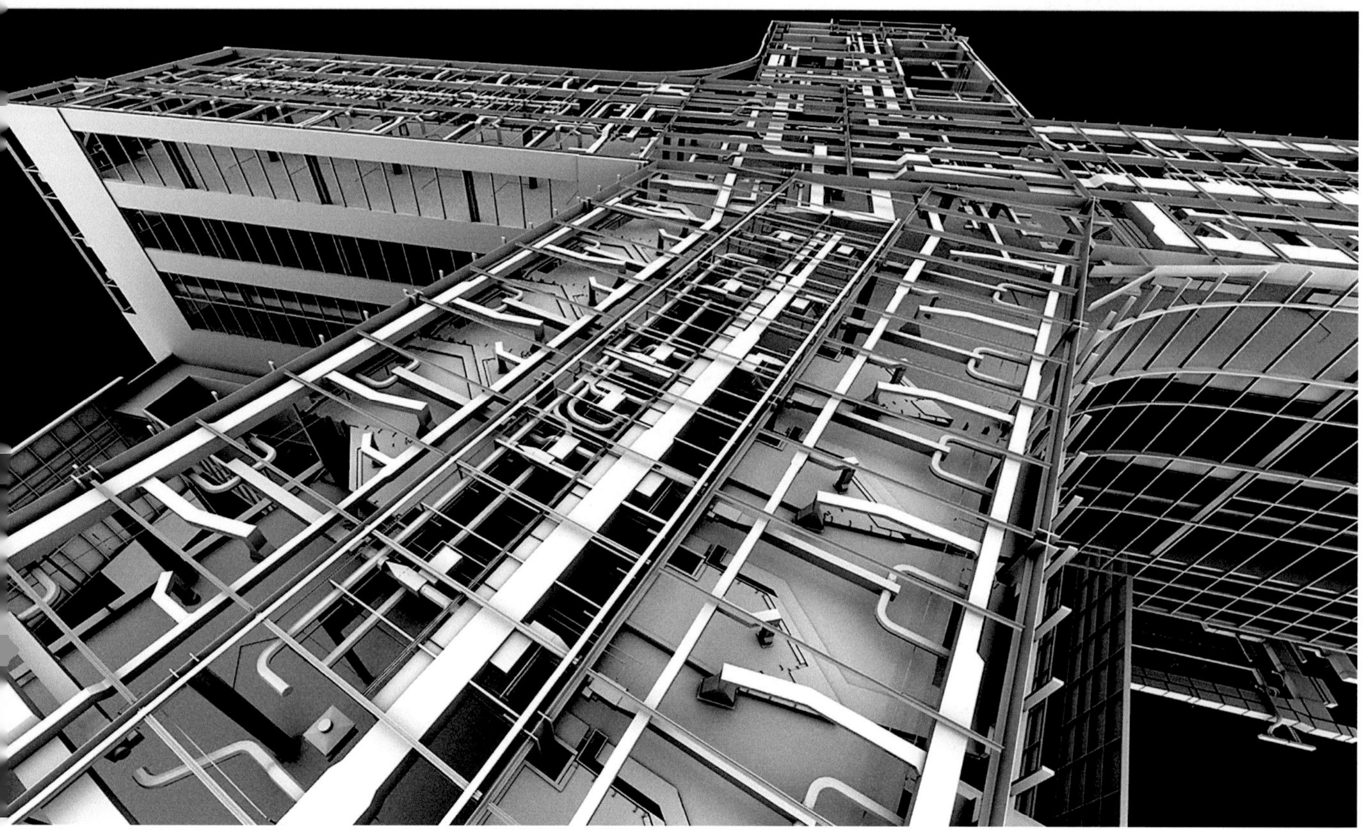

6.14.6a–h
Components were built in a rented manufacturing plant a few miles from the construction site, then installed in sequence inside the superstructure

6.14.7 View of a nurses' workstation, adjacent to an inpatient room

breakthrough occurred when it was realized there was no need to prefab the entire module in one fell swoop, but instead as a kit of interlocking components. The result was what NBBJ refers to as the *blade*—178 modules each housing the headwall and all medical gases, IT data ports, toilet compartment, and vestibule entry as a single unit, including plumbing, a caregiver workstation and an audio-visual data port (Figure 6.14.5a–b).

This component-based approach broke from conventional prefab methods, where, in the hotel industry, or in the building of college dormitories, or the case of the voluminous levels of construction occurring in China, the most common prefab strategy is volume-based. That is, a single monolithic element—such as a hotel room— is crafted then repeated *ad infinitum*. By contrast, the offsite prefab strategy at Miami Valley was component-based. Skanska and its subcontractors soon realized that a component's specific shape, size, and weight distribution factors would be critical. In lifting a blade up off a flatbed, for instance, its center of gravity had to be precisely ascertained beforehand.

Normally, there would not have been any interior construction onsite until after the ironworkers finished. But ironworkers were able to erect the hospital tower's steel framework in tandem with the prefab work happening at the warehouse. Each toilet module was delivered onto its pre-specified floor, and with a three-quarter inch depression cast into every slab, it was then placed (slid) into its precast footprint. Similarly, each headwall module was dropped into its own pre-scored floor footprint (Figure 6.14.6a–h). Skanska's rented warehouse was, in time, jammed with offsite-built components before the onsite team was able to receive them. This created an inventory challenge, with the contractor ending up renting a second warehouse nearby to keep the manufacturing process moving forward on schedule. Skanska did not possess precise metrics, prior, on how long the various offsite-built parts would take to fabricate, as this was their largest U.S. project of this type to date. The corridor ceiling MEP/HVAC modules and the compartments to receive the racks were subdivided into segments (highlighted in yellow), each eight feet by twenty feet long, and built at the warehouse with all systems onboard including the medical gas distribution system. Sidewalls of the compartments that received the prefab MEP/HVAC modules were then sheathed in smoke-tight sheetrock. When installed, the assembled bulkheads ran continuously in the ceiling plenum. A high degree of spatial dexterity, curvilinearity, in plan, was attainable (Figure 6.14.7). As for the outboard edge of the building envelope, every inpatient room features the aforementioned full-height windows, and the expansive views they provide to occupants (Figures 6.14.8 and 6.14.9).

6.14.8 Offsite-built componentry blends seamlessly at Miami Valley Heart and Orthopedic Center

6.14.9 Inpatient rooms feature full height windows, expansive views, and overnight amenities for families

15 Raptor Prototype, USA

ARCHITECT/ENGINEER: Gregory Swindon, CU/A+H
CLIENT/SPONSOR: American Red Cross
TYPE OF CARE: Emergency/trauma care (RHC/RTC)
NUMBER OF BEDS: 60–120
FEATURED MATERIALS: Steel/fabric panels
METHOD OF ASSEMBLY: Modular/plug-in
SITE CONTEXT: Variable
DEPLOYMENT (MIN/MAX): 1,100–50,000+ square feet
PROPOSAL: 2012

Context/site

Raptor is a self-contained RHC/RTC designed to be functionally autonomous in a multiplicity of site contexts ranging from everyday circumstances for the provision of primary and sickness prevention medical care, to specialty services such as kidney dialysis, to emergency medical care. It can be deployed in a football stadium, a paved parking lot, an unobstructed field, and in irregular natural terrain within a disaster strike zone (Figure 6.15.1). The system is deployable in either its entirety, as illustrated, or as a partial deployment (minimized) mode, with a patient bed capacity ranging from 16 beds up to 120 beds on a single site. A fully deployed installation is a full-service micro-hospital, featuring emergency/triage, intake/admit services, an adjacent tented (outdoor) decontamination unit (not depicted), and exam/procedure rooms, laboratory, clean and soiled utility components, a central supply unit, pharmacy, pre-operative, surgical, and post-surgical units, materials management, administration, and waiting and family support areas. Additional functions include staff dormitory accommodations, full HVAC/MEP support, and power generators. Access to the facility is through a main arrival module, where the emergency/triage unit, decontamination unit, public restrooms, and patient intake services are housed (Figure 6.15.2). When fully deployed, this system requires a relatively flat, rectangular site and effective natural drainage, unobstructed by overhead utility wires, poles, or natural rock outcroppings. The system facilitates the provision of courtyards, natural daylight and ventilation to be transmitted into interior spaces as a function of how various modules of differing shapes, in section, are plugged into one another.

Building/unit

Interlocking/plug-in modules are fabricated of lightweight steel sheathed in a tightly pulled, durable fabric membrane 'cover'. The fabric is stretched rigidly over the frame of each module. Modules are arranged in a linear pattern and an A/B A/B rhythm is attainable, with various modules differing in sectional profile, or multiple modules identical in their sectional profile can be assembled, becoming in effect one far larger space with a monolithic, continuous ceiling, and with continuous lighting fixtures horizontally affixed, spanning the top edge the full length of the room's outer walls (Figures 6.15.3 and 6.15.4). This option allows for the creation of large inpatient wards of up to twelve beds each, a main waiting area, pre-operative bays, surgical suites, post-operative bays, and other functions requiring larger, clearspan space. This feature of the system therefore yields multiple footprint options, especially in large installations.

Natural ventilation and daylight bathe interior spaces to an extent not often possible with a containerized portable facility. In full deployment, this system consists of up to eighty modules, each approximately twenty-four feet wide by twelve feet high by six feet in width. The flexibility of its kit-of-parts, in section, allows for compositional variability, where various internal zones can be assembled to differ spatially and in their exterior appearance. This allows for multiple units identical in shape to be assembled together for use, for instance, as a patient ward is a feature that allows an installation to be more customized to local needs, as mentioned. If so desired, a waiting room, laboratory, or inpatient ward can be individually sized, i.e. customized, in the same way as if planning this same type of space in a stationary brick and mortar facility (Figure 6.15.5a–b). Similarly, functions that require less space, such as a clean/soiled utility room, can be housed in one or two modules of the same size/shape, just as in a stationary facility.

In section, a hexagonal, panelized wall system is illustrated, showing how combinations of modules can be assembled in rows, resulting in variable roof pitches, and how clerestories can be

6.15.1 Raptor RTC's flexibility mitigates the deleterious impact of land- or sea-based disasters

modulated to transmit varying degrees of natural daylight. Stabilizer (structural) tubes are located at oblique angles, double functioning to demarcate interior circulation (Figure 6.15.6a–c). The interstitial plenum inside each fabric-sheathed structural frame is injected with polyurethane foam to provide additional rigidity while maintaining the unit's maximum *lightness*. Customization options carry into the fenestration system, a zipper-activated flexible translucent plastic for use as doors and windows. Modules sit on telescopic tube-legs that are pneumatically activated, or activated manually by means of a conventional lift-jack. Structural reinforcement is achieved by means of tension cables that lock rows of modules together, and also anchor the rows to the ground. The system allows for modules to be added or subtracted without disturbing the installation's overall footprint, in the same way that the U.S. Army CSH units are set up and can be modified later, next door to a stationary hospital in Iraq. Modules are stackable, if pre-built (as illustrated) with stabilization, in-transit, provided via tension cables anchored to the upper deck of the transport ship. The system can also be shipped in flat-pack mode then assembled on site, including the injection of the 'structural' foam, or it can deploy in either pre-built modular or flat-pack mode via large air cargo transporters.

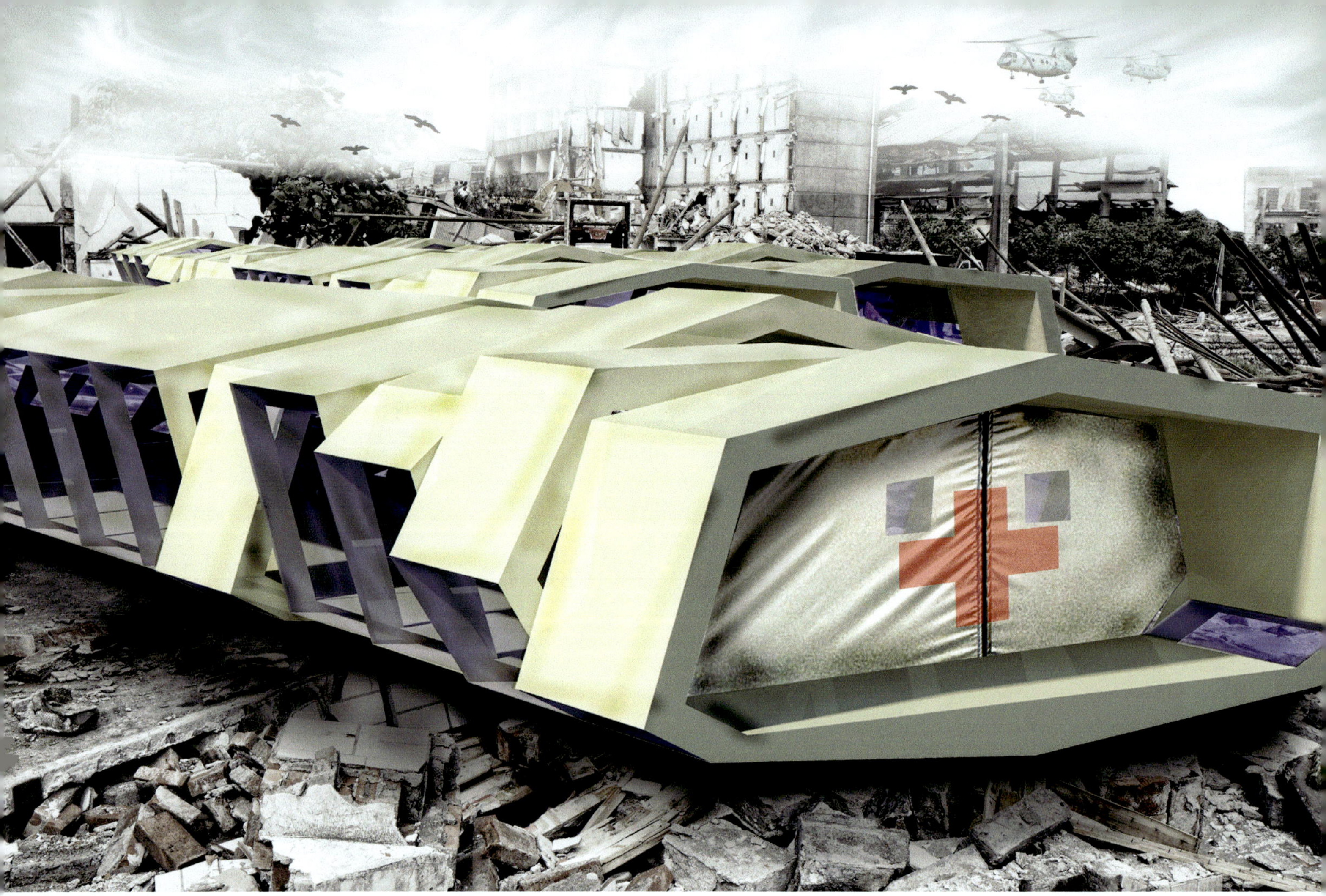

6.15.2 Raptor's kit-of parts allows for modules in a variety of sizes and shapes within a contiguous installation

6.15.3 Modules allow for varied spatial sequencing compared to most conventional containerized portable hospitals

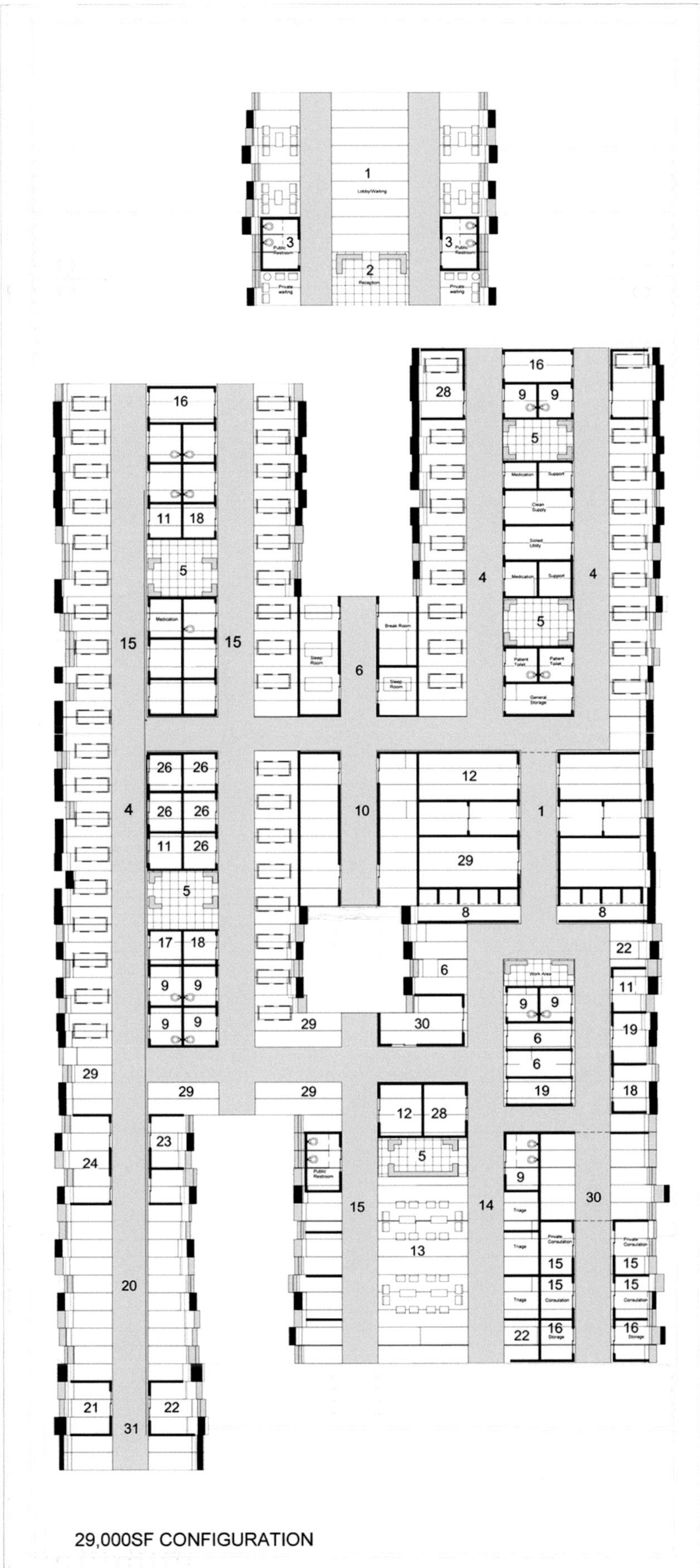

6.15.4 The footprint of this civilian RTC is relatively conventional, in plan, however inspired by the functional amenity of the military-sector CSH

Key:
1 lobby/waiting
2 sign in/intake
3 public restrooms
4 med-surgical unit
5 nurses station
6 staff support
7 radiology
8 changing room
9 patient restrooms
10 staff shower/locker
11 medication
12 laboratory
13 family support
14 triage
15 consultation
16 storeroom
17 clean utilities
18 solid utilities
19 nursing administration
20 medication management
21 telecommunication
22 electrical mechanical
23 housekeeping
24 biohazardous waste hold
25 bulk storeroom
26 examination/procedure
27 administration
28 physicians
29 waiting
30 conference
31 service/supplies

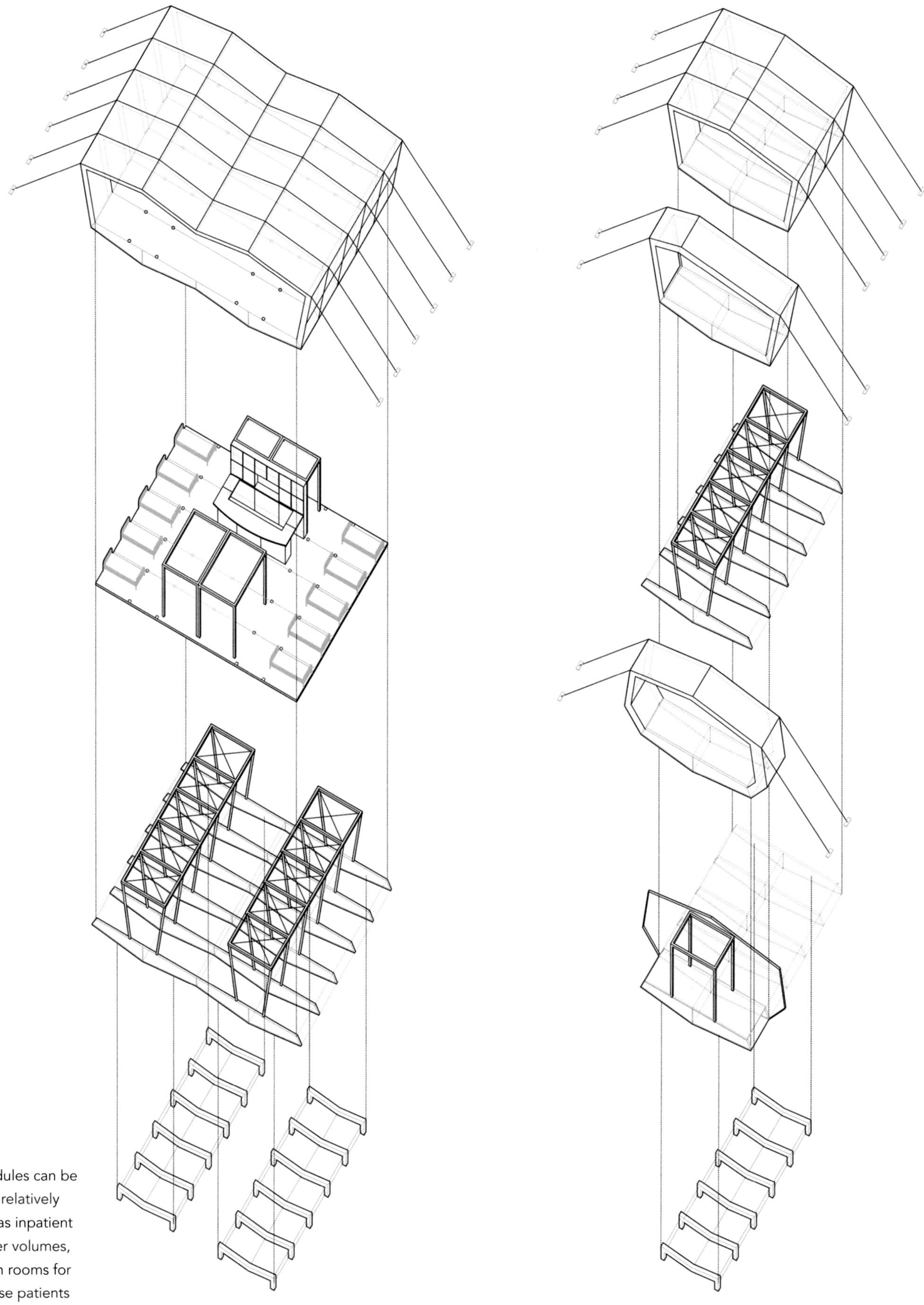

6.15.5a–b Modules can be assembled into relatively large volumes, as inpatient wards, or smaller volumes, such as isolation rooms for infectious disease patients

Cross section

Longitudinal section

6.15.6a–c The telescopic feet beneath modules are visible in these sectional views, as are their HVAC/MEP plenums. The system can be shipped pre-assembled (as shown here) or in flat-pack mode

16 SmartPOD Prototype, USA

ARCHITECT/ENGINEER: George Hughes, CU/A+H
CLIENT/SPONSOR: American Red Cross
TYPE OF CARE: Emergency/trauma care (RTC)
NUMBER OF BEDS: 48 (base configuration)
FEATURED MATERIALS: Stainless steel/tensile-fabric
METHOD OF ASSEMBLY: Modular/plug-in
SITE CONTEXT: Urban (variable)
DEPLOYMENT (MIN/MAX): 1,500/55,000 square feet
PROPOSAL: 2013

Context/site

SmartPOD is a hybrid RTC capable of operating remotely, or tethered to a stationary medical center. It is inspired by the affordances of the generic ISO intermodal container as much as by the classic tent systems of the past century. Its hybridity aspires to synthesize the best qualities of both types of offsite prefab precursors. Its custom-built containers meet international ISO design standards—each container is forty feet in length and conforms to the standard width and height of ISOs. The containers are stackable while in transit, and can be stacked right alongside generic ISOs. This system requires forty-five units for a full base deployment of forty-eight inpatient beds. The exterior of each container is adorned with the logo of their organizational sponsor, i.e. the *International Red Cross*, so as to avoid confusion and the possibility of routing snafus while in transit. Each container is loaded and unloaded by means of highboy lift equipment and is built to be somewhat lighter than a conventional ISO container of comparable size. Units can be airlifted by helicopter into a dense forest or a dense urban neighborhood. The system is designed for deployment in four baseline conditions: urban streetscape, an urban or suburban parking lot, i.e. a shopping mall or hospital parking lot, a football pitch or similar open, flat sports playing field, or an airport tarmac.

This system is designed, manufactured, and outfitted for deployment in cold weather climates for an extended period of time if necessary (Figures 6.16.1 and 6.16.2). As depicted here, it is owned and operated by the U.S. Army, and would be transported from a military base to its deployment site (Figure 6.16.3a–l). The site depicted here is a dense urban neighborhood with a triangular-shaped pocket park, with the modules set up along two of the streets and a third street remaining open to emergency/EMS vehicles only. The park's open green space would function as a triage and decontamination staging area. The system is depicted here as it might be fully deployed, for example, along Pennsylvania Avenue, four blocks from the White House, in Washington D.C. and in close proximity to George Washington University, in the aftermath of a bioterrorist attack on the United States capital. In this scenario, the area's conventional hospitals hit by the biological chemical attack remain decommissioned (Figure 6.16.4).

Building/unit

The system is a hybrid in terms of its construction technology and methods of assembly. Fifty percent of the shipping containers are reused on site as occupied space in the fully commissioned facility, with the remaining 50 percent of the facility comprised of assembled flat-pack panels, assorted modularized clip-on/plug-in flooring, wall panels, and ceiling grid componentry. The roof is comprised of a tensile structure tent membrane that double functions as roof and sunscreen device, with the tension cables and structural masts rising above the flat roofs of the container modules (Figures 6.16.5a–b to 6.16.7a–b). The intent of this hybridity is to imbue the SmartPOD with 'best of both worlds' versatility. In other words, the aim is to make the best use of a custom-designed ISO strategy by repurposing it as inhabitable space and in the process furthering its amenity. This aspect of the system draws its inspiration from aforementioned military field hospital precursors including the MASH units of the Korean conflict and, more recently, the technological advances expressed in the CSH's structural rigidity and its mixture of soft walled modular tents with hard walled containerized modules.

Assembly commences with staking out a site, ensuring it is properly leveled and prepped, then positioning the inhabitable/pull-out ISO units, functioning as 'anchors' at various endpoints of the facility's eventual built-out footprint. Each ISO has a pop-out bay, effectively doubling its size. These form the perimeter of the

6.16.1 SmartPOD was developed in response to the growing threat of bioterrorist attacks globally since 9/11

installation. The tensile tent masts are erected in a grid, situated between assembled flat-pack componentry. These elements house all internal circulation, public areas, transition zones, and support spaces that can benefit from natural ventilation and daylight. The option exists on larger sites to configure the footprint so as to create one or more open courtyards at the center. The internal circulation is a racetrack (continuous loop) and is completely internalized. It can be fully weatherproofed. Environmental control systems are powered by state-of-the-art diesel generators to ensure uninterrupted 24/7 operations of all critical functions. The containers' ship-like, operable portal windows allow natural light and the transmission of fresh air.

Interiors feature an array of ceiling types and heights—a direct reaction to the often oppressively low ceiling heights of most conventional ISO-based portable field hospitals currently in use. This variability in ceiling height allows for numerous clerestories, with potentially therapeutic benefits for patients and staff alike, particularly in post-operative inpatient wards (Figure 6.16.8a–c). In addition, the pop-out inpatient care bays allow for multiple bed placement options, providing options to situate patient beds along the outer perimeter wall or, if more direct nursing observation is called for, closer to the central nurse's workstation. Most medical equipment is specifically designed, or adapted for, the SmartPOD and these devices plug directly into adjacent floor and wall panel grids. MEP/HVAC systems run throughout the installation's undercarriage.

6.16.2 SmartPOD is a hybrid tent-containerized system

6.16.3a–l Structural components, non-fixed equipments and furnishings, and supplies are shipped in custom-fabricated intermodal containers

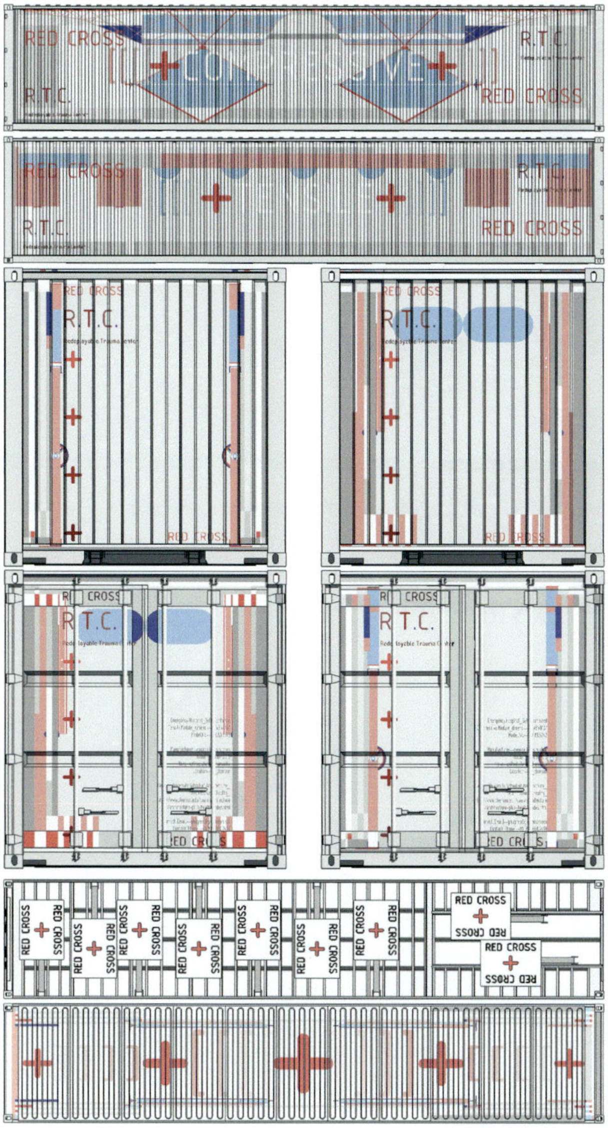
RED CROSS
R.T.C.

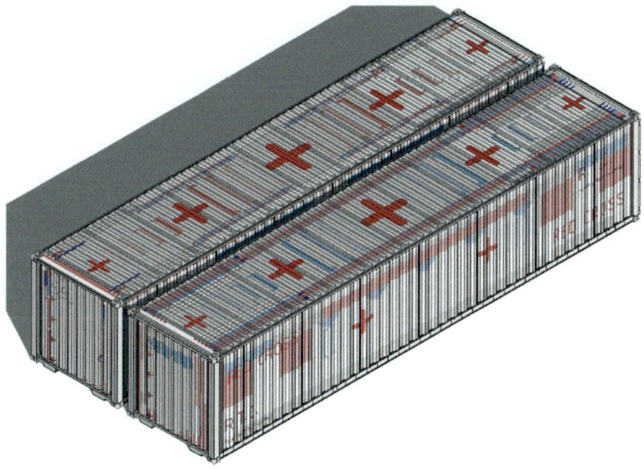

R.T.C.
RED CROSS

MAERSK LINE

RED CROSS
COSCO

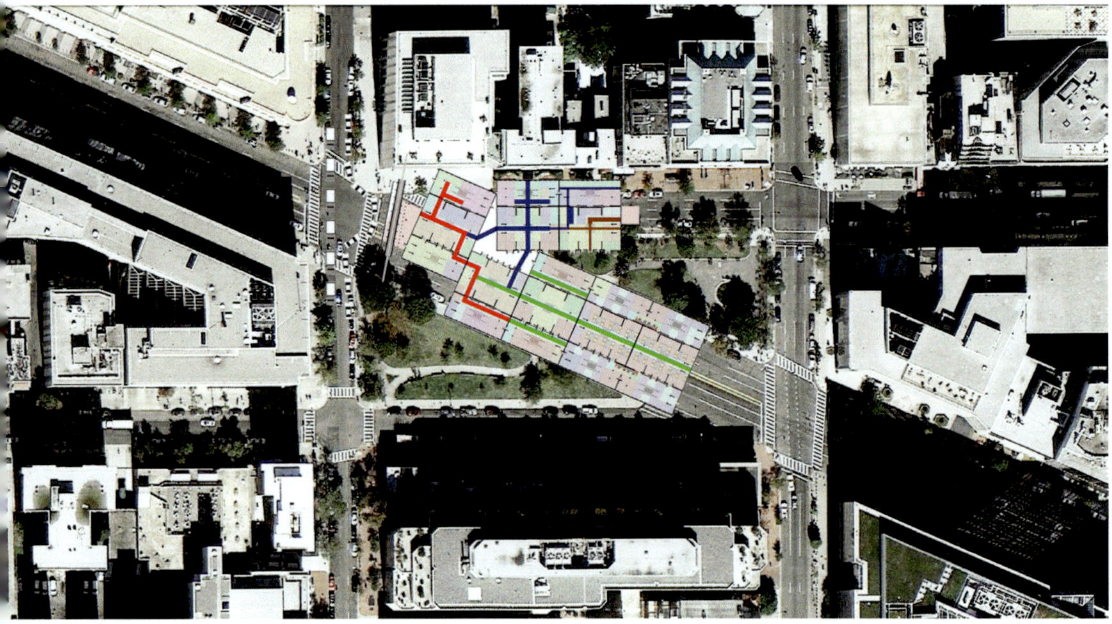

6.16.4 Site plan of installation in Washington D.C. across the street from George Washington University Medical Center

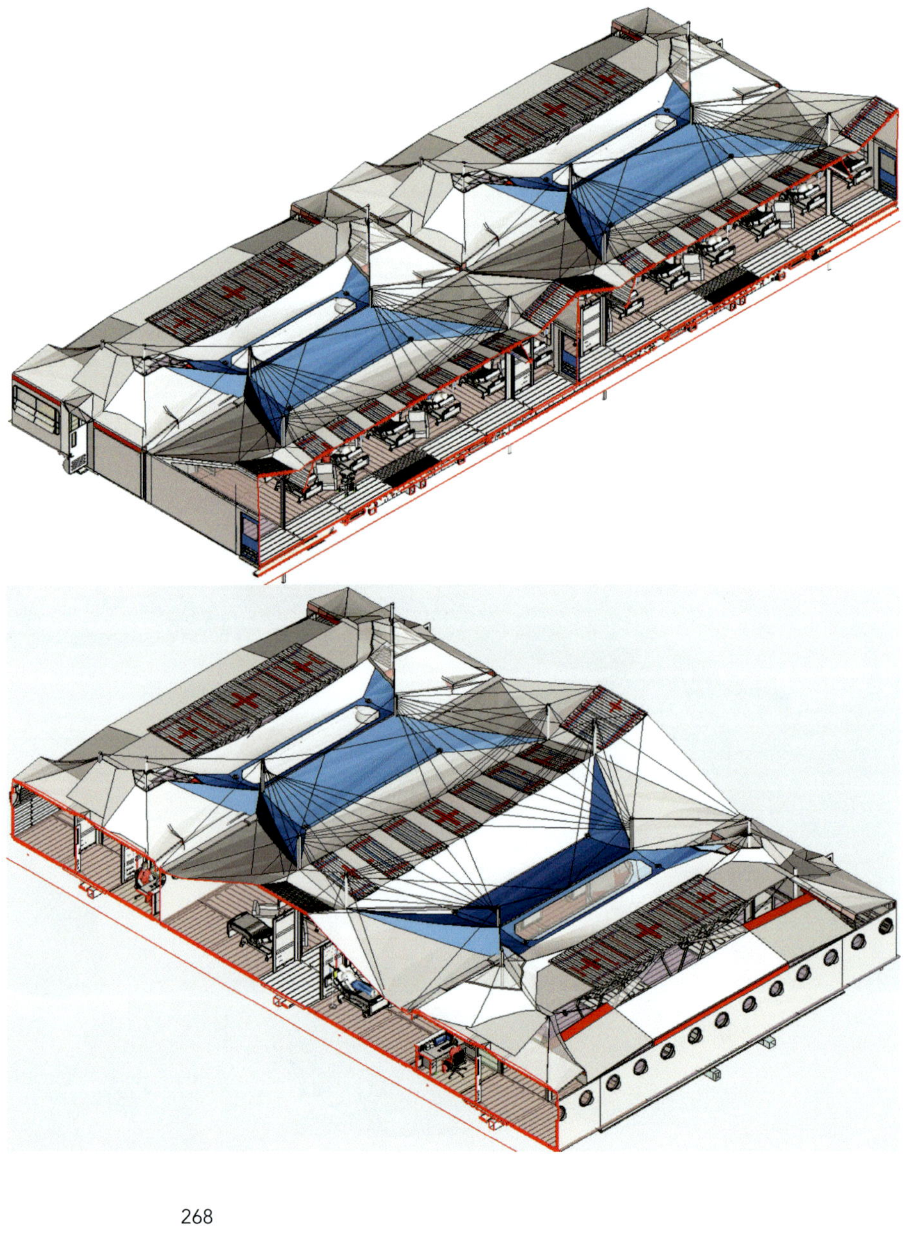

6.16.5a–b Cutaway views into a patient housing wing. This installation is a mixture of containers, rigid panels affixed to a platform, and tentage

6.16.6a–e The combination of containers, panels, and tents allows for varied ceiling heights and interior spaces, and provides options for natural ventilation and daylight

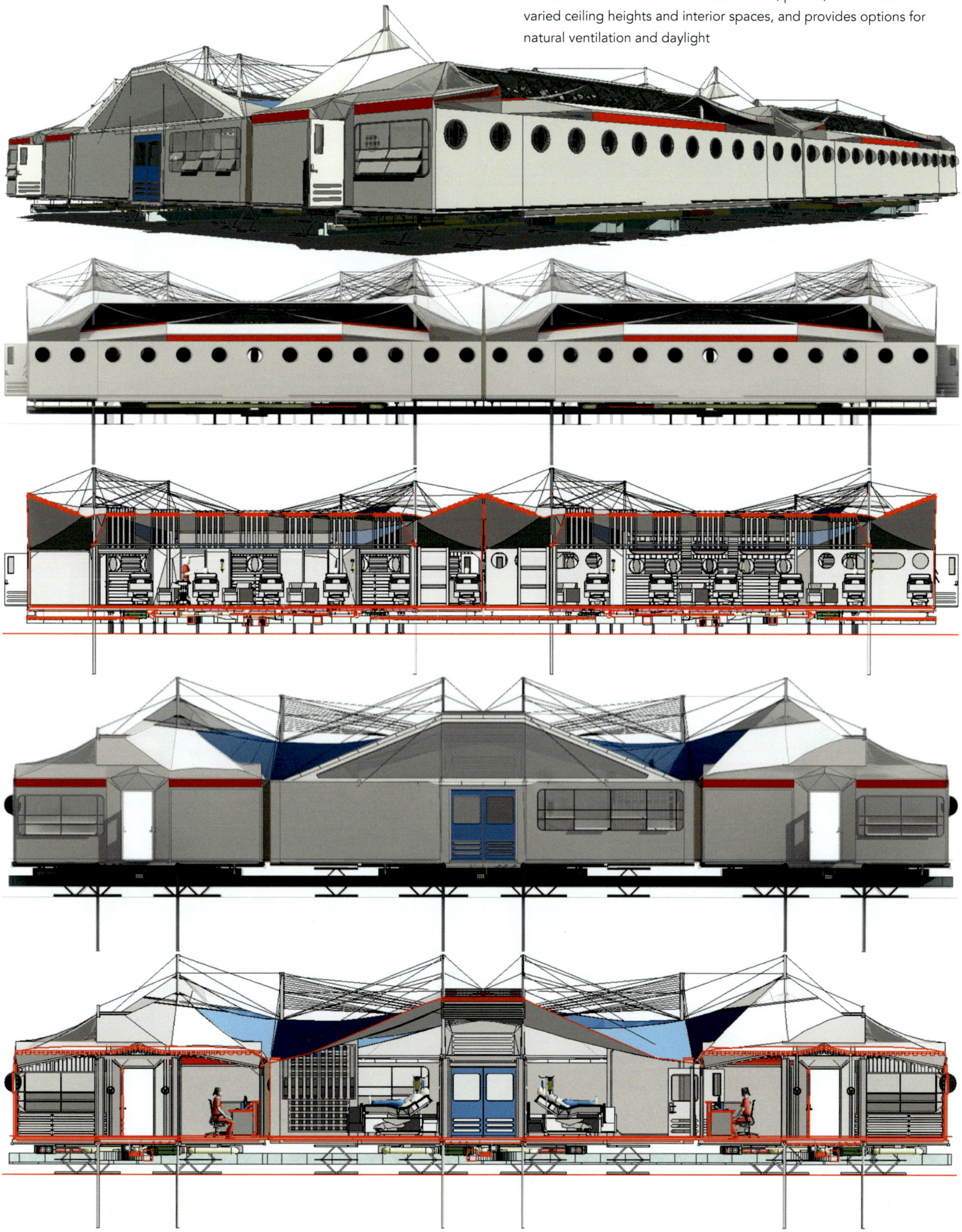

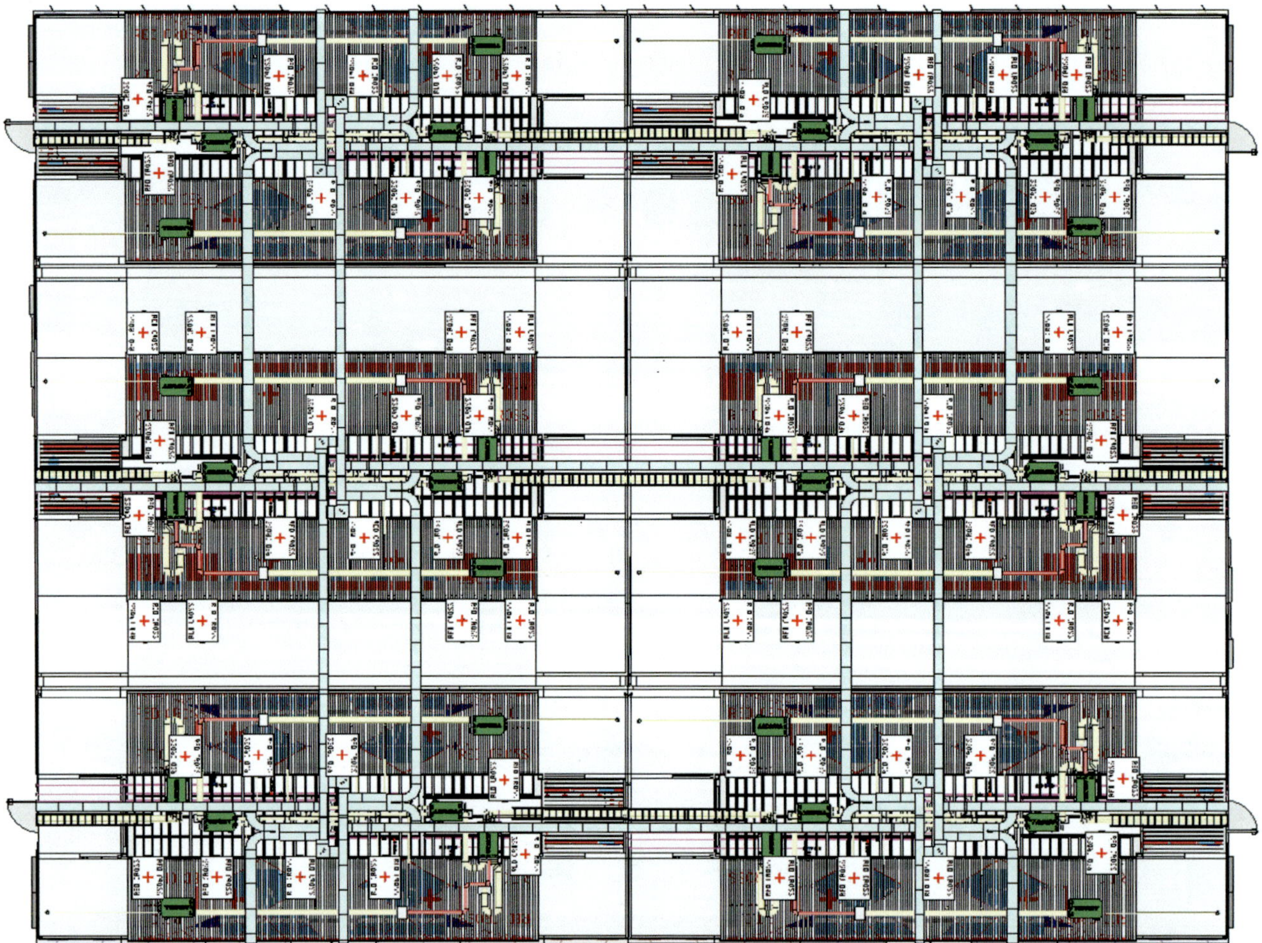

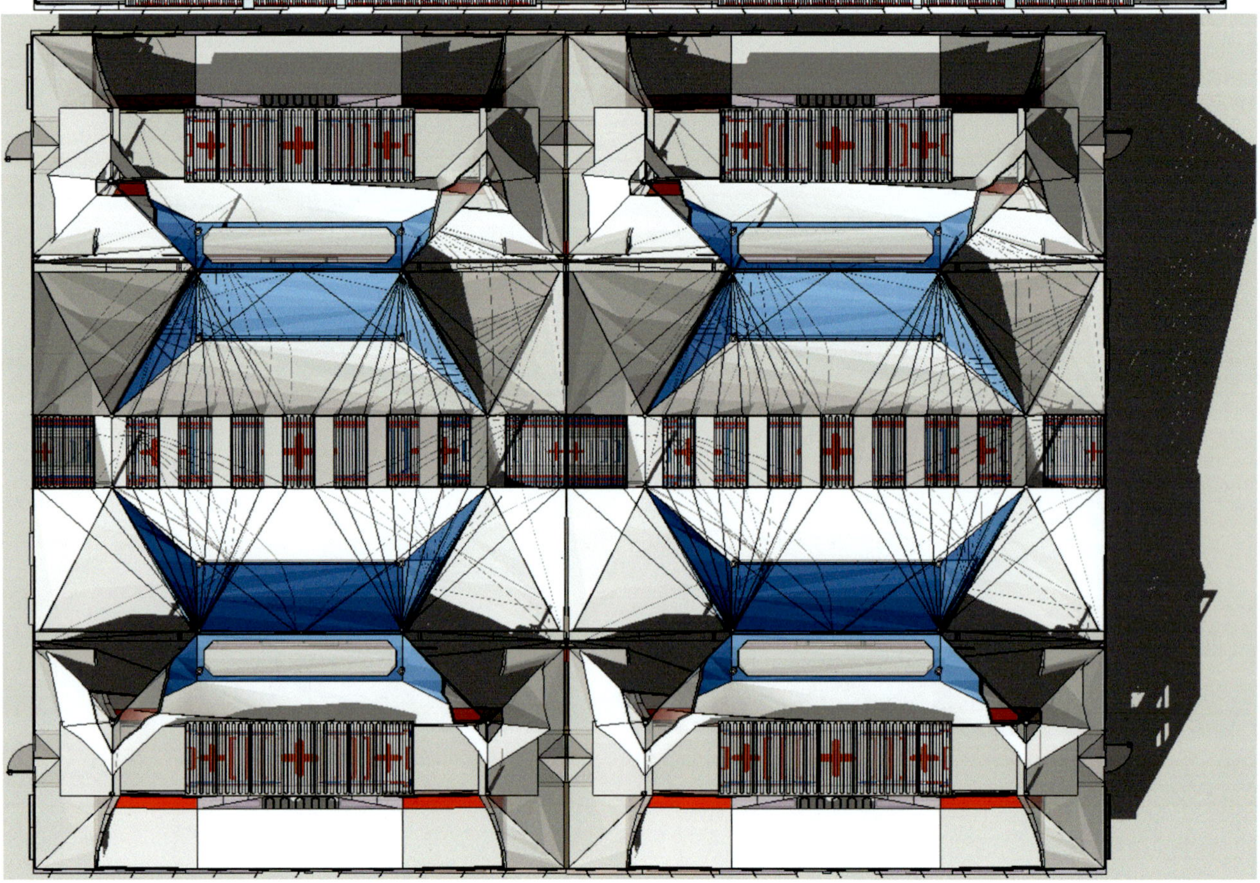

6.16.7a–b View of the HVAC/MEP system racks (top) and the roof plan indicating the tents and cable-mast structural system (bottom)

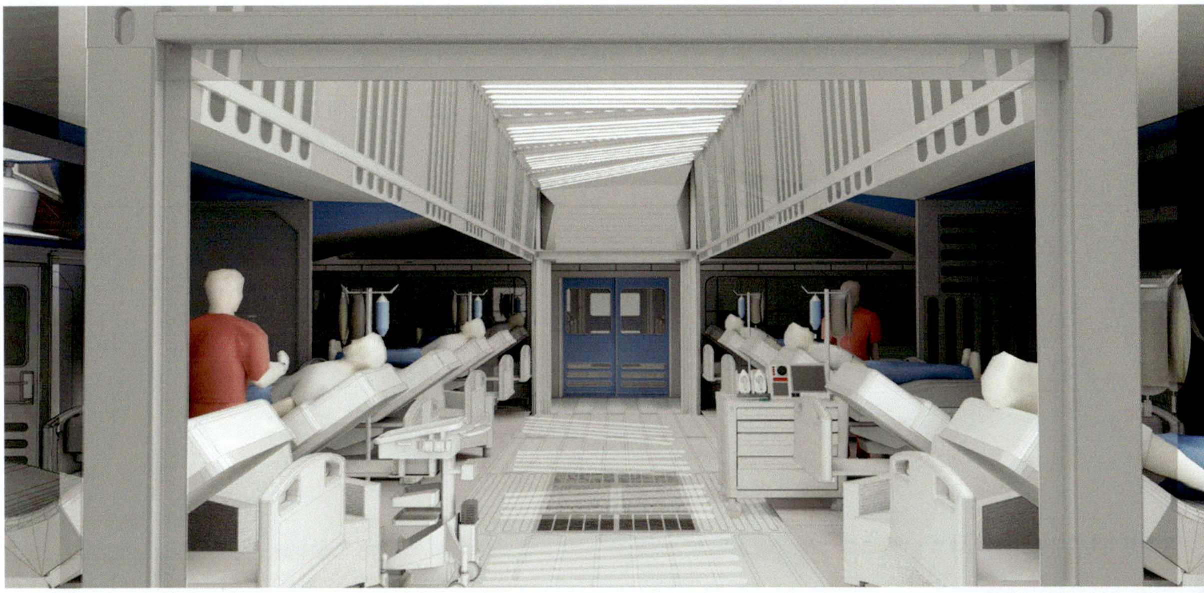

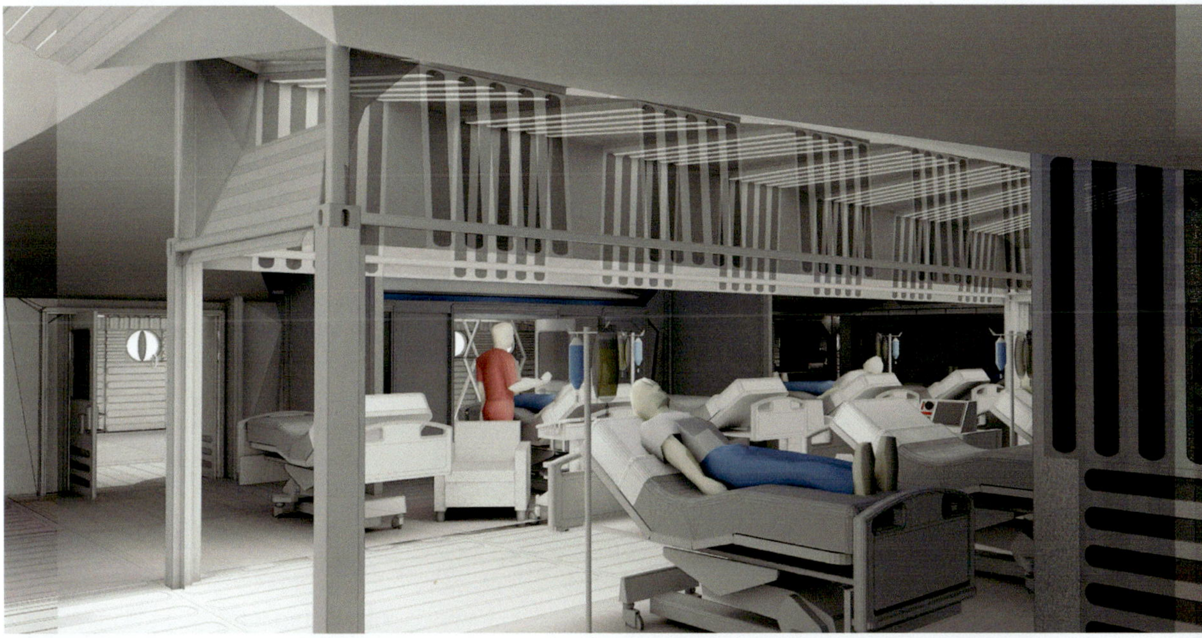

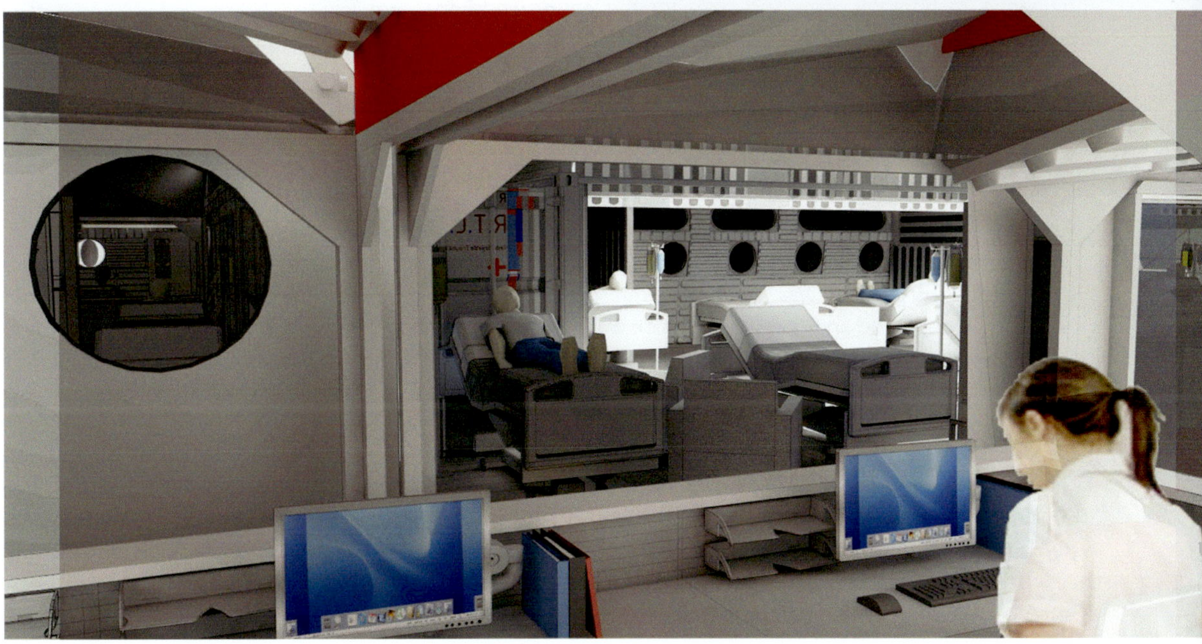

6.16.8a–c Variable ceiling heights establish spatial hierarchy throughout the interior zones of SmartPOD

17 Seagull Prototype, USA

ARCHITECT/ENGINEER: Ryan Ramsey, CU/A+H
CLIENT/SPONSOR: Doctors Without Borders
TYPE OF CARE: Emergency/trauma care (RTC)
NUMBER OF BEDS: 10 (min.)/unit
FEATURED MATERIALS: Polymers/stainless steel
METHOD OF ASSEMBLY: Modular/plug-in
SITE CONTEXT: Sea/land
DEPLOYMENT (MIN/MAX): 1,200/65,000 square feet
PROPOSAL: 2012

Context/site

On the evening of 20 April 2010, a massive explosion occurred in the Gulf of Mexico sixty miles off the coast of Louisiana. An immense ball of fire erupted high into the clear night sky as eleven men lost their lives. An over-budget, problem-plagued deepwater oil exploration platform had exploded—a platform now known globally as the *BP Deepwater Horizon*. The limitations of extreme engineering technology were laid bare for the entire world to witness as this rig fell 150 meters to the ocean floor, collapsing in ruins. For three months thereafter, its ruptured wellbore spewed more than 200 million barrels of crude oil directly into the ocean. The unprecedented damage inflicted upon the region's delicate aquatic ecosystems garnered extensive media scrutiny and the attention of environmental advocacy organizations worldwide, including *Greenpeace* and the *Ocean Conservancy*.

In response to this and other water-borne and shoreline disaster events, *Seagull* prototype was designed. This prefab modular system can be deployed and commissioned on water (or land) as a rapid response facility, with its buoyant ship-like framework. It is an additive system, expandable to up to seventy-five modules, in deep or shallow water, and in shoreline site conditions on dry land. It was developed as a specific response to the aforementioned BP disaster, the Tohoku earthquake and tsunami, and the strife in 2012 along the coast of Libya in the Mediterranean. This prefab system features photovoltaic panels and lightweight rigid structural shells that interlock. Its thermoplastic exterior shell was developed in accord with prefab manufacturing methods perfected in the automotive industry. The shells will not rust or corrode, compared to steel, and the unit is designed to be built on an assembly line similar to an automobile (Figure 6.17.1).

As mentioned, configuration options range from a single amphibious module to as many as seventy-five on a single water-borne 'floating platform'. Options exist, as mentioned, for land-tethered water-borne sites, or dry shoreline sites. This allows for greater flexibility in diverse situations such as when, for example, an installation must be put in service for emergency/triage care first, for immediate patient stabilization, until that point in time when coordinated MEDIVAC operations with land-based hospitals can commence. Each module is in effect, a boat, transported by means of helicopter or barge. Floating modules can be airlifted in and then assembled together sequentially. When deployed in floating clusters, an installation site takes on an organic biomorphism. These amphibious modules can be added or subtracted as care needs dictate and in accord with site determinants.

Building/unit

The Seagull's six module types are: triage-injury assessment (F-Unit); acute care and treatment (TR-Unit); the pre-operative, operative, post-operative suite for relatively minor procedures (OR-Unit); staff support spaces, i.e., break room and administrative functions (Br-Unit); staff overnight dormitory accommodations (H-Unit); and public areas including a main waiting area (E-Unit). Individual modules are expandable, with a footprint allowing for various arrangements in plan (Figures 6.17.2a–i and 6.17.3a–f). An individual module, in its base configuration, is twenty-five feet in length, but for purposes of transiting logistics can be shipped as five separate panels, each five feet in length, that are then connected to one another upon arrival at the deployment site. In section, the ceiling system and interior proportions of a typical module are discernable. All equipment and furnishings are locked or clipped into place due to the need to control the effects of wave motion within the modules in nautical site contexts.

An axonometric diagram depicts the primary componentry of a typical module, including its waterproof exterior skin, flooring system, structural apparatus, panels, and the rooftop photovoltaic

6.17.1 The Seagull prototype is an alternative to the land-bound limits of both stationary and traditional prefab portable hospitals

panels. Modules come equipped with a roof-mounted searchlight, thereby making it easier to locate the installation at night with respect to arrivals and departures. This allows for the units to be identified from a distance by air or ship in situations where an offshore accident has occurred, and the installation is sited perhaps fifty miles away from the disaster site in order to ensure the safety of its inhabitants (Figures 6.17.4–6.17.7). The scope of care provided by the *Seagull* is to be limited to triage and immediate patient stabilization. The uncertainties associated with being located on water render any more acute level of care infeasible due to the lightweight attributes of the modules and their relative compactness. By contrast, large hospital ships such as the USS *Mercy* are able to maintain exponentially greater equilibrium while at sea. Regardless, the Seagull, for its rapid response capabilities, lightweight attributes, and adaptability, is well suited as an adjunctive prosthetic device in terms of its ability to extend the reach of a large floating hospital as well as land-based, stationary, medical institutions.

6.17.2a–i Clusters of modules can be grouped together in non-orthogonal patterns forming biomorphic, *nautical villages*

MICRO_config.

12units | **10,500**SF

01 with the micro configuration, site specific design is mostly obsolete. a string of connection nodes will allow for a dozen units to flex around just about any site.

02 the next step determines how the units will connect. accordian-like connection portals will expand outward linking each "illuminAID" with a node

03 one by one the units will arrive via helicopter or truck. the micro configuration will mostly stay linear but works well with wrapping around city blocks in a more urban setting

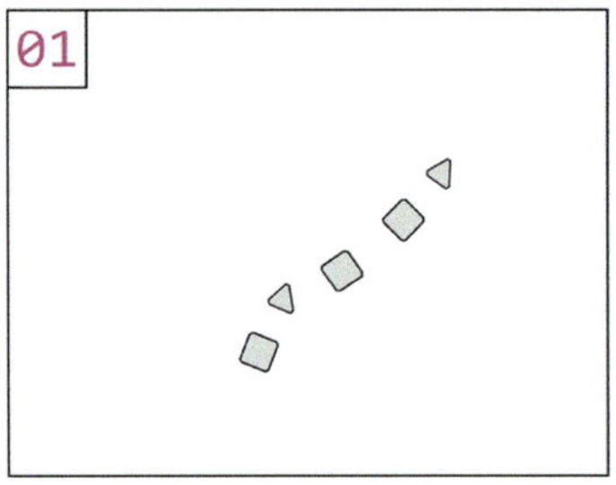

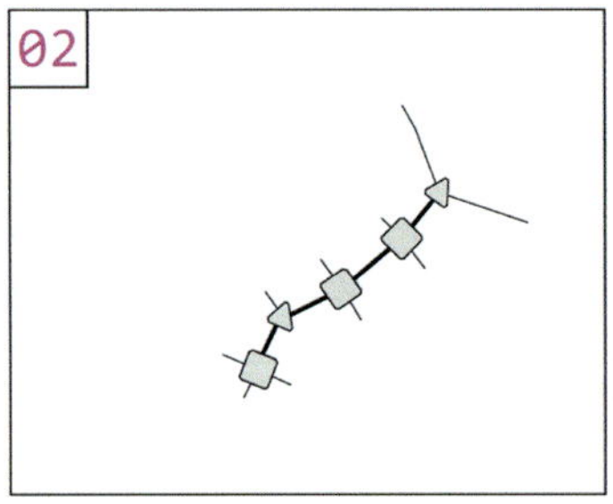

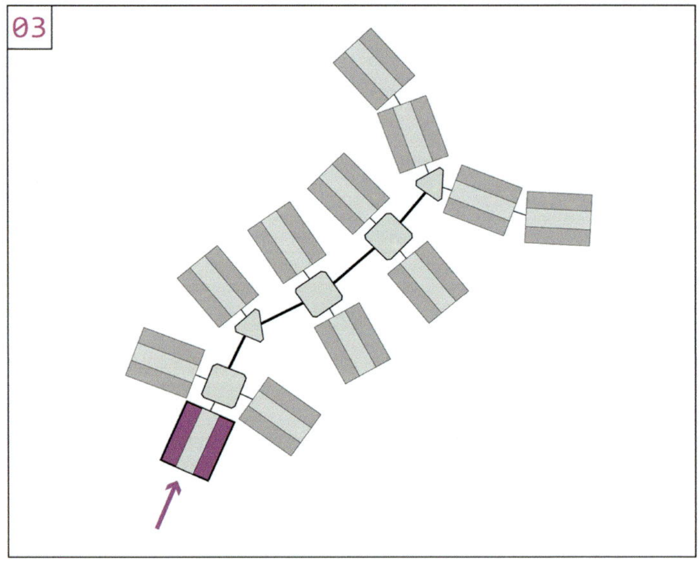

SPATIAL_config.

33units | **29,000**SF

01 the spatial configuration is used in settings without site limitations or boundaries. a string of connection nodes are laid out with the idea of maximizing views and creating open courtyards where possible

02 next, the connection partals branch outward. along the outside nodes the units diverge more, creating split circulation for staff housing

03 one by one the units will arrive via helicopter or truck. the spatial configuration will begin to resemble a sprawling suburban plan, in this case more room equates to more order

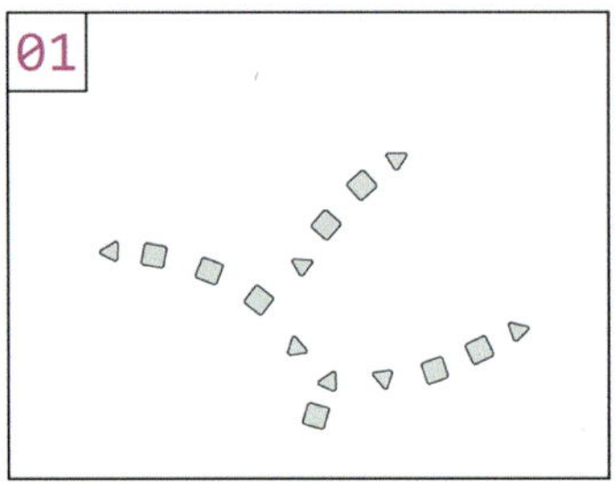

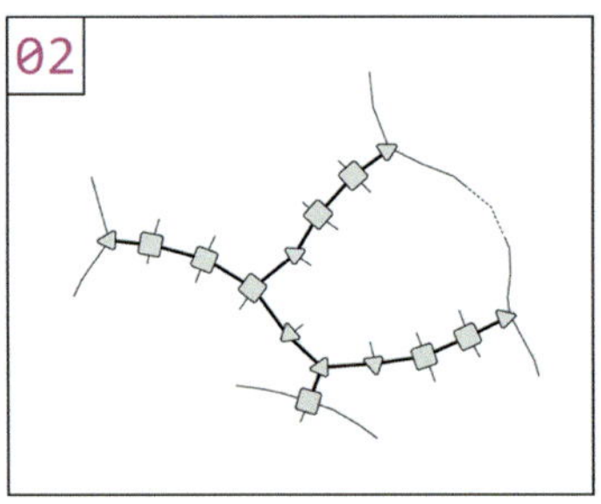

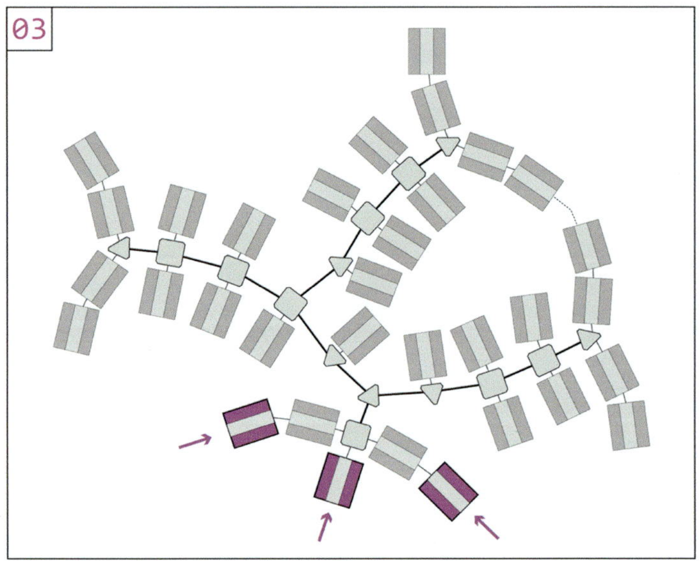

EFFICIENT_config.

33units | **29,000**SF

01 the efficient configuration is used in high disaster settings where a replacement hospital is needed and space is limited. connection nodes are dropped close together and appear mostly linear

02 next, the connection partals branch outward. to create the most efficient plan, majority of the nodes will connect to 3 additional nodes

03 one by one the units will arrive via helicopter or truck. this configuration calls for inner units that connect to nodes on both sides creating a more grid-like plan

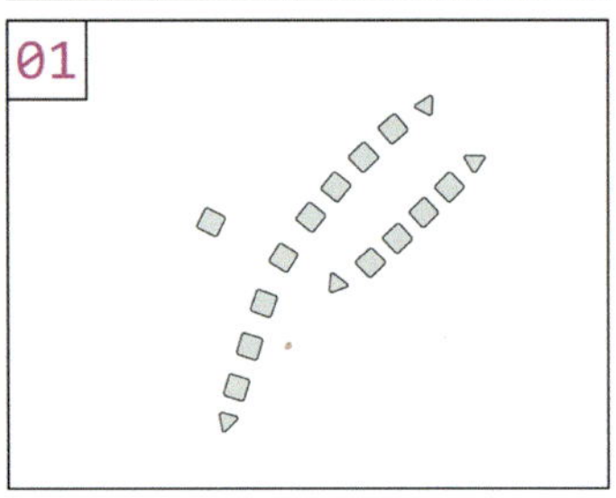

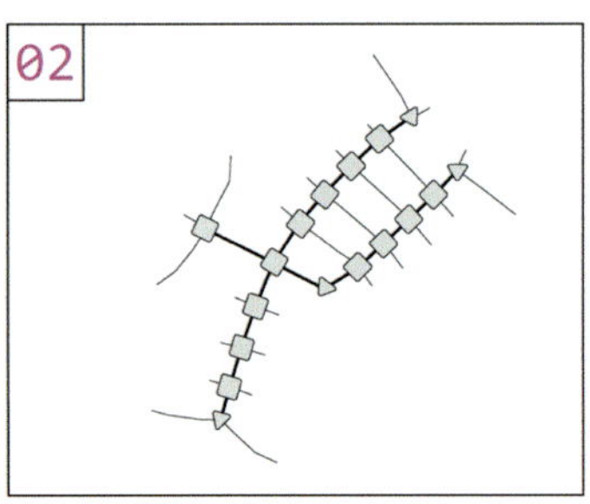

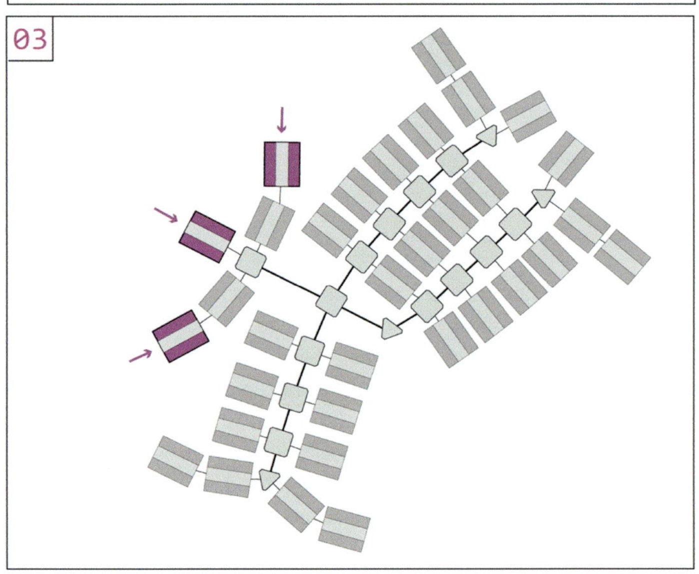

6.17.3a–f Modules' biomorphic polymer shells are watertight, and their interiors are manufactured to comply with extreme performance requirements

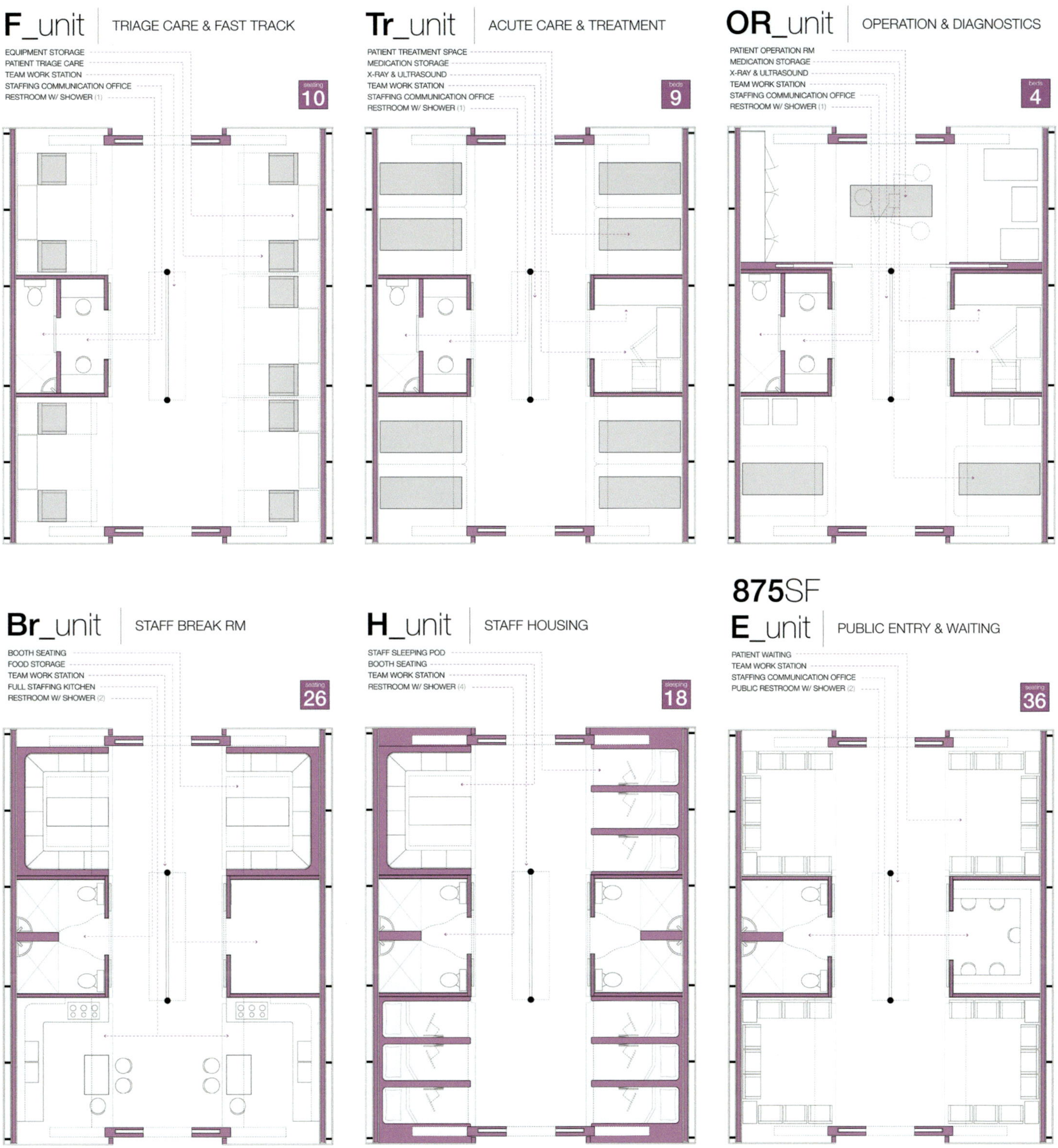

6.17.4 Seagull units en route via a conventional air cargo transporter

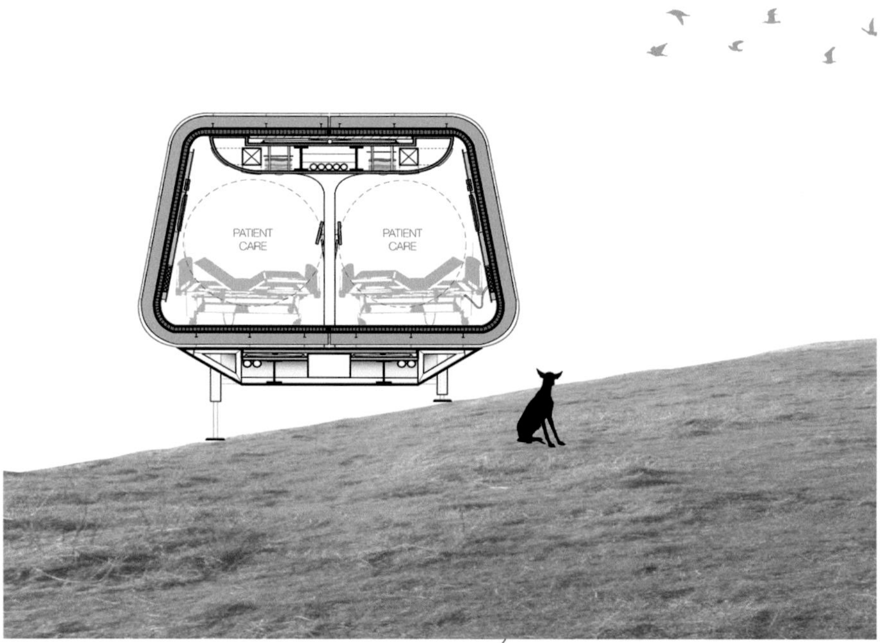

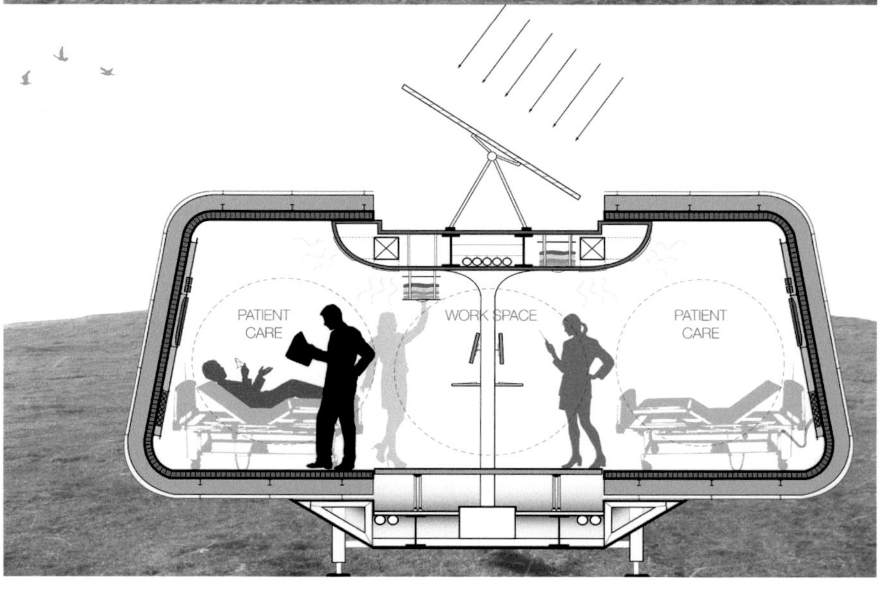

6.17.5a–b Modules' HVAC/MEP systems run both in the ceiling plenum (for nautical deployments) and below the floor (land-based deployments) with one or the other able to be deactivated, accordingly

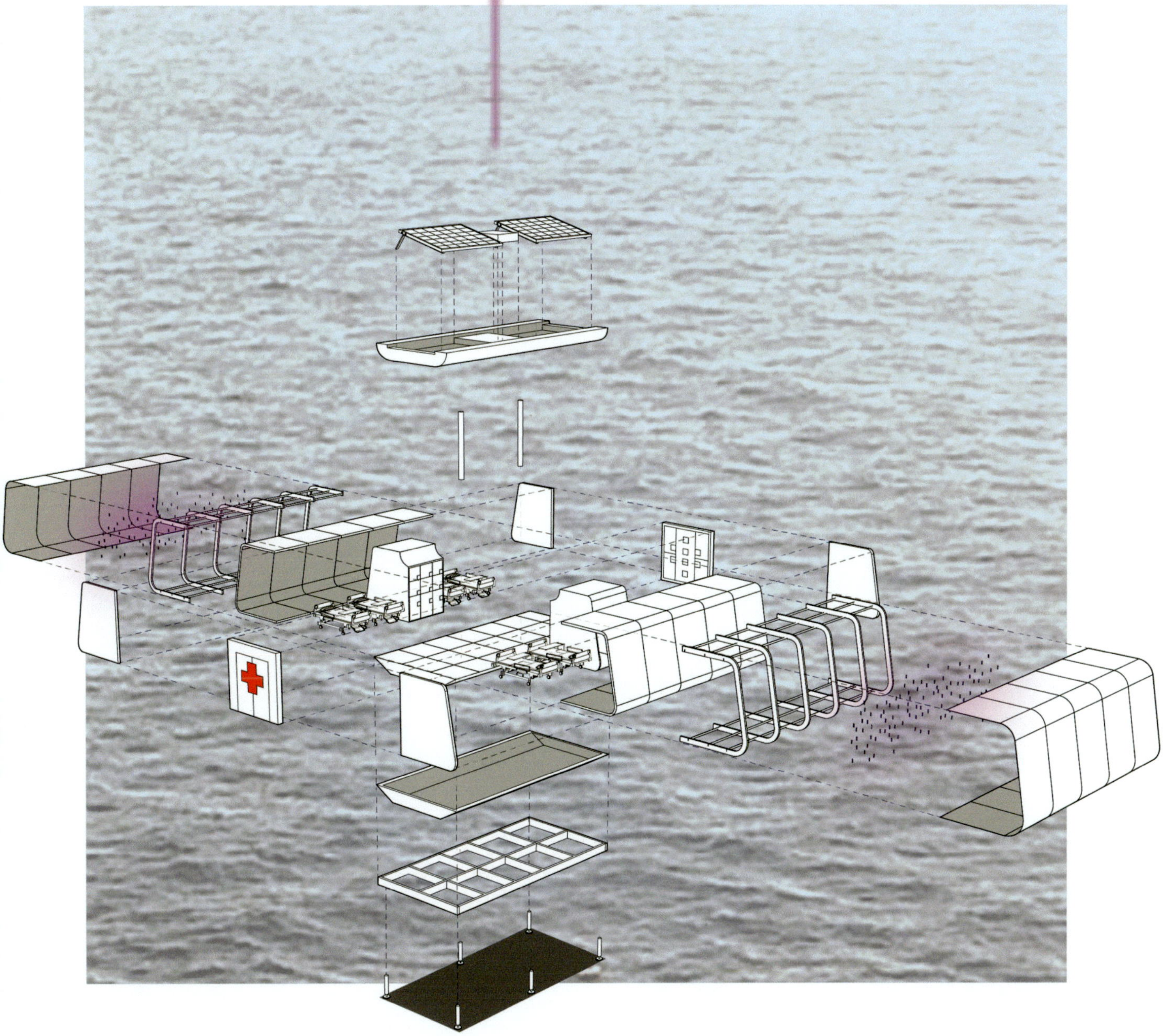

6.17.6 Blow-apart axonometric view (nautical deployment)

6.17.7 Land-based installation with modules' searchlight beacons, probing the night sky

18 RDoC Pop-up Pavilion-Clinic, San Francisco, USA

ARCHITECT/ENGINEER: Perkins+Will (Michael Bardin, Coordinator), Degenkolb Engineers, Mazzetti Engineering, San Francisco.
CLIENT/SPONSOR: Public Architecture/Alliance Health
TYPE OF CARE: Primary/emergency care (RHC/RTC)
NUMBER OF BEDS: N/A (Outpatient)
FEATURED MATERIALS: Aluminum/fabric/solar cells
METHOD OF ASSEMBLY: Flat-pack
SITE CONTEXT: Urban
DEPLOYMENT (MIN/MAX): 150–20,000+ square feet
PROPOSAL: 2013

Context/site

Disaster events and the havoc they wreak are stark reminders that despite wealthy nations' sophisticated, supposedly state-of-the-art building standards, and arsenal of advanced technologies, communities and entire nations remain extremely vulnerable. The general public, unfortunately, has become immune, lulled into complacency in often blindly assuming that first responders will be there to adroitly react to each and every disaster event. Misperceptions such as this remain the status quo. From a major forest fire decimating hundreds of thousands of acres in the American West, to the catastrophic effects of Superstorm Sandy on the Eastern Seaboard and the subsequent flooding in the New York metro area, to the effects of prolonged drought in California, the general public remains vulnerable. New York City's experience during Sandy in 2012 exposed the extreme threat posed by a 'non-hardened' urban infrastructure. After a disaster such as an earthquake, the sick and injured survivors, out of habit, will immediately turn to the existing local medical care network. For this reason, any breakdown or systemic failure of a stationary healthcare network during an emergency poses a significant threat to the public's health—with caregivers severed from the victims—not unlike what occurred in New Orleans in 2005 (see Chapter 1).

Against this backdrop, a prefab modular pavilion-clinic was developed. The *RDoC* portable prefab module can be used in normal everyday contexts for the provision of primary care, cancer screening, nutritional education, immunizations, and related health services (Figure 6.18.1). However, a fundamental mission of this system is to provide triage and emergency care following a disaster event. The modules are designed and manufactured to be sited in tightly packed clusters but are not necessarily intended to plug directly into one another. They can be erected side by side on a flat site such as a lawn or paved surface. A prototype installation of this system is depicted along a street in the center of San Francisco (Figure 6.18.2). If the local hospitals are knocked offline and can no longer provide critically needed services, these modules can be activated and deployed citywide on short notice. Staffed by personnel from local hospitals trained beforehand to operate the equipment to be staged at the *RDoC* modules, these miniature clinics can be set up either in clusters or as one-off installations for use until the local stationary medical centers are repaired and are back online or until additional RTCs are brought into the strike zone. The ability to be adequately predisposed to address public health needs in these extreme situations, first, requires a public education and awareness campaign to foster the necessary level of political support, which in turn would translate into the funding support so essential to manufacturing this and similar rapid response architecture.[28]

Building/unit

Each prefab module is designed and transited as a flat-pack, kit-of-parts. Interlocking flooring, sidewall, and ceiling components provide a rigid structural envelope (Figure 6.18.3). Each module features its own photovoltaic solar panel to ensure continuous functioning and independence from conventional power sources. A fabric sunscreen is provided beneath the solar panel to filter out unwanted ultraviolet exposure. Each module is oriented to optimize its solar amenity and the polyurethane wall panels are rigid yet lightweight and easy to install. A small backup emergency power generator, a rainwater cistern, and a wastewater-recycling tank are provided. Daylight is transmitted *vis-à-vis* screen panels, as is natural ventilation, as these are open-air structures. A module can be erected in two hours by a team of three to four persons. Two small folding canvas pup tents (for staff use) are provided in each

6.18.1 RDoC wellness screening installation in a neighborhood park in San Francisco (pre-disaster)

module's assembly kit. In everyday circumstances, a number of modules can be set up in Union Square and elsewhere in the city. Here, they are depicted in Union Square in the heart of the city, serving as portable public health units on a typical weekday, with various modules providing, in this scenario, routine sickness prevention information, cancer screening, and pediatric immunization vaccines (Figure 6.18.4). A series of quakes jolted the Bay Area in 2014, and seismologists regard this activity as a prelude to further seismic activity in the future.[29] The RDoC pavilion-clinics are therefore designed to function both as primary and wellness care modules, and alternatively, as units capable of rapidly being transformed into portable emergency care/triage stations in the unfortunate event of an earthquake in the San Francisco region (Figure 6.18.5).

6.18.2 RDoC installation, Union Square in San Francisco (pre-disaster)

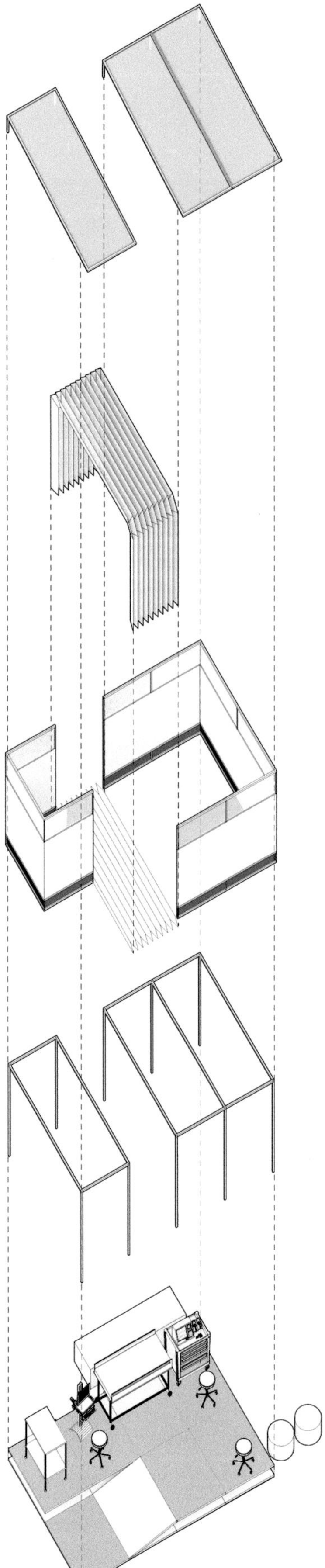

6.18.3 Axonometric view, typical RDoC module illustrating its lightness, transparency, and energy self-sufficiency

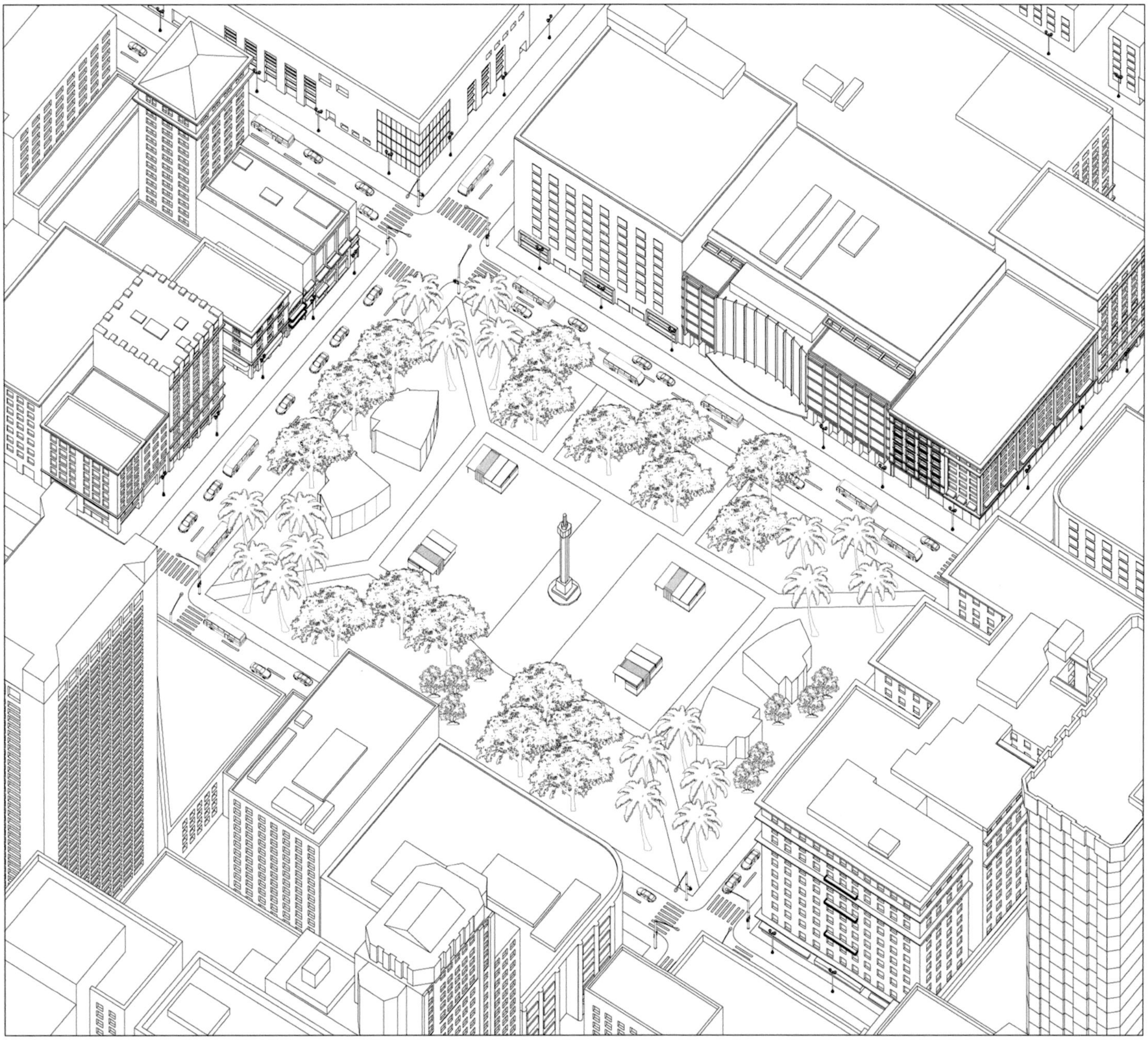

6.18.4 Union Square, San Francisco, RDoC modular installation (pre-disaster)

6.18.5 (overleaf) RDoC triage installation, San Francisco (post-disaster)

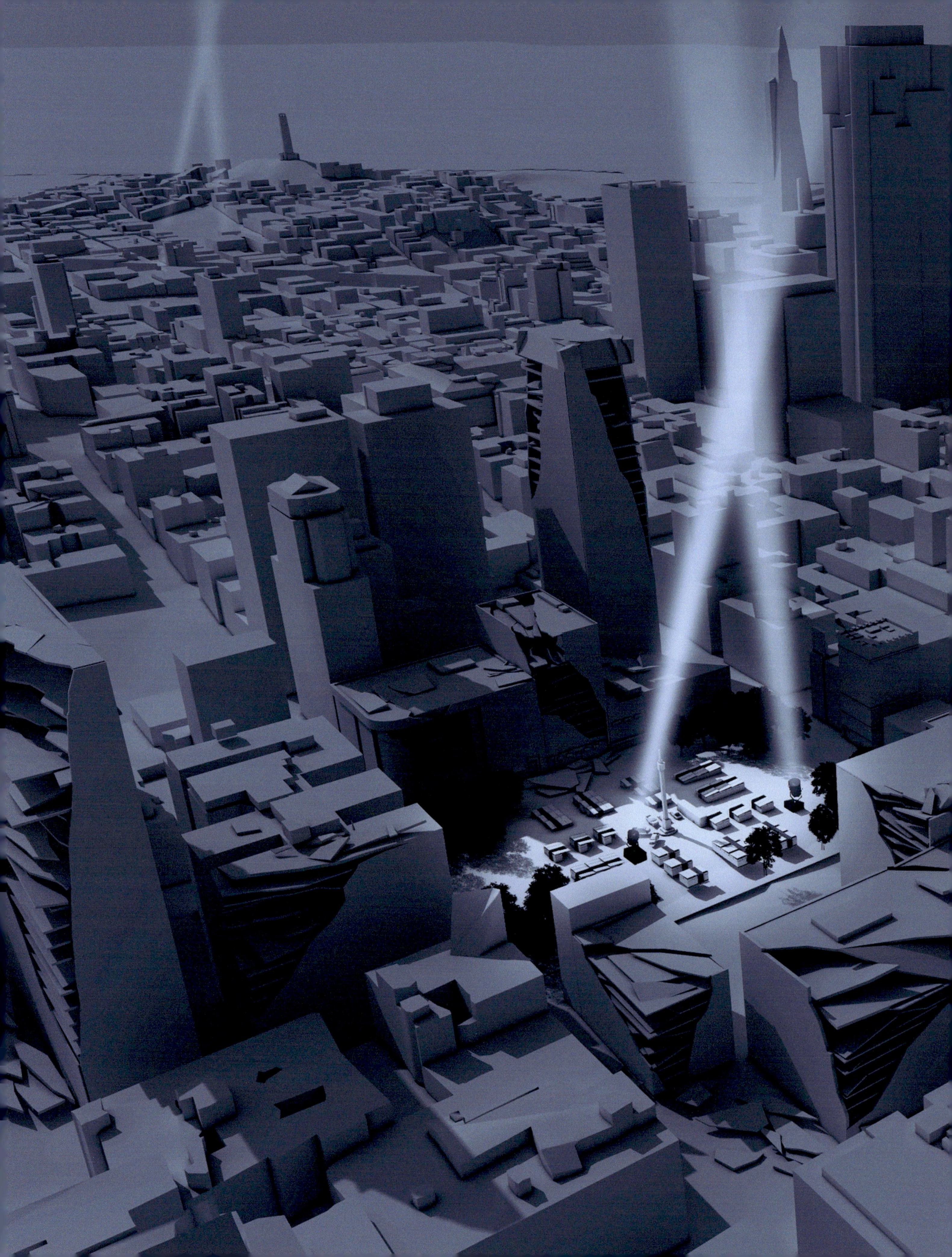

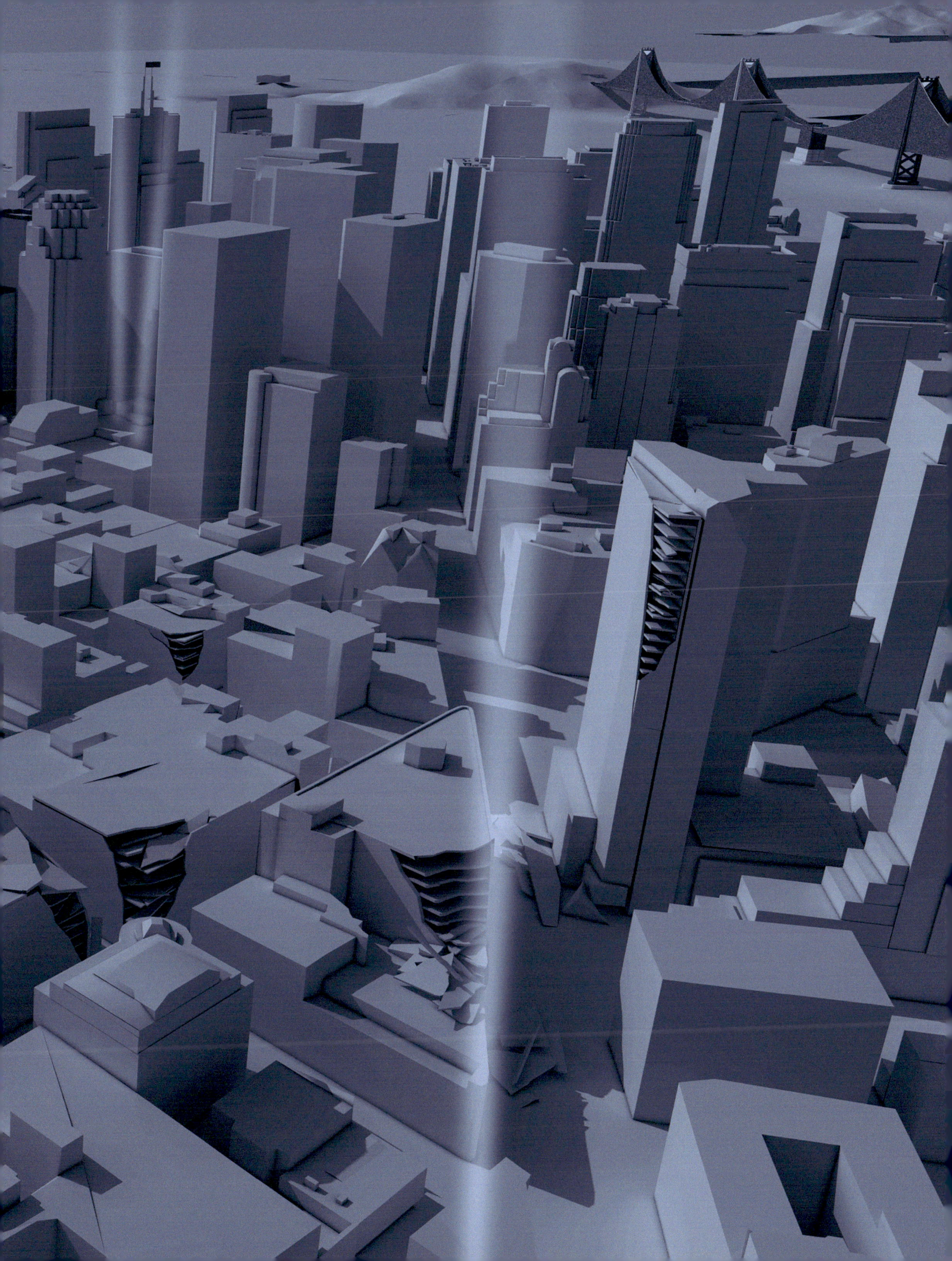

Notes and references

1 Introduction

1 Straub, Peter (2005) *Lovecraft: Tales*, New York: The Library of America, 823. 'The Call of Cthulhu' is a short story by American writer H.P. Lovecraft. Written in the summer of 1926, it was first published in the pulp magazine *Weird Tales*, in February 1928. French literary theorist Michel Houellebecq, in his 2005 book *H.P. Lovecraft: Against the World, Against Life* (San Francisco: McSweeney's, Believer Books), described the story as the first of Lovecraft's 'great texts.' Also see Joshi, S.T. (ed.) (1999) *The Call of Cthulhu and Other Weird Stories*, New York: Penguin Classics.

2 Van Young, Adrian (2014) 'Santeria and voodoo all mashed together', *Slate*, 4 March. Online. Available at www.slate.com/articles/arts/culturebox/2014/true_detective_louisiana_is_more_than_just_the_setting_it_s_the_inspiration.html (accessed 5 March 2014).

3 Verderber, Stephen (2008) 'Evidence-based design for healthcare in post-Katrina New Orleans: current dilemmas', *Health Environments Research and Design Journal*, 1(2): 71–79.

4 Ibid.: 73.

5 Verderber, Stephen (2009) *Delirious New Orleans: Manifesto for an Extraordinary American City*, Austin: University of Texas Press.

6 Verderber, Stephen (2009) 'The unbuilding of historic neighborhoods in post-Katrina New Orleans', *Journal of Urban Design*, 14(3): 257–277.

7 Verderber, Stephen (2009) *Health Environments Research and Design Journal*: 75.

8 Wombwell, James A. (2009) 'Army support during the Hurricane Katrina disaster: occasional paper 29', *U.S. Army Combined Arms Center*, Fort Leavenworth, Kansas: Combat Studies Institute Press. Also see Brown, Matthew H. and Kilar, Steve (2012) 'Navy moving hospital ship Comfort to Virginia', *The Baltimore Sun*, 14 February. Online. Available at http://articles.baltimoresun.com/2012-02-14/news/bs-md-comfort-moves-20120214_1_hospital-ship-navy-secretary-ray-mabus-naval-station-norfolk (accessed 8 November 2014).

9 Verderber, Stephen (2009) *Health Environments Research and Design Journal*: 72.

10 Franco, Crystal, Toner, Eric, Waldhorn, Richard, Maldin, Beth, O'Toole, Tara, and Inglesby, Thomas V. (2006) 'Systemic collapse: medical care in the aftermath of Hurricane Katrina', *Biosecurity and Bioterrorism*, 4(2): 66–79. Online. Available at http://online.liebertpub.com/doi/pdfplus/10.1089/bsp.2006.4.135 (accessed 25 February 2014).

11 Ibid.: 67.

12 Fink, Sheri (2009) 'The deadly choices at Memorial', *The New York Times*, August 25. Online. Available at www.nytimes.com/2009/08/30/magazine/30doctors.html (accessed 25 February 2014). A grand jury in New Orleans declined to indict her on second-degree murder charges. Since then, Pou has helped write and pass three laws in Louisiana that

offer immunity to healthcare professionals from most civil lawsuits, although not in cases of willful misconduct, with respect to their work in future disasters, from hurricanes to terrorist attacks to pandemic influenza. The tale of this hospital and others like it raises many questions: Which patients should receive aid when resources are extremely limited? What is the purpose of trying to provide the greatest 'good for the greatest numbers?' How should physicians and nurses be held accountable in the most harrowing of circumstances, especially when their employer and government has failed them?

13 Foster, Mary (2006) 'Nursing home owners charged with negligent homicide, cruelty in LA', *Insurance Journal*, 22 September. Online. Available at www.insurancejournal.com/news/southcentral/2006/09/22/72665.htm (accessed 8 November 2014). The owners of the nursing home mounted a defense centered on the claim that then-Governor Kathleen Blanco and a litany of public officials utterly failed to mount an evacuation plan to transport medically at risk individuals to a healthcare facility on high ground, as required by state law.

14 Nossiter, Adam (2007) 'Nursing home owners acquitted in deaths', *The New York Times*, 8 September. Online. Available at www.nytimes.com/2007/09/08/us/nationalspecial/08nursing.html (accessed 27 February 2014).

15 DeBoisblanc, James (2005) 'Blackhawk, please come down: reflections on a hospital's struggle to survive in the wake of Hurricane Katrina', *American Journal of Respiratory and Critical Care Medicine*, 172(4):1239–1240.

16 Stern, Jeffrey (2009) 'Hurricane Katrina and 9-11', *Aftermath Dynamics in Critical Incidents*, ACIA Case Conference at Virginia Tech, July 2009. Online. Available at www.spring2009.aciajj.org/proceedings/hurricane-katrina-and-9-11/html (accessed 8 November 2014).

17 Anon. (2005) 'Katrina medical help held up by red tape', *CNN-The Associated Press*, 4 September. Online. Available at www.freerepublic.com/focus/f-news/1477432/posts (accessed 26 February 2014).

18 Parker, Mary G. (2006) 'LSU in the eye of the storm: a University model for disaster response', *Proceedings of the SWASFAA Annual Conference*, November 2006. Online. Available at www.lasfaa.org/docs/news/disaster/SWASFAAPresentation.ppt (accessed 6 November 2014). Also see McCullar, Steven Lee (2011) *Crisis Management Post Hurricane Katrina: A Qualitative Study of a Higher Education Institution's Administrator's Response to Crisis Management*, Ph.D. Dissertation, Baton Rouge: Louisiana State University.

19 Dentzer, Samuel (2005) 'Hurricane hospital challenges: a report from Baton Rouge, Louisiana, about how makeshift hospitals are coping with a surge of patients', *Public Broadcasting System*, September 8. Online. Available at www.pbs.org/newshour/bb/weather-july-dec05-hospitals_9-8/ (accessed 26 February 2014).

20 UNFCCC (2014) *First Steps to a Safer Future: Introducing the United Nations Framework on Climate Change*, Geneva, Switzerland: United Nations Framework Convention on Climate Change. Online. Available at http://unfccc.int/essential_background/convention/items/6036.php (accessed 21 October 2014).

21 Environment Canada (2013) *Contribution to Intergovernmental Panel on Climate Change*, Ottawa: Environment Canada. Online. Available at www.ec.gc.ca/sc-cs/default.asp?lang=En&n=DDCFB594-1 (accessed 8 November 2014).

22 Intergovernmental Panel on Climate Change (2014) *Fifth Assessment Report: Climate Change 2014—Impacts, Adaptation, and Vulnerability*, Cambridge, U.K.: Cambridge University Press. Online. Available at www.ipcc.ch/report/ar5/wg2/ (accessed 8 November 2014).

23 Associated Press (2013) 'Global warming likely to make bad things worse, scientists forecast', *The Times-Picayune*, 3 November. Online. Available at www.nola.com/environment/index.ssf/2013/11/global_warming_likely_to_make.html (accessed 12 December 2013).

24 IPCC Working Group III (2014) *Special Report on Renewable Energy Sources and Climate Change Mitigation*, Geneva, Switzerland: Intergovernmental Panel on Climate Change. Online. Available at http://srren.ipcc-wg3.de/ (accessed 15 October 2014).

25 Suzuki, David (2014) 'Fighting climate change offers many health benefits', *Straight.com*, 9 September. Online. Available at www.straight.com/news/724561/david-suzuki-fighting-climate-change-offers-many-health-benefits (accessed 10 November 2014). Also see Gillis, Justin (2014) 'Scientists trace extreme heat in Australia to climate change', *The New York Times*, 29 September. Online. Available at www.nytimes.com/2014/09/30/science/earth/human-related-climate-change-led-to-extreme-heat-scientists-say.html?_r=0 (accessed 10 November 2014).

26 Raloff, Janet (2012) 'Warming indicted for extreme weather', *Science News*, 11 July. Online. Available at www.sciencenews.org/article/warming-indicted-extreme-weather?mode=magazine&context=4536 (accessed 10 November 2014).

27 Gillis, Justin and Chang, Kenneth (2014) 'Scientists warn of rising oceans from polar melt', *The New York Times*, 12 May. Online. Available at www.nytimes.com/2014/05/13/science/earth/collapse-of-parts-of-west-antarctica-ice-sheet-has-begun-scientists-say.html?_r=0> (accessed 12 May 2014).

28 Lang, Ian (2014) 'Science grossly underestimates rate of upper ocean warming', *Daily Digest News*, 7 October. Online. Available at www.dailydigestnews.com/2014/10/science-grossly-underestimates-rate-of-ocean-warming.html (accessed 12 October 2014).

29 McDonnell, Tim (2013) 'Natural disasters have cost $3.8 trillion since 1980, World Bank says', *Mother Jones*, 18 November. Online. Available at www.motherjones.com/blue-marble/2013/11/natural-disasters-cost-38-trillion-1980-world-bank-says (accessed 25 November 2013).

30 Kahn, Brian (2013) 'Floods may cost coastal cities $60 billion a year by 2050', *ClimateCentral.org*, 18 August. Online. Available at www.

climatecentral.org/news/floods-may-cost-coastal-cities-60-billion-annually-by-2050-16356 (accessed 25 November 2013).
31 Klein, Naomi (2014) *This Changes Everything: Capitalism vs. the Climate*, New York: Simon & Schuster.
32 Prothero, Donald R. (2011) *Catastrophes!: Earthquakes, Tsunamis, Tornadoes, and other Earth-Shattering Disasters*, Baltimore: Johns Hopkins University Press.
33 EM-DAT (2014) 'Recent global trends', *The International Disaster Database*. Online. Available at www.emdat.be (accessed 25 October 2014).
34 Ebi, Kristie L. and Semenza, Jan C. (2008) 'Community based adaption to the health impacts of climate change', *American Journal of Preventive Medicine*, 35(5): 501–507.
35 Guha-Sapir, Debarati, Hoyois, Philippe and Below, Regina (2014) 'Annual Disaster Statistical Review 2013', Centre for Research on the Epidemiology of Disasters (CRED), Institute of Health and Society (IRSS) and Université catholique de Louvain, Brussels. Online. Available at www.cred.be/sites/default/files/ADSR_2013.pdf (accessed 25 October 2014).
36 Horne, Jed (2008) *Breach of Faith: Hurricane Katrina and the Near Death of a Great American City*, New York: Random House.
37 Brinkley, Douglas (2007) *The Great Deluge: Hurricane Katrina, New Orleans, and the Mississippi Gulf Coast*, New York: Harper Perennial.
38 Brooks, Janet (2006) 'MED-1: hospital on wheels', *Canadian Medical Association Journal*, 12 September, 175(6): 569–573.
39 Farmer, Paul (2012) *Haiti after the Earthquake*, Reprint Edition, Malden, MA: Public Affairs.
40 Reitman, Janet (2011) 'Beyond relief: how the world failed Haiti', *Rolling Stone*, August 4: 35–39.
41 Garamone, Jim (2010) 'USNS Comfort arrives in Port-au-Prince', DoD News, *U.S. Department of Defense*, 2 January. Online. Available at www.defense.gov/news/newsarticle.aspx?id=57631 (accessed 11 July 2014).
42 Levy, Gad, Blumberg, Nehemia, Kreiss, Yitshak, Ash, Nachman and Merin, Ofer (2012) 'Application of information technology within a field hospital deployment following the January 2010 Haiti earthquake disaster', *Journal of the American Medical Informatics Association*, 17(11): 626–630.
43 Barkan, Noam (2010) 'Israel hospital in Haiti ends operations', *Ynetnews.com*, 26 January. Online. Available at www.ynetnews.com/articles/0,7340,L-3839561,00.html (accessed 11 December 2012). Also see Berrin, Danielle (2010) 'Israel's Haitian tent hospital boosts IDF image', *Jewish Journal.com*, 11 May. Online. Available at www.jewishjournal.com/community/article/israels_haitian_tent_hospital_boosts_idf_image_20100511/ (accessed 11 December 2012).
44 Newton-Small, Jay (2010) 'Haiti's medical crisis: treating crushed survivors', *Time*. 21 January. Online. Available at http://content.time.com/time/specials/packages/article/0,28804,1953379_1953494_1955525,00.html (accessed 5 December 2012).
45 de Córdoba, José (2010) 'Aid spawns backlash in Haiti', *The Wall Street Journal*, 13–14 November: A1; A10.
46 Author's interview with Allison Howard-Berry, July 2013. See Interview 2 in the Appendix.
47 Verderber, Stephen (2013) 'Zombie housing for the displaced in the aftermath of disaster', in Sen, Arijit and Johung, Jennifer (eds.) *Landscapes of Mobility: Culture, Politics and Placemaking*, Surrey, U.K.: Ashgate: 47–72.
48 Juhasz, Antonia (2011) *Black Tide: The Devastating Impact of the Gulf Oil Spill*, New York: John Wiley and Sons.
49 Ibid.: 8.
50 Birmingham, Lucy and McNeill, David (2012) *Strong in the Rain: Surviving Japan's Earthquake, Tsunami, and the Fukushima Nuclear Disaster*, London: Macmillan.
51 Ibid.: 11.
52 Lum, Thomas (2013) *Typhoon Haiyan (Yolanda): U.S. and International Response to Philippines Disaster*. Washington, D.C.: Congressional Research Service.
53 Mulles, Albert (2014) *Typhoon Haiyan the Untold Story: A Story of Hope and Survival*, Portland, OR: Amazon Digital Services.
54 Anon. (2014) 'Philippines marks Typhoon Haiyan anniversary', 8 November. *Aljazeera*. Online. Available at www.aljazeera.com/news/asia-pacific/2014/11/philippines-marks-typhoon-haiyan-anniversary-201411835744828320.html (accessed 10 November 2014).
55 Editorial (2013) 'Worse than hell', *The Economist*, 16 November. Online. Available at www.economist.com/news/asia/21589916-one-strongest-storms-ever-recorded-has-devastated-parts-philipines-and-relief (accessed 11 November 2014).
56 Eamer, Gwen (2013) 'Post-typhoon field hospital welcomes baby Fiona Haiyan', *Reliefweb*. Online. Available at http://m.reliefweb.int/report/618290 (accessed 2 December 2013).
57 Ross, Monique (2013) 'Typhoon Haiyan: field hospital medics seeing "horrific injuries" in wake of Philippine storm', *ABC News*, 21 November. Online. Available at www.abc.net.au/news/2013-11-21/philippines-typhoon-medics-seeing-horrific-injuries/5107764 (accessed 2 December 2013).
58 Bradsher, Keith (2013) 'At a Philippine hospital, survivors face quiet despair', *The New York Times*, 13 November. Online. Available at www.nytimes.com/2013/11/14/world/asia/at-a-philippine-hospital-survivors-face-quiet-despair.html (accessed 14 November 2013).
59 Humanity Road/Animals in Disaster (2013) 'Social media report for clinics, mobile medical units and fixed field hospitals. Timeline: report period ending November 24, 2013,' *Humanity Road/Animals in Disaster*. Online. Available at www.reliefweb.int/sites/reliefweb.int/files/resources/HumanityRoad%20SMHosp%20Sitrep%20Nov%2024.pdf (accessed 24 November 2013).
60 Ibid.: 14.

61 Specific measures are required to increase the region's resilience in the face of future disaster events such as Haiyan. First, the standard of living and quality of housing must be improved. Politicians' empty promises have been repeated for generations and many citizens long ago became apathetic but somehow, systemic improvements must become mandatory. Second, far better early warning systems are needed to fully alert citizens and communities of impending danger well before it strikes.

62 Holling, C.S. (1973) 'Resilience and stability of ecological systems', *Annual Review of Ecology and Systematics*, 4(2): 1–23.

63 Walker, Brian and Salt, David (2012) *Resilience Practice: Building Capacity to Absorb Disturbance and Maintain Function*, Washington, D.C.: Island Press.

64 Lee, James H. (2012) *Resilience and the Future of Everyday Life*, Shelbyville, KY: Wasteland Press.

65 Ibid.: 26.

66 Downes, Barbara J., Miller, Fiona, Barnett, Jon, Glaister, Alena and Ellemor, Heidi (2013) ' How do we know about resilience? An analysis of empirical research on resilience, and implications for interdisciplinary praxis', *Environmental Research Letters*, 8(2): 1–8.

67 Walker and Salt (2012): 42.

68 Fisher, Thomas (2012) *Designing to Avoid Disaster: The Nature of Fracture-Critical Design*, London: Routledge.

69 Hollinagel, Erik, Woods, David D., and Leveson, Nancy (eds.) (2006) *Resilience Engineering: Concepts and Precepts*, Surrey, U.K.: Ashgate. Also see National Climatic Data Center (2013) *Billion Dollar Weather/ Climate Disasters: Overview*, Washington, D.C.: U.S. National Oceanic and Atmospheric Administration; and Solnit, Rebecca (2012) 'Solnit on Hurricane Sandy: stop ignoring climate change', *Mother Jones*, 8 November. Online. Available at wwwmotherjones.com/environment/ 2012/11/rebecca-solnit-sandy-climate-change?page=2 (accessed 1 December 2012). The *Superstorm*—a relatively new term, similar to the term *Haboob*, which is now used to describe intense sandstorms in the U.S. desert Southwest—obliterated the New Jersey shore and heavily damaged lower Manhattan's subway system due to flooding. Fifty people were killed and more than eight million left without power. This storm caused more than $68 billion in damage, a U.S. total only surpassed by Katrina.

70 The National Academies (2012) *Disaster Resilience: A National Imperative*, Washington, D.C.: The National Academies Press.

71 Wilson, George A. (2012) *Community Resilience and Environmental Transitions*, London: Routledge.

72 Carlson, Scott (2013) 'After catastrophe', 6 May, *The Chronicle of Higher Education*. Online. Available at http://chronicle.com/article/ After-Catastrophe/138927/ (accessed 15 June 2013).

73 Fiksel, Joseph (2006) 'Sustainability and resilience: towards a systems approach', *Sustainability: Science, Practice & Policy*, 2(2): 14–21. Online. Available at http://sspp.proquest.com/static_content/ vol2iss2/0608-028.fiksel.pdf (accessed 12 September 2014).

74 Walker and Salt (2012): 54.

75 Mehaffy, Michael and Salingaros, Nikos A. (2013) 'Toward resilient architectures I: biology lessons', *Group Resources: Building a World of Resilient Communities*, 25 March. Online. Available at www.resilience.org/stories/2013/03-25/toward-resilient-architectures-i-biology-lessons (accessed 9 May 2013).

76 Zolli, Andrew and Healy, Anne Marie (2012) *Resilience*, New York: Free Press, 5.

77 Ibid.: 6–7.

78 Ibid.: 8–9.

79 Ibid.: 37.

80 Ibid.: 9.

81 Ibid.: 11.

82 Lewis, Michael and Conaty, Patrick (2012) *The Resilience Imperative: Cooperative Transitions to a Steady-State Economy*, Gabriola Island, British Columbia: New Society Publishers.

83 Zolli and Healy: 12.

84 Ibid.: 13–14.

85 Vanderwerker, Earl E. (1976) "A brief review of the history of amputations and prostheses," *The Association of Children's Prosthetic-Orthotic Clinics*, 15(5): 15–16. In many societies, even up to the present, the infant is disposed of to hide the evidence. Others with deformities are warehoused in state-run institutions for the developmentally disabled. Also see Katoch, Roger and Rajagopalan, Samuel (2010) "Warfare injuries: history, triage, transport and field hospital setup in the armed forces," *MJAFI*, 66(44): 304–308.

86 Norton, Kim M. (2007) 'A brief history of prosthetics', *inMotion*, 17(7): 11–13. Online. Available at www.amputee-coalition.org/inmotion/ nov_dec_07/history_prosthetics.html (accessed 10 November 2014).

87 Herodotus, as translated by Grene, David (1987) *The History*, Chicago: University of Chicago Press. Pliny the Elder (23–79 A.D.) wrote of a General in the Second Punic War (218–210 B.C.) who had a right arm amputated. Celsius, who lived at the time of the birth of Christ, described amputation as a necessary procedure to combat gangrene. This practice continued through the Middle Ages, proliferating in the 14th century due to the invention of gunpowder. It was common for tradesmen, including armorers, to design and fabricate artificial limbs. Diverse trades contributed; watchmakers were instrumental in adding functionality to devices by means of intricate springs and gears.

88 Wilson, Brian B. (1972) 'The modern history of amputation surgery and artificial limbs', *Orthopedic Clinicians of North America*, 3(7): 267–285. During the U.S. Civil War, a patented device called the 'Hanger Lomb' was fabricated from whittled barrel staves and was used to produce prosthetic devices to thousands of wartime amputees. Few advancements were made in World War I. At the conclusion of World War II in 1945, it is noteworthy that many returning amputees were dissatisfied with the strikingly low technology of their devices, so they demanded improvements.

89 Ibid.: 31.

90 Norton (2007): 15.

91 Hurley, Amanda K. (2014) 'Exhibition review: designing for disaster', *Architectural Record*, 13 May. Online. Available at http://archrecord.construction.com/news/2014/05/140513-Exhibition-Review-Designing-for-Disaster.asp?WT.mc_id=rss_archrecord (accessed 12 June 2013).

92 Preiser, Wolfgang and Vischer, Jaqueline (2004) *Assessing Building Performance*, London: Routledge.

93 World Health Organization (2012) 'United States of America: Health Profile', *World Health Organization*. Online. Available at www.who.int/gho/countries/usa.pdf (accessed 29 September 2014). A medically underserved area is defined as an entire 'county or a group of contiguous counties, a group of county or civil divisions or a group of urban census tracts in which residents are confronted with a shortage of personal services. This type of population typically faces economic, cultural, or linguistic barriers to healthcare.' Also see World Health Organization (2012) 'Linkages between health and human rights', *World Health Organization*. Online. Available at www.who.int/hhr/HHR%20linkages.pdf (accessed 21 October 2014). Regardless, much of the world's population continues to suffer from pronounced health inequities in the everyday milieu.

94 Health Resources and Services Administration (2012) 'State Population and Health Professional Shortage Areas Designation Population Statistics', *Health Resources and Services Administration*. Online. Available at www.hrsa.gov/ReportServer?/HGDW_Reports/BCD_HPSA/BCD_HPSA_State_Summary&rs:Format=HTML3.2.html (accessed 20 October 2014).

95 Rickets, Thomas, Goldsmith, Laurie, Holmes, George, Randolph, Randy, Lee, Richard, Taylor, Donald and Ostermann, Jan (2007) 'Designating places and populations as medically underserved: a proposal for a new approach', *Journal of Health Care for the Poor and Underserved*, 18(6): 567–589.

96 Fortney, John C., Burgess, James F., Bosworth, Hayden B., Booth, Brenda M., and Kaboli, Peter J. (2011) 'A re-conceptualization of access for 21st century healthcare', *Journal of General Internal Medicine*, 26(11): 639–647. In the case of South Carolina, the percentage of the population who live in poverty (17 percent versus 14 percent in the national overall) indicates its citizens are rather likely to suffer from poor access to healthcare, versus the Nation as a whole. HRSA statistics confirm this pattern.

97 Anon. (2014) 'Key health data about South Carolina', *Trust for America's Health*. Online. Available at http://healthyamericans.org/stats/?stateid=SC (accessed 1 November 2014).

98 These vehicular clinics consist of Clemson University's mobile unit, based in the Upstate region on the Clemson University campus, the Med/Mission (Mission of Hope Ministries) unit, based in Lexington, the New Horizon Family Dental CAREs Team Mobile Unit, based in Greenville, the Spartanburg Regional/Bearden-Josey Center for Mobile Mammography Unit, based in Spartanburg, and the Department of Veteran Affair's Mobile Outreach Unit, based in Columbia. These units provide a wide range of care including cancer screening, immunizations, and primary care, i.e. child and maternal health, and nutritional education, dental care, and mental health counseling. The Clemson mobile unit travels regularly to outlying rural districts to serve illegal migrant farmworkers and their families. It is not uncommon for migrant workers to walk miles after sundown to the unit. The units have been a success and more are needed. By bringing services closest to where people live and work, health inequities can, it is hoped, be significantly reduced if not eradicated.

99 Mittelman, Sharyn (2012) 'Israel—A leader in disaster planning', *AIJAC: Australia/Israel & Jewish Affairs Council*. Online. Available at www.aijac.org.au/news/article/israel-a-leader-in-disaster-planning (accessed 24 April 2012).

100 Verderber, Stephen (2012) 'Redeployable trauma centers for post-disaster response', *World Health Design*, 5(10): 56–61.

101 Fisher (2012): Chapter 1.

102 Klein, Naomi (2008) *The Shock Doctrine: The Rise of Disaster Capitalism*, New York: Picador.

103 Verderber (2012): 57.

104 Verderber, Stephen (2003) 'Compassionism and the design studio in the aftermath of 9/11', *Journal of Architectural Education*, 56(3): 48–62.

105 Verderber (2012): 60.

106 Steinhäusler, Friedrich and Edwards, Frances (eds.) (2005) *NATO and Terrorism—Catastrophic Terrorism and First Responders: Threats and Mitigation. NATO Security Through Science Series B: Volume 2*, Berlin: Springer.

107 World Health Organization (2012) *Handbook for Emergency Field Operations*, Geneva: World Health Organization. Online. Available at www.who.int/hac/techguidance/tools/7661.pdf?.ua=1 (accessed 14 July 2014); World Health Organization (2013) *Compendium of Innovative Health Technologies for Low-Resource Settings: Assistive Devices, e-Health Solutions, Medical Devices*, Geneva: World Health Organization. Online. Available at http://apps.who.int/iris/bitstream/10665/108781/1/9789241564731_eng.pdf (accessed 14 July 2014); World Health Organization (2009) Gaza Strip Health Cluster Weekly Bulletin, No. 2, 4 February, *World Health Organization*. Online. Available at www.who.int/hac/crises/international/wbgs/sitreps/gaza_health_cluster_4feb2009/en/ (accessed 14 July 2014): discusses two inflatable tent clinics; World Health Organization (2012) 'Quake victims reach help too late to save crushed limbs', *Bulletin of the World Health Organization*, 83(12). Online. Available at www.who.int/bulletin/volumes/83/12/news31205/en/ (accessed 14 July 2014).

108 UNHCR (2002) *Resettlement Handbook*, New York: United Nations High Commissioner for Refugees. Online. Available at www.unhcr.

org/3d98623a4.html (accessed 10 September 2014). Also see Gojer John and Ellis, Ann (2014) 'Post traumatic stress disorder and the refugee determination process in Canada: starting the discourse', *United Nations High Commissioner for Refugees Technical Report*, March 2014; also UNHCR (2012) 'Second Revision—Syria Regional Response Plan', *United Nations High Commissioner for Refugees*, September. Online. Available at www.unhcr.org/5062c7429.html (accessed 1 July 2014).

109 Wilkinson, Ray (2003) 'After two decades of war, Sri Lanka is on the mend', *Refugees*, 1(130): 5–15.

110 Peer-reviewed publications include *Disasters, International Journal of Disaster Risk Reduction, Journal of Emergency Management*, and *Asian Journal of Environment and Disaster Management.*

111 Forsythe, David P. (2005) *The Humanitarians: The International Committee of the Red Cross*, Cambridge, U.K.: Cambridge University Press.

112 Bortolotti, Daniel (2010) *Hope in Hell: Onside the World of Doctors Without Borders*, Richmond Hill, Ontario: Firefly Books.

113 Four days after Hurricane Katrina, I stood in the sweltering Texas heat and humidity for hours in Austin, Texas, waiting to withdraw funds from my New Orleans-based bank. The bank's entire central operations in downtown New Orleans had been knocked off grid. The bank's management decided to relocate the entire operation to Shreveport, Louisiana in a convoy of ten 18-wheelers. Meanwhile, the sole Austin branch had no online access to any New Orleans customers' bank records. The branch relied on trust and goodwill, and yet, those of us in that long line went slack jawed as the tellers handed each of us, one at a time, a mere $100.00 bill. We each then signed a handwritten withdrawal note. That was the maximum allowed. With hundreds in that line—most having evacuated with scant cash, what remained was quickly running out. Two days later the bank's database was up again in a true test of resilience in the face of total system disruption.

114 Boseley, Sarah (2014) 'World Health Organization admits botching response to Ebola outbreak', *The Guardian*, 17 October. Online. Available at www.theguardian.com/world/2014/oct/17/world-health-organization-botched-ebola-outbreak (accessed 12 November 2014).

2 Transportables for health: a brief modern history

1 McLaughlin, E., and Papadopoulo, A. (2008) 'An introduction to portable field hospitals', *Rural and Remote Health*, 8(830): 1–12. Also see Kronenburg, Robert (2002) *Houses in Motion*, Second Edition, West Sussex: Wiley-Academy.

2 Schwartz-Clauss, Mathias and von Vegesack, Alexander (eds.) (2002) *Living in Motion: Design and Architecture for Flexible Dwelling*, Stiftung gGmbH, Weil am Rhein: Ultra Design Museum, 144.

3 Kronenburg, Robert (2002) *Flexible: Architecture that Responds to Change*, London: Laurence King, 14, 95–100.

4 Tarr, Laszio (1969) *The History of the Carriage*, Georgetown, CT: Arco Publishing.

5 Kronenburg, Robert (2008) *Portable Architecture: Design and Technology*, Fourth Edition, Berlin: Birkhauser.

6 Connell, Christopher (2007) 'Is war good for medicine?', *Stanford Medicine Magazine*, Summer. Online. Available at http://sm.stanford.edu/archive/stanmed/2007summer/main.html (accessed 1 October 2014).

7 Kronenburg (2008): 42–46.

8 Lanktree, Graham (2008) 'Canadian MDs risk life and limb in Afghanistan', *National Review of Medicine*, April, 5(4): 14–16.

9 Gibbon, Edward (1996) *The History of the Decline and Fall of the Roman Empire, Volume 1*, New York: Penguin.

10 Brice, Lee L. (2014) *Warfare in the Roman Empire: From the Etruscan Wars to the Battle of Actium*, Santa Barbara, CA: ABC-CLIO.

11 Margotta, Roberto (1968) *The Story of Medicine*, New York: Golden Press. An excellent source for a deeper examination of the extensive medical writings of Hippocrates is to be found in Jones, W.H.S. (1868) *Hippocrates Collected Works I*, Cambridge Harvard University Press. Also see Schneider, Dona, Lilienfeld, David E., and Winkelstein, Warren (2008) *Public Health: The Development of a Discipline, From the Age of Hippocrates to the Progressive Era*, New Brunswick, NJ: Rutgers University Press.

12 Horstmanshoff, Manfred (ed.) (2010) *Hippocrates and Medical Education (Studies in Ancient Medicine)*, Leiden, The Netherlands: BRILL.

13 Sherry, Eugene, Trieu, Lawrence, and Templeton, John (eds.) (2003) *Trauma*, Oxford, U.K.: Oxford University Press, 2–9.

14 Singer, Charles and Underwood, E.A. (1962) *A Short History of Medicine*, Second Edition, Oxford, U.K.: Oxford University Press.

15 Ibid.: 77.

16 Ibid.: 94.

17 Ibid.: 13.

18 Margotta (1968): Chapter 1.

19 Keegan, John (1994) *A History of Warfare*, New York: Vintage. Also see Keegan, John (2000) *The Book of War: 25 Centuries of Great War Writing*, New York: Penguin.

20 Thompson, John, and Goldin, Grace (1975) *The Hospital: A Social and Architectural History*, New Haven: Yale University Press.

21 Parenti, Michael (2004) *The Assassination of Julius Caesar: A People's History of Ancient Rome*, New York: The New Press.

22 Winston, Henry (2009) 'Medicine and surgery in ancient Rome.' *Crystalinks*. Online. Available at www.crystalinks.com/romemedicine.html (accessed 29 April 2012).

23 Thompson and Goldin (1975): 77.

24 Risse, Guenter B. (1990) *Mending Bodies, Saving Souls: A History of Hospitals*, Oxford, U.K.: Oxford University Press.

25 Huff, Toby E. (2003) *The Rise of Early Modern Science: Islam, China and the West*, Cambridge, U.K.: Cambridge University Press.

26 Savage-Smith, Emille (1994) *Islamic Culture and the Medical Arts: An Exhibit at the National Library of Medicine*, Exhibition Catalogue, Bethesda, MD: National Library of Medicine.

27 Tschanz, David W. (2007) 'Medieval Islamic hospitals and medical schools', *IslamOnline.net*, 6 April 2007. Online. Available at www.onislam.net/english/health-and-science/faith-and-the-sciences/429558-medieval-islamic-hospitals-and-medical-schools.html?the_Sciences= (accessed 25 April 2013).

28 Noushirawy, A.R. (2004) 'The Islamic Bimaristans of the Middle Ages', Arabic translation by Badra, M. Kh., *The Arab Legacy Bulletin*, 21(4): 202.

29 Kaf-Al-Ghazal, Sharif (2007) *The Origin of Bimaristans (Hospitals) in Islamic Medical History*, Manchester, U.K.: Foundation for Science Technology and Civilization. Online. Available at www.muslimheritage.com/uploads/The_Origin_of_Bilaristans_in_Islamic_Medical_History.pdf (accessed 20 July 2014). Also see Bey, Isa A. (1939) *The History of Bimaristans in Islam*, Damascus: 20–40.

30 Thompson and Goldin (1975): 153.

31 Ibid.: 8.

32 Gillet, Mary C. (2002) *The Army Medical Department: 1775–1818*, Honolulu, HI: University Press of the Pacific. Also see Anon. (2012) 'The History of Medicine: The Revolutionary War,' *International Wellness Directory*. Online. Available at www.mnwelldir.org/docs/history/history02.htm (accessed 14 July 2014).

33 Thompson and Goldin (1975): 155.

34 Devine, Shauna (2014) *Learning from the Wounded: The Civil War and the Rise of American Medical Science*, Chapel Hill, NC: University of North Carolina Press.

35 Goldin, Grace (1994) *Work of Mercy*, Erin, Ontario: The Boston Mills, 185. Also see Schroeder-Lein, Glenna R. (1994) *Confederate Hospitals on the Move*, Columbia, SC: University of South Carolina Press.

36 Verderber, Stephen (2014) 'Exploring healthcare through the medium of film: motives and techniques', *International Journal of Architectural Research (Archnet-IJAR)*, 8(1): 29–49.

37 Nightingale, Florence (1859) *Notes on Nursing: What It Is and What It Is Not*, Glasgow and London: Blackie & Son. Also see Nightingale, Florence (1859) *Notes on Hospitals*, London: Parker & Son.

38 Adams, George (1952) *Doctors in Blue: The Medical History of the Union Army in the Civil War*, New York: Henry Schuman.

39 Johnson, Charles (1874) 'The Regimental Hospital', *The Civil War*. Online. Available at www.civilwarhome.com/regimentalhospital.html (accessed 14 May 2013).

40 Wilbur, C. Keith (1998) *Civil War Medicine 1861–1865*, Old Saybrook, CT: The Globe Pequot.

41 Price, Angel (2010) 'Whitman's "drum taps" and Washington's Civil War hospitals', *Whitman's Wartime Washington*. Online. Available at www.civilwarhome.com/fieldhospitals.html (accessed 27 April 2013).

42 Schroeder-Lein (1994): 101.

43 Devine (2014): 74.

44 Manning, M.M., Hawk, Alan, Calhoun, Jason, and Anderson, Rommey (2009) 'Treatment of war wounds: a historical overview', *Clinical Orthopedics and Related Research*, 467(8): 2168–2191.

45 Manning, et al. (2009): 2169.

46 Davis, William C. and Wiley, Bell I. (eds.) (1981) 'Caring for the men: the history of Civil War medicine', *In The Image of War: 1861–1865, Volume V*, Washington, D.C.: The National Historical Society. Online. Available at www.civilwarhome.com/medicinehistory.html (accessed 14 May 2013).

47 Schroeder-Lein (1994): 41.

48 Devine (2014): 85.

49 Marble, Sanders (2012) *Meatball Surgery and Hip-Pocket Hospitals: The Origins, Evolution and Demise of the M.A.S.H.*, Washington, D.C.: Office of Medical History, U.S. Army Medical Command: 1–72.

50 Ibid.: 34.

51 Ginn, Richard V. (1997) *The History of the U.S. Army Medical Service Corps*, Washington, D.C.: Office of the Surgeon General and Center for Military History.

52 Dumas, Samuel (1923) *Losses of Life Caused by War*, Oxford, U.K.: Oxford University Press.

53 United States Army Medical Department (1916) *Manual for the Medical Department. United States Army*, Washington: General Printing Office. Online. Available at http://collections.nlm.nih.gov/catalog/nlm:nlmuid-14210890R-bk (accessed 12 May 2013).

54 Ginn (1997): 44.

55 United States Army Medical Department (1916): 42–54.

56 Stokesbury, James (1980) *A Short History of World War II*, New York: William Morrow.

57 Cowdrey, Albert (1994) *Fighting for Life: American Military Medicine in World War II*, Toronto: The Free Press.

58 Bingham, Lt. Col. Harral A. (1969) *Greater Flexibility for Combat Zone Hospitals*, Carlisle Barracks, PA: U.S. Army War College, 3 March, 1–71.

59 Cowdrey (1994): 77.

60 Greenwood, John T. (1947) 'Portable surgical hospitals', *Office of Medical History*, Washington, D.C.: Office of the Surgeon General, U.S. Army Headquarters. Online. Available at http://history.amedd.

army.mil/booksdocs/wwii/surgicalhosp/PortableSurgicalHospitals.html (accessed 25 May 2013).

61 Ibid.: 4.

62 Ibid.: 5.

63 Cowdrey (1994): 78.

64 Marble (2012): 56.

65 Greenwood (1947): 5.

66 Fishbein, Morris (1945) *Doctors at War*, New York: E.P. Dutton & Company.

67 Apel, Otto F. and Apel, Pat (1998) *M.A.S.H: An Army Surgeon in Korea*, Lexington, KY: University of Kentucky Press.

68 Ibid.: 14.

69 Department of the Army (1959) *Field Manual 8–10: Medical Service—Theatre of Operations*, 3 November, Washington, D.C.: Department of the Army Headquarters.

70 U.S. War Department (1945) *Field Manual 8–5: Medical Department Units of a Theatre of Operations*, Washington, D.C.: U.S. Government Printing Office, 31 May. The three CZ transportables in the AMEDD inventory as of 1950 were the Evacuation Hospital (EH), the Convalescent Hospital (CH), and the PSH. The EH was a semi-mobile 400 to 500-bed facility that was erectable in four to six hours and meant for far forward, front line definitive treatment and to prepare casualties for evacuation to base hospitals. Services there consisted of triage, intake, ward, pharmacy, laboratory and X-ray functions. The CH was designed for care and observation and for rehabilitation cases that were to be returned to duty (RTD) within 120 to 180 days, or relocation to an EH. Its standard capacity was 3,000 patients, although bed capacity was expandable to 5,000 beds if required, but this was only to be sustainable for a short duration of time. Services consisted of patient administration (PAD), surgery, ENT (ear, eye, nose and throat), orthopedic, laboratory, dental, X-ray and pharmacy. Lastly, the PSH provided definitive care for seriously wounded casualties where delay due to further transport would be fatal. The PSH provided temporary hospitalization for isolated combat units prior to establishment of more comprehensive facilities. Equipped with portable U-packs to last an estimated ten days, loaded packs were not to exceed forty pounds, bringing their total weight to approximately 1,000 pounds.

71 Marble (2012): 14.

72 Woodward, Capt. Scott C. (2003) 'The AMSUS history of medicine Assay Award: the story of the Mobile Army Surgical Hospital', *Military Medicine*, 168(7): 503–513.

73 Jones, Charles (1955) 'Part V: Medical Corps', *Combat Support in Korea*. Online. Available at www.history.army.mil/books/korea/22_1_5.htm (accessed 27 May 2013).

74 Terhune, Lea (2006) 'U.S. Army converts last Mobile Army Surgical Hospital', *IIP Digital*, 16 October. Online. Available at http://iipdigital.usembassy.gov/st/english/article/2006/10/20061016152704mlenuhret0.346615.html#axzz3Zx1LwdCm (accessed 12 July 2014).

75 Ibid.: 3.

76 OTSG History Division (1998) '8076th MASH history', *Korean War Project*. Online. Available at http://the45thsurg.freeservers.com/8076th_MASH.html (accessed 26 May 2012).

77 Bingham (1969): 64–71.

78 Winchester, James H. (1967) 'The medical miracles in South Vietnam', *Popular Science*, July: 70–73. Online. Available at www.vietnam.ttu.edu/virtualarchive/items.php?item=2250111039 (accessed 14 May 2013).

79 Ginn (1997): 312.

80 Verderber, Stephen and Fine, David J. (2000) *Healthcare Architecture in an Era of Radical Transformation*, New Haven, CT: Yale University Press, 112.

81 Ginn (1997): 313.

82 Whelan, T.J. (1975) 'Surgical lessons learned and relearned in Vietnam', *Surgery Annals*, 7(1): 1–23.

83 Ginn (1997): 313.

84 Taylor, S.F., Kopchinski, B.J., Schreiber, M.A. and Singleton, L. (2000) 'Trauma patient outcome in an Army deployable medical systems environment compared with a medical center', *Military Medicine*, 165(11): 867–869.

85 Ross, James W. (1990) *Study of Vehicle Transportation Requirements for Hospitals at the Corps Level*, Montgomery, AL: Air University, Maxwell Air Force Base, 50–51.

86 Yawitz, Aubrey A. (1976) *Medical Unit, Self-Contained, Transportable Non-Medical Components (MUST-NMC): A System Assessment Technical Memorandum, System Assessment No. 8*, St. Louis, MO: U.S. Army Troop Support Command.

87 Department of the Army (1990) *Training Circular 8–13: Deployable Medical Systems—Tactics, Techniques and Procedures*, Washington, D.C.: Headquarters, Department of the Army. Also see Department of the Army and Air Force (1986) *Technical Manual 10-5411-200-14: Operator, Organizational, Direct Support and General Support Maintenance for Shelter, Tactical, Expandable, Two-Sided*, Washington, D.C.: Department of the Army and Air Force.

88 Horn, William, Brown, Douglas, Colaianni, Albert, Slyman, George, and Lindstrom, Kenneth (1987) *Improving the Army's Field Medical Capability, Volume 1—Report AR602R1*, Bethesda, MD: Logistics Management Institute.

89 Ibid.: 17–22.

90 Ginn (1997): 135.

91 Montgomery, Nancy (2004) '31st CSH care for servicemembers, Iraqis shattered by war injuries', *Stars and Stripes*, 9 May. Online. Available at www.stripes.com/news/31st-csh-care-for-servicemembers-iraqis-shattered-by-war.html (accessed 11 June 2014).

92 Department of the Army (1997) *Field Manual 8-10-25: Employment of Forward Surgical Teams—Tactics, Techniques and Procedures*, Washington, D.C.: Headquarters, Department of the Army.

93 Gawande, Atul (2004) 'Casualties of war—military care for the wounded from Iraq and Afghanistan', *New England Journal of Medicine*, 351(24): 2471–2475.

94 Sherry, et al. (2003): 3. World War I was characterized by a high incidence of gangrene in the trenches. Motorized ambulances were first introduced, and Dakin's solution was first used as an antiseptic. In World War II (1939–1945) wounds were fully debrided and left open, and whole blood transfusions were first used at the battlefront. Antibiotics and intramedullary nailing of the femur were practiced for the first time, and air evacuation was first introduced. During the Korean conflict (1950–1953) MASH units were field-tested and modified, along with the first helicopter air transport over rough terrain and relatively longer distances, vascular repair in limb injuries, advancements in the use of antibiotics, the treatment of early renal failure, and treatment with hemodialysis. In the Vietnam War (1964–1975) further advancements in air evacuation were developed along with laboratory backup in the field, and the first use of the artificial kidney. In the Iraq War (2003–2013) the extensive use of air evacuation was further refined.

95 Verderber, Stephen (2010) *Innovations in Hospital Architecture*, London: Routledge, 32.

96 U.S. War Department (1945).

97 Crowley, Roger (2009) *Empires of the Sea: The Siege of Malta, the Battle of Lepanto, and the Contest for the Center of the World*, New York: Random House.

98 Verderber (2010): 33.

99 Verderber (2010): 34. From 1990 to the present, throughout the Iraq War and in Afghanistan, U.S. forces deployed military infirmary ambulances and medical supply vehicles.

100 U.S. War Department (1945).

101 McGinnis, K.L. and Judge, T. (2006) *Air Medicine: Accessing the Future of Health Care*, Alexandria, VA: Foundation for Air-Medical Research and Education.

102 Marble (2012).

103 Anon. (2013) 'Armbruster tents for U.S. defense', *Armbruster Corporation*. Online. Available at www.armbrustertentmaker.com/tents.html (accessed 14 June 2014).

104 Anon. (1884) 'New inventions: Doecker's patient portable hospitals', *The London Medical Record*, Article 3166, 15 September 419. Not many portable 'huts' were sold. But by the late nineteenth century this alternative to the rising cost of stationary hospitals in the non-military sector, in emergencies, was now beginning to be taken seriously by hospital superintendents.

105 John, Richard R. (2013) 'How the Post Office made America', *New York Times*, 8 February. Online. Available at www.nytimes.com/2013/02/09/opinion/how-the-post-office-made-america.html (accessed 1 October 2014). For example, if a forest fire destroyed a town's municipal water supply, perhaps a week would pass before emergency aid could be sent in from neighboring towns.

106 Smith, Thomas (1837) *The Origin and History of Missions*, Boston: Kendal. Some missions lasted years, but this often required months of preparation.

107 Dunant, Henry (1911) *The Origin of the Red Cross: Un Souvenier de Solferino*, 2009 Edition, Whitefish, MT: Kessinger Publishing. The standard emblem would be a red cross on a white background. In 1864, the Geneva Convention was adopted, making it compulsory for all armies to care for all casualties regardless of what side they are on. Since then, this has been made a requirement in modern humanitarian aid law, enshrined in the 1949 Geneva Convention and in two additional manifestos (1977 and 2006).

108 Anon. (2012) *Founding and Early Years of the ICRC (1863–1914)*, Geneva: International Committee of the Red Cross. Online. Available at www.icrc.org/eng/who-we-are/history/founding/overview-section-founding.htm (accessed 14 May 2014).

109 Anon. (2014) 'Red Cross retrospective: the 1906 San Francisco earthquake', *American Red Cross*. Online. Available at www.redcross.org/news/article/Red-Cross-Retrospective-The-1906-San-Francisco-Earthquake (accessed 21 July 2014). Also see Bronson, William (1996) *The Earth Shook, The Sky Burned*, San Francisco: Chronicle Books. Also Gibson, Christine (2006) 'Our 10 greatest natural disasters', *American Heritage*, August/September: 24–36. By 2014, the American Red Cross supplied nearly 40 percent of the nation's blood, provided extensive domestic and international humanitarian aid, and as a NGO, continued to rely entirely on private donations.

110 Joffe-Walt, Chana (2012) 'The cost of free donuts: 70 years of regret', *This American Life*, Washington, D.C.: National Public Radio. Online. Available at www.npr.org/blogs/money/2012/07/13/156737801/the-cost-of-free-donuts.html (accessed 4 February 2013).

111 Moser Jones, Marian (2012) *The American Red Cross from Clara Barton to the New Deal*, Baltimore: Johns Hopkins University Press.

112 Anderson, James (2011) *Public Policymaking*, Seventh Edition, Boston: Wadsworth, Cengage Learning. Also see Anon. (2007) 'A public health emergency from the perspective of the U.S. NDMS', *National Defense Medical System*. Online. Available at www.semp.us/publications/biot_reader.php?BiotID=417.html (accessed 12 December 2013).

113 Ibid.: 4.

114 Verderber, Stephen (2009) *Delirious New Orleans: Manifesto for an Extraordinary American City*, Austin: University of Texas Press. Also see Verderber, Stephen (2008) 'Evidence-based design for healthcare in post-Katrina New Orleans: current dilemma', *Health Environments Research and Design Journal*, 1(2): 71–79. Also Verderber, Stephen (2008) 'Emergency housing in the aftermath of Hurricane Katrina: an assessment of the FEMA travel trailer program', *Journal of Housing and the Built Environment*, 23(4): 367–381.

115 Dunlop, A.L., Isakov, A.P., Compton, M.T., White, M., Nassery, H., Frank, E. and Glanz, K. (2007) 'Medical outreach following a remote disaster: lessons learned from Hurricane Katrina', *American Journal of Disaster Medicine*, 2(3): 121–132.
116 Verderber, Stephen (2005) *Compassion in Architecture: Evidence-Based Design for Health*, Lafayette, LA: The Center for Louisiana Studies. In the mid-1950s, the State of Louisiana Department of Health owned six mobile vehicular units, providing TB testing, polio screening, and immunizations.
117 Anon. (2010) 'Medical Coaches: history'. *Medical Coaches, Inc.* Online. Available at www.medcoach.com/company/history.html (accessed 12 December 2013).
118 Santana, Julieta (2005) 'Going out to the community: mobile clinics bring health care to families of migrant farmworkers', *Mobile Health Clinics Association*. Online. Available at www.mobilehca.org/featured.html (accessed 12 June 2014).
119 Ibid.: 289.
120 Ibid.: 290.
121 Verderber and Fine (2000): 289.
122 Anon. (2012) 'Medcoach: history', *Medcoach Corporation*. Online. Available at www.medcoach.com/company/history.html (accessed 10 July 2014).
123 Brooks, Janet (2006) 'MED-1: hospital on wheels', *Canadian Medical Association Journal*, 175(6): 569. Also see Riddle, Eric R. (2009) *Watershed: Service in the Wake of Disaster*, Bloomington, IN: AuthorHouse, 97; also James Spring (2014) 'Carolinas MED-1: a mobile hospital for disasters, hospital outages, community and sporting events', *Carolinas HealthCare System*. Online. Available at www.carolinashealthcare.org/carolinas-med-1 (accessed 10 August 2014).
124 What began in 1997 as Charlotte-Mecklenburg County's *Advanced Local Emergency Response Team* (ALERT) evolved into a multi-agency first response team. In 2000, under the leadership of Dr. Tom Blackwell, it shifted from a singular emphasis on mass casualty, treatment, transport, and quarantine capabilities to the provision of mobile, autonomous units deployed quickly to a disaster site to be tethered to provide auxiliary support in lieu of or in tandem with local stationary healthcare facilities. In 2003, with a $1.85 million grant from the U.S. Department of Homeland Security, the Carolinas MED-1 project began construction of two truck-based mobile response units, whose function was to provide first response healthcare in the aftermath of acts of terrorism and major disasters, to facilitate rural populations' access to healthcare, and to aid in disaster strike zones afflicted with damaged infrastructure.
125 Williams, George (2011) 'History of MED-1', *MED-1 Partners*. Online. Available at www.med-1partners.com/about/history/html (accessed 12 July 2014). In Waveland, Mississippi, the 102-bed Hancock County Medical Center was obliterated, with six inches of mud in its *second-floor* operating room. MED-1 took up residence in the parking lot of a nearby K-Mart for a seven-week deployment as the sole medical facility in a three-county area. It soon was receiving 350 patients daily, hosted multiple surgeries, and treating severe cases including heat attacks, strokes, and lung disease.
126 Anon. (2011) 'MED-1 deployments', *MED-1 Partners*. Online. Available at www.med-1partners.com/about/deployments/html (accessed 12 July 2014). In New Orleans, when the U.S. Army Corps of Engineers' federal levee system failed in twenty-four locations, LSUHSC's Charity Hospital was shuttered and the local healthcare network left in shambles. The MED-1 mobile unit was deployed for a second time, during the height of the Mardi Gras season. More than 550 patients were treated, and its 60-bed ward provided backup to meet surge needs. A mobile clinic typically costs at least $500,000 to purchase and operate in the first year and approximately $250,000 to staff each year thereafter. Often, partnerships are set up with a nearby hospital for referrals or more intensive diagnosis and treatment. In terms of spatial amenity, a unit may have at least one intake/interview station, unisex restroom, a nurses charting area, two sinks, one bathroom, refrigerator(s), built-in storage cabinets, one or more general examination areas each with an exam table, fold-down chairs, tabletop work areas, telecommunications equipment, a space for dental care, and a power generator. Recent innovations include Medcoach's 2011 mobile unit with twin expandable pop-out components. Drawbacks of nomadic clinics include their small windows and restrictive views to the outdoors, their frequently tight, narrow circulation spaces, small rooms, and minimal storage space. Pullout awnings, pop-out and pop-up elements, and interesting color palettes have been proven to yield more commodious space, and a more aesthetically attractive, less spatially confining interior environment.
127 Burnham, Kelly (1951) *The Prefabrication of Houses*, London: Chapman & Hall/Cambridge, MA: MIT Press/New York: Wiley.
128 Hunter, Rebecca (2012) *Mail Order Houses: Sears Homes and Other Kit Houses*, Westminster, MD: Shire USA. After World War II, acute housing shortages required quickly built prefabrication technologies and this accounts for why architects in Japan, and Europe became leaders.
129 National Research Council of the National Academies (2009) *Advancing the Competiveness and Efficiency of the U.S. Construction Industry*, Washington, D.C.: The National Academies Press.
130 Levinson, Marc (2006) *The Box: How the Shipping Container Made the World Smaller and the World Economy Bigger*, Princeton, NJ: Princeton University Press.
131 Ibid.: 44.
132 Craven, Jackie (2008) 'Architecture for Humanity: building a HIV/AIDS clinic for Africa,' *Architecture: About*. Online. Available at http://architecture.about.com/cs/socialconcerns/a/humanity_3.htm (accessed 5 February 2014).

133 Anon. (2008) 'OUTREACH: mobile Health clinics to combat HIV/AIDS in Sub-Saharan Africa', *Worldchanging*. Online. Available at http://openarchitecturenetwork.org/node/503 (accessed 12 June 2014).
134 Verderber, Stephen (2003) 'Architecture for health: an international perspective', *The Journal of Architecture*, 8(3): 281–302.
135 Neder, Federico (2008) *Fuller Houses: R-Buckminster Fuller's Dymaxion Dwellings and Other Domestic Architecture*, Zürich: Lars Muller.
136 Sergeant, John (1984) *Frank Lloyd Wright's Usonian Houses: The Case for Organic Architecture*, New York: Whitney Library of Design.
137 Brynjolfsson, Erik and McAfee, Andrew (2012) *Race against the Machine: How the Digital Revolution is Accelerating Innovation, Driving Productivity, and Irreversibly Transforming Employment and the Economy*, Richmond, VA: Digital Frontier Press.
138 Montgomery (2004): 4.
139 Barger, James (2009) *A Brief History of the Army Medical Department*, Unpublished Report, Fort Sam Houston, TX: U.S. Army Medical Department. The history of portables for healthcare in the military remains underdocumented.
140 Rowland, Ingrid D. (ed.) (2001) *Vitruvius: Ten Books on Architecture*, Cambridge, U.K.: Cambridge University Press.

3 Offsite

1 Terzich, Alexander (2012) 'Atlantic Yards high-rise modular', Keynote Lecture, *Offsite: Theory and Practice of Architectural Production*, Association of Collegiate Schools of Architecture Fall Conference, Philadelphia, September 2012.
2 Steadman, Philip (2014) *Building Types and Built Forms*, Leicester: Troubadour Publishing, Ltd.
3 Silver, Christopher (2007) *Renkioi: Brunel's Forgotten Crimean War Hospital*, London: Valonia Press. Also see Shepard, John A. (1991) *The Crimean Doctors: A History of the British Medical Services in the Crimean War, Volumes 1 and 2*, Liverpool: University of Liverpool Press. Also see Thompson, John and Goldin, Grace (1975): Chapters 3 and 4, and Silver, Christopher (2004) 'Renkioi: a forgotten Crimean War hospital and its significance', *Vesalius*, 10(2): 55–60.
4 Verderber and Fine (2000): Chapters 4 and 6.
5 Anderson, Mark and Anderson, Peter (2007) *Prefab Prototypes*, New York: Princeton Architectural Press.
6 Gössel, Peter (2014) *PreFab Houses*, Berlin: Taschen.
7 Woudhuysen, John (2004) *Why is Construction so Backward*? London: Academy Press.
8 Willett, Megan (2013) 'Japan's experimental "micro apartments" look pretty dilapidated after 41 years', *Business Insider*, 2 October. Online. Available at www.businessinsider.com/kisho-kurokawas-nakagin-capsule-tower-2013-10?op.html (accessed 10 September 2014).
9 Wheeler, Carolynn (2012) 'World's tallest tower plan raises eyebrows', *The Globe and Mail*, 28 September, B-24. Also see Ephgrave, Oliver (2012) 'Engineer to retire if China achieves super-quick tower', *Design Middle East*, 16 July. Online. Available at www.Designmena.com.html (accessed 12 August 2014). The builder had, prior, completed only two towers, neither over thirty floors. A tower of such height normally requires an enormous concrete and steel structural frame and a lengthy period of time for its settlement. Plus, code officials asserted the lack of structural stiffness and proper elasticity would make the tower structurally unsound. Other problems cited were improper egress, soil subsidence issues, and 'elevator crawl' as the floor to elevator ratio was deemed unsustainable.
10 Chaban, Mark (2013) 'Barclays at 1: taking the next step', *New York Daily News*, 22 September. Online. Available at www.nydailynews.com/new-york/brooklyn/building-barclays-article-1.1461562 (accessed 10 September 2014).
11 Post, Nadine M. (2014) 'Skanska, Forest City Ratner sue each other over tallest modular building-to-be', *Architectural Record*, 3 September. Online. Available at www.archrecord.construction.com/news/2014/09/140903-Skanska-Forest-City-Ratner-Sue-Each-Other-Over160-Tallest-Modular-Building-To-Be.asp?WT.mc_id=rss_archrecord (accessed 5 September 2014).
12 Anon. (2014) 'Products overview', *Western Shelter Corporation*. Online. Available at www.westernshelter.com/products/commercial/complexed-shelter-systems.html (accessed 3 March 2014).
13 Verderber, Stephen (2008) *Journal of Housing and the Built Environment*, 367–381.
14 Anon. (2014) 'Fast Response Shelter Systems', *STAR-TIDES Corporation*. Online. Available at http://startides.net/resource/dd-frb-fst-response-buildings-disaster-response-building (accessed 14 March 2014).
15 Anon. (2012) 'Yasutaka Yoshimura Architects: ex container project, anywhere in Japan', *Designboom Architecture*, 4 May. Online. Available at www.designboom.com/architecture/yasutaka-yoshimura-architects-ex-container/ (accessed 18 August 2014).
16 British Antarctic Survey (2005) 'Futuristic design wins competition for new Antarctic research station', *British Antarctic Survey*. Online. Available at www.antarctica.ac.uk/press/press_releases/press_release.php?id=63 (accessed 24 August 2014).
17 Slavid, Ruth (2012) 'Halley VI Antarctic Research Station by Hugh Broughton Architects, Brunt Ice Shelf, Antarctica', *The Architectural Review*, July. Online. Available at www.architectural-review.com/essays/halley-vi-antarctic-research-station-by-hugh-broughton-architects-brunt-ice-self-antarctica/8603050.article (accessed 10 September 2014). Also see Bloom, Daniel (2010) 'British scientists stranded in freezing Antarctic research station when power failed as

temperatures hit a record low of –55C', *The Daily Mail*, 8 August. Online. Available at www.dailymail.co.uk/news/article-2719796/British-scientists-stranded-freezing-Antarctic.html (accessed 10 September 2014).

18 Herbert, Gilbert (1978) *Pioneers of Prefabrication: The British Contribution in the Nineteenth Century*, Baltimore: Johns Hopkins University Press. Also see Vale, Brenda (1995) *Prefabs: A History of the UK Temporary Housing Programme*, London and New York: Spon Press; and White, R.B. (1965) *Prefabrication: A History of its Development in Britain*, London: HMSO.

19 Bogardus, James, Badger, Daniel D. and Thompson, John W. (1970) *The Origins of Cast Iron Architecture in America*, New York: Da Capo Press.

20 Sears, Roebuck (1991) *Small Houses of the Twenties: The Sears, Roebuck 1926 House Catalogue*, New York: Dover Publications.

21 Anon. (2009) 'Taking care of business', *Dwell*, 12(2): 100.

22 Smith, Ryan E. (2010) *Prefab Architecture: A Guide to Modular Design and Construction*, New York: Wiley.

23 Le Corbusier (1935) *Aircraft: The New Vision*, New York: The Studio Publications.

24 Benton, Timothy and Benton, Charlotte (1975) *Form and Function: A Source Book of the History of Architecture and Design 1890–1939*, London: Crosby Lockwood Staples.

25 McCoy, Esther (1977) *Case Study Houses: 1945–1962*, Santa Monica: Hennessey & Ingalls. Also see Smith, Elizabeth A.T. (1998) *Blueprints for Modern Living: History and Legacy of the Case Study Houses*, New York: Museum of Contemporary Art, and Smith, Elizabeth A.T. (2009) *Case Study Houses*, Koln: Taschen.

26 Cherner, Norman (1957) *Fabricating Houses from Component Parts: How to Build a House for $6000*, New York: Reinhold.

27 Herbert, Gilbert (1947) 'House in "industry": a system for the manufacture of industrialized building elements', *Arts and Architecture*, 644(11): 3–28. Also see Herbert, Gilbert (1959) *The Synthetic Vision of Walter Gropius*, Johannesburg: Witwatersrand University, and Gropius, Walter (1961) 'True architectural goals yet to be realized', *Architectural Record*, 129(6): 147–152.

28 Neder, Federico (2008) *Fuller Houses: R. Buckminster Fuller's Dymaxion House and Other Domestic Adventures*, Zurich: Lars Muller.

29 Sergeant, John (1984) *Frank Lloyd Wright's Usonian Houses: Designs for Moderate Cost One-Family Homes*, New York: Watson-Guptill.

30 Fetters, Thomas T. and Kohler, Vincent (2006) *The Lustron Home: The History of a Postwar Prefabricated Housing Experiment*, Jefferson, NC: McFarland & Company. Also see Dieta, A.G.H. and Cutler, Laurence S. (eds.) (1971) *Industrialized Building Systems for Housing*, Cambridge, MA: MIT Press.

31 Knerr, Douglas (2004) *Suburban Steel: The Magnificent Failure of the Lustron Corporation, 1945–1951*, Columbus, OH: Ohio State University Press.

32 Herbert, Gilbert (1984) *The Dream of the Factory-Made House: Walter Gropius and Konrad Wachsmann*, Cambridge, MA: MIT Press.

33 Adamson, Marty and Braun, Ernest (eds.) (2002) *Eichler/Modernism Rebuilds the American Dream*, Salt Lake City: Gibbs-Smith. Also see Ditto, Jerry (1995) *Eichler Homes: Design for Living*, San Francisco: Chronicle Books.

34 Anderson and Anderson (2007): 10.

35 Kieran, Stephen and Timberlake, James (2004) *Refabricating Architecture*, New York: McGraw-Hill.

36 Ibid.: 44.

37 Ibid.: 7.

38 Le Corbusier (1923) *Towards a New Architecture*, 1985 Edition, Mineola, NY: Dover Architecture.

39 Kieran and Timberlake (2004): 11.

40 Ibid.: 18.

41 Woudheysen (2004): 44.

42 Gann, David M. (1996) 'Construction as a manufacturing process? Similarities and differences between industrialized housing and car production in Japan', *Construction Management and Economics*, 14(5): 437–450.

43 Kieran and Timberlake (2004): 42.

44 Ibid.: 113.

45 Kensek, Karen and Noble, Douglas (2014) *Building Information Modeling: BIM in Current and Future Practice*, New York: Wiley.

46 Kieran and Timberlake (2004): 120.

47 Verderber and Fine (2000): 109.

48 Ibid.: 112. A referral system was set up where patients were referred from rural public health units (Type 1) to inpatient hospitals for more intensive care (Type 4). Type 4 facilities were 25,000 square feet or larger. Type 1 public health units were the foundation of the network. Ten riverboats were purchased to transport staff to the various clinic sites. The modular units could be repaired with a screwdriver, and building materials, components, and connections were designed and built to mitigate infestation from insects. Each unit was equipped with an emergency power generator. The main impediment was staff recruitment for the forty-two facilities and to this day staffing is a serious challenge in remote, extreme locales.

49 Ibid.: 114.

50 Anon. (2014) 'Mobile space frontier', *Sankyo Frontier Corporation, Ltd.* Online. Available at www.sankyofrontier.com/eng/ (accessed 12 September 2014).

51 Verderber and Fine (2000): Chapter 6.

52 Trinkoff, Alison M., Geiger-Brown, Jeanne M., Caruso, Claire C., Lipscomb, Jane A., Johantgen, Meg, Nelson, Audrey L., Sattler, Barbara A., and Selby, Victoria L. (2008) *Patient Safety and Quality: An Evidence-Based Handbook for Nurses*, Rockville MD: Agency for Healthcare Research and Quality. In Chapter 39, 'Personal Safety for Nurses,' recent research is reported on the trials and tribulations of

nursing staff in the lifting and transferring of obese patients, and it is a call for ergonomically designed devices to ameliorate the high rate of nurses' workplace injuries.

53 Anon. (2014) *Modular Services Company*. Online. Available at www.modularservices.com (accessed 12 April 2014).

54 Anon. (2009) 'Eggrock enters hospital construction market with order for 500 pre-built bathroom pods for large hospital expansion', *Business Wire*, August. Online. Available at www.businesswire.com/news/home/20090505006207/en/Eggrock-enters-hospital-construction-market-order-500#.VVJS6k3QNaQ (accessed 12 September 2014).

55 Anon. (2014) 'Eggrock modular solutions: overview', *Eggrock Modular Solutions*. Online. Available at www.eggrock.com (accessed 27 June 2014). Units are delivered to the site, hoisted by crane then slid in from the side (in concrete buildings) or dropped in from above (in timber framed buildings). The module is positioned a few feet from its final position while plumbing risers and sheetrocking is completed, then it is slid into its final position using air casters. Protective wrapping is then removed and the door latch is secured. Then all remaining sheetrocking (along with adjacent spaces) occurs and permanent connections are made with the floors above and below.

56 Anon. (2013) 'New cancer center to open April 1 at Swedish/Edmonds: outpatient facility to provide medical oncology infusion services close to home', *Swedish Health Network*. Online. Available at www.swedish.org/about/blog/march-2013/new-cancer-center-to-open-april-1-swedish-edmonds (accessed 25 June 2014).

57 Author's interview with Ryan Hullinger and Farah Rahman, of NBBJ, Columbus, Ohio, in August 2014. In this interview, they recounted their firm's experience as the lead A/E team for the two prefab hospital projects, both located in Ohio, featured in this chapter.

58 Wartenberg, Steve (2013) 'Riverside's new neuro combines function, form', *Columbus Dispatch*, 21 July. Online. Available at www.dispatch.com/content/stories/business/2013/07/21/mastered-design.html (accessed 21 June 2014).

59 Brzezinski, Robert (2014) *HIPAA Privacy and Security Compliance Simplified: Practical Guide for Healthcare Providers and Practice Managers*, 2014 Edition, North Charleston, SC: Create Space Independent Publishing Platform.

60 Henry J. Kaiser Family Foundation (2013) *Summary of the Affordable Care Act*, Menlo Park, CA: The Henry J. Kaiser Family Foundation. Online. Available at http://kff.org/health-reform/fact-sheet/summary-of-the-affordable-care-act/ (accessed 12 September 2104).

61 Goldman, Marc (2011) 'Landscape information modeling', *Design Intelligence*, 3 May. Online. Available at www.di.net/articles/landscape_information_modeling/ (accessed 1 September 2014).

62 Author's interview with Hullinger and Rahman (2014).

63 Ibid. The federal government remains lukewarm towards prefab modularity for its healthcare facilities and this stance is fundamentally tied, politically, to the way government projects are bid and awarded. NBBJ has had no success thus far in convincing the U.S. Department of Veterans Affairs, for instance, to adopt prefab to any meaningful degree because subcontractors are unwilling to take on the perceived risk, unless financially incentivized to do so.

64 Hanley, William and Mirviss, Laura (2013) 'nARCHITECTS wins NYC micro-unit competition', *Architectural Record*, 22 January. Online. Available at http://archrecord.construction.com/news/2013/01/130122-nArchitects-Wins-NYC-Micro-unit-Competition.asp (accessed 30 July 2014).

65 Webb, Mick (2009) 'Shipping container to solar powered restaurant in 90 seconds? Meet the Muvbox portable restaurant', *Gizmag*, 7 July. Online. Available at www.gizmag.com/muv-box-portable-restaurant/12162/ (accessed 13 August 2014).

66 Kieran and Timberlake (2004): 112.

67 Illman, James (2013) 'Basildon builds prefab ward to mitigate winter A&E challenge', *Health Services Journal*, 12 July. Online. Available at www.hsj.co.uk/hsj-local/acute-trusts/basildon-and-thurrock-university-hospitals-nhs-foundation-trust/basildon-builds-prefab-ward-to-mitigate-winter-ae-challenge/5061058.article (accessed 29 August 2014).

68 Anon. (2012) 'm-ch: micro compact home', *openarchitecturenetwork.org*. Online. Available at http://openarchitecturenetwork.org/node/753 (accessed 15 December 2013).

69 Anon. (2012) 'Push button house by Adam Kalkin', *Treehugger.com*. Online. Available at www.treehugger.com/sustainable-product-design/push-button-house-by-adam-kalkin.html (accessed 10 December 2013).

70 Anon. (2014) 'Shipping container is transformed into a sauna by Castor Canadensis', *Designboom*. Online. Available at www.designboom.com/architecture/shipping-container-is-transformed-into-a-sauna-by-castor-canadensis/ (accessed 10 May 2014).

71 Anon. (2013) 'Das Park Hotel—Berne Park', *Go Unusual.com*. Online. Available at www.unusualhotelsoftheworld.com/dasparkhotel (accessed 12 May 2014).

72 Anon. (2010) 'Fincube: new sustainable modular dwelling from Studio Aisslinger', *Designcurial*, 1 April. Online. Available at www.designcurial.com/news/fincube-new-sustainable-modular-dwelling-from-studio-aisslinger (accessed 22 May 2014).

73 Kotnik, June (2013) *New Container Architecture: Design and Sustainability*, Barcelona: Links International. Also see Buchmeier, M., Slawik, H., Tinney, S., and Bergman, J. (eds.) (2010) *Container Atlas: A Practical Guide to Container Architecture*. Berlin: Gestalten. For additional examples of adapted containers, see the *busyboo.com* archives, where offbeat, experimental structures (although not healthcare facilities) are presented, i.e. homeless shelters, multi-level office buildings, dormitories, and restaurants.

74 Facility Management Institute (2012) *Modularization and Prefabrication—Role Development and Evolution*, Raleigh, NC: FMI

Management Consulting. Online. Available at www.fminet.com/media/pdf/article/ModularizationandPrefab_Trends2012.pdf (accessed 17 March 2014).

75 Kovacs-Silvis, Jennifer (2013) 'Putting the pieces together: a Q&A with Tom Hardiman, Executive Vice President, Modular Building Institute', *Healthcare Design*, 11(3): 46–47. Online. Available at www.healthcaredesignmagazine.com/article/modular-building-institute-qa-putting-pieces-together (accessed 5 April 2013). Also see Poechmann, Lee (2012) 'Promising prefabrication', *Healthcare Design*, 10(12): 29–32. Online. Available at www.healthcaredesignmagazine.com/blogs/lee-poechmann/promising-prefabrication (accessed 15 March 2013) and Horwitz-Bennett, Barbara (2009) 'High marks for modular', *Healthcare Design*, 9(12): 32–34. Online. Available at www.healthcaredesignmagazine.com/article/high-marks-modular (accessed 15 March 2013).

76 Anon. (2010) 'Christian Susana designs a futuristic two-piece caravan', *Trendhunter.com*. Online Available at www.trendhunter.com/trends/christian-susana (accessed 22 August 2014).

77 Fortmeyer, Russell (2012) 'Pixel: Studio 505', *GreenSource: The Magazine of Sustainable Design*, July. Online. Available at www.greensource.construction.com/green_building_projects/2012/1207-pixel.asp (accessed 12 August 2014).

78 Shinal, John (2013) 'New tech economy: 3D printing's promise in prosthetics', *USA Today*, 17 March. Online. Available at www.usatoday.com/story/tech/2013/03/17/autodesk-phillips-electronics-3d-printing/1990703/ (accessed 29 March 2014).

79 A significant percentage of construction in China and throughout the Pacific Rim is prefab modular, consisting of modules stacked atop one another and plugged into a support superstructure. Also see Kaye, Leon (2012) 'Modular building could lead way in China's commercial construction', *The Guardian*, 26 July. Online. Available at www.theguardian.com/sustainable-business-modular-building-china-commerical-construction (accessed 15 September 2014). One builder in China in 2014 used 3D printing to print-build ten houses in a single day. See Blain, Loz (2014) 'Chinese company uses 3D printing to build 10 houses in a day', *Gizmag*, 23 April. Online. Available at www.gizmag.com/china-winsun-3d-printed-house/31757/ (accessed 15 September 2014). Also see Quirk, Vanessa (2012) 'How 3D printing will change our world', *Archdaily.com*. 12 July. Online. Available at www.archdaily.com/253380/how-3d-printing-will-change-our-world/ (accessed 29 March 2014).

80 Verderber and Fine (2000): Chapter 4.

81 Anderson and Anderson (2007): 12.

82 Kovacs-Silvis (2013).

4 Pop-up clinics

1 Kronenburg, Robert (1995) *Houses in Motion: The Genesis, History and Development of the Portable Building*, Chapter 1.

2 Erickson, Amanda (2013) 'The world's biggest pop-up city,' *The Atlantic Cities*, 74(1): 44–47. Online. Available at www.citylab.com/work/2013/01/worlds-biggest-pop-city/4402/ (accessed 7 February 2013).

3 Pradhan, Sharat (2013) 'Hindus enter River Ganges in Maha Kumbh Mela, worlds largest religious festival,' *The Huffington Post*, 14 January. Online. Available at www.huffingtonpost.com/2013/01/14/hindus-enter-river-ganges_n_2470862.html (accessed 7 February 2013).

4 Ibid.: 3.

5 Taylor, Alan (2014) 'Burning Man 2014', *The Atlantic*, 1 September. Online. Available at www/theatlantic.com/photo/2014/09/burning-man-2014/100802/ (accessed 22 November 2014).

6 World Health Organization Center for Health Development/United Nations Human Settlements Program (2010). *Hidden Cities: Unmasking and Overcoming Health Inequalities in Urban Settings*, Kobe, Japan: World Health Organization/UN-HABITAT. Online. Available at www.who.int/kobe_centre/publications/hidden_cities/en/ (accessed 14 February 2013).

7 Gouverneur, David (2014) *Planning and Design for Future Informal Settlements: Shaping the Self-Constructed City*, London: Routledge.

8 Verderber, Stephen (2005) *Compassion in Architecture: Evidence-Based Design for Health in Louisiana*, Lafayette, LA: The Center for Louisiana Studies.

9 Groth, Paul (1997) 'Frameworks for cultural landscape study', in Groth, Paul and Bressi, Todd W. (eds.) *Understanding Ordinary Landscapes*, New Haven: Yale University Press, 1–21.

10 Verderber (2005): 2.

11 Verderber, Stephen (2009) *Delirious New Orleans: Manifesto for an Extraordinary American City*, Austin: University of Texas Press.

12 Appleton, Jay (1997) 'The Integrity of the Landscape Movement,' in Groth, Paul and Bressi, Todd W. (eds.) *Understanding Ordinary Landscapes*, New Haven: Yale University Press, 189–199. Appleton, a cultural geographer, was among the pioneers in this field. Groth extended Appleton's reasoning in that the interdisciplinary study of the phenomena of the everyday milieu need not be focused on any particular building type or socio-economic group. It is, nevertheless, a bona fide 'field' whose members are interconnected disciplinarily, if only remotely. But a double-edged sword it is: systematic cultural landscape analysis still remains somewhat peripheral to the mainstream.

13 Verderber (2005): 4.

14 Yost, Mark (2006) *Tailgating, Sacks, and Salary Caps: How the NFL Became the Most Successful Sports League in History*, London: Kaplan Business.

15 In New Orleans, the owner of the New Orleans Saints NFL team went so far as to buy a vacant shopping mall next to the Mercedes Benz Superdome and then proceeded to demolish one third of it just to provide a setting for pop-up tailgating events. On the occasion of each fan pilgrimage, a large paved plaza becomes filled with multiple temporary music stages and food stands whose offerings are consumed by thousands of rabid devotees.

16 Techentin, Warren (2005) *Dead Malls*, Forum for Architecture and Urban Design, Santa Monica, CA: Ram Distribution. Also see Dunham-Jones, Ellen and Williamson, June (2011) *Retrofitting Suburbia: Urban Design Solutions for Redesigning Suburbs*, New York: Wiley. Also Stephen Verderber (2012) *Sprawling Cities and Our Endangered Public Health*, London: Routledge.

17 Kaydo, Chad (2014) 'Why pop-ups are getting even more popular', *BIZBASH*, July. Online. Available at http://trendwatching.com/media/bizbash-why-pop-ups-are-getting-even-more-popular/ (accessed 17 November 2014).

18 Elejalde-Ruiz, Alexia (2014) 'Retail matchmaker service Storefront launches in Chicago', *The Chicago Tribune*, 15 July. Online. Available at www.chicagotribune.com/business/breaking/chi-storefront-launches-chicago-20140715-story.html (accessed 17 November 2014).

19 Bradburn, Jamie (2014) 'Pop-up goes the museum', *Torontoist*, 29 August. Online. Available at http://torontoist.com/2014/08/pop-up-goes-the-museum/ (accessed 17 November 2014).

20 Anon. (2013) 'Pop-up retail', *Trendwatching.com*. Online. Available at http://trendwatching.com/trends/POPUP_RETAIL.htm (accessed 7 February 2013).

21 Ibid. Vacant Club members sometimes know about a pop-up store's opening only moments before it happens. The Guerrilla Store, in Berlin, was open for one year, located in a remote neighborhood in what was once East Berlin, in a 750 square foot bare bones warehouse space. The concept's success and its chic aesthetic was rooted in its sheer exclusivity. This retailer has since opened stores in other eastern European cities including Warsaw, Ljubljana, and Vilnius.

22 Ibid.: 4.

23 Ibid.: 5. The London Fashion Bus nomadic pop up was launched in 2003. It is a continually touring showroom stocked with over 1,400 items from emerging designers. This retrofitted bus travels throughout the U.K. to places far from the fashion center of London, and instant 'tour dates' are posted on its website. As for the success of pop-ups far from urban areas, the Brazilian cosmetics firm Oceanic decided to equip its franchisees with Fiat Doblo minivans, which it refers to as shops-on-wheels. These mobile stores travel to universities, schools, hospitals, parks, and trade shows. In Milan, APE Malandra, a mobile pop-up clothing retailer, caters to women and children. Its stores have three wheels in the form of an APE Piaggio, a small vehicle that can be set up wherever it is parked. Besides Milan, in summer it visits resort towns such as Forte dei Marmi, the seaside resort near Florence. Ironically, Trendwatch.com suggested they add an element of genuine need, 'empathy, by actually showing up when and where your customers need you most.'

24 Online auctioneer eBay in 2004 first opened its eBay Showhouse in New York. It invited eight designers to each 'make over' a different room. Each designer was required to make all purchases through its online auction website only. All of the furnishings were resold on eBay during the one week the showroom was open in June 2004. Other pioneering retailers to more recently via a pop-up format include Method Products (open ninety days), Crown Royal Whiskey (open one month), *Self* magazine's spa (one month), a collaboration between Levi's and alife (forty-five days), Creative Time (one week), Sharp Electronics (one month), Suave shampoo's pop-up salons in New York, Chicago and Minneapolis (five weeks), the retailers Umbro and Shotgun, in London (one week each), Havaianas sandal brand, in Sao Paulo, Brazil (one month), and the Nike Runner's Lounge, a pop-up where athletes can test out new items, located strategically along Vancouver's Seawall, a major jogging route (one month, then extended for four more months), and the mass fixed-site retailer J.C. Penney for one week in New York, for the express purpose of introducing a new bridal collection.

25 Schneider, Gary (2014) *Electronic Commerce*, Boston, MA: Cengage Learning. Also see Bourne, Leah (2012) 'How e-commerce killed shopping as a sport', *Forbes*, 78(3): 44–49. Online. Available at www.forbes.com/sites/leahbourne/2012/03/30/why-e-commerce-killed-shopping-as-a-sport/ (accessed 23 November 2014). Online retailers relentlessly gain market share, each year.

26 Jordan, Jeff (2013) 'The death of the American Shopping Mall', *The Atlantic Cities*. Online. Available at www.citylab.com/work/2012/12/death-american-shopping-mall/4252/ (accessed 12 February 2013).

27 U.S. Census Bureau (2012) *Health Insurance Highlights*, Washington, D.C.: United States Census Bureau. Online. Available at www.census.gov/hhes/www/hlthins/data/incpovhlth/2012/highlights.html (accessed 7 November 2014).

28 La Veist, Thomas A. (2005) *Minority Populations and Health: An Introduction to Health Disparities in the U.S.*, New York: Jossey-Bass/Wiley.

29 Barr, Donald A. (2008) *Health Disparities in the United States: Social Class, Race, Ethnicity, and Health*, Baltimore: Johns Hopkins University Press.

30 Shi, Leiyu and Stevens, Gregory D. (2010) *Vulnerable Populations in the United States*, New York: Jossey-Bass/Wiley.

31 Bolano, Vanessa (2012) 'Pop up grocery store provides temporary relief to residents of the Lower 9th Ward', *The Baltimore Sun*, 17 October. Online. Available at www.baltimoresun.com/videogallery/72932187/News/Pop-Up-Grocery-Store-Provides-temporary-Relief-

To-Residents-Of-The-Lower-Ninth-Ward.html (accessed 21 February 2013).

32 American Anthropological Association (2000) *Social and Cultural Aspects of Health*, Public Policy Briefing Sheet. Online. Available at www.ameranthassn.org/pphealth.html (accessed 14 February 14).

33 Verderber (2005): Chapter 7. Also see Carpman, Janet R. and Grant, Myron (1994) *Design that Cares: Planning Health Facilities for Patients and Visitors,* Second Edition, Chicago, IL: American Hospital Publishing.

34 Verderber, Stephen and Refuerzo, Ben J. (2003) 'Research-based architecture and the community health care consumer: a statewide initiative', *Journal of Architectural and Planning Research*, 20(1): 57–67.

35 Farbstein, Jay (1993) 'The impact of the client organization on the programming process', in Preiser, Wolfgang F.E. (ed.) *Professional Practice in Facility Programming*, New York: Van Nostrand Reinhold, 121–135.

36 Verderber, Stephen and Fine, David J. (2000) *Healthcare Architecture in an Era of Radical Transformation,* New Haven, CT: Yale University Press. Also see DeNavas-Walt, Carmen, Proctor, Bernadette D. and Smith, Jessica C. (2012) *Income, Poverty, and Health Insurance Coverage in the United States: 2011*, Current Population Reports: P60-243, U.S. Department of Commerce, Economics, and Statistics Administration, Washington: U.S. Census Bureau, September. Online. Available at www.census.gov/prod/2012pubs/p60-243.pdf (accessed 20 December 2013).

37 Keith, Katie, Lucia, Kevin W., and Corlette, Sabrina (2012) 'Implementing the Affordable Care Act: state action on early market reforms', *The Commonwealth Fund Quarterly*, 6(22): 47–55.

38 Verderber, Stephen (2013) 'Community health centers for the medically underserved: an American case study', *Urbanism+Architecture*, 6(11): 6–15. The State of Louisiana has achieved success over the past two decades in replacing the majority of its community-based outpatient clinics, over a twenty-four-year period. The Strategic Facility Improvement Initiative (SFI) was created to assess, redefine, and redevelop Louisiana's network of 132 freestanding program sites across sixty-four parishes (counties). The SFI program stands as the longest running health agency-sponsored Evidence-Based Research and Design (EBR&D) effort of its kind in North America. Also see Verderber, Stephen and Refuerzo, Ben J. (1993) 'Empowerment on Main Street: implementing research-based design', in Feldman, R., Hardie, G., and Salie, D. (eds.) (1993) *Power by Design: Proceedings of the 24th Annual Conference of the Environmental Design Research Association,* Oklahoma City: Environmental Design Research Association, 114–121. Also see Moffit, David (2006) 'Compassion in architecture: evidence-based design for health in Louisiana', *Places*, 18(4): 13–18 and Verderber, Stephen (2012) 'Evidence-based architecture, health promotion, and the medically underserved', Paper presented at *Promoting Environmental Justice through Effective Education, Collaboration, and Mobilization Annual Conference*, Atlanta: U.S. Environmental Protection Agency.

39 Gaylin, Dan, Goldman, Sidra, Ketchel, Alana and Moiduddin, Adil (2005) *Community Health Center Information Systems Assessment: Issues and Opportunities. Final Report,* Chicago: NORC at the University of Chicago. Online. Available at http://aspe.hhs.gov/sp/chc/chc.pdf (accessed 15 September 2014).

40 Verderber (2009): Chapter 2.

41 Bourne, Joel K. (2007) 'New Orleans: a perilous future', *National Geographic,* 112(8): 16–37. Online. Available at http://ngm.nationalgeographic.com/print/2007/08/new-orleans/new-orleans-text (accessed 12 February 2012). The $14 billion spent by the U.S. federal government in the decade since Katrina to rebuild and fortify the ring of levees and seawalls that encircle the area is meant to provide further protection. As the land experiences further subsidence, however, the network of 'improved' levees and seawalls themselves sink faster into the spongy soil. All this places the city and metro area in a perilous predicament.

42 Miller, Robert (2007) *Reassessing the Effects of Climate Change in Charleston*, Charleston, SC: Clemson University Architecture Center. Based on a recent report issued by the Intergovernmental Panel on Climate Change, a direct-hit hurricane's impact in Charleston would be at level four magnitude. Major sections of the historic core of the city and beyond would be destroyed. The Clemson team's report was awarded the National Council of Architectural Accreditation Boards (NCARB) National Prize for Creative Architectural Inquiry in University-based programs in architecture, in 2009.

43 Borenstein, Seth (2007) 'Rising seas are predicted to reshape U.S coasts', *The Milwaukee Journal*, 8 October, 4A, 4G.

44 Barnett, Jonathan and Beckman, John (2007) 'Coastal cities face rising seas', *Planning*, 54(8/9): 47–57.

45 Booth, Thomas C. (2006) 'The storm lingers on: Katrina's psychological toll', *Time*, 14 June, 56.

46 Fothergill, A., Maestas, E.G., and Darlington, J.D. (1999) 'Race, ethnicity and disasters in the United States: a review of the literature', *Disasters*, 23(2): 156–173.

47 Brunker, Mike (2006) 'FEMA trailers—toxic tin cans?' *Rising from Ruin: Two Towns Rebuild after Katrina.* Online. Available at http://risingfromruin/msnbc.com/2006/07/are_fema_traile.html (accessed 24 February 2013).

48 Henry J. Kaiser Family Foundation (2013) *Who Benefits from the ACA Medicaid Expansion?* Menlo Park, CA: The Kaiser Commission on Medicaid and the Uninsured. Online. Available at http://kff.org/medicaid/quicktake_aca_medicaid.cfm (accessed 12 February 2014). In the case of Louisiana, Governor Bobby Jindal asserts that Louisiana could not afford its 10 percent share of the state's cost to insure its more than 400,000 low-income citizens who would newly qualify for

health insurance. Report from the Kaiser Family Foundation tagged the cost for Louisiana at only about $1 billion, over a period of 10 years. This estimate was far less than the State's own in-house, politically driven $3.7 billion estimate.

49 Editorial (2013) 'Medicaid expansion is essential for Louisiana residents', *The Times-Picayune*. Online. Available at www.nola.com/opinions/index.ssf/2012/11/medicaid_is_essential-for_loui.html (accessed 12 February 2013). This is particularly ironic as health clinics that opened their doors in poor, medically underserved communities after Katrina chronically face closure due to lack of operational funds. Widely praised as cost-effective, and popular with the public, they have provided some measure of healthcare resiliency. They provide services on a sliding, pay-what-you-can scale.

50 Beam, Adam (2012) 'Keck: South Carolina should not expand Medicaid', *The State*, 29 November. Online. Available at www.thestate.com/2012/11/29/2536202/keck-sc-should-not-expand-medicaid.html (accessed 14 February 2013). There, a similarly recalcitrant governor, Nikki Haley, also refused to allow 'her state' to become part of the ACA's Medicaid expansion and as such both of these states remain in non-compliance with the federal ACA. When translated into its lost impact on real people, South Carolina continues to turn down $3 billion in new federal money, which would add 513,000 citizens to that State's existing Medicaid program.

51 This is according to the Washington, D.C.-based Corporation for Enterprise Development, a private think tank. Nearly half of the state's residents are living on the financial precipice, with almost no savings to fall back on in the event of a job loss, health crisis, or other income-depleting emergency. Also see Corporation for Enterprise Development (2013) *Assets & Opportunity Scorecard*, Washington, D.C.: Corporation for Enterprise Development. Included in this at-risk group are those who live below the poverty line of $23,050 (2013) for a family of four. Also included in this 'asset poor' category are the 19 percent of households with incomes between $47,593 and $71,580 but with less than three months of savings in reserve. The report stated that 28 percent of South Carolina jobs are classified as low-wage, the ninth worst in the nation. The majority of these persons and households do not have health insurance. Louisiana ranked fortieth nationally in this same regard and fiftieth (dead last among all fifty states) in 2012 in the family income to poverty rate (19.7 percent versus 14.6 percent nationally).

52 The Graduate Program in Architecture + Health at Clemson University was established in 1968, and stands as the first M.Arch. degree curriculum of its kind in North America. Each year, a cadre of eight to ten post-baccalaureate students enter a two-year track that prepares graduates for careers in the health sector of the architectural profession.

53 Abhas, Jha, Miner, Todd W. and Stanton-Geddes, Zuzana (2013) *Building Urban Resilience: Principles, Tools, and Practice*, Report Number 75845, Washington, D.C.: The World Bank.

54 Verderber, Stephen (2008) 'Asleep at the switch: architectural education for disaster response in the 21st century', Poster Presentation, *The Oxford Conference 2008: 50 Years On—Resetting the Agenda for Architectural Education*, Oxford, U.K.: University of Oxford.

55 Jones, E.W. (2012) 'Community health centers and the Affordable Care Act: increasing access to affordable, cost effective, high quality care', *HealthCare.gov*. Online. Available at www.healthcare.gov/news/factsheets/2010/08/increasing-access.html (accessed 23 September 2012). A sum of $11 billion has been targeted to bolster and expand the nation's network of outpatient community health centers to better serve the thirty million-plus individuals who recently became eligible for health insurance coverage under the ACA. In addition, $9.5 billion was earmarked to construct new community outpatient health centers in federally designated underserved areas.

56 Christensen, Julia (2008) *Big Box Reuse*, Cambridge, MA: MIT Press. The pattern is by now well known: a mass retailer such as Wal-Mart descends on a community and proceeds to construct a massive big box, only to soon abandon it when it builds a larger one just down the road, or elects to close down, and simply leave town.

57 Hamilton, D. Kirk (2008) *Evidence-based Design for Multiple Building Types*, New York: Wiley.

58 Hamilton, D. Kirk (2003) 'The four levels of evidence-based practice', *Healthcare Design*, 3(4): 18–27. Also see Mallory-Hill, S., Preiser, Wolfgang F.E., and Watson, C.G. (2012) *Enhancing Building Performance*, New York: Wiley-Blackwell.

59 Ulrich, Roger S., Zimring, Craig, Zhu, Xuemei, DuBose, Jennifer, Seo, Hyun-Bo, Choi, Young-Seon, Quan, Xiaobo and Joseph, Anjali (2008) 'A review of the research literature on evidence-based healthcare design', *Health Environments Research & Design Journal*, 1(3): 101–165.

60 Fitzpatrick, Mary (ed.) (2006) *New Orleans: Life in an Epic City*, New Orleans, LA: Preservation Resource Center of New Orleans.

61 Davidson, Debra J. (2010) 'The applicability of the concept of resilience to social systems: some sources of optimism and nagging doubts', *Society and Natural Resources*, 23(2): 1135–1149.

62 Morello-Frosch, Rachael, Brown, Phil, Lyson, Mercedes, Cohen, Alison, and Krupa, Kimberly (2011) 'Community voice, vision, and resilience in post-Katrina recovery', *Environmental Justice*, 4(1): 71–80.

63 Davidson (2012): 1145.

64 LaLone, Mary B. (2012) 'Neighbors helping neighbors: an examination of the social capital mobilization process for community resilience to environmental disasters', *Journal of Applied Social Science*, 6(2): 209–237. Also see Ebi, Kristie L. and Semenza, Jan C. (2008) 'Community-based adaptation to the health impacts of climate change', *American Journal of Preventive Medicine*, 35(5): 501–507. Also see Olaris, Kristine (2008) 'Community health services and climate change: exploring the sector's capacity to respond', *Environmental Health*,

8(2): 8–41. Also see Bell, Erica (2011) 'Readying health services for climate change: a policy framework for regional development', *American Journal of Public Health*, 101(5): 804–813 and Adelson, Jeff (2012) 'Louisiana ranks poorly on latest income, health insurance statistics', *The Times-Picayune*, 12 September, A2. Online. Available at www.nola.com/politics/index.ssf/2012/09/louisiana_ranks_poorly_on_late.html (accessed 13 September 2012).

65 Wasserman, Barry and Sullivan, Patrick (2000) *Ethics and the Practice of Architecture*, New York: John Wiley and Sons. Also see Fullinwider, Robert K. (1998) 'Civil society and democratic citizenship', *Philosophy and Public Policy Quarterly*, 18 (3): 2–4 and Jones, Jeffrey M. (2012) 'Texas widens gap over other states in percentage uninsured,' *Gallup Wellbeing*, March. Online. Available at www.gallup.com/poll/153053/texas-widens-gap-states-percentage-uninsured.aspx (accessed 23 September 2012). In Louisiana approximately 947,000 residents lived below the poverty line in 2011, the state's poverty rate was 21.1 percent (second highest in the nation), and the median family income was $40,658 (ranking forty-six out of fifty states). Worse, 20.8 percent of its residents, or 938,000 persons, did not have private health insurance of any sort.

66 Hill, Jonathan (ed.) (1998) *Occupying Architecture: Between the Architect and the User*, London: Routledge.

67 Verderber, Stephen and Kimbrell, Joseph J. (2005) 'The role of the architectural environment in community health: an evidence-based initiative', *Journal of Public Health Management and Practice*, 11(1): 79–89.

5 Planning and design considerations for transportable healthcare

1 Verderber, Stephen (2010) *Innovations in Hospital Architecture*, London: Routledge, 118.

2 Berk, Michael (2003) 'Architects address the Sub-Saharan AIDS crisis', *Competitions*, Fall, 41(3): 36–51.

3 McLaughlin, E. and Papadopoulou, A (2008) 'An introduction to portable field hospitals', *Rural and Remote Health*, 8(830): 41–54.

4 Manabe, Tsunehiro, Nishiyama, Akihiko and Sakuma, Takumi (1996) 'Research on systematization of moveable building constructions', *Journal of Architecture, Planning and Environmental Engineering*, 486(7): 117–123.

5 Bricknell, M.C. (2001) 'Organization and design of regular field hospitals', *Journal of the Regular Army Medical Corps*, 147(4): 161–167.

6 Anon. (1999) 'Turkey: Earthquake Situation Report No. 34', *ReliefWeb*, 17 December. Online. Available at http://reliefweb.int/report/turkey/turkey-earthquakes-situation-report-no-34 (accessed 12 March 2006).

7 Meinhold, Bridgette (2008) 'Prefab Friday: Reaction Housing emergency shelters', *Inhabitat*, Online. Available at http://inhabitat.com/prefab-friday-reaction-housing-emergency-shelters/ (accessed 12 January 2010).

8 Guenther, Robin and Vittori, Gail (2012) *Sustainable Healthcare Architecture*, Second Edition, New York: McGraw-Hill.

9 Markham, Derek (2013) 'This prototype turns a pallet of water bottles into a disaster shelter', *Treehugger*. Online. Available at www.treehugger.com/clean-technology/prototype-turns-pallet-water-bottles-disaster-shelter.html (accessed 18 March 2014).

10 Williams, Scott (2011) *Bug Out Vehicles and Shelters: Build and Outfit your Life-Saving Escape*, Berkeley, CA: Ulysses Press.

11 Ross, Kenneth G. and Matthews, Robert W. (eds.) (1991) *The Social Biology of Wasps*, Ithaca, NY: Cornell University Press.

12 Burns, Jim (1972) *Arthropods: New Design Futures*, New York: Praeger.

13 Editors (2011) 'Zombie safe house competition winners 2011... ARRRGGH!!', *Bustler*. Online. Available at www.bustler.net/index.php/article/zombie_safe_house_competition_winners_2011.....arrrggh/ (accessed 11 November 2011).

14 Thompson, John, and Goldin, Grace (1975) *The Hospital: A Social and Architectural History*, New Haven: Yale University Press.

15 McCallum, Jack E. (2008) *Military Medicine: From Ancient Times to the 21st Century*, Santa Barbara, CA: ABC-CLIO.

16 Dutch Health (2011) 'Hospital train design presented September 2011', *Dutch-Health.com*. Online. Available at www.dutch-health.com/news/id1611/hospital-train-design-presented-sept-2011.html (accessed 5 December 2014).

17 Kossman, Sienna (2012) 'A vision to improve vision: ORBIS Flying Eye Hospital to replace aircraft by 2013', *Airventure.org*, 28 July. Online. Available at www.airventure.org/news/2012/120725_ORBIS-to-replace-aircraft-by-2013.html (accessed 19 December 2013).

18 Yengkhom, Sumati (2013) 'Hi-tech flying hospital a hit in Kolkata', *The Times of India*, 14 September. Online. Available at http://timesofindia.indiatimes.com/city/kolkata/Hi-tech-flying-hospital-a-hit-in-Kolkata/articleshow/22564557.cms (accessed 19 December 2013).

19 Kirby, Mary (2011) 'FED-EX donates MD-10-30F to non-profit ORBIS', *Flightglobal*, 3 August. Online. Available at www.flightglobal.com/news/articles/fedex-donates-md-10-30f-to-non-profit-orbis-360321/ (accessed 19 December 2013).

20 Lanks, Belinda (2011) 'A house for refugees, made from 100 shipping pallets', *Co-Design*, 19 December. Online. Available at www.fastcodesign.com/1665676/a-house-for-refugees-made-from-100-shipping-palets (accessed 15 December 2013).

21 Garber, Megan (2014) 'This jet was transformed into an Ebola quarantine unit', *The Atlantic*, 5 August. Online. Available at www.theatlantic.com/technology/archive/2014/08/this-jet-was-transformed-into-an-ebola-quarantine-unit/375584/ (accessed 4 December 2014).

22 McCraken, Harry (2013) 'Home, smart home', *Time*, August 26–September 2: 14.

23 Gruber, Petra (2010) *Biomimetics in Architecture: Architecture of Life and Buildings*, Berlin: Springer Vienna Architecture.

24 Verderber (2010).

25 Anon. (2013) 'Pediatric clinic/4of7 Architecture', *ArchDaily*. Online. Available at www.archdaily.com/48188/pediatric-clinic-40f7-architecture/ (accessed 29 July 2014).

26 WHO-PAHO (2003) *WHO-PAHO Guidelines for the Use of Foreign Field Hospitals in the Aftermath of Sudden-Impact Disasters*, Washington, D.C.: Department of Emergency and Humanitarian Action, World Health Organization/Pan American Health Organization.

27 USAID (2010) *USAID Post-Disaster Assessment Checklist*, Washington, D.C.: USAID. Online. Available at www.usaid.gov/hum_response/ofda/fog/ch2ctxt.html (accessed 12 July 2013).

28 Blackwell, Thomas and Bosse, Michael (2007) 'Use of an innovative mobile hospital in the medical response to Hurricane Katrina', *Annals of Emergency Medicine*, 49(5): 580–588.

29 Nordic Corporation (2013) *Nordic Shelter AS Military and Emergency Services Command Posts*. Online. Available at www.naval-suppliers.info/supplier/nordic-shelter (accessed 12 February 2013).

30 City of Philadelphia (2010) 'New portable EOC showcased at LibertyRAD Exercise in Philadelphia', *City of Philadelphia Department of Emergency Management*. Online. Available at https://cityofphiladelphia.wordpress.com/2010/04/27/new-portable-eoc-showcased-at-libertyrad-exercise-in-philadelphia/ (accessed 12 December 2014).

31 Kelly, Peggy (2012) 'Mobile command unit: disaster scenario no match for new portable EOC', *Santa Paula Times*, 15 June. Online. Available at www.santapaulatimes.com/news/archivestory.php/aid/25429/Mobile_Command_Unit:_Disaster_scenario_no_match_for_new_portable_EOC.html (accessed 12 December 2014).

32 Price, Scott (2007) 'The U.S. Coast Guard & Hurricane Katrina', *United States Coast Guard*, Washington, D.C. Online. Available at www.uscg.mil/history/katrina/docs/DarkestDay.pdf (accessed 5 December 2014).

33 World Bank and United Nations International Strategy for Disaster Reduction Secretariat-Central Asia (2009) 'Central Asia and Caucasus Disaster Risk Management Initiative', *UNISDR-CA*. Geneva: UNISDR-CA. Also see Penuel, K. Bradley and Staller, Matt (eds.) (2011) *Encyclopedia of Disaster Relief*, Thousand Oaks, CA: Sage Publications, 27.

34 MegaDeck Corporation (2014) 'Landing site matting', *MegaDeck Corporation*. Online. Available at www.megadeckrigmats.com/portable-airfield-mats.php (accessed 12 December 2014).

35 Solarline, Ltd. (2014) *Solarline Solar Generators*. Online. Available at www.solarlinepower.com/products/portable-solar-generator (accessed 30 January 2014).

36 CSafe Corporation (2014) 'CSafe Offers Cool Chain Solutions to Typhoon Haiyan Disaster Relief Agencies', *CSafe Corporation*. Online. Available at www.csafeglobal.com/csafe-offers-cool-chain-solutions-to-typhoon-disaster-relief-agencies (accessed 30 January 2014).

37 Baseel, Casey (2013) 'The amazing disaster relief equipment of Japan's Self Defense Force', *Rocket News 24*, 12 September. Online. Available at http://en.rocketnews24.com/2013/09/12/the-mazing-disaster-relief-equipment-of-japans-self-defense-force/ (accessed 30 January 2014).

38 Schmidt, Thomas (2013) 'How it's built', *Triumph Modular Systems*. Online. Available at www.triumphmodular.com/temporary-modular/how-its-built (accessed 20 August 2013).

39 Cabot, Sandra S. (2012) 'Disaster field hospitals: triage and treatment in times of crisis', *Homeland Security*, 6(4): 23–26.

40 Iserson, K.V. and Moskop, J.C. (2007) 'Triage in medicine part I: concept, history and types', *Annals in Emergency Medicine*, 49(3): 275–281.

41 Royal Cornwall Hospital NHS Trust (2012) 'Decontamination Policy', April 2012. *National Health Service*. Online. Available at www.rcht.nhs.uk/DocumentsLibrary/RoyalCornwallHospitalsTrust/Clinical/InfectionPreventionAndControl/DecontaminationPolicy.pdf (accessed 12 November 2014).

42 Pro-Guard Environmental Solutions (2013) *Axiom Oilfield Solutions*. Online. Available at www.fas.org/nuke/guide/usa/doctrine/army/mmcch/decontam.html (accessed 12 November 2014).

43 Savatech Corp (2013) *Inflatable Decon Shower Unit*. Online. Available at www.savatech.eu/environmental-protection-and-rescue/fire.html (accessed 12 December 2013).

44 DRASH (2013) 'Specialty shelters', *DRASH*. Online. Available at www.drash.com/Products/Shelters/SpecialtyShelters/MobileHygieneSystem.aspx (accessed 21 April 2013).

45 Harris, Andy (2013) 'What is a decontamination unit?' *Site Showers, Ltd*. Online. Available at www.site-showers.com/what-is-a-decontamination-unit/ (accessed 12 December 2013).

46 Attguard, Ltd. (2013) '3-stage mobile decontamination shower unit', *Attguard, Ltd*. Online. Available at www.attguard.com.au/decon-mobile.html (accessed 12 December 2013).

47 Verderber (2010): 135.

48 Lijas, Per (2014) 'Tacloban survived the world's strongest recorded storm, but only barely', *Time*, 7 November: 45–46.

49 Verderber, Stephen and Refuerzo, Ben J. (2006) *Innovations in Hospice Architecture*, London: Routledge/Spon Press.

50 Magill, Shelley S., Edwards, Jonathan R., Bamberg, Wendy, Beldavs, Zintars, Dumyati, Ghinwa, Kainer, Marion A., Lynfield, Ruth, Maloney, Meghan, McAllister-Hollod, Laura, Nadle, Joelle, Ray, Susan M., Thompson, Deborah L., Wilson, Lucy E., and Fridkin, Scott K. (2014) 'Multistate point-prevalence survey of health care—associated

infections', *New England Journal of Medicine*, 27 March, 370(4): 1198–1208.

51 Verderber (2010): 167.

52 Escombe, A. Roserick, Oeser, Clarissa C., Gilman, Robet H., Navincopa, Marcos, Ticona, Eduardo, Pan, William, Martinze, Carlos, Chacaltana, Jesus, Rodriguez, Richard, Moore, David A.J. Friedland, Jon S., and Evans, Carlton A. (2007) 'Natural ventilation for the prevention of airborne contagion', *PLoS Medicine*, 4(2): 309–317.

53 Ulrich, Roger S., Zimring, Craig, Zhu, Xuemei, DuBose, Jennifer, Seo, Hyun-Bo, Choi, Young-Seon, Quan, Xiaobo and Joseph, Anjali (2008) 'A review of the research literature on evidence-based healthcare design', *Health Environments Research & Design Journal*.

54 AGER Industries (2013) 'Mobile field hospital modular design for military and civilian applications', *AGER Industries*. Online. Available at www.ager.com. (accessed 14 July 2013).

55 Ibid.

56 Verderber (2010): 152.

57 Ibid.: 154.

58 SAAB (2014) *Medical Care Solutions—Flexible Field Facilities*, SAAB Industries. Online. Available at www.saabgroup.com/Global/Documents%20and%20images/land/Integrated%20.html (accessed 5 December 2014).

59 Verderber and Refuerzo (2006): 71.

60 Global Defense Systems (2013) 'GDS supplies everything from field hospitals to the kitchen sink', *Global Defense Systems*. Online. Available at www.shoalhavendefence.com.au/SiteFiles/shoalhavendefencecomau/GDS.pdf (accessed 5 December 2014).

61 OR Technology (2014) 'X-ray systems for disaster management in field hospitals', *OR-Technology*. Online. Available at www.or-technology.com/disaster-management-field-hospital.html (accessed 5 December 2014). Also see Anon. (2014) 'Transmodular hospitals'. Online. Available at www.transmodularhospitals.com (accessed 5 December 2014). This manufacturer produces a containerized expandable portable field hospital that transits with a full diagnostic imaging unit.

62 Centers for Disease Control and Prevention (2015) '2014 Ebola outbreak in West Africa—case counts', *U.S. Centers for Disease Control and Prevention*. Online. Available at www.cdc.gov/vhf/ebola/outbreaks/2014-west-africa/case-counts.html (accessed 1 January 2015).

63 Centers for Disease Control and Prevention (1995) 'Outbreak of Ebola viral hemorrhagic fever—Zaire', *MMWR Weekly*, 26 May, 44(20): 399.

64 Hinshaw, Drew (2014) 'Deadly disappointment awaits at Ebola clinics due to lack of space', *The Wall Street Journal*, 7 September. Online. Available at www.wsj.com/articles/deadly-disappointment-awaits-at-ebola-clinics-due-to-lack-of-space-1410137713 (accessed 8 December 2014).

65 Freeman, Colin (2014) 'British Ebola clinic opens for patients in Sierra Leone', *The Telegraph*. 5 November. Online. Available at www.telegraph.co.uk/news/worldnews/ebola/11212080/British-Ebola-clinic-opens-for-patients-in-Sierra-Leone.html (accessed 8 December 2014).

66 World Health Organization (2014) 'An Ebola treatment center', Geneva, Switzerland: World Health Organization.

67 Angelle, Amber (2010) 'How Doctors Without Borders set up field hospitals in Haiti', *Popular Mechanics*, 22 January. Online. Available at www.popularmechanics.com/science/health/a5039/4343363/ (accessed 1 February 2014).

68 Aitken, Peter, Leggat, Peter, and Leclercq, Muriel (2012) 'Logistic support provided to Australian disaster medical assistance teams: results of a national survey of team members', *Journal of Emerging Health Threats*, 5(10): 45–62. Online. Available at www.eht-journal.net/index.php/ehtj/article/view/9750 (accessed 1 February 2014).

69 College of Physicians and Surgeons of Ontario (2006) *Confidentiality of Personal Health Information, Policy Number 8-05*, Toronto, Ontario: College of Physicians and Surgeons of Ontario. Online. Available at www.cpso.on.ca/policies-publications/policy/confidentiality-of-personal-health-information.html (accessed 8 December 2014).

70 Shepley, Mardelle M. (2014) *Design for Pediatric and Neonatal Critical Care*, London: Routledge.

71 Verderber, Stephen and Fine, David J. (2000) *Healthcare Architecture in an Era of Radical Transformation*, New Haven, CT: Yale University Press, Chapter 8.

72 Connors, Chris (2009) 'Containers 2 Clinics', *Make Magazine*. Online. Available at www.makezine.com/2009/03/15/containers-2-clinics.html (accessed 29 January 2014).

73 Lynch, Kevin (1960) *The Image of the City*, Cambridge, MA: MIT Press.

74 White, Edward T. (2004) *Site Analysis: Diagramming Information for Architectural Design*, Tallahassee, FL: Architectural Media, Ltd.

75 LaGato, James A. (2008) *Site Analysis: A Contextual Approach to Sustainable Land Planning and Site Design*, Second Edition, Hoboken, NJ: John Wiley and Sons.

76 Anon. (2014) 'Patient services', *Memorial Hospital of Tampa*. Online. Available at http://www.memorialhospitaltampa.com/ (accessed 29 January 2014).

77 Gruver, Deb (2010) 'Hospitals for Hope converts shipping containers into clinics', *The Wichita Eagle*. Online. Available at www.kansas.com/news/local/article1021575.html (accessed 29 January 2014).

78 Centers for Medicare and Medicare Services (2012) *HIPAA—General Information*, Washington, D.C.: Centers for Medicare and Medicaid Services. Online. Available at www.cms.gov/Regulations-and-Guidance/HIPAA-Adminstrative-Simplification/HIPAAGenInfo/index.html?redirect=/HIPAAGenInfo/ (accessed 12 December 2014).

79 Connors (2009).

80 Verderber, Stephen (2012) *Sprawling Cities and Our Endangered Public Health*, London: Routledge.

81 Christensen, Julia (2008) *Big Box Reuse*, Cambridge, MA: MIT Press, 196–213.
82 Capps, Kriston (2014) '12 disaster relief projects by Shigeru Ban Architects', *Architect*, 24 March. Online. Available at www.architectmagazine.com/design/12-disaster-relief-projects-by-shigeru-ban-architects_o (accessed 12 December 2014).
83 Meinhold, Bridgette (2013) 'Reciproboo: A simple reciprocal bamboo frame emergency shelter', *m.inhabitat.com*. Online. Available at http://inhabitat.com/reciproboo-a-simple-reciprocal-bamboo-frame-emergency-shelter/ (accessed 25 August 2013).
84 Dantherm Corporation (2013) 'AC-M18 Tent Cooling', *Dantherm Corporation*. Online. Available at www.dantherm.com/uk/mobile-heating-cooling/product-range/ac-m18-tent-cooling.html (accessed 12 July 2014).
85 Jones, Walter (2013) 'Haiti domes', *World Shelters*. Online. Available at www.worldshelters.org (accessed 10 April 2013).
86 Editor (2014) 'Abeer Seikaly weaves shelters for disaster relief using patterned fabric', *Designboom*. Online. Available at www.designboom.com/architecture/abeer-seikaly-weaving-a-home-disaster-relief-03-06-2014/ (accessed 14 December 2014).
87 Stohr, Kate and Sinclair, Cameron (2012) *Design Like You Give a Damn 2: Building Change from the Ground Up*, New York: Harry N. Abrams.
88 Cannefax, Dinah (2010) 'Texas Health Resources Field Surge Program', *Texas Health Resources/Presbyterian, Harris Methodist and Arlington Memorial Medical Centers*. Online. Available at www.ehcca.com/presentations/emsummit2/cannefax_pc2.html (accessed 14 December 2014).
89 This region of the central United States includes the Texas Panhandle and the states of Oklahoma, Nebraska, Kansas, Missouri, and Arkansas.
90 Buban Charles E. (2012) 'Floating house could help PH tackle flooding crisis', *Philippine Daily Inquirer*, 10 August. Online. Available at http://business.inquirer.net/76079/floating-house-could-help-ph-tackle-flooding-crisis (accessed 12 December 2014).
91 Decker, Julie (2005) *Quonset Hut: Metal Living For the Modern Age*, New York: Princeton Architectural Press.
92 DRASH (2013) 'J Series Shelter', *DRASH*. Online. Available at www.drash.com/Products/Shelters/JSeries.aspx (accessed 21 April 2013).
93 Minuru, Yashushi (2013) 'Quick Space 72 Disaster Relief Clinic'. Online. Available at www.qs72.com/index.html (accessed 14 August 2013)
94 Verderber (2010): 264.
95 Diep, Francie (2012) 'Multitouch floor may someday detect your heart attack', *NBC News*. Online. Available at www.nbcnews.com/id/46968862/ns/technology_and_science-tech.html (accessed 19 June 2013).
96 Ball, John (2013) 'The adaptation of 3D printing technologies to the production of intelligent building façade panels', *Herberger Institute for Design and Art, Arizona State University*. Online. Available at http://herbergerinstitute.asu.edu/degrees/phd_environmental/images/ball_john.pdf (accessed 15 December 2013).
97 DeFreitas, Susan (2012) 'Cheap, green, and custom: 3D printing in green building', *earthtechling.com*, 10 August. Online. Available at http://earthtechling.com/2012/08/cheap-green-and-custom-3d-printing-in-green-building/ (accessed 20 December 2013).
98 Hsu, Jeremy (2013) '3D printed organs may mean end to waiting lists, deadly shortages', *LiveScience*. 25 September. Online. Available at www.huffingtonpost.com/2013/09/25/3d-printed-organs_n_3983971.html (accessed 19 December 2013).
99 Mings, Josh (2010) 'How big is the biggest freeform 3D architecture print? This big', *SolidSmack.com*. Online, Available at www.solidsmack.com/fabrication/enrico-dini-big-freeform-architecture-3d-print-sardina-villa-rocce/ (accessed 10 October 2012).
100 Jones, Shelby (2012) 'Printing a room on demand', *Wall Street Journal*, 13 October: C4. Also see European Space Agency (2013) 'Building a lunar base with 3D printing', *European Space Agency*, 31 January. Online. Available at www.esa.int/Our_Activities/Space_Engineering_Technology/Building_a_lunar_base_with_3D_printing (accessed 12 January 2015). Also Gaitan, Daniel (2014) 'Volunteers use 3D printers to create inexpensive prosthetics', *Reuters*, 25 September. Online. Available at www.reuters.com/article/2014/09/25/us-3d-printing-prosthetics-idUSKCN0HK1X520140925 (accessed 25 September 2014).
101 Kleiman, Jacob (2012) 'Amazing innovations: 3D printer can build a house in 20 hours', *International Design Times*. Online. Available at www.idesigntimes.com/articles/1997/20120813/contour-crafting-behrokh-khoshnevis-3d-printer-ted.htm (accessed 19 December 2013).
102 Ulrich, et al. (2008): 13.
103 Sackett, D.L., Rosenberg, W., Gray, J.A., Haynes, R.N. and Richardson, W.S. (1996) 'Evidenced-based medicine: what it is and what it is not', *British Medical Journal*, 312(4): 71–72.
104 Hamilton, D. Kirk (2004) 'Four levels of evidence-based practice', *AIA Newsletter*. Online. Available at www.arch.ttu.edu/courses/2007/fall/5395/392/students/garay/Research/Research.pdf (accessed 4 December 2014).
105 Partners in Health (2013) 'Partner's in Health's work in Haiti', *Partners in Health*. Online. Available at www.bu.edu/haitihelp/cause/partners-in-healths-work-in-haiti/ (access 12 January 2015). Also see Anon. (2014) 'Chief nursing officer raises the bar for nursing in Haiti', *Partners in Health*. 15 May. Online. Available at www.pih.org/blog/chief-nursing-officer-raises-the-bar-for-nursing-in-haiti (accessed 12 January 2015).
106 Childs, Peter and Storry, Mike (eds.) (2002). 'Ambient Music', *Encyclopedia of Contemporary British Culture*, London: Routledge.
107 Hill, Stephen (2013) 'Definition of Spacemusic', *History of Spacemusic*. Online. Available at www.hos.com/history.html (accessed 22 August 2013).

108 Reynolds, Simon (1995) 'Chill: the new ambient', *ArtForum* 74(1): 45-48. Also see Holmes, Thom (2008) *The Techno Primer: The Essential Reference for Loop-Based Music Styles*, Milwaukee: Hal Leonard Publishing.

109 Kim, C.S., Spahlinger, D.A, Kin, J.M., and Billi, J.E. (2006) 'Lean health care: what can hospitals learn from a world-class automaker?' *Journal of Hospital Medicine*, 1(3): 191–199.

110 Spear, S.J. (2005) 'Fixing healthcare from the inside', *Harvard Business Review*, September: 1–14.

111 Anon. (2014) 'First, let's describe what modular construction is', *Modular Building Institute*. Online. Available at www.modular.org/HtmlPage.aspx?name=why_modular (accessed 29 January 2014).

112 Ramtech Corporation (2014) *Ramtech Building Systems*. Online. Available at www.ramtechmodular.com/floorplans.html (accessed 29 January 2014).

113 IMS Corporation (2014) *Modspace Modular Solutions*. Online. Available at www.modspace.com/modular-solutions/modular-buildings/healthcare/ (accessed 29 January 2014).

114 Ibid.

115 Satellite Corporation (2014) *Satellite Corporation Products*. Online. Available at www.satelliteco.com/products/ (accessed 29 January 2014).

116 Anon. (2014) 'Disaster relief structures', *Alibaba.com*. Online. Available at www.alibaba.com/showroom/mobile-clinic.html (accessed 30 January 2014).

117 Jones, Wesley (2014) 'Shelters', *ThomasNet.com*. Online. Available at www.thomasnet.com/ (accessed 30 January 2014).

118 Weatherhaven Corporation (2014) 'Portable Medical Shelters', *Weatherhaven Corporation*. Online. Available at www.weatherhaven.com/medical/ (accessed 30 January 2014).

119 Fort USA (2014) 'Fort Portable Medical Clinics', *Fort USA*. Online. Available at http://fortsusa.com/models/emergency/medical-clinic/ (accessed 30 January 2014).

120 Spring, Stacie (2013) 'Portable medical clinic designed as ASU student project seeks funding', *East Valley Tribune*, 28 June. Online. Available at www.eastvalleytribune.com/money/article_faae3808-ac80-11e2-9036-0019bb2963f4.html (accessed 30 January 2014).

6 Case studies 1–18

1 Anon. (2010) 'Major earthquake causes hospital to collapse', *The Telegraph*, 12 January. Online. Available at www.telegraph.co.uk/news/worldnews/centralamericaand the caribbean/haiti/6977308/Major-earthquake-off-Haiti-causes-hospital-to-collapse.html (accessed 30 July 2013). Also see Anon. (2010) 'Only one hospital open in Haiti's quake-hit-capital', *NewsComAU*, 14 January. Online. Available at www.news.com.au/breaking-news/only-one-hospital-open-in-haitis-quake-hit-capital/story-e6frfku0-1225819044634 (accessed 30 July 2013).

2 Tamarin, Nicholas (2010) 'Anshen + Allen turns containers into clinics', *Interior Design*, 25 March. Online. Available at http://www.interiordesign.net/projects/detail/1254-anshen-allen-turns-containers-into-clinics/ (accessed 8 August 2013).

3 Verderber, Stephen and Fine, David J. (2000) *Healthcare Architecture in an Era of Radical Transformation*, New Haven, CT: Yale University Press, 296.

4 Anon. (2012) 'Shipping container art school in Korea by LOT-EK', *designboom architecture*, 18 December. Online. Available at www.designboom.com/architecture/shipping-container-art-school-in-korea-by-lotek/ (accessed 24 November 2014).

5 Anon. (2013) 'Shipping container library and clinic in Indonesia designed by dpavilion architects', *DZine Trip Online Design Magazine*, 7 August. Online. Available at www.dzinetrip.com/shipping-container-library-and-clinic-in-indonesia-designed-by-dpavilion-architects/ (accessed 6 March 2014).

6 Constantineau, Bruce (2013) 'Vancouver social housing built from shipping containers', *Vancouver Sun*, 2 August. Online. Available at www.vancouversun.com/Vancouver+social+housing+built+from+shipping+containers/8739234/story.html (accessed 24 November 2014).

7 Anon. (2011) 'Missouri DMAT mobilizes BLU-MED hospital to Joplin', *BLU-MED*. Online. Available at www.blu-med.com/index.php?cID=238.html (accessed 23 June 2013).

8 NHK (2011) 'March 11 tsunami a record 40.5 meters high', *NHK*. Online. Available at www.nhk.or.jp.html (accessed 5 July 2014).

9 National Police Agency of Japan (2014) 'Damage situation and police countermeasures', *National Police Academy of Japan*, 9 August. Online. Available at www.npa.go.jp/archive/keibi/biki/higaijokyo_e.pdf (accessed 15 August 2014). Also see NPR (2011) 'Millions of stricken Japanese lack water, food, heat', *National Public Radio*, 12 April. Online. Available at www.npr.org/2011/03/18/134527591/millions-of-stricken-japanese.html (accessed 10 August 2014).

10 Jiji Press (2012) 'Disaster donations top $520 billion', *Japan Times*, 8 March, 1.

11 Asada, Eiki (2011) 'Overcoming contradictions—QS72 at the disaster site', *International Council of Societies of Industrial Design*. Online. Available at www.icsid.org/feature/current/articles/1562.html (accessed 12 August 2014).

12 Amundsen, Denise (2012) 'History of deployable medical systems (DEPMEDS)', *Olive-Drab*. Online. Available at http://olive-drab.com/od_medical_other_depmeds.php (accessed 16 January 2013).

13 Odulair Corporation (2014) 'Ebola virus outbreak isolation unit', *Odulair Corporation*. Online. Available at www.odulair.com/mobile-

ebola-isolation-treatment-center-portable-ebola-lab.html (accessed 24 November 2014).

14 People for the Ethical Treatment of Animals (2014) 'PETA's mobile clinics division', *PETA*. Online. Available at www.peta.org/about-peta/learn-about-peta/helping-animals-in-hampton-roads/snip/ (accessed 24 November 2014).

15 Anon (2009) 'The mobile health clinic', *Family and Community Medicine*, The University of Arizona. Online. Available at www.fcm.arizona.edu/mobile-health/mobile-clinic.html (accessed 5 August 2014).

16 Cilento, Karen (2010) 'Mobile hospital/Hord Coplan Macht + Spevco', *ArchDaily*, 1 April. Online. Available at www.archdaily.com/?p=54890.html (accessed 20 August 2014).

17 Meinhold, Bridgette (2010) 'The MONARCH system for a mobile and modular hospital', *Inhabitat.com*. Online. Available at http://inhabitat.com/the-monarch-systems-mobile-modular-hospital/ (accessed 20 August 2014).

18 Crouch, Thomas D. (2009) *Lighter than Air: An Illustrated History of Balloons and Airships*, Baltimore: Johns Hopkins University Press.

19 Barnes, C.H. (1989) *Shorts Aircraft since 1900*, New York: U.S. Naval Institute Press/Putnam Aviation Series.

20 Aboitiz, Christa (2004) 'Mobile HIV AIDS health clinic', *Open Architecture Network*. Online. Available at http://openarchitecturenetworknetwork.org/node/497 (accessed 4 May 2014).

21 Philip, Donald N. and Aziz, Mehwish (2012) 'Science outreach through the iDAPT Centre for Rehabilitation Research', *Research Gate*. 44(1): 12–23. Online. Available at www.researchgate.net/publication/230881977_Science_Outreach_through_the_iDAPT_centre.html (accessed 2 December 2014).

22 Editorial (2012) 'About Toronto Rehab', *The Journal of Spinal Cord Medicine*. 35(5): 273–274.

23 Teotonio, Isabel (2011) 'Rehab revolution', *The Toronto Star*. 26 February. Online. Available at www.thestar.com/life/health_wellness/2011/11/24/rehab_revolution.html (accessed 12 November 2013).

24 Editor (2014) 'An interview with United Libyan Holdings', *Hospital Build & Infrastructure Middle East Exhibition & Congress*. 4 June. Dubai: UAE: Dubai International and Exhibition Centre. Online. Available at www.hospitalbuild-me.com/en/MediaZone/Resource-Centre/Interviews/An-Interview.html (accessed 14 November 2014).

25 Miller, Rosalind (2011) 'Revolutionizing healthcare for the poor', *The Guardian*, 21 January. Online. Available at www.theguardian.com/global-development/2011/jan/21/india-low-cost-healthcare (accessed 24 November 2014).

26 Anon (2013) 'India's 1st prefab hospital', *Speed 4 Prefab*. Online. Available at www.speed-4.com/prefab-hospital-in-construction-architecture-update.htm (accessed 24 November 2014).

27 Zeit, Kristin D. (2012) 'Citation of merit winner: Miami Valley Heart and Orthopedic Center.' *Healthcare Design*, 20 September. Online. Available at www.healthcaredesignmagazine.com/article/citation-merit-winner-miami-valley-heart-and-orthopedic-center (accessed 14 June 2014).

28 Bardin, Michael (2013) 'Building resilient communities through design', *Perkins+Will*. Online. Available at www.perkinswill.com/building_resilient_communities_rdoc.html (accessed 12 February 2014).

29 Knickmeyer, Erin and Thanawala, Sudhin (2014) 'Strong California quake shakes famed wine country, injures dozens', *Global News*, 25 August. Online. Available at www.globalnews.ca/news/1523921/earthquake-shakes-californias-san-francisco-bay-area-wine-country/ (accessed 24 November 2014).

Appendices

APPENDIX 1

Installation sites 7–18 in New Orleans and Charleston

7.Bowling Alley Charleston

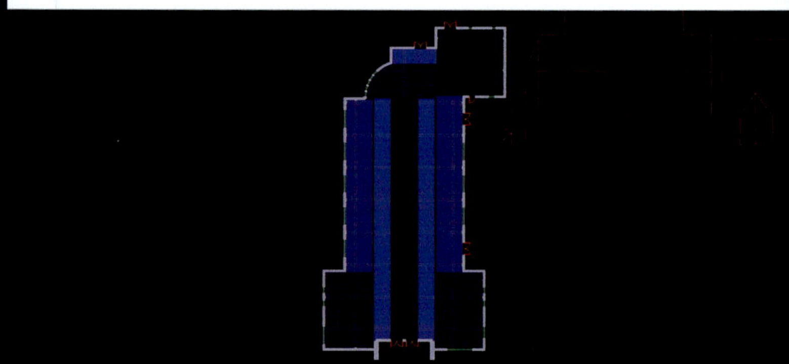

8.Greater St. Luke AME Church Charleston

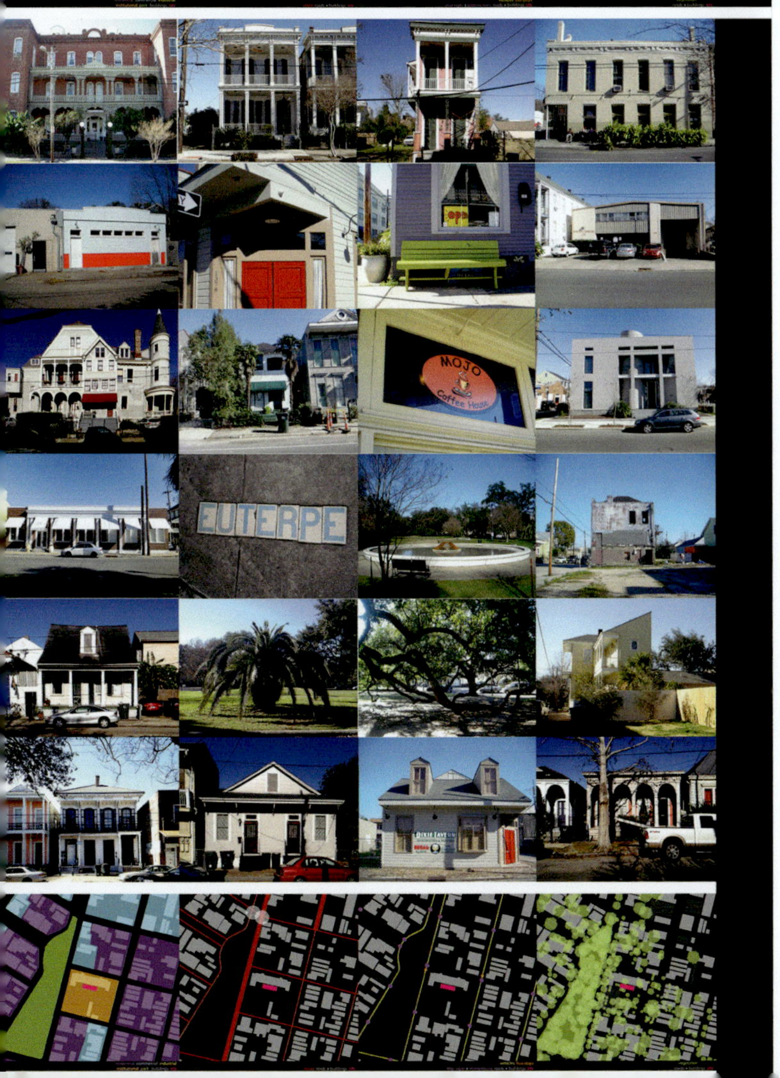

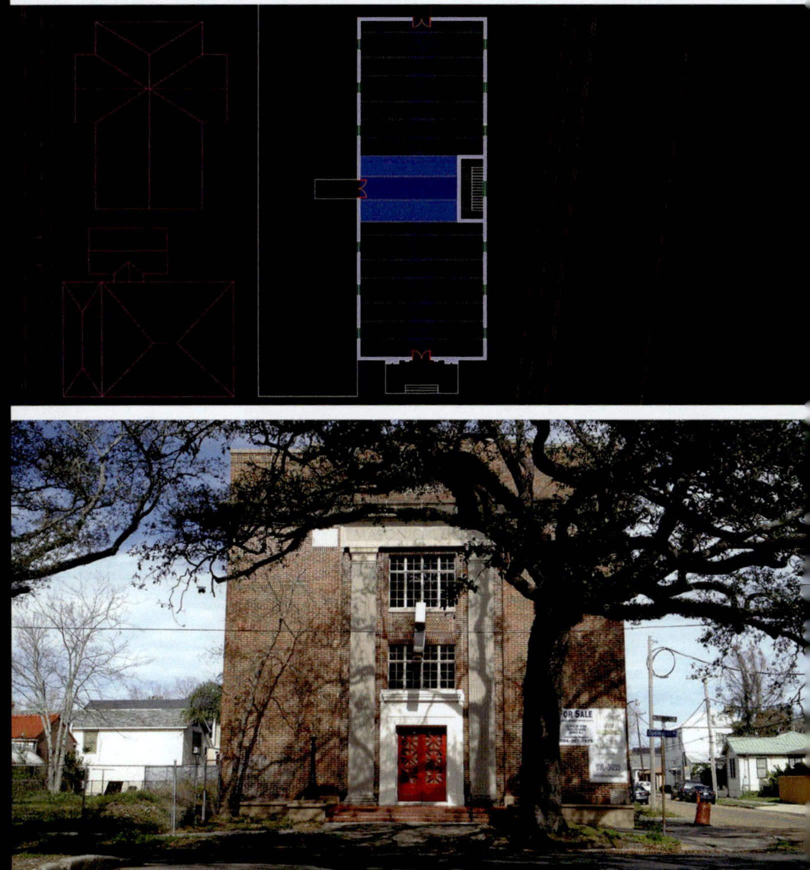

9. Masonic Temple New Orleans

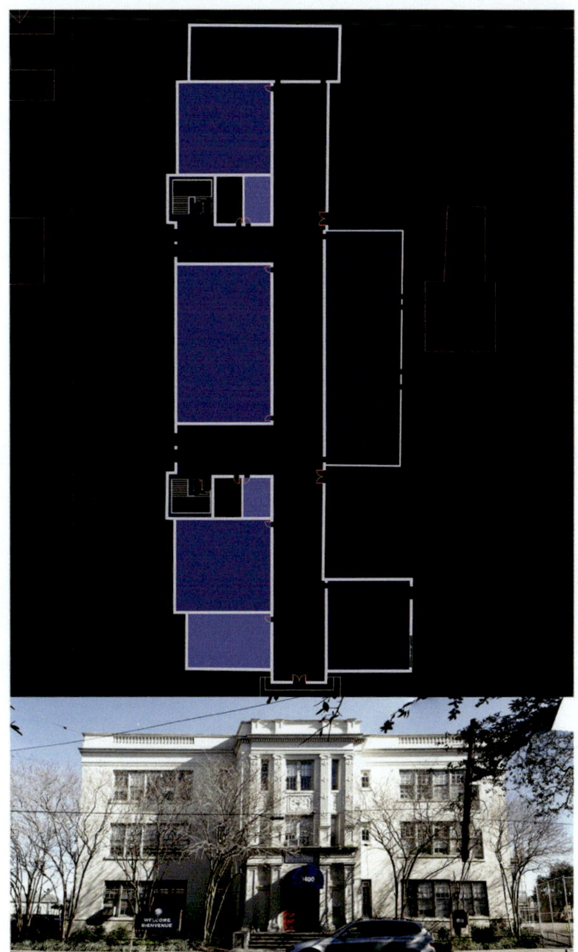

10. International School of Louisiana New Orleans

11. College of Charleston Library Charleston

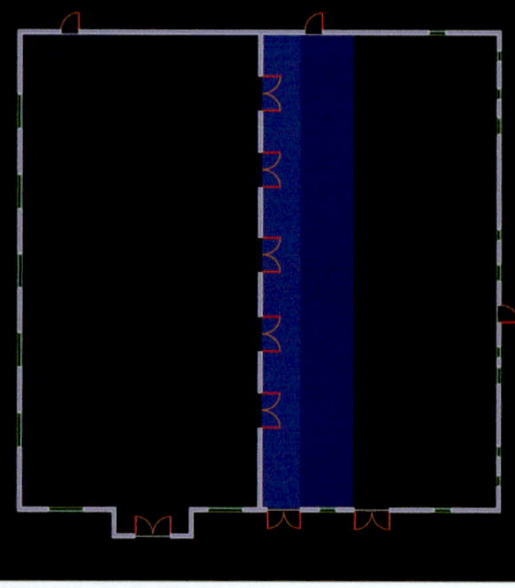

12. Mt. Carmel Baptist Church, Lower Ninth New Orleans

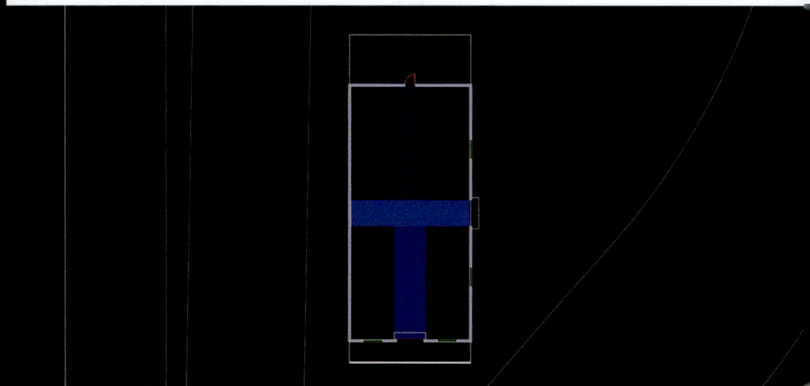

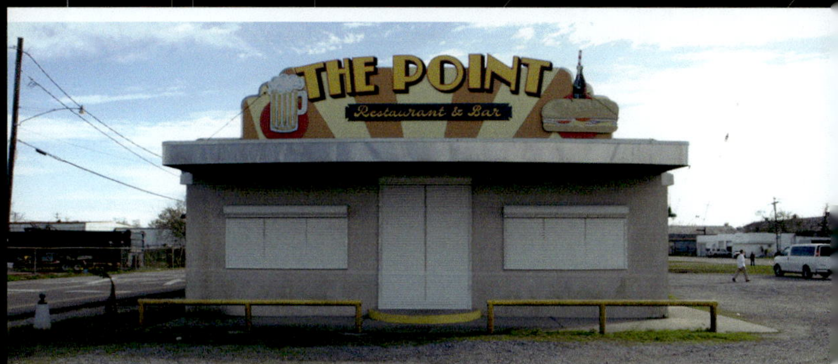

13. The Point New Orleans

14. Fire Station 20 New Orleans

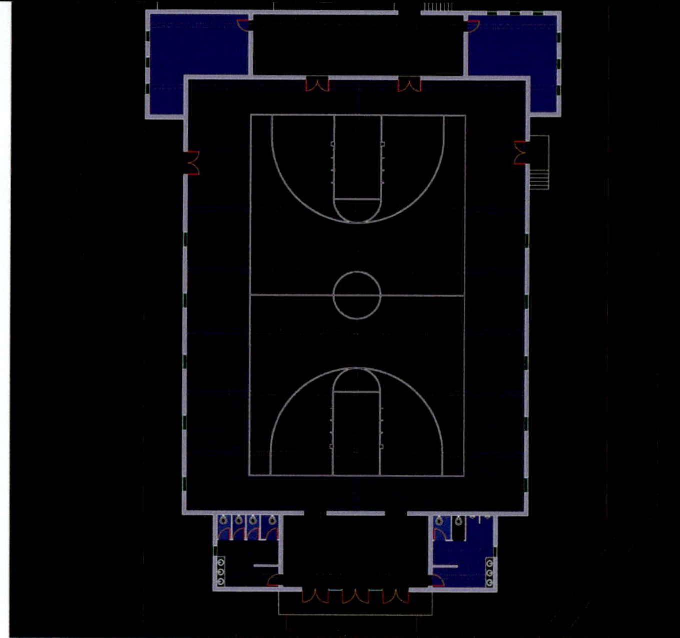

15. Ursuline Academy Gymnasium New Orleans

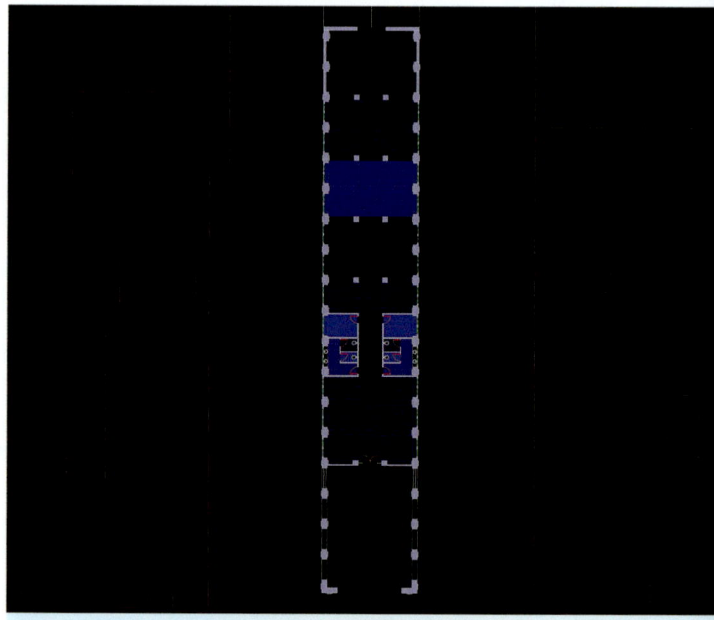

16. Charleston City Market Charleston

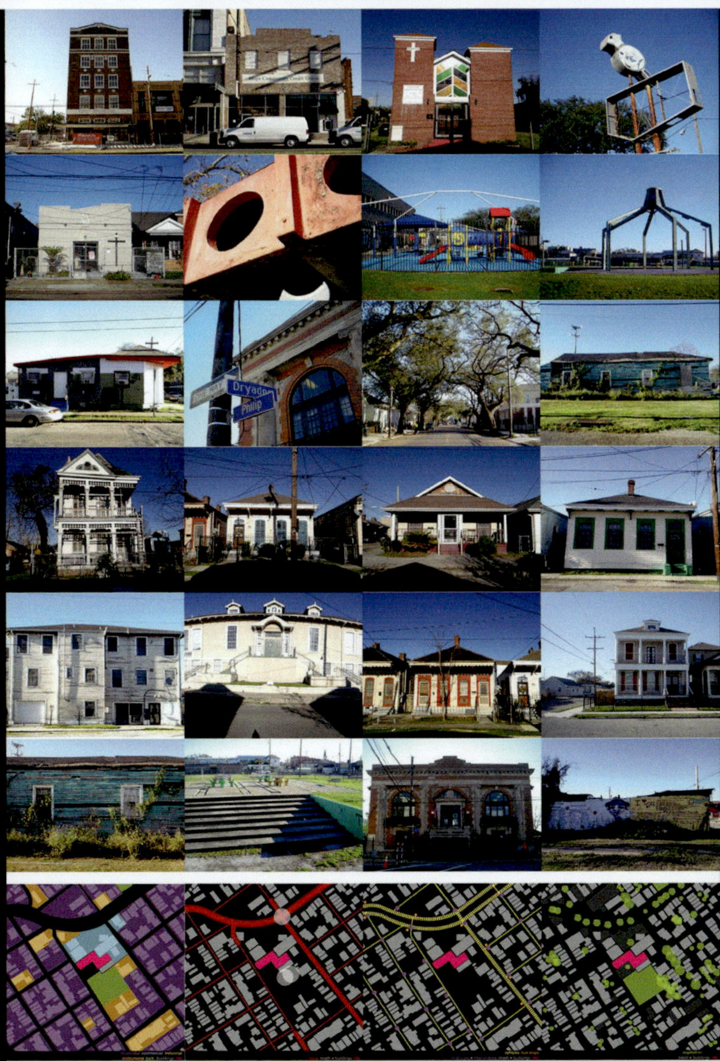

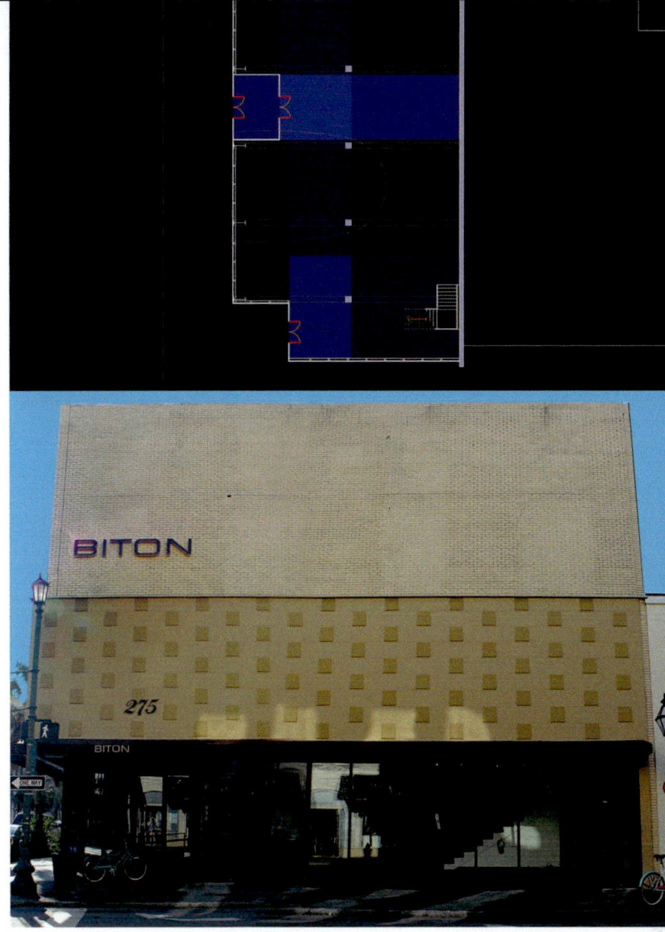

17. Biton Storefront Charleston

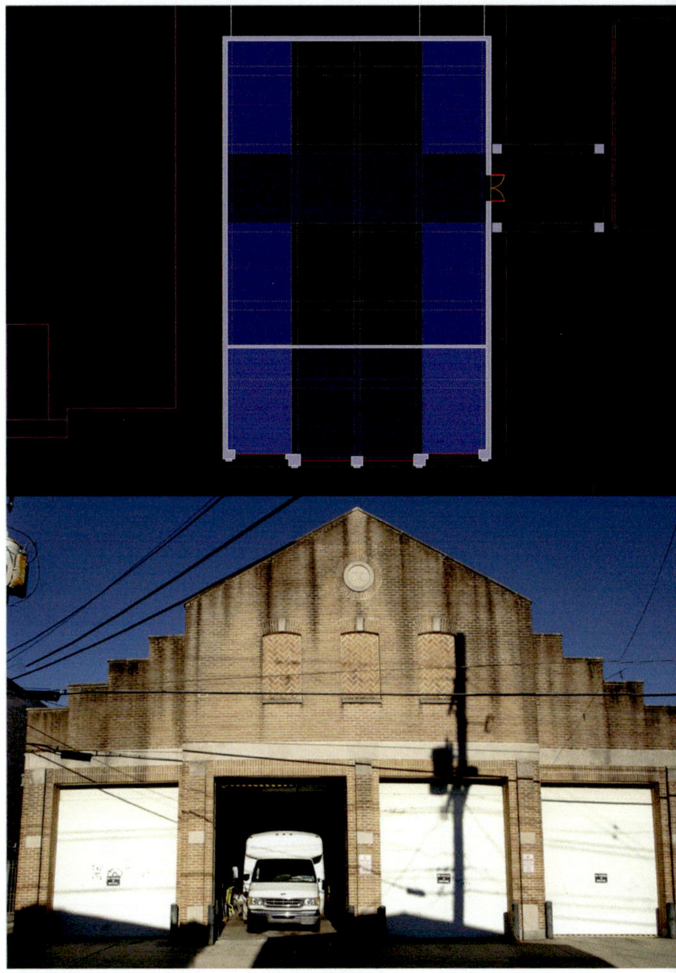

18.EOC Senior Citizens Center New Orleans

Four interviews

APPENDIX 2

Interview 1

View from the nursing director of a pop-up clinic in the aftermath of Hurricane Katrina—interview with Gail Gibson, RN, February 2014

In the harrowing days after Katrina's devastation of New Orleans in 2005, the Louisiana State University Health Science Center (LSUHSC) needed temporary quarters, quickly, to consolidate its outpatient clinics. With few buildings left undamaged, the LSUHSC Interim Clinic settled on the vacant Lord & Taylor department store next to the Louisiana Superdome. Gail Gibson, RN, is currently the Stateside Consulting Nursing Coordinator with the State of Louisiana Department of Health and Hospitals, Office of Public Health. She served as the Assistant Director at the LSUHSC Downtown Clinic from its opening in November 2005.

SV: Please discuss the origin of the LSUHSC Interim Clinic.
GG: We needed a location in close proximity to where we were prior to Katrina, one large enough to house all of our medical services plus room for expansion. We knew we might be there for a few years before we could move to a permanent location. As we explored potential sites, one particular building [the vacant department store] came up as the best option and we immediately asked the LSUHSC Facilities Director to meet with the State Facilities Planning and Control Office [part of the State of Louisiana Division of Administration, based in Baton Rouge]. Due to the large size of this space we were worried that converting it for use as a temporary clinic would take far too long.

SV: Where were you housed before this?
GG: Within a week after Katrina we set up in four open-air tents in the parking lot at the LSUHSC University Hospital a few blocks away. The U.S. Army set up these tents, and they housed triage, urgent care and a small laboratory. Surgical services were not provided. We were there from September to the end of November. By early October the USS *Comfort* [hospital ship] had arrived. It was docked at the [Mississippi] riverfront next to the Riverwalk [mall]. I was one of the many hundreds of first responders still displaced. When the [pop-up] clinic opened on Poydras Street in the empty Lord & Taylor store, the staff working in the tents moved in and many of them were still living on the hospital ship.

SV: Did the State of Louisiana sign a lease with the owner of the mall in order to gain access to this space?
GG: Yes, originally, it was a five-year lease and it was renewed for a second five years in 2011. So they are currently in the period of the second lease, with the expectation the Interim Clinic will be out of the building by the time the second lease ends [in 2016]. In laying out the spaces for this clinic we made sure there was enough space for everything we needed plus room to expand on the assumption that everything takes much longer than first expected in terms of [permanent] facility construction. Bob Arnold, the LSUHSC Director of Facilities at the time, was instrumental. He was very good to work with because he was patient, listened carefully when we were conveying our space needs, and he coordinated the pre-move construction work. He carefully translated our space needs on a line item basis for all of our programs. He developed the layout and [circulation] flow plan including the locations of all newly installed portable sinks, water supply lines, all signs, the cubicles, where and how far apart, and the medical equipment—even including the large hyperbaric chamber we disassembled at the closed Charity Hospital a block away and rebuilt at the Lord & Taylor site.

SV: What types of outpatient services were provided?
GG: When we opened it was strictly a Level 1 Urgent Care Center. Later, we added a general primary care clinic, internal medicine, and gradually numerous specialty clinics. Soon, we were providing everything from ophthalmology to orthopedics. This was followed by minor outpatient surgical procedures, and still later, neurology and cardiac care. Any specialization we added was dependent upon getting our physician specialists back to New Orleans. Our personnel was widely dispersed everywhere after the disaster, including all of the medical students and interns. This made it extremely difficult for them to simply pick up and come back right away. The timing of this ramping-up process was critical.

SV: If you were to do this again, what would you do differently?
GG: A three-level department store with a large central atrium is not set up to suddenly become a high-volume [pop-up] healthcare clinic. The biggest challenges included having nowhere near enough private, lockable rooms with walls all the way up to the ceiling. You always had to be cognizant of patient privacy and confidentiality because everyone could basically hear everything. Other pressing facility issues revolved around establishing Internet support, to staffing, to setting up a somewhat logical patient movement system throughout the clinic's three floors. It simply was not designed for the high volume of people who needed to use it daily and especially the intense level of use it had to support on the major clinic days. The two escalators were extremely narrow and unreliable. There was only one public elevator and it was small. In no way did the clinic comply with Americans with Disabilities Act (ADA) minimum requirements in the way of bathrooms or other accommodations for the disabled. There were stairwells, but these were too remote from where the patients traveled within the clinic and far out of the way, so no one could ever find them. As a result, they were for emergency use, and little else. The stairwells were designed for fire escape use and not for regular public use so they weren't public stairwells at all. The big atrium in the center of the store took up too much space and the circulation system wrapped around it. The escalators were in plain sight in this massive open space that took up all three levels. From the escalators you could see from the top floor all the way up to the bottom floor because it was entirely open. This was a pain, because we really had to take that into consideration when deciding where things were going to be—where things were going to be in relation to the escalators because while going up and down the escalators you could see right into the open cubicles in direct view below. So we had to be really careful about the arrangement of all diagnostic and treatment cubicles from a privacy standpoint.

SV: Did the elderly have particular problems with its openness?
GG: This was a challenge, especially for the aged patients dependent on canes, walkers, and wheelchairs. The escalators were always breaking down, there was only one freight elevator, and the fire stairs were remotely located and out of sight. We had many issues with wheelchair-bound patients, regardless of their age. Worse, the staff and patients always had to share the same set of escalators in the open central atrium as well as the same elevators and bathrooms.

SV: What was it like to always transport medical records from floor to floor?
GG: Unfortunately, with only a single public elevator to serve a three-level clinic, it was always being used to transport patient

medical records. Luckily, the trash could be removed using the industrial-grade freight elevator. It was useful when we needed to move real freight, but it could not ever be used as a second public elevator for patients because it had huge garage doors.

SV: Describe the directional signage.
GG: The staff and patients were forced to share the same circulation paths from day one. One of the biggest challenges from the opening day was poor directional signs. We really, really had to work on making the signage more effective to assist people in finding where everything was. It could get very confusing. Going from one level to another was so hard for so many—directing people to the right floor for their appointment. It would have been far less complicated if the clinic were on two floors or on only one floor. There were so many waiting rooms because we had to set up numerous ones on each floor. We constantly strove to improve the signage. In time, we placed a large board inside the main entry on the main level and it listed what was located on each floor. Signs were created to show how to use the escalators and stairs—anywhere patients needed to get to. As a matter of fact, it seemed like we studied this day in and out. On different days—sometimes on the same day—we had three or four high volume clinics going on at the same time in the same part of the clinic. For example, in Third Floor Section A, internal medicine was scheduled in the morning and endocrinology scheduled as the evening clinic. What I did was have generic sign holders created so you could slide into a slot what was going on any given weekday or night in every part of the clinic on all three floors. This alone required a lot of staff coordination. Soon, we color-coded discrete sections—those clusters of partitions that comprised each major clinical area. If there were, for example, eight exam rooms clustered together these were coded in a certain color. On each floor, there were color-coded sections labeled A, B, C, D, and so on. The red section was Section A and the blue one was Section B, and this helped patients get to their destination. The color-coding concept remained constant although the type of clinic occurring in a given section would change, as mentioned, from day to day or even within the same day. Because the overall volume of clinic space was immense, but with only very few lockable rooms, we were forced to create offices in the former dressing rooms areas tucked away in the far corners on each level. The condition of the (inherited) carpeting came up every time we were surveyed by the accreditation agency. It was worn out and fraying and this posed a tripping/fall hazard. We replaced all the carpet twice. The entire roof was also replaced because we endured chronic leaks that would drip on the shiny floors right down throughout the clinic and this caused mold and accident issues. During the first year the leaky roof was a big problem.

SV: How was the lighting throughout the clinic?
GG: The lighting wasn't great at all. We had to supplement the existing ceiling fixtures with adjustable (task ambient) portable lights, and also specially designed high-wattage light fixtures versus the existing fixtures from when it was a department store. Six months are after we moved in we had to open a satellite clinic nearby (at University Hospital) for those services most dependent upon more intensive lighting requirements such as dermatology. Because we were in a shopping mall (built in 1987) it was windowless. This lack of windows was an ongoing problem for the staff, in general, and no one raved about the lack of windows and daylight. But when you have to, you adjust. However, perhaps the atrium had some positive effect in maybe taking peoples' minds off of their own workspace because they had that larger space to look at in the middle. At least one could look out or walk out briefly into this larger area away from one's small exam room cubicle or office. The only area where we could see outside was at the main entrance on the street level.

SV: Was a break room provided for the staff or any places for respite?
GG: Yes, but it had to be added later—a full kitchen with sink, microwave, refrigerator, and storage cabinets.

SV: In the clinic were the plumbing lines run vertically? Did they have to drill holes in the floors in order to run these lines?
GG: It was a little of both and it was a chronic problem. So many sinks, probably sixty, overall, had to be added.

SV: How was the heating and air conditioning?
GG: For the most part, it was fine. We never had any major complaints about the heating or air conditioning systems. But we were always aware that we did not have an emergency backup generator if and when another Katrina should strike.

SV: If you were to do this again, would you rather have opened up in a place like an empty grocery store where everything could be on one level?
GG: I would have to say definitely yes. Definitively. One level would have been far better for so many reasons. Also, it would have been better to have backup power generators on site in the parking lot, and for the public to be able to more effectively find their way around inside the facility. But no space like that was available in early 2006 in a ruined New Orleans, nothing that wasn't already badly ruined by the flood. Because we needed to be as close to the inpatient services and emergency room at University Hospital this Lord & Taylor space was best suited. Everything was flooded in the immediate area around the hospital that would have otherwise been a candidate. As it was, we were forced to send our laboratory specimens for testing and analysis down to Houma, an hour south of the city. We used a courier system for this and three pick-ups and three deliveries were scheduled daily. Interestingly, the temporary lab set up in Houma was in a vacant grocery store. This was designated the LSUHSC main lab and it was there for a year before it could be relocated back to University Hospital in downtown New Orleans, near us.

SV: Did you ever imagine this pop-up clinic would be operating in an abandoned former department store for ten years?
GG: Yes, I expected it might be this long. But we had no way to know when it was first set up whether it would be for one year, two, or more because no one really knew at the time. It took what seemed like forever to get all the approvals for the replacement hospital to begin construction [the 425-bed LSUHSC replacement hospital opened in 2015 in Mid City New Orleans, five blocks away].

SV: Was parking a problem?
GG: Parking for patients was available in the parking lot next door at the Superdome. About a year after we opened we began to offer valet parking for our patients who were immobile and/or elderly because they needed assistance in getting in and out of the clinic. Luckily, there was a covered drive at the main entrance on Poydras Street. This worked out reasonably well and there were also accessible public bus transit stops and routes.

SV: How do you think patients regarded the clinic? Did they accept it, or otherwise?
GG: They did well, overall, while some consistently struggled. Above all, most were relatively comfortable with the place because there was a lot of love conveyed by the staff from day one. In the waiting rooms, you know, we tried to make it as comfortable as possible, and everyone got to watch television. I think the patients have done well with it and I can't complain about what we were able to provide in the way of patient support. This applied to staffing, the equipment, furnishings, or whenever supplies were needed. The care itself was provided on a sliding scale based on one's ability to pay. There were minimum Medicaid and Medicare base level requirements one had to qualify for in order to receive free care and the fee scale slid down to zero. More than 80 percent were provided care for free because they could not otherwise pay for it on their own. Many patients with chronic conditions continued to come back to the clinic for many years. This is pretty amazing in and of itself.

SV: How well has the staff hung in there all these years in a temporary facility? Has there been much turnover?
GG: Actually, no. Our staffing was very stable during the first seven years. But when Children's Hospital took over the management of LSUHSC University [Interim] Hospital and its network of outpatient clinics [in 2013], we began to experience high staff turnover. Strangely, our location was still called the LSUHSC Interim Clinic and the main acute care hospital was still called the LSUHSC Interim Hospital even though Children's [Hospital] technically now ran both.

SV: What will happen with the Lord & Taylor space when this pop-up relocates to its permanent home?
GG: Tom Benson, the owner of the New Orleans Saints of the National Football League, wants to turn the entire shopping mall into a glittering sports entertainment venue. As for us, we had to make our own best guesses from the very beginning. It was a constant process of trial and error with no roadmap or owner's manual of any type.

Interview 2

View From a global healthcare NGO provider—interview with Allison Howard-Berry, July 2013

Non-governmental organizations (NGOs) are taking on a more prominent role in sponsoring prefab primary health clinics in medically underserved places worldwide. One such organization, C2C (Containers to Clinics), based in the Chicago area, assists medical care providers by providing staff and facilities in post-disaster strike zones.

SV: How was C2C founded and how long it has it been in existence?
AH-B: Elizabeth Sheehan founded C2C in 2008 on the premise of providing what we call *last-mile medicine*—bringing basic primary and sickness prevention healthcare services to medically vulnerable communities. Our special emphasis is on women and children because they are the most vulnerable inhabitants in these communities. Our flagship clinic is currently in operation in Haiti. C2C is a long-term redevelopment organization, as opposed to a first responder disaster relief organization. As an NGO, we occupy a specific niche. Dr. Sheehan is a physician by training and has spent several decades working abroad in Africa and in Asia. The founding of the organization was the culmination of her life's work in medicine, public health, and global development. We spent 2009, our first full year, working on a prototype containerized clinic. We devoted much effort on ensuring its financial sustainability over the long term, as this differentiates us from the broader disaster relief community.

SV: Did you have any affiliation with the Clinton-Bush Relief Fund for Haiti in 2010?
AH-B: No, no direct affiliation. They work at higher levels such as relations with the Haitian government, and multilateral organizations like the World Health Organization, so they do not generally work directly with private sector NGOs.

SV: Is the C2C facility in Port-au-Prince?
AH-B: Yes, we sponsor one unit in Port-au-Prince, a second unit further north and a third clinic in Namibia, in Southern Africa. We operate all three. In the Port-au-Prince clinic we work directly with Grace Children's Hospital. This clinic works in tandem with a hospital that lost 80 percent of its buildings in the earthquake. They needed a special solution for women's services. We partnered to provide physical space and funding for women's health education and prenatal care and the doctors and staff in the clinic are, technically, employees of the partner hospital. In the case of Namibia, the C2C clinic is a partnership with the Ministry of Health. We therefore plugged in directly to the public health system there, and the staff is part of the Namibian health system.

SV: C2C always offers its services to a local provider?
AH-B: Yes, that's right. We definitely look for local partners within communities, and determine if it can be successful. We conduct extensive due diligence before we approach an organization so we already know something about its history, track record, viability, and the quality of care it generally provides. We're most interested in their broad-based mission and goals and in their historical performance but we also understand that by virtue of seeking out some support from C2C they will have gaps in their performance record. In the case of Grace Children's Hospital, they had a specific aim to improve the care provided to pregnant women. In the case of Namibia, the local government sought a solution to their crisis-level infant mortality problem. Namibia has a very severe infant mortality problem and in fact it had doubled in only ten years. Women are dying at childbirth there due to an acute lack of prenatal care. These deaths are avoidable if problems are identified early. It was a strategic, targeted intervention. We are providing prenatal care that catches early-stage complications. In the case of this clinic, our due diligence revolved around precise market research, making sure that, first, a need existed, and second, to understand the health economics at the village level. Before, people paid for health services but received low quality care in return. C2C now provides a higher level of care for roughly the same cost they paid before.

SV: Does C2C make a minimum or maximum commitment to a community?
AH-B: Yes. With the Port-au-Prince clinic it is a five-year commitment. With the Namibia clinic it is a three-year commitment. The time frame varies based on the needs of the local partner. In the case of Haiti it was very clear that three years would not be enough. Our second Haitian clinic is a joint venture with a private sector provider we hope will assume ownership, in time. We do not aspire to be in any community forever, only to fill an interim need

in capacity. A physical site needs to be furnished by each partner organization. So far, so good. Our strategy is to build credibility early on. We form a local steering committee so key stakeholders, whether religious leaders, teachers, village elders, or businesspersons, are part of the local planning process.

SV: Shifting gears a bit, how does C2C commission its architects? How did the organization contact Anshen + Allen, and Stack?
AH-B: It has been a journey. From the organization's inception, we focused on containerized solutions; as we evolved and grew we developed a longer-term strategic plan. Now, we have more expertise but it is interesting to think back to when we worked to 'solve' the ISO modular container. We learned quickly, as we found architects interested in adapting shipping containers as building modules. We didn't seek to reinvent the wheel. One can go online and buy any number of various generic, containerized modular clinics. The challenge isn't really the box itself, but getting the box there, making sure it is full of the right things, and making sure the right local partnerships are in place so that the facility fulfills our vision for its performance. At the time C2C was based in Boston, where there are many specialists in global health, and a lot of energy and expertise in this area. We approached our advisory board, together with local experts, to learn what the various options were and the most strategic direction going forward. We hosted a public lecture and it attracted a lot of attention. Instantly, architecture firms approached us offering their services, pro-bono, to internally plan and design a prototype modular clinic for us. It's interesting, because shipping containers come in a few sizes, i.e. eight feet by twenty feet or eight feet by thirty feet with few other options. Designing a facility really wasn't that hard, because you don't have that much space to work with in the first place. We found the interesting part was the transition from design to fabrication. It was all well and good on paper; because there were literally only so many ways you can situate a bed, sink, and a medical cabinet. The real challenge was in the fabrication process—actually manufacturing the building components in the U.S. for shipment to other countries. We knew we were going into very hot and humid climates where electricity, water, and sanitation are always major challenges. Those were among the biggest issues we had to solve. We built each of our prefab clinics with different fabricators, so we have been experimenting. We haven't built with the same manufacturer twice.

SV: Is that so C2C can garner new ideas?
AH-B: Each time we learn as we search for ways to lower costs. We strive to provide the asset for the lowest cost while maintaining high quality. We focus on construction materials: it has to be well insulated; the power source must work because it is going into a tough environment, and it must be durable. There can be no compromising on materials; there must be a laser-focused priority on construction quality. As we get better and better at what we do, this is happening in a more streamlined manner. We are continually in talks with our vendors to keep capital costs down. The first prototype, done with Stack Design Build [stackdb.com] in Rhode Island, was the hardest. We had to make tough decisions along the way but they were terrific to work with. We built the second clinic with LS Industries, a large company that builds everything out of ISO shipping containers. And the third time, we worked with a group based in Miami, a much smaller company, with expertise in working with containers. Of course, the main benefit of being in Miami was that it was the nearest U.S. port to Haiti. We were able to efficiently transport the two clinics from Miami to Haiti.

SV: You worked with Anshen + Allen on the first clinic. Did you work with different architects on the second and third facilities?
AH-B: No, we found we really didn't need an architect. Anshen + Allen had some great ideas about the layout of the first designs, but because it's only eight feet by twenty feet, there were relatively few ways they could arrange things internally. We learned from patients the second time around, and our doctors and nurses about how they needed the limited space to be configured. They provided great feedback, things like 'we don't need this window,' or 'we need shutters here,' or 'we need an extra sturdy lock over here,' or 'the sink should be over here.' It was a user-focused process the second time around. We relied on Anshen + Allen and StackDB very heavily at the beginning, however, because we were a new organization and didn't have any operations abroad. Once we were operational abroad, we then obtained feedback from our own direct users. Thus far, our two-container facility configuration works well with one for patient consultations, and a second housing a laboratory, pharmacy, and staff workspace. We always configure the two containers in an L with a connecting canopy—an open-air roof—a patio roof fabricated of corrugated metal with seating and a deck provided beneath. It offers protection from the elements. In the rainy season it rains late in the day after the clinic has closed,

but the heat is the major challenge nearly every day. This siting provides direct access to patient treatment spaces and the pharmacy window, and patients can wait outside for their lab results. This outdoor space needs to be safe and protected, especially from the heat and sun. This is where health education consultation, such as HIV prevention and reproductive health education, is provided because patients may wait for a while on the busiest days.

SV: Do you use video monitors?
AH-B: We do. We equip each clinic with at least one television for global health education videos presented in the local language, such as Haitian Creole, at the Port-au-Prince clinic.

SV: Are there normal hours of operation?
AH-B: The hours are approximately 9:00am to 3:00pm, but this depends on local norms. In Namibia, people get up very early and are lined up outside the clinic as early as 8:00am. In Haiti, things tend to close down by 2:00pm. It just gets so hot, but the staff works later on administrative tasks such as inventory management. The clinics are open Monday through Friday and all onsite volunteers are trained, paid clinicians. Restroom facilities are provided outside the containers. Before the containers arrive at the local port, we prepare the site to ensure it is level with a solid (usually concrete) pad, piers provided for the containers to be installed on, and the fresh water supply is in place. The Namibia site was basically a desert, and we had to prepare the site from scratch, whereas in downtown Port-au-Prince, it was much easier to come in with the containers, because there was already a basic infrastructure in place. We always provide either repurposed existing toilets or build two toilets on the site for use by patients and staff.

SV: What are C2Cs goals for the next five years?
AH-B: Our strategic plan is for three or four new containerized portable clinics each year for the next five years. We are headed into a growth phase and this involves raising additional capital to launch new clinic sites. The idea is that each clinic will financially break even after three years. We see no real need to set up any clinics domestically in the United States. We remain focused on our work abroad, and committed in particular to Haiti in part because it is the nearest clinic site to the U.S.

SV: Have you looked at tents or any way to combine tents with a containerized facility?
AH-B: We have carefully studied other types of prefab solutions. There are many types of post-disaster relief tents and things such as modular POD clinics, different kinds of things, and especially after the earthquake in Haiti. The organization Safer Children used different building materials [from us] so we have seen other prefabricated options. I think a lot of them are great. It really depends on the long-term goals of the operation. If the goal is immediate disaster relief, other types of NGOs will provide water purification tablets and food distribution to meet victims' short-term needs. I think some type of a POD could be terrific. We have the goal of being in place for so long, however, so we really prefer a sturdier, containerized, solution as opposed to a tent, fiberglass panel building, or an air-inflated fabric structure.

SV: Are tents more appropriate for a first responder organization, in your view?
AH-B: For first responders, probably yes. A fully containerized clinic may not be ideal for a first responder if you need to have full electricity, air conditioning, and water and sanitary services up and operational quickly. A first responder must get in there fast with the aim of saving lives, and because of this they are probably better off in something significantly more flexible. It is not terribly challenging to bring containers in but we have to deal with customs at the port, and each loaded container weighs 6,000–7,000 pounds, so you need flatbed trucking, and a crane and forklift. This requires precise logistical support in order to get it to the right destination, and this alone can be extremely challenging in a first responder situation.

SV: Do you have any advice for architects as to how they can become more involved with this type of work?
AH-B: The organization Architecture for Humanity [now defunct] is better able to answer that question. We worked, early on, with Anshen + Allen [now part of STANTEC], a firm with a keen sense of pro-bono social responsibility. I find that progressive architecture firms will do pro-bono health-service driven projects. We had many different architects interested in 'building in' this kind of expertise into our mission at the founding of our organization. There certainly is interest out there among architectural professionals in the United States but I can't speak directly to the expertise they need to ideally have. Of course, many architecture firms have considerable

experience in healthcare design so there already exists a natural synergy between architecture firms designing hospitals and clinics, and NGOs seeking to transfer this expertise to emergency care facilities in developing countries. The NGO Partners in Health is a large Boston-based organization that is also working in Haiti. They recently opened a first world, state-of-the-art hospital in central Haiti that was designed by Western architects—American architects. I believe there are many architects who would wish to contribute their expertise to socially responsible projects in post-disaster situations.

SV: Do you think a North American survey of healthcare architects on this subject would be of interest to NGOs at this point in time?
AH-B: Yes, this would be very interesting and helpful. Anecdotally, I think there would be much interest in such a survey. At present there is no way to know in what part of the country [within the U.S.] interest among architects might be greatest, or the commitment to devote X number of hours per week greatest, or how a firm would best go about donating its services. Right now it seems to be a very individualized proposition, depending on the interests of a particularly motivated individual within the context of the firm he or she works in or leads. It seems the smaller the firm, the easier it is to have the leeway to take on a project like this. On the other hand, the larger firm would seem to have the deepest financial and staffing resources to be able to dedicate its energies to this important work.

Interview 3

View from the military sector—interview with Colonel (retired U.S. Army) Richard Gullickson, May 2013

This interview explores the U.S. Army Military Health System (MHS), the National Disaster Medical System (NDMS), and the deployment of portable hospitals worldwide. It was conducted at Fort Gordon, Georgia, and included a tour of the CSH unit stationed there. This portable hospital is used at present for training and education and yet remains at 24/7 readiness. Colonel Gullickson served as the U.S. Army MHS Chief Commander in Bosnia, where he oversaw the 249th CSH, a 476-bed installation that treated over 9,500 casualties.

SV: What is the National Disaster Medical System?
RG: The NDMS is operational throughout the U.S. It grew out of the Federal Emergency Management Agency (FEMA). FEMA's experience in post-disaster mitigation greatly influences the scope and type of support currently provided by the U.S. military in post-disaster civilian contexts. Our military-based teams have equipment that is prepackaged and preloaded for rapid deployment to any disaster site, anywhere. The NDMS consists of specially trained medical assistance teams and mortuary support teams. The primary operating (facility) system for the U.S. Army is the Combat Support Hospital, or CSH, and over time it has morphed significantly into an autonomous support unit. Each CSH has, on hand, always, 248 beds staged for use in the field, wherever needed. In Hurricane Katrina in 2005, the 115th CSH, out of Fort Polk, Louisiana, was deployed to provide immediate assistance and the 21st CSH followed soon thereafter.

SV: In what types of post-disaster settings are U.S. Army CSH units most effective?
RG: When you look at the entire post-disaster mitigation system under FEMA, first off, all disasters are defined as local in nature. If the capabilities of the local authorities, followed by state-level authorities, become overwhelmed, then they turn to the federal government. This most often results in a Presidential Declaration, where a specific geographic area is declared a federal disaster area. And this is when FEMA comes in—FEMA sets up its Federal Coordinating Office and proceeds to manage the disaster both locally and at the federal response level. The deployment of a military CSH system is the most expensive option. FEMA's role is first to stabilize and set up subcontracts to help get the local economy up and running again. The U.S. military is a costly proposition because every expense item must be borne by the military. The unit deployed to New Orleans after Katrina was on site a total of ninety days and it was set up on the uppermost level of the Superdome's parking deck.

SV: How do FEMA and the MHS coordinate personnel and resources?
RG: FEMA will pump a lot of money in up front to get the local community back up on its feet. FEMA's role is to gradually disengage once it has completed its first response mitigation mission. The MHS and FEMA will meet regularly, and they

designate key liaisons for all communications throughout the mitigation process. For example, if FEMA asks the MHS for emergency evacuation vehicles the MHS will translate that request into the delivery of say, twenty-four or thirty-six vehicles. What does that equate to? It equates to a full EMS ambulance company. So, we will activate a ground ambulance company, drawing from either local active National Guard Reserve Units, or from one or more active regular Army components stationed at nearby military bases. It is strictly a capabilities-based response. FEMA's Federal Coordinating Office and the MHS orchestrate all operations.

SV: Does the state where the disaster occurred figure much in this process?
RG: Within the affected state, its statewide Department of Public Health normally will handle the emergency medical response, and staff its own Statewide Emergency Operations Center (EOC). In the case of Hurricanes Katrina and Rita in 2005 the EOC was based in Baton Rouge. Since then, FEMA constructed a huge emergency medical evacuation shelter in Alexandria (Louisiana). It is a permanent, year-round facility on call 24/7. Thousands of cots are stored there, for instance. All kinds of equipment and supplies are prepositioned there in the event something suddenly happens along the [Gulf] coast. The Centers for Disease Control and Prevention (CDC) maintains its own National Stockpile of post-disaster equipment and pharmaceuticals in the event of an outbreak of communicable disease after a disaster.

SV: What are the key physical features of a CSH facility?
RG: The CSH is entirely containerized prior to deployment. This applies to every single function we take into the field – from a containerized radiology unit to a complete OR (operating room) unit. Shipping containers store the medical equipment and these conform to conventional ISO container standards. Certain of these expand outward on two sides from a baseline-shipping configuration. And within an OR-ISO we can ship two procedure tables and therefore two surgical operations can occur simultaneously. As for traditional brick-and-mortar facilities—we provide the same capabilities as an Eisenhower Medical Center—although we operate our hospital as a mix of tents and rigid containers. We have a laboratory, pharmacy, radiology unit, and the Army's Medical Field Feeding System (MFFS)—it is truly a system of systems. For the hospital to be operationalized you have to have all full electrical support system, water distribution system, the staff and patient internal flow systems in place, and all medical logistics systems online in order to operate the hospital on a 24/7 basis. If any one of these systems is not fully functioning it will have a detrimental impact on the patient. Upon deployment to a disaster site, and after installation, the CSH can accept its first patient within eight to twelve hours. But you're usually not going to be fully operational for another forty-eight to seventy-two hours, depending on the proficiency of the medical and administrative personnel.

SV: Do you have predetermined scenarios for deployment? For instance, does the MHS have a small-size CSH unit, mid-size, and maximum-size unit?
RG: We normally deploy an initial entry package—a forty-four-bed facility. This is the basic configuration. It can be ramped up to an eighty-four-bed facility although beyond eighty-four beds you're probably going to be there a long while. A 248-bed facility is the largest CSH configuration possible at this time. Normally they will divide its day-to-day operations, on the administrative side, into an Alpha Company and Bravo Company. Normally we deploy our Bravo Company as a forty-four-bed, early-entry package. In Afghanistan, the MHS utilized a combination of existing brick and mortar facilities, together with adjacent portable CSH facilities. Brick and mortar hospitals and clinics are termed 'hardened facilities.'

SV: What happens to a CSH unit after it returns from a combat theatre?
RG: As a theater matures – and this happened repeatedly in Iraq—the units deployed early stay there and in time new units will continue to fall in 'underneath' the existing CSH on site. It then becomes a matter of personnel replacement rather than equipment replacement. Over time, as equipment wears out, replacement procurement processes determine if 'We've got to reorder this suction equipment' for instance, and this will happen as normal procedure. The 86th CSH is famous for the Baghdad ER with Casper Jones—he was its commander at the time. They actually fell in on Saddam's (Hussein) private hospital in Baghdad—and operated more out of that fixed-site permanent facility than from the CSH itself. Iraq became (by 2013) a 'mature theater.' When I was in Bosnia in the late 1990s we operated out of a facility called the Blue Factory. It was basically a truck stop, to be honest. The locals called

it the Blue Factory because it was painted blue on the exterior. The MHS commander simply walked in one day and said, 'This is where the hospital's going and you've got ninety days to make it happen.' Within ninety days we built a wooden facility and moved the hospital in and all its support capabilities—probably across a distance of fifteen miles—into this new facility because the decision was made to shut down the CSH at the airfield site. The Blue Factory CSH was therefore a combination of tents, containers, and a fixed-site building. It housed a radiology unit, with the OR housed next door in the adjacent 'permanent' building. So it combined adapting an existing facility right beside a portable facility. This wooden facility's shell—not unlike the old World War II barracks—was constructed of just plywood and two-by-fours, and then we inserted our equipment into it to set up the inpatient wards. We derived the maximum advantages of both types of shelter. Whenever possible, it is best to set up a CSH inside a permanent preexisting facility. That strategy possesses many advantages, including not having to simultaneously fight the elements such as blinding dust storms or intense monsoon rainstorms.

SV: Was this a problem with the older, inflatable MASH (Medical Army Surgical Hospital) and MUST (inflatable) units?
RG: All it took was one mortar strike and the hospital would go down. In Bright Star, 1983, with the 5th MASH, they actually had deployed the old MUST system. We were at the Cairo West Airfield, where they had established elements of a MASH. No units are housed in inflatables like that anymore. None. A subsequent report identified more than twenty-five flaws with the inflatable facility. Basically, they had elected to too hurriedly field-test it in the Vietnam War in actual combat zones. The last one deployed was in 1987.

SV: So if Bravo Company requires a forty-four-bed configuration, what does Alpha Company require—is there a different facility bed capacity for Alpha?

RG: Alpha normally will require an additional bed count and medical support capacity. Depending upon how its Commander wants to set it up, it could be a forty-four-bed, eighty-four-bed, or larger configuration. The basic authorization is for an eighty-four-bed package, but they probably wouldn't set it all up at first. They would set up the forty-four-bed package. It can be enlarged later to 164 beds and up to 248 beds. In the future, it may make sense for every disaster-prone region in the U.S. to deploy its own civilian-owned mobile field hospital unit although having a fully deployable unit on 24/7 standby can be expensive. This can consume tremendous overhead because of the up-front purchase of the equipment. Once the equipment is on hand, however, packed and ready to go, the meds (medications) onboard may become problematic. Many meds are time-dated, as they require year-round climate control to maintain potency. Otherwise, they must be on preorder so with a flip of a switch or one call they are delivered prior to deployment. Next, all med supplies must be transited in the correct shipping container. And—most significantly—proper training is essential.

SV: What is the optimal mode of transport to a disaster strike zone, and how many containers are required to deploy a typical CSH installation?
RG: The hospital normally is floated (via ship) and it takes a number of days. The priority of air cargo transports is to quickly maneuver troops, as troops require smaller pieces of equipment. However, you can still move out via air transport smaller elements not as bulky as a full combat-support hospital, such as an Area Support Medical Company (ASMC). An ASMC requires a smaller 'logistical cube,' or package, because it possesses less capability compared to a full-scale CSH. Its forward surgical team would provide far-forward surgery, with the ability to stabilize the injured, and then rely on the MEDIVAC system to get that soldier back to a more definitive mode of medical care. U.S. Army Ready Brigades are on constant alert as well but this provides only minimal capability at first within a combat theater, as the first troops hit the ground. On poor roads, with eight flatbed trucks traveling 200 miles or more to the installation site, a lot of things can go wrong. This takes two to three days depending on the relationships you have within the country—and it may take longer. Prior to this, six days in transit on the boat and at least one day in logistical staging at the port upon arrival, and two more days for travel—then another 24 hours for set up. More realistically, it can take up to thirty days, from the time of notification to when the boat is being loaded. A shipment at sea can take up to twenty days. In humanitarian missions, transport timelines become a huge logistical challenge. Ever since the Vietnam War, helicopters have been used because they can quickly fly in across long, difficult terrain—flying everything in to the naval port or the site—wherever the CSH is deployed. Above all, the

MHS is 100 percent focused on rapid triage—getting the IV started and within one hour getting the individual into surgery.

SV: What if a CSH were to be deployed to an American city, such as the Medical University of South Carolina (MUSC) in Charleston, after its main hospital has gone down in a disaster?
RG: We would get the CSH to the site there within five days, with another twenty-four to forty-eight hours to set it up. I would also try to acquire a nearby gymnasium or something similar. Tents alone, to me, are the least feasible option. For a humanitarian mission within the United States it is best, as mentioned earlier, to move into a preexisting facility, with a minimum number of tents and containers erected on site in close adjacency. One limiting feature of [non-tent] containerized units is essentially they are nearly five feet off the ground with a ladder leading up to them. Just the physical lifting of a patient on the ladder, especially for people not used to lifting 150 pounds over their heads, can be a challenge although every container is fully climate-controlled, with air-conditioning, heating, and a full plumbing system. In the field, normally, there is one anesthesiologist, one nurse and a nurse's aide monitoring each patient together with the surgeon and an additional OR nurse—one for each procedure station—plus medical support techs...up to twelve personnel at one time in a container. The hours are 24/7 to ensure proper management and to provide them with proper food, rest, and hygiene amenities. As for triage, we set tents up ASAP. Large refrigeration containers must become morgues in the event of any deceased persons. Another container houses the central laundry because it is essential to have clean linens. Two such units are shipped typically with a CSH. These, and the refrigeration units, are each twenty feet long with (the aforementioned) pullout side modules.

SV: How is the site prepared?
RG: The tent-staking procedure is extremely important. This is accomplished with strings because every tent must be carefully and accurately staked out...and the top ridge of each tent must be perfectly centered with all others. Tents are laid out and connected by vestibules. If staking is off by even more than a few inches everything will be off and then rain will get inside. In training this point must be repeatedly emphasized because once the thing is staked down it doesn't move. But even before staking, everything will be arranged on the ground in accord with the field operations manual. Simulated scenarios are used in training exercises. This requires three days of classroom instruction, followed by one to two days for field staking exercises where the team actually lays it out and builds it in its entirety. Intense coordination is critical otherwise it is just one tent or container at a time, and construction will be slow as molasses. Incidentally, the EMT (Emergency Medical Tent) must be the first tent up and running. Unfortunately, some guys will invariably not really know what they are doing. They usually just open it all up, pour the stuff out and then try to put it together. Depending upon how many teams are staking, the first step is to stake out the EMT. From there, next is the pre-op, then the OR in order to establish the basic sequence of diagnosis and treatment. As soon as they get these units and the EMTs staked then the [pop-out] sides of the boxes are activated...classic multitasking is essential during set up. Then, the first patients can be admitted. It is possible, sometimes, to construct the OR container and the EMT, and pre-op tents at the same time. For this you must have multiple staking teams that can work simultaneously. Then there comes the moment where...if you build it they will come. And as soon as the EMT is able to accept its first casualties, guess what? But before we can accept the first patient to the CSH itself we set up what we call 'tailgate medicine.' If somebody rolls up before we get it [the hospital] running, we can treat the casualty right there on the spot on the ground, outside, if we have to. We set the stretchers with the patients on them right on the open ground. The hospital is dysfunctional until it has power. It is dark. The doctors, nurses, and technicians do have a jump-bag staged in a designated area just in case, say, someone goes into heart attack stage before the hospital is fully up.

SV: What other systems must be operational?
RG: Power distribution boxes provide mainline feeds for power and are routed and subdivided to reach every area of the CSH. Thick black cables snake throughout the site in seemingly all directions. Assembly diagrams depict how to set up the central power distribution system, including the proper length of every cable. The tents are air-conditioned and equipped with padded floors and tubular light fixtures are suspended from the ceilings and these are plugged into modular junction boxes. 'Alaskan' means that the CSH and its interior components can handle cold weather and this calls for a somewhat different layout configuration versus more temperate, or tropical, conditions. In cold climates,

tents may be vaulted (with curved roofs) although all configurations have zippered connections, windows, and entry vestibules. They are very sophisticated designs because their tent-wall 'portals' can be unzipped to allow for daylight and natural ventilation and screens keep insects out.

SV: How many patient beds are housed within a typical tent?
RG: Normally, twelve ICU beds are housed within a tent. These beds are configured with six on one side and six on the other.

SV: Describe the CSH water distribution system.
RG: The dark grey pipes are for gray water and sewage disposal. The sewage water system is set up around the entire field hospital. There is also a comprehensive potable water supply system, with its own portable pumping station. Freshwater is pumped though light-colored pipes. A hospital without a water supply system is dysfunctional. Freshwater is stored in large bladders and the Quartermaster is in charge of the water supply.

SV: What are the most pressing challenges once a CSH unit arrives at its installation site?
RG: First, because a CSH is fully containerized in transit, the biggest challenge is to get all the containers to the right place at the right time, undamaged. Whenever possible, it is a single cargo shipment. Where the CSH containers are staged, there may be perhaps a thousand different containers stored in that staging yard. Every container must be loaded on the same ship, and tracking must ensure every single container is headed to the right place at all times. Sometimes things do not get sent at the right time or to the right place and sometimes some containers are left behind, sitting on the dock. Second, as for selecting an installation site, it is critical to not set up in a wetland or on a site with poor natural drainage. Otherwise, what you thought was a dry area on Day One can turn out to be a major floodplain on Day Two. Successful troubleshooting requires knowing who is in charge at all times.

Interview 4

View from an architect-specialist in healthcare—interview with David Lopez, July 2013

North American architects are developing innovative transportables for medically underserved communities and for post-disaster contexts. David Lopez is an Associate with the Baltimore-based firm, Hord/Coplan/Macht (HCM). HCM's staff totals 120 and the firm specializes in education, housing, and healthcare.

SV: Describe the project proposed for Morocco (Chapter 6).
DL: In 2010, the firm set up a studio devoted to modular architecture. Its focus was on disaster relief. We developed a portfolio of conceptual proposals for a company called *Spevco*—which stands for Special Vehicles Company, based in Winston-Salem, North Carolina. They build merchandising modular trailers—mostly NASCAR trailers—huge eighteen-wheelers that pull into NASCAR venues and then fold out, transforming into merchandise trailer-stores. These trailers feature expandable sides, with flip-down and flip-up stage-rig technology onboard a classic eighteen-wheel platform chassis. Spevco presented to FEMA a prototype for an expandable trailer. Soon thereafter, FEMA scheduled a meeting with Spevco at Johns Hopkins University Medical Center in Baltimore. FEMA suggested our firm, as they were already aware of our prefab modulars for post-disaster uses. When we met, our ideas melded together. Next, we developed the prototype forty-eight-bed hospital configuration. The design is a flatbed trailer capable of multiple interior layout options, foldout and pop-up components, and multiple docking options with other modules. We solved how they are to be powered, their mechanical systems, potable water supply system and sanitation infrastructure. We developed three types of modules within a single system plus a mechanical system-intensive module, an electrical generator module, and a trailer-based desalination module. It is a system for use anywhere, anytime: plug it in and tie it into a solar power grid or to the local conventional power grid.

SV: The forty-eight-bed configuration appears to be self-sufficient but also capable of installation in a parking lot and docked to an existing medical center.
DL: Yes, that was the idea. It features everything a functional forty-eight-bed stationary hospital would have including triage,

emergency trauma care, radiology, surgery, and post-surgical holding bays. We applied what we already knew about hospital architecture to Spevco's core skill sets and we simply pushed that envelope as far as we could take it. Initially, the government in Morocco expressed interest because at the time Morocco was looking at portable healthcare facilities and deployed them to the sixteen governances that comprise that nation. This also explains the desert context for the renderings depicted in our firm's promotional literature. At this same time we were receiving positive feedback from potential clients in other parts of the world. After the forty-eight-patient bed hospital was posted online so much positive feedback was coming back to us, such as 'Well, I'd like just a five-unit [truck] configuration for women's healthcare' or, 'a five-unit clinic for kidney screening and dialysis treatment.'

SV: The three prototypes in the brochure are a children's clinic, a women's clinic, and a kidney dialysis clinic. Were these developed after the initial forty-eight-bed hospital prototype?
DL: Yes, we developed multiple floor plans for various uses after the initial proposal. For example, it was necessary that the nurse's station, blood-draw stations, processing labs, and other critical support functions were immediately adjacent to the patient examination bays. All adjacencies were carefully worked out in a process that took about three months. Then we studied linking them together in various configurations. Meanwhile, we were receiving a lot of questions about pricing, logistics, and transport options to various countries overseas. Each of these 'offshoot designs' took about a month to develop. We realized interest was heating up and we needed something more to further promote the idea. This was accomplished by means of a branding exercise. We called it *Monarch*, or Mobile Nomadic Architecture. We developed a logo—all done in-house—and an accompanying video. We posted it online in four different languages along with a booklet.

SV: Was international interest stronger than domestic (U.S.) interest?
DL: At first, yes. But we encountered problems with Spevco, the vehicle manufacturer, because they just could not meet the needed price point to make the system genuinely cost effective from a client's viewpoint. Mexico, for instance, was very interested, and their government was quite far ahead of the curve with respect to portable clinics for disaster relief. They wanted to order twenty fully equipped mobile clinics capable of traveling to various regions throughout the country. The problem was that each trailer averaged out to somewhere between $800,000 to $1.8 million to produce, depending on the level of technology onboard. A few years earlier we had proposed for a client a modular educational classroom project that featured a clerestory and a roof that lifted up, and we had spoken with a few manufacturers. It was a fairly simple concept, assembled with bottle jacks and cranks, and so we proposed something similar to Spevco. Spevco has a great deal of know-how, and a can-do attitude but custom solutions require higher up-front costs.

SV: So, is cost the main impediment?
DL: Cost is the main issue. Actually, cost is the sole limitation at this point in time. In every other way it is very feasible and attractive as a transportable modular system. We even proposed a *hub-and-spoke* model with a main clinic and smaller, remote, one or two-module clinics stationed in outlying areas, comprising a multi-site network. Some clients were interested in configurations with a traditionally constructed component with numerous plug-and-play portable modules connected to it in various ways. For example, the doctor's offices, examination rooms, and support spaces, including the main lobby and waiting room, would be housed in the stationary structure. This 'anchor' would be a permanent building, in other words, and adaptable to different sites. This enabled the addition of elements varying in number and function, such as wherever fewer (or more) emergency treatment bays and operating suites were called for to increase surgical capacity, or when a CT scan unit was needed at a specific site. Spoke modules would unplug and then be driven about locally or elsewhere further out within the network. We believe it is an effective strategy to reduce healthcare costs, because far more people than would otherwise be the case can attain access to high quality healthcare. The hospital comes to them instead of their having to always travel to a distant hospital. This addresses a huge problem of access to medical care in developing nations and in post-disaster contexts. A hybrid system such as this can travel ten, twenty, thirty miles out from its mothership hub, and then return at night to re-dock and recharge. Flyers could be distributed in a community saying the clinic will be in a given neighborhood for the next two, three, four or five days.

SV: What did FEMA ultimately say?
DL: Unfortunately, FEMA right now concentrates on setting up food and rations distribution tents, and they do not own anything like

this. In addition, their housing modules were never meant to be adapted to healthcare uses. They are poorly insulated, do not have many windows, and are just not healthy spaces for people to live in or be in at all. The initial idea was that we would be able to improve upon that idea dramatically and thereby fill a void in the FEMA toolkit following a disaster. They do bring housing in but have never done *anything* in terms of providing emergency healthcare facilities. This is a major weakness, I believe, in their first response system. This is why FEMA passes off healthcare to other organizations right now such as the American Red Cross. I think it may be a liability issue for them and they realize they are not set up to deal with it. They know that the American Red Cross, Doctors Without Borders, and other NGOs will be there to provide healthcare.

SV: Where do you think all this is going right now?
DL: Over the past three years we received nearly seventy-five inquiries about how much our prefabricated modular truck-based system would cost, what it could do, and how long it would take to deliver a system. There definitely is a lot of interest, but our price points remain probably 30–40 percent too high for the target market. If the manufacturing costs were to be whittled down somewhat I think it would quickly take off. Also, new prefabrication manufacturing technologies are being developed, onboard computerization capabilities, and green products including low-cost solar panels. Perhaps we are a bit ahead of the market but we do believe the time is right for this *right now*. I don't think any of the ideas we are promoting are necessarily ahead of the curve. In its essence, it is about adapting and equipping trucks with sophisticated expandable sides—an idea that has been around for more than twenty-five years. This basic feature has been around for a while in the recreational vehicle industry so it is not new. It will require, however, a rethinking of what we already know and to use this to feed our vision to achieve beyond the status quo. Our proposal is for healthcare to travel. Just this single aspect of the vision will require a shakeup of the healthcare industry, local building codes, and accreditation agency minimum standards in an industry controlled by increasingly fewer, larger, ever more powerful healthcare organizations. This applies to the public governmental sector and to private, for-profit, sectors of the healthcare industry in North America and elsewhere. As for the latter, the Cleveland Clinic, and Johns Hopkins, for instance, are but two examples of organizations in a prime position to dictate the standards of mobile healthcare globally. They are in a position to set the standards and means of healthcare delivery although unfortunately, they tend to still prematurely dismiss [prefab transportable facilities] and yet many more providers are getting interested in it, in theory at least. It is really a matter of price pointing. Johns Hopkins has an organization, a not-for-profit arm that serves low-income underserved populations in Africa and in other underdeveloped parts of the world. They were interested in commissioning a mobile truck clinic to travel throughout Ghana. Hopkins represents the cutting edge in the sense of always looking at new ways to provide basic healthcare services including primary care, pre-cancer screening, immunizations, and child and maternal health care. For instance, they developed an implementable test in the field—a 95 percent accurate pap smear assessment. At the same time, on American soil, Johns Hopkins operates traditional fee-for-service tertiary care hospitals and works closely with conventional third-party private payers [for-profit insurance companies]. Currently, mobile healthcare calls for a unifying, holistic vision to get beyond the point where it is today. Progressively minded healthcare providers must devote more attention and resources to meet global populations' needs within geographic catchment areas reachable through mobile facilities—it is an immense opportunity that remains virtually unexplored.

SV: What can architects do to become better first responders?
DL: I teach a class at a local University, where we have looked at shelter housing in post-disaster scenarios and I brought a group of students down to Haiti. We got involved with a build-out down there, talked to a lot of people building shelters there, and concluded we could build better shelters than what was being constructed at the time. Our team that worked on the modular truck clinic project for North Africa possessed this same investigative inquisitiveness: research must come before the design, and deliberative design must occur before the build. To many architects, disaster relief is just a knee-jerk response, simply sending plywood and studs down there and building some boxes to get people into transitional shelter. Few architects are really ahead of the curve, genuinely thinking ahead, and *nobody* is investing the proper amount of money *before it needs to be spent*. Climate change continues to spiral upward with weather patterns getting more and more extreme just as architects are falling further and further behind. The status quo is insufficient. As for the prototype we

developed with Spevco, nettlesome design challenges include the reality that in many foreign countries, different regulations exist for wheel axels on semi-trailers. This requires some structural modifications to the chassis that have to be considered on a country-by-country basis. When an order is received, we would literally need to set up shop overseas to construct them within the given country, or as close by as possible, and we seriously studied this option in North Africa (Morocco). European-based manufacturers would produce the units in Europe and then ship them to North Africa. This strategy would be cost effective from a quality control perspective because we would manufacture multiple orders from a single plant then ship them 'turnkey' to clients in more than one country. The advantage in the U.S. is we have a lead-time edge on the requisite prefab manufacturing technology. The chassis does take some time to build (two or three weeks) then it is skinned and fitted out in another three weeks. It is built on an assembly line, once one chassis is built and receives its finishes, another is in line right behind (or alongside it). This is how architects can turn something around in considerably less than six months time from the signing of the manufacturing contract to the in-plant construction start date to opening day.

Postscript

In June of 2013, the U.S Army Corps of Engineers handed over the keys to the $14 billion hurricane protection system it had to rebuild around metro New Orleans in the years following Hurricane Katrina. Right after the disaster, the former, byzantine patchwork quilt of independent levee authority agencies was rolled into a single, two-part agency. One of these former entities now operates under the aegis of the *South Louisiana Flood Protection Authority—East* (SLFPA-E). This is the jurisdictional body now responsible for paying the bill for the repaired/rebuilt system that protects the city. But it does not have the money. Worse, any likely funding solutions making it possible to pay this bill continue to be blocked by state and congressional political antics. And this figure does not even include the perpetual need to raise the levees in order to mitigate the effects of chronic land subsidence and rising sea levels. This sum could rise from $14 million in 2015 to as much as $20 million or more annually over the coming years. This sum represents the state's cost-share portion for maintaining the federal levees. If SLFPA-E can't find a workable solution, the only alternative will be to issue bonds at rates that would be catastrophically exorbitant for local residents in the three parishes impacted, and particularly for the residents of St. Bernard Parish. St. Bernard sits smack in the bull's eye of the wrath of the Gulf of Mexico and Hurricane Alley. The other two neighboring parishes on the financial hook don't have the money, either.

In the wake of the levees' widespread collapse in 2005, when engineers looked at the best way to protect the metro area east of the Mississippi River from future storm surge, they didn't consider the political sovereignty of the three parishes—but they knew water doesn't recognize geographic boundaries, or that all three parishes sit on the same flat, sinking delta surrounded by the same bodies of water. A grade school child will tell you that previous storms have repeatedly demonstrated that water that pours into one parish can and will eventually pour into others. The engineering solution was obvious—to construct a perimeter defense around the entire area—but its governing political structure is absurd. If there is no money to operate and maintain any one part of the system, then there is no coordinated system whatsoever. Anyone who says differently—that one parish can be protected without protecting the others—doesn't know what they are talking about.

Meanwhile, in Washington, D.C., a panel of scientists testified during a Senate committee briefing in February 2013, that New Orleans will probably be mostly underwater anyway by the end of the twenty-first century. James McCarthy, a Harvard University biological oceanography professor, testified that human activities and climate change will cause global sea levels to rise from three to six feet by then if the temperature rises by eight degrees or so, as substantial scientific research indicates will happen. This will have a major impact not only on the Gulf of Mexico but on all North American coastal cities and low lying coastal cities everywhere. In his words that day, "New Orleans is gone." As for Charleston, its main predicament is having been built in another low-lying coastal zone, and even in that city, public indifference continues to rule the day. Minimal public discourse is occurring in Charleston as time begins to run out. In Louisiana, recently, the SLFPA-E tried to at least do something to restore its vanishing coastline. It boldly sued ninety-six oil and gas exploration companies for their having destroyed the Louisiana delta over the past seventy-five years, by their dredging of more than 10,000 miles of canals and pipelines that now crisscross the wetlands. This case is pending in the federal courts, at this writing, and the governor of Louisiana, Bobby Jindal, has strenuously tried everything he could to kill this lawsuit.

Grandstanding, non-climate-denier politicians who attended the hearing in Washington called it a "shocking wake up call." As the oceans rapidly warm, helping to fuel immense weather events of increasing ferocity, the United States (and Canada) lags behind the developed world in adopting policies that will yield resilient defenses to counter the ramifications of what is to come. John Balbus, a U.S. National Institute of Environmental Health Sciences senior advisor for public health, has stated that so long as China and other high-polluter nations see the U.S. as not taking serious action, it opens the door for them to do nothing.

Index

For Product Safety Concerns and Information please contact our EU representative GPSR@taylorandfrancis.com Taylor & Francis Verlag GmbH, Kaufingerstraße 24, 80331 München, Germany

Batch number: 10745682

Printed by Printforce, the Netherlands